The Ultimate Insider's Story
of Five Presidents and
How They Won the Cold War

SIMON & SCHUSTER

From the Shadows

ROBERT M. GATES

SIMON & SCHUSTER
Rockefeller Center
1230 Avenue of the Americas
New York, NY 10020

10   9   8   7   6   5   4   3   2   1

Library of Congress Cataloging-in-Publication Data

Gates, Robert Michael.
   From the shadows : the ultimate insider's story of
five presidents and how they won the Cold War /
Robert M. Gates.
      p.   cm.
   Includes index.
      1. United States—Foreign relations—Soviet
Union.   2. Soviet Union—Foreign relations—
United States.   3. Gates, Robert Michael.
4. Intelligence service—United States—History—
20th century.   I. Title.
E183.8.S65G39   1996
327.73047—dc20   95-51704   CIP
ISBN 0-684-81081-6

Acknowledgments

Above all, I wish to thank the five Presidents I served and their National Security Advisers and Directors of Central Intelligence for giving me the opportunity to participate in and observe the dramatic events described in this book. Further, I want to express my appreciation to the countless colleagues with whom I worked in government for their help and friendship. At a time when respect for public servants seems on steady decline, I am proud to say that nearly all of those with whom I worked over more than a quarter century were people of enormous skill, ability, and personal integrity. Americans should be proud to have people of such quality serving them and the country.

In writing this book, I relied almost entirely on my personal papers at CIA and from the NSC, as well as the memoirs of those for whom and with whom I worked. Thus, I want to thank the Executive Secretariat at CIA, especially Jim Pittman; my longtime secretary and assistant, Diane Edwards; and the staff of the National Archives and several presidential libraries.

Documents that I quote are either from my Agency or NSC files and have been cleared for use in this book, or have been declassified and are available to the public. Where I quote individuals in conversations or meetings, the source is either a memorandum of conversation or record made immediately after the event or, if I was not present, from one of the participants. To keep this book of manageable length, I have deleted from the text citations from a number of documents and records, as well as descriptions of some second-level officials of successive administrations. A complete, unedited manuscript has been given to the Historical Intelligence Collection at CIA and to the John F. Kennedy School of Government at Harvard University for the use of scholars.

Under the terms of my employment with CIA, the manuscript was reviewed by the Agency's Publications Review Board, and I want to thank them—and especially Molly Tasker—for their cooperation and promptness, particularly in light of the massive number of classified documents and Agency activities that I describe. Their review was eminently fair and consistently reflected good common sense both in terms of what could be declassified and what had to remain secret. Similarly, I received good cooperation from the reviewers at the National Security Council.

I asked a number of people to review parts or all of the manuscript, and want to thank all of them for taking the time and effort to help me: Richard Helms, William Colby, Frank Carlucci, Admiral B. R. Inman, John McMahon, Richard Kerr, Zbigniew Brzezinski, Brent Scowcroft, Richard Armitage, Grey Hodnett, Kay Oliver, George Kolt, Barry Stevenson, Condoleezza Rice, Don Oberdorfer, and Professor Ernest May. Obviously, responsibility for any errors or mistakes is mine alone.

Special thanks go to Wayne Kabak of International Creative Management, Inc., who began this process as my representative but soon also became my friend, adviser, and counselor. I also want to express appreciation to the remarkable Alice Mayhew of Simon & Schuster. I join her long list of students and admirers.

I owe special thanks to the men and women of the DCI security staff for their support, help, and friendship over many years.

Finally, this book would not have been possible without my wife, Becky, whose patience and understanding as I was writing was surpassed only by her patience and understanding during the quarter century that the book describes.

To Becky,
Eleanor, and Bradley

Contents

INTRODUCTION   15

PART ONE
1969–1974: Détente—
THE YEARS OF SMOKE AND MIRRORS
1 Washington and Moscow: 1969   27
2 So This Was "Détente"?   39

PART TWO
1975–1980: THE MASK OF SOVIET ASCENDANCY
3 American Paralysis   53
4 The "Third World" War   64
5 Planting Lethal Seeds   85
6 MUTS, Spies, and Dissidents   97
7 Defense and Arms Control: Advantage USSR   105
8 1979: Cold War, Hot War—East War, West War   118
9 Carter Turns to CIA   135
10 The Mask of Soviet Ascendancy, the Reality of Vulnerability   170

PART THREE
1981–1986: THE RESURGENCE OF THE WEST
11 The Reawakening   183
12 Reagan's Sword: Casey at CIA   198
13 Turning the Tables   226
14 1983: The Most Dangerous Year   258

15 The War in Washington, 1983: Shultz Against the Field 278
16 Central America, 1983–1984: Our Own Worst Enemy 293
17 Passages: Last Gasp of the Soviet Old Guard 317
18 1985: Reagan and Gorbachev—the Best of Enemies 327
19 The Third World Competition, 1985–1986: Washington
   Pours It On 346
20 Intelligence Wars 357

PART FOUR
1986–1991: LIBERATION AND HISTORY'S DUSTBIN
21 Gorbachev's Uncertain Trumpet, 1986–1987 375
22 Diversions 390
23 Geneva to Washington 404
24 Ending the "Third World" War 427
25 Gorbachev: Destroying the Soviet System 438
26 The "Velvet Revolutions" of 1989: The Avalanche
   of Liberation 449
27 Together at Last: Bush and Gorbachev 472
28 Destruction of the "Evil Empire" 508
29 A Joyless Victory 532
   Reflections 553

NOTES 577
INDEX 581

Reminiscing with President Nixon, long after I worked briefly for him on the National Security Council at the White House.

With President Ford in 1976. He never got the credit he deserved, especially in foreign policy.

Bidding President Carter farewell in December 1979, with Brzezinski looking on. The Soviets saw Carter as a dangerous adversary, quite contrary to the view of his foreign policy at home.

Briefing President Reagan before the November 1985 Geneva Summit with Gorbachev. Casey, Shultz, and Chief of Staff Don Regan all keep a wary eye.

At Kennebunkport, Maine, in August 1990 with President Bush and Jim Baker preparing for Desert Shield/Desert Storm. A key issue was getting the Soviets into the coalition and keeping them there.

My wife, Becky, and I greet Prime Minister Thatcher. After Deputy Secretary of State Larry Eagleburger and I twice visited her to propose reductions in U.S. forces in Europe, she took to calling us "Tweedledum and Tweedledee." On this occasion, I had no bad news for her.

Mikhail Gorbachev and I encounter one another again in May 1991, at the White House. On this occasion, we exchanged only smiles.

As the first Director of CIA to visit Moscow, I met in October 1992 with Yevgeniy Primakov, head of the Russian Foreign Intelligence Service, successor to the KGB. We were old adversaries trying to move our organizations into a new era.

In October 1992, I met with President Yeltsin in the Kremlin. We discussed both the past and the future. There were a lot of ghosts in the room, on both sides.

A miniature copy of *The Gulag Archipelago*, Solzhenitsyn's great book about the Soviet concentration camps, similar to many printed by CIA and smuggled into the Soviet Union.

WANTED

Robert Gates
Director of CIA

For violation of
international law and
human rights violations.

CIA OFF CAMPUS

Public esteem: one of the rewards of being head of CIA.

Introduction

LOOKING BACK, it all seems so easy, so painless, so inevitable—the collapse of Soviet communism, the breakup of the Soviet Union, the liberation of Eastern Europe, the reunification of Germany. After forty-five years of stalemate, wars hot and cold, and the threat of nuclear annihilation, the breakneck speed with which history was made after 1988—the liberation of Eastern Europe in less than six months, the collapse of the Soviet Union in less than a year—was stunning, almost miraculous.

Very, very few predicted that these revolutionary events would happen in this century. No one foresaw that they would happen so fast. And so the search began for the hows and the whys.

The first step in answering the question "How did it happen?" is to remind ourselves what really did happen, and the second step is to ask why it happened. I try to do both in this eyewitness account of the last half of the Cold War, from Vietnam to the collapse of the Soviet Union, as seen from CIA and nearly nine years on the National Security Council staff at the White House under four Presidents.

Drawing on personal experience at CIA and the White House, as well as knowledge of CIA documents and activities never before revealed or declassified, I want to tell what really happened, how people and leaders really felt—of dangers, fears, conflicts, and miscalculations; of leadership and courage on both sides; of sacrifices for freedom around the world, including in the Soviet Union; of wisdom and folly; of purposeful strategies and policies, and awesome unintended consequences; of patriots and scoundrels and patriotic scoundrels; of egos as big as all outdoors. I want to challenge the proliferation of myths and revisionism, and to challenge conventional wisdom on important events and personalities of the period.

This book offers a perspective on the entire period from 1969 to 1991 by someone who was there throughout. The memoirs of the key players through all these years now either are available or soon will be. But they are written from the vantage point of four- or eight-year (or less) windows into events. They usually are written by people with records to defend, axes to grind, or, too often, scores to settle. Not a single book has been written by a nonpartisan, senior career official who was present throughout this remarkable time, who knew and watched all of the senior decision-makers, and who could write from the convenient perch of the White House and CIA, and with a post-Soviet vantage.

With some unease, I want to write also a book about CIA from the inside and about its activities and culture over the span of a career, to open the doors of that uniquely closed society to public scrutiny—operations, covert actions as seen from inside, assessments, and, perhaps most intriguing, its bureaucratic politics and leaders. It is time to let in a little sunshine and let people see CIA as an integral part of the government. As the only Director of Central Intelligence to rise from entry level to the top, I believe I have a unique perspective on this story.

Most readers of this book presumably are interested in learning about the real CIA, and that surely includes interest in Aldrich Ames, the CIA officer who spied inside the Agency for the Soviets from 1985 to 1994. Throughout this book, the reader will find observations about the CIA bureaucracy and culture that help explain how Ames could have continued his sordid treason for so long. These passages were written *after* Ames's arrest, even though they are often based on events and documents that long predate his betrayal.

Because of the enormous publicity surrounding the Ames case, and despite the very minor part he plays in the quarter-century story I have to tell, I want to summarize here what Aldrich Ames did and did not do. Then, the reader can place this information in context while reading about this extraordinary period of history. I also want to make clear at the outset that when writing about events during the last years of the Soviet Union, I was fully cognizant of Ames's activities.

There can be no doubt that the Agency's greatest counterintelligence failure, and perhaps its greatest operational failure, during the last half of the Cold War was Aldrich Ames's treason and his work as a Soviet mole in the heart of CIA's clandestine service for nearly ten years. During this period, he devastated CIA's human intelligence and counterintelligence effort against the Soviet Union, betraying the identities of a number of American agents in the USSR and, as a result, causing the executions of at least nine. He disclosed much about U.S. human and technical intelligence capabilities and made possible a number of KGB double-agent operations against us—operations in which the KGB controlled agents CIA had recruited and passed both valid and misleading information through those agents. In short, a significant number of CIA human intelligence operations inside the USSR during its final years were known to, and often controlled by, the KGB. It was a tragic and sad final chapter in the Cold War for a clandestine service that, as the reader will see, had played so important a role in acquiring critical Soviet military secrets and in keeping pressure on the USSR around the world for so long.

In 1995, as part of the effort to assess the extent of the damage done by Ames, the issue arose whether the Soviet double-agent operations he facilitated had influenced U.S. government perceptions or decisions during 1985–1991—whether U.S. decision-making was influenced by the thirty-five clandestine reports known to have come from double agents (and sixty other reports from "suspected" double agents) that were sent to policymakers over the ten-year period. Most of the double-agent reporting concerned the technical characteristics of Soviet weapons systems, and thus it likely was aimed primarily at the U.S. Defense Department. Yet, according to the publicly released summary conclusions of the December 1995 official Ames "damage assessment," the impact of the reporting on Defense acquisition decisions ranged from "on the margin" to "negligible." "[C]lear-cut damage" to analysis relating to Defense research-and-development and procurement programs "may have been limited to a few cases." No major instance of the reporting influencing U.S. arms control positions or negotiations was identified. Altogether, then, it would appear that early, highly publicized claims that the double-agent reporting had resulted in Defense wasting billions of dollars were wrong and that specific damage was very limited—at least insofar as the decision-making process can be reconstructed.

However, damage was severe in one area: during these years, the Directorate of Operations broke faith with both CIA and Defense analysts and with U.S. policymakers by failing in a number of instances to alert them that the clandestine reports they were receiving were from controlled sources. Rebuilding their confidence could take the DO a long time.

A broader, more politically charged issue arising out of the 1995 damage assessment was whether the double-agent reporting and the Soviet effort at "perception management" led the United States to overestimate Soviet military capabilities during the late 1980s and early 1990s, as alleged by some. I strongly believe that it did not, the most important reason being that—as will become evident—by 1987–1989 (when much of this reporting reached Washington), CIA's assessments of future Soviet military capabilities were influenced predominantly by the rapidly accelerating Soviet economic crisis, a crisis I will show was well documented at the time by the Agency.

It is possible that double-agent reporting during this period led to an overestimate of Soviet progress on a few specific military programs. However, the notion that a few dozen clandestine reports over nearly seven years—a small fraction of the total clandestine reporting from the USSR—led the U.S. intelligence community to overestimate Soviet military capabilities is wrong, betraying little understanding of intelligence community perceptions of the growing weakness of the USSR after 1986–1987 and the multisource nature of intelligence analysis. It also betrays ignorance of what CIA and the intelligence community actually said at the time. Finally, the notion that fewer than a hundred reports over a decade altered or shaped the views of senior policy officials reflects little grasp of how decisions are made and how senior officials read, use, and react to individual raw intelligence reports—something I saw firsthand in the White House over many years. In sum, the popular impression in 1995 that, because of Ames, the Soviets were able to influence Defense Department decisions and the views of senior U.S. decision-makers through double-agent reporting was quite mistaken.

The reader needs to know right at the start of this book that CIA's failure to find Aldrich Ames for a decade did grievous harm, but mostly to the U.S. intelligence community, and especially to

CIA itself, its agents, and its operations. Above all, the Agency's long failure to identify Ames, especially in light of his mistakes and obvious personal weaknesses, made apparent serious problems not just in CIA counterintelligence, but also in the management and culture of CIA's Directorate of Operations and in the Agency chain of command. These problems would, in the mid-1990s, result in both sweeping internal soul-searching and irresistible outside pressures for thoroughgoing change and reform in the clandestine service—a cultural revolution. This book makes clear that both the problems and the need for such a cultural revolution in CIA were recognized long before Aldrich Ames betrayed his colleagues and his country. And it makes clear why efforts to bring change failed.

I worked for six Presidents, from Lyndon Johnson to George Bush, and eight Directors of Central Intelligence. I served on the National Security Council staff in the White House under four Presidents during this quarter of a century—Richard Nixon, Gerald Ford, Jimmy Carter, and George Bush. I was CIA's head of analysis (Deputy Director for Intelligence), Deputy Director of Central Intelligence (and for nearly six months Acting Director) during the Reagan administration. I served as Deputy National Security Adviser and then as Director of Central Intelligence under George Bush. No one had longer uninterrupted continuity in senior or key national security positions during this period. Because of the opportunities my positions offered, I knew and observed firsthand virtually all of the principal figures in both the American and the Soviet national security structures. I was, during the remarkable events from the late 1960s to the early 1990s, there in the shadows, the proverbial fly on the wall in the most secret councils of government, listening, watching, observing many of the greatest events of the century.

My journey through this history began with a meeting with a CIA recruiter on the campus of Indiana University in the fall of 1965. That was in the days when CIA recruiters were welcome on campuses, especially conservative ones like Indiana. I saw the recruiter on a lark because I thought I could get a free trip to Washington. Six months later, after that trip to Washington to be tested, probed, and polygraphed, I was invited to join the mystical brotherhood of CIA. I reported for work in August 1966, knowing that—because CIA offered no draft deferments—I would be entering the U.S. Air Force under CIA sponsorship in only a few weeks.

CIA headquarters in the Virginia suburbs is surrounded by

trees and a high chain-link fence with strands of barbed wire. The huge gray, concrete structure, its roof covered with antennas, was a forbidding sight in those days for a new recruit. As I rode through the gate in an Agency bus, I thought, So this is where the coup plots are hatched, where agents are dispatched to the remote corners of the world, where fabulous technical devices collect information from the most unlikely places and enable CIA's version of James Bond to thwart insidious communist plots, so this is the location of the American "secret government." Or so I thought or had heard. I was twenty-three and I had a lot to learn.

The inside of the building was deceptively bland. Long, undecorated hallways. Tiny cubicles to work in. Linoleum floors. Metal, government-issue furniture. It was like a giant insurance company. But, then again, it wasn't. Every desk had a safe. Every office had a row of safes and a rainbow of telephones—red, black, green, gray, each with a different level of classification protection. Briefcases and purses were searched on departure, sometimes to the great embarrassment of people trying to take work home—and getting a security violation for their efforts.

In those days, armed guards and turnstiles separated the analytical and operational sides of the Agency, and you could not go back and forth without a special marker on your security badge. As a friend gave me a tour of the building, we tiptoed down the seventh-floor hallway where the director and the most senior officers of the Agency had their offices. We spoke in hushed tones, and worried that someone would come out one of the always-closed doors and demand to know why we were snooping around the executive suites. Not even in my fantasies did I dream that I would one day occupy most of those suites, including the director's.

With CIA help, I entered Air Force Officer Training School in Texas in October 1966. Upon my commissioning in January 1967, and with a very brief interruption to get married, I reported for duty at Whiteman Air Force Base in Missouri, an intercontinental ballistic missile base. There were two of us in the intelligence office, and we briefed the missile crews on international political and military developments. Their lack of interest was awesome.

For a very green second lieutenant, I had a number of unusual opportunities to hobnob at higher levels in the Air Force because I was the only person in our outfit who could pronounce the names of our targets. This was still Curtis LeMay's Strategic Air Command, and one of my most memorable briefings was for the lieutenant general who commanded 8th Air Force. I briefed him on our targets, including the fact that 120 of our 150 Minuteman missiles were targeted on Soviet ICBMs. The general, a LeMay "wannabe" smoking a huge cigar, went ballistic. He jumped up and shouted that it was a "goddamn outrage" to be targeting what would in war be empty missile silos. He demanded that I—a second lieutenant—change the targeting strategy, proclaiming that "when the balloon goes up, I want to kill some fucking Russians, not dig up dirt." He was not to be my most sophisticated audience, but certainly he was one of the most unforgettable.

My views on Vietnam were much influenced by my year at the missile base. There, I caught a glimpse of the impact of the Vietnam War on America's overall strategic strength, and it was depressing. Money was scarce because of the resources going to Vietnam, and we watched with dismay as pilot losses in the war resulted in white-haired lieutenant colonels being reassigned from our base to fly in Southeast Asia. We knew then we would not win the war. After a year of targeting the USSR with American ICBMs, I returned to Washington in January 1968 to begin my CIA career in earnest, still focused on the same target, but in very different ways.

As soon as my wife and I arrived in Washington, I entered the Career Training Program at CIA, which meant six months of learning the realities of the intelligence business and putting aside forever fantasies about fast cars, loose women, and the other stuff of fiction. We learned about writing intelligence reports, setting up meetings with agents, dead drops, studying the Soviet Union, learning clandestine tradecraft, becoming familiar with satellite collection systems, learning about the intelligence bureaucracy, and conducting surveillance. (I never realized how few people are on the streets of Richmond, Virginia, at eight o'clock in the morning. Our team's surveillance target, the "rabbit," was a woman from the Agency, and a good citizen of Richmond alerted the police that several disreputable-looking men were stalking this woman. Happily—if professionally unsatisfying—I had lost contact with the rabbit almost immediately and therefore missed my colleagues' encounter with the local gendarmes. It was not an auspicious start in the spy business for any of us.)

In those days, everyone going through the Career Training Program had to be under "cover"—that is, because you might go overseas in a clandestine assignment, you could not be identified with or known to work for CIA. Therefore, each of us was assigned a cover story or "legend," a false story of assignment to another agency of government and another line of work. My cover was that I worked for the Department of Defense. The Agency didn't work too hard in those days at cover for most new employees, and this led to another test of my aptitude for clandestine work. At a cocktail party, a man came up and asked where I worked. I mumbled vaguely something about working for the government (a dead giveaway in Washington that you work for CIA). He pressed me on what department and I replied, "Defense." His face brightened and he said that he did as well. Where did I work? I replied, "The Naval Munitions Building on Constitution Avenue." He said, "So do I— where are you?" I gave him my legend office number. He paused, then frowned and said, "They tore that wing down about two months ago." With an ease and suaveness Sean Connery would have envied, I—totally undone—muttered that "I don't get into the office much" and simply fled the conversation.

For several of us, our newness was no hindrance to suggesting to the instructors that there were better ways to do some things. Not surprisingly, veterans of Vienna, Berlin, the Congo, and Vietnam—of the darkest corners of the Cold War—were not much interested in the ideas of new recruits, and not much impressed with us either. Truth to tell, the ideas probably weren't all that terrific, anyway. But speaking out and discontent with the old ways of doing business for me and for my friends began early—and it is to the Agency's credit that we weren't sacked right away. I concluded quickly that I wasn't cut out for the clandestine service, a conclusion I am certain was shared by all of the operations instructors. And so, in August 1968, I began my career as an analyst working on the Soviet Union.

Time thankfully has dimmed the memories of those of us who are old enough to remember 1968, for I believe it was one of the worst years in modern American history. The year opened in January with North Korea's seizure of the *Pueblo*, a U.S. signals intelligence collection ship operating in international waters. Also in January 1968, unknown to the American people or government, a U.S. Navy chief warrant officer named John Walker made contact with the KGB in Washington to volunteer his services as a spy. He would be, as far as we know, the KGB's premier agent in the United States for nearly seventeen years—until CIA's Aldrich Ames volunteered to commit treason. According to a senior KGB defector, Walker's information about U.S. encryption devices allowed the

Soviets to decode nearly a million American military messages. Another invaluable KGB agent providing signals intelligence information, British citizen Geoffrey Prime, volunteered to the KGB only a few days before Walker.

The Tet Offensive in Vietnam also came in January. Lyndon Johnson's dreams of progress and reconciliation at home shattered, he announced on March 31 that he would not run for reelection. Four days later, the Reverend Martin Luther King, Jr., was assassinated and the ensuing rioting engulfed numerous American cities in flames, including the nation's capital. A few weeks after that tragedy, on June 6, Robert F. Kennedy, too, was assassinated. At the Democratic Convention in July, the nation saw yet another spectacle of violence as demonstrators and police clashed outside the nominating hall in Chicago, and what was later described as a police riot resulted in more scenes of bloodshed and horror on the streets. In November, Richard Nixon at last achieved his life's ambition. He won the right to govern a nation trapped in an expensive, unwinnable, and dirty war; a society deeply divided racially and generationally, where hatred and crude insults dominated political dialogue; a nation that because of Vietnam already had come deeply to mistrust its own government, including especially the Agency I had just joined.

Soviet leaders, in 1968, could look with satisfaction on the problems facing the United States. Indeed, they also could see generational conflict creating an atmosphere of crisis elsewhere in the West, particularly in West Germany and France. But the Soviets could view problems in the West only as a respite from their own. The most pressing challenge for the Soviets was the political crisis in Czechoslovakia that began in January 1968. At that time, Alexander Dubcek replaced the old Stalinist Antonin Novotny as Party First Secretary and proceeded to try to improve and reform the system. The power struggle that followed escalated to the point where the foundations of the system were challenged.

On the night of August 20–21, 1968, the Soviet army and forces from all the East European states except Romania and Yugoslavia invaded Czechoslovakia. The invasion took place on the second day after I began my career as an analyst. In just a few short days, I learned a lot about intelligence work, crisis management, about the Soviets, and about the dangers of spurious or unsubstantiated intelligence reports. All in all, it was an extraordinary initiation into my new world.

PART ONE

1969–1974: Détente—
the Years of Smoke and Mirrors

CHAPTER ONE

Washington and Moscow: 1969

VIETNAM. The war dominated everything by 1969. The passing of the Johnson administration and obvious commitment of the new President to leave Vietnam did not still the antiwar demonstrations.

It is hard to imagine two groups of people more distant in outlook than many of the demonstrators and us button-down, "preppy," mostly middle-class men and women whom Richard Nixon inherited in the government bureaucracy. The contrast seemed especially stark among us "twenty-somethings" in government and our counterparts on the streets. The two groups seemed to be from different planets.

But we had more in common than either side realized at the time. For inside the government there were many, especially young people—and middle-aged parents influenced by their college-age kids—who shared hostility to the war and to the so-called Establishment. I was now twenty-five, had served in the air force, and was a CIA analyst working on Soviet policy in the Middle East and Africa. I and virtually all of my friends and acquaintances in CIA were opposed to the war and to any prolonged strategy for extracting us. Feelings among my colleagues—and nearly all of the men in those days were military veterans—were strong. Many from CIA marched in antiwar demonstrations on the Mall and at the Pentagon. My one and only was the May 9, 1970, demonstration after the U.S. military offensive in Cambodia.

Popular impressions then and now about CIA—especially as a

conservative, Cold War bureaucratic monolith—have always been wrong. In the late 1960s and early 1970s not only was antiwar sentiment strong at the Agency, we were also influenced by the counterculture. There is not a doubt in my mind that some of my older colleagues and supervisors, presumably influenced in some measure by their college-age children, experimented with marijuana and perhaps even other drugs. Antiwar and anti-Nixon posters and bumper stickers festooned CIA office walls.

While facing this not inconsiderable fifth column within his own government, Richard Nixon set about finding a strategy for extricating the country from the war in a way that would, in his view, preserve American credibility and honor. In his first months in office, a dual strategy emerged that involved (1) turning the fighting in Vietnam over to the Vietnamese (Vietnamization) so U.S. troops could be brought home and thus lance the domestic boil, and (2) taking advantage of the Soviet interest in closer relations with Washington to elicit Soviet help in influencing North Vietnam to negotiate an honorable exit. Several of Nixon's closest advisers believe that détente was, in fact, born out of Nixon's determination to end the war.

With antiwar, antimilitary protesters at the front door of the White House and strong antidefense sentiment in the Congress, the Nixon administration faced a serious challenge in preserving a viable defense budget and programs to modernize American strategic weapons. Nineteen sixty-nine was the first year that the defense and intelligence budgets were seriously challenged in Congress. For intelligence, it marked the beginning of more than ten years of budget cuts that would reduce our manpower by 50 percent and money by some 40 percent—with commensurate reductions in capabilities. For defense, every aspect of the program was challenged—overseas presence, strategic doctrine, and virtually all weapons programs (especially strategic offensive weapons).

Nixon saw the need for U.S. strategic modernization through the prism of one of the most significant failures in the history of American intelligence. At the time of the Cuban Missile crisis in 1962, the United States had a very large advantage over the Soviet Union in both land- and sea-based intercontinental ballistic missiles. President Kennedy was aware at the time that the United States had about a four-to-one lead in ICBMs (over four hundred to the Soviets' seventy–eighty or so); a significant lead in submarine-launched ballistic missiles; and a huge advantage in strategic bombers (some 1,300 to less than 200).

Humiliation in Cuba galvanized the Soviets into action. The USSR proceeded to undertake the largest military buildup in history over a twenty-five-year period, with profound consequences for the international balance of power, for the United States, and ultimately, and fatefully, for the Soviet economy and state. The Soviets increased the number of their ICBMs from fewer than a hundred to more than 850 by 1968 and to more than 1,500 by 1972, while the U.S. number remained constant at 1,054. They began a vast expansion of their submarine ballistic missile force and laid the foundations for qualitative improvements to their strategic forces—such as MIRVs—as well.

No matter how accurate CIA was in identifying what was actually happening on the ground, the reality is that in the mid- to late 1960s and early 1970s, the Agency did not foresee this massive Soviet effort to match and then surpass the United States in strategic missile numbers and capabilities—and did not understand Soviet intentions. Thus surprise magnified the impact of the change in the global balance of power and elimination of American strategic superiority—and had a profound impact on U.S. domestic perceptions of the Soviet threat. CIA paid a high price for this failure in terms of its credibility, most especially in the eyes of the new President and his Secretary of Defense, Melvin Laird.

As if finding a respectable way out of Vietnam and sustaining the national defense in the most antimilitary climate in Washington since the 1930s were not challenge enough, the new administration was alarmed by the unseemly rush in the latter half of the 1960s of America's key allies to reach separate accommodations with the Soviets. This had a profound impact on Nixon and Henry Kissinger, his National Security Adviser, and their approach to the Soviets. Already disposed to establish a more stable, less volatile relationship with the Soviet Union and to lean on it to help extricate the United States from Vietnam, Nixon apparently decided that unless he publicly accepted the European notion of a "détente" with Moscow, the United States would become isolated in the alliance and would see the Russians and key U.S. allies cutting separate deals—"separate détente"—with Moscow holding the high cards.

Contrary to longstanding conventional wisdom, Nixon's embrace of détente was not motivated primarily by the desire for a new kind of relationship with the Soviet Union. Rather, it seems to have been a tactical response to (1) deal with the Soviet military buildup, (2) improve crisis management during a dangerous time, (3) manage pressures at home relating to Vietnam and the defense budget that threatened the President's ability to formulate and implement his foreign policy in Washington, and (4) counter pressures in Europe to kiss up to Moscow in a way that threatened the President's ability to maintain U.S. leadership of the Atlantic Alliance.

NIXON AND CIA

The views of the Central Intelligence Agency counted for little as the Nixon administration developed policy strategies for Vietnam, Europe, arms control, defense, the Soviet Union, and China —the issues that would dominate Nixon's first term. The President, Kissinger, and later Defense Secretary Mel Laird all personally attached little importance to what CIA thought. Nixon's antipathy to CIA was deeply rooted, originating with his belief that former director Allen Dulles had been responsible for candidate John F. Kennedy's exploitation of the "missile gap" with the Soviets in the 1960 election, thereby costing Nixon the election. He had a long memory.

Further, aware of CIA's failure to forecast accurately Soviet missile deployments in the 1960s, Nixon disdained its assessments, believing the Agency had been wrong or, worse, "soft" in its estimates on the Soviet Union and Vietnam, and he infrequently read them. Indeed, as then–CIA director Richard Helms recalls, Nixon never missed a chance to needle or gouge the Agency on its estimates of Soviet military strength. The President paid little attention to the *President's Daily Brief,* CIA's morning intelligence publication designed and intended for the President alone. Nixon saw the Agency as politically liberal, and made no secret of his view that too many of its officials—including Helms—were closely tied into the "Georgetown social set." Right off, CIA stumbled with Nixon in its assessments on Indochina, first by underestimating how much supply was reaching the North Vietnamese troops through the Cambodian port of Sihanoukville. Nixon also held against the Agency its failure to predict the 1970 Lon Nol coup in Cambodia ("What the hell do those clowns do out there in Langley?" he asked Secretary of State William Rogers), forgetting that under congressional pressure, all CIA officers had by then been withdrawn from Phnom Penh. Then, in 1971, the Agency underestimated the anticipated resistance to the South Vietnamese offensive against the Ho Chi Minh Trail in Laos (the operation known as Lam Song 719).

Another important battle involving CIA—and ending to its political detriment—early in the Nixon Presidency was over whether the three warheads on the Soviet blockbuster ICBM, the SS-9, were independently targetable (the Defense view) or would, when released, simply take ballistic paths like bombs (CIA's view).

Helms stood his ground against Defense on the technical capabilities of the SS-9 and CIA was later shown to have been correct. But the Agency won a battle and lost a war: the fight made an adversary out of the tough and combative Laird, who is said to have asked, "Whose team is CIA on?" Laird was a formidable bureaucratic adversary, one of the most skilled in-fighters in modern American government. Helms recounts the story of going into the Oval Office to see Nixon just as Laird was leaving and having Nixon point to the departing Laird and say, "There goes the most devious man in the United States." Some accolade, considering the source.

In Johnson's last years, CIA had been held in high esteem by the President and by his closest advisers. But the air quickly went out of CIA's balloon with the arrival of Nixon and Kissinger, with the former's biases against the Agency and both of their reactions to the Agency's unfortunate early mistaken assessments. With the new administration, CIA had no special cachet, no special access. Helms participated in meetings but was never a confidant of Nixon's as he had been of Johnson's.

More than any other government department, CIA's influence and role are determined by its relationship to the President and the National Security Adviser, a relationship that finds expression almost exclusively in the CIA director's personal relationship with those two individuals. Nixon's attitude toward the Agency and toward Helms, reinforced by Kissinger's and Laird's unhappiness with its estimates, weakened CIA, reinforced its already strong insularity, and ultimately made the Agency more vulnerable to the devastating attacks to come.

Inside the Agency, though, the late 1960s and early 1970s represented the last hurrah of those who had helped build the organization and still ran it. Helms was widely respected, consid-

ered the consummate professional and one of the most adept politi-
cal operators in Washington. CIA's leaders then—Helms, William
Colby, James Jesus Angleton, and others—were the stuff of legend
inside the Agency. They and their cohorts had been blooded in the
OSS in World War II and tempered in the fires of the high Cold
War of the late 1940s and the 1950s—Berlin and Germany, Austria, France, Italy, the Balkans. They had gone face-to-face with the
Beast—"the evil empire"—and won far more times than they lost.
Some, like Angleton, were mysterious, even weird—sitting in a
darkened office with a single desk light, chain-smoking, a figure
from another world. Others were very Ivy League, very establishment, very well connected. The people who ran the rest of the
government at the highest levels were their personal friends and
often their tennis partners. For these reasons, and because the critical views of Nixon and Kissinger were unknown to most of us at
CIA in those days, there was a general aura of confidence, power,
and influence about the place that made us proud and independent
—and, many would say, very arrogant.

CIA, then as now, comprised four directorates: the Directorate
of Operations (DO)—the clandestine service; the Directorate of
Intelligence (DI)—analysis; the Directorate of Science and Technology (DS&T); and the Directorate of Administration (DA). They
represented four distinct, very different bureaucratic cultures. The
Agency in 1969 was totally dominated by the clandestine service.
Its division chiefs (Near East, Soviet Bloc, etc.) were powerful figures in their own right and not afraid to run their own shows
independent of both the DCI and the head of the clandestine service (the Deputy Director for Operations—DDO). They would
decide what to share with their boss and he would decide what
would be given to the director. While this independence was curtailed under Helms because he had run the clandestine service and
was one of the club—indeed, he ran the club—both before and
after Helms the clandestine service aggressively asserted its unique
place and its independence in the Agency.

The Directorate of Operations (formerly Plans) was and still
is the heart and soul of CIA. Many different organizations in Washington have analysts who study the international scene. Satellites
can be and are designed in several institutions. But only CIA runs
spies, develops the technologies to support them, and has carried
out covert actions at the behest of the President. And in CIA, only
the clandestine service and its support elements routinely place

officers in dangerous and risky situations abroad, where they live and succeed by their wits—and expose their families often to extraordinary hardship. State and Defense Department officers face hardship and death as well, but the work of spies makes risk routine and danger the companion of every day's work. For them, secrecy is not a convenience or a bureaucratic matter, but the essential tool of their craft—without it, sources are executed, operations fail, case officers' careers are cut short, and sometimes they and their agents die. Their culture, their ethic were CIA's in 1969. They ran the Agency bureaucratically and dominated it psychologically. And few questioned the rightness of that.

The other leading element of the Agency was the Directorate of Intelligence (DI), the analytical branch of the house. Filled with scholars and specialists of every discipline, from the hard sciences to the social sciences, the DI was rooted in the tradition of the Research and Analysis branch of the OSS, the most successful part of that wartime organization.

CIA's analysts gathered information from spies, embassies, the world's press, and satellites, integrated it, and kept the President and Congress informed of what was going on around the globe. And they did it better than anyone else on earth. In forecasting the intentions of foreign governments or how many missiles the Soviet Union would have in five years, their record was spotty, dotted with spectacular successes (e.g., the 1967 Middle East war) and spectacular failures (the Soviet missile buildup of the 1960s). But the failures were not yet acknowledged and there was a sense of superiority not just to other intelligence agencies but to the policymakers themselves, most of whom were regarded as parvenus. What was real, however, was an unparalleled ability by CIA to describe existing military capabilities and the technical characteristics of weapons, as well as to gather and offer (understandably and usably) massive amounts of information and to do so unswayed by departmental programs or the need to defend policy. The analysts often brought their own biases—most especially a mind-set opposed to nearly any view or proposal offered by the Department of Defense—but still they represented for the President a vital, independent view. And, what's more, in bureaucratic terms, they were his like no other part of the government. Still, Nixon and Kissinger more often than not disdained this asset.

Clandestine operators and analysts had little contact with one another in 1969, except at the topmost level. As a young Soviet analyst, I—like my colleagues—had one point of contact in the clandestine service's Soviet Bloc Division, a low-ranking officer responsible for processing incoming reports from the field and disseminating them to the great unwashed, which included us.

The consequences of this bureaucratic Berlin Wall were minimal at that time only because, thanks to the excessive zeal of Angleton and his counterintelligence staff, during this period we had very few Soviet agents inside the USSR worthy of the name. As Angleton's power eroded within the Agency, his level of suspicion and even paranoia perhaps grew. After James Schlesinger became DCI, he developed serious concern about Angleton, not knowing exactly what to make of him. Schlesinger asked one of his special assistants, Sam Hoskinson, a friend of mine, to talk to Angleton and see what was going on—including about the relationship with the Israelis, which remained under Angleton's control. Hoskinson years later told me that he had gone downstairs to Angleton's office for this discussion and found him seated behind his desk, blinds drawn, a single desk light on. Chain-smoking. Over a forty-five-minute period, according to Hoskinson, Angleton spun out a long and convoluted explanation of Soviet conspiracy that concluded with the declaration that Schlesinger (the DCI) was one of "them." Hoskinson, until then lost in this Byzantine tale, reacted with shock and told Angleton that he would have to tell Schlesinger what he had just alleged. Sam told me that Angleton then glared at him and said simply, "Well, then, you must be one of them, too."

Angleton by the end of his career had become a caricature of a counterintelligence officer, so much so that his personality and behavior became an obstacle to serious consideration of the very real problem of determining whether CIA or the U.S. government had been penetrated by a foreign intelligence service or whether a recruited spy was real and his information valid. Under Angleton, suspicion finally went too far, but when he left, in reaction to him and to his methods, the bureaucratic pendulum swung too far in the other direction. CIA would pay a heavy price in the 1980s for not taking counterintelligence seriously enough after he left.

We in CIA worked terrible hours, but we had a lot of fun, too. We collected outrageous reports for a "Great Moments in Intelligence" file—items such as the Cambodian situation report from the Commander-in-Chief, Pacific, to the Chairman of the Joint Chiefs that said, "The situation becomes clearer—although still not too good, by the same token it is not too bad." Or a

1968 report from Iran graphically detailing visiting Soviet Premier Aleksei Kosygin's success at a state dinner in caressing the inner thighs of the wife of the Iranian governor-general and her corresponding "Iranian dance of hands, head and bosom." Or the note from the Agency's Operations Center describing the movement of Cambodian troops toward the Bassac River as moving "Bassacwards." We, like the President we served, may have been isolated and even besieged, but we didn't know it then and, with our level of hubris, wouldn't have cared if we did. It was the calm before the investigatory storm.

The CIA in 1969 had not yet been traumatized by a multitude of investigations that exposed ill-fated or ill-conceived operations, nearly all undertaken at presidential direction. Most of us then had only a glimpse—mainly through *Ramparts* magazine—of Agency involvement in U.S. institutions and activities, or in collecting information on Americans. That was yet to come. We were at the end of an era, and we didn't even know it.

Moscow's Problems

Fortunately, the other superpower had its own troubles. Washington's need, for domestic purposes and alliance politics, to establish a better understanding with the USSR was paralleled in Moscow. Above all, by 1969 the Kremlin's problem with China had become acute.

As political relations deteriorated, small-scale border clashes began and increased in frequency. CIA learned in early 1969 that the Chinese had become especially offended by the aggressive patrolling of a unit led by a particular Soviet lieutenant of the border guards, whom the Chinese regarded as very pushy. CIA found out from several sources that at one point a number of Chinese soldiers lined up on the bank of the Ussuri River, turned their backs on the Soviet soldiers on the opposite shore, dropped their pants, and "mooned" the Soviets. The next time it happened, the Soviet soldiers were prepared and when the Chinese mooned them, they held up pictures of Mao so that the Chinese were making this gesture to their own leader. It ended the practice.

The situation boiled over on March 2, 1969, when some 300 Chinese soldiers ambushed the "pushy" lieutenant's patrol on Damansky Island (Chenpao on Chinese maps) in the channel of the Ussuri River and killed dozens of Soviet border guards. The Soviets retaliated against the Chinese on the island with a furious counter-attack on March 15, involving both armor and artillery. The results of the battle were apparent to our satellites. One photo interpreter told us that after the battle the Chinese side of the river was so pockmarked by Soviet artillery that it looked like a "moonscape." The Soviets, having proved their point, then left the island and the Chinese resumed control.

The most costly aspect of the rivalry with China and the border confrontations in 1969 was the impetus given China's leaders to reach out to the United States. Soon, the first steps were under way that in 1971 would lead to a historic diplomatic revolution, the reconciliation between the United States and China.

After toying with Nixon for two years, Moscow suddenly found itself outmaneuvered and disadvantaged. The Soviet leaders simply could not allow the United States and China to develop a relationship independent of and hostile to the Soviet Union. Since reconciliation with Mao was out of the question, the Soviets found themselves compelled also to reach out to Washington for a new kind of relationship.

It was all an extraordinary turnabout in the strategic equation. Nixon had pulled off a strategic coup of historic proportions in a way that greatly strengthened the American position in the world and dramatically complicated the Soviet position precisely where they felt most vulnerable—and where they had, from 1969 on, hoped for U.S. help. It was, for Moscow, a nightmare come to pass.

The second motive for Soviet interest in improved relations with the West was the sorry state of the Soviet economy. That the Soviets had serious economic troubles came as no news to anyone. From the late 1950s forward, CIA had documented the chronic and growing economic weakness of the Soviet Union as well as its growing military power.

There was no debate in Washington in the late 1960s over CIA's assessments of the Soviet economy. CIA provided to the policymakers and to the public a generally accurate portrayal of trends in the Soviet economy and its serious weaknesses. And every President from Johnson onward would base his policies and attitudes toward the USSR, at least in part, on the belief that it was a country in increasing economic difficulty—and, later, in crisis.

The Soviet leaders' unwillingness to make basic changes in economic priorities—heavy industry and the military were consistently given top billing—or in the economic structure left them with little choice by the late 1960s but to turn to the West both for technology and to buy grain because of their inability to meet their own needs. This, then, required an improvement in political relations with the West. Thus, by the end of the 1960s, First Secretary Leonid Brezhnev and his colleagues had high hopes that détente would yield economic benefits to them without any sacrifice of their broader political ambitions around the world. They were right—for a while.

Moscow's Other Headaches

There is no question that China and the economy were the primary motives for the Soviets to seek a changed relationship in the West. But there were other problems that weighed on Brezhnev, Kosygin, and the other leaders as well.

The political consequences of the invasion of Czechoslovakia were transitory almost everywhere except in Eastern Europe. The Soviets were especially concerned about continuing problems in Czechoslovakia, Poland, and even East Germany. Economic troubles continued to grow in Poland during the late 1960s, with little increase in wages and perennial shortages of consumer goods. Two bad harvests compounded these problems with real shortages of food. Wladyslaw Gomulka, the Polish party leader, decided in December 1970 to take advantage of the popularity of the just-signed treaty with West Germany to raise food prices, especially meat. The lid came off. There was rioting in Gdansk (the future birthplace of Solidarity) which spread to other cities. Tanks had to be used to suppress the disturbances, and on December 20 Gomulka was replaced by Edward Gierek. A new prime minister was appointed and his first action was to freeze food prices for two years. The situation calmed, but the Soviets had been reminded now in Poland as well as Czechoslovakia that Eastern Europe remained a tinderbox.

Prior to 1969, the Soviets had always spoken positively about an anti–ballistic missile system, and Soviet research and development on ABM and the construction and modernization of ABM sites would continue to be a high Soviet priority until the end of the Cold War. Nonetheless, they hated and feared the idea of the United States developing such a strategic defense, and Nixon's decision in August 1969 to proceed with ABM came as very bad news. All intelligence reporting indicated that the Soviets were worried because, aware how primitive their own system was, they believed the United States could build a far more sophisticated system than they could and, worse yet, do it faster. Their fear of unleashed U.S. technology was evident. After resisting the inclusion of ABM in strategic arms negotiations consistently, the Soviets changed their tune after August 1969. Henceforth, stopping the U.S. ABM (and later the Strategic Defense Initiative) would be the centerpiece of Moscow's negotiating position in arms control—and would remain so until the end of the Soviet Union.

It is apparent that by 1969–1970, Brezhnev, Kosygin, and the rest of the Soviet leadership had ample motive to pursue a better relationship with the United States—China, a troubled economy, Eastern Europe, the prospect of an American ABM. A comprehensive Soviet strategy for approaching the West, the "Peace Program," was put forward on March 30, 1971, in Brezhnev's main address at the 24th Party Congress. Brezhnev made clear then, as he would repeatedly in the future, that détente and improved relations with the West meant no change in Soviet support for "national liberation movements" or any sacrifice of ideological principles. The Soviet leaders plainly believed that they could achieve their goals—and deal with their nightmares—without paying a price.

CHAPTER TWO

So This Was "Détente"?

DÉTENTE WAS BORN in Europe and, realistically, never had meaning or consequence outside of Europe. Notwithstanding overblown political rhetoric about "working together to build a peace," "a new road of cooperation," and "a new age in the relationship between our two countries," throughout the non-European world and in bilateral relations, the Soviet Union and the United States after 1968 continued the same intensely competitive struggle that had characterized their relationship since the late 1940s. This was vividly demonstrated by developments during the "best" days of détente.

After December 1969, the USSR was able to set Vietnam aside as a factor in the bilateral relationship. The Soviets took Nixon and Kissinger to the mountaintop, showed them the wide array of issues on which there could be progress—SALT, Berlin, the Middle East, a summit meeting—and the President chose to go forward without Soviet cooperation on Vietnam. Détente and the Soviets were irrelevant to the outcome in Vietnam. CIA had warned repeatedly that the Soviets wouldn't help the United States, and that "linkage"— no progress on other issues without Soviet help in getting the United States out of Vietnam—would not work. We said the United States was on its own, and we were right.

Nowhere was the rivalry between the two superpowers, their competition for advantage, more unbridled and intense than in the Middle East. Nowhere was the new relationship supposedly taking shape more irrelevant. In two separate crises in the Middle East in 1970, in Egypt and Jordan, the Soviets played for advantage at the risk of confrontation with the United States and independent of other issues on the bilateral agenda. I do not believe that the Soviets had any grand strategy in this, except for the broad objective of seizing any opportunity that might come along and promise geopolitical gains. What is also apparent is that they felt they could pursue such opportunities without jeopardizing détente in Europe or the developing bilateral relationship with the United States.

The secret Soviet effort to build a support base for their ballistic missile submarines (SSBNs) in Cuba in 1970 is an important further example of their willingness to act aggressively even when the target of opportunity was one of the most neuralgic and sensitive problems in U.S.-Soviet relations. Nixon and Kissinger successfully faced down the Soviets, and the confrontation ended with Soviet reaffirmation of the 1962 understandings and assurances that operational ballistic missile submarines would never again call at Cuban ports.

In the 1971 war between India and Pakistan, Nixon and Kissinger both believed that Moscow had played a perfidious role in supporting India that ultimately threatened a Sino-Soviet war and U.S. involvement on the side of Pakistan and China against the USSR and India. During the entire crisis, the government had been deeply split—mainly between the State Department and the White House. The media and the Congress were bitterly critical of the U.S. "tilt" toward Pakistan (whose government had started the whole problem). We in CIA remained throughout pretty much in the dark about the machinations of our own government. We just puttered along, eager to stay out of the war downtown and trying to track as best we could the war in South Asia.

If the faceoffs with the Soviets in 1970–1971 over Egypt, Jordan, Cuba, and the Indo-Pakistani war took place in the early stages of détente, the third Middle East crisis and ensuing dangerous U.S.-Soviet confrontation occurred at the very height of détente. That crisis was, of course, the Yom Kippur War in October 1973.

The outbreak of the war was a major embarrassment for CIA and the occasion of my worst personal intelligence embarrassment. I was an intelligence adviser to the U.S. SALT delegation in Geneva, and on the morning of October 6 took the morning intelligence summary in to Paul Nitze, a senior delegate, for him to read.

The cable version of CIA's *National Intelligence Daily* that morning reported on developments in the Middle East but again suggested that there was not likely to be a conflict. Nitze read that, looked up at me from his desk, and asked if I spoke French and listened to the radio. I replied "No" twice and Nitze proceeded to inform me that had I answered "Yes" I would have known that war had already broken out—because he had found out from the radio news. I slunk out of his office.

Despite all the rhetoric about new rules for engagement and a new kind of bilateral relationship between the United States and the USSR because of détente, the reality is that the Yom Kippur War demonstrated that none of it counted for much. Nixon believed that the Soviets even encouraged the war. In retrospect, it appears that the Soviets did know about President Anwar Sadat's intentions—probably well before October 3 through penetrations of the Egyptian military—and perhaps tried to dissuade him but, failing that, took no steps to warn the United States or otherwise to head off war. So much for a new approach to international affairs.

It is to Nixon's and Kissinger's lasting credit—and a tribute to their nerves of steel—that they so completely outmaneuvered the Soviets in the Middle East during and after the Yom Kippur War, even as our government was enduring one of its greatest political crises—Watergate, Nixon's firing of Special Prosecutor Archibald Cox (the "Saturday Night Massacre"), and the resignation in disgrace of Vice President Spiro Agnew. Once again, détente had proven no deterrent to hardball global competition. This time, the United States had shown itself to be every bit as unconstrained by the new relationship as the Soviets had been.

THE SOVIET MILITARY BUILDUP

Simultaneously with arms control negotiations and treaties, summit meetings and "Basic Principles" to govern a new U.S.-Soviet relationship, the Soviet military buildup continued without interruption or slackening. The number of Soviet ICBM launchers first matched and then exceeded the U.S. number until the Soviets had nearly 50 percent more than the United States—some 1,500-plus to 1,054. Coming in the wake of that effort was modernization of the entire ICBM force, with four new ICBMs under development, at least three of them equipped with MIRVs. New submarines equipped with missiles of such range that they could be launched at the United States from Soviet ports were under construction, and scores of other new weapons—conventional and strategic—were moving from research and development to deployment.

CIA analysis of Soviet strategic intentions began to take on a new, more worried tone, especially after the arrival in February 1973 of James Schlesinger as DCI. Helms, never close to Nixon, had been fired in late 1972, some believed because he deflected Nixon's effort to have CIA block the investigation of Watergate. The three and a half months Schlesinger was at CIA were a bad time. Senior officials went from a DCI who was one of them, understood the heart and soul of intelligence, and was a gentleman of the old school, to a DCI who had a mandate from Nixon to shake things up, and who intended to toughen analysis, reduce the size of the clandestine service, and cut the budget. Unlike Helms, he had Nixon's total support. But what reached us at lower levels was that senior Agency officials were especially bothered by Schlesinger's abrasive, abrupt treatment of people. He was, we were told, crude, demanding, arrogant, and dismissive of experience. Shirttail out, hair uncombed, in appearance and in manner Schlesinger was most definitely not "old school."

Above all, Schlesinger wanted to rid CIA of people he called "dead wood," especially the "old boys" of the clandestine service that he felt were blocking the way upward for younger, fresher people. He also thought that the Agency as a whole was overstaffed. And so began what the entire Agency came to call "the massacre." In all, Schlesinger in his short stay purged about 7 percent of CIA. People in all directorates were fired, forced to resign or to retire. Nor was it done gently. The largest hit, by far, was taken by the Directorate of Operations—the spies, the collectors of intelligence from human sources, the planners and implementers of covert action. I was later told that on a trip abroad, Schlesinger told one of our chiefs of station, "I'm going to break up Helms's Praetorian guard." That word got around pretty fast, even if apocryphal. Nearly all of us feared for our jobs in the apprehensive atmosphere all this created, but for many of us, there was also some sympathy for Schlesinger's attempt to break the DO's grip on the Agency and to restore energy, zest, and relevance to the CIA. With few exceptions, though, even those who generally supported Schlesinger's goals liked neither him nor his methods. To this day, despite a tenure of only fourteen weeks, among those who were in the

Agency then, Jim Schlesinger remains the most unpopular director in CIA's history.

The new director felt strongly that CIA analysis was too academic, too often irrelevant to the needs of policymakers. He would acerbically remind us, "CIA *is* a part of the American government, you know." He was especially intent on making our analysis of Soviet strategic developments more tough-minded and realistic.

It was in this environment in the spring of 1973 that a new national intelligence estimate was commissioned that would strike a more skeptical tone toward the USSR and Soviet intentions. I did the first draft of this estimate ("Soviet Strategic Programs and Détente: What Are They Up To?"—Special National Intelligence Estimate 11–4–73), and it was then handed over for a rewrite to one of the assistants Schlesinger had brought into the Agency, Fritz Ermarth from the Rand Corporation. The estimate was published on September 10, 1973.

This national intelligence estimate told U.S. policymakers less ambiguously than usual estimates that the Soviets were going to try to have it both ways—the advantages of détente (which were real for the Soviets) and an unconstrained strategic buildup; that, for the first time, because of internal U.S. problems, they actually saw a chance that the military buildup could bring real strategic advantage (by U.S. default); and that they would not moderate their buildup unless persuaded it would provoke a U.S. reaction that would jeopardize their gains or that they could attain their objectives through arms control.

The estimate accurately captured the full momentum of the Soviet military buildup and portrayed a much more aggressive Soviet Union seeking whatever advantages it could obtain. It reflected the kind of Soviet behavior the United States had seen in the Middle East in 1970 (and would see again in October 1973, only a month after publication of the estimate), Cuba in 1970, and India-Pakistan in 1971. With this estimate's preparation—reflecting Schlesinger's intellectual legacy—and its publication in September 1973, CIA and the U.S. intelligence community fell to the back of the détente parade.

A LITTLE GOOD NEWS

The one issue where linkage worked was Berlin, and it was there (and only there) that détente had meaning for a regional problem.

Of the Europeans racing to cut their own deals with the Soviets during this period, the West Germans were the swiftest. The West German government, led by the new chancellor, Willy Brandt, on November 16, 1969, made a formal proposal to the USSR to begin talks on an agreement for the mutual renunciation of force. Nixon had little choice but to support Brandt's policies toward the East *(Ostpolitik)*. But he and Kissinger also knew that Brandt needed an agreement on Berlin to get his treaties with the Soviet Union and other communist states ratified at home. They thus used the so-called Eastern treaties as leverage (or linkage) with Brandt to keep him under control and with the Soviets to make clear to Moscow that the gains it sought through agreements with West Germany could be realized only with agreement on Berlin.

The Berlin negotiations were at last successful and the Quadripartite Agreement on Berlin signed on September 3, 1971. The Berlin agreement essentially eliminated the city as a flash point in the Cold War, which was far from over. Nixon's effort to link the border guarantees the Soviets sought from West Germany to successful conclusion of the Berlin agreement had worked. Although a less flashy achievement than the opening to China or the summits in Moscow and Beijing, the Quadripartite Agreement was of historic importance. It not only brought an immediate improvement in the lives of many people; combined with the Eastern treaties it created a climate in Central Europe that I believe contributed mightily to the profound changes to come in Eastern Europe.

CIA was on the sidelines for the Berlin agreement, but from the beginning of the strategic arms limitation talks (SALT), the Agency was an integral and constant participant. It is no exaggeration to say that there would have been no SALT, no arms control at all, without CIA's active involvement.

With Helms's steadfast support, the head of the CIA team at the negotiations, Howard Stoertz, brought about a quiet cultural revolution in CIA, the intelligence community, and in the U.S. government generally as day by day he steadily broadened the kind of intelligence information we shared with the Soviets. There was little, if any, internal opposition in CIA. For a bureaucracy that had to be pushed to share information within the same Agency, this truly was revolutionary. And, by the time the negotiations were proceeding intensively, virtually all of the data on Soviet systems under discussion by the two sides were CIA information.

There were risks in this approach and we probably paid a certain price. We plainly gave the Soviets good insight into how much we knew about their weapons programs—and what we did not know. They undoubtedly learned a great deal about both our satellite photographic capabilities and our signals intelligence. We probably helped them improve their capability to deny us information and, perhaps, in some limited areas, to deceive us.

Participation in SALT and arms control delegations would impose other, more political costs on CIA. Just as the Agency would come under attack, especially from liberals, for its involvement in covert action, so too would involvement in arms control increasingly subject CIA to criticism from the political right—from those opposed to arms control in principle and from those who concluded that CIA was biased toward arms control and that this skewed its strategic analysis.

From the date of signature, SALT was controversial, and it would become more so over time as the Soviets continued to expand their strategic offensive capabilities. Conservatives would highlight Soviet noncompliance and cheating on the terms of the agreements and Soviet military developments seen to be inconsistent with them. Liberals would argue that the offensive agreement did not go nearly far enough—that it merely codified the existing programs of both sides and simply channeled the arms race from quantitative to qualitative grounds. I believe these criticisms from both sides were mostly valid.

Even so, I believe SALT and the SALT process were important and made a genuine contribution to keeping the superpower competition under control. The process itself was probably the most useful part. For the first time, the two sides sat down and began a dialogue about their nuclear weapons and, implicitly, their nuclear strategies. Military and civilian experts on both sides were able to take the measure of one another and, at the same time, engage their political leaders in an unprecedented way in learning about the balance of terror.

In concrete terms, SALT began a process of regulating the nuclear arms race. SALT, like détente, would be oversold and pretensions would be made on its behalf that were wholly unwarranted.

It was certainly not disarmament—to the contrary, the number of weapons on each side increased hugely during the negotiations. Even so, the negotiations and agreements put some loose bounds for the first time on what had seemed an open-ended competition. The race became more predictable both in numbers and in kinds of weapons.

Additionally, while critics along all points of the political spectrum would call the negotiations and resulting agreements a deception and a ruse, in reality they provided a certain anchor to windward in the rough seas of the global struggle. Both governments developed a huge political stake both at home and abroad in keeping the talks going, and thus certain bounds were placed on how bad relations could get. Even in the most antagonistic days to come, with the sole exception of 1983, the talks would continue.

Participation in SALT both in Washington and overseas was a real education for me. I saw that the internal negotiations in both our government and the Soviets' were probably tougher and dirtier than between the two countries. The more complicated the issues became, the more senior officials—especially Presidents—found themselves deferring to the experts. Four of the five Presidents I worked for were bored to tears by the details of arms control. And, too often, we not only lost sight of the forest but mistook tiny shrubs for trees. All this was an eye-opening experience. I would forget none of it.

"Détente" was a double-edged sword when it came to the defense budget. On the one hand, the climate of perceived reductions in tensions with the Soviets strengthened the battle cry of reordering national priorities away from defense and toward domestic affairs. On the other hand, when weapons systems were being negotiated with the Soviets, most members of Congress were unprepared unilaterally to eliminate weapons programs which, if traded, could obtain reductions on the other side. This helped keep certain new strategic weapons programs alive in the face of an extremely antimilitary mood in Congress.

Nixon and the country were lucky in these circumstances to have as Defense Secretary Mel Laird, one of the canniest, most deceptive, toughest in-fighters ever to grace the nation's capital. Laird was a double threat bureaucratically because if he couldn't beat you in the Executive Branch, he would go to his former colleagues in the Congress and nail you there. He was an awesome force and during the worst years of antimilitary sentiment was largely responsible for preserving not only our force structure overseas, but also the Trident submarine and missile, the B-1 bomber program, the Minuteman III MIRVed ICBM, a new ICBM (MX), and the Safeguard ABM.

Most of these programs were funded at relatively low levels in their early stages simply to keep them alive. Laird and others in the administration hoped to fund them more fully and accelerate them in the "outyears"—the budgetary future where the Office of Management and Budget promises that all your dreams will come true. The outyears would be a long time in coming, but thanks to détente, the SALT negotiations, and Laird's legerdemain, the programs were there to build on. It would be one of history's little ironies that détente—flawed in so many ways—would play a major role in saving America's strategic modernization programs.

DÉTENTE: THE BALANCE SHEET

Twenty years after Watergate, after Nixon's departure, the era of détente is still controversial. Conservatives still contend that Nixon and Kissinger gave away the farm to the Soviets, that they were led around by the nose by skilled Soviet negotiators, that they were bamboozled in a multitude of ways—that America was the loser. Liberals tend to disdain the cold-hearted balance-of-power approach to the Soviets and an approach that neglected human rights and did not reflect a more idealistic face of America to the world. Conservatives and liberals alike complain that Nixon and Kissinger conceded equality and respect to the Soviet Union without trying to change an internally repressive system. And specific agreements like SALT are still criticized for their shortcomings or failures.

So, from the vantage point of more than twenty years, what is the balance sheet on détente?

On the positive side, as a means of dealing with the U.S. public and the Congress, détente must be counted a success. Détente, and especially its arms control component, was successfully exploited to defend a number of strategic weapons programs from the budget knife on the Hill—from ABM to Trident, cruise missiles, and the B-1 bomber. Engagement with the Soviets and their reluctant acquiescence to negotiations about conventional military forces in Europe finally beat back the Mansfield Amendment and other congressional initiatives to cut U.S. forces in Europe unilaterally. The defense programs that were deployed in the 1980s amid applause from conservatives could not have been started or sustained politically in the Nixon years without détente. During the 1970s, on defense programs, the conservatives were never able to put congressional votes where their mouths were.

Détente—along with the opening to China—also gave the administration a popular and sometimes dramatic vehicle in the early 1970s to sustain a very active foreign policy and to maintain national credibility around the world in the wake of losing a major war and strong domestic sentiment for turning inward.

Nixon and Kissinger further exploited détente effectively to maintain a reasonable degree of alliance cohesion in dealing with the Soviet Union. Linkage in the context of détente produced a genuinely important agreement on Berlin that would essentially eliminate the city as a flash point for the last half of the Cold War. The opening to Eastern Europe under the umbrella of détente and inter-German agreements began a process of engagement there— of planting seeds—that before the decade of the 1970s was out would open the first cracks in the Iron Curtain. Détente also opened a dialogue on strategic arms that would prove more significant than the agreements that resulted, at least until the late 1980s. And it began a process of at least channeling the arms race, or regulating it, in ways that made it more predictable and therefore less dangerous.

At the same time, however, in terms of the U.S.-Soviet struggle, apart from Berlin and the strategic dialogue, very little changed. Contrary to their pious public pledges, each superpower tried to secure "unilateral advantage" over the other whenever the opportunity arose, in the Middle East, South Asia, the Caribbean, and China. Each was willing to go to the brink of major crisis or confrontation to achieve its ambitions in regional disputes. Each was willing to take very real risks to gain an advantage over the other. Neither was prepared to give up a single major new strategic offensive weapon in arms negotiations, even those in research and development, although both embraced the opportunity to avoid spending tens of billions of dollars to build a nationwide antiballistic missile system. And the Soviets, for all their talk, never spent a chip with the North Vietnamese to help the United States get out of Indochina less painfully.

On balance, in the midst and aftermath of America's greatest defeat in war in 160 years, détente helped the President avoid national humiliation, maintain some semblance of a responsible defense budget, aggressively pursue continued American international leadership and engagement, and lead the Atlantic Alliance (and especially Germany) in a disciplined approach to Soviet enticements—with long-term benefits for Berlin and Eastern Europe.

Contrary to the views of conservatives, neither Nixon nor Kissinger had any illusions about the Soviets. They were not "soft" toward the Soviets and in fact played hardball with Moscow on a number of occasions—with considerable success. Nor did they give away any weapons system in SALT. They had few good cards to play in the late 1960s and early 1970s, but in China, the Middle East, Cuba, and elsewhere they often played them very skillfully— and occasionally with genius. At times, they had few options or choices but to take the course they did. They could not realistically be expected to achieve at the bargaining table a one-sided reduction in Soviet strategic weapons or restructuring of Soviet strategic decisions, especially absent any soon-to-be-deployed comparable U.S. capabilities.

Détente's greatest achievement was the opening of consistent contact between the United States and the USSR in the early 1970s —a gradually intensifying engagement on many levels and in many areas that, as it grew over the years, would slowly but widely open the Soviet Union to information, contacts, and ideas from the West and would facilitate an ongoing East-West dialogue that would influence the thinking of many Soviet officials and citizens.

At the same time, détente was discredited after 1974 because, by then, it was readily apparent that neither power was prepared to change its basic adversarial approach to the competition. Further, neither party could get from détente what it most wanted. The United States wanted to stop the Soviet arms buildup and to obtain Soviet help in extracting itself from Indochina. It was unsuccessful on both counts. The Soviets wanted an ally against China and help in dealing with its increasingly severe economic problems. It, too, was unsuccessful on both counts.

From 1969 to the end of 1974, American policy toward the Soviet Union and U.S.-Soviet relations generally were characterized by smoke and mirrors—obscuring the reality of continued competition and enmity, as well as détente's limits and failures, magnifying its modest successes, a time of secret deals and public obfuscation (and deception), all reflecting more accurately than they imagined the personalities of its principal architects.

As the reality of continued superpower competition—and Soviet aggressiveness—became apparent, disillusionment resulted. And disillusioned, Americans denied their leaders the confidence and the means to respond to Soviet opportunism. Americans turned inward, exhausted by domestic crisis and shamed by their own government. Now the price would be paid.

PART TWO

1975–1980: The Mask of Soviet Ascendancy

CHAPTER THREE

American Paralysis

To the White House

I felt like a deckhand on the *Titanic*. I had been interviewed months earlier for the National Security Council staff at the White House, but when the great day to report for work finally arrived, it was July 8, 1974, just one month before President Nixon would announce his resignation. Although the most senior Nixon appointees were mostly gone by then, and several were in or on their way to jail, everyone else around the Old Executive Office Building and the White House still was a Nixon loyalist. The photos on the walls portrayed the "glory days" of the Nixon Presidency and seemed to me as remote from the present as the paintings of his long-departed predecessors. By the time I arrived, Nixon and his Presidency were zombies and the atmosphere at the White House was funereal. The "circle the wagons" defensive crouch of every White House under attack had largely dissipated with the final realization that the President himself had created the mess. There continued to be resentment of the press—I never worked in a White House where that was absent—for their determination to "get" Nixon, but even that seemed halfhearted.

My supervisors at CIA had been unenthusiastic about my accepting an appointment on the NSC staff. Some outright opposed it and warned me I was making a serious career mistake—interestingly (and parochially) not because Nixon's Presidency was going down the drain but because at CIA any assignment outside the

Agency at that time was frowned upon and discouraged. So my move was, from a personal standpoint, somewhat risky professionally. Especially since none of us had any idea when Nixon's and the country's agony over Watergate would end and whether Gerald Ford would keep any of us on.

Even when a Presidency is politically besieged, there is nothing comparable to working at the White House. The pace is frenetic and the hours impossible. Intrigue. Backstabbing. Ruthless ambition. Constant conflict. Informers. Leakers. Spies (at the White House from inside the U.S. government). Egos as big as the surrounding monuments. Battles between Titans. Cabinet officers behaving like children. High-level temper tantrums. I would ultimately work in the White House for four Presidents and I saw it all. The struggles for pride and place, the preoccupying quest for "face-time" (personal encounters) with the President or even his most senior advisers, the cheap thrill of flashing a badge and walking through those massive gates as tourists look on and wonder who you are, young and not-so-young staffers calling friends (or the service station) and having a secretary say, "The White House is calling."

The constant pushing and shoving to get on lists. Lists for NSC meetings, Oval Office meetings, to get on *Air Force One* or the presidential helicopter (*Marine One*), State Dinner guest lists, participation in presidential foreign trips, access to the White House tennis court, the list of those authorized to use White House cars, the White House Mess, parking lists, White House Christmas parties, the South Lawn for Fourth of July fireworks, White House concerts, and countless more lists. Given the effort at every level on a daily basis to get on lists or improve one's position on lists, it is amazing that as much work got done as it did.

The ease with which egos at every level are bruised—these feelings and experiences are common to every person and each administration I would serve in the White House. The embarrassing self-abasement—even by senior people—to get on lists and the tears that accompanied failure were awesome and a little scary to behold. One senior NSC staffer notorious for the time and energy he spent to get on lists and to get face-time with the President was nicknamed by the Secret Service "the Ferret." The directive among the agents was that if one of them saw a lump under the carpet moving in the direction of the Oval Office he was to step on it—it's the Ferret. The Secret Service would joke about checking the identification of the waiters at a State Dinner if the Ferret was not on the guest list.

Yet while all of the personal clashing, climbing, and game-playing went on (and I am confident always will), the real thrill of working at the White House is not the power trip—you don't have to be there long to know how little real power anyone but the President has—but the chance to be at the center of events, to participate in them, and perhaps even make a difference. There is also the sense of history and pride in being chosen to help the President govern the country and, in the case of the NSC, protect our national security. I knew few people in the White House over a twenty-year span who did not share these feelings going far beyond personal achievement or ambition—no matter how many or how few lists they were on.

When I joined the NSC staff, Henry Kissinger was still both Secretary of State and National Security Adviser (technically, Assistant to the President for National Security Affairs). Lieutenant General Brent Scowcroft was his deputy. Kissinger's right-hand man on Soviet and European affairs, Helmut "Hal" Sonnenfelt, had accompanied Kissinger to State as counselor, and had been replaced by A. Denis Clift, a member of Sonnenfelt's office. William Hyland, also a Soviet expert, had gone to State with Kissinger as well, and after a long hiatus, I was appointed to take Hyland's position.

Kissinger was riding high when I joined the staff, by then a remote, world-famous figure. Writing memos for him in his dual role was like writing for the Wizard of Oz. We hardly ever saw him in person, but the occasional growl or thunderbolt would hurtle down from clouded mountaintops to remind us of his presence and our shortcomings. Neither Clift nor I had any illusions that we had acquired our predecessors' influence along with their offices. Clift was the most competent senior staff officer I ever knew and, over time and as Kissinger's political star waned and Scowcroft became more of an independent force, Clift—with me in his train—through steady, reliable and capable performance, and a low-key, good-humored style, also attained greater influence.

Our work was diverse, ranging from high policy in preparing papers and talking points for the President for important meetings with European and Soviet leaders, to the less cosmic tasks of preparing presidential responses to letters concerning our area, drafting questions and answers for press conferences, preparing press releases on foreign visits, and doing first drafts of speeches and even dinner toasts. We and our colleagues were the President's personal foreign policy staff. He needed one. A common thread of our days was the fruitless effort to persuade the bureaucracy, and especially the State Department, that they worked for the President and might occasionally make time in their busy schedules to support his requirements and implement his policies. One State desk officer once told me, "If I could just get the goddamn President and Secretary of State off my back, I could get my work done."

The experience of supporting the President in the foreign policy arena was a revelation to me as an intelligence officer. I realized quickly that CIA knew how foreign policy was made in every country in the world except one—our own. Analysts and their supervisors were oblivious to how information reached the President. They had no idea of the sequence of events preceding a visit by a foreign leader or a presidential trip abroad, or even the agenda of issues the President and his senior advisers would be working on during a given week. In short, the distance from CIA's headquarters at Langley to the White House was vastly greater than the drive down the George Washington Parkway. I realized the Agency could do a lot better in supporting the policy-making process if it made an effort to know more about how it really worked.

Clift and I tried to help CIA when we could. For example, we offered advice on the timing of some of their current intelligence. We told them that running the profiles of foreign leaders the very day they were to meet with the President meant the profiles often went unread. After all, that morning the President had to shave, shower, and dress just like other humans, cut his grapefruit and toast his English muffin, and so on. In short, they had to think of the user of their work—they needed to get information to him or to his staff in time for him to be able to read it and use it. The battle for timeliness and relevance of intelligence would be one I would fight for the next twenty years.

CONGRESS TAKES ON THE PRESIDENCY

There was nothing fun about being in the White House in the summer of 1974. Apart from the inevitability of Nixon's demise as President, the Presidency itself was under assault. Our system of "checks and balances" by which each of the three branches of government keeps the other two from becoming too powerful works wonderfully, but it is neither a gentle nor a subtle process. Nor does it function normally as a routine, frequent series of minor adjustments. It is more comparable to the swings of a pendulum than a balancing scale—and one branch (or the mood of the country as a whole) reacts usually only when another branch has acted so stupidly or so egregiously to expand its power as to compel a response. Vietnam and the way Lyndon Johnson escalated and fought the war provoked the congressional attack on the powers of the Presidency. Dislike of Nixon, the way in which he and Kissinger negotiated secretly and deviously, and finally Watergate and Nixon's cover-up greatly magnified the intensity of the attack.

In this period of presidential weakness, Congress sought to capture for itself and from the President a coequal (and, at times, dominant) role in foreign affairs that it had not had since before World War II and America's emergence as a superpower. Congressional attempts to wrest away the initiative on defense matters from the President began soon after Nixon's inauguration.

The first target was defense spending. Because there was no overarching strategy behind myriad congressional decisions and budget cuts, and because the internal budget-cutting process at Defense was so driven by tactical compromises, maneuvering with Congress, and military service politics, the entirety of the defense budget and program lacked rationality and coherence. As a result, our military capabilities and morale were severely degraded over the 1970s. Most force structures remained and a number of weapons programs survived, but training, logistics, communications, operations and maintenance, readiness, and benefits for the troops were starved.

Congress basically left Nixon alone on Vietnam for almost a year. But then, losing faith in the President's willingness to end the war quickly, provoked by the U.S. military campaign against Cambodia in May 1970, and pushed along by the outrage of the media and huge demonstrations targeted on the Cambodian operation, Congress acted to limit Nixon's military options in Southeast Asia by statute. Congressional limitations on Executive authority to conduct military operations in Indochina became especially severe after the Peace Accords were signed.

By 1973, with Vietnam in the background and Watergate in the headlines sapping the President's political strength, the floodgates were open for congressional initiatives in diverse areas to constrain the authority of the President. Nor would this erosion of

Executive authority in national security matters diminish after Nixon was gone. To the contrary, it would gather momentum. Indeed, election of the "Watergate" Congress in November 1974 would intensify congressional activism in trying to establish legislative authority to approve or determine broad policy and strategy and even tactics in diplomacy, defense, and intelligence.

Of all of Johnson's and Nixon's successors, Gerald Ford would shoulder the greatest burden of and pay the highest price for this congressional resurgence. In dealing with the Soviet Union, North Vietnam, another Cyprus crisis involving Greece and Turkey, the civil war in Angola, and other foreign policy challenges, Ford—lacking an electoral mandate or sanction and weakened by his pardon of Nixon—would be the modern President most constrained by Congress. And during this time, 1974–1976, significant new opportunities would arise for the Soviet Union, which, seeing American paralysis, would seize them aggressively.

TARGET: CIA

Because CIA served principally as an instrument of the President, and had no constituency and little support in either the Legislative or Executive branches apart from him, the President's vulnerability after 1973 in turn made CIA vulnerable. His weakness became CIA's. And the unwillingness of Nixon and inability of Ford to shield CIA, the past instrument of Presidents, left it extraordinarily exposed. CIA had been in trouble before—inaccurate estimates, the Bay of Pigs, other flaps—but the support of strong Presidents had enabled it to weather the storm, even if its directors sometimes did not. But beginning in 1973, in the midst of Watergate and at the end of Vietnam, CIA confronted a new kind of investigative journalism, a newly aggressive Congress, and a President who both disliked the Agency and was himself dying a slow political death. CIA now had to face its past, a past of acting at the direction of Presidents, without them. Alone.

The Agency's time of troubles can be dated from early May 1973, when a newspaper account alleged that the White House "plumbers' " break-in at the office of the psychiatrist of Daniel Ellsberg (the leaker of the Pentagon Papers) had been carried out by former CIA employee Howard Hunt, using CIA equipment, and that the files were to be turned over to CIA for evaluation. This surprised both Schlesinger and his successor as DCI, William Colby. To avoid future such surprises, Schlesinger issued a directive on May 9 to all current and former CIA employees asking them to come forward with any information they might have on previous CIA activities that might have been illegal or at least outside its charter. The subsequent compilation of "potential flap activities" by the Agency's Inspector General ran to 693 pages of possible violations of or questionable activities in regard to CIA's legislative charter. The compilation soon became known as the CIA "family jewels."

According to Colby, the "family jewels" included Operation Chaos, directed against the anti–Vietnam War movement; surveillance of U.S. journalists to determine the sources of leaks; all connections to the Watergate conspirators; Agency experimentation with mind-control drugs; and involvement in assassination attempts against Castro, Patrice Lumumba, Trujillo, and more. The same day Schlesinger issued his directive, May 9, Colby was told by White House Chief of Staff Alexander Haig that Schlesinger would be going to Defense and he, Colby, would become DCI.

While Colby was given a rough time in his confirmation hearings, the Senate committee members—apart from the chairman—were unaware as yet of the "family jewels," and so that very sensitive subject did not come up. CIA's skeletons in the closet would remain there for a while longer.

But only until December 18, 1974. On that date, investigative reporter Seymour Hersh telephoned Colby to inform him that he had uncovered Operation Chaos, the surveillance activities undertaken by CIA against antiwar activists. Colby's efforts to explain ended up confirming some of what Hersh had learned and therefore did not deter or mitigate the front-page *New York Times* story on December 22. There was an explosion of press and political outrage.

The first congressional hearing on the family jewels, a joint hearing of the intelligence subcommittees of the Senate Armed Services and Appropriations committees, was on January 15, 1975. When the transcript of the hearing was released to the public, there was another firestorm and deep suspicion that there were still important improprieties that were being kept secret. On January 21, the Senate voted to create a Select Committee to Study Governmental Operations with respect to Intelligence Activities, and Senator Frank Church was named chairman. With Daniel Schorr's report of purported CIA involvement in assassinations on the "CBS Evening News" on February 28, what had been an anti-CIA frenzy became hysteria.

Nineteen seventy-five was the worst year in CIA's history. During a year in which South Vietnam was conquered by the North, the Khmer Rouge took over Cambodia, there was a revolution in Portugal and civil war in Angola, where tens of thousands of Cubans would be sent to fight, the *Mayaguez*, SALT, a crisis with Turkey, and more, CIA's senior officers were preoccupied with the multitude of investigations. Colby was constantly testifying, often several times a week, before a number of congressional committees on virtually the entirety of CIA's history.

At the end of the investigations, CIA had few secrets left other than the names of sources and some of its technical collection capabilities. Certainly, there were few secrets about its operational activities. And when, by the end of the year, the investigations were over or winding down, the conclusions of the Church committee were not far from what Colby had reported at the beginning of the year. Both the Church and Pike committees had to concede that CIA had not operated independently as a "rogue elephant," that it had in fact been an operating arm of Presidents, and that its misdeeds—while real and at times egregious—had been far less horrific than portrayed in the rhetoric of congressmen or foreshadowed by news accounts earlier in the year.

Unfortunately, a pattern had been established. Any allegation against CIA was automatically credible, no matter how farfetched, always good for a headline for a journalist, a legislator, or even the occasional crook. But when the facts relating to most allegations were established by congressional, Executive, or legal investigators, they were usually either far less malign or showed innocence of wrongdoing. Somehow, though, the more balanced account or absolution never got much play. Just like the full final conclusions of the Church committee.

With the murder of Richard Welch, CIA's station chief in Athens, in December 1975, and a reawakened awareness that the Soviet Union was still out there and that the world was still hostile, came recognition that a secret intelligence service—and secrets—were still necessary. Yet, even though the furor died down, CIA's status and role had changed forever. If CIA had been acting as the President's agent in many of its improper actions, then the way to control CIA was to dilute the President's heretofore nearly absolute control over the Agency. And that would be done by a much more aggressive congressional oversight mechanism, one not dominated by old congressional lions who would protect CIA, but rather by permanent committees representing the full political spectrum that would review not just budgets, but the entire range of agency activities from analysis to covert action. At a time when Congress was taking flexibility, authority, and power from the President in other areas of foreign policy, so, too, would it take away his unique power over CIA.

Steadily, during and after 1975, CIA would move from its exclusive relationship with the President to a position roughly equidistant between the Congress and the President—responsible and accountable to both, unwilling to act at presidential request without clearance from Congress. And after 1975, most of CIA's senior professional career officers would accept this reality and do their best to serve two masters, however awkward.

After experiencing the Schlesinger purge in 1973 and the many changes Colby instituted in 1973–1974, the people in CIA spent a year in public purgatory. We all had told ourselves before 1975 that we were unique in our skills, in the quality of our people and of our work, and in our bureaucratic status in Washington and abroad. If people "on the outside" had any view of CIA, it was one of a place of power and mystery, that not a leaf fell anywhere in the world that CIA didn't know about it—or cause it. Those illusions were stripped away in 1975. Our pride, however based on a fiction, took a blow from which we never recovered. We all would go home at night and face spouses and children who had watched news of poison dart guns and assassination attempts and other nefarious activities and question whether that was a place they wanted a spouse or father or mother to work. Some colleagues became estranged from their college-age children, who couldn't understand how a parent could work in a place like CIA. There was intramural bitterness inside the Agency as analysts and others complained about the clandestine service bringing disrepute onto the Agency.

There was considerable criticism at the White House and in CIA of Colby and his cooperation with the investigations. Colby to this day remains controversial in CIA circles, especially for his revelations to the Congress and his at least implicit role in the eventual indictment of Dick Helms for misleading Congress on CIA's Chilean operations. I met Colby only after he became Director and when he would meet weekly with the national intelligence officers to discuss estimates and global developments. He looked like a stereotypical teacher, slicked-back hair, glasses with clear plastic frames, thoughtful and low-keyed, constantly fidgeting with a couple of yellow pencils. He was friendly and treated us with courtesy. I was once asked to join several other junior officers to have lunch with him and share our thoughts about the Agency and its direction. He seemed to me to be open to new ideas and approaches.

I saw Colby then, and now, as a reform Director—as someone from the inside prepared to make changes in order that CIA do its job better and as a person who saw sooner than others that, after Nixon and Watergate, CIA's role would not be the same. Facing the investigations, he was very much alone. The White House—especially Kissinger and Scowcroft—was consistently critical of his willingness to accede to congressional demands for information, though I am convinced they would never have been able to persuade Ford to instigate a constitutional crisis only months after Nixon's resignation to try to prevent the Congress from getting CIA's documents. The White House and people inside the Agency criticized Colby for preparation of the "family jewels," forgetting that it was Schlesinger who had ordered employees to report. Colby made some tactical mistakes—like taking to the Hill for "show and tell" a dart gun for administering poison—but I believe he had no choice in 1975 but to cooperate.

Colby did not have many allies among Agency retirees and senior DO officers, especially after Helms ran into difficulty. He was regarded by many as having sacrificed his former colleague and patron. And many thought his cooperation with the investigators was destroying the Agency. Perhaps it is because I was Acting DCI during the most intense period of the Iran-Contra investigations that I am sympathetic to Colby's actions during 1975. No one knows whether CIA would have survived had he taken a much tougher tack, had he resisted. Because I believe President Ford would not have backed such a course to the extent that would have been needed—a constitutional confrontation—and would have been forced ultimately to give way to Congress either politically or legally, I believe resistance to the investigations would have been useless and very costly to CIA. The forces Colby faced—a new and different kind of Congress, an aroused press, public outrage, and a weak President—were overpowering. It is to his credit that, whether or not he recognized all this at the time, he eventually placated these forces or accommodated to them in a way that made possible CIA's continued effectiveness as an intelligence service— even if now under joint presidential-congressional management.

Despite Colby's efforts, CIA was, for all practical purposes, traumatized and weakened for most of the rest of the 1970s. Schlesinger's purge, the congressional investigations, a huge turnover of professionals because of retirements and resignations, continued budget reductions, and a new administration in 1977 openly hostile to CIA and intelligence (many of whose appointees served on the Church committee)—all affected morale. There was little interest inside the Agency in advancing bold new operational ideas even as the Soviets charged ahead in the Third World. After the mid-1970s, to a large extent CIA became just another Washington bureaucracy, and self-protection—conscious or not—would be its hallmark. And this just at a time when successive Presidents would again look to CIA to bear the primary burden of countering new Soviet aggressiveness in the Third World.

CHAPTER FOUR

The "Third World" War

WHEN GERALD FORD, the first appointed Vice President, became President on August 9, 1974, he was weakened by lack of electoral sanction and by his pardon of Richard Nixon. These inauspicious circumstances were made the more so by a Congress on the rampage against Executive prerogatives and authority (including over CIA). To make matters worse, the new Congress elected in November 1974 (the "Watergate Congress") quickly turned against not just Executive authority but the authority of their own leadership in the legislature as well. Unfortunately, the rest of the world —and, most particularly, the Soviet Union—noticed our disarray and weakness. And if Soviet policy during that period is regarded, in the best light, as ruthlessly opportunistic, the next several years would present them with a number of opportunities—which they seized ruthlessly.

VIETNAM

As if fate demanded the fullest measure of American humiliation in Vietnam before it would free the United States of this tragedy, the first disaster awaiting Ford was in Indochina. The final North Vietnamese offensive in Cambodia began on January 1, 1975. A week later the final offensive in South Vietnam began. Ford asked the Congress on April 10, 1975, for $722 million for ammunition for the Saigon government. The request was rejected out of hand. The Cambodian capital of Phnom Penh fell to the

Khmer Rouge the next day and Saigon to Hanoi's army less than three weeks later, on April 29.

The Soviets remained consistent to the end. They refused to approach Hanoi to request time for an orderly evacuation of refugees, the Soviet Ambassador to the United States, Anatoliy Dobrynin, saying that they couldn't help because of the hard-line attitude in the North. In response to threats from Kissinger, the Soviets did, apparently, help arrange a brief pause in the final offensive, but only to allow the hasty evacuation of Americans.

ANGOLA

Spring 1975 marked an ending and a beginning of the superpower struggle in the Third World. It saw the end of the Vietnam War for the United States, and final communist victory and American defeat there. The U.S. experience in Indochina, and the domestic travail it entailed, seemed to say to politicians and military officers alike "Never again!" The perception quickly grew that it would be a cold day in hell before the United States again involved itself militarily in a Third World struggle. This near-universally accepted conventional wisdom, shorthandedly termed "the Vietnam Syndrome," would have profound implications for CIA, because even as the benediction was being pronounced on Vietnam in the spring of 1975, a new arena of superpower competition had opened, in Africa.

A new, significant opportunity for Soviet involvement in Africa came in 1974 with a military coup in Portugal that brought to power a leftist military regime with close ties to the Portuguese Communist Party. The new Portuguese government quickly announced its intention to divest Portugal of its colonial empire and grant independence to the former colonies—most importantly, Angola. A successful right-wing countercoup in Portugal in March 1975 did not alter the decision in Lisbon to let Angola go and independence day for Angola was set for November 11, 1975.

There were three factions in Angola vying for control of the country when it became independent: the Popular Movement for the Liberation of Angola (MPLA), a communist group close to Cuba and the Soviets and led by Angostinho Neto; the National Front for the Liberation of Angola (FNLA), led by Holden Roberto, who had been supported earlier by both the United States and China; and the National Union for the Total Independence of

Angola (UNITA), led by Jonas Savimbi, who also had had a long relationship with the Chinese and later would be supported by South Africa. These three had fought Portugal separately for Angolan independence and, based on an agreement among them with Portugal—the Alvor Accords—reached in January 1975, were to form a coalition government to prepare for elections.

Although the Soviets had provided a small subsidy to Neto for many years, at the beginning of the 1970s they had not yet decided which of the three factions to support. Soviet sources later told us that they had suspected Neto of having ties to the West and they also knew that he had a serious drinking problem. They once again threw their support to him after 1973, primarily because China was supporting the other two factions.

For some time, before and after the 1974 radical coup in Lisbon, communists in the Portuguese army had been facilitating the shipment of Soviet and Cuban arms deliveries to the MPLA. Staging areas had been established by 1974 in the Congo Republic, with training centers and transshipment points in Brazzaville, the capital. The Soviets, in October 1974, stepped up the supply by air and sea of Soviet weapons to the MPLA in anticipation of the struggle for control of the newly independent country. And, in December, they began to provide training on the new weapons for MPLA troops in the USSR.

Shortly after the January 1975 agreement between the Portuguese and the three factions—all of which were tribally based, lending an ethnic aspect to their conflict—CIA proposed to the White House that a very limited amount of money be provided to Holden Roberto's FNLA for political organization. The suggestion was considered by the "40 Committee," the NSC group that weighed and monitored covert actions, and it approved $300,000 for political assistance—a printing press and campaign materials—to the FNLA, to be infiltrated from Zaire. It was a trivial gesture compared to the longstanding and now rapidly growing Soviet military help to the MPLA. The notion that this minuscule CIA assistance was even noticed at the time, much less that it provoked the massive Soviet and Cuban buildup that followed, as alleged by some, is silly.

The MPLA asked the Soviets in January 1975 for more assistance, and soon additional weapons and military support began arriving by airlift through Congo-Brazzaville and by ship. A contingent of Cuban military advisers also was sent to help Neto, and in May some Cuban mercenaries and regular troops. Thus reinforced, the MPLA launched a full-scale offensive on July 9, and succeeded in driving both the FNLA and UNITA out of Luanda.

The U.S. response to this activity was not to jump in but, more typically, to dither. As usual, the State Department detested any covert action that wasn't its idea and wrote a paper recommending diplomatic measures to deal with the situation.

Also as usual, CIA didn't like the idea of getting further involved either. Beyond the fact that covert action rarely has been "career enhancing" in the clandestine service—as opposed to recruiting agents—and thus was generally unpopular within the Agency, another real-world consideration not of interest to the grand strategists downtown was CIA's limited capability at that point to carry out a major covert operation. CIA had been shedding covert assets and capabilities with near-abandon since closing down its activities in Vietnam. Added to that was the Schlesinger massacre, which had focused in particular on getting rid of covert action officers. The cumulative effect of these factors—and the conviction that a CIA covert program could not counter a massive, overt Soviet assistance program and thus could not succeed—all led CIA to hang back on Angola.

With both CIA and State lukewarm to hostile to further involvement, nothing happened until summer 1975. At that point, Kissinger became actively involved and pushed the issue, in no small part because of the juxtaposition of a possible communist takeover of Portugal and of Angola at nearly the same time. At his urging, CIA finally came forward with a proposal for weapons and other help for the FNLA and a reduced version of the same for UNITA. This program and some $14–$17 million in military assistance to the FNLA was approved by the "40 Committee" and then by President Ford in early July. Another $10 million or so was added in late August for a total covert program in Angola by September 1975 of about $25 million. It is worth noting that the governments of both Zaire and Zambia—Angola's neighbors—supported the covert program of military assistance to the MPLA's opponents. Joseph Mobutu agreed to let Zaire be the staging base for arms shipments to the FNLA, and Zambia's Kenneth Kaunda permitted transshipment bases in his country for help to UNITA. The first planeload of arms left the United States on July 29.

The FNLA and UNITA—now with United States, Chinese and South African logistical help and several thousand South African troops—took the offensive that summer and moved toward the capital, Luanda. At this point, the MPLA again asked Moscow for more help. The Soviets told Neto to approach Castro. He did so in early August and shortly thereafter Castro agreed; an extraordinarily well coordinated Soviet-Cuban air- and sealift of troops (from Cuba) and equipment for them (from the USSR) soon followed. Indeed, it represented the largest Soviet deployment of matériel to a non–Warsaw Pact country we had seen up to that time. By November, some 4,000 Cuban troops were in Angola and Castro himself would later admit that by the end of 1976 there were some 36,000 Cubans in Angola. CIA estimated that by February 1976, the Soviets had sent 38,000 tons of supplies and weapons at a cost of about $300 million. The record suggests rather strongly that the Soviets were not as reluctant to become involved in Angola as they would later claim—just clever.

As the Ford administration watched the Soviet and Cuban buildup in the fall of 1975, and the reversals suffered in November by the FNLA and UNITA, it asked CIA for a new options paper. The Agency responded with alternative programs at different levels of funding. Approximately another $30 million in military and other support to Holden Roberto and Savimbi was approved. Unable to fund this out of the Agency's contingency funds, Colby went to the Congress to secure additional money.

The DCI's effort to get more money aroused opposition in Congress, and criticism that we were getting involved in another Vietnam. The entire Angola operation was leaked to investigative reporter Seymour Hersh of the New York Times, and it became public in a page-one story on December 13. This, together with Colby's request for more money, prompted Senator Dick Clark to submit an amendment to cut off all covert assistance to any faction in Angola. His amendment passed the Senate on December 19. A bitterly resentful President signed the Clark Amendment into law on February 9, 1976.

Thus, U.S. involvement in the Angolan conflict ended for a decade, after spending some $30 million—at most one-tenth the estimated Soviet spending to that point. As Cuban forces flooded into Angola and U.S. assistance ended, Holden Roberto's FNLA collapsed, the South Africans withdrew, and Savimbi's UNITA was forced back into the bush of its tribal homeland in southeastern Angola.

As Arkady Shevchenko, the seniormost Soviet defector to the United States, later wrote, the Soviet leaders were overjoyed by this ignominious end to U.S. involvement in Angola. The next time an opportunity presented itself, in Ethiopia, the Soviets would not hesitate to take the lead themselves, regardless of how provocative, bringing the Cubans along. The Soviet leaders did not seem to mind that with each such step, the U.S.-Soviet relationship was deteriorating and in Washington that détente was quickly becoming tarnished and a political liability.

Round one in the "Third World" war, Angola, went to the Soviets and Cubans. The next round would involve a new American team. A more aggressive Soviet role in Africa and elsewhere in the Third World was just beginning, and would dog the new administration throughout its four years. Internal divisions in the new administration over how to respond, evident within weeks, would make the Soviet challenge in the Third World even more difficult to meet.

CARTER AND COMPANY

After the 1976 election, I decided to return to CIA from the NSC, largely because I assumed that the new team would replace all of us anyway and I wanted to leave under my own steam. After nearly three years at the White House, I had a hard time readjusting to the Agency bureaucracy. So when David Aaron, deputy to the new National Security Adviser, Zbigniew Brzezinski, called me on May 5, 1977, to ask if I was interested in returning to the NSC to work for them, I quickly said yes. I was later told by one of the secretaries in the office that Brzezinski and Aaron had been complaining that they had fired everyone who knew how to make the NSC bureaucratic process work and that another secretary had mentioned my name as someone who could help. I met with Aaron the next day, had a brief conversation with Brzezinski, and was hired. Well, almost. The new Director of CIA, Stansfield Turner, apparently was concerned that I might assist Brzezinski in circumventing the DCI's proper role and delayed my departure from CIA until his concerns were allayed. I reported to my new office in the West Basement of the White House on May 23, 1977. I would eventually occupy four different offices in the West Wing under three Presidents.

Unlike many others, I took an immediate liking to both Brzezinski and Aaron—although it is hard to imagine two more different people. Brzezinski was organized and neat to the point of fastidiousness. I especially liked Brzezinski because he treated the support staff—secretaries, security people, the Situation Room staff, baggage handlers—with respect and dignity. He might be hard on the professional NSC staff—as Kissinger had been—but they were there by choice and could defend themselves. Toward others he was a gentleman. He infrequently swore and, though something of a flirt, was prudish in his own behavior and his view of the behavior of others. He had a good sense of humor, though I don't believe I ever heard him tell a joke at his own expense.

Brzezinski relished outmaneuvering others. When Turner became DCI, he noticed on the President's schedule that Brzezinski was listed as giving an intelligence briefing at 6:30 A.M. He told Brzezinski that, as DCI, *he* should be giving the intelligence briefings. Brzezinski loved recounting how he told Turner he agreed with him and the next day showed the DCI the President's schedule that now listed at 6:30 A.M. a "national security briefing" —thus no DCI. During the energy crisis one summer, Carter ordered all the thermostats in the White House set several degrees higher to reduce energy consumption by the air-conditioning. Maintenance people were sent around periodically to make sure people had not reset the gauge—we called them the "thermostat police." Brzezinski moved a lamp under his thermostat so that the heat from the light would cause the air-conditioning to cut on. He really didn't care about the temperature; beating the system was what gave him pleasure.

Brzezinski had a disciplined mind, had thought and written extensively about the Soviet Union and Eastern Europe, had a strategic approach, and was in my view very realistic about the Soviets. He was articulate to the point that many thought him glib. A lifelong professor, he relished verbal dueling and gave no quarter to the professional staff or others in the government. He debated like he played tennis—to win and to win all the time. The intellectually weak or deficient or slow merited no sympathy. Sometimes his combative instincts overcame his good judgment and he would reject ideas or approaches simply in the course of winning a debater's point. Accordingly, whenever I had a controversial problem or issue to raise with him, I would do it in writing. I advised others to do likewise. His reactions to the written word were always more considered, more reflective, and better balanced. Then, and now, I considered him by far the most realistic, experienced, and balanced of Carter's foreign policy team. He also was a pleasure to work for.

Toward the end of the Camp David process, when Carter was to go to Cairo and Jerusalem, Brzezinski preceded him by two days to Egypt for preliminary talks with Sadat. I went with Brzezinski. It was my only meeting with the Egyptian president. Zbig finished his work with Sadat quickly and so we had the next day free. We played tourist and went out to the pyramids and Sphinx at Giza. While we were there, an ABC television crew found us and began filming. Somehow getting the notion that Brzezinski wanted to be left alone with his thoughts in that remarkable place, I positioned myself between him and the cameraman twenty or so yards away. When we returned home and he saw the tapes from the news, he put his hand on my shoulder and told me that I was a bright young man who would undoubtedly go far, but not if I ever again got between him and a TV news crew.

He wore his ego lighter than most, however, despite all the talk of his wanting to be as significant a figure as Kissinger had been and his supposed rivalry with Kissinger—which, frankly, I never saw. He and Aaron were always mildly critical of each other's protégés on the NSC staff. Once, at a morning meeting of the three of us, as they were arguing about this, I told them that the staff actually was divided into three parts—Brzezinski protégés, Aaron protégés, and a tiny number of us hired on merit.

For all that has been written about the divisions in the Carter national security team, on a personal level Zbig had a cordial if not close relationship with all most of the time. Until near the time of Secretary of State Cyrus Vance's resignation, the two of them played tennis periodically. And while Brzezinski could be cutting about Vance's views on issues, I don't think I ever heard him say an unkind word about Vance in a personal sense. In fact, the Soviet Union aside—granted, no small exception—it seemed to me that Vance and Brzezinski agreed on a number of issues.

Brzezinski's struggle with Vance was not personal in the sense of ambition, power, and the perception of influence—their differences were deep, philosophical, and were centered, in the first instance, on how to deal with the Soviet Union. They agreed on the desirability of SALT, but Vance believed that arms control was so overridingly important that no action should be taken that might jeopardize negotiations or the political relationship necessary for their ultimate success. On one regional dispute after another, Vance saw each as a local conflict and feared that Brzezinski and others would turn it into an East-West issue imperiling his first priority.

For Brzezinski, SALT had to be embedded in the overall relationship, a relationship that was potentially cooperative but inherently confrontational—and he was convinced that neither aspect could be managed in isolation from the other. At minimum, public opinion would not allow it.

David Aaron was a counterpoint to Brzezinski in almost every respect. He was one of the most personally undisciplined and disorganized people I ever met. In contrast to the very efficient Brzezinski, Aaron hated paperwork and did it at all only under great duress. He had a volcanic temper and a rich blue vocabulary which he exercised routinely. Indeed, one time he was cursing so loudly that Vice President Mondale—his mentor and friend—walked down the hall from his office and slammed Aaron's door.

All that said, David Aaron was one of the smartest people with whom I ever worked. He also had a great sense of humor—was in fact quite funny. I had met him in Vienna in 1971 when we were both on the SALT delegation and he, like so many others, had worked on Kissinger's NSC. He could master complex issues and briefing books faster than anyone I knew. He could cut through all the bureaucratic bull to the heart of an issue quickly and incisively. He was something of an intellectual and policy bully, but if you stood your ground, you always got a hearing. Though considered very liberal politically, actually he was very tough-minded when it came to the Soviets and provided strong support to Brzezinski at critical times. In the two and a half years I spent in the Brzezinski-Aaron front office, the only time I remember the two of them disagreeing vehemently was over Nicaragua in the last days of Somoza. Early in the Reagan years, some right-wingers were very critical of me for my association with Aaron. It was clear that they really knew neither of us or anything about our views, at least on the Soviet Union.

Carter was difficult to fathom. There has probably never been a smarter President in terms of sheer brain power. He had in common with Nixon a cold demeanor even around White House staff and little sense of humor—although Robert Strauss, who ran his 1980 campaign and held several senior positions, once told me that, in private with intimates, Carter had a good sense of humor. I think few, other than intimates, saw it.

President Carter would make individual decisions based on the technical merits, but—as with decisions on weapons systems—somehow failed to grasp that those decisions taken together conveyed a political philosophy or direction. He read voraciously. Brzezinski would send in a long document and explicitly tell the President he needed only to read the summary or the first few pages, but we would get it back later with annotations and even corrections in the remotest annexes. We sometimes referred to him as the nation's "chief grammarian." He even corrected CIA's *President's Daily Brief*, and once wrote Brzezinski a special note to remind him that Mrs. Carter's name—Rosalynn—was spelled with two *n*'s.

This, then, was the team I joined in a junior capacity in May 1977.

ETHIOPIA

In 1974, a communist faction headed by Colonel Mengistu Haile Mariam overthrew Ethiopian Emperor Haile Selassie. Facing a Somali-supported insurgency in the Ogaden desert and a secessionist movement in Eritrea, the new Ethiopian government turned to the Soviets for help. Forced to choose between its old client, Somalia, and a new opportunity in Ethiopia, the Soviets unsurprisingly opted for the latter—with ten times the population and an even more favorable strategic location overlooking sealanes for oil shipments from the Persian Gulf to the West. After the Soviets and Ethiopians signed a military assistance agreement in May 1977, the Somalis turned to the United States for help.

Cuban troops first showed up in Ethiopia at the beginning of July. The presence of those troops was not uniformly welcomed by the people of Ethiopia. The Cubans, like the Soviets, were overbearing, insulting, and disregarded the cultural sensitivities of their hosts. We received a report in May 1978 of increasing evidence of friction between Ethiopians and the Cubans. There were reports in particular of Cuban military abuses against the Ethiopian population, including "charges of theft, rape and mayhem." The most serious accusation against the Cubans, according to one authoritative report, was that of sodomy with Ethiopian goats and sheep. In the latter case, Cubans had been caught in the act of abusing the livestock by Ethiopians who, not surprisingly, characterized the Cubans as "devils."

The crisis in the Horn was the occasion of the first serious clash between Brzezinski and Vance. Brzezinski had believed that an insurgent incursion from Angola into Shaba province of Zaire in

March 1977 had been a Soviet test of the new administration, and he was equally persuaded that the Soviet and Cuban intervention in Ethiopia was part of a larger Soviet strategy to challenge the United States in the Third World. Where Vance wanted to handle Angola, Shaba, and the Horn in isolation from the overall U.S.-Soviet relationship, and SALT in particular, Brzezinski was convinced of the need to link Soviet behavior in Africa and elsewhere to other aspects of the relationship, including arms control.

In the end, the Carter administration took no military or political actions in response to Soviet intervention in the Horn, and the intervention had no impact on the broader U.S.-Soviet relationship. However, the United States had lost a major ally in the Horn of Africa (Ethiopia); our friends in the region—Saudi Arabia, Sudan, Kenya, and North Yemen—felt threatened; and the Soviets had gained an important foothold in a geographically and politically important country.

SUMMER 1978: INTELLIGENCE PUSHES POLICY

Even as the Ethiopian crisis was heating up, President Carter was briefed on June 1, 1978, by Turner and senior intelligence community experts on a new national intelligence estimate, "Soviet Goals and Expectations in the Global Power Arena." The secret assessment (now declassified), published only three weeks before the meeting, signaled a perceptible shift in the intelligence community's thinking about the Soviet Union—a shift toward a more somber assessment of the main thrust of Soviet military policy and of likely Soviet behavior, especially in the Third World. It was not an alarmist estimate, but it was sobering, a cold shower. And it hit the administration just at a time when Brzezinski and others were deeply concerned about Soviet aggressiveness around the world.

Because of the White House actions that flowed from that estimate, it is worth citing certain of its principal conclusions:

• "Soviet military assistance and support to proxies have come to be an effective form of bringing Soviet power to bear in distant areas.

• "Soviet leaders themselves see their foreign policy as essentially revolutionary, resting on the expectation of fundamental changes in the international system and within the states that constitute it, and deliberately seeking—though cautiously and intermittently—to help bring these about.

• "Soviet international behavior in the 1980s is likely to include a purposeful, cautious exploration of the political implications of the USSR's increased military strength. Soviet policy will continue to be competitive and assertive in most areas of engagement with the West."

I am confident that Brzezinski saw the estimate and the briefing of the President as an opportunity to galvanize U.S. government action in response to the Soviet intervention in Ethiopia, their and the Cubans' growing role in Angola, and assertive Soviet behavior elsewhere. Something had to be done.

Brzezinski's next move was to schedule a Policy Review Committee meeting chaired by Vance on August 15, 1978. The consensus of the meeting was that the United States would, in fact, continue to encounter an assertive Soviet Union in foreign policy, and the Third World would be the most dynamic area. Brzezinski and Aaron told us after the meeting that the conclusions of the principals had been much influenced by the realization of growing Soviet military strength and the general decline of U.S. competitiveness.

In the aftermath of the meeting, with Carter's approval, Zbig took several new initiatives to begin to deal with the Soviet challenge. First, he signed on August 24 Presidential Review Memorandum 42, "U.S. Strategy for Non-Military Competition with the Soviet Union," addressed to Mondale, Vance, Defense Secretary Harold Brown, General David Jones, and Turner. It said that the President, pursuant to the August 15 meeting, had directed preparation of options for enhancing the U.S. position vis-à-vis the USSR in the global competition—how to counter Soviet actions in the Third World and how best to take advantage of U.S. economic and technological advantages in the superpower competition. Brzezinski's memorandum also directed development of a broad concept to guide U.S. strategy in key geographic areas; examination of places where there might be specific problems or opportunities for the United States or the USSR relating to political, trade, or military influence; and a study of how to galvanize public and congressional support for administration initiatives.

The same day, August 24, Zbig also signed Presidential Review Memorandum 43, "United States Global Presence." Also a follow-up to the August 15 meeting, it said that the President directed the examination of U.S. military presence abroad from the standpoint of maintaining and enhancing our political and military position vis-à-vis the Soviets and of providing reassurance and confidence to key countries of concern to us. It also directed the development of options for "U.S. military presences" in various areas. This study was to be chaired by the NSC and also was due on October 2.

This is one of the few instances I can recall where a national intelligence estimate provoked such a strong reaction on the part of a President and senior policymakers and led to actions being taken—the two PRMs. Clearly, against the backdrop of events earlier in the year in Africa, the conclusions had hit a nerve.

But the bureaucracy's nerves were shot. Zbig's initiatives ran into bureaucratic obstructionism, again from State and CIA. Opposition to PRM 42 was couched in substantive terms, but I believed then—and still do—that hostility to a more aggressive posture toward the Soviets lurked behind the other arguments. Typical of the objections was a September 26 memo on PRM 42 to State from Arnold Horelick, CIA's national intelligence officer for the USSR, which described the White House guidance as "fuzzy" and the problem as "ill-defined." He said the scope of the paper requested was enormous, "as broad as the scope of U.S. foreign policy," and complained that the way the study was structured plainly focused the PRM on the competition in the Third World.

At the end of the process, in late March 1979, Horelick wrote, "The venture [PRM 42] was doomed from the start and the problem has been how to terminate the exercise with the least damage and visibility, taking into account its originator [Brzezinski]."

SOUTH YEMEN, RHODESIA, AND LIBYA

Angola and Ethiopia would draw the greatest international attention between 1975 and 1978, but the Soviets and Cubans were actively involved elsewhere as well. For example:

• A coup in the People's Democratic Republic of Yemen (PDRY) resulted in an even more pro-Soviet government coming to power. This led to a further expansion of Soviet influence and military presence on the Arabian peninsula, thereby raising the potential for troublemaking in the volatile Middle East.

• In Rhodesia, the Soviets provided arms, training, money, and political support to the Zimbabwe African Peoples Union (ZAPU) and Zimbabwe African National Union (ZANU) guerrilla movements, both of them black nationalist organizations trying to overthrow the white supremacist government.

• During the mid-1970s, the Soviets also established a closer relationship with Colonel Muammar al-Qaddafi in Libya. The real breakthrough came in 1974 when Qaddafi's right-hand man, Major Abdul Salam Jallud, visited Moscow and signed the first of a series of arms deals that would, over a decade, earn the Soviets some $20 billion in hard currency. By the end of 1978, Libya's aggressive policies would bring it to the brink of war with Egypt. Tripoli would have troops in Uganda helping Idi Amin, become militarily engaged in Chad, and try to overthrow the government of Sudan —where one of Qaddafi's planes tried to bomb a major Sudanese broadcasting facility.

It will come as no surprise that I agreed with Brzezinski's general analysis of the situation. After watching from the Ford NSC the Soviet role in the final collapse of Vietnam, their actions in Angola, and their behavior earlier in the 1970s, it seemed apparent to me as I observed from the Carter NSC that the Soviets were continuing to press ahead in the Third World—tactically seizing opportunities, strategically exploiting U.S. unwillingness to become involved again after Vietnam. Whether one agreed with Zbig's proposed actions to raise the costs to the Soviets of this aggressive behavior, his analysis of the consequences—Soviet consolidation of their gains and leaping at the next opportunities—seemed obvious and irrefutable. He understood that Soviet use of Cuban surrogate troops in the Third World represented a new and different kind of challenge which, if left unmet, would inevitably lead to further interventions.

By the same token, Vance's determination to isolate Soviet actions in the Third World from all other aspects of the bilateral relationship; to avoid any U.S. action that might turn regional conflicts into East-West conflicts, long after the Soviets had done just that; to believe that diplomacy could reverse Soviet and Cuban power plays and the realities of force on the ground—all of this struck me as idealistic and naïve. Coming immediately after Vietnam, Vance's approach signaled weakness and invited further Soviet aggressiveness in the Third World—and that's what we got.

Intelligence assessments from January through April 1978 provided indirect support to Brzezinski. A national intelligence estimate in late January on the Soviets, Cubans, and Ethiopia said that the Soviets believed they couldn't afford *not* to react in Ethiopia after a succession of setbacks in the Middle East—Sudan, Lebanon, and Egypt, and expulsion from the port at Berbera, Somalia. They saw a threat to the credibility of their claimed status as a great power with an expanding presence in the world. The estimate went on that the Soviets saw an opportunity in the Horn to consolidate their influence in the most populous East African state, to restore their naval position on the coast of the Horn, to shore up an ideologically sympathetic regime, and possibly to bring about the overthrow of Somali leader Siad Barre.

In April 1978, National Intelligence Officer Arnold Horelick wrote Turner an even gloomier assessment. He pointed out that since 1975, the Soviets had found it possible to intervene on a large scale in Angola and Ethiopia and to secure victories for ideologically congenial forces and, in their view, hoped to secure an enduring presence for themselves. He noted that each intervention had set new precedents: the scope of the Soviet logistical effort, the quantity of military hardware deployed, the size of the proxy Cuban forces, and the severity of political constraints hindering a Western response. Further, he wrote that the most valuable Soviet discovery was the political advantage of the extensive use of Cuban proxies. It was a farsighted and accurate assessment.

CUBA: SURROGATE IN CHIEF

Late in the 1970s, CIA concluded that the Soviet-Cuban military relationship had entered a new phase in 1975. A major Soviet program had begun then to upgrade Cuba's defenses but also to give it the capability to conduct military operations in the Third World. This far-reaching decision apparently was made before the Cuban involvement in Angola became a major intervention. Our conclusion was that some of the weapons provided after the Cuban intervention may have been added to the original modernization program as a "reward" for Cuba's actions in Angola and in Ethiopia. Nonetheless, the program clearly reflected a mutual desire to enhance Cuba's capabilities in future Third World conflicts. The Agency judged in 1979 that the weapons provided since 1975 had transformed Cuba's forces from essentially a home defense force into a military power with "formidable offensive capabilities relative to its Latin American neighbors as well as all but the largest Third World countries."

Soviet-Cuban intelligence cooperation increased as well. The vast Soviet signals intelligence facility at Lourdes, Cuba, was significantly expanded at about this same time. As a joint State-Defense report stated: "From this key listening post, the Soviets monitor U.S. commercial satellites, U.S. military and merchant shipping communications, and NASA space program activities at Cape Canaveral. Lourdes also enables the Soviets to eavesdrop on telephone conversations in the United States."

The modernization of Cuba's armed forces led in late 1978 to yet another flap between the Carter administration and the Soviets —this time over whether the Soviets had provided to Cuba new variants of MiG-23 aircraft that were nuclear-capable—and therefore theoretically capable of serving as an offensive weapon potentially threatening the United States, in contravention of the 1962 and 1970 U.S.-Soviet understandings.

The Special Coordination Committee first met on this issue on November 13, shortly after policymakers received intelligence from CIA that the new MiGs had been sighted through satellite reconnaissance. There was a consensus at the meeting that these airplanes constituted a violation of the 1962 and 1970 understandings with the Soviets, and all agreed to approach the Soviets to register U.S. concern. Vance called in Ambassador Anatoly Dobrynin and conveyed the message on the evening of November 14.

As so often happens to complicate U.S. diplomatic endeavors, the story of the MiG-23s was leaked and published the next morning, November 15, in a column by Roland Evans and Robert Novak. On November 16, the Soviet leadership responded publicly. Kosygin told a delegation of U.S. congressmen that the USSR had never violated the 1962 understandings and that the MiG-23 hullabaloo was "a trumped-up issue." There was no question of a violation of the 1962 understandings.

After weeks of negotiations and publicity—of "understandings," "assurances," and "clarifications"—the U.S. ambassador in Moscow, Malcolm Toon, was instructed by Vance on January 4, 1979, to let the matter stand "as is." The Soviets never wavered from their position that they could provide ground-attack aircraft to Cuba "in unlimited numbers."

The bottom line: The United States had blown the issue up into a major diplomatic face-off with the Soviets, and came away with no change in the situation on the ground. The outcome made Carter look weak, the administration ineffectual, and heightened

the sense—in the wake of the Soviets' Angolan and Ethiopian interventions—of a successfully aggressive Soviet Union. It would not
be the last time. And press leaks during the entire episode made it
impossible to handle the issue discreetly—which at least would
have minimized the damage.

Soviet and Cuban intervention in Angola and Ethiopia, elsewhere in Africa and on the Arabian peninsula, their growing advisory role in the Third World, and the strengthening of Cuba's
capabilities to provide combat advisers as well as to intervene with
its own military forces began a period of years of challenge to the
security and political interests of the United States in the Third
World. Sometimes dismissed at the time in the press and in Congress, and by some in the administration, this aggressive Soviet-
Cuban opportunism to expand their presence and influence (soon
augmented by the complementary efforts of Libya and Vietnam)
was a problem for Ford and bedeviled both Carter and Reagan. And
because all three Presidents chose CIA as their primary weapon to
meet the Soviet-Cuban challenge in the Third World, it would
bedevil us, too.

AGAIN THE CHINESE

If anything, CIA—and the U.S. government generally—underestimated Soviet paranoia about China, and the degree to which
Beijing constantly filled the thoughts of Soviet leaders. Moreover,
I think we also underestimated the degree to which Soviet aggressiveness in the Third World—at least in the mid-1970s—was initially directed as much at China as at the West and the United
States in particular.

The Soviets were absolutely terrified that the U.S.-Chinese
reconciliation in 1971–1972 would be followed by a military relationship—either arms or an alliance or both. On one occasion, CIA
learned that Kosygin had plaintively asked a Danish political leader
in a meeting, "What does all this mean? Is everyone ganging up on
us?" The Soviets knew that exploitation of the triangular relationship gave the United States important strategic advantages. And
they never ceased looking for ways to neutralize that advantage.

One opportunity they looked to for this purpose was the death
of Mao Zedong. The Soviets saw him as the architect of anti-Soviet
policy in China, and hoped and believed that there were other
Chinese leaders more amenable to improved ties with the USSR.

Thus the Soviets saw Mao's death late in 1976 as presenting a chance to alter nearly twenty years of increasing enmity.

Even so, they just couldn't help themselves from jabbing at the Chinese. After Mao died, they spread a story with ghoulish glee that the Chinese had botched the embalming job. According to the Soviet story, the Chinese had sought expert help from the Vietnamese—who had recently embalmed Ho Chi Minh—but it turned out that Hanoi had relied on Soviet assistance. When the Vietnamese asked the Soviets if they could pass along to the Chinese information on the embalming process they had used on Ho, the Soviets refused, saying the Chinese had to come to them directly. The Chinese refused, according to the Soviets, and "self-reliantly" embalmed Mao. However, when they permitted the masses to file by the open casket, they inadvertently exposed the remains to bacteria and an "embarrassing decomposition" occurred.

In December 1976, after Mao went to his reward (presumably unaware that the Soviets continued to vex him after death), the Soviets sent their ambassador and deputy foreign minister Ilichev back to Beijing to assess the position of the new Chinese leadership on Sino-Soviet issues. Ilichev remained until February, and returned to Moscow with extremely pessimistic conclusions. He said, we learned from human sources, that the Chinese were totally unyielding, perhaps even more negative than before Mao died. By the summer of 1977, according to CIA's information, Soviet pessimism about China had further deepened. Post-Mao China was actually tougher and more menacing toward Soviet interests than Mao. The men in the Kremlin looked at the world and saw a Chinese challenge everywhere—Indochina, Eastern Europe, Africa, and even among West European communist parties.

Where Soviet concerns in the spring and summer of 1977 had focused on their political vulnerabilities, by fall they also saw worrisome developments relating to China's strategic military capabilities: a decision to opt for orderly economic growth, thus providing more resources for the military; a turn to the West for basic technology to build up a Chinese defense industrial base; Chinese reception of Western and Japanese officials with military or intelligence expertise (including former U.S. Defense Secretary and DCI Schlesinger, former Chief of Naval Operations Elmo Zumwalt, and former DCI George Bush); continued development and testing of China's nuclear and strategic weapons capability and the development of prototype photoreconnaissance and signals intelligence satellites; and Chinese deployment of about a hundred missile delivery vehicles (our much more accurate estimate was that the Chinese had less than a tenth that number).

Soviet concerns would continue to build, fed by their paranoia and Chinese actions. On April 3, we learned that Brezhnev had told the leaders of the Trans-Baikal Military District during his cross-country rail trip with Defense Minister Ustinov that China was now "the primary enemy," "the number-one enemy."

Just as the Soviets were exploiting new opportunities in the Third World at a time of U.S. political weakness and lack of interest in involvement in such situations, so, too, were they attempting to preempt the Chinese, especially in Indochina and Africa. Thus one of many ironies during this period was the reality that while members of the U.S. Congress, Secretary Vance, others in the administration, and various pundits were stressing the importance of not turning local or regional conflicts into international or East-West conflicts, it was already a done deal—these "local" conflicts in Angola and elsewhere already had become internationalized, often as "East-East" conflicts before becoming "East-West" conflicts.

THE MIDDLE EAST: ADVANTAGE UNITED STATES

There was a bright spot for the United States in the Third World during this period. The progress Nixon and Kissinger had made in reducing Soviet influence in the Middle East at the end of the 1970 war of attrition and crisis in Jordan, and further after the Yom Kippur War in 1973, continued after Nixon left office. Kissinger began another round of shuttle diplomacy in August 1975 and, after a prodigious effort, on September 1 concluded an agreement between Israel and Egypt for a further pullback in the Sinai.

President Carter was also determined to pursue the cause of peace in the Middle East. Many volumes have been written about his efforts, culminating in the Camp David Accords, and I will not try to shorthand such a complicated business here. Suffice it to say that the signing of the accords on March 25, 1979, was a dramatic moment and an important success for American diplomacy and prestige.

The intrinsic merits of peacemaking aside, an important side effect of the leading role of the United States from 1970 to 1978 in serving as the go-between, facilitator, and negotiator with Arabs and Israelis was the near-total exclusion of the Soviet Union from political developments in the region. Relegated to arms supplier for Syria and lacking significant political influence in any Arab capital, the Soviets became bystanders.

THE "THIRD WORLD" WAR

In pursuit of advantage against the United States and China, and to expand their own influence and presence, by 1978 the Soviet leaders had moved massively and quickly to exploit opportunities created by the American defeat in Vietnam, as well as the collapse of the Portuguese empire in Africa and the overthrow of Haile Selassie in Ethiopia. At the same time, they had begun a major expansion and modernization of Cuban military capabilities, in the process significantly enhancing Castro's ability to intervene in other Third World conflicts. And so there would be other, significant Soviet-Cuban advances in the Third World in 1979.

By 1978, the impression was growing around the world of Soviet and communist advances in the Third World, our success in the Middle East notwithstanding. The United States was perceived to be paralyzed by its defeat in Vietnam and the weakness of two successive Presidents. Defense and intelligence budgets were still being reduced, and the "hollow army"—inadequately trained, inadequately supplied, inadequately manned, and inadequately armed —became a reality. Amid Western economic troubles and lack of direction, and steadily growing Soviet military power and international influence, these were flush times in the Kremlin.

But with each new intervention abroad, with the strengthening of client relationships with Vietnam and Cuba and others, the Soviet Union was making new commitments of its resources and prestige. It is more obvious in hindsight than it was at the time that in each place the Soviets and Cubans intervened—and, to a lesser extent, the Vietnamese and Libyans—there were resistance forces lying in wait, waiting for an opportunity to emerge from hiding to challenge the Soviets, their surrogates, and their local clients. And as these Soviet gains were one by one challenged in the late 1970s and 1980s, the costs for a severely strapped Soviet economy would become exorbitant.

The early rounds of the "Third World" war beginning in

1974–1975 went to the Soviets. Misinterpreting transitory American and Western problems and weakness as long-term crises and vulnerabilities, the Soviets moved aggressively and quickly in one Third World country after another. They discovered too late that they had ended up in a long and grueling slugfest where overall national strength—not just military power—would prove decisive. And thus, their "ascendancy" in the Third World during the last half of the 1970s and early 1980s would prove transitory—contrary to their and our expectations at the time.

CHAPTER FIVE

Planting Lethal Seeds

THERE WERE TWO REASONS the Soviets liked doing business with Nixon. First, he was willing publicly to acknowledge Soviet equality —they sought this acknowledgment shamelessly and often, and plainly regarded it as legitimizing both at home and abroad. Second, Nixon and Kissinger never tried to cause the Soviets trouble at home, to question seriously their internal policies or the legitimacy of their rule. As then–Soviet Foreign Minister Andrei Gromyko recalled about Nixon: "I cannot remember an occasion when he launched into a digression on the differing social structures of our states. He always presented himself as a pragmatist uninterested in the theoretical aspects of an issue, a man who preferred to keep discussions on a purely practical level." With Nixon's departure, this U.S. approach began to change.

THE HELSINKI ACCORDS: A BASKET OF TROUBLE

To get Western agreement to participate in the Conference on Security and Cooperation in Europe (CSCE), the Soviets not only had to agree to make progress on Berlin, but also to include as part of the Helsinki Declaration language concerning human rights. Similar subjects of the Declaration were grouped—at British suggestion—in "baskets" and, in the draft Declaration, "Basket III" included "free movement" of people and ideas. According to Hyland, Basket III essentially was "invented" by the Western participants to counter the idea that the conference was being held only to ratify the post–World War II political and military status quo in Europe.

In early summer 1975 I went on the advance trip to Helsinki to prepare for the President's participation. Ford intended also to visit Eastern Europe to highlight that he was not abandoning their interests at the conference. The stops included Poland, Romania, and Yugoslavia.

In Romania, the security services wanted to make sure I knew they knew I was from CIA. Once my official passport was in the hands of Romanian security officials, it "mysteriously disappeared." During the night, I received a number of phone calls in my hotel room, in which a heavily accented voice would ask if I had my passport and describe luridly what might happen if I did not. This both worried and angered me, and during the business sessions the next day, I was extremely hostile to the senior Romanian security officials attending our meetings—so much so that a senior State officer advised me that if I didn't ease up, it might affect the visit. I did not get my passport back, and the embassy had to issue me a tourist passport to get out of the country. Just before the door to our presidential jet closed upon our departure, in a regrettable but immensely satisfying display of pique and immaturity, I bade farewell to Romania's security police with an uplifted middle finger from the doorway of *Air Force Two*.

By the time the Helsinki Conference was held, considerable time had passed since the original blush of European enthusiasm for it in 1969. Attitudes had changed, and now the idea of holding a conference at the summit level to ratify the territorial status quo in Europe had become quite controversial in Europe as well as in the United States. In the United States especially, East European émigrés and conservatives more generally saw this as a one-sided concession by the West to keep détente alive. It was seen as a sellout of Eastern Europe by Ford. Nearly everyone saw Basket III, on human rights, as hortatory window dressing, a paper exercise of no consequence.

The political problem was very real for Ford, as conservatives already critical of détente were making their unhappiness widely felt, and because the relationship with the Soviets was already deteriorating over Angola, Vietnam, SALT, and more. Indeed, Ford's own staff was telling him the relationship was going downhill. Within the White House, some of the President's closest advisers believed Kissinger was leading Ford down a wrong path with the Soviets and trying to salvage a failed détente policy. Tensions between these staffers and Kissinger would grow steadily through 1975 and 1976.

Ford describes in his memoirs some of the political pressures on him not to go to the conference. There were editorials in major newspapers like the *Wall Street Journal* ("Jerry, don't go") and the *New York Times* (a "misguided and empty" trip), conservatives like Ronald Reagan and Senator Henry M. Jackson were critical, and Americans of East European descent were especially outraged.

I mention this opposition because, in retrospect, the results of the Helsinki Conference and Declaration were so different from what was anticipated at the time. Bill Hyland, years later, would write, "If it can be said that there was one point when the Soviet empire began to crack, it was at Helsinki." In retrospect, it is indeed apparent that CSCE provided the spark that kindled widespread resistance to communist authority and the organization of numerous independent groups throughout Eastern Europe and even in the Soviet Union determined to bring change. This spark of resistance would burst into flame in Poland only months later, and spread throughout the Soviet Empire within a short time. No one expected this, least of all the Soviets.

The first country to experience the consequences of CSCE was Poland. According to Lech Walesa, the year 1976 was a turning point "on the road to change in Gdansk," as organizations totally independent of the Communist Party—such as "the Movement in Defense of Human and Citizen Rights," dedicated to "publicizing human wrongs, violations of individual rights guaranteed by the Helsinki Accords"—began to appear. Walesa states that this movement also gave rise to the idea of an independent trade union to defend the rights of workers. These nongovernmental political activities were strengthened by the Gierek government's failed attempt to raise consumer prices in June 1976.

There was also trouble in East Germany soon after the Helsinki Accords were signed. CIA reported to us at the White House that by late summer 1976 there had been new restiveness in East Germany, prompting complaints from party boss Erich Honecker to the Soviets on the need to crack down. CIA further learned from East German sources that Honecker had griped to the Soviets that the growing number of dissidents in East Germany was receiving great attention in the West German media and that dissident messages were being broadcast back into the GDR. He reported new trouble with the Lutheran Church. Finally, he cited increased numbers of East Germans, spurred by the Helsinki Accords and expanded inter-German contacts, putting in immigration papers at the West German mission in East Berlin.

Through its spies in East Germany, CIA found out that in June 1976, Honecker and Gromyko agreed to take measures to reduce inter-German contacts, but deferred action at Gromyko's insistence until after the October election in West Germany—the Soviets did not want to hurt the election chances of Chancellor Helmut Schmidt. CIA also reported that the Soviet ambassador in East Berlin, Pyotr Abrasimov, was painting for Moscow a picture of growing threats to East German stability.

In promoting CSCE, and agreeing to the human rights provisions, no matter how qualified, the Soviets made a historic miscalculation. Helsinki stimulated dissident activity to a far greater degree than Moscow expected, not just in Eastern Europe, but at home—and not only among Jews and intellectuals, but among national minorities and Christian sects with broad support. By signing the Helsinki Declaration, the Soviets and their East European minions gave legitimacy to efforts by their own citizens and the West to try to implement the document's principles concerning human rights and freedom of movement. This in turn stimulated the growth of movements and nongovernmental organizations in Eastern Europe and in the Soviet Union that would help change the course of history.

CIA explained to the new Carter administration why the Soviets were so sensitive about its aggressive human rights approach in a February 18, 1977, memorandum to Brzezinski. It said, "Recent public and private Soviet signals of displeasure with the U.S. human rights campaign reflect anxieties much broader than Soviet dissidence." It went on to note that the Soviets were even more disturbed about trends in Eastern Europe, seeing Western criticism of official behavior there as compounding an already serious problem. The memorandum added: "The emergence of dissident activity throughout Eastern Europe since the beginning of 1976 has added a new dimension to the problems of East Germany and Poland. It is linked in the Soviet view with the behavior of dissidents in the USSR as a single challenge which the West is encouraging against the existing order in the East."

The Agency paper concluded that the Soviets plainly saw common elements in the antiregime activities throughout Eastern Europe. Just one example was the emergence of the "Charter 77" movement in Prague involving less than five hundred intellectuals but endorsed by Hungarian and Romanian intellectuals. The Agency paper ended with the statement that the Soviets undoubtedly believed what was happening was a sign that CSCE—the Helsinki Conference—was causing dissidence to spread.

And how about the reaction in the West? Ford's decision to go to Helsinki and put the American stamp of approval on the Accords was both wise and farsighted. It was not inadvertent or ill-considered, as his 1979 memoirs make clear. In fact, the newspapers, conservative critics, and Americans of East European descent were wrong in 1975. CSCE was perhaps the most important early milestone on the path of dramatic change inside the Soviet empire. The most eloquent testimonials to its importance come from those who were on the inside, who began their political odyssey to freedom at that time, and who became the leaders of free countries in Eastern Europe in 1989.

The Soviets desperately wanted CSCE, they got it, and it laid the foundations for the end of their empire. We resisted it for years, went grudgingly, Ford paid a terrible political price for going—perhaps reelection itself—only to discover years later that CSCE had yielded benefits to us beyond our wildest imagination. Go figure.

CARTER AND HUMAN RIGHTS: DID IT MATTER?

From the beginning of his campaign for President, Jimmy Carter had been critical of the realpolitik approach of Nixon-Ford-Kissinger, which he believed improperly and unnecessarily relegated matters of principle such as human rights to subordinate status. Committed to pursuing improved relations with the Soviets and to progress on arms control, Carter believed he could carry out these policies even while highlighting the importance of human rights. When he first met with Ambassador Dobrynin on February 1, 1977, Carter stated that he would not interfere in the internal affairs of the Soviet Union "but would expect all existing agreements to be carried out, including those relating to human rights. . . . When the Soviets signed these documents, they had placed the subject of human rights firmly on the agenda of legitimate discussions between our two nations."

In mid-February, the eminent Soviet physicist Andrei Sakharov wrote to President Carter describing his plight. On the joint recommendation of Vance and Brzezinski, Carter decided to respond and did so, informing Sakharov of his personal commitment to promote human rights in the Soviet Union.

On February 14, Carter sent a comprehensive letter—drafted by Vance and Brzezinski—to Brezhnev with the intention of using it to begin a dialogue with the Soviet leader. It addressed various aspects of arms control, arms sales, Berlin, and human rights. Brezhnev's reply, on February 25, was scathing, especially on human rights. He referred specifically to Carter's exchange of letters with Sakharov. The relationship was off to a bad start.

I believe we all underestimated just how sensitive—paranoid—the Soviets were about the dissidents. They were more aware than we by that time of the consequences of the Helsinki Accords and the spread of human rights monitoring groups in Eastern Europe and in the Soviet Union itself. Hyland later wrote, "The human rights issue struck at the very legitimacy and survival of the Soviet political structure."

In response to Carter's policies and the problem of spreading dissidence in the empire, the Soviets acted in February–March 1977. The regime launched a wave of arrests of the Helsinki Watch Group, including its founders, Yuri Orlov and Aleksandr Ginzberg, and then in March arrested Anatoliy Shcharansky.

CIA clandestinely obtained in early spring, 1977, a Hungarian leader's description of the Soviet leadership that underscored the impact of the human rights campaign on the Soviet leadership. The Hungarian said, "The picture is one of a grim, remarkably insecure, almost paranoid Soviet party leadership, worried to death about what it perceives as a genuine threat or challenge to its power—from the U.S. human rights campaign, and incredible as it may seem, believing that the U.S. stand on human rights is a deliberate strategy designed to overthrow the Soviet regime." Indeed, Gromyko in his memoirs notes Carter's personal role "as Washington engaged more and more actively in ideological subversion against the USSR."

The effort to promote human rights, support dissidents, and stir up the nationalities—all efforts that had the effect of attacking the legitimacy of the Soviet government—went far beyond presidential statements and letters. Beginning early in the administration, and going beyond the human rights campaign, Brzezinski initiated, and Carter approved, an unprecedented White House effort to attack the internal legitimacy of the Soviet government.

Zbig wasted no time, though bureaucratic opposition at State and CIA would significantly constrain and delay his ambitious anti-Soviet agenda. As early as March 1977, Carter approved several of Brzezinski's proposals for covert propaganda actions inside the USSR. Due to bureaucratic inertia, and even resistance inside CIA, nothing much came of the effort. On May 10, 1977, Brzezinski tried again, chairing a meeting of the Special Coordination Committee (the members included Vance, Brown, and Turner as the core) at which a working group was established to generate and review proposals for both overt and covert activities targeted on the Soviet Union. The working group, chaired by Aaron, met later the same day. At that meeting, Aaron told the participants that Brzezinski was "distressed" at the low level of activities aimed at the Soviet Union and therefore wanted task forces formed to develop both covert and overt proposals for action.

The Soviet homeland (or even Eastern Europe) had never been central to CIA's war against the Kremlin—the preferred battleground was in other countries. Indeed, the DO's Soviet/Eastern Europe (SE) division level of covert activity—as distinguished from clandestine collection of information—had declined from low to nearly nonexistent. It was in SE division where the covert activities approved by Carter in March 1977 had languished. Accordingly, after the May SCC meeting a different part of the clandestine service, the Covert Action Staff (CAS), picked up the action. CAS refurbished four moribund SE proposals from March and presented them to the covert working group. The proposals included:

• enhanced clandestine distribution in the USSR of Russian-language books and periodicals by dissident authors and of Soviet "samizdat" (dissident writings by authors in the USSR circulated privately in-country), a measure pushed by émigrés;

• an enhanced book publishing program involving subsidies of East European–oriented journals (primarily Polish and Czech) with distribution in cultural circles in Eastern Europe;

• a minorities program aimed at infiltrating written materials focused on the culture of and conditions in diverse ethnic regions of the USSR, primarily Ukraine. The proposal called for the transfer of one such ethnic group supported by CIA from the United States to Europe with an expanded charter; and

• support to groups in Western Europe promoting Soviet observance of human rights and democracy through press articles and other means.

The last of these was opposed by the State Department, always uneasy about covert action in Western Europe, even if targeted elsewhere, and, surprisingly, also by Walt Slocombe, representing the Defense Department.

Despite Brzezinski's support, these measures, modest as they were, moved excruciatingly slowly through the interagency process and through CIA. It was not until October 26, 1977, almost five and a half months later, that the SCC met to review the working group's proposals. At that meeting, the expanded covert book production and distribution programs were approved and forwarded to the President.

Prior to the SCC meeting, the working group had resuscitated the idea of a covert program targeting Soviet Muslims and Ukrainians, and forwarded to the SCC the Muslim and expanded minorities programs as well as efforts aimed at supporting human rights activists. State, then and later, found the idea of supporting ethnic minorities in the Soviet Union abhorrent and "slow-rolled" the proposals. Similarly, covert programs aimed at supporting human rights activists encountered very rough weather in the department. Covert action programs to stir things up inside the USSR were controversial in CIA as well as in State.

Apart from increasing the scale of covert infiltration of books and periodicals, the bureaucracy was gagging on Zbig's effort to turn up the heat on the Soviets internally. This just wasn't done; it wasn't within the parameters of the rules of the game as it had been played for many years. The National Intelligence Officer for the Soviet Union, Arnold Horelick, wrote the head of CIA's analytical directorate, Robert Bowie, on November 18, 1977: "This march of proposals was precipitated by Brzezinski's expression of interest last May on what more could be done via CIA against Soviet and East European targets. It is not clear to anyone in this building [CIA] what Zbig may have had in mind; I do not exclude the possibility that he had not thought that much about it beforehand. . . ." Three days later, on November 21, Horelick wrote Bowie, "In present circumstances, U.S. policy interests in fostering greater East European worker discontent, especially in Poland, are at least ambivalent (some would say that they are directly contradictory)."

Throughout this period, CIA stayed clear of direct support for or contact with Soviet dissidents. While CIA aggressively worked to feed dissident writings back into the Soviet Union and give them wider circulation, everyone recognized that any operational connection could do grievous harm to a dissident movement zealously monitored by the KGB.

State was also wary of moving covertly (or overtly, for that matter) into the nationalities area, for example, Central Asia, because they felt the United States simply was not well enough informed to be able to make appropriate decisions. Brzezinski, on the other hand, was deeply interested in exploiting the Soviets' nationalities problem. He wanted to pursue covert action in that arena and forced State, after a long delay, to produce a paper on nationalities in the USSR and proposed U.S. policy alternatives. That paper was the subject of an SCC meeting on June 20, 1978.

The State paper claimed that the United States didn't know enough about Soviet nationalities and asserted that a tighter, more focused effort was clearly needed to increase our knowledge. State then proposed a vast U.S. information-gathering effort on Soviet nationality groups. It was a classic bureaucratic stalling tactic. The department also wanted to study all programs targeted on Soviet nationalities since World War II, as well as obtain answers to a raft of other questions that plainly would take a long time to assemble —and then would probably never be complete.

Only after saddling CIA with enough bureaucratic paperwork to keep it busy for years did State turn to the policy issues *they* had been asked to address. The department described two schools of thought on the Soviet ethnic issue. The first view was that the nationalities problem was contributing to the economic slowdown, weakening of the armed forces, the possible breakup of the Soviet state, and weakening Soviet power and its capacity to wage war. If this view were accepted, these trends would be desirable and should be promoted. The other view was that Soviet power was capable of containing the ethnic forces within its borders and that little could be done from outside to diminish their capability to do so. In short, was ethnic assertiveness potentially disruptive to the Soviet state or was it a manageable problem?

State also raised several broader considerations: First, nationalism was at least as divisive in Eastern Europe as in the USSR and there were possible negative consequences to efforts to help centrifugal forces among Soviet nationalities or in Yugoslavia and Czechoslovakia, "each of which could disintegrate." Furthermore, ethnic and nationalist forces were likely to be among the most violent and divisive forces in the world over the coming decades and had brought separatism and violence to every continent. State also appeared concerned over the relationship of promoting these divisions to U.S. human rights policy, as well as the U.S. domestic political connection. I must admit State was quite farsighted in its concerns relating to the first two of the above considerations.

State's adamant opposition—however artfully and indirectly presented bureaucratically—to any covert action touching on the nationalities was clear. What was surprising to the NSC was that State's view had strong support on the analytical side of CIA. For example, the National Intelligence Officer for the USSR wrote the head of the Covert Action Staff in June 1978 that State's paper seemed to be a reasonable line of march and that a hold on new covert programs also was reasonable.

To the chagrin of the DO and the NSC, State and the intelligence analysts carried the day. Throughout the remainder of the Carter administration, and even in the Reagan administration, efforts to promote covert actions stirring up the Soviet nationalities problem would consistently fail inside the U.S. government. (As it turned out, such efforts proved unnecessary. Ethnic minorities inside the USSR needed little encouragement.)

In sum, Brzezinski, with Carter's support, had set forth an ambitious agenda of covert action to stir up trouble inside the USSR. While State and CIA were able to whittle down his covert program substantially, still there was a significant increase in the quantity of dissident and Western information and literature smuggled into Eastern Europe and the USSR.

Brzezinski, again with Carter's support, also had an overt weapon available to communicate with a much larger audience inside the Soviet Union than could be reached by CIA's covert publications program—the U.S. government–supported radios, especially Radio Liberty and Radio Free Europe. Zbig moved early to strengthen the radios. In Carter's "Report on International Broadcasting," submitted to Congress on March 22, 1977, at Brzezinski's urging, the President recommended additional transmitters to overcome the intense jamming efforts by the USSR and East European governments. He called for sixteen new 250-kilowatt transmitters, five for the Voice of America and eleven for Radio Free Europe and Radio Liberty.

The radios were effective. In a 1977 interview, the noted Soviet dissident Andrei Amalrik, who was forced into exile, said of the radios: "Foreign broadcasts into Russia play an enormous role. It is the only alternative information available to millions of Soviet citizens. The role of the radio is continually growing for two reasons. One is simply physical; the number of transistor radios in the Soviet Union keeps on growing. And second, the activity of Soviet dissidents is itself continually growing, and the growth of that activity is communicated and becomes widely known." Brzezinski would later write about his motives: "While the Radio should not be used to foment insurrections in the East, it should, in my judgment, serve as an instrument for the deliberate encouragement of political change."

Thus, after the Helsinki Final Act, and with the revival of the dissidents and proliferation of organizations dedicated to monitoring compliance with the Final Act, Western newsmen would obtain the writings of Soviet dissidents or interviews with them and publicize them in the West. The U.S. government radios would broadcast them back into the Soviet Union and CIA would clandestinely smuggle written versions back into eastern Europe and the USSR. In short, through the public policies and pronouncements of the President, and significantly more aggressive use of the radios and of CIA's clandestine distribution network in Eastern Europe and the Soviet Union, the Carter administration waged ideological war on the Soviets with a determination and intensity that was very different from its predecessors. This challenge would continue throughout Carter's term and be sustained and broadened further by his successor. Greater access to information from the West played an important part in the growing Soviet domestic crisis. I believe that the propaganda and covert endeavors of the Carter administration produced their share of the tiny fissures in the Soviet structure that ultimately helped bring about its collapse.

Carter had, in fact, changed the long-standing rules of the Cold War. Through his human rights policies, he became the first president since Truman to challenge directly the legitimacy of the Soviet government in the eyes of its own people. And the Soviets immediately recognized this for the fundamental challenge it was: they believed he sought to overthrow their system. In a departure from the Nixon-Kissinger-Ford approach of avoiding ideological issues in the relationship, other than to placate specific constituencies at home on emigration, Carter injected himself into Soviet domestic affairs from the outset with his letter to Sakharov and subsequent open support for dissidents. The Soviet leaders knew the implications for them of what Carter was doing, and hated him for it.

While Carter's human rights policies were derided at home as naïve and counterproductive, in later years Soviet dissidents would be virtually unanimous in their praise of those policies and the importance to the democratic dissidents of the publicity those policies brought to their cause. Carter's actions and policies gave encouragement to the nascent human rights groups that sprang up throughout Eastern Europe and in the Soviet Union after the signing of the Helsinki Final Act in 1975. His approach marked a decisive and historic turning point in the U.S.-Soviet relationship. Too bad for Carter that the important impact of his policies would only become known years later as dissidents fled the East and those affected by his policies would become leaders as their nations became free.

The Helsinki Accords. Carter's human rights campaign. The election of Karol Cardinal Wojtyla as Pope. The first two were disparaged and belittled when they happened, especially by those who considered themselves as hardheaded realists in foreign policy. Few grasped the significance of the election of this Pope for Eastern Europe, for Poland, and for the Soviet Union itself.

Walter Lippmann many years ago wrote that we must all "plant trees we will never get to sit under." The efforts of Gerald Ford and Jimmy Carter to plant and nurture the seeds of change on behalf of human rights in the East, and to challenge the communist governments' treatment of their own people, in my view, gave new heart, resolve, and courage to those inside the Soviet "prison house of nations," people who would challenge not just governments' treatment of their citizens but the legitimacy and the very existence of those governments. The fragile seeds of change planted between 1975 and 1978, so scorned and controversial at the time, would bear lethal fruit and help destroy an empire that was more vulnerable than either its own rulers or the West understood at the time.

CHAPTER SIX

MUTS, Spies, and Dissidents

DURING THE UPS AND DOWNS of the U.S.-Soviet relationship after 1975—and there were mostly downs—the intelligence services of the two countries could be counted on to make an already difficult-to-manage relationship even more complicated. Each had an assigned role from its government, but the unpredictability of intelligence operations and the seeming reality that a fundamental law of intelligence work is Murphy's Law repeatedly created tensions and, on occasion, crises in the relationship.

THE MOSCOW UNIDENTIFIED TECHNICAL SIGNAL (MUTS)

In the early 1960s, the United States first verified an unidentified microwave signal of very low intensity being beamed at our embassy in Moscow. Over the years, various such signals were detected and judged harmless to the health of people in the embassy. Then, in 1973 and again in 1975, two new and persistent signals were picked up. The signals were aimed at the upper floors of the central wing of the embassy—where the ambassador and intelligence functions had their offices—and because of their duration and peculiar characteristics they were regarded as posing a greater health hazard.

We knew that these signals were directional microwave beams —ultra- and super-high frequency radiowaves—coming from transmitters located in the vicinity of the embassy. Clearly the signals were related to intelligence activities. What was not clear was whether they were intended to jam our electronic radio waves or represented collection efforts by the Soviets against the embassy. On January 31, 1976, Walter Stoessel, U.S. ambassador to the USSR, protested to the Soviets about the MUTS emanations. The MUTS story leaked to the press soon thereafter.

During a meeting with Kissinger, Scowcroft, and Hyland on February 13, Ford decided to pursue reciprocal U.S. and Soviet reductions in electronic collection efforts, as well as elimination of the Soviet signals aimed at our embassy. Although the United States dismantled one of the antennas on the roof of our embassy in Moscow, there was no Soviet reciprocal action in the United States and only a slight decrease in the MUTS signal. In early April 1976, the Soviet chargé d'affaires in Washington, Yuli Vorontsov, presented Hyland a note saying that instructions had been given to "appropriate competent services" to take steps for the maximum possible decrease in the level of the electromagnetic field caused by industrial installations in Moscow, and these measures had been taken. Hyland told Vorontsov that there was "nothing encouraging" in this reply. There were no further U.S.-Soviet negotiations on MUTS.

The MUTS story ended with a United Press International dispatch from Moscow on May 29, 1979, which reported a U.S. embassy statement that the Soviets had halted the microwave bombardment of the embassy building.

With MUTS, the United States had identified a problem and raised it with the Soviets. However, leaks to the press and the desire to exploit the problem by one or another politician or political faction in Washington blew the matter up into a major confrontation, and then the United States had to back down or find some face-saving formula. There would be more such episodes in the years to come. None of these periodic tempests would be resolved on the terms demanded by the United States at the outset, with varying political costs at home. But such crises would become a regular and disruptive feature of the relationship for the rest of the Cold War. And, like the microwave radiation attack in Moscow—MUTS—all too often these crises involved intelligence.

DISSIDENTS, SPIES, AND NEWSMEN

Neither John le Carré nor any other novelist of the twists and turns of the Cold War could have concocted a plot as complicated, cynical, and as full of misunderstanding and miscalculation as the series of events during the first half of 1978 involving real spies, dissidents, and their Western journalistic contacts.

As described in Chapter 5, the Helsinki Accords had a significant impact inside the Soviet Union, leading not only to the founding of the Helsinki Watch Group to report on human rights abuses in the USSR, but also to the formation of new nationalist/ethnic groups in a number of the non-Russian republics of the Soviet Union.

This flowering of dissidence after CSCE became a problem the Kremlin could not let alone. The Soviet leadership moved to squelch the challenge. A number of dissidents were arrested between 1975 and 1977, including those seized right after Carter took office. Some, like Anatoliy Shcharansky, were accused of being agents of CIA.

Soviet problems associated with human rights and non-Russian nationalist dissidents were magnified by President Carter's strong support for their efforts, but also—and importantly—by the dissidents' ready access to Western newspaper reporters and other journalists who carried their message and information to a world-wide audience. Thus the Soviet leadership acted to break the connection between the dissidents and journalists—especially American journalists—with a new round of arrests of dissidents. This campaign involved the arrest of dozens of prominent dissidents during May and June 1977.

Trials for two of the most prominent dissidents, Ginzberg and Shcharansky, both arrested right after Carter entered office, were announced in early July 1978. The two of them, and an accused spy, Anatoliy Filatov, were tried and sentenced in mid-July.

At the same time, the dissidents' Western newspaper contacts were also under attack. On June 13, 1978, the KGB tried to stage a provocation against the bureau chief of the *New York Times,* David Shipler, but they backed off when he failed to take the bait. We heard that he had been notified that he had lost a package and that he should pick it up at a certain militia office. Unaware of any lost package, Shipler did not appear. On the 27th, a slander suit was filed by the Soviets against Harold Piper of the *Baltimore Sun* and

Craig Whitney of the *New York Times*, and they had to appear in court the next day. (On May 25, the *Sun* had published a story by Piper on the situation in Soviet Georgia.)

Simultaneous with this Soviet campaign against dissidents and efforts to break their contacts with American newsmen, there was a major—and genuine—spy crisis under way. The spy story begins, for our purposes, on May 17, 1978, just after the KGB began rounding up dissidents. That day, Brzezinski was informed by DCI Turner that the FBI proposed to arrest three KGB officers resident in New York. The Bureau intended to declare persona non grata the only one of the three with diplomatic immunity and expel him, and to arrest the other two.

On May 20, the FBI arrested Valdik Enger and Rudolf Chernayev in New Jersey on charges of espionage. They had fallen for an FBI "dangle" operation, a U.S. Navy officer under FBI control offering to sell them military secrets. (A dangle operation in intelligence is similar to a law enforcement "sting": a controlled subject with known access to secrets offers to sell or pass them to the other side—he is "dangled" in front of them.) The two were brought before a federal court where the judge set bail at $2 million each. (The previous high bail set for a captured Soviet spy had been $500,000 in 1963, which was subsequently reduced to $100,000.) This was the first espionage case involving Soviets without diplomatic immunity since the 1960s, and the high bail—set independently by the judge—clearly exceeded anything either side had experienced in the past.

Five days later, U.S. experts discovered a sophisticated technical penetration of our embassy in Moscow—a chimney had been used as access for pervasive bugging of the embassy, with a wire going up the chimney to serve as an antenna. It was a major Soviet intelligence operation and it looked like a very successful one. The same day, May 25, the Soviets handed over their second protest note in Washington concerning the arrest of and high bail for Enger and Chernayev.

You just had to give the Soviets credit for audacity when their embassy in Washington on May 28 presented a note to the State Department protesting the "unlawful" penetration by the U.S. embassy staff in Moscow into the chimney of the adjacent Soviet apartment building—where the bugging system was discovered. At the same time, the Soviet embassy noted to State that there had been no publicity about the discovery of American bugs in their embassy and installations in Washington, and then warned the United States to behave with similar restraint. The bugging of the U.S. embassy leaked a week later.

At my request, CIA did an analysis for Brzezinski on how the Soviets were looking at all this. The Agency thought that the Soviets probably saw the arrests of Enger and Chernayev (and attendant publicity), along with the flap over bugging the embassy, as an excessive reaction by the United States and as part of an anti-Soviet campaign. The Agency said that the Soviets presumably saw the very high bail and all of the publicity about the arrest—usually spies are quietly expelled—as a breach of the "rules" and, further, the leaking only a week after the arrests of the "discovery" of the complex technical penetration of the embassy as part of the same anti-Soviet operation. CIA noted the coincidence in Soviet eyes between these events and the troubled nature of the bilateral relationship at that time—Soviet activities in Africa, remaining SALT II issues, renewed interest in Sino-Soviet relations, and a strengthening of NATO resolve—and concluded that all this probably looked to the Soviets like a deliberately orchestrated policy of increased hostility to the Soviet Union. But it wasn't. The Soviets had a legitimate gripe on the high bail, but the discovery of the embassy bugging system was pure serendipity.

The Soviets now took the initiative. CIA learned that the KGB's First Chief Directorate (foreign operations) in late May sent cables to all its posts—"residencies"—describing the arrest of three of its officers and saying that the $2 million bail, which they said had been set by the administration, was "unrealistic and impertinent." Finally, a KGB order was sent to its officers in Moscow to humiliate U.S. citizens there. It said that additional measures were planned and that residencies should plan a new campaign of anti-American actions in their host countries, to include blackmail and slander. The KGB was definitely annoyed.

On June 9, Soviet Ambassador Dobrynin met with Vance and warned that severe retaliation and public consequences would follow soon if bail for Enger and Chernayev was not reduced. He charged that the United States had changed the rules of the game and "if we are on a new basis, consequences will follow."

Three days later, on June 12, the KGB followed through on its threats and arrested an American businessman, Jay Crawford, on the charge of currency speculation. The next day, June 13, the U.S. embassy protested an *Izvestia* article on U.S. spy activities in

Moscow and the KGB staged its provocation against *New York Times* correspondent David Shipler. Things were getting hot.

On June 17, Dobrynin was instructed to return to Moscow because of increased political tensions. At about this time, CIA learned from a source that the Soviets had reacted strongly to Carter's speech at the U.S. Naval Academy on June 7, a toughly worded address that offered the Soviets "either confrontation or cooperation" and indicated that the United States was ready for either choice. According to the source, the Soviets until then had dismissed much of the administration's anti-Soviet rhetoric as coming only from Brzezinski, whom they correctly perceived as hostile to them. After Annapolis, the Soviets came to believe that the President personally was behind the move toward confrontation. The fact that the speech came within two weeks of Brzezinski's return from China also raised Soviet concerns that the United States was actively seeking a military alliance with Beijing. These developments together made for a chilly June.

Negotiations proceeded between June 22 and 26 for release of the two Soviet spies and Crawford to the custody of their respective ambassadors in Washington and Moscow. This took place on Monday, June 26. Now the two sides were ready to begin negotiating a swap.

The U.S. side took the initiative in trying to arrange an exchange that would return the two spies to the Soviet Union and thus ease the crisis in the relationship. On June 30, Vance met with Dobrynin to pursue the idea of an exchange involving Enger and Chernayev. He proposed trading the two Soviets for Anatoliy Shcharansky, plus several additional Soviet prisoners. It was a rare —perhaps unprecedented—offer to swap Soviet spies for Soviet political prisoners. It was also just the beginning of a secret negotiation that would last for months.

Feelings ran high in both governments. CIA learned that on July 29, KGB head Yuri Andropov met with Georgi Korniyenko of the Foreign Ministry to review the progress of the swap negotiations. Andropov was angry at Western "interference" in Soviet internal affairs and only reluctantly concurred in the idea of negotiations at all. Andropov complained that the West would continue to interfere and that any swap resulting in a "clean slate" would be only temporary—the Soviet Union would continue to enforce its laws. He instructed Korniyenko to play down interest in Enger and Chernayev for bargaining purposes.

As the negotiations dragged on, Brzezinski on November 8 raised with Turner the idea of a "code of conduct" for intelligence, saying that Dobrynin had raised it with him several times and he needed to be prepared to discuss it. Zbig wondered about an agreement that both sides would use only people with diplomatic passports for espionage activities.

The reaction to the "code" at CIA was strongly negative. One veteran operations officer captured the overall CIA view of a "code." He wrote on one of the papers, "When I was a spy, I assumed that if caught I would be executed. When I thought about it—as I often did—I only hoped it would be over quickly and before I was forced to tell too many secrets. This was a clear-cut approach, and I rather prefer it, but if now we are to have a code of rights for caught spies, I hope someone takes down the statue of Nathan Hale [at CIA]—perhaps to put Tony Lapham in his place." Tony Lapham was CIA's General Counsel—its top lawyer.

The quibbling and negotiating over a swap continued for several more months until agreement was reached, with the Soviets probably deciding finally to act because of the impending U.S.-Soviet summit and signing of SALT II. On April 27, 1979, five leading dissidents boarded a plane in Moscow bound for New York. The same day, Enger and Chernayev boarded a plane in New York for Moscow.

From the arrest of Enger and Chernayev to completion of the exchange had taken almost a year. Relations between the United States and the USSR, already troubled, deteriorated significantly during that time. But the U.S. side had played a tough hand reasonably well and had extracted a considerable price from the Soviets for its efforts—though not its preferred outcome, the release of Shcharansky. That would have to wait for years. CIA did its best to help those who had spied for it, learning in the process that one, Ogorodnik ("Trigon"), almost certainly had been executed and finding out nothing about another—a defector named Shadrin. (CIA would learn from a senior KGB defector years later that Shadrin had died in Vienna in 1975 when the KGB tried to kidnap him and threw him in a car trunk to exfiltrate him back to the East. We heard later that his death had been accidental, either from suffocating in the trunk because of a hole that admitted carbon monoxide from the car's exhaust pipe, or because they tried to knock him out with chloroform and overdosed him.)

These events in 1978 illustrate how intelligence operations on both sides could and did complicate the U.S.-Soviet relationship, at times seriously. At the same time, they demonstrate that the Soviets were so concerned by the spread of the dissident movement by 1977–1978 that the Kremlin was prepared to risk the relationship with the United States to break the connection between dissidents and the Western correspondents who published their views all over the world.

CHAPTER SEVEN

Defense and Arms Control: Advantage USSR

BY THE LATTER HALF of the 1970s, Soviet and American observers could agree on at least one thing: the Soviet star seemed to be ascending while the American one was falling. Watergate. Communist victories in Indochina. Soviet-Cuban interventions in Ethiopia and Angola and elsewhere in the Third World. Cuban rearmament. Western economic problems and loss of confidence. A politically weak U.S. President. The list of Soviet advances and American problems seemed to grow with each passing month.

But what truly gave the impression to a global audience of a change in the balance in favor of the Soviet Union was the strategic arms race. There had been voices for years raising concerns about the Soviet strategic buildup, but the antidefense, antimilitary spending attitude in the country, and especially in the Congress, had caused these warnings to fall on pretty barren ground—certainly in terms of doing anything about the situation. While few strategic programs were killed outright, even as détente soured, all were starved for funds, stretched out, and deployments often delayed and curtailed. The perception at home by the mid-1970s was one of American strategic lassitude compared to surging Soviet programs.

While the Soviets clearly closed the strategic gap in the 1970s, and surpassed the United States in several measures of strategic offensive capability, the United States had begun strategic modernization programs of its own as early as the Johnson administration that, if deployed as planned, even hard-line conservatives recognized would remedy U.S. vulnerabilities by the mid-1980s. Programs begun in the Johnson or Nixon administrations included putting three independently targeted warheads (MIRVs) on each of 550 Minuteman missiles; replacing the single-warhead Polaris ballistic missile with the ten-to-fourteen-warhead Poseidon missile; developing the Trident ballistic missile submarine (construction of the first began in 1975) and new associated missile; development and testing of air-launched cruise missiles; beginning development of a new U.S. ICBM, the MX; modernizing the aging B-52 bombers; and developing a new strategic bomber, the B-1.

Still, budget cuts slowed many of these programs, some survived by a thread in Congress (Trident survived the Senate in 1973 by two votes), and deployment schedules were stretched out. Strategic weapons always had strong and very vocal critics and, for many of the programs, their history looked a lot like "the perils of Pauline" as they narrowly avoided again and again the fatal buzz saw.

THE SOVIET MILITARY JUGGERNAUT: OUR "WINDOW OF VULNERABILITY"

The USSR's economic weakness and ultimate political collapse in the late 1980s and early 1990s have clouded the memories of many people as to the relentlessness, magnitude, and fearsomeness —indeed, the very reality—of the Soviet military buildup from 1962 until 1987. Indeed, a critical factor in the Soviet economic crisis in the late 1980s was the mammoth investment the country had made in the military over a twenty-five-year period and the leadership's decision to sustain that level of investment even as the economy plunged into crisis. But the resources poured into defense had formidable results in terms of increased military power.

DCI George Bush, in approving National Intelligence Estimate 11–3/8–76, "Soviet Forces for Intercontinental Conflict Through the Mid-1980s," attached to it a cover letter that characterized its contents: "To the extent that this *Estimate* presents a starker appreciation of Soviet strategic capabilities and objectives, it is but the latest in a series of estimates that have done so as evidence has accumulated on the continuing persistence and vigor of Soviet programs in the strategic offensive and defensive fields."

The estimate did present a "starker" portrayal of the threat. Its now declassified key conclusions told the tale:

• "The Soviets had 1,556 ICBM launchers at operational complexes as of 1 November 1976." (The United States had 1,054.) The Soviets had four new ICBMs being deployed, three of which were equipped with MIRVs, ranging from four warheads on the SS-17, six on the SS-19, and up to ten on the huge SS-18. All of the ICBMs had better accuracy than their predecessors and were being deployed in silos "several times harder" than their predecessors and thus less vulnerable to attack. All had more throwweight (the useful weight that could be delivered to a target) than their predecessors, three to four times as much in the case of the SS-17 and SS-19. These two missiles also uniquely used a "cold launch" technique in which they were "popped up" out of the silo before igniting, thus allowing the silo to be reloaded in a relatively short time. The estimate went on to say that yet another generation of ICBMs was in development and likely would have even further improved accuracy.

• "The Soviets have been steadily increasing the size and overall strike capability of their submarine-launched ballistic missile force since the mid-1960s. As of 1 November 1976, they had 799 SLBM launchers on 60 nuclear-powered ballistic missile submarines (SSBNs) which had reached operational status." (The United States at that time had about forty SSBNs.) The estimate reported that the Soviets were launching new SSBNs at a rate of about six per year, and had launched four units of their newest sub, the Delta-III. The estimate also warned that the Soviets were developing a much larger class of SSBN, about the size of the U.S. Trident, that could be operational by 1980. (This was the Typhoon submarine, made famous by author Tom Clancy in his novel *The Hunt for Red October*.) While two Soviet submarines still were patrolling off each U.S. coast, the estimate advised that the new subs had missiles of such long range that they could be launched against targets in the United States from their home ports in the USSR.

Based on its forecasts of Soviet ICBM and SLBM capabilities and evident plans, the estimate focused on several alarming possibilities. While it concluded that the Soviets did not "hold as an operative, practical objective the achievement of clear strategic superiority over the U.S." during the next ten years, it did say that "the Soviets are striving to achieve war-fighting and war-survival capabilities which would leave the USSR in a better position than the U.S. if war occurred." The estimate also said that the Soviet leaders saw "politically useful advantages" in larger strategic forces and, further, that their strategic capabilities would give them "wider latitude" than in the past for vigorous pursuit of foreign policy objectives, and that "these capabilities will discourage the U.S. and others from using force or the threat of force to influence Soviet actions."

Another conclusion of the estimate that would draw much comment was its judgment that the strength of the Soviet offensive strategic forces might be at its greatest relative to the U.S. forces in the early 1980s and would pose an increasing threat to U.S. missile silos. This was what came to be known then as "the window of vulnerability" projected for the early 1980s, that is, a limited period of time—several years—when a theoretical possibility existed that the Soviets might be able to launch a disarming first strike against the United States, destroying enough of our ICBMs in their silos to cripple a retaliatory strike and either prevent a U.S. response or allow the USSR to emerge from a war in significantly better condition than the United States.

You didn't have to believe that the Soviets actually might start a war for this to be of concern. In fact, very few in Washington thought there was even a remote chance that the Soviets would suicidally throw the dice that way. But a lot of people worried that if the Soviets had a significant advantage over us in strategic capabilities, including the perception that they could substantially destroy our ICBM force before we launched, this would give them the confidence to be even more assertive in their foreign policy ambitions and actions—and that other countries would act on the basis of perceived Soviet superiority. Further, there was the worry that in a real crisis, the Soviets might actually be tempted to attack if they thought they could come out ahead by destroying our ICBMs. Thus, the window of vulnerability came to be accepted by a substantial part of the political spectrum interested in such matters—both Republicans and Democrats—and greatly influenced the strategic debate for a number of years.

CARTER AND DEFENSE: PERCEPTION AND REALITY

Conventional wisdom holds that, as the Soviets built up in the late 1970s, President Carter began cutting the defense budget and pursued an antidefense policy that weakened the country. The conventional wisdom is misleading.

By 1977, U.S. defense spending had been declining for nearly a decade, especially if Vietnam operational expenses are set aside. Carter says in his memoirs that the defense budget, measured in real dollars (i.e., not counting inflation), had declined 35 percent over the preceding eight years even as the Soviet budget had been growing at about 4 percent per year. Intelligence capabilities suffered badly.

When the Carter administration arrived, there was no discounting the magnitude or importance of the Soviet strategic or conventional military buildup. The Carter administration's view of the Soviets, their military gains of the preceding years, and their likely behavior was quite consistent with the estimates prepared by the intelligence community in 1976—in the Ford administration. A dozen years of single-minded Soviet effort and a huge expenditure of resources had enabled the Soviets to close the strategic gap and establish a favorable military balance in Europe, and offered them the potential to gain superiority in a number of areas—depending on what the United States did. Those who, after the Soviet collapse, would argue that the Soviet military threat was overstated would have found few in either political party or in the American government generally in 1976 or in 1977 who would have agreed. In fact, in retrospect, it is quite clear that the sober assessments of Soviet military power—the forces they actually had—in both the Ford and Carter administrations were quite accurate.

Despite his own administration's realistic assessment of Soviet military strength and capabilities, Carter's approach to defense looked decidedly negative (or weak) up close:

• In January 1977, he cut his first defense budget, already bare bones, by more than six billion dollars.

• Carter canceled the B-1 bomber development program in June 1977.

• Early in the administration, as part of a new SALT proposal, he authorized Vance "to offer to scrap" both the B-1 and the Trident ballistic missile submarine program if an agreement on deep reductions seemed possible.

• Carter initiated a number of new arms control negotiations with the Soviets, including limiting conventional arms sales in sensitive areas and military deployments in the Indian Ocean. All were controversial inside the administration and, after negotiating efforts with the Soviets of varying duration, virtually all sputtered out.

• Against the advice of Vance, Brown, and Brzezinski, Carter decided in April 1978 to defer production of the Enhanced Radiation Weapon (ERW). In so doing, and in the way he did it, he deeply antagonized Chancellor Schmidt of West Germany and other allies. (Carter's perception that the Europeans didn't want the ERW, and indeed public criticism in Europe itself of ERW, probably were influenced by one of the most aggressive covert operations ever mounted in Europe by the Soviets. The KGB undertook a massive propaganda campaign in Europe against the so-called neutron bomb in July and August 1977 to create just the impression of the broad unpopularity in Europe of the bomb that so bothered Carter.)

• Carter called for U.S. troop reductions in South Korea to the consternation of the South Koreans, Japanese, and other Asians.

• Carter was most unenthusiastic about going forward with a new ICBM for the United States, the MX. (According to Brzezinski, Carter during this period kept asking Brown if keeping the triad—ICBMs, SLBMs, bombers—was still necessary, and at one meeting complained that the perception of Soviet superiority had been created by "this group"—referring to his own senior advisers.)

These major decisions, and a number of lesser ones, including some on the budget, formed (and still form) the basis for the view that Carter was weak on defense. As in the case of the B-1, he took a great deal of time to study the issues, including the technical aspects, and, I am convinced, made up his mind on each one based on the facts. Somehow, though, he seemed unable to stand back and see that a number of these decisions all in the same direction formed a pattern—and that pattern established the basis for the attacks on him as antidefense. He seemed not to understand the cumulative political impact of discrete decisions.

Further, I think his reputation for weakness was due to his rhetoric, his deep-seated ambivalence toward the Soviet Union, his lack of support for defense budget increases, several of his unilateral initiatives, and because he turned down two major weapons programs that came to him during his term—the enhanced radiation weapon (neutron bomb) and the B-1 bomber. What he did ultimately support, and it was a great deal, he supported grudgingly, often under enormous pressure and usually only after agonizing indecision.

With the atmospherics now so far distant, the reality is that Carter's record on defense looks more robust today than it did at the time. The peaks and valleys of the day-to-day struggle fade from view, as do the occasions when the President made a decision not because he wanted to but because his hand was forced or when he yielded to the counsel of his senior advisers.

Whatever may have been Carter's attitude or rhetoric, he continued the strategic modernization programs begun under his predecessors for the air-launched cruise missile, the MX, completion of the MIRVing of Minuteman, and the Trident ballistic missile submarine and new submarine-launched missile. He approved and funded development of stealth aircraft technology that led to wholly new kinds of tactical and strategic attack aircraft. Indeed, with the sole exception of the B-1, Carter sustained virtually every major U.S. strategic modernization program and began an important new one. The perception of new U.S. strategic power and strength that emerged in the first half of the 1980s as new weapons were built and deployed was, in fact, Ronald Reagan reaping the harvest sown by Nixon, Ford, *and* Carter.

There was more.

The Carter administration took seriously the adverse military trends in Europe—and the Europeans' related concerns—from the very beginning. In May 1977, the NATO heads of government, with Carter in the lead, agreed in London to develop a long-term defense program to strengthen both the conventional and nuclear military capabilities of the alliance.

The really contentious issue for the alliance was how to redress the balance in terms of nuclear capabilities—specifically how to respond to the 1977 Soviet deployment in the European theater of the new SS-20 intermediate-range ballistic missile, a highly accurate weapon with three warheads. To address this issue, Carter arranged a summit meeting with British Prime Minister James Callaghan, French President Giscard d'Estaing, and West German Chancellor Schmidt on the French island of Guadeloupe on January 5–6, 1979.

I and two others from the White House had the good fortune to do the advance planning for this meeting, and we flew in an Air Force plane to Guadeloupe in mid-December. We arrived at the hotel in business suits and were told that our French hosts were waiting for us in a small pavilion on the beach. So we walked down to the pavilion, looking only slightly out of place wearing suits on a Caribbean beach.

But the situation was even worse than that. The pavilion was open-sided, and our meeting with the *chef de cabinet* of the French president (sort of a chief of protocol/senior staff officer) and his colleagues was situated right in the middle of a topless beach, heavily populated with young women from France taking full advantage of the Caribbean sun. In such a setting we planned a historic summit meeting on one of the most critical issues in NATO's history —the deployment of new nuclear weapons to Europe. I was terribly grateful that the Guadeloupe summit took place without a hitch or surprise because I confess the notes I made in that pavilion were somewhat disjointed.

I accompanied Carter and Brzezinski to the Guadeloupe summit. The informal nature of the discussions there contributed to very frank talk among the four leaders concerning how NATO should respond to the SS-20s. It was in these talks that the "dual-track" approach to TNF (later known as Intermediate Nuclear Forces, or INF)—was born, that is, that deployment of U.S. missiles to Europe would take place only after an effort to negotiate limits on such weapons had been made and only if it failed.

Despite an intensive and massive Soviet effort, overt and covert, to thwart the initiative, NATO agreed upon and issued the final plan on December 11–12, 1979. It called for deployment of 108 Pershing II missiles to replace a like number of Pershing Is and 464 new ground-launched cruise missiles. To demonstrate that NATO was not trying to increase its dependence on nuclear weapons, the plan called for one thousand older warheads to be withdrawn from Europe. And, of course, there was much stress on pursuing negotiations with the Soviets.

The decision in December 1979 based on the discussions at Guadeloupe the preceding January, was the most important NATO initiative in many years and reaffirmed the military and political vitality of the alliance at a time when the Soviets were very much on the offensive diplomatically and had a remarkable array of military modernization programs under way. The decision was one of the earliest signs that the West had turned a corner with the Soviets and was on the way back from the malaise that had dominated U.S.-European relations for several years. And it was Jimmy Carter who had done the lion's share of the work and provided the leadership that shaped an alliance consensus.

Carter did more in the defense arena outside the strategic competition and strengthening of conventional and nuclear forces in Europe. A new strategic doctrine provided new flexibility on targeting, as well as new emphasis on military targets, the military-industrial complex, and Soviet command and control. This directive and the others gave the United States an improved ability actually to fight a war that lasted more than a few hours. Ironically, Reagan's implementation of measures originated during the Carter administration to improve U.S. war-fighting capabilities would cause him to be branded a crazy warmonger, viciously attacked by critics in the United States and by the Soviets. The latter were, in fact, deeply worried by these improvements in U.S. strategic posture.

Carter approved creation of the Rapid Deployment Force, a strengthened successor to Strike Command and the forerunner of Central Command—the military organization that commanded and fought the Persian Gulf War more than ten years later. In his State of the Union address on January 23, 1980, Carter asserted that "Any attempt by any outside force to gain control of the Persian Gulf region will be regarded as an assault on the vital interests of the United States of America and such an assault will be repelled by any means necessary, including military force." This statement of U.S. policy, which became known as the Carter Doctrine, would be enforced by both Presidents Reagan and Bush. (Vance wanted to cut this portion of the speech and deleted it in the State draft returned to the White House. Brzezinski told press secretary Jody Powell there was nothing to the speech without the passage and Powell persuaded Carter to leave it in. Thus are issues of historic importance often determined.)

Regardless of Carter's enthusiasm or lack of it for some (or even most) of these measures, the cumulative impact was to provide a strong foundation for Ronald Reagan to build upon. Indeed, I believe the Soviets saw a very different Jimmy Carter than did most Americans by 1980, different and more hostile and threatening. In addition to Moscow understanding the longer-range implications of the strategic and conventional weapons programs Carter approved, I think by 1980 the Soviets were feeling increasingly isolated. They were stunned by U.S.-Chinese normalization and the immediate announcement thereafter that the United States would not oppose Western arms sales to Beijing; with the Sino-Japanese treaty, they saw Asia's greatest economic power and its largest country put aside more than half a century of hostility and declare their desire to work together, implicitly to prevent Soviet hegemony; and they saw new resolve in NATO to strengthen the alliance militarily.

We received a small insight into Soviet paranoia about the United States in mid-1980. On at least three occasions, there had been failures of the U.S. early warning computer system leading to combat alerts of U.S. strategic forces. CIA later learned that during the first half of June 1980, the KGB had sent a message to all of their residencies reporting these failures and saying that they were not the result of errors but were deliberately initiated by the Defense Department for training. The KGB circular stated that the Soviet government believed that the United States was attempting to give the Soviet Union a false sense of security by giving the impression that such errors were possible, and thereby diminish Soviet concern over future alerts—thus providing a cover for possible surprise attack.

Two of these false alarms did produce scares, but under circumstances far different from what the KGB was reporting. During one, Brzezinski's military assistant, Bill Odom, overheard on his communications net a dialogue between the National Military Command Center (NMCC) at the Pentagon and the North American Air Defense Command (NORAD) in which they were describing a missile being tracked from the Soviet Union toward the Oregon coast. As Odom later described the event to me, NORAD and the NMCC debated whether this was really a missile attack long past the time when they should have notified the Secretary of Defense. Ultimately, they concluded that it was a false alarm, a computer glitch.

The second incident was even more dramatic. As he recounted to me, Brzezinski was awakened at three in the morning by Odom, who told him that some 220 Soviet missiles had been launched against the United States. Brzezinski knew that the President's decision time to order retaliation was from three to seven minutes after a Soviet launch. Thus he told Odom he would stand by for a further call to confirm a Soviet launch and the intended targets before calling the President. Brzezinski was convinced we had to hit back and told Odom to confirm that the Strategic Air Command was launching its planes. When Odom called back, he reported that he had further confirmation, but that 2,200 missiles had been launched—it was an all-out attack. One minute before Brzezinski intended to telephone the President, Odom called a third time to say that other warning systems were not reporting Soviet launches. Sitting alone in the middle of the night, Brzezinski had not awakened his wife, reckoning that everyone would be dead in half an hour. It had been a false alarm. Someone had mistakenly put military exercise tapes into the computer system. When it was over,

Zbig just went back to bed. I doubt he slept much, though. Such were the terrors and nightmares of the Cold War, now faded so far from memory.

From my nonpartisan perch, and especially with the passage of time, the Carter record—continuing nearly all U.S. strategic development and modernization programs, working with NATO to strengthen the conventional military capabilities of the alliance and to respond to Soviet theater nuclear force improvements (the SS-20), and making far-reaching improvements in U.S. strategic war-fighting capabilities—is far stronger than conventional wisdom would have us believe. In both the conventional and strategic military arenas, Carter laid the foundations for much of what Ronald Reagan would undertake in the defense area, albeit with a vastly increased budget and genuine presidential enthusiasm. That's a fact, despite how distasteful partisans on both sides of the political fence might find it.

CARTER AND SALT II: THE BEST OF INTENTIONS

If President Carter's principal advisers were in substantial agreement on the strategic balance and outlook, they were badly divided over what to do about the problem—and Carter himself was ambivalent. The very public disagreements between Vance and Brzezinski on how to deal with the Soviet challenge and Carter's equally public inability to decide between them or even reconcile their views for himself was very damaging to the administration and to the country.

The one exception to this picture was SALT. There was agreement in the administration from the President on down in support of arms control in general and SALT in particular. Vance, Brown, and Brzezinski were all committed to success and worked together reasonably well to achieve it. They did succeed in negotiating a new agreement with the Soviets, but their handling of the treaty after signature, as well as domestic politics and Soviet actions, virtually eliminated any hope of ratification by the Senate.

CIA complicated the administration's efforts on SALT by insisting that the treaty go even further than had been agreed to address satisfactorily the issue of telemetry encryption. Every missile being flight-tested sends signals back to the ground that provide measurements of performance. U.S. intelligence over the years learned not only how to acquire these signals from Soviet missiles, but also how to derive a great deal of information about the capabilities of the missiles from the signals. Over time, however, the Soviets increasingly encoded these signals, thus denying the United States the information it needed both to inform our military and to monitor SALT agreements. In the final months of the SALT II negotiations, Turner insisted that U.S. intelligence had to have access to unencoded telemetry signals necessary to monitor Soviet compliance with the treaty provisions. He had the administration over a barrel. Unless the DCI could assure the Senate that U.S. intelligence could adequately monitor Soviet compliance with a SALT treaty, it had no chance of being ratified.

The telemetry issue was made harder by the fact that the Iranian revolution had eliminated U.S. access to its Tacksman monitoring sites in northern Iran and significantly reduced the quality and quantity of telemetry we could collect. Those in the Senate skeptical of the treaty knew this and used it to full advantage. The senior intelligence community leadership, the SCC, and the Congress spent an extraordinary amount of time and effort in the spring of 1979 figuring out how to replace the Tacksman sites. The answer was found in China.

Despite tensions inside the administration, in a brief upturn in the relationship with the Soviets, SALT II was completed in May, setting the stage for a summit and signing ceremony in Vienna on June 18, 1979.

In preparation for the summit, CIA provided a great deal of material to the White House and a major briefing on June 6. The CIA briefers made the following two points:

• As the summit approaches, Brezhnev and the Soviet leadership "can view their position in the world with considerable satisfaction. Part of the Soviet mood is a sense of momentum in the USSR's favor in the Third World."

• "The Intelligence Community is largely agreed that the outlook for the Soviet economy over the next five to ten years is more bleak and the prospects for policy choices more uncertain than at any time since Stalin's death."

Briefings carried out, preparations complete, we headed to Vienna. The meetings took place in the U.S. and Soviet embassies in Vienna, alternating between them. As Brzezinski's assistant, I attended several of the meetings and lurked around the periphery of the others.

I couldn't get over how feeble Brezhnev was by then. Going in and out of the embassies, two huge—and I mean *huge*—KGB officers held him upright under his arms and essentially carried him. Odom, a Soviet expert, and I were trapped in a narrow walkway at one point, and as the KGB half-carried Brezhnev by we were nearly steamrollered. At another point, Colonel C. G. Fitzgerald, an old Soviet hand, saw Brezhnev's bodyguards literally carry him up the stairs without his feet touching the ground. When Fitzgerald was shouldered aside (as Odom and I had been) on the steps, he began to fall and one of the massive guards, still carrying Brezhnev with his left arm, reached out with his free right arm and, with a "Careful, Mr. Colonel," broke Fitzgerald's fall and lifted him to an upright position.

During the meetings, Gromyko and Defense Minister Ustinov did not hesitate to correct Brezhnev when he misspoke or made a mistake, and he would often turn to them with questions or for them to comment. More than once after finishing a presentation, Brezhnev would turn to Gromyko and ask, "Did I do all right?" He was still clearly in charge, they clearly still deferred to him, but he was enormously dependent upon them for support. He was a very infirm old man, with a shuffling walk, slurred speech, and a puffy appearance. A doctor who observed Brezhnev in Vienna said, "He looked eerily like a zombie being wheeled from point to point, with only minimal comprehension of his surroundings."

The Vienna summit was just a brief interlude in a four-year relationship marked by confrontations, harsh rhetoric, aggressive opportunism by the Soviets, and, largely behind the scenes, an increasingly tough U.S. reaction. The Carter administration's military and covert response to the Soviets was overshadowed by the President's decisions on B-1 and the neutron bomb and the rising tide of criticism that he and his colleagues were failing to react to the Soviets at all. Even as SALT II was being completed and then signed, events were under way around the world that would, by the end of 1979, make SALT II irrelevant politically and—somewhat unfairly—forever seal Jimmy Carter's reputation as a weak President.

CHAPTER EIGHT

1979: Cold War, Hot War—
East War, West War

THE YEAR 1979 was a significant turning point in the last half of the Cold War. Soviet (and, in some cases, Cuban) actions in Africa, the Middle East and Southwest Asia, Central America, the Caribbean, and, finally, the Soviet invasion of Afghanistan—all hard on the heels of their interventions in Angola and Ethiopia and against the backdrop of a continuing Soviet military buildup—at last got the attention of the administration, the Congress, and the American people. Moscow's assertiveness, compared to American impotence in Iran and apparent lack of response elsewhere, kindled growing resolve in Washington to counter the Soviets, to again strengthen the U.S. military and CIA as the most suitable instruments to combat Soviet ambitions.

For all the same reasons, 1979 was a very tough year for Jimmy Carter and his national security team. The challenges and problems rolled in from all parts of the globe. Indeed, it seemed at the time like the Soviets or their clients, repeating the pattern of their actions in the Third World in the preceding several years, were asserting themselves and expanding their influence and presence worldwide without constraint. Little did we (or they) know then that that year would represent the high-water mark of the Soviet empire.

CHINA INVADES VIETNAM: A CARTER GO-AHEAD?

For Carter, 1978 had ended with a grand flourish and an important achievement—the normalization of diplomatic relations between the United States and China. This historic development was announced at 9:00 P.M. on December 15.

There are few experiences as exhilarating as being in the White House between the time a major, historic agreement or event has been decided or arranged in deepest secrecy and when it is announced. In nearly a decade at the White House under four different Presidents, I can recall only a few such occasions. They have much in common, and the atmosphere in the White House inner circle surrounding such events is worth describing. Most of the White House staff—in fact nearly all of it, including very senior people who will later obscure (or outright fib about) their lack of knowledge to preserve their status—is still in the dark. Yet there is a quietly frenzied air surrounding the National Security Adviser's office, where closed-door meetings take place all day as the final arrangements or language of announcements or letters and messages to foreign leaders are completed. The National Security Adviser and one or two of his senior helpers go to the President repeatedly throughout the day, walking out of the adviser's office, twenty steps straight down the hall, making a left turn where the Vice President's office is on your right and the Chief of Staff's office directly ahead, and then another ten steps to the hidden door on the right offering admission to the special inner sanctum, the President's study, where he does his real work—as opposed to the ceremonial Oval Office. An alternative access is a few steps farther, squeezing through the stewards' tiny galley where they prepare coffee or tea for the President and his visitors.

In the Carter administration, only Brzezinski, Chief of Staff Hamilton Jordan, and Powell could routinely use these private entrances. Only at special times could others escape the terrible wrath of the President's secretary or gatekeeper for using these doors to reach the President, because they could not record the times individuals entered and left. (It also diminished their control.) Others, even the most senior staff, were expected to enter the study through the Oval Office under the watchful eyes of the gatekeeper. Such unscheduled access to the President in the years I was at the White House was exceptional. And it was permitted only two or three people, and rarely a few others—in the latter case during times of great crisis or in the midst of great events.

The study is a small room, accommodating only three or four people and usually a place to sit for only one or two. The President has a desk, an easy chair or two, a small television, sometimes a stereo. Here the final approvals are given, the President puts his final personal touch to the papers. And those in the know, not more than three or four in the entire White House complex, pity the rest who must go through their day unaware that history is about to be made.

Once the last word is drafted, the last decision made, the waiting is the hardest, as you vainly try to pass the time until the hour of the announcement by pretending to yourself you will do routine paperwork—when you can't even sit still in your chair. Nervous energy has you careening off the walls but careening must be done discreetly and quietly so no one—often not even your secretary—will know. It is an unforgettable experience.

Thus it was the afternoon and evening of December 15, until we gathered just before nine in the Roosevelt Room just outside the Oval Office to watch the President make his announcement. By now the other staff know something really big is up since the television networks need several hours' notice to set up for an Oval Office telecast, and the curiosity about the subject is intense. Usually someone too eager to show off his "insider" status by an hour or so before the announcement will have leaked at least the subject, and then the buzzing and the speculation starts.

However many times I experienced this sequence, it never lost the edge, the excitement of being a part of history. It is one of the great natural highs. And you tell yourself at the time, I will tell my children and my grandchildren I was there that day. I had a part, even if only a small one, in events that historians will write about long after all the participants are dead. And the intensity of the experience compensates for the long hours, the frustrations, the middle-of-the-night phone calls, and even, to some degree, the days and nights that sometimes passed without seeing one's wife and children.

In keeping with the invitation extended by Carter in early December 1978 during the final stage of the normalization discussions, Deng Xiaoping visited Washington and the White House January 29–31, 1979. Deng had one item of business that he asked to raise with the President privately at 5:00 P.M. on January 30.

With the Vice President, Vance, and Brzezinski also present, Deng informed Carter that China intended to "put a restraint on the wild ambitions of the Vietnamese and to give them an appropriate limited lesson." The Chinese could only have been encouraged by the response from the moralistic Carter, who, the next day, met alone with Deng, summarized the possible consequences of China's actions, and simply encouraged restraint.

This had to have been the best signal Deng could have hoped for. No mention of disruption of normalization. No mention of a change in the direction of economic and military cooperation. No principled objection to the invasion of another state. Just the mildly —albeit firmly—expressed worry that it might create problems. Further, no indication that the secret just shared would be violated to warn the intended victim or complicate Chinese plans. And, I suspect, but can't prove, that there were comments made by Brzezinski and others that the Chinese found even more encouraging, however subtly expressed.

On February 2, forty-eight hours later, CIA reported to the White House that there were fourteen Chinese divisions on the Vietnamese border, and that a second echelon of forces was moving south to reinforce them. On the 18th, these forces moved south across the Vietnamese border. The number of forces involved led CIA to worry initially that the Chinese might decide to press on all the way to Hanoi, especially since the White House—consistent with Nixon and Kissinger's practice—had kept CIA wholly in the dark about Deng's comments to the President, Mondale, Vance, and Brzezinski. Even so, before too many days passed it became apparent through our overhead collection systems that the Vietnamese were giving a good account of themselves and that the Chinese were having problems maintaining command and control, that their equipment was outdated, and that Hanoi's troops were seasoned veterans compared to the Chinese. Whether the Chinese intended to go farther we still do not know (although Deng had told Carter the action would be of limited scope and duration). In any event, they stayed within a few tens of miles of the border.

Apart from China's intentions once across the border, the big unknown was what the Soviets would do. In briefings for Carter the preceding November and subsequently, CIA was fairly consistently reassuring—that the Soviet response depended in no small part on how far into Vietnam the Chinese went, but that Moscow, ever the dependable ally, would do as little as it could get away with and take little risk of a direct military clash with the Chinese. The only source of real concern about Soviet actions, according to the Agency, was if the Chinese pushed south so far as to threaten the Hanoi regime.

On this, CIA was right on the money. When the danger was high, the Soviet response was minimal. A Soviet "airlift" to Vietnam began on February 22, four days after the "lesson" started. Yet in the first two weeks there were only ten flights. (Compare that to Soviet flights landing every twenty minutes for three months in Ethiopia.) Moscow's authoritative "warning" to Beijing maintained a calculated ambiguity on what the USSR would do to live up to its treaty commitment with Vietnam if the Chinese did not desist. All in all, while Soviet political and propaganda support was strong, their practical efforts were modest and focused on helping Vietnam within its own borders.

We didn't know for sure how the Soviets would respond, however, and neither did the Chinese. So, as part of the new U.S.-China relationship, each evening during the Sino-Vietnamese conflict Brzezinski would meet with the Chinese ambassador or his representative and provide the latest American intelligence on what the Soviets were doing.

By the time the Chinese pulled back, Vietnam had learned a lesson, all right. They moved quickly to strengthen their military and security relationship with the Soviet Union. During the last half of March, the Vietnamese allowed Soviet naval warships to use the American-constructed navy base at Cam Ranh Bay for the first time, a facility that ultimately would become the Soviets' only enduring (non–Warsaw Pact) overseas base. In addition, the Vietnamese allowed the Soviets to construct a large signals intelligence facility near Cam Ranh Bay. This SIGINT facility, paralleled worldwide only by the Soviet SIGINT facility at Lourdes, Cuba, substantially improved Soviet intelligence capabilities against Southeast Asia, southern China, U.S. forces in the western Pacific, and against U.S. ships in the East and South China seas.

Beyond the forewarning of the Vietnamese lesson and encouraging U.S. response, Deng's visit to Washington in late January 1979 produced another major step forward in the security relationship between the two countries—an offer by Deng to cooperate in collecting and sharing intelligence on the Soviet Union. The United States had lost two of its most valuable sites for collecting information about Soviet missile tests when the new revolutionary

Islamic government of Iran closed the U.S. collection stations (known as Tacksman) in northern Iran. This left a real gap in U.S. collection, a gap that was sure to be used by critics of the anticipated SALT agreement as evidence that Soviet compliance with important provisions of the treaty could not be adequately monitored by the United States. In discussions between Deng and Brzezinski, agreement was reached in principle to pursue a joint effort to establish new collection facilities in western China. The effort would be exceptionally sensitive.

The negotiations culminated at the very end of December 1980–early January 1981, with a never-before-revealed secret visit to Beijing by DCI Turner. I accompanied him. We left Andrews Air Force Base on December 27 and returned on January 7. The visit took place in utmost secrecy. Turner even grew a mustache for the visit.

The talks included technical discussions and exchanges on developments in the Soviet Union—that's why I was along, since I was, by then, National Intelligence Officer for the USSR. We spent a lot of time on Soviet military developments. There were a number of high-level meetings and it was clear that the Chinese leadership, Deng especially, regarded this cooperation as a major strategic decision for them. It was for us, too, as we sat down with people with whom we in intelligence had been at war since 1949. At times we had to pinch ourselves to make sure it wasn't all a dream. Contrary to my expectations, it would not be my only trip to the People's Republic.

Thus, normalization and Deng's visit to Washington marked dramatic steps forward in the relationship between the United States and China. Not only did they change the political content and level of the relationship; they also encompassed security discussions and agreements that would form a strong and lasting foundation for a relationship that would suffer a variety of political ups and downs in both Beijing and Washington. It was all at the expense of the Soviet Union but, at the same time, certainly opened the way for the Soviet Union to establish a strong security relationship with and military presence in Vietnam.

CUBA

By spring 1979, Cuba was really starting to get on people's nerves in the Carter administration, no one more so than Brzezinski. Brzezinski and Aaron were both concerned by the growing number of examples of Soviet-Cuban military cooperation, including the interventions in Angola and Ethiopia, delivery of MiG-23s to Cuba, information on Soviet troop training activity in Cuba, submarine and barge activity at the naval base at Cienfuegos, and more.

Intelligence information provided by Admiral Turner to Brzezinski in the summer of 1979 portrayed a close military relationship between the Soviet Union and Cuba, not just for the purpose of strengthening and modernizing Cuba's own military capabilities, but also a partnership for intervention in a number of places in Africa, Latin America, and the Middle East.

The assertiveness of the Soviets and Cubans, and the scale of their activities, were not denied, questioned, or dismissed by anyone in the administration. However, Vance wanted to shield arms control and especially SALT from these Soviet activities. Brzezinski, and ultimately Carter, believed that unless the administration showed a willingness to tackle this Soviet behavior and unless the Soviets stopped or curtailed it, SALT ratification would be highly problematical.

Carter, Vance, and Brzezinski that summer considered possible ways to take on the Soviet-Cuban problem and, in the absence of any good overt options, decided first to see if they could split Cuba off from the Soviets. The idea was to let Castro know authoritatively that the administration would be prepared to lift the embargo and other punitive measures against Cuba if Havana would back off in Angola, Ethiopia, and elsewhere in the Third World.

The FBI had a contact high in Cuban intelligence and close to Castro whom they had used as a conduit for information about Mariel refugees and other practical law enforcement problems where a quiet communications channel between U.S. and Cuban authorities was required. The decision was made to arrange a meeting in New York between David Aaron and this Cuban intelligence officer and for Aaron to pass Carter's sensitive message. David approached such missions with a certain panache and decided that the meeting should be over lunch, and he chose one of the poshest restaurants in New York City as the site.

The FBI, Brzezinski, and Aaron also decided that I would accompany Aaron and, further, that I would be "wired" to record the entire conversation. About an hour before the lunch, I met the FBI in a room in the Essex House Hotel facing Central Park and stripped to the waist so the FBI technicians could tape a recorder to the small of my back, with a wire and microphone over each shoulder and taped to my chest. I remember them telling me it was a very sensitive, very expensive device. I dressed and was taken by the Bureau agents to the restaurant where I met Aaron. The Cuban intelligence officer, accompanied by a guard, arrived a few minutes later.

Beginning a conversation with an archenemy is never easy, especially in exceedingly awkward circumstances (it was clear that both Cubans were armed and the restaurant was full of well-armed FBI agents). So we did the inevitable and started by talking about baseball. As the courses came and went, Aaron steered the conversation to Cuban adventurism in the Third World and made the administration's pitch—end your overseas games and we'll get rid of the embargo. Rarely had such a historically significant proposal been made so simply or straightforwardly. Aaron was tough with the guy, unrelenting in detailing their activities, the cost to their homeland, and the obvious exploitation of Cuba by the Soviets. The only difficulty was that the Cuban was having none of it. After nearly three hours, we wrapped it up.

It was clear to Aaron and to me right after the meeting that the initiative had been worthwhile but had failed utterly. I strongly recommended against any further meetings. I'm pretty sure that Aaron agreed. But, typically, State wouldn't let go and Peter Tarnoff, then Vance's executive secretary, accompanied by the NSC's Robert Pastor, held several additional meetings with the Cubans—all with similar negative results.

GRENADA

Castro's reluctance to make a deal probably was greatly influenced by the fact that things were going very much his and the Soviets' way at this point. For an example, he needed to look only south and east to the little island of Grenada, less than a hundred miles from the Venezuelan coast.

On March 13, 1979, Maurice Bishop, who had had a close relationship with Cuba for six years, seized power in Grenada. Two days later, the State Department advised the NSC that they were not prepared to characterize Bishop as a Cuban puppet, despite his long ties to the Cubans. State suggested that Bishop was still "co-optable" by either the United States or the Cubans. The department could not have been more wrong. Just short of a month later, on April 14, a Cuban ship off-loaded a large quantity of trucks, arms, ammunition, and at least fifty Cuban military advisers. This got the attention of the White House, and on May 8, Brzezinski sent Turner a memorandum expressing the President's concern about the growing Cuban presence on Grenada.

By September, we had learned from Grenadian police that earlier that month nearly four hundred Cuban regular troops had arrived on the island to train a special force of 3,000 Grenadians for Bishop. In December, the Cubans began the construction of the Port Salinas airport, involving three hundred Cuban "workers" at a cost of $50 million. In short, within six months of Bishop's seizure of power—and long before even a hint of concern from the United States—hundreds of Cuban soldiers and a large supply of weapons had been sent to the small island with the purpose of entrenching this committed authoritarian Marxist.

NICARAGUA

The Carter administration saw a similarly activist Cuban role in the victory of the Sandinista guerrillas in Nicaragua that same year. As late as May 1979, CIA thought the Sandinistas had little chance of seizing power. Indeed, when, on June 8, the analysts prepared a memorandum for senior policy officials suggesting that the Sandinistas were now likely to succeed, Deputy CIA Director Frank Carlucci complained with exasperation that the analysts had been reporting right along that President Anastasio Somoza's position was secure. The "Alert Memorandum" on the situation in Nicaragua was not distributed until June 11. Thus the Carter administration had little warning, at least from CIA, of a prospective Sandinista victory in Nicaragua.

I am struck by the fact that neither Carter, Vance, nor Brzezinski devote more than a passing glance in their memoirs to the victorious Sandinista revolution that summer of 1979. However, I remember—and the record confirms—that they took Cuban-supported developments in Central America quite seriously at the time and the SCC met often on these developments after midsummer 1979.

Brzezinski convened the Special Coordination Committee on June 25 to discuss developments in Nicaragua, just before Carter departed for the Tokyo economic summit. The SCC met again on

July 2, and again on the 10th. During and after these meetings, different options were explored as to how the United States could affect the outcome of events in Nicaragua, with some arguing there should be no such effort and others that the Sandinistas should be stopped or at least a strong signal sent to the Cubans. After one meeting where the possibility of sending such a signal by way of a significant reinforcement of U.S. fighter aircraft in Panama was discussed, Aaron rushed into Brzezinski's office shouting his opposition to sending the aircraft to Panama. Zbig was more than a little nonplussed and reacted quietly but sharply. They argued for a few minutes, and Aaron stormed out of the office. The planes were never sent. This was one of the few times I witnessed a serious substantive disagreement between Brzezinski and Aaron.

On the 18th, CIA warned the White House that Somoza's National Guard was faltering and probably would cease to exist in a few hours. The Sandinistas took power on the 19th.

On July 20, the SCC met to discuss the broader situation in Central America after the Sandinista victory. An important focus was the state of U.S. intelligence in the region. All agreed it wasn't very good. There was unanimous agreement on the need to improve human collection. CIA's resources were so short that most stations in the region had been cut back and we had come within a hair's breadth of closing more than one station entirely. Turner was pessimistic about the chances for improved collection, especially in El Salvador, where we knew very little about what was going on. He noted somewhat sardonically the speed with which the SCC had accepted both State and Defense papers that called for relaxing the administration's human rights stand in Central America.

CIA and the Carter White House knew at the time that the Cubans had played a role in the Sandinista victory. The Cubans had provided substantial arms supplies to the Sandinistas, and tactical combat guidance had been provided by twenty-four Cuban military advisers based in Costa Rica. The overall judgment of the intelligence community was that these advisers had played an important role in helping the Sandinistas oust the Somoza regime. Further, immediately following the Sandinista victory, according to the intelligence assessment, Cuban military advisers moved quickly into Nicaragua and a military communications network was soon established linking Havana with Managua. By the beginning of August 1979, the intelligence experts forecast that the new Nicaraguan government would likely look to the Cubans to send additional military advisers "to help transform the guerrilla forces into a conventional army." The assessment further predicted, "The Cubans can also be expected in the months ahead to begin using Nicaragua to support guerrillas from countries in the northern tier of Central America."

This was Stan Turner's and Jimmy Carter's CIA—not Bill Casey's and Ronald Reagan's. The circumstances of the Sandinista takeover and the future Sandinista-Cuba strategy were identified accurately from the beginning. But what to do?

IRAN

The overthrow of the Shah and what followed warrants attention because the events proved a great, unexpected benefit for the Soviets as the United States lost its primary ally in the Persian Gulf area—and because fears of Soviet gains in Iran would influence attitudes and decisions in both the Carter and Reagan administrations. On Iran, as on so much else, there had been a bitter dispute within the administration, and especially between Vance and Brzezinski, on how to deal with the crisis.

With the departure of the Shah in mid-January and the return of Ayatollah Khomeini to Tehran on February 1, 1979, a reign of terror soon settled over Iran. There was enormous confusion in Washington at this point about who was in charge in Tehran, or if anyone was in charge. CIA wasn't much help. At an SCC meeting on February 12, Turner reported that the situation was out of the control of Khomeini and Mehdi Bazargan, the premier. CIA's difficulty in penetrating the fog in Iran was underscored again in late February by an assessment that doubted Khomeini and Bazargan had sufficient control to remain in power.

The next months were characterized by alternating unrealistic optimism about Khomeini and crises in the U.S.-Iranian relationship. Throughout the summer, the question of whether to admit the Shah to the United States was argued, with Brzezinski the primary advocate inside the government (supported by Kissinger and David Rockefeller on the outside), and Vance objecting. The issue percolated until October, when we learned that the Shah was ill, perhaps terminally so. Under these circumstances, and after State checked with the Iranian government, explained the circumstances, and received assurances that Americans in Iran would be protected, Carter agreed to admit the Shah and he entered the United States on October 23.

A few days later, Brzezinski flew to Algiers to represent the United States at the twenty-fifth anniversary of the Algerian revolution—a gesture of reconciliation. I accompanied him. It was an extraordinary experience. A highlight of the celebrations was a reception for the foreign guests and a lavish banquet. The reception was an intelligence officer's dream come true. All the principal thugs in the world were present—Assad of Syria, Qaddafi of Libya, Yasir Arafat of the PLO, General Giap of Vietnam, Admiral Gorshkov of the Soviet navy (wearing a red medallion around his neck with a giant diamond in the middle), and a remarkable collection of lesser-known terrorists, guerrilla leaders, and representatives of various national liberation movements. I ventured from Zbig's side and moved around the room observing and meeting most of these characters. I kept silent about both my national and institutional affiliation—it seemed the wisest course. Zbig was maneuvered into a reception line where he was virtually forced to shake hands with Arafat—to his distaste and subsequent political discomfort, but avoidable only by causing a huge and unpleasant uproar.

Interspersed with a guided tour of the Algiers Casbah, an impressive (and long) military parade, and other festivities, Brzezinski had a number of substantive meetings. The most dramatic was with the Iranian delegation, which sent word they wanted to meet with him. He agreed and on November 1 walked down the hall of the hotel to their suite—with me in tow as notetaker—for the session. Our hosts were Prime Minister Bazargan, a wizened little guy with wisps of white hair floating around his head; Foreign Minister Ibrahim Yazdi; and Defense Minister Mustafa Ali Chamran. Their greeting and the tone of the entire meeting were surprisingly friendly under the circumstances.

Zbig assured them of American acceptance of their revolution, discussed the reality of a common foe in their Soviet neighbor to the north, the need to cooperate on security matters relating to the Soviets, and left open the possibility of resuming military sales. They raised the return of the Shah to the United States the week before and demanded that he be turned over to Iran for trial. The issue was batted back and forth for a long time and then Brzezinski made an eloquent statement about America's history of providing refuge. At last he stood up and told the Iranians flatly, "To return the Shah to you would be incompatible with our national honor." Even with that, the meeting broke up amicably. However, three days later, our embassy in Tehran was seized and a crisis began that would dominate the remainder of Jimmy Carter's days as President. Two weeks later, the Bazargan government fell, in large part because of the meeting with Brzezinski.

The Soviets must have watched all of this with glee. A major U.S. ally in a critical region of the world virtually overnight had become an implacable enemy. While internal developments offered little encouragement to the Soviets either, in the global competition the U.S. loss of Iran was in itself an important strategic gain for the USSR.

Nor did they just watch and wait. CIA learned that within a few weeks of the November 4 seizure of our embassy, the Soviet General Staff had prepared contingency plans to occupy all of northern Iran should Moscow conclude that developments in Iran posed a threat to Soviet security or in case the United States were to intervene militarily. Further, during the first four months of 1980, activities involving Soviet forces opposite northwestern Iran suggested that the Soviets were improving the posture and readiness of those forces, including an unusual amount of field training.

A special national intelligence estimate produced in August 1980, reflecting on Soviet activities seen in the preceding several months, concluded on an alarming note: ". . . it is evident that the Soviets are indeed developing plans for military contingencies in Iran." We had learned that Soviet planning involved a large-scale invasion moving as far as Esfahan in south-central Iran. The effort included objectives on the Persian Gulf. Indeed, a major Soviet exercise that same August suggested that Soviet contingency plans called for an invasion on two fronts, one in the Transcaucasus and one from Turkestan and Afghanistan, with the objective of seizing all of Iran. The Soviet plans specified twelve divisions to come from the Transcaucasus Military District, three or four divisions from Turkestan, and part of the 40th Army in Afghanistan. The estimate observed that the overall preparedness of the units involved had undergone relatively modest upgrading.

While there was little dispute among the intelligence agencies about the evidence of Soviet contingency planning, there were bitter divisions over what it meant and whether military action was contemplated by the Soviets. The majority view was that the Soviets had not made any decision to invade Iran, though they were taking steps to strengthen the ability of their forces to do so "should Soviet leaders so decide." The U.S. military intelligence representatives were more worried than the rest that the Soviets might act, whereas the State and CIA officials involved thought that the chances of a "low-risk" opportunity for the Soviets were very remote. Further, they argued, the Soviets were far more likely to react militarily to actions by the United States to reestablish its position.

The bottom line, however, was that beginning within a month after the U.S. embassy was seized in Tehran, and within weeks of the Soviet invasion of Afghanistan, the United States observed worrisome military activity by Soviet forces on Iran's northern border and learned about contingency plans for a Soviet invasion of Iran if conditions warranted. In the wake of Soviet assertiveness elsewhere in the Third World in recent years, and the just-completed invasion of Afghanistan, these worries did not seem at all exaggerated. Soviet interest in Iran concerned the Carter administration, though not as much as it would the next administration.

AFGHANISTAN

If ever there was a crisis foreseen well in advance it was the gradual but unmistakable growing Soviet involvement in Afghanistan. As early as March 28, 1979, the National Intelligence Officer for the Soviet Union, Arnold Horelick, wrote Turner to alert him to the possibility of difficult choices ahead in Afghanistan. He sketched a plausible scenario in which the Taraki regime disintegrated to such an extent that: (1) only extensive and direct external military assistance could save it; (2) the Soviets would decide to provide such assistance; (3) this would evoke overt political and barely disguised covert military assistance to the insurgents from Pakistan, Iran, and perhaps even China; and (4) this would lead to a sharp deterioration of Soviet relations with Pakistan and possibly a call from Islamabad for the United States to deter or oppose Soviet military intervention in Pakistan and provide military assistance to states aiding the insurgency. After describing the possible scenario, Horelick concluded that "the Soviets may well be prepared to intervene on behalf of the ruling group."

Horelick then posed the sixty-four-dollar question: how far would the United States go in responding to Pakistani or Iranian appeals for U.S. support of the cause of the Afghan rebels against Soviet intervention? He noted that such help offered the opportunity to turn the tables on the Soviets for their actions in Africa and Southeast Asia, would encourage a polarization of Muslim and Arab sentiment against the USSR, and might offer an opportunity to establish relations with the Iranian government. While Horelick's forecast was not accurate in every detail, he was remarkably far-sighted.

Less than a month later, on April 24, Horelick again wrote Turner, advising that the entire intelligence community watching Afghanistan agreed that the Soviets were gradually increasing their involvement there. The intelligence experts saw more advisers and more matériel going in. Meanwhile, the Soviets were stepping up accusations that the United States and China were instigating the rebellion. (A fascinating demonstration of bureaucratic tunnel vi-sion and compartmentation was the fact that that very spring CIA surveyed Afghanistan as a possible replacement site for its Tacks-man SIGINT collection facilities in Iran, just closed by Khomeini.)

As the weeks went by, the Soviet role grew. A classified CIA paper issued on August 20 stated that the Soviet involvement was by then so extensive that the Soviets might believe they had the assets to stage a successful coup—though it was not clear they would launch one soon. CIA concluded, "We see few signs the Soviets are so wedded to leftist rule in Afghanistan that they will undertake an operation of this magnitude." Another report to key policymakers on August 24 declared that the majority of analysts "continue to feel that the deteriorating situation does not presage an escalation of Soviet military involvement in the form of a direct combat role."

As the situation on the ground in Afghanistan worsened, strains in the Kabul government also mounted. On September 11, President Nur Mohammad Taraki stopped in Moscow on his way home from the nonaligned summit to discuss with Brezhnev the replacement of Prime Minister Hafizullah Amin. Two days later, Amin preempted Taraki's power play against him and on the 16th, Taraki's "resignation"—he was murdered by Amin—was an-nounced. The Soviet congratulatory telegram to Amin was notably cool.

Turner again warned the President and other senior officials of a possible major Soviet move in an "Alert" memorandum on September 14. The memo said, forthrightly, "The Soviet leaders may be on the threshold of a decision to commit their own forces to prevent the collapse of the regime and to protect their sizable stakes in Afghanistan." After stating a straightforward and rather bold position, however, the intelligence warning memorandum once again pulled back. It predicted only that the Soviets, well aware of the open-ended military and political difficulties that could flow from any expanded role against the Afghan rebels, were likely to increase their military role incrementally rather than dramatically—increasing the number of advisers, expanding combat activities, possibly bringing in special battalions or regiments to provide security in key cities.

However hedged, the "Alert" memorandum did galvanize action at the White House. On September 20, a week after the paper was issued, there was an interagency meeting at the Old Executive Office Building to discuss contingency planning against the possibility of Soviet military intervention in Afghanistan. The focus was on actions that might be taken—diplomatic, political, and propaganda—in advance of an intervention to sensitize the countries most concerned.

CIA regularly reported on the increasing Soviet presence and role in Afghanistan, including in the late fall evidence of a buildup of Soviet forces on the border. On December 19, Turner signed yet another "Alert" memorandum to the President and his senior advisers, warning that "The Soviets have crossed a significant threshold in their growing military involvement in Afghanistan." It informed the leadership that the Soviets were "building up . . . more substantial forces near the Soviet-Afghan border" and advised that preparations for much more substantial reinforcements might also be under way. Still, the clearest warning to policymakers came from the Director of the National Security Agency, Vice Admiral B. R. Inman, who telephoned Brzezinski and Brown on December 22 and told them there was no doubt the Soviets would intervene in a major way within seventy-two hours. He called again on December 24 to say the Soviet move would be within fifteen hours.

Starting on Christmas Eve and Christmas Day, 1979, Soviet troops poured into Afghanistan, some 85,000 of them in a period of weeks. A KGB special team dressed in Afghan uniforms attacked the presidential palace and shot Amin and his mistress in a bar on the top floor.

CIA had tracked the growing Soviet involvement with great precision and conveyed to policymakers in a timely way Moscow's growing presence and combat role in Afghanistan. And CIA provided good tactical warning to the President that the invasion was about to happen. But between summer and December, CIA's Soviet analysts just couldn't believe that the Soviets actually would invade in order to play a major part in ground combat operations. They saw all the reasons why it would be foolish for the Soviets to do so —the same reasons many in the Soviet leadership saw—and simply couldn't accept that Brezhnev or the others might see the equation differently. The analysts thought that the Soviet leaders thought as they did. It was not the first or the last time that they would make this mistake.

CHAPTER NINE

Carter Turns to CIA

CIA UNDER STANSFIELD TURNER

The call from the director's office came at about 4:30 on a Friday afternoon. It was January 25, 1980, and I had been back at the Agency from my job as Brzezinski's executive assistant just three weeks. I had come to dislike working in the Carter White House intensely and had first approached Zbig about returning to CIA early in 1979. I liked and respected Brzezinski, and agreed with his views nearly across the board, but his office seemed to me a lonely island of sanity in an otherwise very screwed up White House. I had been offered my first senior managerial position as director of the Strategic Evaluation Center in CIA's Office of Strategic Research and I wanted badly to take it. It took nearly nine months to get out of the NSC.

When Turner asked to see me that January afternoon, I thought it was just a courtesy to welcome me back to the Agency. Our paths had crossed periodically down at the White House when he would come in to see Zbig or drop by before a meeting. I had been in the director's office only a couple of times in my whole career up to that point, both while Colby was there.

As I walked in to see Turner, I took a good look around. By the standards of most departmental and agency heads in Washington, the CIA Director's office is pleasant but not particularly impressive. It is rectangular, probably forty feet by twenty feet, with a corner walled off for a small bathroom and shower. It is paneled in a light wood veneer with a number of recessed lights in the ceiling. Legend has it that at least one of the recessed lights over the sitting area had a bug in it, variously described as intended by the DCI to tape conversations with visitors or, more ominously, installed by the Agency careerists to monitor the DCI. I never believed there was a bug, but then I never checked.

Turner, wearing a cardigan sweater, greeted me in a friendly way, asked me about my new assignment, and made small talk for a few minutes. Then he threw me a curve. He asked me to become his executive assistant. I was horrified. I had just escaped such a job at the White House with Brzezinski and was eager to get back into analytical work and gain experience as a manager. I had finally persuaded Zbig to let me return to CIA based on my desire to work on substantive issues and do what I could to help improve CIA's analysis. To accept Turner's offer would suggest to Brzezinski, whom I valued as a friend, that I had either misled or double-crossed him. I told Turner all of this, and declined his offer. He told me to think about it over the weekend and see him again Monday morning.

At Monday morning's session, the same scenario repeated itself, and he said he wanted to see me again at lunchtime. In that third meeting, he finally indicated that he didn't think I understood the situation. The light dawned and I realized he had made up his mind. With great strength of character, I responded, "Admiral, I'd be happy to work with you." Thus I found myself working directly for the man regarded with deep hostility and dislike by many in and out of the Agency and intelligence community, then and now.

The Carter administration, from the top down—except for Brzezinski—arrived in Washington suspicious and distrustful of CIA. The new President had campaigned against CIA, accepting at face value allegations of "CIA's role in plotting murder and other crimes." The new Vice President, Walter Mondale, had been a liberal member of the Church Committee investigating the Agency. His protégé, David Aaron, the new Deputy National Security Adviser, had been on the staff of that committee, as had Rick Inderfurth, Brzezinski's first executive assistant. Others on the NSC had served on the Church Committee staff as well. Moreover, salted throughout the White House, State, OMB, Justice, and elsewhere were other new officials antagonistic to U.S. intelligence generally and CIA in particular.

Turner arrived at CIA leading with his chin and with a chip

on his shoulder. He was a disappointed man. He wrote in his memoirs that he would have preferred appointment as Vice Chief of Naval Operations and then moving up later to CNO. Now he found himself in a world that was alien to him, one of the most closed bureaucracies in Washington, an agency hostile to "outsiders" at any level, a complex and clannish organization deeply averse to change. An Agency that had been pummeled and punched by press and Congress for nearly two years, had seen its funds and personnel cut and its secrets—good and bad—exposed. It was an agency nearly thirty years old. A large number of those who had been present at its creation were nearing retirement age and a generational change of extraordinary proportions was in the offing.

Thus the stage was set. A new DCI committed to change, appointed by a President with the charge to get control of CIA. A bureaucracy still dominated by the clandestine service, resources depleted, reputation savaged, and on the verge of a demographic revolution.

Turner arrived skeptical and suspicious, and soon found reasons to remain so. He quickly decided his deputy DCI, a career man, was likely to be disloyal. The briefing books were too long, too detailed, and off the shelf rather than tailored to his needs. They offered one-sided views of difficult issues. The jargon was all new and hard to follow. Answers to his questions lacked specificity and clarity. He found no "warm welcome or a sense of great competence."

In short order, he cut himself off from the organization. He brought with him several naval officers who had been a part of his coterie for some time. At one point, there were rumors that he would bring as many as sixty, but even the handful who did come sent a very negative signal to the organization. And when one of them refused to take the standard polygraph for new appointees, Turner signed him up anyway—though he was fenced off from sensitive information in an office downtown.

From the outset, Turner was determined to assert his authority over the Agency quickly and completely. He believed that one reason George Bush had been so popular as CIA director was that he had let the professionals run it the way they wanted. Turner wanted to be in charge of CIA the way a captain is in charge of a ship, and this extended to every aspect of its activities.

Turner further alienated himself from the Agency by appointing a number of new senior officials from outside. He brought in

Frank Carlucci, the then-ambassador to Portugal, as DDCI. He replaced Sayre Stevens as DDI with Robert Bowie, whom he brought to the Agency from Harvard. In addition, in an apparent effort to distance CIA's analytical work from operations and even "intelligence," Turner abolished the Directorate of Intelligence, as the analytical arm of the Agency had been known for decades, and renamed it the National Foreign Assessment Center, with Bowie as its director. Turner also soon replaced the head of the clandestine service, William Wells, with John McMahon, a CIA career officer whose background had not been in human intelligence but on the technical collection side (he had a major part in the SR-71 program). While McMahon was a CIA officer, he was not from the clandestine service career track and thus was not regarded by them as one of them. There were other changes in senior positions as the new DCI sought to put his stamp on the Agency, sought to take charge.

The cultural and philosophical gap between Turner and the clandestine service was simply too wide to be bridged. One episode after another would poison the relationship. Turner early on assigned one of the special assistants he had brought in with him, a civilian, to investigate the DO. He traveled around the world looking into corners in CIA stations, trying to determine if the rules were being followed and procedures were satisfactory. While the assistant gave the DO generally good marks, his efforts prompted a legion of stories about his reporting to Turner on case officers' having affairs and other evidence of immoral or unethical behavior by DO officers. It really didn't matter whether these stories were true. They simply were accepted as true. Similarly, Turner's desire to make CIA "open" to the public, for the Agency's role to be more visible, made the DO recoil. And when Turner repeatedly used the DO's improper treatment of a defector as an example of disgraceful behavior, his continued picking at the scab—long after his point was made—seemed to reflect his distaste for the DO, its work, and its people.

The event that really soured the relationship between Turner and the clandestine service, though, was his decision to reduce the size of the Agency, with particular focus—like Schlesinger—on the DO. He cut 820 positions in the DO, a reduction both then-current and retired DO officers regarded as crippling and unwise. Subsequent intelligence failures would be laid at the doorstep of this action. As if the cuts weren't bad enough, they were carried out in an unnecessarily cold-blooded manner that seemed to all a slap in the face to men and women who had served their country long and well.

Again, the perceptions became more important than the facts. Perhaps that is because the facts cast a more sympathetic light on Turner's actions, and people preferred to believe the worst. The DO itself in mid-1976 had examined its personnel needs in a post-Vietnam environment and concluded that the staffing level should be reduced by 1,350 positions over a five-year period. No action was taken before Turner's arrival and when he subsequently asked the DDO, William Wells, what he thought about the earlier recommendation, Wells did not strongly resist a cut. Accepting the recommendations of the Agency comptroller, Turner reduced the cut to 820 but decided to carry it out over two years rather than five. This meant a number of people were forced to retire or retire early. Actually, fewer than twenty people were outright fired and less than 150 forced to retire early. The rather heartless notice to those affected was the result of Agency administrative and legal officers' advice to Turner that the kind of sympathetic note he intended could open the Agency to lawsuits by people trying to get their jobs back.

If Turner's relationship with the clandestine service was sour, just the opposite happened with the DI (or NFAC). Because he was interested in analysis and needed substantial support for his frequent briefings for the President, Turner spent a lot of time with analysts from every subject area and at all levels of seniority. Being listened to is an analyst's bread and butter, and Turner listened a lot. He was demanding but he was interested. He would, from time to time, impose his views and his approach on analyses and estimates, but that was generally regarded as Turner wanting his own way and his prerogative rather than as politically motivated. Again, perceptions counted for a lot.

Turner was an agent of change. Frustrated by four different personnel systems in one agency, he thought they should be consolidated. He wanted to break down the barriers between the four directorates and his concept of "one Agency" became an epithet for many managers who thought the DCI just didn't understand the organization. He was full of ideas for improving training, career management, strategic planning, budgeting, the system of security compartmentation, and more. There was no aspect of managing the vast enterprise that did not interest him or bring his involvement. His attempts to improve communication with employees, especially junior officers, further earned him the dislike of senior managers as he broke the chain of command and called seniors on the carpet based on what he was told by their subordinates.

Overall, CIA was not a happy shop under Turner. He was essentially at war with his senior managers, often the same people he appointed. There was a mutual lack of loyalty and trust. They would often stall when he called for change and find ways to circumvent his wishes. He, in turn, would find ways to override or go around them. He was a reformer, a man of high integrity, a believer in the rule of law and congressional oversight, a smart man. But he was also an impatient man and, confronted with bureaucratic obstructionism inside CIA and in the intelligence community, he would just charge forward and try to force through change. Where his authority was unchallengeable, in CIA, many of the changes were implemented. He won partial compliance where his authority was not complete. But in nearly every case, his failure to build a substantial internal constituency for his changes led to the reversal of his initiatives very quickly after his departure.

By the time I arrived in Turner's office, in February 1980, he had learned a lot and mellowed some. And the Agency had settled down under him. The passage of time had dulled memories of earlier clashes and problems. He remained committed to reform, to change. I agreed with much of what he wanted to do in terms of breaking down the walls among different parts of the organization, giving younger people more opportunities (I especially liked that one), rationalizing collection management, and more. Believing that senior people want to hear the unvarnished views of their close associates, I was often brutally candid with Turner about his management style—as well as the problems I saw in the Agency. I was, from time to time, quite insubordinate. But Stan Turner never closed me out, never shut me up. He was, in fact, quite tolerant of some pretty harsh criticism. Coming at the end of Turner's time in office, I quickly came to appreciate what he was trying to do, understood the bureaucratic resistance to that, and gained considerable respect for him. Watching the way the Agency bureaucracy obstructed his efforts, I once told him I had learned a valuable lesson working for him. I now knew that I never wanted to be DCI—anyone who wanted the job clearly didn't understand it.

I made at least one contribution to Turner that year. He and

Brzezinski had treated each other warily from the beginning. I soon came to realize that Turner and Brzezinski agreed on a number of substantive issues and that they were natural allies on many. The problem was that in an administration as riven with internecine warfare as Carter's, all of the various bureaucracies looked for ways to provoke conflict between their bosses. Mostly it was to advance parochial agendas, partly it was a clash of personalities at lower levels, and partly I think it was simply blood sport on the part of the permanent bureaucracy. In any case, a close friend of mine, Les Denend, had replaced me as Brzezinski's executive assistant, and we worked together to prevent or at least mitigate the troublemaking by the NSC staff and CIA bureaucracy. We also tried to reduce the level of suspicion and paranoia toward each other on the part of the two principals. We were largely successful, and in that last year of the Carter administration, Turner and Brzezinski worked together usefully and productively. I had believed since I first went to the NSC under Nixon that the National Security Adviser and the DCI were natural bureaucratic allies in Washington—the former provided access to the President and information on the national security agenda, the latter provided manpower and critical information on the world. Working for Turner was my first chance to help make that alliance work better.

Turner's relationship with Carter was curious and ambivalent. He was Carter's choice. They went back a long way—they had been at the Naval Academy together. Zbig told me that on one occasion, Carter discussed Turner with Vance, Brown and Brzezinski, praising him in nearly adulatory terms and telling them that "Some day, Turner might make a Secretary of State in the mold of George Marshall." (I wonder how that made Vance feel.)

At the beginning, Turner briefed Carter at least once a week on subjects of his own choosing. After a while, the briefings went to every two weeks and then even longer intervals. Turner devoted tremendous effort to preparation of the briefings, but Brzezinski told me that Carter often found them boring. Most indicative of Carter's attitude toward Turner was the DCI's exclusion throughout Carter's term from the regular Friday morning foreign policy breakfast, attended by Carter, Mondale, Vance/Muskie, Brown, Brzezinski, and later several other senior White House advisers. I think Turner may have been invited once or twice, but not more. I always thought Turner blamed Brzezinski for his exclusion, but I know that Zbig suggested to Carter on several occasions that

Turner be invited, and Carter turned him down—on one occasion firmly telling him to drop the subject.

This, then, was CIA under Stan Turner. But it is also a fact that, despite all the turmoil and conflict, both Turner and CIA continued to do their work—both analysis and operations. And despite allegations both then and subsequently that CIA was crippled under Carter, much good analysis was produced and some very imaginative covert action and intelligence collection programs were implemented, both human and technical.

Most importantly, contrary to conventional wisdom, the Carter administration turned almost from the outset to CIA to carry out covert actions. As Jimmy Carter soon learned, to use Dick Helms's expression, "It is *his* CIA." However, by 1977, CIA's covert action capability already had been seriously weakened. Most of that weakening was the result of reductions in covert action infrastructure (people and equipment) after Vietnam, Schlesinger's purge in 1973, the impact of the 1974–1975 congressional investigations of previous Agency covert activities, and broader Agency-wide budgetary losses. In short, CIA's covert action capability had been weakened significantly *before* the Carter administration by decisions and events of the preceding four years.

Indeed, as Carter turned to covert action within weeks after his inauguration and increasingly frequently thereafter, the most constant criticism of CIA that I heard from both Brzezinski and Aaron was its lack of enthusiasm for covert action and its lack of imagination and boldness in implementing the President's "findings" (legal shorthand for presidential decisions authorizing covert actions). As described earlier, Carter and company turned to CIA for covert actions aimed at the Soviet internal scene as early as March 1977. Throughout that year and the next, CIA was asked to step up its activities targeted inside the USSR. As early as September 1977 CIA had identified a massive Soviet covert campaign in Europe against deployment of the ERW, and had been authorized by the SCC to begin a countercampaign publicizing that the Soviets had developed their own neutron bomb.

Beyond the covert actions focused inside the USSR, the Carter administration turned to CIA also to counter Soviet and Cuban aggression in the Third World, particularly beginning in mid-1979. Because Vance was unwilling to use diplomatic leverage against the Soviets, and Brown and others wanted no part of U.S. military involvement in the Third World, their standoff gave Brzezinski an enormous opportunity to put forward covert action—which was under the purview of the NSC—as a means of doing something to counter the Soviets. That is just what he did, and until now virtually all of those efforts—like those inside the USSR—have remained shielded from public view.

GRENADA

I described earlier the seizure of power in Grenada by Maurice Bishop, a pro-Cuban Marxist, in March 1979, and the arrival of Cuban weapons and advisers on the island within a month. This resulted in a memorandum from Brzezinski to Turner on May 8, 1979, expressing the President's concern about the growing Cuban presence on Grenada and suggesting a covert effort to focus international press attention on it. Turner responded on May 14 with a political action program going beyond Brzezinski's suggestion and intended to counter the Cubans on the island. Carter signed a "finding" on July 3, 1979, that authorized a covert effort to promote the democratic process on Grenada and also to support resistance to the Marxist government there.

All hell broke loose when Carter's finding was briefed to the Senate Intelligence Committee on July 19. The committee expressed its "strong displeasure" with the finding and pointed to the divergence between the covert proposal and the administration's position on human rights and noninterference. The committee sent a letter the next day telling the President that they "cannot support the projected covert action directed at Grenada." Although the committee had no legal authority to stop the covert action, in the wake of the congressional investigations, to the chagrin of the White House, and contrary to public and political perceptions, CIA was responsive to the congressional position and on July 23 ceased all covert activity relating to Grenada. Carter's effort to respond covertly to the Cuban encroachment on Grenada was thwarted by Congress. Now the problem would fester until President Reagan's use of military force four years later.

AFGHANISTAN

The Carter administration began looking at the possibility of covert assistance to the insurgents opposing the pro-Soviet, Marxist government of President Taraki at the beginning of 1979. On

March 5, 1979, CIA sent several covert action options relating to Afghanistan to the SCC. The covering memo noted that the insurgents had stepped up their activities against the government and had achieved surprising successes. It added that the Soviets were clearly concerned about the setbacks to the Afghan communist regime and that the Soviet media were accusing the United States, Pakistan, and Egypt of supporting the insurgents. The SCC met the next day and requested new options for covert action.

The DO informed DDCI Carlucci late in March that the government of Pakistan might be more forthcoming in terms of helping the insurgents than previously believed, citing an approach by a senior Pakistani official to an Agency officer to discuss assistance to the insurgents, including small arms and ammunition. The Pakistani had stated that without a firm commitment from the United States, Pakistan "could not risk Soviet wrath."

Meanwhile, in Saudi Arabia, a senior official also had raised the prospect of a Soviet setback in Afghanistan and said that his government was considering officially proposing that the United States aid the rebels. The DO memo reported that the Saudis could be expected to provide funds and encourage the Pakistanis, and that possibly other governments could be expected to provide at least tacit help. The memo conceded that the Soviets could easily step up their own resupply and military aid, although "we believe they are unlikely to introduce regular troops." Further, if they decided to occupy the country militarily there was no practical way to stop them, but such a move would cause them serious damage in the region.

On March 30, 1979, Aaron chaired a historic "mini-SCC" as a follow-up to the meeting some three weeks earlier. At the mini-SCC, Under Secretary of State for Political Affairs David Newsom stated that it was U.S. policy to reverse the current Soviet trend and presence in Afghanistan, to demonstrate to the Pakistanis our interest and concern about Soviet involvement, and to demonstrate to the Pakistanis, Saudis, and others our resolve to stop the extension of Soviet influence in the Third World. Newsom continued, however, that we didn't know enough about the real potential for reversing the current trend or the Soviet response to such an effort. He worried about an increased Soviet role in Afghanistan in the wake of an abortive U.S. intervention and the risk that they might stimulate the Baluchi tribes against the Pakistani government. Walt Slocombe, representing Defense, asked if there was value in keeping the Afghan insurgency going, "sucking the Soviets into a Vietnamese quagmire?" Aaron concluded by asking the key question: "Is there interest in maintaining and assisting the insurgency, or is the risk that we will provoke the Soviets too great?" If the interest exists, he said, we need to consult with others and be prepared to make a limited commitment. The second question was what could be done to help the Pakistanis deal with the situation? State was directed to develop the articulation of U.S. policy, and CIA was directed to prepare a paper on possible Soviet reactions.

In anticipation of an April 6 SCC meeting on Afghanistan, all of the relevant bureaucracies were "papering their principals." I learned that at State, the Near East Bureau was telling Vance that, at this stage, the United States shouldn't go beyond a modest effort to publicize Soviet actions and intentions, both through diplomatic contacts and publicly. Further, the State bureaucracy was urging Vance to wait for the Pakistanis to react to a recent U.S. approach on their nuclear program before pursuing consultations with them on Afghanistan, and asserting that intelligence liaison contacts should be limited to exchanges of information on Soviet activities and insurgent capabilities.

The day before the SCC meeting on April 6 to consider Afghan covert action options, Soviet NIO Arnold Horelick sent Turner a paper on the possible Soviet reactions. Horelick said if the Soviets were determined to keep Taraki in power, covert action could not prevent it, and external assistance would be used to justify their own deepening involvement. But, he added, they would take this line anyway and were already making such charges. His bottom line: covert action would raise the costs to the Soviets and inflame Moslem opinion against them in many countries. The risk was that a substantial U.S. covert aid program could raise the stakes and induce the Soviets to intervene more directly and vigorously than otherwise intended.

The SCC met at 11:00 A.M. on Friday, April 6, to consider a wide range of options. These included:

- a small-scale propaganda campaign publicizing Soviet activities in Afghanistan;
- indirect financial assistance to the insurgents;
- direct financial assistance to Afghan émigré groups to support their anti-Soviet, antiregime activities;
- nonlethal material assistance;

- weapons support; and
- a range of training and support options.

At the meeting, these options were discussed and there was a general preference for an active role, but only for nonlethal assistance. CIA was charged with preparing a finding for coordination and the President's signature. It did so quickly and returned the paperwork to the NSC.

After moving quickly, the proposed finding now languished for some weeks. In the interval, one of the Afghan insurgent leaders traveling abroad made contact with a CIA official and asked that the Agency provide some direct aid to the rebels. Turner reported this to Brzezinski and recommended that we do what we could to get the Pakistanis to move unilaterally. We learned on April 4 that the Chinese had informed the Afghans that they might supply arms to the Afghan Mujahedin. Two months later, Carlucci observed the turbulent situation in Afghanistan and suggested at a morning staff meeting that the covert action finding be considered expeditiously. Turner responded that it was still with Brzezinski, awaiting a final SCC meeting.

The meeting was finally held on July 3, 1979, and—almost six months *before* the Soviets invaded Afghanistan—Jimmy Carter signed the first finding to help the Mujahedin covertly. It authorized support for insurgent propaganda and other psychological operations in Afghanistan; establishment of radio access to the Afghan population through third-country facilities; and the provision either unilaterally or through third countries of support to the Afghan insurgents, in the form of either cash or nonmilitary supplies. The Afghan effort began relatively small. Initially, somewhat more than half a million dollars was allocated, with almost all being drawn within six weeks.

The Afghan finding was briefed to the SSCI on July 19, at the same time as the Grenada finding. While it did not evoke the same opposition, members of the committee were very nervous.

By the end of August, Pakistani President Mohammad Zia ul-Haq was pressuring the United States for arms and equipment for the insurgents in Afghanistan. He called in the U.S. ambassador to make his pitch and indicated that when he was in New York for the UN General Assembly session in September, he would raise the issue at higher levels in the Department of State. Separately, the Pakistani intelligence service was pressing us to provide military equipment to support an expanding insurgency.

When Turner heard this, he urged the DO to get moving in providing more help to the insurgents. They responded with several enhancement options, including communications equipment for the insurgents via the Pakistanis or the Saudis, funds for the Pakistanis to purchase lethal military equipment for the insurgents, and providing a like amount of lethal equipment ourselves for the Pakistanis to distribute to the insurgents.

On Christmas Eve and Christmas Day, 1979, the Soviets massively intervened in Afghanistan. A covert action that began six months earlier funded at just over half a million dollars would, within a year, grow to tens of millions, and most assuredly included the provision of weapons.

There is no doubt that the invasion of Afghanistan was a watershed not only for the Soviets but also in resolving disagreements in the U.S. government about what the Soviets were up to and how the United States should deal with them. The administration imposed a wide range of sanctions on the Soviets, often without much consultation with the allies, who were dragged along on many measures and simply balked on others—like boycotting the 1980 Olympic Games.

As senior U.S. officials looked at Soviet behavior after the invasion, the key question was what it meant in terms of longer-range Soviet goals in the region. Turner addressed this issue in a sensitive "Eyes Only" memo he sent to the President and other members of the National Security Council on January 16, 1980. The paper, "Soviet Options in Southwest Asia After the Invasion of Afghanistan," made the following points:

- "It is unlikely that the Soviet occupation is a preplanned first step in the implementation of a highly articulated grand design for the rapid establishment of hegemonic control over all of southwest Asia.

- "The occupation may have been a reluctantly authorized response to what was perceived by the Kremlin as an imminent and otherwise irreversible deterioration of its already established position in a country within the Soviets' legitimate sphere of influence.

- "However, they do covet a larger sphere of influence in southwest Asia and probably believe that the occupation improves their access to lucrative targets of opportunity.

- "Of all the objectives that the occupation of Afghanistan may have placed within easier Soviet reach, a pro-Soviet Iran is the most tantalizing. The occupation emplaces Soviet forces on Iran's eastern and northern borders, and has created the possibility for large-scale Soviet aid to the Baluchi as well as Azeri and Kurdish separatist movements. Iran may be on the brink of political, social, economic chaos. At a time when the Soviets are about to encounter significant shortfalls in domestic energy production, it is probable that expansion of its influence over Iran will rank at or near the top of the Kremlin's hierarchy of regional priorities."

In February 1980, Brzezinski traveled to Pakistan where, alone with President Mohammad Zia, they discussed an expanded covert action program. From Pakistan, Brzezinski went on to Saudi Arabia, where he cemented the arrangement that the Saudis would match the U.S. contribution to the Mujahedin.

At the end of March, Brzezinski asked Turner to assess whether the invasion of Afghanistan was an aberration in Soviet behavior or a symptom of a change in the global balance that would see further such Soviet aggression. The reply, prepared by Horelick, went back to Zbig in mid-April. While the analysis came down firmly on both sides of the issue ("Each view captures important aspects of reality, but omits important considerations"), it concluded, "The possibility that Afghanistan represents a qualitative turn in Soviet foreign policy in the region and toward the third world should be taken seriously."

What was more interesting was Turner's personal cover note to Brzezinski in forwarding the Horelick paper. Turner wrote:

> I would only add a personal comment that I would be a bit more categoric than the paper in stating that the Soviets' behavior in Afghanistan was not an aberration. I agree we do not have the evidence that the Soviets are firmly committed to continuing as aggressive a policy in the third world as was this Afghan example. Yet, I do believe that the Soviet track record over the past five or six years indicates a definitely greater willingness to probe the limits of our tolerance. "Détente" was not a bar to this greater assertiveness in Angola, Ethiopia, Kampuchea and Yemen. It need not be so again, even if we return to détente. As the paper concludes, how assertive the Soviets will be in the future will very likely depend upon how "successful" the Soviet leadership views their intervention in Afghanistan to have been.

Turner had it exactly right.

By July 1980, the covert program had been dramatically expanded to include all manner of weapons and military support for the Mujahedin. On July 23, Turner briefed the President that the insurgents were becoming ever more dependent on Pakistan, which had agreed to step up arms deliveries.

The last act on Afghanistan in the Carter administration was a meeting between Turner and Brzezinski on October 29, where the latter complained "over and over" that he didn't think CIA was providing enough arms to the insurgents and wanted the Agency to increase the flow. Back at the Agency, the DCI said that he sympathized with this point of view and wanted to be able to reassure Brzezinski when they next met that CIA was pushing everything through the pipeline that the Pakistanis were willing to receive.

Most observers since the Carter administration have applauded what was seen as a "late in the day" awakening to Soviet aggressiveness and the strong U.S. reaction to the invasion of Afghanistan. In fact, Carter and Brzezinski saw the Soviets beginning to increase their role in Afghanistan almost a year before the invasion, initiated work on a covert response nine months before, and implemented a covert finding to help the insurgents resist the Soviets almost six months before the massive Soviet move. U.S. help was nonlethal and modest in size until the invasion, but it was a start. The key alliances were established with Saudi Arabia and Pakistan, and the first elements of an extraordinary logistics pipeline from suppliers around the world were assembled. The stage was set for the vast future expansion of outside help, all run by CIA.

THE ARABIAN PENINSULA

Another Third World conflict that drew Carter administration attention was on the Arabian peninsula, where the radical Marxist government of the People's Democratic Republic of Yemen (PDRY) attacked the Yemen Arab Republic (YAR) to its north in late February-early March, 1979. From the beginning there was suspicion that the Soviets, Cubans, and/or the Ethiopians were involved with the PDRY in the attack.

This issue was discussed at the same mini-SCC on March 30 where Afghanistan was on the agenda. In the papers prepared for Carlucci for that meeting, the DO advised that the concept of a defensive counterinsurgency had been overtaken by events and that future discussion of covert action in the area should focus on steps to prevent Abd-Al-Fattah Isma'il, the PDRY leader, from fomenting a Marxist revolution throughout the Arabian peninsula. The options put forward by the DO were aimed at shoring up the shaky political and security situation in the YAR and aiding the Omanis to stave off PDRY-backed disorder. These efforts were described as interim measures that ultimately would fail unless executed in conjunction with a broader U.S. program aimed at dealing with the basic problem posed by Isma'il's regime. The basic proposal was to create dissension in the PDRY to impede Isma'il's ability to destabilize other Arabian peninsula countries, to undermine his authority and perhaps lead to his fall from power.

At the March 30 meeting, there was considerable discussion of what to do about the situation. The State Department was particularly concerned about the role of Saudi Arabia and whether they were prepared to stand by the YAR. CIA was authorized at that meeting to pursue with the Saudis the question of their resolve, their views on the current leadership in the YAR, and alternative courses of action.

Overall, the meeting was quite forward leaning in terms of possible covert action to help the YAR. Aaron asked if we could help the YAR improve its intelligence and security services, and CIA was authorized to discuss this with several friendly intelligence services in the region. Similarly, there was general support for helping the Omanis deal with subversion sponsored by the PDRY.

Covert assistance to the YAR was discussed and agreed upon at the April 6 SCC meeting after yet another debate about possible Soviet reactions. The President signed a Middle East finding on July 3, 1979, at the same time he signed the findings on Afghanistan and Grenada.

CENTRAL AMERICA

Developments in Grenada, Nicaragua, and El Salvador during the summer of 1979 caused great concern in the Carter administration. The reaction to the building Cuban position on Grenada has already been described. But now the administration faced a Sandinista victory in Nicaragua and a related upsurge in the Marxist insurgency in El Salvador. The U.S. response was inhibited in part because of a lack of good intelligence on what actually was happening.

Once again, Carter turned to CIA and to covert action. The President signed findings on both Nicaragua and El Salvador in

late July—less than two weeks after the Sandinistas seized power—
and the House intelligence committee was briefed on the Nicaragua
finding as early as August 1. (So much for the notion that covert
action in Central America was the brainchild solely of the Reagan
administration.) This finding was focused primarily on propaganda,
exposing what the Sandinistas were all about, and the Cuban role
in supporting the Nicaraguan revolution. The El Salvador finding
was more directed at helping the government deal with the insurgency. In both countries, there was a parallel, crash effort to improve intelligence collection.

Because of Cuba's central role, there was also a major effort to
devise a strategy to deal with Havana's "adventurism" in both Africa and Latin America. On September 20, Aaron chaired a mini-
SCC concerning national intelligence priorities regarding Soviet
and Cuban assertiveness worldwide. As a result, the NSC levied a
requirement on Turner to produce a list of proposals, by priority,
for improving CIA coverage and activities.

On October 19 there was another meeting with the President
on Central America and the Caribbean. By this time, covert action
had been authorized in Grenada (though stopped by Congress),
and there were covert actions authorized and under way in El Salvador and Nicaragua. At the meeting, the State Department, often
eager to promote both military action and covert action—vice diplomacy—to deal with problems, made a strong pitch for even
more assertive covert actions in the region. There was a particularly
spirited debate over whether Jamaican Prime Minister Michael
Manley was "retrievable" from Soviet influence. Some five weeks
later, on November 24, 1979, the President signed a broader finding authorizing CIA actions to counter the Soviets and Cubans
throughout Latin America.

In August 1980, CIA sent the policy agencies and departments
a report on Soviet and Cuban military activity in Central America
and the Caribbean. After a six-page, single-spaced listing of Cuban
military activity in Central America, the paper observed that Cuba
was the principal source of military training and aid to the Nicaraguan armed forces. It reviewed a variety of fragmentary reports of
Cuban military assistance to insurgent groups elsewhere in Central
America, especially in El Salvador and to a lesser extent in Guatemala and Honduras.

Specifically, the memo reported that the Cuban advisory presence in Nicaragua was steadily increasing, was estimated at 3,400–

4,000, and that Cubana Airlines was now making a daily round trip from Havana to Managua. It went on to say that the Cubans were delivering Soviet-made weapons, that Sandinistas were receiving military and security training in Cuba, and that seventy Sandinista pilots had been sent to Cuba for MiG flight training. With respect to El Salvador, the Cubans continued to train, advise, and arm the Salvadoran insurgents, with more than five hundred trained since late 1978. The paper concluded that over the next few months, "the Soviets will probably continue a policy designed to expand their influence in the region, particularly with the Nicaraguan regime." Outside of Cuba, though, there was little evidence of direct Soviet military activity in Central America—the Soviets were clearly letting the Cubans take the lead in providing military assistance to leftist groups.

By October 1980, despite the covert actions, clearly the Sandinistas were consolidating their power in Nicaragua with Cuban help, and the insurgents were becoming more active in El Salvador. The issue of supporting the resistance to the Sandinistas came up, and Turner expressed concern to Brzezinski that an attempted counterrevolution or even a report that there might be one would be used by the Cubans as an excuse to increase their presence. He also advised Brzezinski that the covert action in El Salvador was well under way, that Defense was being supportive, but that he hoped Defense would be sure to coordinate with CIA anything they were thinking of doing to interdict the arms supply.

Five days before the U.S. election, Brown advised Turner and others that Defense was looking at two military scenarios in Nicaragua in the event of a coup attempt against the Sandinistas. The first was to insert U.S. forces more rapidly than the Cubans could insert theirs. The second was to intercept Cuban forces in flight to Nicaragua.

An interagency report issued on November 24 spelled out the Soviet strategy in the region:

> The Soviets seek to propitiate conditions for leftist advances and their own influence in the region. The Soviets regard political strife in Guatemala and El Salvador as opportunities, and we have limited indications that the Soviets have assisted leftists in the latter country and are considering policies to assist leftists in Guatemala. The Soviets have continued to support the leftist front in El Salvador through a major propaganda campaign against alleged U.S. interference, re-

ported financial payments, clandestine arms shipments via Cuba, and periodic advocacy of violent revolution. . . . Cuban military influence in Nicaragua is evident in the construction of military camps at Villa Nueva and Matagalpa about 70 miles north of Managua. They are similar in layout and building construction to the most modern military camps in Cuba and not typical of Nicaraguan camps currently in use.

In sum, the U.S. government's preoccupation with communist advances in Central America and the Caribbean, and Cuba's role in fostering those advances, did not begin with the Reagan administration. Nor did the use of covert action throughout the region as the preferred means of stopping Cuban-sponsored, violent revolutions aimed at installing Marxist governments. The foundations of U.S. policy and actions in Central America in the 1980s were put in place by Jimmy Carter—and well before the invasion of Afghanistan.

IRAN: RESCUING HOSTAGES

Two of the most daring and courageous clandestine operations during my career took place in the first four months of 1980, and both involved efforts to rescue Americans taken hostage in Tehran after our embassy was seized on November 4, 1979.

As the embassy was being taken, six Americans managed to escape the U.S. compound and flee to the Canadian embassy, where they were hidden. When the Canadians advised us of the predicament, CIA set about devising a way to bring these people out. A very brave CIA officer, using a commercial cover, entered Iran with false identities for the six and, using techniques that ought to remain secret so they can be used again, managed to get the six out of Iran.

The second rescue effort was, of course, the larger operation undertaken by the U.S. military, with intelligence in a supporting role. The basic plan was to fly helicopters into a desert airstrip inside Iran, where they would rendezvous with C-130 transport planes bringing troops and fuel. The helicopters would then fly into Tehran where special forces would rescue the hostages and carry them out under protective air cover. The military part of this operation has been described (and criticized) elsewhere, so I will focus on the CIA part.

CIA had two key roles in the rescue attempt. The first was to scout a landing place in the desert (Desert One) for the C-130s and helicopters, and emplace landing lights for a runway in the middle of nowhere. The second was to obtain information from inside the embassy compound on the precise locations of the hostages and also to provide trucks to move the hostages to the helicopter landing site near the embassy.

We used our imagery satellites to scout the Iranian desert for a suitable landing site—one where the planes could land and yet be hidden from roads and possible witnesses. Our photo interpreters identified such a site. Meanwhile, the wizards in CIA's Office of Technical Services devised battery-powered landing lights that could be emplaced easily and switched on remotely from the air. When all this was done, about two weeks before the actual rescue mission, a CIA Twin Otter propeller plane flew low over the coast into Iran, evading radar detection. Those few of us at Headquarters aware of the operation had a very long day as we waited to hear that our team had completed their incredibly risky mission and returned to safety. They found the designated site, a relatively level remote area, and landed the plane. While one pilot emplaced the landing lights, the other rolled a motorcycle out of the plane, fired it up, and took off to scout the area and assure that traffic on a nearby road was sufficiently infrequent to provide a significant chance that the rescue force wouldn't be spotted. Mission successful and completed, they flew back out of Iran without detection.

CIA's role in Tehran was not so successful, but we did develop a good source inside the embassy compound and we were able to rent a warehouse and acquire trucks for the rescue. Nonetheless, this part of the effort was constantly criticized by the military as being inadequate, and a lot of bad blood built up in the period before the actual mission. The efficacy of CIA's preparations in Tehran was never tested because of the tragedy in the desert when a helicopter crashed into one of the C-130s.

The evening of the rescue attempt was a long one. I was with Turner the whole time, including at the White House. We knew by late afternoon about the trouble with the helicopters and the decision not to proceed. News of the further tragedy in the desert came later. Carter and most of his senior national security team were in the Cabinet Room and the Oval Office, placing secure phone calls—the only secure telephone around was in the Oval Office—and making notifications to the Congress and others. We finally left the White House at about 1:30 in the morning. I was driven back to the Agency where I picked up my car. I turned on the radio and caught the 2:00 A.M. news reporting the disaster in Iran. Convinced that the mission could have succeeded, depressed at the deaths of our servicemen, and realizing the likely cost to Carter for having acted boldly and failed, I had a long, sad drive home.

Fiasco: The Soviet Brigade in Cuba

Even as Carter leaned more and more heavily on CIA and covert action as the action arm of his efforts to cope with Soviet and Cuban aggressiveness around the world, in the last half of 1979 intelligence would be responsible for one of the most embarrassing episodes in Carter administration foreign policy.

It all began with Brzezinski's request in April 1979 for an intelligence community assessment of the Soviet-Cuban military relationship. One of the agencies of the intelligence community researching its files to develop a comprehensive report was the National Security Agency. It issued a summary report to the other intelligence agencies on Friday, July 13, 1979, that concluded, among other things, that a Soviet military formation observed in Cuba "is a brigade," consisting of subordinate motorized rifle, artillery, armor, and support elements, some at the battalion and company level. Turner was informed promptly and the following Monday, the 16th, warned his senior staff of likely high interest in the days to come of reports of a Soviet brigade in Cuba. An interagency intelligence assessment dated July 19 was fairly low-key. It reviewed NSA's evidence as well as recent imagery and concluded that the "evidence does not indicate any suspicious change in recent years."

At this point, early on, politics and the media entered the picture. Turner learned on July 19 that newsman Ted Koppel intended to do a broadcast that day on the Soviet military presence in Cuba. Turner met with Vance, who brought in his press spokesman, Hodding Carter, to go over a press release. The statement mentioned that Soviet troops had been in Cuba for a long time for training purposes, and Turner wanted to add "and for conducting electronic spying for themselves." Vance said he agreed with the point, but demurred at adding it, saying that he didn't want to heat up the atmosphere with the Soviets during Senate consideration of the SALT II treaty, which had been signed only three weeks before

—a reflection of Vance's desire throughout the episode to play down the brigade so as not to endanger ratification of SALT II. Turner responded that he "continued to remain concerned . . . at the fact that the Soviets stick it to us with abandon regardless of SALT." He told his colleagues when he returned to CIA that he wanted to pull together a list of what the Soviets were doing to the United States so that he could show it to Vance as balance.

Now politics intruded. Senator Richard Stone of Florida had asked both Vance and Brown during their separate testimony before the Senate Foreign Relations Committee respectively on July 10 and 11 about Soviet activities in Cuba and how they fit into the 1962 and 1970 U.S.-Soviet understandings on Cuba. Vance sent a letter to Stone reviewing the history of those understandings and, in essence, concluding that current Soviet naval and other military activities in Cuba did not violate the 1962 understandings. But the Congress was getting aroused.

Vice President Mondale had lunch with Senator Stone on July 24. The lunch didn't slow Stone down at all. The same day, he sent President Carter a letter asking that the 1962 understandings with the Soviets be made public: "It is important during the SALT II debate to know whether or not the Soviet Union has lived up to these commitments concerning Cuba." He referred to news stories in recent days citing senior administration officials receiving intelligence that the Soviets were setting up a high-ranking command structure in Cuba able to handle a brigade-size force. Stone concluded that such a command structure—"in my view"—constituted a Soviet effort to establish a military base, and he asked Carter to take "appropriate steps" to effect its removal.

Throughout August, the intelligence community became more confident about the existence of the Soviet brigade. On August 29, there was a White House meeting on what to do about it. Dave Newsom of State reported that Vance's special counsel on the USSR, Marshall Shulman, had told the Soviet chargé on July 27 that the United States would regard the presence of organized Soviet combat units in Cuba with "deep concern." A new démarche to the Soviets was prepared at the meeting, to be coordinated with the principals. It was decided at the meeting that the démarche had to be made in the next day or two in anticipation of congressional inquiries and the expectation of an eventual leak.

Predictably, the leak came first and forced action with respect to Congress. On August 30, the next day, State learned that the magazine *Aviation Week and Space Technology* had the brigade story, and all began to think about how to brief congressional leaders before their return from the Labor Day recess. State was especially sensitive because they, like Vance at the outset, understood the negative implications for SALT ratification of this development.

The temperature plainly was rising on the issue. There was a meeting at State on August 30 to review proposed papers on strategy for dealing with the brigade and press guidance and congressional strategy. All understood that the United States had almost no direct leverage on the Soviets and that the maximum realistic U.S. goal could only be to induce the Soviets to agree not to increase their ground forces in Cuba and not to introduce any additional combat units. We could hope to get the Soviets to characterize the unit as nonoffensive, assure us that it was not a "coherent" unit, and make observable changes in the unit itself. In short, there already was a vast gap between what members of Congress were demanding and what the administration believed, as of August 30, it could get from the Soviets.

The discussion of congressional strategy focused almost entirely on how to limit the damage to SALT. As one participant said, "If the brigade issue tips the votes of even a few Senators, it could cause a defeat or delay on SALT. The negative linkage to SALT may be reinforced by charges that our intelligence capabilities have proven inadequate 90 miles from our shores. More important is the perception of our ability to deal with the Soviets effectively over their combat unit in Cuba. Some may call for confrontation and demand its immediate removal."

Once it was clear that *Aviation Week* had the story, State congressional liaison officials recommended informing Senate Majority Leader Robert Byrd and Minority Leader Howard Baker, who were apparently in Washington; telephoning Senators Frank Church in Idaho and Jacob Javits in New York; and briefing Speaker Tip O'Neill and Minority Leader John Rhodes. They suggested a meeting also with Stone. All agreed that whatever briefings took place had to be done promptly.

Senator Church was in the middle of a desperate reelection campaign. He had visited Cuba and had been photographed with Castro, and his opponent was using this against him in the election. Since he had been assured by State that there was nothing there to worry about, Vance and Newsom thought he should be brought up to date on what the administration had learned—before it was published in the press. Vance called Church and briefed him. Church asked if State would be making a statement and, when told that it probably would not, the Senator responded that the information was so sensitive that he couldn't "sit on it." The Secretary did not explicitly object to Church going public, and so he did. And the administration's challenge in managing the brigade issue became significantly tougher.

CIA and Turner were right in the middle of all of this. At the August 30 meeting to develop administration strategy to deal with both the Congress and the Soviets (sometimes it was hard to keep straight which was the more challenging adversary on the brigade issue), Horelick's assistant NIO, Robert Dean, figuratively rolled a grenade into the room by noting evidence that the troops in question had been in Cuba well before 1975–1976.

And, within days, information began to surface showing that the brigade, in fact, had been in Cuba a long time. Admiral Inman, the director of NSA, on September 3 provided a more complete chronology concerning the brigade. It showed that the first reference to a brigade in intelligence information had come in mid-1968, and that there had been other information about ground forces in late 1968, 1969, 1970, and 1971. A few days later, CIA's Directorate of Operations discovered in its files human source reporting from 1968–1971 corroborating the NSA information developed during the preceding two weeks. The reports provided convincing evidence that the troops in question had been in Cuba since at least 1968, and probably before.

In discussions with Vance, Soviet Ambassador Dobrynin was unyielding on the brigade, saying that, in his view, withdrawal of the Soviet unit from Cuba would not be acceptable. Further, he said there had been no significant change in numbers in the unit since 1962, and no change in the mission of training Cuban officers on Soviet equipment.

When, in a subsequent meeting, Vance handed over a diplomatic note with a number of detailed additional questions about the brigade and the Soviet presence in Cuba, Dobrynin responded, "We have a crisis on our hands. If the Soviet Union presented such questions to the U.S. about its installations around the world, the U.S. would tell the Soviets to go to hell. These questions do not lead to a way out—they lead to a deadlock."

How to proceed with the Soviets resulted in a major blowup between Vance and Brzezinski at a breakfast with the President on

September 21. The two of them and Brown reviewed two papers on what to do next, one by State and one by the NSC. The issue was how tough to be in dealing with the Soviets. As Horelick described the debate for Turner:

> The dispute is basically between (1) those who attach central priority to saving SALT and preserving some semblance of "détente" in our relationship with the Soviet Union, (2) those who see the Brigade negotiations failure as providing a point of departure for restoring a U.S. foreign policy consensus behind which a more vigorous U.S. competitive stance against the Soviet Union could be mounted (with SALT if possible, but without it if necessary), and (3) those who are primarily concerned with salvaging the Carter presidency, a preoccupation which for the most part inclines them toward the second rather than the first posture.

Vance and Gromyko discussed the brigade several times during their meetings in New York in late September. Gromyko at one point asked why the Soviets would send some "unit" to threaten U.S. security, why this would be done. Vance replied that Castro could have said to the Soviets that he had deployed Cuban forces in Africa and therefore wanted reassurance at home, and had asked the Soviet Union to send its forces there. At that point Gromyko became very sarcastic, saying, "The Secretary must have read a mystery story that was very artistic. Are you addicted to mystery stories? . . . When I return to Moscow I will have to tell the Soviet leadership and Brezhnev personally that something had occurred that had never been contemplated by Soviet authorities— that the Secretary and the U.S. administration were laboring under a delusion."

Four days later, Carter personally brought this embarrassing episode to a close with a speech in which he accepted Soviet assurances that "they do not intend to enlarge the unit or give it additional capabilities." He also announced that the United States would increase its surveillance of Cuba, establish a Caribbean Joint Task Force at Key West, expand military maneuvers in and economic assistance to the region, and would assure that Soviet troops in Cuba were not used as a combat force to threaten the security of any nation in the hemisphere. And, on October 31, Vance said publicly that the Soviets had taken steps in Cuba to reduce U.S. concerns about Soviet troops there. He added that "some factors have changed and the changes are not unpleasant."

The "Soviet brigade" fiasco began with intelligence agencies failing to do their homework before rushing into print and to brief, raising an alarm about a situation that in fact had long existed, and responding too quickly to the demand of policymakers for information *now*—often before it had been vetted. These errors were compounded by the subsequent leak of the intelligence warning, and then a politically motivated, quick and excessive reaction by the Congress. Because the administration could not extract from the Soviets any real concession to help it save face, this chain reaction of blundering jeopardized the fate of SALT II well before the Soviets invaded Afghanistan. It was all a self-inflicted wound.

But the episode had focused attention on two serious problems. First, it alerted both the administration and the Congress to the real impact on both human and signals intelligence capabilities of the long years of budget cuts. From 1968 through 1975 there had been minimal collection on Cuba and a major reduction in resources. By 1979, U.S. intelligence simply did not know what "ground truth" was on the island.

The second problem highlighted by the flap was the real Soviet and Cuban subversive threat in Central America and the Caribbean, and the brigade episode focused serious attention on this for the first time. During September, with the help of the intelligence community, Lloyd Cutler of the White House had put together an unclassified "white paper" addressing Soviet and Cuban involvement in Central America. It said the brigade issue shouldn't be viewed in isolation but had to be seen against the broader background of a pattern of Soviet/Cuban military activity and interventionism in the Third World, "particularly the continued expansion of this activity in Latin America and the Caribbean. The uninterrupted continuation of these developments poses a threat to global stability, peace in the western hemisphere, and to U.S. security."

The White House paper stated that some forty thousand Cuban military personnel were by then stationed outside of Cuba, receiving their entire support—logistical, transport, military weapons, and more—from the Soviet Union.

> Most importantly, as a result of the recent Soviet buildup in Cuba since 1975, the Cubans now have a lift capability to pursue their adventures throughout the Caribbean and Central America. . . . This increased military cooperation between the Soviet Union and Cuba, coupled with the growth of Soviet/Cuban military capabilities in our

own backyard and Cuban support for revolutionary movements and covert action in a number of Latin American countries, is a matter of grave concern to the United States. It was undertaken in disregard of long-standing U.S. sensitivities, and its continuation could pose a serious threat to stability in an area that has historically been considered important to U.S. national security.

This was the Carter administration's description of the problem in Central America in the fall of 1979—not a Reagan administration broadside in the mid-1980s.

POLAND

The final act in U.S.-Soviet relations for the Carter administration was in dealing with the crisis in Poland. Both the administration and CIA ended 1980 with a flourish—and a success.

The decade of the 1970s had been hard on Poland. The protests and riots in December 1970 that brought Edward Gierek to power were followed by another crisis in 1975 when the government attempted to cut wages, and still another in mid-1976 with one more attempt to raise the price of food. Once again, in 1976 in response to worker protests, the government had to back down.

As a reaction to these events, and mindful of the pledges the Soviet and Polish governments had made at the Helsinki conference in 1975, new organizations and publications began to appear. In the summer of 1976 the "Committee for Defense of Workers" (KOR) was founded in the hope that such an organization could protect workers. Also in 1976 the "Movement in Defense of Human and Citizen Rights" first appeared with the purpose of monitoring human rights violations in keeping with the Helsinki Final Act. Other organizations, like the "Young Poland Movement," soon also emerged. Discussions among worker activists about a free trade union began in the fall of 1977. The problems and obstacles facing workers, however, remained great. Walesa said of that time, "I remember the mid and late 1970s as a time of defeat and failure, on every level: social, professional, and moral."

According to Walesa, "the decisive moment" came on May 3, 1980, when members of the Young Poland Movement and the Movement in Defense of Human and Citizen Rights were arrested and others, including Walesa, began to circulate leaflets demanding political and economic concessions by the government—recognition of political rights of Poles, immediate overhaul of the economy, an end to price increases and inflation, and more. The government ignored the demands, sent the militia, and there was a stalemate between representatives of the workers and the soldiers.

CIA was watching all of this very closely. On July 19, 1980, we issued an "Alert" memorandum to senior government officials warning that labor disturbances in the Polish city of Lublin—which began on July 2 over an increase in meat prices—could become more intense and spread to other parts of the country. We expressed concern that tensions were increasing throughout Poland and that some of the agreements settling disputes between workers and management were coming "unglued." The memo raised the possibility that the strikes could degenerate into a violent confrontation with the regime. Just three days later we relaxed as the disturbances ended and the regime continued to take a conciliatory approach. The Soviet hands-off approach was continuing.

This all changed when 100,000 workers at the Gdansk shipyard went out on strike on August 14 after a worker, Anna Walentynowicz, was dismissed five months short of retirement for distributing the Free Trade Union newspaper. The demands of the strikers included permission to raise a monument to those killed in December 1970, a pay raise, and, most importantly, the right to organize trade unions independent of both management and the government.

The demands for the pay raise ultimately were granted and the strike was near settlement on August 17, but the leaders decided to remain on strike. According to Walesa, "Solidarity" was born at the moment when the shipyard strike "evolved from a local success in the shipyard, to a strike in support of other factories and business enterprises, large and small, in need of our protection: moral reasons impelled us toward solidarity with our neighbors and our coworkers in every line of endeavor." An interenterprise strike committee was formed and on August 22 published a list of twenty-one demands, including recognition of an independent Free Trade Union, a guaranteed right to strike, guaranteed freedom of expression, restoration of the jobs of those dismissed for defending workers' rights, access to the mass media, and a number of economic demands. Negotiations began with the government.

Meanwhile, we at CIA were busy. On August 29, the Acting NIO, Robert Dean, sent a memo to Turner saying that the crisis had entered perhaps a decisive phase. The strike actions were continuing to spread, raising the possibility of a nationwide work stoppage. Dean acknowledged that we couldn't predict how it would all turn out because even near-term containment measures by the government would have a high potential for unraveling and escalating. He concluded, with considerable insight, that any concessions on free trade unions would result in the de facto weakening of the party's monopoly of power: "This will produce a fundamental change in the distribution of political authority and will set the stage for the evolution of a pluralistic system." Even so, the government signed the list of demands and overall agreement on August 31. Gierek resigned shortly thereafter.

At a meeting with Turner on September 3, Brzezinski expressed his concern at the possibility of a Soviet invasion of Poland because the agreement with the workers so undermined the foundations of the Polish political structure. He asked us to do a paper on the prospects of Soviet intervention.

He received a less hypothetical paper than he expected. On September 19, Turner sent to the President and the other principals of the NSC an "Alert" memo stating that "Soviet military activity detected in the last few days leads me to believe that the Soviet leadership is preparing to intervene militarily in Poland if the Polish situation is not brought under control in a manner satisfactory to Moscow." The memo cited military activity in the USSR's three westernmost military districts and other military developments as well as manifest Soviet leadership concern over the developments in Poland. The paper concluded that the Soviets likely would give the new leader, Stanislaw Kania, additional time to regain control, "but if current trends continue unabated against the Polish Party's control over the nation or Poland's role in the Warsaw Pact is called into question, the Soviets will threaten or employ military force."

The memo mentioned also our growing problem in learning what was going on inside Poland and in the western part of the Soviet Union. Much of the area was cloud-covered, thereby impeding our ability to monitor the activities of both Polish and Soviet military units. Embassy Warsaw reporting was, as one report said, "fragmentary because of Foreign Service personnel transfers and personnel limits generally." The budget cutbacks of the 1970s were being felt everywhere.

On September 23, the SCC met with Brzezinski in the chair and Brown, Warren Christopher (then Deputy Secretary of State),

Acting JCS Chairman General Lew Allen, and Turner attending. Turner began the meeting by briefing that the unrest in Poland was spreading and that the Soviet military was taking some preparatory steps similar to those taken in Czechoslovakia in 1968. He said that he thought the Soviets had not yet made up their minds to invade Poland. He added that it would take some thirty Soviet divisions to invade and that we would have two to three weeks of warning time. All agreed the Poles would fight if the Soviets invaded.

At the meeting, the overall situation in Eastern Europe also was reviewed. Turner said that it was clear that the Polish Communist Party was in disarray over reform, with some members resigning. The Polish Church had made gains. Elsewhere in Eastern Europe, the economic picture was equally gloomy, with growing anxiety about spillover from Poland. The East Germans, Romanians, and Czechoslovaks were plainly the most nervous.

Turner continued that the Soviets viewed the developments in Poland as a threat to the entire communist system. They saw a ripple effect elsewhere in Eastern Europe and eventually in the Soviet Union itself as a real danger. Turner suggested that the Soviets saw the current situation as potentially more contagious than previous crises in individual countries in that the working class had demonstrated a strategy to extract fundamental concessions from a communist government. He concluded that the developments in Poland threatened the fabric of the Warsaw Pact and therefore Soviets couldn't let it spread. But he added that the Soviet leadership was divided on what to do.

At another meeting on September 29, the question of AFL-CIO financial support of the Polish trade unions was raised. Zbig said he was going to meet with the head of the AFL-CIO, Lane Kirkland, and try to make him aware of the sensitivity of the situation. As usual, State was the most nervous and worried that AFL-CIO support would afford the Soviets a propaganda target and cause the Soviets genuine concern. Christopher asked if there were any appropriate steps that could be taken to persuade U.S. trade unions to take a low profile on assistance to the Polish unions.

In a meeting with Turner on October 30, Brzezinski offered his own view of what was most likely to happen. He said he thought the Russians would try to pull off a coup involving right-wing elements, Russia supporters inside Poland, Polish police, and other security elements rather than try an outright invasion. Turner said he thought that was high-risk in view of the possibility that the Polish army would be against them. Brzezinski responded that the Polish army would only react in a unified way if they were ordered from the top, and the top would be subverted by the Soviets.

The Polish crisis entered an especially dangerous phase in late November. I became the National Intelligence Officer for the Soviet Union and Eastern Europe on November 24, in the middle of this crisis. I remembered that my first day in CIA had been the day before the invasion of Czechoslovakia in 1968. It seemed like déjà vu all over again. I knew and respected the Assistant NIO for the USSR, Bob Dean, and he continued to carry the heaviest burden of watching Poland. We oversaw the preparation of another "Alert" memorandum, which we issued on November 25. It told the President, "The Polish leadership is facing the gravest challenge to its authority since the strikes on the Baltic Coast ended in August." We advised that the Warsaw leaders of Solidarity had issued six political demands and threatened large-scale strikes if the regime failed to begin talks on the demands by noon on November 27. We thought it would be difficult for the regime to acquiesce in the demands, especially in light of a Soviet warning on the 24th against a railroad strike. "Thus the present situation moves us closer to coercive measures by the regime or possibly a Soviet military invasion."

On November 28, four days after becoming NIO, I sent Turner my first personal analysis of the situation. I wrote, "The situation in Poland is intolerable to the Soviet Union." I described the divided and demoralized state of the Polish party and its steady weakening under the weight of concessions to Solidarity. I said that the demands of Solidarity had reached the point where they struck at the foundations of communist power in Poland, the security forces. The party was increasingly not in control and the economic situation was grim. "Even were no further demands or concessions to be made, I believe the Soviets cannot and will not settle for the status quo." I concluded that "in the next few weeks the tone of Soviet propaganda will harden and the Soviets will pressure Kania to draw the line with Solidarity. Failure to do so would bring his replacement. Before Christmas, the regime will be under great Soviet pressure to take coercive measures. . . . If this fails, the Soviets will step in. The cost of re-establishing Polish party control will be great; the cost of failure to do so would be incalculable by Soviet reckoning." I was right on the mark in what the Soviets would do —but I was almost exactly a year too early.

During the following days, though, it looked like I would be right—right then. CIA reported on December 1 that the Soviet exercises near Poland were "unscheduled and unprecedented for this time of year." Our apprehension was increased by continued poor weather, which adversely affected our collection of information on Soviet troop movements.

We issued yet another "Alert" memorandum on December 2, which Turner covered with a dramatic note to the President: "I believe the Soviets are readying their forces for military intervention in Poland. We do not know, however, whether they have made a decision to intervene, or are still attempting to find a political solution. . . ." The memo described Soviet military preparations in and around Poland that "are highly unusual or unprecedented for this time of year." There were preparations for an imminent unscheduled exercise involving the Soviets, East Germans, Polish, and possibly Czechoslovak forces, and large areas of East Germany along the East German–Polish border were to be closed between November 30 and December 9. A substantial buildup of forces "could now be under way" in the western military districts of the Soviet Union. In the awkward and hedged language characteristic of too many intelligence forecasts, the memo concluded: "On balance, this activity does not necessarily indicate that a Soviet invasion is imminent. We believe that these preparations suggest, however, that a Soviet intervention is increasingly likely."

Now the crisis machinery swung into high gear. On December 3, there was a meeting of Brzezinski, Ed Muskie (who had replaced Vance as Secretary of State in April 1980), Brown, and Turner to discuss contingency measures in response to Soviet activities, including a public statement warning against intervention. As the debate went back and forth on whether to issue such a public statement, Zbig observed, "Wouldn't it be odd if Governor Reagan and [his adviser] Richard Allen appeared to make the stronger statements."

They then discussed whether to precede a public statement with a Hotline message to Brezhnev. Muskie thought perhaps that should be reserved until there was "something imminent." Brown said he thought it would cause Brezhnev to take the public statement more seriously and at the same time allow us to be both tougher and more reassuring at the same time. Zbig said he was coming around to that view and added, "One has to think about history. We will have to ask ourselves whether we had done all we could do to prevent an invasion."

Brzezinski then dictated a Hotline message from Carter to Brezhnev and all agreed to it. In final form, the public statement warned of "very grave consequences to U.S.-Soviet relations" if the Soviets acted militarily in Poland. Further, messages were sent to Giscard d'Estaing, Schmidt, the Chinese, and Indira Gandhi, urging them to speak out as forcefully as possible against a Soviet move into Poland. Brzezinski also called the Pope with a similar message.

The mini-SCC met the same afternoon at three in the Situation Room. The intelligence briefing reviewed military activities, and the State Department representative agreed that the Soviets were ready to go into Poland but had not decided to do so. We then turned to military contingencies and the JCS representative noted that SACEUR (the Supreme Allied Commander in Europe) had requested authority to take certain preparatory actions, including measures for heightened vigilance, activating the alliance's wartime headquarters and other measures to improve readiness. Aaron also urged JCS to consider proposing some highly visible measures, such as increasing war reserve munitions, for the SCC to consider. All agreed. On economic sanctions, Aaron said that we should make clear to the Europeans that if there is an invasion, we believe "(1) major turnkey projects should be canceled and (2) the gas pipeline deal should be held in abeyance. We should also seek allied agreement on how to characterize the invasion, what non-provocative measures could be taken to strengthen allied defense, and more on economic sanctions."

On Sunday afternoon, December 7, the NSC met with the President in the Cabinet room to discuss the Polish situation. The Carter national security team subsequently was joined by the congressional leadership so they could be brought up to date on events and the administration's plans. I accompanied Turner and sat behind him. Several members of the leadership expressed concern that we were not doing enough. Both Brown and General David Jones several times expressed concern about "getting out in front of the allies." At one point, the House Minority Leader, John

Rhodes of Arizona, sat back in his chair, hooked his thumbs in his belt, and said, "What you all call getting out in front of the allies, in my part of the country we call leadership."

We learned within days that on December 5 there had been a Warsaw Pact summit in Moscow at which Kania had persuaded the other bloc leaders to give him some more time. He also agreed to avoid a policy of continuing concessions to Solidarity. Subsequently, it became clear in Poland that the country had been close to a Soviet intervention, and that knowledge imposed new sobriety on Solidarity, the party, and the Church. (Years later, former Warsaw Pact military leaders would write that intervention was, in fact, planned for December 5, to include fifteen Soviet divisions, two Czech divisions, and one East German division, with nine more Soviet divisions to arrive within days. A hold was put on the order to invade at 6:00 P.M. on December 5.)

Despite the lull, in a report to Turner on December 22, we stated that the Soviets were unlikely to accept the status quo as a long-term solution—virtual dual power, fragmentation, and the potential de-Leninization of the party.

As the crisis eased temporarily, Turner told his senior officers at CIA that the Agency had played a major role in shaping the policymakers' reactions to the events in Poland. A good part of the White House statement on the situation in Poland had been the result of the DCI's meetings with analysts on December 6, prior to the SCC and NSC meetings.

In fact, the Agency had performed well during the Polish crisis, despite cloud cover that greatly inhibited a clear picture of the state of Soviet military readiness and activities, little embassy reporting, and little clandestine reporting on the activities or thinking of Solidarity leaders, the Polish government or party, or on Soviet intentions or thinking. Quality analysis had been based mostly on fragmentary information, experience, and skill. Similarly, based on fragmentary information, the Carter administration—even while preoccupied with the Iran hostage crisis—had played its cards with the allies and with the Soviets well. The President's statement and Hotline message, along with strong warnings from European leaders, probably were not decisive, but they were well-timed and undoubtedly at least conveyed to the Soviet leaders a huge additional cost if they invaded: the relationship with the West. And CIA had begun clandestine activities in support of dissident Poles.

For all the internal turmoil in CIA under Turner and initial wariness of the Agency by the new administration, CIA ended up as the administration's primary weapon in trying to cope with Soviet and Cuban aggression in the Third World and as an important asset in challenging Soviet abuses at home. Both the President and the DCI had come a long way since early 1977.

CHAPTER TEN

The Mask of Soviet Ascendancy, the Reality of Vulnerability

To THINK that between 1973 and 1979 we could fight and lose the most divisive war in our history, nearly impeach and ultimately force from office a President for the first time in our history, suffer two economically catastrophic increases in oil prices, and somehow not grasp that these epochal developments would profoundly affect us and global perceptions of us has always struck me as unbelievably naïve.

Even more striking, and dangerous, is that this period of great national political weakness—paralysis—coincided with unique opportunities for the Soviet Union to expand its influence and presence internationally against the backdrop of a strategic military buildup at that time unparalleled in the history of the world. The Soviet collapse in 1991 should not obscure the reality of their challenge in the 1970s. Indeed, it was, at least in important measure, the magnitude of that effort that, in the end, bankrupted them and brought down a hollow political shell that had been sustained by military and police power and the willingness to use it at home and abroad.

The Soviets did not establish strategic superiority over the United States during the period, but the psychological balance was totally changed, along with the strategic nuclear balance. While the number of U.S. strategic missile launchers remained relatively stable over a fifteen-year period, the Soviet number grew nearly sevenfold. Through MIRVing, the United States doubled the number of its intercontinental warheads, but the Soviets increased theirs by nearly twenty times. Thus the United States not only lost its overwhelming superiority of the 1960s, but all of the momentum in the strategic race seemed to be on the Soviet side.

Many Americans did not seem to realize at the time that new U.S. strategic capabilities also were in development, including the new heavy ICBM, the MX; the air-launched and sea-launched strategic cruise missiles; stealth aircraft; and more. New Trident submarines were being built. While we had no plans for strategic defenses and virtually all of our programs were under budgetary pressure, we were just introducing the Abrams main battle tank and the Bradley fighting vehicle into the Army; F-15s and F-16s were just going to the Air Force; and the Navy was building more Nimitz-class nuclear aircraft carriers and Los Angeles–class attack submarines. In short, the United States, even in the dark days of the 1970s, continued to modernize its forces and increase their capabilities substantially. Indeed, on several occasions in the 1970s, I heard the President and senior members of Congress ask our military chiefs whether they would trade forces with the Soviets. The answer was always negative.

What was clear, and not much argued, was that the Soviet Union's increasing military power was emboldening it to act and to take risks in advancing its interests and ambitions around the world. As DCI Turner told the Congress in his "Worldwide Briefing" in February 1980, "Under Brezhnev, and especially since the mid-1970s, an assertive, global Soviet foreign policy has come of age."

The intelligence community, reflecting on the 1970s, formally expressed its view of Soviet foreign policy in a national estimate published in mid-1981. The secret estimate, "Soviet Goals and Expectations in the Global Power Arena," began with an unusually candid and unambiguous conclusion:

> As it enters the 1980s, the current Soviet leadership sees the heavy military investments made during the last two decades paying off in the form of unprecedentedly favorable advances across the military spectrum, and over the long term in political gains where military power or military assistance has been the actual instrument of policy or the decisive complement to Soviet diplomacy. . . . This more assertive Soviet behavior is likely to persist as long as the USSR perceives that Western strength is declining and as it further explores the utility of its increased military power as a means of realizing its global ambitions.

With respect to the United States, the estimate stated that "in light of the change in the strategic balance and continued expansion of general purpose forces, the Soviets are now more prepared and may be more willing to accept the risks of confrontation in a serious crisis, particularly in an area where they have military or geopolitical advantages." The conclusions of the NSC-chaired interagency "Comprehensive Net Assessment," prepared during the Carter administration, were strikingly similar.

Overall, then, both the intelligence community and policymakers in the Carter administration believed by the end of the 1970s that, while the Soviet Union had not acquired strategic superiority, maintaining the balance required continuation of U.S. modernization programs—and additional resources. The geopolitical consequences of the extraordinary Soviet military buildup beginning in the mid-1960s were equally obvious: the loss of U.S. military superiority and growth of Soviet military power had given the Kremlin new confidence to pursue its ambitions internationally more aggressively and without much concern for U.S. sensitivities.

MALAISE: WEST AND EAST

Deepening pessimism in the United States about the future in terms of the competition with the Soviets was compounded by deepening problems at home. If too many observers underestimated the impact at home and abroad of the U.S. defeat in Vietnam, so, too, I believe, did too many underestimate the aftershocks of Watergate. The whole sad saga profoundly changed American politics, adding significantly to popular mistrust of the national government—already high because of Vietnam—and increasing mistrust and ill will between the Executive Branch and the Congress.

Even more important than the political malaise of the mid- to late 1970s was a major economic crisis. When Carter became President, inflation was still about 6 percent, unemployment was high at 7.8 percent, and the economy was growing quite slowly compared to past performance. By 1980, both inflation and interest rates were nearing 20 percent, unemployment was growing, and the nation was in recession. And Americans weren't the only unhappy citizens of a Western democracy in the late 1970s.

The overall result was a widespread impression that the West was in trouble, facing tough economic times, low growth, low expectations, and low confidence that its leaders knew what they were doing. The personal relationships among Carter, the new British prime minister Margaret Thatcher, Schmidt, and Giscard d'Estaing seemed to personalize and highlight the perceived disarray of the West compared to the growing power of the Soviet Union. The Europeans needed American leadership and did not find what they were looking for in Jimmy Carter. And when Carter told the American people in July 1979 that the country was suffering from a "crisis of spirit," he was in fact accurate. Unfortunately for Carter, they held him to blame for the malaise.

Preoccupation in the West, and especially in the United States, with difficulties at home, masked the growing crisis in the Soviet Union through the latter half of the 1970s. Policymakers accepted at face value the notion that the Soviet Union had serious economic problems. Indeed, the belief in the Soviet need for Western economic help was a fundamental aspect of Nixon's approach. Still, U.S. leaders viewed Soviet economic problems through the prism of their own economic difficulties and, if anything, thought the Soviet Union had it better. Most did not grasp that the West was passing through a phase, a cycle brought on by very specific causes —including another huge oil price increase in 1979—while the Soviet economic problem was systemic, eventually terminal, and could turn critical soon.

This was not for CIA's lack of trying to portray the Soviet economic crisis. From the late 1950s, CIA had clearly described the chronic weaknesses as well as the formidable military power of the Soviet Union. In the late 1970s, the Agency began to chronicle not only deepening economic difficulty, but also social problems— popular disaffection, ideological erosion, material frustration, and ethnic unrest. In August 1979, CIA published the assessment that "Soviet consumer discontent is growing and will cause the regime of the 1980s serious economic and political problems."

In June 1980, DCI Turner expressed CIA's long-range pessimism about the Soviet economy. He described the economic outlook as "grim" and stated that the size of the military burden would continue to grow relative to the overall economy because it was expanding considerably faster than the economy. The burden of maintaining and expanding the Soviet empire was increasing. Turner went on: "The outlook [for the Soviet economy] is for a continued decline in the rest of the 1980's." Concluding that the Brezhnev leadership would mark time, Turner stated, "By the mid-

1980's, a new, well-established Politburo could be persuaded that more radical policies were necessary." They could then either move toward austerity "by all available means" to support continued growth in military spending, or "Alternatively, the economic picture might look so dismal by the mid-1980's that the leadership might coalesce behind a more liberal set of policies. These policies could include major shifts in resource allocation, structural reforms, or both."

In light of later criticisms of CIA's work on the Soviet economy, the record of its work in the late 1970s merits attention. During that period, and later, CIA presented a series of bleak forecasts for the decade of the 1980s, predicting that slow industrial growth and productivity would continue through the 1980s, might intensify, and that by mid-decade major changes could be under consideration. In 1979, CIA perceived the Soviet economy in a state of crisis, and its forecasts conveyed an impression of substantial pessimism.

Nevertheless, by fall 1980, the sense that the Soviets and their surrogates were "on the march" around the world was palpable in Washington and elsewhere. Vietnam. Angola. Ethiopia. Mozambique. Yemen. Libya. Cambodia. Nicaragua. Grenada. Cuba. Afghanistan. In all of these places, and more, observers saw the Soviets or their minions challenging existing governments, supporting sympathetic movements or governments, and establishing a strong military and intelligence advisory presence.

Even as we contemplated the Soviets' likely next moves, however, forces were at work that would turn most of the symbols of an expanding Soviet empire in the Third World into political liabilities and extraordinary burdens that, coupled with the growing internal crisis, would help bankrupt the regime politically and economically and contribute to its ultimate collapse.

Within two years of Mao's death, Beijing had established diplomatic relations with the United States, and the relationship expanded to include the kind of security cooperation that had so preoccupied and worried Brezhnev in his talks with Nixon, Ford, Schmidt, and others. With what appeared to be U.S. collusion, the Chinese attacked Vietnam, a Soviet client. And China was soon working both independently and with the United States to support the anti-Soviet resistance in Afghanistan. Finally, China's economic reforms promised to provide the resources for modernization of its military and for its further integration with the non-Soviet world.

The "second front" in the East was becoming more a reality than a worst-case nightmare.

In Eastern Europe, economic problems, together with greater political activism by noncommunist elements of society spawned by the Helsinki Conference, had created a full-blown crisis in Poland that threatened to spread. The Polish Communist Party was split and demoralized, discredited in the eyes of both Poles and Soviet authorities. Solidarity was striking heavy blows at the foundations of communist power in Poland. Other East European communist leaders, especially in East Germany and Czechoslovakia, were desperately fearful of "the Polish disease" spreading and demanded action by Moscow. But the Soviets by 1980 no longer could quiet the situation by simply making more goods available, and the prospect of military intervention—the unbelievable political, economic, and military costs—was daunting.

In the Third World, the seeds of counteroffensives directed at the Soviet gains of the 1970s were being planted. Less than a year after the invasion of Afghanistan, the Soviets confronted a Mujahedin resistance supported by Pakistan, Iran, Saudi Arabia, China, and the United States. While the level of assistance was still modest, it seemed certain to grow. In Angola, South Africa continued to support Savimbi in his opposition to the Soviet-backed government, sustaining UNITA and allowing it to expand its military operations beyond the southeastern part of the country. In Nicaragua, Jamaica, Yemen, and elsewhere, modest covert U.S. assistance to those opposing Soviet clients was already beginning to flow, and where the support did not go to the resistance, it was directed at exposing and discrediting the actions of those clients—and occasionally at exacerbating their problems. In every case, this support, too, would only grow.

Meanwhile, the specter of a continuing Soviet military buildup, the impression—and reality—of Soviet aggressiveness in the Third World, national humiliation in Iran, and a sense of growing national weakness finally were turning the tide of public opinion in the United States in favor of more spending on defense and intelligence. When Senate debate on SALT II treaty ratification resumed in late October 1979, after the Cuban brigade fiasco, the focus again was on the defense budget—but now with a new twist: how much *more* should it be?

As the United States approached its presidential election in 1980, these fledgling challenges to the Soviets were scarcely visible to the experts and even less so to the politicians and the electorate. Indeed, none of the efforts in the Third World as yet had matured to the point where they presented a real problem for the Soviets. But Carter had planted seeds, often reluctantly, that Reagan would nurture into full-fledged challenges to the Soviet empire.

Soviet issues became my primary responsibility at CIA in November 1980, when I finally escaped staff work as Turner's executive assistant after persuading him to appoint me as National Intelligence Officer for the Soviet Union. After sitting just outside Brzezinski's office door in the White House, and then Turner's at CIA, for some time, I had thought CIA was sending a mixed and therefore confusing message to policymakers about the Soviets. Because we published our military and strategic analysis independently of our political and economic assessments, I suspected that busy senior officials hadn't been able to fathom the real meaning of a still-growing Soviet military juggernaut continuing to gobble up resources in a country already in dire economic straits. I wrote Turner a memorandum on October 29, 1980, in which I tried to integrate the two.

I said that the Soviets had a different perception of the strategic environment in the 1980s than CIA had been publishing. I believed the Soviets saw themselves as an isolated superpower, facing the combined hostility of the United States, Western Europe, Japan, and China even as they confronted serious problems in Eastern Europe, instability on their southern border, and deep economic problems. Meanwhile, they saw the United States pursuing a number of weapons programs intended to reverse the strategic trends since the mid-1960s and a strategy (again, in their view) aimed at acquiring a U.S. first-strike capability, strategic superiority, or provoking a conflict that would be fought exclusively in Europe and the USSR. Further, they confronted a changing internal situation, including long-range industrial, energy, agricultural, social, and demographic problems, as well as a leadership transition just begun by the death of Kosygin. I wrote, in October 1980, that Soviet aggressiveness internationally and their vigorous military programs masked what they saw by then as very real vulnerabilities.

REEVALUATING CARTER

I believe historians and political observers alike have failed to appreciate the importance of Jimmy Carter's contribution to the collapse of the Soviet Union and the end of the Cold War.

He was the first President during the Cold War to challenge publicly and consistently the legitimacy of Soviet rule at home. Carter's human rights policy, building on the important and then largely unrecognized role of the Helsinki Final Act, by the testimony of countless Soviet and East European dissidents and future democratic leaders, challenged the moral authority of the Soviet government and gave American sanction and support to those resisting that government. Whether isolated and little-known Soviet dissident or world-famous Soviet scientist, Carter's policy encouraged them to press on. The power of the policy is best measured by the shrill reaction of the Soviet leaders who, better than Western leaders, understood the dangers to them of such an American approach. This challenge set the stage for the even stronger ideological gauntlet thrown down before the Kremlin by Ronald Reagan.

Nor was this idle preaching. Carter backed up his rhetorical support for those challenging the Soviet government with practical support. Overtly, he poured new resources into the U.S. government–sponsored radios that could broadcast directly into the Soviet Union and Eastern Europe. Covertly, he approved programs that expanded efforts to smuggle into the Soviet Union literature about freedom and democracy, as well as the writings of the dissidents themselves—titles such as *The Gulag Archipelago,* by Alexander Solzhenitsyn. The administration also covertly worked to keep alive the heritage of ethnic minorities in the Soviet Union by infiltrating written materials about their history and culture.

With respect to the Soviet economic crisis, Carter did not intend to worsen their difficulties through economic warfare, but the policies he pursued in response to other events had that practical effect. After the Soviets decided in 1978 to put the prominent dissidents Shcharansky and Ginzberg on trial, and following a bitter internal battle inside the administration, Carter in July decided to impose selected economic sanctions on the USSR. Much broader sanctions were imposed on the USSR after the invasion of Afghanistan. This new, tougher approach to economic relations and technology transfer—which outraged U.S. farmers and businessmen —set the stage for continuation and intensification of economic measures against the Soviet Union by Reagan.

Under Carter, the United States either continued or began the modernization programs—except for the B-1 bomber—that would form the backbone of American strategic strength in the 1980s and beyond. Major programs for NATO modernization were initiated and the original commitment made to deploy both nuclear cruise missiles and the Pershing II IRBMs—INF—in Europe.

And, finally, Carter began numerous covert actions to counter Soviet advances in the Third World. Well before the invasion of Afghanistan, he approved intelligence findings aimed at countering the Soviets and/or Cubans in Grenada, Jamaica, Nicaragua, El Salvador, Yemen, and even Afghanistan. While often modest and confined—at least before 1980—to nonlethal measures, they were an important start. And, most importantly, Carter's strategy of turning to CIA and covert action to counter the Soviets in the Third World would be continued and vastly expanded by Ronald Reagan—with the agreement and cooperation of Congress.

Nearly all of the foregoing is contrary to the contemporary view of Carter and even the historical perception of his performance. How can this be? First, he did not embrace most of these actions enthusiastically. Some he approved only after bitter fights inside the administration and after long consideration. In other cases, such as human rights, I believe his motives were idealistic and not primarily motivated by the notion of undermining the Soviet government. Also, his equivocation in public addresses and comments in terms of how he saw the relationship with the Soviets conveyed, at best, indecision and, at worst, confusion about how to proceed. His principal spokesman, Secretary Vance, was deeply committed to arms control and in his pronouncements bent over backward to sound conciliatory toward Moscow. Finally, highly visible negative decisions on weapons programs like ERW and the B-1 shaped attitudes toward him and his policies.

Perceptions of Carter's weakness were also greatly influenced by his handling of diverse crises. The administration's inaction when the Soviets and Cubans intervened in Ethiopia created an early negative impression. The hostage crisis in Iran made the United States seem weak and militarily timid and incompetent. This undoubtedly spilled over to influence attitudes on his approach to the Soviets. The administration also badly handled the set-tos with the Soviets over nuclear-capable MiGs in Cuba and then the Soviet brigade in Cuba.

The irony is that relations between the Soviet Union and the United States were more consistently sour and antagonistic during the Carter administration than was (or would be) the case under any other President of the Cold War except for Harry Truman— including Ronald Reagan. Far more than Americans or Europeans, the Soviets saw Carter as abandoning the ground rules that had governed the relationship for decades and striking out boldly on a path of confrontation and challenge.

Contrary to conventional wisdom, I believe the Soviets saw Carter as a committed ideological foe as well as geopolitical adversary—and as a President prepared to act on his hostility in both arenas. And in that he represented a decided change from his predecessors going back to Eisenhower. Further, I think the Kremlin later came to see great continuity between Carter's approach to them and that of his successor, Ronald Reagan. In fact, Carter prepared the ground for Reagan in the strategic arena, in confronting the Soviets and Cubans in the Third World, and in challenging the legitimacy of Soviet authority at home. He took the first steps to strip away the mask of Soviet ascendancy and exploit the reality of Soviet vulnerability. Unfortunately for Carter, until now hardly anyone has known.

PART THREE

1981–1986: The Resurgence of the West

CHAPTER ELEVEN

The Reawakening

The impression of Soviet ascendancy and perception of deep malaise in the West were firmly fixed in the American and European popular mind in the late 1970s and at the beginning of the 1980s. Voters in all of the major countries were ready for a change.

Change came first in Great Britain where, in May 1979, the Conservative Party, led by Margaret Thatcher with a revolutionary economic program, ousted the Labor government of James Callaghan. Thatcher also was dismayed by the growth in Soviet military power and international adventurism and was determined to rebuild Britain's military strength and resist the Soviets.

The British prime minister's views and aspirations—economically, internationally, and psychologically—were shared almost identically in the United States by Ronald Reagan. Like Thatcher, Reagan's views were at odds not only with those of the Democratic President then in office, but also with his Republican predecessors. He, like her, found in the recent leadership of his own party an approach to government that was merely a pale shadow of their political opponents—both in domestic policy and foreign affairs.

The next change came in France, with the end of Giscard d'Estaing's term as president in May 1981, and his replacement by François Mitterrand. While Mitterrand shared little of the economic philosophy of Thatcher or Reagan, as a socialist who had battled the French communists his entire career, the new French president was adamantly anti-Soviet and prepared to play his part in challenging Moscow's gains around the world—especially those in or neighboring former French colonies.

The last of a formidable phalanx of leaders arrived as a result of the fall on October 1, 1982, of Chancellor Schmidt's coalition government in the Federal Republic of Germany, and his replacement by Helmut Kohl, leading a coalition of the Christian Democratic Union and the Free Democratic Party, led by Hans Dietrich Genscher. The change in Bonn was not as dramatic as in the other three countries because Schmidt had been on the conservative end of the Social Democratic Party both on economic issues and security policy.

Thus, within a relatively short time, the principal Western leaders of the last half of the 1970s were out of office, and along with them those who had embraced détente and the preeminent importance of arms control as the best way to deal with an assertive USSR. In the United States and the United Kingdom, the new leaders represented a revolutionary change in both domestic and foreign policy. They both projected a long-absent sense of confidence and optimism about the future of their countries and the West in general. And, in international affairs, they would soon be complemented by new leaders in France and West Germany prepared to join them in challenging the gains of the Soviet Union.

MOSCOW: APPROACHING TWILIGHT

As the Western economies began to recover in the early 1980s, the fact that the Soviet economy continued to spiral downward began to draw increasing attention. We in CIA helped focus that interest because our story on the Soviet economy was a gloomy one (contrary to later allegations).

Typical was the Agency's annual briefing on the Soviet economy to the Joint Economic Committee (JEC) of the Congress in mid-1981. The report, presented by Harry Rowen, chairman of the National Intelligence Council, advised that the Soviet economy's performance during the preceding two years—1979–1980—was even "worse than we anticipated." He observed that shortfalls in industrial production and back-to-back harvest failures had reduced Soviet GNP growth to the lowest level since World War II and that there were few signs of a rebound in 1981. The Soviet economy didn't get any better over the next year.

CIA anticipated—and predicted—that by the mid-1980s a new Soviet leadership would be forced by economic decline to consider drastic changes in the system to alter the downward path. As Western economies recovered, the USSR's problems were worsening due to the nature of the Soviet system, high and still increasing expenditures on the military, and the growing economic drag of the Soviet empire—primarily in Eastern Europe but also in the Third World.

The Soviets faced one other monumental disadvantage. Just as the United States, Britain, France, and West Germany had elected new, vigorous, and aggressive—though not necessarily young— leaders, the aged Soviet leadership literally was dying on its feet.

As leadership change, due primarily to the Grim Reaper rather than politics, began to sweep through the Kremlin in the early 1980s, CIA had little useful inside information on Soviet politics at the highest levels. A few snippets of clandestine reporting and some communications intelligence helped some.

After seventeen long years of Brezhnev's leadership, there would be three successors within three years. Given how little hard information CIA had, it was thanks to experts such as Robert Blackwell, Grey Hodnett, Kay Oliver, George Kolt, and others that we correctly forecast two of the three victorious candidates and, more importantly, helped U.S. policymakers understand what the issues and implications were in each contest.

The last two years of Brezhnev's life and reign are probably better described by a novelist because, regardless of the facts, the maneuvering and stories coming out of Moscow would have done the worst of the czarist courts justice for intrigue and drama.

CIA had little information on the factional struggle under way. We knew who Brezhnev's cronies were, but we did not have a clear picture of the existence of a strong Andropov faction determined to seize control. The core of that faction, in addition to KGB chief Yuri Andropov himself, probably included his close associate Defense Minister Ustinov, Foreign Minister Gromyko, Gorbachev, and Grigory Romanov, the Leningrad party leader whose fealty was based on how much dirt Andropov knew about him and his personal corruption, which was astonishing even by Soviet standards.

The contest for power was worthy of either a CIA or Mel Brooks plot. Andropov appears to have set out to discredit Brezhnev even before the old man died. In early 1982, soon after Mikhail

Suslov—party ideologist and kingmaker—died, the KGB went after several of Brezhnev's closest associates and even his family for corruption. Stories reached CIA, and journalists as well, that the KGB had investigated Brezhnev's daughter Galina, who had been having an affair with a Moscow singer and playboy named Boris Buryata, nicknamed "Boris the Gypsy." The scandal involved a sizable diamond-smuggling ring including members of the Moscow Circus, and Boris the Gypsy was apparently a part of it. In the course of the investigation, the first deputy chairman of the KGB (and Brezhnev's brother-in-law), General Semion Tsvigun, apparently committed suicide. One allegation was that he had tried to cover up the scandal. According to another story, Boris the Gypsy, who seemed in good health when he was arrested, did not survive his first night in jail because either Galina's jealous husband or the authorities killed him. The Deputy Minister of Internal Affairs, General Yuriy Churbanov, Brezhnev's son-in-law and Galina's husband, lost his job. Other Brezhnev associates soon found themselves under investigation for corruption, and there were rumors of other suicides. Regardless of who murdered whom or who committed suicide—and it is possible there were no murders or suicides—the KGB made sure Western intelligence services and journalists had all these lurid stories.

In his dying months, Brezhnev apparently tried to arrange for Konstantin Chernenko to succeed him, but death came too soon for him and his circle to lock up the succession for the longtime aide. Andropov, on the other hand, had the support of Ustinov and the military, as well as the KGB. That, together with Chernenko's lack of stature, made Andropov hard to beat in 1982. According to several sources, the leadership had resolved by the spring of 1982 that Andropov would succeed Brezhnev. Indeed, one report indicated that Chernenko actually had been the one to put his name forward.

On September 18, 1981, some fourteen months before Brezhnev died, the new CIA director, William Casey, asked for a thorough analysis of the succession—not just the players, but their capability and standing, the kind of following they had, where they had institutional clout, their sources of support, and the posture toward each of them of the critical forces in Kremlin politics (the KGB, the army, the rest of the Politburo). On November 6, the DCI requested another paper, this one on Soviet nationalities and dissidents. And, on November 23, Casey asked for yet another paper reviewing the relationship between the Soviet government and the Soviet people. He wanted more on nationalism, the minorities, health, alcoholism, problems in Central Asia, separatist forces, prison and psychiatric camps, and slave labor.

All these tasks came at the end of a decade and more of U.S. defense and intelligence budget cuts, and, frankly, CIA's capabilities to respond were limited. Because of the long dry spell in Soviet politics and internal affairs, that had seemed to managers one of the places where resources could be cut, both in analysis and collection. And cut they had. We needed new capabilities to answer properly many of Casey's questions. But they certainly were the right questions.

The DCI wouldn't wait for us to rebuild. In addition to the papers he requested in the fall of 1981, on May 10, 1982, he asked me to have a talking paper prepared on the policy implications of the Soviet succession and the views of each contender.

Though much of what Casey wanted to know was unknowable —a mystery rather than a secret—we gave it our best shot four days later.

- On the economy, we thought that proposals endorsed by even the most "reform-minded" leaders would not be sufficiently radical to bring any major improvement.
- On arms control, none of the leaders were secure enough, in our view, to suggest concessions, though, over the long haul, Chernenko seemed more inclined to bargain and had stressed the economic benefits.
- On adventurism in the Third World, it looked to us as if the leadership was fairly united in support of efforts to expand Soviet influence and project Soviet power. However, we thought possibly Chernenko and Andropov might believe expansionism should be tempered by economic needs at home. In reality, there wasn't much of a range of views.
- On the military buildup, our information suggested that all in the leadership had supported the increase in military power in the Brezhnev years, and no one seemed prepared to reduce the level of commitment.
- Finally, with respect to internal problems, we thought Andropov was the most experienced, although Chernenko had attempted to portray himself as attuned to popular aspirations and seemed somewhat more sensitive to the country's social problems than the other leaders.

On July 20, 1982, the Reagan administration began contingency planning for the Soviet succession with a Crisis Pre-Planning Group (CPPG) meeting in the Situation Room. (The CPPG was an NSC-chaired interagency committee charged with preparing policy options and contingency plans, and with crisis management.) By then Deputy Director for Intelligence, I attended for CIA. I was asked to prepare a new, more detailed biography of Andropov, one that would offer some insights into a man we all thought would represent a serious new challenge.

On August 3, Casey sent a report to President Reagan that provided a sense of the atmosphere in Moscow in the waning days of Brezhnev's long tenure. According to information from inside the Communist Party Central Committee, there was a feeling of malaise brought on by corruption, violent crime, and economic hardship. Some, even then, believed the whole party system had to be done away with. Rampant corruption and theft by Communist Party officials had encouraged others to see what they could steal from the system, and there had been a big increase in crime. An agent told us a remarkable story about how some miscreant had stolen six fine fur hats belonging to important visitors from the hat stand right outside Andropov's office—in the Lubyanka, yet. Discontent had led to many brief strikes by workers over the years, but there had been two major strikes in 1981, in Gorky and Togliatti. We were told by human sources that within the KGB, there was a strong feeling that something had to be done to put the country in order.

We concluded our report to the President as follows: "The influence of détente and the general erosion of discipline in Soviet society have led to growing criticism of Soviet institutions and the regime in general. *To embark on reform in any circumstances would be to court disaster* [emphasis added]. In Eastern Europe, some experimentation can be tolerated because if the situation gets out of hand there, Soviet troops are on hand to reassert control; if things go wrong in the Soviet Union itself, however, no one will protect the Party."

Brezhnev died on November 10, and Yuri Andropov was quickly announced as his successor. After the "long good-bye," the prolonged death watch on Brezhnev, the Soviet Union had a new leader. In Moscow for the Brezhnev funeral, Vice President Bush and Secretary of State George Shultz met with Andropov. When they returned, Shultz told us that he had come away with the feeling that Andropov could escalate a situation quickly and "take us on." The Secretary said Andropov was very good at disinformation and that he had misrepresented the context of his meeting with the American delegation in the morning when he met with the Germans in the afternoon. He said that while Andropov had been friendly to Bush and him, with the Germans his tone had been threatening and he had laid on the line how he saw things. Shultz described Andropov as seemingly vigorous, pale, steely-eyed, with a quite unrevealing expression. Andropov seemed to have an easy and relaxed relationship with Gromyko, and the two occasionally whispered and laughed between them. When Bush said that he and Andropov had had the same jobs in intelligence, Andropov replied, "Yes, we are men of peace, but they [referring to Gromyko and Shultz] are the men of problems." Shultz told us there was no question that Andropov was completely in charge. It also appeared obvious that he had been running things for some time—he was not just taking the baton upon the death of Brezhnev.

Brezhnev's funeral offered CIA a unique opportunity to have a ringside seat in Moscow with the U.S. delegation. Vice President Bush headed the U.S. contingent and invited Robert Blackwell, a superb CIA expert on Soviet leadership politics, to accompany him on the plane to Moscow and then to be close at hand for interpretation of events. It was a rare opportunity for a CIA analyst, and Blackwell made the most of it. He did a great job for Bush—little did he know that his performance and a dying Soviet leadership would enable him to repeat the experience twice more within a little over two years.

Many people both in the United States and in the USSR had high hopes that, after the paralysis of the late Brezhnev period, Andropov would bring change to the Soviet Union and to U.S.-Soviet relations. So he did, but not in the way anyone expected.

Andropov had spent fifteen years as the top cop for one of history's most repressive regimes, and he did his job well. If he saw the need for change, for reform, it was simply to make the totalitarian machine run better. Yuri Andropov was not some kind of proto-democrat or free-marketeer. Hardly. A CIA study on Andropov in April 1978 had concluded, "For the outside world, including the U.S., Andropov constitutes a formidable adversary, whose intelligence, pragmatism, subtlety and sophistication make him the more dangerous."

A few days after Andropov became General Secretary, I wrote

a personal memorandum on what we should expect. On November 29, Casey sent it to the President and other top officials. I suggested that Andropov would move quickly to tackle Soviet problems—there was wide agreement on the need for renewal, to get the economy moving, to get rid of corruption, to restore discipline, to reaffirm Russia's missionary role at home and abroad. My view was that, in Andropov, the party sought Stalin's toughness, decisiveness, and ability to move the country—"believing they can have all of that without the old dictator's less welcome attributes (such as a tendency to shoot his colleagues)."

I wrote that we probably would see new resources for the military and KGB to respond to a perceived increase in the threat from the United States (and reflecting Andoprov's political debts and institutional loyalties). On the economy, I predicted reform and limited experimentation but with focus also on internal discipline, the anticorruption campaign, and vigilance to avoid the "Polish disease." In the Third World, I thought we would see a continuation of the Soviets' destabilizing activities, and perhaps an increase.

What we did not know then—what the Soviets probably did not know then—was that Andropov, too, was dying. And for a country in a growing economic and social crisis, fifteen months wouldn't be enough—especially not with Andropov in the hospital for most of that time.

The political, economic, and psychological initiative by the end of 1982 had passed already to a reawakened West.

ADVENT IN WASHINGTON

The last thing on anyone's mind in Washington on January 20, 1981, was continuity. The Democrats had lost the Presidency and control of the Senate. While it was bad enough in their eyes that the Republicans had taken over the Senate, what was worse was that a "right-wing" Republican had won the Presidency. The disdain of most Democrats and most of the press for the former movie actor and his ideas about foreign policy—especially the Soviet Union—and how to revive the domestic economy was evident. Only slightly less evident was the discomfort of many traditional, middle-of-the-road Republicans in Washington. Ronald Reagan was as different from them as Margaret Thatcher was from the "me-too" Tories of the preceding two decades.

That the Reaganites saw their arrival as a hostile takeover was apparent in the most extraordinary transition period of my career. For the first time in decades, an incoming President orchestrated a comprehensive battle plan to seize control of a city long believed to be in enemy hands. Main force political units, flanking maneuvers, feints, sappers, and psychological warfare all played their part as Reagan and company between November and January deployed their forces for a political blitzkreig.

During the transition, every department and agency became a political and ideological battlefield. Some, like Defense, controlled against their will by a Democratic President and Congress, went over to the Reagan forces eagerly, without a struggle, before January 20. Others fell after brief skirmishes. And a few, especially on the domestic side, would wage partisan warfare for eight years— subdued by overwhelming political forces but never giving up to the conservative ideology of Reagan and his cohorts.

CIA had had political transition teams before, but the Reagan transition at CIA was something else again. While several CIA old hands were part of the transition team (John Bross, George Carver, Walter Pforzheimer), the "politicals"—Angelo Codevilla, Ken de-Graffenreid, Mark Schneider, and others—dominated the effort and set the tone. As hard-line conservatives and Republican members of the staff of the Senate Intelligence Committee, they found little they liked at CIA. The range of views on what needed to be done to "fix" intelligence was radical and across the board, from wholesale structural and personnel changes to dismantling the Agency entirely.

The prognosis for us on the inside was bleak. In the view of many incoming Reaganites, and not just the radicals on the transition team, CIA had badly underestimated Soviet military capabilities and political intentions for years. They believed the Agency had been crippled by Carter and Turner, who—they said—gutted its budget and destroyed its covert action capabilities. CIA had passively accepted Turner's changes (news, I'm sure, to Turner). The Reaganites thought that CIA over the years had been politicized by the détentist policies of the 1970s and that its performance even in non-Soviet areas had been characterized by failure. Like Nixon in 1969, Reagan's men in early 1981 believed deeply that CIA was dominated by political liberals very much out of touch with the real world and the worldview of the President. Counterintelligence, technical and especially human collection, analysis, and more had all declined or been coopted in their view.

The reaction inside the Agency to this litany of failure and incompetence, together with rumors of impending purges of senior officials, was a mix of resentment and anger, dread and personal insecurity. We had heard that the radicals on the transition team had recommended that the top several hundred Agency officials be fired or retired, with special emphasis on anyone in a senior position who had had anything to do with Soviet affairs. John McMahon, then the DDO and senior Agency professional, was said to head the list, with a lot of company from the Directorate of Intelligence and the National Intelligence Council.

Thus I thought my career was over. I was three times cursed in the eyes of the transition team. I had worked for Brzezinski and Aaron in the Carter White House for three years. I had been Stan Turner's executive assistant for almost a year. And I was then the senior Soviet analyst as National Intelligence Officer for the Soviet Union. Nearly as bad, I also had worked for Nixon, Ford, and Kissinger, who were almost as much of an anathema to the transition radicals as the Carter team. It didn't matter that during the 1970s, under Nixon, Ford, and Carter, I had been regarded as something of a hard-liner toward the Soviets. Guilt by association overrode any substantive views. My personal unease was widely shared in the Agency.

I didn't know anyone on the transition team except George Carver, and it was not at all clear that the CIA retirees on the team had much influence in any case. Nor did I know William Casey, who was soon announced as Reagan's choice to be DCI. Thus it was with real relief that I heard the early rumors that Vice Admiral B. R. (Bob) Inman, director of NSA, might be appointed Deputy DCI. I had gotten to know Inman while I was working for Brzezinski, liked him, and had a lot of confidence in his professionalism as an intelligence officer. It seemed to me that he would be invaluable to CIA and to the intelligence community to guard against the radicals' agenda and politicization of the Agency. This was a special worry with the likely appointment of Reagan's campaign manager as DCI. I called Inman at NSA and, aware of rumors he was resisting the appointment, urged him to accept and told him of the need for him to help the professionals.

Casey's appointment had raised many an eyebrow around the Agency, but most people withheld judgment. After all, George Bush had been Republican National Chairman and he had not played politics at the Agency. And, after a long period of budget cuts and public pummeling, many in the Agency saw, with the new administration, a chance to rebuild lost capabilities and once again for CIA to be an important player on the President's team. Finally, Casey won some early sympathy and support when, upon arriving in office, he simply threw out the transition team and its report. Nor did he fire a single senior career officer. Conservatives, and others, would criticize Casey for that.

Elsewhere in the national security arena, the reaction to the transition campaign was similar. The new Secretary of State, Alexander Haig, also threw out the transition team, and, working with the White House, filled the policy-making jobs at State with a traditional mix of loyalists to the new President and career diplomats. At Defense, Secretary Caspar Weinberger made it three for three, as he, too, ousted the transition team. In fact, he wrote White House counsel Edwin Meese, "Because the transition team had an agenda of its own, it was not useful to me in developing the President's program; it was, in fact, the source of a number of problems." At the same time, he appointed throughout the department Reagan supporters or at least those who supported Reagan's desire to strengthen Defense. He also easily won admirers in the Pentagon by outlining a tremendous increase in defense spending.

Most worrisome to me was the fate of the National Security Council. Its role, prestige, and importance were downgraded, as was the position of National Security Adviser Richard Allen. Symbolic of this was his ouster from the large, bright corner office on the first floor of the West Wing of the White House—which Kissinger had acquired over a decade earlier and Brzezinski had kept—to a basement office just outside of the Situation Room. In a city where symbols of power are well-known and count for much, Allen's relegation to the basement spoke volumes about the downgrading of the NSC. It soon also became clear that the NSC adviser no longer had the open access to the President his predecessors had enjoyed, nor their independent role. I think this change was intended in part to overcome the internecine warfare of the Nixon, Ford, and Carter administrations occasioned at times by the highly visible National Security Adviser. This derogation of NSC function and place would not prevent even more vicious internal conflict in the Reagan administration and, I believe, weakened and isolated the National Security Adviser in a way that led to some of the serious problems of the Reagan Presidency in foreign affairs.

The transition complete, the new team in place, the "Reagan Revolution" was ready to begin.

CHALLENGING THE SOVIETS

The Reagan administration's approach to national security issues was based on several assumptions, asserted as facts. To wit: American military strength and international prestige had been in decline for more than a decade. Many key players thought that détente had been a ruse that allowed the Soviets to expand their presence and influence abroad virtually without opposition, especially in the Third World. Arms control was deemed a fraud that had permitted the Soviet Union to race ahead with their strategic programs while our strength declined. The Soviets were bent on achieving strategic military superiority and using it as a shield behind which they intended to drive the West out of the Third World, replacing Western influence and presence with their own, and over time isolating and surrounding the United States.

However, even in this administration, at least at senior levels, Ronald Reagan probably was alone in truly believing that these trends could be reversed while he was President *and* that the Soviet Union itself could be defeated. His determination to reverse the apparent flow of history underpinned the entirety of his foreign policy.

ECONOMIC PRESSURE

While Reagan's view of the economic failings of the Soviet Union may have been rudimentary, even primitive, it also happened generally to conform to Soviet reality. Thus he was highly receptive to the content of the briefings he received on the Soviet economy. Reagan was convinced that the United States, and the West more generally, could bring serious economic pressure to bear on the Soviet Union that would adversely affect their ability to keep the system going while maintaining their ambitious military programs. As he later wrote, "The great dynamic success of capitalism had given us a powerful weapon in our battle against Communism— money. The Russians could never win the arms race; we could outspend them forever."

Reagan's effort to increase the economic pressure on the Soviets had three elements. First, in his mind, the U.S. military buildup

—in addition to increasing our military power—also served to force increased spending by the Soviets even as their economic performance spiraled downward. Second, the administration—with only a few exceptions—worked hard to prevent an expansion of Western trade relations with the USSR that might help strengthen the latter economically. And third, the administration greatly intensified its predecessor's efforts to stem the transfer of technology to the Soviet Union, whether intended for military purposes or to make their economy more efficient.

The administration did not begin with a comprehensive policy to wage economic warfare against the Soviets. It began with a broad consensus to make things as difficult as possible for the Kremlin. As opportunities arose to put the squeeze on economically, they were seized enthusiastically, if not always effectively. Each of the three approaches described above was pursued more or less independently, on its own merits, with the combined impact occasionally asserted rhetorically but not articulated as policy until late in 1982—and even then carefully couched. In part, this was because declaring economic war per se against the USSR would have aroused great political opposition both in the United States and in Europe. Further, most experts, including in CIA, would have argued—and did—that such a campaign would not work, that despite Soviet economic problems they were not vulnerable to outside pressure. Indeed, the handful of people who wrote that the United States could spend the Soviets into the ground on defense and thereby speed bringing the system to its knees were dismissed by most in Washington as right-wing kooks. And, I must admit, I, along with my Agency colleagues, agreed with that conventional wisdom. Finally, even the Reagan administration was careful not to push the Soviets too hard toward open confrontation, even in the early days. But, at the end of the day, the President believed a tottering regime could be pushed further off balance by such pressures. So he pushed—hard.

MILITARY PRESSURE

From the standpoint of the new Reagan team, the Carter administration had gutted defense, ignored the Soviet military buildup, and neglected critical military needs. Carter, in their view, had failed to respond to Soviet aggression in the Third World, and had been weak in dealing with important challenges such as the revolution in Iran, the hostage crisis, and the Cuban military buildup. Indeed, "weakness" was the watchword applied to every aspect of foreign and defense policy, and intelligence, during the preceding four years.

But, as I have described, the budget cuts that so impaired our defense and intelligence capabilities by 1981 were a legacy of more than a decade of congressional and other pressures through three presidential administrations, two of them Republican. While the three Presidents of the 1970s had been able to keep strategic modernization programs alive, and began to make some improvements in Europe, in reality the cuts had had a devastating impact. The need for money for highly visible new weapons, both strategic and conventional, was clear. But what was absolutely critical was the need to restore all of the other elements of an effective defense capability—logistics, communications, pay, training, stockpiles, maintenance, and more.

Reagan's first priority, then, was to increase significantly the resources for defense and to make clear to the Soviets and to Americans alike that expanding U.S. military power was at the top of his agenda. The impact of the increased resources on our military capabilities was real, as we would see in Operation Desert Storm early in 1991. But the impact was also psychological, both in terms of the confidence and attitude of the men and women of the armed forces, and also on the American public and internationally. Almost immediately, years before the concrete results of the increased investment would be visible, there was a sense at home and abroad —especially in the Soviet Union—of growing American military strength and political resolve. Reagan's confident, even aggressive rhetoric began to reap the international harvest of the military buildup before the ink was hardly dry on the first checks.

Soviet leaders had fretted to one another from time to time in the 1970s about the dangers of unleashed American industrial might and technology in the military sphere. As Brezhnev and other senior members of the leadership were dying, and the Soviet hierarchy contemplated an economy spiraling downward, they saw their worst nightmare coming true in America. For the first time since the Soviets began their huge military buildup in the mid-1960s, an American military juggernaut was getting under way. And it scared the hell out of them.

CHALLENGING THE SOVIETS IN THE THIRD WORLD

Carter's efforts to counter Soviet aggressiveness in the Third World had been wide-ranging, as described in Chapter 9, but they also had been largely covert. None was known to the American public—except for aid to the Afghan Mujahedin, which eventually leaked. The appearance of inaction was only reinforced by the administration's preoccupation with the Iranian hostage crisis and then the reelection campaign.

Under these circumstances, Reagan's rhetoric before and after his election and inauguration threw down the gauntlet to the Soviets. Repeatedly, he denounced Soviet support for "wars of national liberation" and their efforts to subvert and destroy noncommunist governments in the Third World. He also was clear in saying that the United States would no longer simply observe these developments from the sidelines.

So, from the outset, the Reagan administration targeted covert action, foreign assistance, diplomacy, and even direct military intervention on Third World battlegrounds in opposition to the Soviets, Cubans, Libyans—and anyone else perceived to be a surrogate of the Soviet Union. At first, the efforts were defensive, reacting to Soviet and Cuban gains and new threats to Third World governments. Over time, the United States would seize opportunities to challenge and then try to reverse past Kremlin successes. But the surrogate wars in the Third World under Reagan were not just visible, but openly characterized as the cutting edge of a broader challenge to the Soviet Union.

Economically, militarily, politically, ideologically, and in the Third World, Reagan made clear from day one that he intended to reverse "the correlation of forces" with the USSR—to reverse both the reality and the perception of which country was stronger and which represented the future. He seemed not to doubt in the slightest that he could change the decade-long trend of apparent Soviet ascendancy. Reagan, nearly alone, truly believed in 1981 that the Soviet system was vulnerable, not in some vague, long-range historical sense, but right then. And he was determined to move the United States and the West from defense to offense.

CHAPTER TWELVE

Reagan's Sword: Casey at CIA

THE OLD MAN, nearly bald, tall but slightly hunched, yanked open his office door and called out to no one in particular, "Two vodka martinis!" Without waiting for a response, he slammed the door shut. It was February 11, 1981, and this was the first time I had seen the new DCI since his appointment. Casey, in the job less than three weeks, was having lunch with John McCone, his predecessor under President Kennedy. Panic in the outer office. The DCI's suite had been dry under Admiral Turner and there was no liquor. Finally, a bottle was produced—no doubt from someone's desk drawer—and a vague semblance of a martini was carried in to the thirsty pair.

I was visiting the DCI secretaries with whom I had worked under Turner and just happened to be standing there when Casey briefly emerged. He cast a quick, baleful glance in my direction and disappeared. It was only the second time I had laid eyes on him.

Years later, I would think about the martini episode and realize that, however trivial, it foreshadowed how Casey would approach CIA on consequential matters. He would demand something be done immediately which the Agency no longer had the capability to do. He would fire instructions at the closest person regardless of whether that person had anything to do with the matter at hand. And he would not wait around even for confirmation that anyone heard him. People would fumble around trying to figure out who had the action. And the Agency would eventually respond in a minimally satisfactory way but then go create the capability to satisfy the requirement better the next time—if there was a next time.

A great deal has been written about Casey, most of it demonizing him and burdening his memory with suspicion of criminal behavior and as the éminence grise behind Iran-Contra, the belief among many that he disregarded the truth, and a broadly accepted reputation for playing fast and loose with ethics and the law—of living on the edge. I probably spent more time with Bill Casey over the six-year period he was Director of Central Intelligence than anyone outside his family. I was not his close friend, he did not confide personal matters to me—or invite me to confide such in him. I was rarely in his home, and I knew little about him prior to his arrival at CIA. All that said, I believe I was closer to him professionally and knew him better than anyone else at CIA or in government. Because Casey is central to Ronald Reagan's war against the Soviet Union, understanding him and the part he played at CIA is critically important. The public record on Casey at this point tends to have focused solely on his role in the Iran-Contra affair and on covert action (Bob Woodward's book *Veil*), and therefore—apart from a biography by Joseph Persico—is singularly shallow and uninformed about his time as DCI. And so I want to describe here the Casey I knew.

CASEY, DONOVAN, AND THE OSS: HOW TO WAGE WAR

William Joseph Casey, nearly sixty-eight years old, was sworn in as DCI on January 28, 1981. He had been confirmed 95–0 by the Senate. He was a unique DCI in many respects—Cabinet rank, wealth, age, the only DCI to have served with the OSS in World War II who did not go on to make a career with CIA, and more.

What truly set Bill Casey apart from his predecessors and successors as DCI, though, was that he had not come to CIA with the purpose of making it better, managing it more effectively, reforming it, or improving the quality of intelligence. What I realized only years later was that Bill Casey came to CIA primarily to wage war against the Soviet Union. And his approach to waging that war was shaped preeminently by events and a personality that entered his life thirty-eight years earlier.

I believe Casey had only one real hero: William J. Donovan. Donovan had pretty much single-handedly created the U.S. wartime intelligence service, the Office of Strategic Services (OSS).

Both Casey and Donovan had the same first and middle names. Both were Irish Catholics. Both were Wall Street lawyers. In many ways, good and bad, I think Casey tried to model himself on Donovan. If Donovan speed-read countless books and documents, so would Casey. If Donovan was willing to cut a few corners to accomplish the mission, so was Casey. If Donovan was a bull in Washington's bureaucratic china shop, then Casey would be as well. If Donovan was a risk-taker, unafraid to take the point, then that was for Casey. The preeminent place on Casey's office wall as DCI was reserved for an autographed black-and-white photograph of Donovan. You couldn't go in or out without seeing it. He couldn't move without passing it. He spoke to us of Donovan rarely, but for Casey, Donovan's example was before him every day.

CASEY AND CIA'S ANALYSTS: TWO DIFFERENT WORLDS

Casey's approach to intelligence analysis was shaped by his experience in the OSS. Early in his OSS experience, he had taken aboard the value of the work done by the Research and Analysis branch and the emphasis Donovan gave to the accumulation of basic data for use by military planners. An alumnus of the Research Institute of America, where he worked for Leo Cherne in the 1930s, author of several books on tax law, amateur historian, and author of a book on the American Revolution, Casey was himself an analyst and writer of no mean accomplishment.

So, by personal inclination and interest as well as OSS experience, Casey—like Donovan in the OSS—would pay much attention to reading intelligence analysis; asking questions; quarreling with conclusions; sending the researchers back for more data, more evidence; seeking out new and different sources of information; probing and listening to obscure and not-so-obscure outside experts; quizzing anyone who seemed to have a good idea; reaching out to businessmen with international experience. He was enormously impatient and frustrated with the career analysts' unwillingness to follow his lead in aggressively looking beyond the walls of CIA for new information and insights, in being willing to question their own assumptions and always challenging conventional wisdom. What had happened, he would wonder, to the entrepreneurial experts of OSS days?

Above all, Casey wanted information and analysis that informed or provoked action. Not for him assessments that simply were "interesting" or educational. He wanted information that would help target clandestine operations better, or be useful for U.S. propaganda, or assist military operations, or put ammunition in the hands of negotiators. For Casey, the United States and CIA were at war—just like when he was young and in the OSS—and speed and relevance to action were his benchmarks for effective analysis.

Casey was appalled at the lackadaisical approach to key issues. He wrote Harry Rowen, chairman of the National Intelligence Council, and me an indignant note in the spring of 1982 demanding that intelligence estimates be more aggressive and more timely. As usual, he had done his homework. He informed us that the last national intelligence estimate (NIE) on the prospects for international communism had been done in 1964—eighteen years before; the last one on prospects for nuclear proliferation in 1976; on the reliability of Moscow's East European allies in 1966; on CIA's capability to monitor limits on Soviet strategic weapons systems in 1965; and so on. It was time to get relevant.

Casey's interests were eclectic, and our economic analysis certainly drew his attention, but the real pressures to perform were in those subjects pertinent to the war against the Soviet Union. It was Donovan's way.

The Soviet economy. The most intricate details of their military-industrial complex. Internal demographic, social, ethnic problems. The full scope of Soviet military developments. Soviet science. The Soviet propaganda apparatus. Soviet subversion, deception, and covert activities. Any kind of information on Soviet surrogates—Cuba, Libya, Vietnam, Eastern Europe. Economic, political, and social developments in the Third World that might provide opportunities for the Soviets or for us to exploit. Technology transfer. Terrorism. Catholic liberation theology. These were the kinds of subjects that really got him fired up. His appetite in these and related areas was insatiable. This kind of broad-range research was what Research and Analysis had done in the OSS. And it was as important for the war against the Soviets as it had been against the Nazis.

More than any other DCI, Turner had paid attention to the analysts in the Directorate of Intelligence, used them, listened to them, for the most part deferred to them. Now, more than any other DCI, Casey drove them, pushed them to do more on the subjects that he considered important to his war against the Soviets.

Casey's attention to analysis was highly focused. He almost never second-guessed or criticized day-to-day, "current" intelligence reporting to the President and his senior team. In the more than four years I was Deputy Director for Intelligence, I only rarely consulted him about what I intended to publish each day in the *President's Daily Brief* and can count on the fingers of one hand the number of times I showed him an article in draft before we ran it —in each case because I knew our analysis would stir up Shultz, Weinberger, the National Security Adviser, or some other administration pooh-bah. Nor did Casey complain about technical analyses on weapons capabilities or force estimates.

The analytical products that drew Casey's intense interest and active participation were NIEs—the interagency intelligence forecasts of what the Soviets or others intended to do—all of which, incidentally, traditionally had been issued in the DCI's name and in which his predecessors also had taken an active interest and role. His primary focus was on the USSR and the Third World, where the war was under way. He paid relatively little attention to China or the rest of Asia, South Asia, or developments in the Third World that did not somehow relate back to opportunities or challenges vis-à-vis the USSR or its surrogates.

As DCI, Casey quickly put his finger on a serious deficiency in CIA's collection and analysis on the Soviet Union. Surprising as it may seem—shocking, in fact—while the Directorate of Operations collected information on Soviet covert actions around the world, the Soviets' espionage activities against others (non-NATO), and their propaganda networks, these reports were regarded as "operational"—not substantive—and were rarely shared with the analysts; even more rarely was this information circulated outside the operations directorate. These were the tools of Soviet subversion, their efforts to destabilize Third World countries, and we hardly paid attention. We tracked military and economic assistance and Soviet diplomatic activities pretty thoroughly, but CIA analysts neglected the seamier side of Soviet activities around the world. This reflected, all too often, a lack of background in Soviet history, a mind-set about Soviet behavior, and a lack of information from the clandestine service.

The new DCI was determined to change this, and within five

weeks of his confirmation in the job, on March 4, 1981, he wrote DDCI Inman calling for two initiatives:

• First, to pay attention to the worldwide "intangible threat" to U.S. interests—propaganda attack, subversion, terrorism, espionage, "with special attention to the degree to which it may be organized, supported, directed and coordinated by forces hostile to us in the world."

• Second, he wanted a new intelligence estimate on (a) economic forces in the world either as a threat to our security or in terms of the political leverage they might afford for or against us; and (b) "instabilities and the potential for developing instability in those areas of the world which are of geopolitical importance and other areas of special interest to us."

Others in the Reagan administration were interested in these issues as well. In late April, Secretary of State Alexander Haig asked for an interagency assessment of Soviet KGB and other Soviet bloc subversion around the world—what the Soviets and their allies were doing, the results, the vulnerability of these efforts to attack and exposure. The Secretary also wanted to know the Soviets' major current targets, principal operational techniques, the scale of their effort (the number of agents and cost). And he wanted it by June 1.

It was in the context of this interest in the "underside" of Soviet behavior that Haig also asked for a national intelligence estimate on Soviet support for terrorism. Unfortunately, he asked only after he had asserted publicly that the Soviets were behind much of international terrorism. Everyone knew he wanted an answer that would support what he had said—after all, policymakers always want that from intelligence when they go too far out on a limb. The assignment for drafting the estimate fell to the Office of Soviet Analysis (SOVA).

The struggle over this estimate inside the intelligence community is worth examining because it would poison the relationship between the DCI and some of the Agency's Soviet analysts for the rest of his tenure. It was also the first instance in which allegations were made that Casey had changed an estimate to meet his preconceptions and administration desires. This estimate also helped form Casey's suspicion that CIA's analysts working on Soviet activities in the Third World were detached from and seemingly oblivious to the dirty realities of Moscow's behavior. As usual, there was some merit on both sides of the dispute, but historical perspective suggests that Casey had the better of the argument, though he handled the matter poorly, to say the least.

The first draft by the analysts proved beyond a shadow of a doubt that Haig had exaggerated the Soviet role—that the Soviets did not organize or direct international terrorism. The draft essentially argued that the Soviets disapproved of terrorism, discouraged the killing of innocents by groups they trained and supported, did not support or help free-lance Third World terrorist groups like the Abu Nidal organization, and under no circumstances did Moscow support the nihilist terrorist groups of Western Europe—the Red Brigades, the Red Army Faction, and so on. It cited Soviet public condemnations of such groups and carefully described the distinctions the Soviets made between national liberation groups or insurgencies and groups involved in out-and-out terrorism.

At that time, the major argument on the analysts' side was the absence of direct evidence of Soviet or East European involvement with terrorism or terrorist groups. There were rumors, and occasionally a very indirectly sourced clandestine report would suggest that one or another terrorist had gotten some help. But it was pretty thin stuff. What it boiled down to was the basic outlook of the observer toward Soviet behavior. Some believed the Soviets would support terrorists if it served their interests and others believed they would not—not from scruple but because of the costs if found out. The irony to me was that the same analysts who complained constantly about the lack of good human intelligence on Soviet activities in effect argued that the absence of such reporting proved their case.

Casey was very unhappy over the draft. He sent a memorandum to McMahon, then head of the analytical directorate, on March 26, 1981, saying he was "greatly disappointed" and that he "would not be willing to put his name on it." He said that the problem had been improperly defined and that the draft was too narrowly focused on whether the Soviets exercised direct operational control of terrorist groups. He said the draft had the "air of a lawyer's plea" that an indictment should not issue because there was not enough evidence to prove the case beyond a reasonable doubt.

Casey went on to say that there were two things wrong with this approach. First, "[T]he practical judgments on which policy is based in the real world do not require that standard of proof, which is frequently just not available." Second, "The real question is the extent to which the Soviets either directly or indirectly through their satellites train, supply and otherwise support these groups, what it tells us as to their political and strategic objectives and how Soviet policy with respect to terrorism might be altered or otherwise dealt with." But he didn't stop there. He added, "I find it [the Office of Soviet Analysis—SOVA—draft] deficient in intellectual and semantic rigor and over-reliance on Soviet statements. I do not wish to ask those who prepared this draft to correct its faults or otherwise alter it." The very next day, he asked the Defense Intelligence Agency to prepare a completely new draft.

The Defense Intelligence Agency wrote an alternative draft estimate and sent it to Casey, who liked it much more than the CIA draft. But now everyone was preparing new drafts. The result was something of a donnybrook inside the intelligence community, with CIA and DIA analysts ranged on opposite sides. The issue was finally resolved many weeks later when an old hand in the estimates business crafted a text that both sides grudgingly (and mainly because they were fed up and exhausted with the fight) accepted. It described "The Soviet Role in Revolutionary Violence."

The estimate didn't finally hit the streets until the end of May, and it actually wasn't too bad. It acknowledged that the Soviets were deeply engaged in support of "revolutionary violence" worldwide in an effort to weaken unfriendly societies, destabilize hostile regimes, and advance Soviet interests. The Soviets were indifferent to whether terrorist tactics were used, and had no scruples against such tactics. There was conclusive evidence that the Soviets directly or indirectly supported a large number of national insurgencies and some separatist-irridentist groups, many of which carried out terrorist activities as part of their larger program of revolutionary violence. The estimate went on to say that many groups that employed terrorism did not accept Soviet control and direction, though some did. With respect to the nihilistic, purely terrorist groups, the estimate said the evidence was thin and contradictory but noted that some individuals in such groups had been trained by Soviet friends and allies that also provided them with weapons and safe transit. It also observed that the Soviets had often publicly condemned such groups and considered them uncontrollable adventurers whose activities on occasion undermined Soviet objectives. It noted that some such nihilistic terrorists had found refuge in Eastern Europe.

Casey, DIA, the National Intelligence Council, and CIA's So-

viet analysts all had wrestled for the steering wheel of this controversial estimate, and together they took the entire effort into the
ditch. It had taken weeks to put things back together again, but
the damage to Casey's relationship with a number of CIA's Soviet
analysts was irreparable. And a larger number who had not been
involved were disconcerted by the manner and vigor with which he
had verbally eviscerated their colleagues. As Casey's chief of staff at
the time, I was on the sidelines in this fight and thus underestimated
the damage that had been done.

For all the blood on the floor at the end, and for all of the
careful compromise drafting to get the damn estimate out, we
would learn a decade later that it had been too cautious. After the
communist governments in Eastern Europe collapsed, we found
out that the East Europeans (especially the East Germans) indeed
not only had provided sanctuary for West European "nihilist" terrorists, but had trained, armed, and funded many of them. (For
example, during the late 1970s–early 1980s, the East German Stasi
(intelligence service) supplied the West German Red Army Faction
with weapons, training, false documentation, and money. The
training and weapons were put to use in the RAF car bomb attack
against Ramstein Air Force Base in West Germany on August 31,
1981, which injured seventeen people. The same group also was
involved in the unsuccessful rocket attack against the car of General
Frederick Kroesen in Heidelberg in September 1981.) It was incon-
ceivable that the Soviets, and especially the KGB, which had these
governments thoroughly penetrated, did not know and allow (if not
encourage) these activities to continue. As it turns out, Casey had
been more right than the others.

In keeping with this struggle, and others like it, getting the
CIA bureaucracy to do more on Soviet covert action and subversion
was painfully hard and eventually took on a political edge. Only at
the end of November 1981 were all CIA stations finally tasked to
submit a monthly report on Soviet covert action ("active measures") in their respective countries as a way of permitting more
aggressive counteroperations. And only after I became Deputy Director for Intelligence in January 1982 did we at last establish on
the analytical side an organization to study Soviet and other foreign
covert actions and deception activities around the world. The "Foreign Intelligence Capabilities Group" came into being in the spring
of 1982, not in the Soviet office but in the office responsible for

monitoring terrorism on a global basis. Only a handful of CIA's Soviet analysts took this work seriously.

To establish a data base of Soviet covert activities, I finally was able to persuade the Deputy Director for Operations, John Stein, to allow a team of analysts to pore through the operational files on the USSR and, with exhaustive effort, to extract the nuggets of information they found buried there on Soviet covert activities worldwide. A CIA ability to monitor Soviet covert action in an organized and thorough manner at last was born—thirty-five years into the Cold War. It was this kind of slowness and conventional thinking that exasperated—and more than occasionally infuriated —Bill Casey.

Casey complained bitterly and often graphically when the analysis he got seemed fuzzy-minded, lacked concreteness, missed the point, or in his view was naïve about the real world, when it lacked "ground truth." At the same time, while he had strong views, he was willing to change his mind (or to learn) when presented with good evidence or a cogent argument.

However, an analyst had to be tough and have the courage of his or her convictions to challenge Casey on something he cared about and knew about. He argued, he fought, he yelled, he grumped with the analysts in person and on paper. He pulled no punches. Some thrived on it. Many were put off by his abrasiveness, his occasional bullying manner, his presumption in questioning their work and their judgments, and his determination to channel their work into relevance for action and for his war. For a cadre of analysts accustomed to "gentlemanly discourse" and even more to a hands-off approach to their work from their own senior managers in the analysis directorate, such intrusiveness and assertiveness on the part of the DCI was unprecedented, and unwelcome. It laid him wide open to accusations that his effort to channel and focus analysis—especially in the Soviet arena—for relevance and action extended to shaping the conclusions to support his war.

Casey's belief that CIA's analysis was too flabby, unfocused, and "academic" prompted him to look outside the Agency for people to bring on board in order to provoke greater intellectual ferment and offer a different perspective. The results were mixed. He was wise enough not to place any of these people in the strongholds of the CIA career service, such as the Directorate of Intelligence. Rather, he assigned them to the National Intelligence Council, where various national intelligence officers in the past had been brought in from the outside to oversee the preparation of inter-agency intelligence estimates.

Most prominent among these was also the most successful—Professor Henry (Harry) Rowen of Stanford, whom Casey appointed as chairman of the National Intelligence Council. Harry had been the head of the Rand Corporation and had been in and out of Washington over the years. A thoughtful, provocative, and thoroughly likable intellectual with many contacts both in government and the academic community, Harry was reasonably well accepted by the career Agency people. He presided over the NIC with a light touch for more than two years before resigning to return to Stanford.

Others from the outside whom Casey brought to the NIC were a mixed bag. Some, like Rowen, were successful and respected. Still others were excessively policy-oriented, ideological, and arrogant—though often asking what I thought were insightful, even piercing, questions and offering useful insights and suggestions for doing our work better. Most CIA career professionals couldn't stand most of the outsiders, and the feeling was often reciprocated.

As with so many Casey initiatives, the difficult question surrounding some of these appointments was whether the gain outweighed the costs.

CASEY AND THE DO: FRUSTRATION AND TROUBLE

Casey's approach to clandestine operations was shaped even more by his OSS experience than his approach to analysis. By the time he became DCI, CIA's Directorate of Operations (DO) had become a guild of sorts. There was no room for amateurs, for those who had not grown up in the spy business, even from within CIA. The DO had become like the military, and each officer had to check off certain boxes in order to advance. For an operations officer, going outside that directorate for an assignment elsewhere in the Agency, with rare exceptions, did not help one's career and often harmed it. More and more, the recruitment process for the clandestine service had led to new officers looking very much like the people who recruited them—white, mostly Anglo-Saxon; middle and upper class; liberal arts college graduates; mostly entering in their mid to late twenties; engaging hale fellows well-met. Few non-Caucasians. Few women. Few ethnics, even of recent European background. In other words, not even as much diversity as there was among those who had helped create CIA and the clandestine service in the late 1940s.

By 1981, the Directorate of Operations had become a closed circle, and a bureaucratic one at that. No one who failed to fit the mold could get in. Few could get out to broaden their experience either within CIA or elsewhere in Washington. And, with too few exceptions, they resented and dismissed anyone from outside their ranks who had the temerity to offer insights or advice on how to do their job better. Outside critics? What could someone who has never recruited an agent or made a dead drop or lived in some godforsaken hellhole in the Third World know about operations? New kinds of information and new ways to get it? If information isn't stolen, it isn't worth having. Counterintelligence? Can't beat the polygraph and, besides, Angleton went too far and paralyzed operations.

In 1981, burdened by years of bureaucratic encrustation and the lessons of the investigations of the mid-1970s, the DO was hard-pressed for resources, unimaginative, a blindered fraternity living on the legends and achievements of their forebears of the 1950s and 1960s. There were still bold and successful operations, there were still recruitments of extraordinary foreign agents, and there were still individual officers who distinguished themselves with courage and imagination. But the institution was a pale reflection of its past. Even Carter administration officials had been disappointed by the lack of imagination and boldness.

This was not the way the OSS had been. Nearly everyone there had been an amateur, including Casey. Yet they had helped fight and win a world war. They had recruited agents, infiltrated behind German lines, run successful operations. People who had never spied before showed that with leadership, direction, motivation, and the pressures of war much could be accomplished. Casey was determined to reshape the operations directorate, even more dramatically than the analytical side of the Agency. He was frustrated by its ponderous bureaucratic ways, the amount of time it took to accomplish straightforward tasks, its reluctance to look outward, its timidity, its lack of diversity. The veteran of OSS arrived at CIA to wage war and found, instead of a clandestine dagger, a stifling bureaucracy. His Donovan-like approach to changing that bureaucracy—and too often, out of frustration and impatience, his inclination to bypass it—would bring Casey to grief time and again.

Indeed, it was his belief that new blood, new ideas, new energy, and a less establishmentarian approach was needed in the clandestine service that led to Casey's first major mistake as DCI. He had brought with him to CIA from the presidential campaign a scrappy little New Englander named Max Hugel. Max had made a lot of money as a risk-taking businessman, and he had brought to the Reagan campaign what Casey saw as true "street smarts." Now CIA as a whole is generally intolerant of outsiders coming in, much less in senior positions. And, while by 1981 a great deal of the Eastern Establishment elitism of the place had eroded, certain appearances and style were still important. Short Max, with his toupée and mannerisms, his style of speech and dress, was put down by the Agency hierarchy—apart from Bill—as soon as he arrived. When Casey made him Deputy Director for Administration in the early spring of 1981, everyone gulped, saluted, and tried to make the best of it.

When Casey, after weeks of begging by Max to get involved in operations, on May 5, 1981, made him Deputy Director for Operations—the most elite and closed union of all in CIA—people were horrified. Casey genuinely believed that Hugel would bring some freshness into the DO, liven things up, stimulate creativity, and perhaps even teach the pin-striped suit set a little about the street.

Casey wrote to Reagan the next day, May 6, to give a report on what he had found at CIA and to explain his unorthodox choice to be DDO. He told the President that "CIA had been permitted to run down and get too thin in top level people and capabilities. . . . The analysis and operations units are the most in need of improvement and rebuilding. . . . The analysis has been academic, soft, not sufficiently relevant and realistic. . . ."

On operations, he said that the paramilitary, counterintelligence, and covert action capabilities also had been permitted to run down. On human collection, he advised the President that "The future of human intelligence will, in my view, depend more heavily on using agents under non-official cover and drawing on the American ethnic community, friendly foreigners visiting and working in this country and American businessmen working, trading and financing abroad." He informed the President that he was going to reorganize the Directorate of Operations into two sections—(1) a worldwide clandestine service, and (2) a clandestine support unit encompassing CIA's paramilitary, counterintelligence, covert action, domestic collection, and nonofficial cover operations, all of which needed to be built up. He then told the President that Hugel would lead the entire directorate.

It was the appointment from hell. Max lacked any experience in clandestine activities. While the DO desperately needed a sprinkling of outsiders as a fresh source of ideas and new approaches, even I—an advocate of more outside appointments to CIA—did not think a neophyte from outside the Agency should be boss of all overseas operations. Hugel made mistakes and certainly did not represent the clandestine service effectively in or out of CIA. But it is also true that the Directorate never gave him a chance. The result was a punishing embarrassment for the Agency. Leaks to the press about Hugel's mistakes, mannerisms, and faux pas began nearly immediately. Everyone was embarrassed to have him go to the Hill to testify or to the White House to meetings, and all kinds of stratagems were employed to keep him out of sight. His deputy, John Stein, was a good soldier and appeared to do everything he could to make the appointment work. But even if Hugel had not gotten into a public scandal in early summer over some earlier business dealings (involving allegations relating to insider trading), Casey would have been forced to move him. As it turned out, Hugel was wrongly accused in the scandal, but tape recordings of his phone conversations were published in the *Washington Post* and so besmirched his image that he could not have survived. He resigned on July 14, just seventy days after becoming DDO. The deputy, Stein, was moved up to take his place—a career operations officer and a safe choice.

Casey was pilloried in the press for the appointment, and the criticism from the Congress was intense. Even the White House wondered what in the world was going on at CIA. His first attempt to put a brash newcomer into the Directorate of Operations in order to open it up and to diminish the bureaucracy failed utterly and cost him dearly. It was the first and last time Casey would challenge the DO institutionally. Badly burned, from then on he would work around the operations bureaucracy rather than try to change it. This would have dreadful consequences. Now he would indulge his instincts and play Donovan—he would reach down into the clandestine service to kindred spirits and work directly with them.

He would do so because he still found the Directorate of Operations as an institution an inadequate instrument for his war against

Moscow. He plainly wanted CIA to become much more aggressive in countering the Soviets and was eager to exploit previously untapped opportunities for recruiting agents and for the conduct of covert action.

Bill Casey the investor also knew that the American private sector—especially business—had a great deal of information on developments around the world that would be useful to CIA. The Agency for decades had contacted businessmen, scholars, and scientists traveling abroad to solicit, on a voluntary basis, information of value they might have picked up. But Casey had in mind something different. He intended to plug in at the highest levels of big companies to establish contact and to get information. But he also wanted to go a step further. The DCI wanted to use these business executives as access agents—as independent channels the administration (or he) could use to contact foreign leaders, e.g., Qaddafi, unreachable through official means. He didn't believe that those in the clandestine service charged with dealing with the private sector could get access to the very top people or that our officers could make the right impression on the heads of the biggest companies. So, at first, he did much of this on his own, although he did send me—as DDI—to New York and to California to establish a couple of these relationships. I focused solely on the information-gathering aspect.

It soon became clear that neither he nor I had the time to do this and so, as became his practice, he bypassed the DO structure, reached down and found an individual case officer he liked and trusted, and gave him the task of making these contacts. The officer's improbable pseudonym was "Lawless." McMahon, Stein, and later I all were extremely uneasy about Casey running this man without checks or supervision. McMahon finally succeeded in corraling this operation—mostly—and bringing Lawless and some of Casey's other independent operators back into the bureaucratic tent under a new Associate Deputy Director for Operations, a position established essentially for overseeing Casey's private-sector initiative.

This and other such activities were all manifestations of Casey's unhappiness and frustration with the Directorate of Operations. By fall 1981, he no longer bothered to sound positive. He wrote Stein on October 15, "Despite months of discussion of areas for rebuilding, neither the DCI nor the DDCI know what is being done." He demanded a report on the closer integration and expansion of the effort to obtain information from the business community into the Directorate, the rebuilding of the covert action and paramilitary capabilities, the expansion and improvement of the nonofficial cover officer program, and the strengthening of counterintelligence. It was easy to see he was fed up with the DO. It was just too cautious, too bureaucratic, too slow, too timid, and too unimaginative. Too much a closed shop. Not at all like the OSS.

But 1981 was not 1943. Containment of the Soviet Union—even under the assertive Ronald Reagan—was different from all-out war against Nazi Germany. The kind of imaginative rule-bending, "beat-the-bureaucracy," free-lancing and risk-taking that could be tolerated and even encouraged in wartime, in OSS, was unacceptable in the fourth decade of the Cold War. Such an approach was an anachronism. Casey was not oblivious to this. He was too smart for that. But his instincts and impulses, the imperviousness of the DO bureaucracy—and his commitment to the war against the Soviets—all inclined him to the old way of operating, to the approach he had learned in OSS and from Donovan.

CASEY, THE CONGRESS, AND THE PRESS: A CASE OF CONTEMPT

I believe Casey's attitude toward the Congress and the press when it came to intelligence matters also was shaped by his OSS experience. When Casey had been an intelligence officer in OSS, there was no congressional oversight, no body of intelligence law, really no rules or regulations. Donovan and his subalterns were able to run whatever operations they thought necessary to achieve victory, with few constraints.

With this as background, Casey was guilty of contempt of Congress from the day he was sworn in as DCI. He had zero patience for what he saw as congressional meddling in operations, and was especially intemperate when he thought Congress was micromanaging. He resented the time he had to spend stroking various members of Congress, the time he spent testifying and briefing, and even the time others of us spent testifying. Casey was convinced the Congress couldn't keep a secret and leaked all the time. He disdained the staffs and wouldn't give them the time of day. While he respected a few members as individuals, most he regarded as egotistical and self-serving. Here he was, just as in the OSS, trying to fight a war against a totalitarian empire, but now with these guys on the Hill taking his time, bothering him and his people, holding him back.

The DCI's attitude was apparent when he was testifying. In giving a briefing on worldwide developments, for example, he would often appear bored, look at his watch, scribble notes, and not work very hard to avoid dripping disdain in answering questions he thought were silly. Casey would periodically go to a hearing and announce at the outset that he had to leave at such and such a time for another meeting, and then leave at that time, turning the chair over to a subordinate.

Despite Casey's overwhelming confirmation, his negative attitude toward the Congress was soon reciprocated. Literally within weeks of his having assumed the job, he was into one scrape after another with the oversight committees, whether over his clearly incomplete financial disclosure or failure to establish a blind trust, or his appointment of Max Hugel or other problems. Truly, the hardest and most frustrating job in CIA was director of congressional affairs for Bill Casey.

Before many weeks passed after his confirmation, Casey had few personal allies on the Hill. Oh, there were a number of conservatives who shared his views of the Soviets and others who grudgingly respected the changes he was trying to make at CIA. But there were very few who would stick their necks out for Bill Casey personally. Republicans and Democrats alike found him hard to take. When real troubles came, beginning in 1982, he would have legion enemies in Congress and hardly a friend. And CIA could not escape guilt by association with its director.

Casey's other nemesis in Washington was the press. Here his problem fell into two categories. First, because he didn't respect the Washington press corps, he didn't pay much attention to it, with the exception of a handful of journalists he found useful or like-minded. (With the exception of the *Washington Post*'s Bob Woodward, to whom Casey gave extraordinary access and time. Apart from trying to influence a book Woodward was doing about him—*Veil*—I never understood why Casey did this, unless he simply relished the game of trying to use Woodward more than Woodward used him.) Casey essentially isolated himself from the press and so, as with Congress, when trouble came, there, too, he had few friends and allies.

A second problem Bill had with the press was his hard-line attitude on leaks. As time went on, and the flow of leaks out of the

Reagan administration became a gusher, Casey became steadily angrier at the administration's failure to do anything to stop it. He wrote countless memos on leaks to the President and other senior officials.

Thwarted in his efforts to deal with the root of the problem, the government leaker, Casey turned to the alternative: trying to pressure and threaten the press with legal action if they printed sensitive intelligence information. Here, as well, he would be frustrated. Casey complained loudly about Justice's unwillingness to pursue press leaks and to take action, and several times went directly to the Attorney General to see if he could make some headway. He got sympathy, but no action.

Casey's lack of success in stopping leaks did not prevent the development of a hostile attitude toward him by most of the press. The media saw his efforts as motivated less by concern over security than by antagonism to them and their criticism of him. As a result, Casey—unlike Inman—had few admirers or contacts in the fourth estate. And even as he survived Agency mistakes and misdeeds in covert action and repeated crises with the Congress, any one of which would have felled another director, his reputation became so sullied that increasingly any accusation against him was believed unhesitatingly.

While Casey was riding high, his contempt of Congress and hostility toward the press were only an inconvenience and an occasional embarrassment. But, as time passed, when real trouble came, they would be there waiting.

A TRUE ORIGINAL

If he patterned his approach to intelligence after Donovan, Casey as a person was an original. Physically, he was tall, somewhat stoop-shouldered, bald with wisps of white hair on the sides and back. He had a receding chin, large lips, a crooked smile, and piercing eyes. He dressed expensively and formally. Even on weekends, when he would come in to the office, he almost always wore a jacket and tie. His shoes were always well-polished. With all of that, he usually looked as if he had just concluded an all-night plane trip. When he walked, it looked like a committee of bones and muscles all trying to amble more or less in the same direction.

Sitting at his desk, Casey was nearly always in motion. He constantly fidgeted with paper clips, bending and unbending them, picking his teeth with them. Disconcertingly, he would often chew on the end of his necktie. He was always punching the buttons on his phone, and nearly always the wrong one. The secure phone system and its buttons baffled him, and when he would be buzzed for a call on the green phone and would push the wrong button, he would swear and shout at the secretary that it wasn't working. After he would call one of us on a direct line, we knew the line would ring again because he had gone on to the next call but without pushing another button. And, sometimes, out of impatience, he would simply give directions on what he wanted to whomever he reached, even if it was the wrong person and even the wrong directorate. We spent a lot of time sorting out his tasking.

He was always impatient. Things he asked for never reached him as soon as he thought they should. More than once, I heard him say he wanted a rubber stamp like Churchill's that said "Action This Day." Papers he was looking for on his desk weren't where he thought they were. He hated long meetings. He was demanding, and usually people didn't react as quickly as he expected. He was impatient with bureaucracy, with the press, with Congress, with others in the administration, and occasionally with Ronald Reagan —though not directly. He was especially impatient with those serving him personally. With the DCI security staff. With secretaries. With doctors. Early in his tenure, he slipped on wet grass playing golf and broke his leg. He didn't miss an hour of work, sitting at his desk with the leg in a cast propped up on a stool. One day an Agency doctor came in to check the leg, lifted it too high, and caused a sharp pain. Casey pushed him back, shouting at him, "Goddammit! Don't you know the damn thing's broken?"

Casey was often careless—perhaps absent-minded—about security. He would take several large briefcases of classified papers home every night and often would read them in bed. The next morning, his security detail would have to search the bedroom for all his papers—looking under the bed, shaking the sheets and blankets. He was often reckless in what he discussed on the phone.

Casey's mumbling attracted much comment and a number of jokes, including the one about him not needing a scrambler phone. Those who knew him reasonably well, I think, had little trouble understanding him in person. I certainly did not and I believe that was true of the other senior officers who were around him a lot. There were times, though, when even those who spent the most time with him had a hard time. On one occasion, one of his secretaries, Debbie Geer, was taking dictation from him while he was eating a sandwich. He took a bite and mumbled something to her. She paused, and then apologetically said she hadn't understood, would he repeat what he said. He mumbled again, and Geer once more had to ask him to repeat himself. This happened a third time and she was really embarrassed by now. Finally, Casey swallowed and said clearly, "I was saying, 'Wait until I finish chewing.' "

It always seemed to me that speaking clearly required a little extra effort on Casey's part, and when he didn't want to put out the effort he was hard to understand. This was especially true when he was dealing with Congress. At the same time, testifying before the House Intelligence Committee on one occasion, as its members fell to squabbling among themselves, Casey turned to the person next to him and stage-whispered as clear as a bell, "Sometimes I fear for the Republic!"

Aside from his personal foibles, most of which those of us around him usually found amusing or endearing rather than irritating, Bill Casey was one of the smartest people I have ever known and certainly the most intellectually lively. Like Donovan, he read voraciously, widely, and quickly. He rarely seemed to read for pleasure. He would go though a book fast—he called his style "skip-reading"—sucking out the essence and moving on. He subscribed to newsletters and information sheets that I sometimes thought couldn't have more than five readers in the world, and then he would ask if I had seen one or another item in them. Bill's office and desk were usually chockablock with books, and he was always handing people one or another volume, urging them to read it.

His intellectual curiosity was deep, and he met with and read an extraordinary variety of people—virtually anyone who he thought might have an interesting idea. Liberals, conservatives, wackos, authors, businessmen. His door was open to them all. He was especially adept at listening to an off-beat point of view and extracting from its obscure depths the one or two ideas or concepts or facts that might be useful. He was well aware of the zaniness of some of what he read. For example, he sent me an article from Lyndon LaRouche's *Executive Intelligence Review* with the comment, "The guys who put this out are crazy, but the [article on] Qaddafi and Khomeini . . . is interesting." With respect to an article he sent me on countering Soviet deception, he wrote, "This is something you should probably know about, but I wouldn't recommend your reading it unless you want to see how easy it is to overcomplicate something."

Too often at CIA (and many other places), people would dismiss an unconventional view or criticism because of the source or because one or another element of a presentation was flawed or mistaken. Casey, more than anyone I ever knew, was able to separate the few grains of wheat from a pile of intellectual chaff and make a conversation or something he read worth his while.

Bill Casey had strong convictions and defended his point of view aggressively. He was something of a bully, and dismissed those who were intimidated or afraid to argue with him. However, he was not dogmatic, and if the other person in an argument had good evidence and strong arguments, Casey would change his mind. In a difficult sort of way, he was open-minded, at least on substantive issues. He would not tolerate sycophants. The people to whom he was closest in CIA were those who argued with him the most—McMahon, General Counsel Stanley Sporkin, and me. McMahon and Sporkin shouted back at him. I just stood my ground. Unfortunately, there were too many unwilling to take him on. Indeed, even when I became DCI, I was disappointed at how few senior people in CIA would tell the DCI exactly what they thought. And I tried to make it easy. Casey didn't, and a price was paid.

Casey, Reagan, and the CIA Team

I always believed that Bill Casey's closeness to Ronald Reagan was exaggerated. I think the relationship was closest in the first months of the administration, while there was still a genuine sense of gratitude on Reagan's part for Casey's successful management of the presidential campaign. They continued to talk about politics and appointments during that early period. Over time, however, their contacts grew less frequent and were focused more on foreign policy issues rather than political or personnel matters. He could always get in to see the President when he wanted to, and could reach him on the phone, but he did so less and less as time passed. Casey had a clear-eyed view of Reagan's strengths and weaknesses. He truly admired Reagan and thought him potentially a great President. But, in private with me and perhaps others, Casey would complain about the President's lack of interest in specifics, his unwillingness to take hard decisions (especially between feuding cabinet members), and his rather simplistic view of the world. The Caseys were not often social guests at the White House, I suspect in no small measure because he wasn't very presentable in Mrs. Reagan's eyes (watching Casey eat was not for the squeamish) and also because she saw him as a growing political liability to her husband after 1982.

Casey maintained a strong personal relationship with Ed Meese throughout the administration, but became estranged from James Baker—whom he had brought into the campaign and then pushed to be Chief of Staff—after their dispute over how the Carter briefing book for the candidates' debate in 1980 came into the hands of the Reagan camp.

Bill had regard for Richard Allen, the first National Security Adviser under Reagan, and considered his successor, Bill Clark, a friend and an ally—although he had few illusions about Clark's lack of knowledge and expertise on foreign policy. Finally, in the White House complex, Casey had little use for George Bush. He thought Bush was weak and rarely had a good word for him. He did not think Bush should succeed Reagan as President.

Weinberger at Defense and Casey would be allies for as long as both were in the administration. They shared a common approach on policy toward the USSR, and Weinberger was supportive in critical ways of the rebuilding of intelligence, especially with money. They had breakfast every Friday when they were both in town, and they disagreed about very little.

Casey had a cordial relationship with Alexander Haig, although the conventional wisdom was that he had wanted the Secretary of State job. At the outset, Casey's relationship with George Shultz was a good one, but within months of Shultz's appointment, antagonism between the two was building fast.

Finally, Casey had recommended his friend Don Regan to be Secretary of the Treasury and, while they had little business with one another, they stayed in touch. Casey especially liked Jeane Kirkpatrick, the U.S. ambassador to the UN, and jokingly referred to her as his "girlfriend." At different times, he pushed her for National Security Adviser, Secretary of State, and in 1986 even spoke of supporting her for President.

At CIA, Casey's relationship with his first Deputy DCI, Bob Inman, was strained from the start. They both knew Inman was there because Barry Goldwater had made clear to Reagan that while he thought Inman should be DCI, he would support Casey if he had the professional intelligence officer Inman at his side. Inman had remarkably strong ties on the Hill, and great respect. Given Casey's view of the Congress, and the knowledge that his deputy was so much more highly regarded than he, tensions were inevitable. The relationship was not enhanced by Inman making clear his unhappiness at being pressured into taking the job. Nor did it help that Inman had been number one at the National Security Agency, running his own show in an organization several times larger than CIA.

The one area in which Casey and Inman were in accord was on the need to rebuild the intelligence community after more than a decade of neglect. Casey worked with Weinberger and others in the administration to make sure that the funds were there, and Inman drew up the five-year plan laying out how the resources were to be used—and did much of the sales job with the Congress. The plan, which focused on new technical and human intelligence resources, creating new collection and analytical capabilities for the Third World and the Soviet military-industrial complex, and modernizing the intelligence community's long-neglected infrastructure, was a sound one and served as the blueprint for the revival of American intelligence.

Inman's opposition to creation of a new and centralized counterintelligence organization located in the NSC and to removal of restrictions on collection against Americans earned him the enmity of some of the more conservative elements of the administration, especially on the NSC staff. They complained often to Casey, and I think fed him gossip prejudicial to Inman—especially that Inman was working the Hill behind his back and to his detriment. In turn, Inman's contacts, who were sprinkled throughout the administration and Congress, told him of negative or snide comments being made by Casey and his friends. This only worsened as the distance between them on covert action and other issues grew.

The Deputy Director for Operations when Casey arrived was John N. McMahon, a career officer who had managed the building of the SR-71 reconnaissance plane and had held a variety of CIA and intelligence community jobs. McMahon was a white-haired, stocky Irishman with a sharp and blasphemous tongue and a wonderfully hearty laugh. He loved CIA, was determined to protect the institution, supported congressional oversight, had no patience for "cowboys" in covert operations, and was intimidated by no man. He had run the DO with an iron hand under Turner, and there had been virtually no flaps while he was in charge. Those who failed to keep him informed or bent the rules paid a heavy price with John. He was a strong manager, and was widely liked and admired. I had known him only slightly before Casey arrived but would come to regard him as a friend and counselor. His common sense and integrity were powerful assets for CIA.

Casey liked him from the beginning. When Bill soon decided he needed stronger leadership in the Directorate of Intelligence to improve analysis, he asked John to take the job. There have been stories that Casey wanted to move McMahon out of the DO in order to make room for Hugel or so he could run operations himself. I can't dismiss those possibilities, but I believe that Casey moved McMahon for the reasons he gave at the time—he wanted a much stronger and bolder leader in charge of analysis, the improvement of which was one of his highest priorities. I think Casey believed McMahon could do anything.

John did make a lot of changes. He totally reorganized the analytical branch along geographic lines, a traumatic change that had been avoided for several decades. But John was bored by analysis after the reorganizing was over. He was an activist, an action-oriented guy, and after only a few months, he started making noises about retiring. To keep him, Casey and Inman reestablished the position of CIA Executive Director, the number-three position, solely as a way to keep John from leaving. He soon made it a real power base.

After the Hugel mess, Casey appointed the loyal John Stein as Deputy Director for Operations, and Clair George as his deputy. Casey didn't know Stein well, but after the Hugel affair felt he had to make a traditional appointment that would quiet both the directorate and the Congress. Stein was a career operations officer, and his appointment was greeted with relief. But Casey knew that Stein would not change much in the directorate. Thus for Casey to accomplish what he wanted through the clandestine service, he would have to go around Stein and the directorate's front office. This was soon apparent throughout the directorate. After one DO division chief met with Casey and received operational instructions, I asked the division chief if he shouldn't walk down the corridor and fill in Stein. He replied that Stein "didn't need to know." If McMahon had still been DDO, by that night the division chief would have been looking for a new job.

Casey had been in office for only a few weeks when it was clear to him that his front office wasn't working very well. He had tried several special assistants but found all inadequate. Furthermore, there was little or no coordination between Casey's staff and Inman's, and the two were going their separate ways on issues without knowing what the other was up to—and this was on activities they weren't even trying to keep from one another. Casey turned to John Bross, an old friend and retired Agency officer, whom Casey persuaded to sign up as a consultant for a few months, for help in finding a solution. I had not known Bross before he retired from CIA but I came to believe that he represented the best of the "old boy network"—Ivy League, wealthy, a well-connected lawyer, veteran of the OSS and CIA's clandestine service, a man of rare good judgment and humor. Totally unintimidated by Casey, representing a tie to CIA's past, the soul of common sense and integrity, Bross was invaluable to Casey during his first several months as DCI.

Observing the front office in chaos, Inman, on the day he was confirmed, suggested to Bross that I be brought up to establish some order. Bross asked if Inman wanted to suggest my name to Casey, and Inman replied, "You take a look at Gates and decide— I don't want Casey to think I'm planting a spy in his office." So Bross asked to meet with me in late February. He asked, in light of my experience as executive assistant to both Brzezinski and Turner, what could be done to sort out the front office. I told him what I thought ought to be done. The next thing I knew I was telling Casey the same thing, and by early March I was no longer NIO for the USSR, but director of a new organization called the DCI/DDCI Executive Staff—in effect, chief of staff for Casey and Inman. So I was back in the DCI suite.

Casey and I hit it off from the beginning. We had similar views about the Soviet Union, and I knew how the national security side of the government worked from my NSC tours. I knew the arms control business, and I believed CIA was in need of rejuvenation. I wasn't afraid of Casey, kidded him, and organized the flow of papers and materials to him in a way that eased his life. During 1981, I sat in on virtually all of his meetings and afterward offered my opinion on what should be done. As I had been with Turner, I was very blunt with Casey about his actions and activities, about what was good and bad about CIA, and about what should be done. I guess he liked what he heard.

I soon realized, however, that one of my main jobs had become the communication channel between Casey and Inman. As the weeks wore on, it became evident that each trusted me more than he trusted the other. So when one heard gossip about the activities or criticisms of the other, I was sent to find out what was up. I advised each on what was annoying the other. I wore a path in the carpet covering that inner corridor between the two offices. It was very uncomfortable because the only way to survive was to be absolutely straightforward with both of them, and that involved saying some things—even if said by the other and not by me—that were pretty ugly.

At the same time, I was writing Casey and Inman memos about what I thought should be done to improve CIA. On analysis, I urged more outside contacts, more CIA sponsorship of conferences and seminars with nongovernment experts, more training and education for analysts, more assignments in the policy community for managers so they had a better understanding of how intelligence was being used, keeping records of analysts' assessments and using those in determining promotions and assignments, creation of an internal evaluation office to look at earlier assessments and estimates to see how we had done and what we could learn, a more rigorous internal review process to improve quality, and more.

From personal experience and my NSC assignments, it seemed to me that CIA had become very bureaucratic. I wrote Casey and Inman on September 23, 1981: "One of management's priority objectives throughout the Agency should be to fight bureaucratic routine and established ways of thinking as absolutely inimical to collecting information and producing the best possible analysis as well as the most effective covert operations. I hardly need point out that one would not now characterize CIA in the above vein. . . ."

I concluded:

As a result of the lack of innovative and creative personnel management, I believe this Agency is chock full of people simply awaiting retirement: some are only a year or two away and some are twenty-five years away, but there are far too many playing it safe, proceeding cautiously, not antagonizing management, and certainly not broadening their horizons, especially as long as their own senior management makes it clear that it is not career enhancing. How is the health of CIA? I would say that at the present time it has a case of advanced bureaucratic arteriosclerosis: the arteries are clogging up with careerist bureaucrats who have lost the spark. It is my opinion that it is this steadily increasing proportion of intelligence *bureaucrats* that has led to the decline in the quality of our intelligence collection and analysis over the past fifteen years—more so than our declining resources . . . or Congressional investigations or legal restrictions. CIA is slowly turning into the Department of Agriculture.

Casey took this aboard, but never did devote sustained and effective attention to remedying CIA's institutional problems.

I was equally blunt with Casey about his view of the centrality of covert action in waging war on the Soviet Union. In September 1981 he sent me a paper on covert action prepared for Nixon in 1968 by Frank Lindsay and asked for my reaction. Lindsay had written, "Covert operations can rarely achieve an important objective alone." I wrote, "More often than not, our covert operations are seen as a way to accomplish a policy objective (if there is one) on the cheap, to cope with a problem where no one has any idea how to obtain public support for the solution to the problem, or to use covert action as a short-term tactic to fend off a problem or disaster—a tactic to be repeated or expanded upon in the absence of the ingenuity, will or money to come up with a viable long-term overt option."

Another point in Lindsay's essay was, "Much greater attention must be paid to clandestinity." I responded, "The DO talks a good game on security and cover; they tend to be far less rigorous when it causes them some inconvenience."

On analysis, operations, covert action, management, and personnel, I told Casey and Inman what I thought and, often, my ideas for remedies. They liked what they read and heard, no matter how close it came to home. And they weren't hearing it from anywhere else. I believed in CIA, but I also believed it could be so much better than it was. Finally, someone was listening to me.

When McMahon indicated he wanted to retire, and Casey and Inman decided to move him up from DDI to be Executive Director, this left the position of DDI open. They debated whether to move up the deputy—Evan Hineman, an old friend and colleague of mine—and make me his number two, or simply to put me in charge. Inman suggested that I become the number two, the Associate Deputy Director for Intelligence, but as Casey looked at the ambitious agenda for change I had recommended and that he wanted implemented, he told Inman, "If he's that good, why waste time?" My appointment as DDI was announced in December

1981 and became effective on January 4, 1982. I was thirty-eight years old.

I quickly implemented an ambitious agenda for change and, with Inman's support, did so all at once rather than piecemeal. I began with an address to all DI managers and analysts in the Agency auditorium on January 7, 1982. I spoke bluntly about shortcomings in Agency analysis, about analytical failures, about intellectual arrogance and resistance to outside views. I laid out in detail the changes that I would be making in a dozen different areas.

If I had been suspected in the past of being too blunt, this talk confirmed it for everyone. While some analysts and managers thought it was about time someone spoke plainly about such matters, and many agreed with the measures I announced to improve analysis, the description of past failures angered a lot of people who might otherwise have been supportive. A tactically smarter—"kinder, gentler"—speech that emphasized the achievements of the past and the need now to build on them would have gone down better. I survived the speech, implemented the measures, and we all got to work.

This, then, was Bill Casey and the CIA he found in January 1981. Two immovable forces. One, Casey. Shaped by World War II, the OSS, and Bill Donovan. Aggressive, inventive, inexhaustible, as unbureaucratic as anyone can be, hostile to Congress and the press, and with a single purpose in mind—to challenge the Soviet empire everywhere. The second, CIA. An Agency in middle age, bureaucratic, scarred by investigations and purges, having had six DCIs in eight years. Resources cut. An Agency in the midst of a profound demographic change as the founding generation retired and huge numbers of new, young, inexperienced people joined. We knew the months and years ahead would not be easy. I had no idea how hard they would be.

CHAPTER THIRTEEN

Turning the Tables

THE REAGAN ADMINISTRATION assumed power in January 1981, breathing fire and ready to confront the Soviet menace. The transition teams had worried, and probed CIA, about the possibility of an early test of the administration by the Soviets. We had told them that a contrived test was unlikely, but that Moscow would be watching the new President's early moves closely. A test came almost immediately, but it was not at all contrived. And it would dominate the national security agenda of the new administration for its first year in power.

POLAND: WORKERS' UNION VS. "WORKERS' PARTY"

The rest of the world did not take a holiday while the United States chose a new President, he selected his team, and they all prepared to take control of the American government. In Poland, new Communist Party Secretary Stanislaw Kania had narrowly averted a Soviet military intervention when he was given more time at the December 5, 1980, Warsaw Pact summit to regain control of the situation in Poland. However, the Soviets continued to watch skeptically and warily, and the Polish regime and Solidarity circled one another during the winter of 1980–1981.

Clearly, Soviet military posturing in November–December 1980 had made the threat of intervention more credible to the workers and to the regime. This resulted in a six-week-long Soli-

226

darity strike moratorium which, in turn, provided some four to five weeks of calm. By early January 1981, though, a harder government line—no doubt at Soviet urging—resulted in more union resistance. At this point, the government in Warsaw had no coherent strategy to limit the unions' political demands or to stem the erosion of party authority.

This, then, was the situation when the Reagan administration arrived on scene. The first interagency meeting on Poland under the new President was on January 23. Still NIO for the USSR and Eastern Europe, I attended and briefed that Solidarity was maintaining pressure on the government with controlled "warning strikes" and that Soviet concern was growing, as reflected in increasing press criticism of Solidarity. State briefed the new Reagan people on contingency plans, all of which were based on the worst-case—a Soviet invasion, resistance, and significant bloodshed—in the belief that the list of U.S. retaliatory measures could be adapted to less dramatic scenarios.

At this meeting, I first briefed the new team that, instead of a Soviet invasion of Poland, there was a good chance that the Poles would enforce coercive measures themselves as a way to keep the Soviets out. I based this on the reporting of a Polish CIA agent, a remarkable and courageous staff officer of the Polish General Staff, Colonel Ryszard Kuklinski. We had been getting information on the Warsaw Pact from him for years, but now we were most interested in his information on preparations for military action in Poland by either the Poles or Soviets. We waited eagerly for each of his reports, recognizing at the same time the added risk to him of our demands for more frequent communication. His information had been important in prompting Carter's tough warning in December 1980 and it would be critical to us all through 1981. Drawing on his reporting, I suggested at the January 23 meeting that the policymakers reconsider their contingency planning to include the internal repression scenario. The chairman, David Newsom of State, agreed.

At that meeting, an additional U.S. response was suggested beyond political and economic retaliation if the Soviets acted. That response, suggested by Richard Burt of State, was to take advantage of the Polish crisis to obtain a long-term strengthening of the NATO alliance (a notion David Aaron had pushed in the last months of the Carter administration) and a restructuring to U.S. advantage of international mechanisms that could make life more difficult for the Soviets—such as COCOM, the organization that determined what technologies could be exported to them.

By the next meeting, on January 30, the contingency planning had been fleshed out. The measures taken in December 1980 to improve NATO's military readiness were reviewed. On technology transfer, all agreed that the Defense Department should prepare a paper on whether the United States should expand restrictions on technology transfer beyond that which was militarily useful to all technology that might be useful to Soviet industry.

Finally, in the event of the use of force by the Poles themselves, we agreed on a menu of political and economic retaliatory actions, such as threatening a severe cutback in the economic arena; recalling our ambassador for consultations; imposing harder terms for repayments to Western banks and other institutions of Poland's massive—and overdue—debt; cutting off agricultural credits; withholding any new Export-Import Bank credits; signaling Western banks that the U.S. government favored their cutting back their exposure in Poland; and so on.

I dwell on these two January 1981 meetings for two reasons. First, they set forth the basic U.S. position on the situation in Poland that would endure in the Reagan administration. For all the tough talk, the conservative new team was wholly focused on stern warnings and possible economic sanctions in the event the Soviets acted in Poland—more dramatic measures weren't even discussed. Second, both in attitude and planning, there was a nearly identical approach to the Polish problem by Reagan's people and the Carter administration.

Throughout February 1981, there was a sense in Washington that tensions were building in Poland and that a crisis was near. CIA published a special national estimate on January 30 that predicted, "Soviet pressure on the Polish regime will increase and this trend is toward the use of coercion by the Polish authorities." Further, the failure of coercive measures by the Poles would "certainly result in the introduction of Soviet forces." The Agency elaborated on this conclusion in its classified "world-wide briefing" presented to various congressional committees early in the year, noting, "The present crisis constitutes the most serious and broadly based challenge to Communist rule in the Warsaw Pact in over a decade," and also noting that recurrent confrontations between the regime and the unions had moved Poland "ever closer" to the edge of Soviet military intervention. The Soviets, we asserted, were less confident than in December that Kania could bring the situation under control. In short, the trends by early February from the Soviet standpoint remained decidedly negative.

The briefing also observed that, compared to the previous October and November, the chances were greater that the Polish regime would respond with force, probably at Soviet urging, if it was faced with a major confrontation. The briefing concluded, "We believe Soviet pressure on the Polish regime will increase, and that if the pattern of domestic confrontation continues, the trend is toward ultimate intervention."

The replacement of Jerzy Pienkowski as Polish premier by Defense Minister General Wojciech Jaruzelski on February 10 and very tough leadership speeches at the party Central Committee plenum had a shock effect in Poland that quieted the situation and bought the regime some more time. Casey told an NSC meeting on February 11 that the Polish party had moved a step closer to the possible use of force. Drawing on another extraordinary clandestine report from Kuklinski, Casey advised the President and his colleagues that the Soviets and Poles would test their martial law procedures on February 13–14—although they still regarded martial law as a last resort because of the great risk of confrontation and widespread violence.

In fact, the Polish government's call for a period of tranquillity gained a good deal of popular acceptance. Solidarity embraced a ninety-day moratorium on strikes, clearly sobered by Jarulzelski's appointment. Even so, CIA predicted that the pattern of the preceding several months would reassert itself, that is, sporadic disputes over local and national issues and the difficulty of either the regime or Solidarity establishing some control over local organizations or militants. We doubted the lull would last ninety days. Longer-range Soviet concerns had not abated at all.

The lull in Poland, which lasted just four weeks, was deceptive. Behind the scenes, as we learned from Kuklinski, joint Soviet and Polish planning for martial law was proceeding. As early as March 4, 1981, in a meeting of the Polish and Soviet leaders, Jaruzelski provided to the Soviets for their review a package of Polish documents dealing with the introduction of martial law.

The next crisis came on March 19, when Solidarity activists in the town of Bydgoszcz urging officials to recognize Rural Solidarity were set upon and beaten. There was evidence that the incident had been provoked by hard-liners in the Polish Politburo in cooperation with the Security Ministry. Solidarity demanded the punishment of the individuals responsible for the brutality in Bydgoszcz, assurances that coercion would not be used in the future, the registration of Rural Solidarity, and the release of all political prisoners incarcerated since 1976. A Polish party Politburo statement on March 22 made clear that the regime wouldn't give much, if any, ground—even though it wanted to defuse the situation.

Just over two months in office, the Reagan administration now got its trial by fire, a test of its nerve. During the last week in March and the first week in April 1981, events in Poland raced to the brink of catastrophe.

The first moment of truth seemed to be coming on the weekend of March 28–29. As tensions mounted in Poland at the end of that week, including a four-hour general strike on Friday, we began to get both technical and human intelligence of the kind that makes an intelligence officer's blood run cold—preparations for military action. In short order, we learned that Polish air space would be closed "for technical reasons" on the night of March 28–29; as of March 23, the East German railroad authorities had been told not to use any flatcars—they were to be held in reserve for an operation conducted by the National Defense Council; the Soviet General Staff initiated a major expansion of command, control, and communications network that would direct an intervention; and at least three Soviet General Staff operations groups were dispatched to Poland. Finally, a series of reports came in, none conclusive, pointing to the likelihood of major developments in Poland during the next weekend (the 28th–29th). There was a general belief in both the U.S. intelligence and policy communities that martial law would be imposed that weekend, possibly involving Soviet military intervention.

We would soon learn from Kuklinski that on March 28 (during the critical weekend when we thought intervention might take place), with the agreement of Kania and Jaruzelski, a group of senior officials from the KGB, Soviet Ministry of Defense, and State Planning Commission (Gosplan) arrived in Warsaw to consult on martial law. The Soviets criticized the Polish plans as inadequate and called instead for the total transfer of power to the hands of the military and introduction of Soviet advisers at all levels of the Polish military. The Polish leadership rejected the Soviet proposal but made some concessions.

From the distance of more than a dozen years, it is easy to

forget the apprehension associated with this and similar crises of the Cold War. Poland's crisis and possible Soviet military action cast a global shadow of tension, the danger of miscalculation, and even possible military conflict between the superpowers. This was a Soviet leadership that had just over a year before invaded Afghanistan and was asserting itself militarily on a global basis. And so radios and TVs were tuned in around the world to see what would happen in Poland. Our allies also thought the imposition of martial law was near, and the North Atlantic Council met in Brussels and arranged to convene a meeting of foreign ministers to consider appropriate NATO responses.

Important and sensitive contingency plans were prepared over the weekend, including implementation of high-priority improvements in NATO, a buildup of U.S. active and reserve forces, and deployment of new, sensitive weapons systems to Europe.

Another contingency plan involved preparation of a proposed presidential statement to be used by President Reagan on national television in the event of a Soviet intervention. The proposed statement ended with the President proclaiming "Polish Patriots Day" and asking the American people for a show of solidarity: "I ask Americans to wear red and white ribbons on that day—Poland's national colors" and ". . . to gather in squares and meeting places of our towns and cities to stand with our Polish brothers and sisters."

There was no need for the President to make a statement. Poland's appointment with repression was postponed again—but who knew for how long. On Sunday, March 29, an agreement was reached between the regime and Walesa in which the government conceded the union's demands on police brutality, and postponed the Rural Solidarity issue as well as the problem of political prisoners. In return, Walesa agreed that Solidarity would postpone the general strike set for Tuesday, March 31. The crisis was not over, just put off.

On April 9, Casey sent the President an Agency assessment of how the Soviets saw the situation in Poland. It said that if the Soviets let the situation drift, they would almost certainly lose control of a key buffer state, "a country vital to their strategic position in Europe." The paper cited Kuklinski to the effect that Soviets were putting the Polish leadership under intense pressure to declare a state of national emergency, but the Poles had rejected a Soviet plan for martial law placing all authority in the hands of the Polish military.

Casey covered the CIA assessment with a note of his own to the President, saying that the Soviets found themselves in a "desperate dilemma." "If they go, they will get economic chaos arising from the debt, a slowdown of the whole Polish work force and millions of Poles conducting a guerrilla war against them. If they don't, they are open to the West and a political force which could unravel their entire system. Before sending divisions in, they will move heaven and earth to get the Poles to crack down themselves."

During the first two weeks of April, as the threat of a general strike still loomed, one of the most melodramatic episodes of the entire Cold War occurred in Warsaw and in Rome. It involved Jaruzelski, the Pope, Walesa, and Polish Cardinal Wyszynski. Casey described the events in two very private memoranda to the President. CIA learned that over the weekend of April 4–5, the regime received information that Solidarity "extremist elements" had begun to prepare for a violent confrontation with the government—preparing Molotov cocktails and planning the occupation of government buildings and destruction of Communist Party offices around the country. Under the circumstances, Jaruzelski believed that a general strike would make it necessary for him to declare martial law on his own authority. He and the Polish generals made every effort during this period to persuade the Soviets not to intervene unless it became apparent that the situation was out of control. At that point, they promised they would invite the Soviets in.

In these circumstances, apparently fearing they were on the verge of losing control and facing Soviet intervention, Kania and Jaruzelski appealed to Cardinal Wyszynski for help, claiming that Poland was on the brink of disaster.

On April 23, the Pope told Casey during a meeting between them in the Vatican that Moscow could not tolerate very much more of the process initiated by Solidarity and that having the union "fall back" was the only way to avoid suppressive measures catastrophic for the Polish people. Under these circumstances, the Pope told Casey, the Church in early April had encouraged a tactical withdrawal by Solidarity that would make it possible to retain some of the advances already obtained. Further, Cardinal Wyszynski had tried to persuade Walesa of his duty to cancel the general strike in order to defuse the struggle.

According to CIA sources, Cardinal Wyszynski, obviously at the Pope's behest, and persuaded by Kania and Jaruzelski that Poland was on the "brink of disaster," had met with Walesa that first week in April and again argued strongly for outright cancellation—as opposed to postponement—of the general strike. Walesa and the other Solidarity leaders refused. As continued deadlock seemed inevitable, the eighty-year-old cardinal, who was dying, knelt before Walesa, grasped the union leader's coat, and said that he would kneel in that position in prayer until his death unless Solidarity abandoned its plans.

The dramatic gesture worked. Walesa reportedly said that there was no way to resist "this emotional blackmail." And when Solidarity called off the general strike, preparations for martial law were suspended, the situation cooled, and Soviet preparations to move subsided. Cardinal Wyszynski died a few weeks later, on May 28.

The Soviets' evident reluctance to intervene prompted me to write Casey a memo on April 30 urging that the Agency begin to think about alternatives: "I believe we must begin to give some attention to the prospect that the Soviets will not intervene in Poland and that the reform movement will continue." The memo mentioned a number of the dramatic changes toward democratization of the Communist Party and went on to say, "In my view, we may be witnessing one of the most significant developments in the post war period which, if unchecked, may foreshadow a profound change in this decade in the system Stalin created both inside the Soviet Union and in Eastern Europe." I suggested that it was time for our analysts to address the implications of Soviet nonintervention for both Poland and its communist allies.

Wyszynski's "emotional blackmail" bought only a few weeks' respite. The reason why was apparent: the Soviets simply could not accept the status quo, for exactly the reasons I had noted in my memo to Casey. In mid-May, Marshal Kulikov, commander of the Warsaw Pact, returned to Poland, where he remained until mid-June consulting with Kania, Jaruzelski, and General Siwicki, the chief of the Polish General Staff. The pressures on the Polish regime continued in early summer as the Polish Communist Party Congress approached. Once again warnings were raised by CIA and the Intelligence Community about the danger of the Soviets acting before or shortly after the congress.

At a mid-June meeting of the Polish party's Central Committee, the Soviets tried to secure the ouster of both Kania and Jaruzelski. They failed. Instead, there was a huge personnel change in the party Politburo and regional party structures, with the old guard being replaced by moderate or liberal members of the party. At the subsequent Polish Party Congress, nearly an entirely new team emerged, with a 90 percent turnover in the Central Committee and only four holdovers of fifteen members of the Politburo.

In midsummer, Jaruzelski and Marshal Kulikov met again, and Kulikov demanded more decisive action regarding the possibility of introducing martial law. Soviet General Staff officers even then were working in Poland with Polish counterparts to produce proposals modifying the Polish contingency plans for the emergency situation. A few days later, the revised Polish plan was presented to the Soviets by General Siwicki, and now dealt with matters such as sealing the borders, additional command and control communications, and more.

The Polish crisis began to pick up steam again in the fall. Kuklinski advised us that, on September 9, General Siwicki informed a small group on the General Staff that Poland was approaching the institution of martial law. They, in turn, asked him whether the regime would receive "help" from the Soviets if the imposition of martial law was unsuccessful. He said yes. Siwicki also advised the group that the martial law proclamations would be printed in the USSR. In mid-September, the Polish political leadership rejected a proposal by the Polish military to institute a state of martial law.

By September 25, Siwicki had come to believe that a political solution might not be possible, and presented two martial law options to the Polish leaders. Neither excluded the possible need to request assistance from the USSR and the Warsaw Pact. Siwicki called for closer cooperation with the Soviet Union and the Warsaw Pact to plan for intervention if it proved necessary. Other sources told us that by September 29, the possibility of a Soviet armed intervention in Poland during the second half of October was being discussed among the Soviet General Staff.

The pace of events began to pick up in October. As of October 7, the martial law proclamations were being printed in the Soviet Union, and Polish officers were acknowledging the "contribution" of the Soviets to the elaboration of the martial law plans. Five days later, under the pseudonym of Petrov, the Soviet leadership published in *Pravda* an extremely harsh criticism of developments in Poland and implied a threat to intervene to set things right.

By mid-October, we knew that Brezhnev had had a number of very unpleasant conversations with Jaruzelski, with Kania being cut out. We also knew from Kuklinski that by this time the Soviets had expanded their influence throughout the Polish government and party, with access to all Politburo and Central Committee members, as well as the provincial authorities. The constant refrain of the Soviets was that Poland must take immediate and firm action against Solidarity. By this time, we also knew that Jaruzelski had been persuaded by his own Ministries of Defense and Internal Affairs, as well as by the Soviet leadership, to favor the introduction of martial law.

Soviet concerns ratcheted up again in light of the outcome of the Polish Central Committee plenum October 16–18, where it was clear that the party was faced with continued hemorrhaging of its authority. In response to increased Soviet pressure to reassert party control, the Polish party replaced Kania with Jaruzelski and talked tough in its public declaration—even while reaffirming its commitment to "renewal." There was a strong attack on Solidarity. This was repeated at a meeting of the Parliament on October 31, where Jaruzelski personally condemned strikes and the "hate campaign" that had been launched against Poland and its allies. A final attempt at reconciliation was made on November 4, when Walesa, Archbishop Glemp, and Jaruzelski met in Warsaw. Jaruzelski had strong demands, and Walesa—a real moderate inside Solidarity—wasn't buying. And that was essentially the end of the line.

On November 3–5, Polish Foreign Minister Czyrek and Party Secretary Stefan Olszowski visited Moscow, where they encountered a rough time. They were told by the Soviets that the Polish leadership had let the situation get out of hand and had endangered socialism throughout the alliance. The Soviets explicitly refused to support Jaruzelski's policy of national reconciliation. Two weeks later, on November 18–19, a commission of nine Soviet General Staff and Warsaw Pact officers headed by C. G. Nikolaev, Deputy Chief of the Main Operations Directorate of the Soviet General Staff, met with the Polish General Staff in Warsaw. The main topic: to discuss documentation regarding the implementation of martial law. The Soviets said that the documents were all prepared and offered to help the Poles implement the measures. The Poles clearly did not want to do anything.

The final act began on November 25, with a sit-in strike at the firefighters' academy in Warsaw. At a Central Committee meeting on November 27–29, Jaruzelski stated that the Polish parliament would be asked to pass legislation outlawing strike activity. Against a backdrop of a Warsaw Pact foreign ministers' meeting in Bucharest and a defense ministers' meeting in Moscow, the striking cadets were expelled from the firefighting academy on December 2 by Polish police and military. The next day, December 3, Solidarity's Presidium, meeting in Radom, declared that the government had destroyed the chances for national accommodation and that Solidarity had decided to consider a general strike. On December 7, the Polish government released tape recordings made at Solidarity's Radom meeting and Solidarity, in turn, announced that it would hold a meeting of its National Commission in Gdansk on December 11–12. By the 7th, we also knew that Marshal Kulikov was back in Warsaw. Polish Archbishop Glemp on December 8 sent a letter to Jaruzelski urging him not to ask the parliament to ban strikes.

The Solidarity National Commission met on December 11–12 and was still in session on the night of December 12–13 as martial law was implemented, and the arrests began. From the Soviet standpoint, the crackdown and defeat (at least temporarily) of Solidarity was accomplished with little cost internationally.

How does the imposition of martial law in Poland while the United States and NATO stood by represent "turning the tables" on the Soviets? First, as in Afghanistan, the Soviets paid a much higher political price than seemed to be the case in the immediate aftermath. Their display of ruthlessness in Poland—because CIA made sure everyone knew the part they had played in the implementation of martial law—brought NATO closer and probably contributed to the alliance's willingness to deploy INF a year and a half later. There were specific retaliatory measures taken, especially in the economic arena. Also, those events in Poland, coming hard on the heels of the Soviet aggression in southwest Asia, left few illusions anywhere about the nature of the Soviet regime.

A second aspect of the developments in Poland was that the Soviet leaders had looked at the political, military, and economic costs of military intervention in Poland and decided not to pay them. In a situation where the entirety of the East European buffer was at risk, the Soviets bent over backward to keep their troops in the barracks, and ultimately did not use them at all. This lack of nerve, or confidence, at a time when so many tiny fissures were appearing in the empire, was not lost on people—especially in Eastern Europe.

Finally, the imposition of martial law resulted in CIA and

American covert action being targeted against Soviet domination in Eastern Europe in a significant way for the first time since the early years of the Cold War. Although there had been some modest activities in support of Solidarity outside of Poland by the Carter administration, as early as March 1981 the notion of enhancing our covert role was discussed in interagency meetings. Nonetheless, Casey was cautious about any covert action planning prior to a Soviet invasion. He told Weinberger that U.S. actions prior to Soviet action would be very risky and promised little benefit.

In keeping with Casey's unease, serious conversations about covert action in Poland did not begin until after the imposition of martial law. Partly this was due to Casey's view that Lane Kirkland and his AFL-CIO were doing a "first-rate" job in Poland helping Solidarity—better, he thought, than CIA could do. Indeed, Casey was worried that if CIA got involved, we might "screw it up."

Much has been written in recent years about a tripartite covert alliance of CIA, the AFL-CIO, and the Vatican to help Solidarity survive underground. I know that there was considerable sharing of information about developments in Poland with the Vatican, sometimes through visits by Casey, at times through roving ambassador and troubleshooter Dick Walters, and perhaps occasionally through our ambassador to the Vatican. I have no doubt that there were discussions at the highest level about the need to assist Solidarity. But I am equally certain that while there may have been a modicum of coordination at the highest levels to avoid tripping over one another, each of these institutions, for important reasons of its own, maintained a clear separation from the others in its activities. I am unaware of any clandestine cooperation between them during the 1980s in terms of helping Solidarity, although some go-betweens representing Solidarity probably did business with more than one and maybe all three.

I was always told that CIA had no direct link with Solidarity and that, in fact, the union did not know in specific terms what, if anything, it was getting from CIA. Our people thought that deniability was important for Solidarity, and so we worked through third parties or other intermediaries in Western Europe. Most of what flowed out of CIA and through the intermediaries to Solidarity was printing materials, communications equipment, and other supplies for waging underground political warfare. There was no lethal assistance.

CIA's effort did not really get rolling until the latter part of

1982. Bill Clark, who had replaced Dick Allen as National Security Adviser, wrote Casey on August 6 seeking advice regarding steps CIA could take "to provide modest support to the moderate elements of Solidarity" in support of U.S. policy "to pressure the Polish and Soviet governments to end martial law, release political prisoners and re-establish a social contract with the Polish people." On September 1, Casey asked Clark to schedule a meeting on an enhanced covert action for Poland, and reported that he had already discussed it with Shultz (who by then had replaced Haig) and Weinberger.

Once the covert action was under way, Casey paid little attention to it. He would be briefed periodically, but he certainly did not devote the attention to it that I would see in other areas, especially in the Third World.

With one exception. Casey would talk to Brzezinski from time to time about developments in Poland. One time Brzezinski complained that funding had been cut off to a very worthwhile project. Casey asked how much it would take to remedy the problem and Zbig replied, "About $18,000." Brzezinski later told me that the next day a man showed up at his office without an appointment and asked to see him. Zbig reluctantly agreed and the man handed him a briefcase full of cash—$18,000 to be precise—for the project Brzezinski had mentioned to Casey. Somewhat nonplussed, he nevertheless took the briefcase and passed it on to a visiting Pole associated with the project who was headed back to Europe. This was indicative of Casey's penchant for "action this day."

As a footnote, CIA was able to extricate Colonel Kuklinski in November 1981, when he became convinced the authorities were closing in on him. The Soviets had learned that we had the plans for the declaration of martial law and when they told Kuklinski this, he knew he had been compromised. He had been one of the most important CIA sources of information on the Soviet military of the Cold War period. Faithful always to his beloved Poland, he provided us with more than thirty thousand Soviet documents over a ten-year period, including Warsaw Pact contingency plans for war in Europe, details on large numbers of Soviet weapons systems, planning for electronic warfare, and much more. His efforts, I am convinced, allowed the United States and its allies to help deter a Soviet invasion of Poland in December 1980 and allowed us to forewarn and then expose the Soviet role in Jaruzelski's declaration of martial law a year later.

All in all, through 1980–1981, under both Carter and Reagan, I believe the United States played its cards well in the Polish crisis. Thanks to good intelligence—to Colonel Kuklinski—we knew what was going on between the leaders of Poland and the Soviet Union and between their military high commands. We were able to speak out strongly at key moments and emphasize to the Soviet leadership the extraordinary costs of intervention. The United States had limited power to affect the course of events in Poland. In retrospect, our government under two Presidents made maximum effective use of that power. And the Soviets' decision not to intervene would have enormous historical consequences.

Nineteen eighty-one was an eventful year for the United States. A new administration. Reagan's tax-cutting and defense buildup legislation. The attempted assassination of the President. The attempted assassination of the Pope. The Israelis' bombing of the Iraqi nuclear reactor at Osirak. The conflict with Libya over the Gulf of Sidra. The assassination of President Sadat. War between Iran and Iraq. And more. But nothing in foreign affairs took as much time and energy as the Polish crisis, which dominated the foreign policy agenda from Inauguration Day nearly until Christmas. And none would have as important consequences for the future as did Poland.

The Attempt to Assassinate the Pope

No discussion of Poland in 1981 would be complete without addressing the attempt by Mehmet Ali Agca to assassinate Pope John Paul II on May 13. We may never know whether the Soviet or Bulgarian intelligence services were involved or at least knew in advance, or whether Turkish right-wingers or others were behind the attempt.

Those who believe the Soviets were involved make the case that the Pope was, in substantial measure, the primary cause of the Soviets' trouble in Eastern Europe and especially in Poland. They point to the Pope's election in 1978 and his subsequent visit to Poland as the spark that caused smoldering Polish nationalism and pride to burst into flame and contributed importantly to the emergence of protests, strikes, and eventually the emergence of Solidarity itself in 1980. They point to the Soviets' fear of the Polish Pope's influence in Lithuania, western Ukraine, and elsewhere in Eastern Europe. In short, the argument is that John Paul II's election and his actions and public posture thereafter threatened to provoke popular reactions not only in Eastern Europe but possibly even in parts of the Soviet Union as well, foreshadowing the beginning of the unraveling of empire. The danger of such a strategic challenge to Soviet hegemony, the argument went, would justify such a drastic step as trying to eliminate the Pope.

The contrary view, and the dominant one among most experts in CIA in 1981–1982, was that the Soviets saw the Pope as a stabilizing element and had been engaged in a secret dialogue with him since early September 1980—shortly after Solidarity was formed. The Soviets initiated the contact with the Pope during mounting tension in Poland over the labor situation in Gdansk. Under the direct supervision of the Pope, Cardinal Casaroli handled the dialogue. Through a series of contacts, the Soviets asked the Pope to restrain the Polish workers and thus ease tensions. They made clear that they would intervene militarily if the situation got out of hand. The Vatican's objective in the talks was to discourage Soviet intervention, which the Pope believed would lead to a bloodbath. He was obviously sympathetic to the workers, but he was also anxious not to provoke the Soviets and eager to get the Soviet government to encourage the Polish authorities to reduce tensions.

By mid-November 1980, both sides were said to be satisfied with the dialogue. Casaroli and the Pope believed that the compromises they achieved had averted Soviet military intervention. By the same token, a Soviet official told an Italian communist leader that the Church was "a stabilizing force in Poland."

During the period of intense Soviet pressure on Poland in early December 1980—when they decided to intervene but held off at the last minute—the Soviets sent a senior official, Vadim Zagladin, from Moscow to assure the Vatican that the Kremlin did not intend to intervene. At this point, the Pope apparently concluded that the chief danger to Poland was no longer a Soviet military move but Soviet pressure on the Polish army to conduct internal repression.

In the weeks just before the assassination attempt, Soviet-Vatican contacts intensified when Warsaw Pact forces conducted "Exercise Soyuz." The Pope and the Soviet ambassador to Rome met alone for two hours on March 28—the same weekend we thought intervention was likely—and afterward the Pope told aides that he had reached agreement with the Soviets on Poland and that a senior Polish official would arrive in Rome in April for discussions on implementation. The Soviets had assured him they would not intervene for six months.

During the next tense period, April 19–25, the Pope and Casaroli met three times with the Soviet ambassador, who told them that the Soviets believed the situation had again stabilized and urged the Church to continue to restrain the Polish workers. Casaroli told others that the Pope was "satisfied" with the Polish situation, and was urging moderation on the Polish unions, government, and military.

Following Agca's attempted killing of the Pope, the dialogue between the Soviets and the Vatican continued. Casaroli observed in June, for example, that the Vatican's efforts to ease the situation and help the Polish government survive the crisis had been undermined by the Pope's slow recovery. Clearly, he was the key intermediary, and the Soviets were uninterested in talking with any lower level in the Vatican. The dialogue continued until the imposition of martial law in December 1981.

As the Italian investigation of the assassination attempt proceeded, CIA was repeatedly asked by policymakers and members of Congress to judge who was behind the assassination. We really didn't know very much during 1981–1982 apart from what we were picking up from the Italians, and that information had more holes in it than a Swiss cheese. With respect to the Soviets, I told Casey in September 1982 that our analysts and operations officers believed that if Moscow had wanted to assassinate the Pope, Agca would have been too risky an instrument. Casey sent a summary of what we knew along these lines to Shultz, Weinberger, and Clark on December 20, 1982. It drew no conclusions.

The papal assassination attempt would dog CIA for years. The criticism came from every direction. Some accused us of trying to cover up the Soviet role, though why we—and especially Casey—would do such a thing I never grasped. Others, then and later, would claim that we were trying too hard to pin the blame on the Soviets. In 1983, Stein and I would testify before the SSCI—the only time the DDO and DDI testified together in my memory—and were agnostic about who was behind the crime, much to the impatience of some senators. This basically remained CIA's position until new information was acquired by the clandestine service in the winter of 1984–1985.

CENTRAL AMERICA: INTO THE BIG MUDDY

As his wars against the Soviet Union grew in number and scale, Casey remained detached from them emotionally. His greatest concern was with Soviet subversion and aggression in the Third World generally, and he was interested in and monitored covert actions in Afghanistan, Poland, Lebanon, Cambodia, Ethiopia, and later Angola and elsewhere. But no individual covert action aroused his passion or significantly occupied his thoughts or even his time, save one. For reasons I never fully comprehended, Bill Casey became obsessed with Central America.

One of the most curious phenomena about Central America in the early 1980s is that there was so little disagreement about what was happening. When we briefed the Congress and the press on the nature of the Nicaraguan military buildup, including the numbers of troops and weapons, and their Cuban and Soviet origin, we found few doubters.

The issue, of course, was not what was happening in Central America and in Nicaragua, but what to do about it. As described earlier, even the Carter administration had reacted strongly to moves by the Sandinistas. After all, Turner had warned as early as 1978 that El Salvador was about to "boil over." I saw a striking similarity between the way Turner, Brown, Brzezinski, and Muskie portrayed the situation and the implications for the United States, and the characterizations of Casey, Haig and then Shultz, Weinberger, and Reagan. And by 1980, small-scale, nonlethal covert actions had been authorized by Carter in Central America and the Caribbean to counter Castro's activities and the ambitions of the Sandinistas.

Thus when Casey proposed a new, broader—but still nonlethal—covert action on February 24, 1981, intended to expose and counter Cuban and Nicaraguan troublemaking in Central America and to staunch the flow of weapons and support from Nicaragua to Salvadoran guerrillas, it seemed to me very much in keeping with the concerns I had witnessed prior to the change of administrations. When Reagan signed new findings on Central America and Cuba on March 9 in an effort to slow the flow of communist weapons to El Salvador, few people—even inside the government—realized that these findings superseded and expanded upon political and propaganda covert actions in Central America targeted against the Sandinistas approved by Jimmy Carter. Only now, force was authorized to interdict the weapons supply. Similarly, when Reagan announced on April 1 that there would be no more U.S. aid for Nicaragua, again he was reaffirming a decision taken some time earlier by Carter.

In sum, the first steps of the Reagan team in Central America were quite consistent with those of their predecessors. But by summer 1981, the Reagan administration would begin to take a much more alarmist view of developments there and begin to shape a much more aggressive response. At that point, consensus inside and outside of the Executive Branch fractured.

Casey's own involvement in Central American matters began to grow soon after he arrived in January 1981. He demanded studies on the flow of weapons from Nicaragua to El Salvador as prelude to sending forward the new finding. On April 6, he approved a national estimate, "Cuban Policy in Latin America," which informed policymakers that the Soviets had changed their approach to the region—that after the Sandinista victory, the Soviet leaders apparently concluded that the prospects for the success of revolutionary forces in Central America were brighter than they had calculated. As a result, local communists began to receive guerrilla training in the USSR and, in particular, the Soviets helped arrange for broader support to the Salvadoran insurgents, especially arms and military equipment, from four East European countries, Ethiopia, Vietnam, and the PLO.

Haig and Casey were of like mind on many issues, but they looked at Cuba and Central America differently. Haig believed that because Cuba was the source of the problem in Central America, the focus of U.S. efforts should be Cuba itself. He told Casey on May 12, 1981, that the administration "has only about six more months to act to get Castro under control." Haig said that it was necessary for the United States "to begin to prepare militarily in the Caribbean and the southeastern U.S. and when Castro observes these actions we might be in a position to persuade him to cease his adventurism." The Secretary disdained covert action in Central America, believing that it could not solve the problem.

Casey, on the other hand, continued to believe that, ultimately, the Soviet Union was the problem, with Cuba only being a piece of it. He thought the chances were nonexistent of actually doing what Haig wanted, whereas covert action at least would engage us in a useful way.

This debate should have been engaged in a more structured

way because it revealed the basic quandary of the Reagan administration. Haig's hope to "go to the source"—Cuba—was impossible politically. By the same token, diplomacy alone would not stop the Soviets, Cubans, and Sandinistas. And few contemplated overt military action against either Cuba or Nicaragua. In fact, Reagan's bold rhetoric belied the limited risks he was prepared to take for Central America.

From the outset, Casey was disgusted with the administration's feeble and failed efforts to attract public support for its policy in Central America. He thought their political efforts inconsistent, unpersuasive, too limited in scope, and too episodic. In his view, the administration was never prepared to go to the American people in a sustained and intensive effort to explain the need for *overt* action in Central America, and never seriously tried to build a political constituency for such action. Thus the only option open to it was covert action. So the primary role fell to Bill Casey and to CIA. And, if CIA was the only game in Central America, then, by God, Bill Casey would give it all he had.

In virtually every covert action other than Central America, Casey was reasonably prudent—often even cautious—grumpily content to work through channels both inside CIA and in the interagency arena. Throughout his nearly six-year tenure, of all of CIA's "secret" wars, only Central America would get him and the Agency into trouble—inside the administration, with the Congress, and with the media and public. Central America was the only covert action where, from the outset, Casey went out of channels at CIA. He plucked a remarkable and flamboyant officer, Duane "Dewey" Clarridge, out of Europe and brought him back to head Latin American operations. Dewey spoke no Spanish and had no experience in Latin America. But he was an operator and an immensely talented manager of covert operations. Told to "Take that hill!," Dewey set about the task with scant regard for convention or regulation. In the Afghan war, he would have been a hero. In the politically charged Central American conflict, he wound up in court. The DDO, John Stein, as well as Inman (and then McMahon), were on the periphery as Dewey would talk, meet, and travel privately with Casey. The die was cast.

In mid-July 1981, Casey visited Southern Command Headquarters in Panama and came back persuaded that Nicaraguan-sponsored insurgencies in Central America were gathering strength more rapidly than had been thought. Through the remainder of the summer, Casey focused more and more on action inside Nicaragua itself, and direct pressure on the Sandinistas as a way to divert them from troublemaking elsewhere—as in El Salvador—but also to counter the consolidation of the regime there. By September, he was taking Clarridge with him to brief Weinberger and Haig on the Central American covert programs and telling them that the United States had not yet faced up to the consequences of the arms buildup in Nicaragua.

By early October 1981, Casey was arguing for a new approach beyond trying to interdict the weapons flow from Nicaragua to El Salvador. He told Weinberger on October 2 that between the extreme alternatives of a purely diplomatic strategy and a purely military strategy there was one "that would make it harder for the Cubans and Nicaraguans—the creation of a third force." Haig remained skeptical. On November 10, in a long discussion with Casey, the Secretary of State said that he "had no desire to get the country committed to halfway measures. Either we are in it to win or we should not get in at all. Rather than go halfway, we should simply accept the country going communist and then deal with the implications of that."

Despite Haig's reservations, by mid-November Casey had sold his new approach and it was tentatively approved at an NSC meeting on November 16. On December 1, Reagan signed a new finding, for the first time authorizing covert support for the Contras, as the opposition to the Sandinistas had come to be known. Nineteen million dollars was authorized to raise a force of five hundred resistance fighters. The two intelligence committees were briefed—only the House committee raised tough questions—and by early 1982, weapons were flowing to the Nicaraguan resistance.

Actually, the Argentine junta had been funding a covert group of Somocistas (former National Guardsmen under the dictator Somoza), many of whom had gone to school in Argentina. The United States basically took over the funding of five hundred of them. The justification still was interdiction of the weapons flow to El Salvador and distracting the Sandinistas as a way of slowing their support to the Salvadoran guerrillas.

The administration's efforts to expose the Sandinista government for what it was got a boost on April 15, 1982, when Eden Pastora, one of the great heroes of the Sandinista revolution (known as "Commandante Zero") openly denounced the regime and went into armed opposition. CIA had gotten word in February that Pastora was considering defecting, and Clarridge flew south and met with him. CIA agreed to provide a rapid flow of arms to Pastora in Costa Rica under the rubric of interdiction. At the same time, Pastora would deny that he was receiving U.S. support.

Soon after the deal was struck, Inman walked in on a meeting between Casey and Clarridge where execution of this plan was being discussed. Inman asked what was going on and, being told, took exception to the plan without a new finding being signed. He argued that it was hard to see how Pastora's actions in Costa Rica could be aimed at interdiction of weapons flowing from Nicaragua to El Salvador—Nicaragua being north of Costa Rica and between it and El Salvador on the north. Inman said that the support of Pastora looked to him like it was intended to try to overthrow the Sandinistas. Casey waved his deputy off, accusing him of being a "goddamn lawyer." It was at that moment that Inman decided to resign. The day Pastora announced his defection from the Sandinistas, Senator Chris Dodd told Inman, "You all will live to regret ever getting involved with Eden Pastora." At that moment, Inman's resignation letter had already been submitted.

By this time, the House Intelligence Committee, which had been nervous when briefed on the Central American covert action in December 1981, was increasingly suspicious that Casey was trying to overthrow the Sandinistas, and its chairman, Edward Boland, was beginning to consider legislation to prevent that. By the end of April 1982, after Pastora had been signed up as part of the Agency program, members of the committee were curious as to how a force based in Costa Rica was going to help stop the flow of weapons to El Salvador—on the other side of Nicaragua (just Inman's point). Skepticism bubbled over.

On April 28, Casey wrote McMahon (now the Executive Director), Stein, and Clarridge that the House committee wanted another briefing on Central America the following week. Casey directed the briefers to say, with respect to Pastora, that CIA had made contact with all dissident forces who might promote pluralism and help stem the flow of arms to El Salvador. "Beyond that, I don't think details should be provided."

When the House committee wrote language into the budget authorization bill prohibiting funds being spent to overthrow the Sandinistas, Casey wrote a note to the Deputy Director for Operations and head of Congressional Affairs that it was necessary to take quick action to avoid the kind of "micromanagement" the House committee would impose.

> It would not be possible to assure that efforts to limit arms shipments or support a political front in favor of a pluralist, democratic Nicaragua would not "directly or indirectly" destabilize or overthrow the government of Nicaragua. Also, it is too much to ask that we be "sure" that funds for paramilitary operations will be used so as to avoid provoking military exchanges between Nicaragua and Honduras. . . . We do not and should not exercise the kind of "sufficient control" of the paramilitary groups to ensure that such fine requirements will be met.

Casey's strategy to deal with Boland's language was first to try to talk it out with the House committee, "but, more urgently, and more importantly, we have to get to the Senate side quickly, today or tomorrow, to explain that this language is impossible and get them to provide in this bill language which would enable all this to be straightened out in conference."

By fall, Casey was again pressing for expansion of the program. By the time Reagan visited Central America at the end of November, CIA had in Nicaragua more than 3,500 fighters—2,300 operating out of Honduras, nine hundred Miskito Indians, and some five hundred under Pastora in Costa Rica and southeastern Nicaragua.

Compliments on Dewey Clarridge's operational achievement notwithstanding (there were few of those from the Hill), Casey's political strategy for blocking the Boland Amendment—prohibiting CIA from trying to overthrow the Nicaraguan government—failed and, on December 8, the amendment passed the Congress. On December 15, Casey told Clark that a House committee hearing he had just attended was "tough" and that some members were concerned that "even if we were not trying to overthrow the Nicaraguan government, some of those we are supporting are." The DCI then said, "We must do some hard thinking about the evolution of the program." When Senator Daniel Patrick Moynihan charged in a letter to Shultz in December 1982 that the administration was breaking the law with its covert Nicaraguan program, Casey told Clark that, while he disagreed with Moynihan, he had to acknowledge that "there is a fine line between our purposes and the purposes of those we support."

Throughout 1981–1982, there also were strains inside the Agency over the Nicaraguan covert program. The analysts consistently complained, with justification, that the DO shared virtually no operational traffic with them and therefore they had little information on what the Contras were up to. (Operational cables, for security purposes, were rarely shown to anyone outside the clandestine service. When CIA was involved in a covert action, this "compartmentation" often left the analysts in the dark.) The analysts believed that the DO was consistently overly optimistic about the prospects for their program in general and the Contras in particular, and that they overstated their accomplishments when briefing policymakers and the Congress.

Both operations officers and Casey often felt that the analysts were too academic, too detached. In July 1982, for example, Casey sent Clarridge the briefing the Directorate of Intelligence had prepared for his use at an NSC meeting with the instruction, "See if you can add some ground feeling and currency into this draft intelligence briefing." The Operations Directorate's Central American Task Force set up their own "war room" where their "analysts" tracked the course of the guerrilla struggle and reported to Dewey and to Casey. They claimed it was in support of the covert program and so, as Deputy Director for Intelligence, there wasn't much I could do about it. But occasionally I would learn that they briefed their views outside of the Agency and I would raise hell with Casey about it. (This wasn't just a turf fight. The people staffing the "war-room" were advocates of the covert program and naturally inclined both to inflate the threat and the success of their efforts.) I also warned Casey that he ran a high risk of embarrassment if he only took operations officers—especially Dewey—to brief the Congress or his administration counterparts. As a result, he started also taking Bob Vickers of the National Intelligence Council as a sort of truth squad. Vickers was a career expert on military matters and had a calm, analytic approach that contrasted with the enthusiasms of his operational counterpart.

There were also stresses over aspects of the covert program itself. Here I was singularly without influence. For example, in September 1982, I was asked to endorse a proposal for use of an AC-47 gunship equipped with infrared sensors to detect and interdict arms shipments from Nicaragua to El Salvador. I objected because of the danger that use of the detectors and rapid-firing guns at night would lead to loss of innocent life. Casey ignored my concerns, approved the proposal, and forwarded it to the NSC, along with other proposed actions for improving the interdiction of arms flowing to the Salvadoran insurgents. McMahon represented CIA at the NSC meeting when these were discussed. When he pointed out the dangers, Jeane Kirkpatrick jumped on this and urged Reagan to turn down the proposal. He did so.

Central America was, in Casey's view, a critical battlefield in the war on the Soviets. He believed that if the United States could not defeat Soviet ambitions in our own backyard, we would be hard pressed to do so elsewhere. And so he waded into "the big muddy."

Deeply suspicious both of diplomacy and of the Congress, from the beginning he behaved on Central America in such a way as to deny himself important allies—from George Shultz, who was no less militant on the region than he was, to some members of Congress who, had they had confidence that the DCI was willing to level with them, might have joined the effort. It was the only covert war where he was politically blind externally and procedurally incorrect internally. For all his criticism of the White House for its lack of a serious political effort in support of its Central American policy, in the one area—the Congress—where political skill was required from him to attract confidence and support, he failed utterly. Already in difficulty on Capitol Hill on Central America by the end of 1982, he hadn't seen anything yet. The real firestorms were still to come.

By the same token, at the end of 1982, the Soviets and Cubans knew that they confronted a new kind of U.S. response in Central America, and that the revolutionaries in Managua now faced their own insurgency.

CASEY AND THE THIRD WORLD

Apart from Central America, Casey's interest in Soviet and surrogate involvement and subversion in the Third World built slowly. While he wanted to wage war against the USSR from the day he set foot inside CIA, it was more than a year before his campaign gathered momentum and began to take shape. The full scope of his intentions and plans did not begin to emerge until March–April 1982. And, as usual, he began with an analytical approach.

On March 29, he sent Inman and McMahon a memo asking for a broad assessment of strategically located Third World coun-

tries—economic pressures on them; subversive and insurgent challenges; security assistance they had received in the past; and their
strategic significance to us and to other developed countries. He
wanted to know how the military sales and foreign assistance policies of the Soviet Union, the United States, and their allies com-
peted and impacted upon these countries; how the United States
and USSR compared in getting foreign advisers to these countries
and in bringing military officers and trainees and civilian students
from them to the United States and USSR; and how this activity
was trending and paying off in influence. Four days later, Casey
sent me—now DDI—a copy of this memo with the note, "High
interest in attached and consider it a very important subject."

Casey's trip to the Middle East—Tunisia, Pakistan, Somalia,
Sudan, and Oman—in April 1982 had a huge influence on him.
When he got back, he wrote the President a long memo saying that
his visits had left him "more concerned than ever about the progress which the Soviets and their proxies are making and can make
in these countries and other adjoining and nearby nations." He
reported that in each country, dissidents were being brought out
and trained, usually in Libya or South Yemen, equipped and sent
back into the country to "organize, propagandize, or practice terrorism against the government." Casey wrote the President that
Libya, Ethiopia, South Yemen, Afghanistan, and Syria, "all working
together or under Soviet influence," in one way or another "almost
completely surround our friends Egypt and Israel and the oil fields
of the Middle East."

Influenced, I think, by the leaders he met with on his trip,
especially Pakistan's Zia, Casey concluded his memo to Reagan
with the following observation:

> Through Libya, South Yemen and Ethiopia, the Soviets have
> mounted subversion and insurgency threats to countries which con-
> trol the most strategic choke-points in the world: Oman at the Strait
> of Hormuz; North Yemen and Somalia at the mouth of the Red Sea,
> the pathway to Suez; and Morocco at the Straits of Gibraltar. In
> the past eight years, the Soviets and their proxies have promoted
> insurgencies in over a dozen countries, five of them successful and
> seven now under way. The Soviets' experience in Afghanistan has
> demonstrated how much more efficient and less costly it is to con-
> quer by subversion than by invasion. Most of these states cannot
> effectively use and do not need sophisticated high-priced weapons.
> What they need is light arms, transport, and communications to deal

with multiple, widely scattered hit and run forces. This security and counter-subversion assistance should be low-profile.

In other words, Casey-managed covert action.

Casey would remain obsessed with Soviet and proxy subversion in the Third World for the rest of his life. Here was the Soviet challenge he had taken the job at CIA to counter and defeat. And from mid-1982 on, the DCI had a crusade. Anchored in Central America and Afghanistan, his campaign would involve CIA on every continent, wherever he could persuade the Reagan administration and the Congress that the Soviets and their proxies were active.

AFGHANISTAN: A SLOW START

Casey devoted little attention or effort to the covert program to help the Afghan Mujahedin in 1981. Funding for the program for the first three years of the Reagan administration—1981–1983 —remained essentially at the level proposed by Carter, about $60 million a year, matched by the Saudis.

On January 14, 1982, however, Casey read a message from the CIA station chief managing the program urging more weapons for the Mujahedin as a means to put additional pressure on the Soviets. In a meeting on February 26, 1982, Casey and Deputy Defense Secretary Carlucci discussed efforts to get another $20 million out of Defense to expedite and expand the Afghan program. Haig also was pushing hard to get more funds for the program. Despite Haig's and Casey's interest, and Weinberger's general support, no more money was forthcoming from DOD, and the program remained at the $60 million level.

But Casey was now engaged. During his meeting on April 6 with President Zia in Pakistan, Zia opened an atlas to a map of the region and laid down a red celluloid template graphically depicting how Soviet possession of Afghanistan would drive a wedge between Iran and Pakistan, with the southernmost tip of the wedge pointed at the Strait of Hormuz in the Persian Gulf—the choke point for oil coming out of the Gulf. Zia reminded Casey that in the nineteenth century, Britain had drawn the line against Russia at the Oxus River, Afghanistan's northern border, and made clear it would contest any move to the south. As a result, the Russians did not move for ninety years. But a vacuum developed after World War II, and the Russians finally moved in 1979. Zia emphasized that the Russians had no intention of giving up their position in Afghanistan and that the United States had a "moral duty" to draw the line at the northern borders of Iran and Pakistan—and make clear that any move south would be contested.

At the end of the history lesson, Casey agreed to find a way to increase the pressure and provide more help to the Mujahedin. Zia then asked for better antiaircraft capability. He said, "The Pathans are great fighters, but shit-scared when it comes to air power."

Casey pushed the issue of more funding when he came back, but still was unable to move the Defense bureaucracy to pony up more money. Reagan might be President and Weinberger Secretary of Defense, but an obstinate bureaucracy can be a formidable antagonist—especially when giving up money is involved. Increased funding for the Mujahedin would have to wait more than another year.

Zia and Casey met again late in 1982, after Brezhnev's death and Andropov's succession. During the meeting, Zia described Soviet long-term objectives in Afghanistan. He told Casey that Nicolae Ceausescu of Romania had told him that the Soviets went into Afghanistan because (1) Iran and Pakistan had raised the cry of Islam, and this was intolerable for the Soviet Union's position with its own Muslim republics; and (2) the Soviets wanted to be in a favorable position militarily to intervene in Iran if the situation required. Zia said to Casey that he agreed with Ceausescu but would add two more objectives: (3) it moved the Soviets closer to the Strait of Hormuz (Casey agreed, saying that he and Zia were in the minority on this), and (4) in the "darkest hours," the Soviets might move through Baluchistan—part of Pakistan—to the Gwadar Coast, gaining access to the sea.

Finally, according to Casey, Zia told him that our objective in Afghanistan should be "to keep the pot boiling, but not boil over" in a way that would provoke a Soviet attack on Pakistan. He said that the present level of arms was about right, but we still needed to give the Mujahedin ground-to-air weapons to use against Soviet and Afghan aircraft.

Between DOD's budgeteers and Zia's concern not to provoke the Soviets, any effort to expand the program significantly would have to wait. But the groundwork had been laid by the end of 1982 so that when money became available and Zia became more aggressive, CIA's Afghan program would expand dramatically.

LIBYA: A BURR UNDER THE SADDLE

Libya's relationship with the Soviet Union had entered a new phase in 1974 with the signing of Tripoli's first major arms purchase from the USSR. While that would remain the heart of the relationship, the Soviets also either cooperated with Qaddafi's adventures in Africa or tolerated them. Further, Libya's role in sponsoring terrorism was well-known, and there were suspicions that the Soviets played some role in training, equipping, and funding some terrorist groups based in Libya.

If the U.S. relationship with Libya was poor before 1981, Reagan's coming to power soon resulted in conflict and a level of overt antipathy between the two countries without contemporary parallel. In the spring of 1981, Libya was implicated in a terrorist murder in Chicago. As a result, the United States ordered the Libyan embassy in Washington closed. In early June, Weinberger urged the President to approve resumption of the Sixth Fleet's annual exercises in the Gulf of Sidra, claimed as territorial waters by Libya. (Various nations around the world make claims of territorial waters in contravention of international law, and the U.S. Navy periodically deploys to these contested waters to demonstrate that the United States does not accept these claims and to assert the freedom of the seas.) Qaddafi had claimed as Libya's territorial limit a line far outside the twelve-mile limit, called it the "line of death," and threatened to attack any intruder crossing the line. Reagan authorized the exercise for August. On August 20, Libyan combat aircraft fired on two U.S. F-14s involved in the naval maneuvers about sixty miles off the Libyan coast. The Libyan aircraft were shot down.

After the incident, CIA received several clandestine reports of Qaddafi's desire to exact revenge. One suggested that he intended to have Reagan killed. Then, in December, we received an even more explicit clandestine report that Bush, Weinberger, and Haig were also being targeted by Libyan hit teams smuggled into this country.

That single clandestine report literally changed the face of Washington. The report seemed credible, and, as a result, security around the President, Vice President, and principals of the national security team was dramatically increased. Construction was begun on barricades around the entrances to key government installations, barricades that were further extended and strengthened after car and truck bombs the next year in Lebanon showed how much damage could be done. In a two-year period, pop-up steel barriers and concrete mazes were built and personal security staffs vastly expanded. In that climate, having a security detail became a highly visible status symbol—if you weren't worth killing, you must not be very important. The paucity of evidence of Libyan plotting against the leaders of the American government in ensuing years suggests that, even granting the accuracy of the original clandestine reports, Washington overreacted to the threat of assassination from Libya.

Meanwhile, the administration was watching Qaddafi's involvement in Chad, to Libya's south, where he was trying to defeat a divided, pro-French government. His main antagonist and the leader of the strongest faction was former Defense Minister Hissen Habre. Casey viewed Libya as a Soviet surrogate everywhere, including Chad, and sought to act against Qaddafi. In fact, five days after the U.S. Navy shot down Qaddafi's planes, Haig urged escalation of these activities, telling Casey he wanted to keep Qaddafi's "nerves jangled." By contrast, the House Intelligence Committee was concerned about such operations, and objected. The administration went forward anyway.

The operation in Chad also was awkward in that Chad was a former French colony and was still considered by Paris to be its ward. Thus we tried hard to get the French to be more active in support of Habre. These efforts were generally successful, and by mid-1982, Habre had taken control of Ndjamena, Chad's capital, and established a transitional government.

Casey saw Chad as only one battle in a multifront campaign against Qaddafi. On September 18, 1982, he told us he wanted an NIE prepared on the "Soviet-Libya-Cuban axis" in Africa. He wanted to focus on the recent Libyan–Ethiopian–South Yemeni pact and the threat it posed to Sudan and Somalia. He also wanted us to look at Soviet and Cuban prospects in Shaba, the implications of the introduction of modern weapons by the Soviets and their surrogates into Namibia and Mozambique, the consequences of Algerian-Libyan support for the Polisario Front in the southern Sahara, and the possible extension of the Libyan–Ethiopian–South Yemeni pact to a campaign against Oman, thus giving them control of the west bank of the Persian Gulf. The estimate was completed in mid-November. To his chagrin, it substantially discounted the impact of the radical "alliances" that worried him.

Some CIA analysts thought that the Reagan administration was making a serious mistake in taking on Qaddafi publicly—that they were creating an Arab hero-martyr inasmuch as Qaddafi was seen standing up to the incredibly powerful United States. They had a valid point, but it was also true that Libya was an incubus for terrorism and for efforts to destabilize a number of African and Middle Eastern governments. To have ignored all this also would have been a mistake, a greater one in my view than responding to his activities.

CAMBODIA: TAKING ON ANOTHER SURROGATE

At the end of December 1978, Vietnam launched an attack into Cambodia with the objective of booting Pol Pot and the Khmer Rouge out of power and replacing them with Vietnamese puppets. Even though it was impossible to regret the ouster of the incredibly barbaric Pol Pot regime, the United States was not happy to see Vietnam further extend its control to the rest of Indochina. But the Chinese were more than unhappy. The Khmer Rouge were Chinese clients and their ouster was a setback for China, made worse by Vietnam's impudence in attacking a government tied to Beijing.

Both the State Department and Casey believed that Vietnamese—and indirectly, Soviet—aggression in Cambodia should be resisted, just as the Soviets were to be resisted elsewhere. While the United States could not support the Khmer Rouge, there were two noncommunist factions in the Cambodian resistance that were politically acceptable and had the support of ASEAN (the Association of Southeast Asian Nations). U.S. help developed slowly. The effort began in the fall of 1981, with protracted discussions of whether the United States should support the resistance at all. Fairly consistently throughout the Reagan administration, the State Department was the primary proponent of covert involvement in Cambodia. As late as December 22, in a conversation with Haig, Casey was cautious, worrying about the costs. Finally, the next summer (1982), a proposal went forward for a $5 million program, but not without reservations. We pointed out that we were uncertain whether the pool of manpower available to the noncommunist resistance would permit the recruitment of the twenty thousand troops called for in the proposal. We also were explicit that these groups were probably not a political alternative to the Vietnamese-sponsored government in Phnom Penh—reminding policymakers that the base of support for the noncommunist resistance was the Cambodian middle class, little of which remained alive. Nonetheless, by late summer 1982, all the key players agreed that it was "worth a few million to show ASEAN we care and support them." But no one expected much from the investment.

TURNING THE TABLES

Push. Push. Push. Casey never stopped coming up with ideas —or forwarding those of others—for waging the war against the Soviets more broadly, more aggressively, and more effectively. From New Caledonia to Suriname, from Afghanistan to Nicaragua, from the Sahara to Cambodia, no report of Soviet, Cuban, Libyan, or Vietnamese activity—no matter how insignificant—escaped his notice and his demands that CIA counter it. Always restless, always flying off to visit "his" war zones. Always poking and prodding, hectoring, demanding. Always frustrated by a DO he found too sluggish, too timid, too business-as-usual. Always impatient with analysts who couldn't see what he saw. And yet, day by day, CIA became engaged ever more widely around the world in taking on the Soviets and their surrogates. Not even in the 1950s had CIA been engaged on so many fronts across the globe. By the end of 1982, Casey's desire on entering office to carry the "Third World" war to the Soviets had become reality.

His wars finally were recognized by Reagan. On May 9, 1982, in a speech at his alma mater, Eureka College, the President declared war on the Soviets in the Third World, pledging that the United States would support people fighting for freedom against communism, wherever they were. His statement became known as "the Reagan Doctrine."

By the end of 1982, the Reagan administration's covert offensive against the Soviet Union was beginning to take shape. In Central America, Afghanistan, Chad, and elsewhere, often building on programs started by Carter, they confronted Soviet clients with resistance forces now funded and often armed by the United States. In Poland, Cambodia, the Caribbean, Libya, the Middle East, Africa, Central America, and elsewhere, the Soviets and their satellites and proxies faced opposition now supported by the United States. The programs would grow, in some cases, hugely. As Yuri Andropov succeeded Leonid Brezhnev in November 1982, it should have been apparent in the Kremlin that the gains of empire during the 1970s were becoming liabilities in the 1980s. And two old men, one in the White House and one at CIA, would ensure that the costs would only increase. The tables were turning.

CHAPTER FOURTEEN

1983: The Most Dangerous Year

THE HOTTEST YEAR of the last half of the Cold War—the period when the risk of miscalculation, of each side misreading the other, and the level of tension were at their highest—was 1983. While we in American intelligence certainly saw the tension in the U.S.-USSR relationship firsthand, we did not really grasp just how much the Soviet leadership felt increasingly threatened by the United States and by the course of events.

Why did we fail to understand that? The answer, I think, lies in the fact that we did not then grasp the growing desperation of the men in the Kremlin, a state of mind that established the framework for how they would look at events that year. By the beginning of 1983, there were no more illusions in Moscow that, relative to the West, Soviet problems were transitory and manageable by modest adjustments to the system. The Western economies had begun their strong expansion, and the boom in technological developments had started. The Soviets' great fear in the 1970s that U.S. industrial and technological prowess might be unleashed in a new military buildup had been realized, and they saw the U.S. defense budget growing at a staggering pace, seemingly without any economic strain. By the early 1980s, they saw strategic weapons being deployed and new programs undertaken that they believed could provide the United States a first-strike capability. The Kremlin saw renewed confidence in the West, and a willingness to use military force.

The Politburo faced its fears and this panoply of challenges with a leadership on its last legs. Within two months of Andropov's elevation to General Secretary, he was in the hospital, and he would combat serious illness throughout his short tenure. His illness meant more stagnation, more time lost in dealing with the crisis of the Soviet economy and society. A bedridden Soviet leader facing the vigorous, confident, and assertive new leaders in the West was a hard-to-miss symbol of the contrast between the societies as a whole.

Soviet defectors for many years had warned us that we had no real understanding of the narrow backgrounds and worldview of Kremlin leaders; how pedestrian, isolated, and self-absorbed they really were; how paranoid, fearful they were both of their own people and of a world they believed relentlessly hostile and threatening. And we now know that those leaders entered 1983 even more paranoid than usual.

THE DEPLOYMENT OF INF: BET, RAISE, AND CALL

One of the most disastrous decisions the Brezhnev leadership made in the 1970s was to deploy the new, three-warhead SS-20 theater ballistic missile to the European theater in 1977. As described earlier, in December 1979, NATO decided to deploy its own new intermediate range missiles to restore the nuclear balance in Europe. The "dual track" decision called for negotiations with the Soviets to see if Moscow could be persuaded to reduce or eliminate the SS-20s. Should such negotiations fail, deployment of ground-launched cruise missiles and Pershing II ballistic missiles would proceed in November 1983.

In the aftermath of the Soviet-mandated declaration of martial law in Poland in December 1981, and the generally poor state of the U.S.-USSR relationship, not much progress was made in the intermediate-range nuclear forces (INF) talks during 1982. The only major sign of life was an informal proposed agreement worked out during the summer of 1982 by the two INF negotiators in Geneva, Paul Nitze and Yuli Kvitsinskiy. Washington went crazy. While many experts liked the compromise, the Secretary of Defense was apoplectic, and his cohorts derided the compromise and called for Nitze's scalp. The President didn't like the idea either. It soon passed into history.

From the day he became Secretary of State, George Shultz

had been preoccupied with NATO's deadline for INF negotiations of November 1983. He understood from personal contacts with the Europeans, and I think instinctively, that the decision to deploy would be a very difficult one politically for nearly all of our allies. Thus he worked steadfastly to clear the air of disputes that might derail the deployment decision and to strengthen the European leaders' case for deployment.

This concern prompted Shultz to seek some flexibility in the U.S. INF position early in 1983. His efforts were very controversial, and both the Defense Department and the NSC opposed him.

As Shultz worked to keep deployment on track, Casey was generally supportive, if mainly by quiet acquiescence. In this case, he listened to Douglas George, the head of CIA's Arms Control Intelligence Staff, and to me. (Indeed, Doug George played an immensely important role in securing Casey's often constructive approach to arms control issues—one of the few areas in which George Shultz had anything positive to say about CIA, and Casey.)

During this period, the Soviets mounted a massive covert action operation aimed at thwarting INF deployment by NATO. We in CIA devoted tremendous effort at the time to uncovering this Soviet covert campaign. Casey summarized this extraordinary Soviet effort in a paper he sent to Bush, Shultz, Weinberger, and Clark on January 18, 1983. We later published it and circulated it widely within the government and to the allies, and, finally, provided an unclassified version for public use.

The vast majority of individuals and groups involved in the European peace movement in the early 1980s were sincere in their beliefs and had no connection with or particular sympathy for the Soviet Union. But that movement was the target of a Soviet campaign extending over a three-year period and involving a major effort to infiltrate, manipulate, and exploit it. Moscow indirectly and covertly provided propaganda themes, organizational expertise, coordination, and materials and financial resources to the anti-INF peace movement. The Soviets mobilized local communist parties and front groups, penetrated local peace groups, used sympathizers and agents of influence, and forged alleged U.S. military documents and policy statements.

Soviet covert action, or "active measures," was the heart of the campaign. Many of the anti-INF active measures employed by the Soviets were adaptations of what had been effective in the neutron bomb campaign in 1977–1978, though on a much larger scale. In

West Germany, the Netherlands, Belgium, and the United Kingdom, communist parties worked directly, through third parties, and in support of independent groups to block INF deployment. The Soviets and East Europeans provided a great deal of financial support to anti-INF efforts. The East German Communist Party (the DKP) provided some $2 million a month to its West German counterpart, and provided financial support to various elements of the peace movement in West Germany. In March 1982, the Danes discovered Soviet funding of the Danish peace movement to the tune of $100,000 annually through cash transfers to the Danish Communist Party Secretary and the Danish-Soviet Friendship Association. There were many such examples. The Soviets also sought to direct the focus of the West European peace movement by providing communist parties and front organizations with propaganda themes keyed to local concerns and U.S. and NATO policies.

Moscow's efforts were also defensive. Given a growing tendency by West European peace activists to blame the USSR as well as the United States for the arms race, the Soviet Central Committee issued a directive in the fall of 1982 to its embassies and departments to collect information on "anti-Soviet phenomena" in Western European countries for use in the propaganda battle over INF. The Soviets told the leaders of the World Peace Council, a Soviet front organization, in late October 1982 to try to limit the effectiveness of a peace group that had criticized Soviet policies.

The Soviets also used forgeries. In May 1982, a forged letter from Secretary of State Haig to NATO Secretary General Luns regarding nuclear arms was circulated in Belgium and the Netherlands. It distorted NATO strategy, and played on the fear of NATO's use of nuclear weapons in limited war situations. In mid-November 1982, the West German Communist Party was involved in fabricating or disseminating a purported official notice in Bonn alerting citizens to measures concerning the transport of nuclear and conventional weapons through the city.

CIA's detailed paper on the Soviet covert campaign made clear the scope and structure of their effort. Our work had two beneficial results. First, as it was publicized, European peace groups became much more attuned to how they were being unwittingly exploited by the Soviets. They became more alert to such efforts, and that made life harder for the Soviets. They also began to couch their protests in anti-Soviet as well as anti-U.S. terms. Second, our efforts largely persuaded a very conservative Reagan administration that the Soviets did not "control" the peace movement, however much they worked to exploit it, and that much of the protest was genuine and therefore a problem to which the European leaders had to be sensitive politically.

Despite Shultz's successful efforts to bring some flexibility to the U.S. position on INF, there was no diplomatic breakthrough before deployment. All of the Soviet jockeying, covert action, and politicking did not deflect NATO. On November 14, 1983, the first U.S. ground-launched cruise missiles arrived in Britain. On the 16th, the Italian parliament voted in favor of INF deployments on their soil, followed by similarly favorable votes by parliaments in Norway and West Germany on November 22. On the 23rd, U.S. Pershing II missiles arrived in West Germany, and on the same day the Soviets pulled out of the INF negotiations in Geneva, promising military countermeasures for the INF deployments.

The Soviets would continue to try to prevent full deployment of NATO's INF, but they would fail. By their actions in deploying SS-20s, the Soviets virtually had forced NATO to respond. In so doing, the alliance demonstrated a measure of solidarity and willingness to modernize nuclear forces that had been weak or absent for many years. And, thanks mostly to Shultz, the United States had shown just enough flexibility to make deployment politically possible for European governments facing strident domestic opposition.

Initiated by Schmidt, pursued by Carter, and completed by Reagan, the INF deployments resulted in a further increase in tensions in the near term with the Soviets, but set the stage for a breakthrough in the INF negotiations later that, in turn, would signal the beginning of a dramatic change in the U.S.-Soviet relationship. However, in 1983, the deployments were a major strategic defeat for the Soviet Union, and tensions between East and West increased significantly.

STAR WARS: AMERICAN SKEPTICISM, SOVIET NIGHTMARE

Just as tensions were mounting and the endgame began on INF deployment in early spring 1983, Reagan flung two challenges at the Kremlin that would dramatically affect the U.S.-Soviet relationship for the rest of the Cold War. They also sent the temperature of the relationship soaring.

On March 8, 1983, Reagan spoke to the National Association

of Evangelicals, a ministers' organization, in Orlando, Florida. His intent was to tackle the nuclear freeze movement then gaining momentum, especially in the nation's churches. In the speech, Reagan spoke these words: "In your discussions of the nuclear freeze proposals, I urge you to beware the temptation of pride— the temptation of blithely declaring yourselves above it all and label both sides equally at fault, to ignore the facts of history and the aggressive impulses of an evil empire, to simply call the arms race a giant misunderstanding and thereby remove yourself from the struggle between right and wrong and good and evil. . . ."

If the Soviet leaders had sought one thing in their political dealings with the United States over the years it had been recognition of coequal status as a superpower and the respect due a legitimate, enduring major power. First Jimmy Carter, and now Ronald Reagan, denied them that respect and sense of legitimacy. Reagan had cast them as an international pariah, an "evil" regime, and to the paranoids in the Kremlin, this was intolerable. The speech in Orlando would stick in their minds and in their craws for years to come. Ironically, many Russians a decade later would acknowledge that, yes, it had been an evil empire.

Two weeks later, Reagan dropped an even bigger bombshell on the Soviets. On March 23, the President went on national television from the Oval Office to talk about the Soviet threat and American defense. He described their aggressive behavior in the Third World, but focused especially on their military buildup and what he characterized as a growing strategic offensive force far beyond what was needed for deterrence. He then described the need for the United States to break out of our long dependence on our retaliatory offensive forces for security and deterrence. Reagan said, "Let me share with you a vision of the future which offers hope. It is that we embark on a program to counter the awesome Soviet missile threat with measures that are defensive. . . . What if free people could live secure in the knowledge that their security did not rest upon the threat of instant U.S. retaliation to deter a Soviet attack, that we could intercept and destroy strategic ballistic missiles before they reached our own soil or that of our allies?" Thus was born the Strategic Defense Initiative (SDI).

Amid countless skeptics that such a defensive umbrella could ever be built, there were two small groups of people who believed it probably could. The first was Ronald Reagan and a small group of his advisers. The second was the Soviet leadership.

SDI was a Soviet nightmare come to life. America's industrial base, coupled with American technology, wealth, and managerial skill, all mobilized to build a wholly new and different military capability that might negate the Soviet offensive buildup of a quarter century. A radical new departure by the United States that would require an expensive Soviet response at a time of deep economic crisis.

As happened so often, Casey's open door exposed CIA to the notion of a U.S. space-based defense more than a year before Reagan's speech. During the first week of January 1982, Lt. General Daniel O. Graham (U.S. Army, ret.), representing "Project High Frontier," had called on Casey and left him a bunch of papers describing a space-based defense for the United States. The papers also described Soviet efforts in this arena. On January 8, Casey asked me for our analysts' evaluation of the materials.

On January 20, he wrote me again on High Frontier, saying that we would be hearing about this from the White House and perhaps from the Hill. He went on, "I want our present assessment of where the Soviets stand on missile defense, on laser and directed energy capabilities and the vulnerability of our spaceborne systems, the threat represented by the possibility of EMP [electromagnetic pulse], the vulnerability of our C3I (command, control, communications, and intelligence) systems, and on the acceleration of the Soviet space program and its possible military dimensions."

We responded on January 26 that the description of Soviet space and antisatellite capabilities described in the "High Frontier" materials was essentially correct. Fourteen months before Reagan's SDI speech, we then accurately predicted the Soviet response to it (or to the High Frontier version). We said they would characterize the United States as a warlike nation engaged in a dangerous and unprecedented expansion and acceleration of the arms race; view the project as a clear violation of the ABM Treaty, thus leading to a further deterioration in relations; undertake to harden their missile boosters and reentry vehicles; and accelerate their own space weapons development program. The analysts concluded by foreshadowing some of the criticisms of SDI in the United States and among our allies, saying that they thought the magnitude of the project was understated, that it could not be implemented before the early 1990s at the earliest, and that it would have a price tag higher than stated in the High Frontier papers.

It was the Soviet contention that SDI wouldn't work that involved CIA in the SDI debate. The Soviets' own programs under-scored their belief that missile defense was possible and, further, they were researching many of the same types of technologies SDI encompassed. They possessed the world's only operational ballistic missile defense system, installed around Moscow, which they had begun to modernize at great cost in 1980. They had built a nation-wide system of extraordinarily expensive large ballistic missile early-warning radars and a network of nine large phased array radars for improved missile tracking—one of which, at Krasnoyarsk, was a clear-cut violation of the ABM Treaty. We saw the develop-ment of ABM components—radars, above-ground launchers, high-acceleration missiles, and other elements—that led us to worry whether the Soviets were establishing a capability that would allow them to expand their ABM defense umbrella significantly and fairly quickly if they chose to do so.

Further, we knew, and reported to the administration and to Congress, that the Soviets were pursuing advanced technologies for strategic defense, including laser, particle beam, kinetic energy, and microwave technologies applicable to strategic weapons. The scale of the effort was impressive. The intelligence community identified, for example, over half a dozen major research and development facilities and test ranges associated with the development of lasers for weapons, a program involving some ten thousand scientists and engineers. While we provided a good deal of specific information on these Soviet programs, we also advised that there were major obstacles to Soviet success—especially their relative backwardness in remote sensing and computer technologies.

American advocates of SDI have contended that it was this program that broke the back of the Soviet Union and contributed critically to its ultimate demise. That overstates an otherwise valid point. SDI did have a significant impact on the Soviet political and military leadership. It was deeply troubling from a military/strategic perspective because it meant that the United States for the first time intended to pursue a strategic defense program of real potential capability; that the United States was launching an incredibly ex-pensive new arms race in an area in which the USSR could hardly hope to compete effectively; and that, if it worked, the Soviet mili-tary efforts of two and a half decades—which had gone far toward bankrupting the Soviet Union—would have been for nought.

For the Soviet political leadership, SDI was symbolic. Their fears during the preceding decade of awakening American industrial and technological power in a new arena of the arms race were being realized. All of the trends in the West that they had seen and worried about over the preceding two years came together symbolically in SDI: accelerating U.S. economic growth that would give Washington the money to build an expensive new capability if it chose to do so; an explosion of technological advances in the West that likely would make SDI feasible; a widely popular and massive U.S. military modernization and expansion under way, of which SDI would be a part; and a confident, assertive American leadership likely to see the project through. And because they believed the United States could build a defensive system that would work (in contrast to their knowledge of the limitations of their own), they were convinced that such a system would give the United States a first-strike capability—allowing us to destroy the USSR while sitting under our defensive umbrella.

It wasn't SDI per se that frightened the Soviet leaders; after all, at best it would take many years to develop and deploy as an effective system. I think it was the *idea* of SDI and all it represented that frightened them. As they looked at the United States, they saw an America that apparently had the resources to increase defense spending dramatically and then add this program on top, and all of it while seeming hardly to break a sweat.

Meanwhile, an enfeebled Soviet leadership, presiding over a country confronting serious economic and social problems, knew they could not compete—at least not without some major changes. In my view, it was the broad resurgence of the West—symbolized by SDI—that convinced even some of the conservative members of the Soviet leadership that major internal changes were needed in the USSR. That decision, once made, set the stage for the dramatic events inside the Soviet Union of the next several years.

At the same time, Reagan's launching of a new arms race two weeks after the "evil empire" speech further increased the levels of tension and suspicion. And, for a leader like Andropov already half-persuaded the United States was preparing for a nuclear conflict with the Soviet Union, SDI likely added to his paranoia.

"The Target Is Destroyed": KAL-007

One of the most horrifying tragedies of the second half of the Cold War was the Soviet shoot-down of Korean Air Lines Flight 007 on September 1, 1983. The plane apparently had strayed off course and crossed into Soviet territory, where it was tracked and then attacked by an SU-15. The shoot-down was viewed in the United States as a stark demonstration of the callous brutality of the Soviet regime. U.S. intelligence agencies provided the evidence that condemned the Soviet government, specifically the conversations between the attacking pilot and his ground controller. We documented the order to fire on the unidentified plane, acknowledgment of the order, and the report of a successful attack.

Under great pressure from Shultz, we agreed to his use of the intelligence in a press conference he gave at 10:45 A.M. on September 1. He provided a chronology of what had happened and expressed this country's righteous indignation. His apparent anger was pale compared to the wave of fury that swept across the United States. Several hundred innocent people had gone to their deaths in a twelve-minute plunge to the sea, thanks to the Soviets, and Americans were just plain mad. It appeared that the Soviet pilot ultimately had identified the plane as a passenger aircraft and was authorized to shoot it down cold-bloodedly anyway.

The intelligence community continued to examine the evidence in the immediate aftermath and, later the same day (September 1), our experts concluded that the story might be a little more complicated. CIA reported in the *President's Daily Brief* on September 2 our conclusion that throughout most of the incident the Soviets had thought they were tracking a U.S. RC-135 reconnaissance plane that earlier had been in the area monitoring an expected Soviet ICBM test. We said that the Soviets had been tracking the RC-135 for at least an hour before detecting the KAL flight. About an hour later, the Soviet SU-15 pilot reported that he had observed the target "visually," and in the next fourteen minutes—until the attack—he reported flying around the aircraft, closing at times to within two kilometers. He never identified the plane as a passenger aircraft.

Later the same day at an NSC meeting with the President, Casey briefed that while there had been no reconnaissance planes in the area of the shoot-down, "That is not to say that confusion between the U.S. reconnaissance plane and the KAL plane could not have developed as the Cobra Ball [reconnaissance] plane departed and the Korean airliner approached the area northeast of the Kamchatka Peninsula." In fact, the majority of CIA and DIA analysts believed that the Soviets on the ground misidentified the plane.

As the days passed, the administration's rhetoric outran the facts that were known to it. In his Oval Office speech to the nation on September 5, the President said, "There is no way a pilot could mistake this for anything other than a civilian airliner." Two days later, at the UN, Ambassador Kirkpatrick said that the evidence established "that the Soviets decided to shoot down a civilian airliner, shot it down, murdering the 269 people on board, and then lied about it."

As more information leaked out about what really appeared to have happened, suspicion grew that intelligence information had been withheld from the policymakers. The notion that the President and Shultz had been unaware of intelligence that the Soviets might not have known the plane was a civilian airliner was suggested in a *New York Times* article on October 7, 1983. Casey was both offended by the piece and worried that his senior colleagues in the administration might believe some of it. Consequently, on October 13, he wrote Shultz, Weinberger, and Clark to express his "distress over the details in the piece and the idea of a gap between administration pronouncements and intelligence reporting." The DCI said that the *Times* article got some of the essentials right, that is, that the Soviets did not take necessary steps to properly identify the plane; they probably did not know they were shooting down an airliner; and the Soviet pilot may well have thought he was engaging an RC-135. But, Casey continued, the contention that all this was determined weeks after the event is "not so." He then recounted CIA's situation reports on September 1.

In addition to the situation reports Casey cited in his memo, the *President's Daily Brief* of September 2 and Casey's NSC briefing the same day, not to mention other reports sent out during those first days, make quite clear that possible Soviet uncertainty about the identity of the airplane was known to everyone in the Reagan administration within twenty-four hours. In reality, with the charged emotions around the country, some U.S. officials got carried away. And some just didn't believe us.

Interestingly, confirmation of that is provided by Shultz in his memoirs. After being briefed on the morning of September 2 by both CIA and DIA on the possibility that the Soviets mistakenly identified the airliner, Shultz later told his staff that a case of mistaken identity was "not remotely plausible." He writes that CIA's advancing such a theory made him suspicious, and he had the feeling he was not being told everything. He told his staff, "They [CIA] have no compunctions about fooling you."

What possible ulterior motive CIA might have had in advancing the notion that the Soviets screwed up rather than intentionally attacked a civilian airliner escapes me. Casey supposedly was the super hard-liner. Why would he give the Soviets a break when they were in a corner and being politically pulverized? Why would the analysts put forward a more benign interpretation of such a terrible act? Shultz's periodically overactive "suspicion gland" was at work here. There was no alternative agenda or motive. CIA was simply reporting the facts—facts that tended to complicate the nice clean case being used to pillory the USSR. The facts were condemnation enough.

In August 1992, the Russian government published the transcript of the September 2, 1983, Politburo meeting on the KAL-007 shoot-down. What is so revealing about the transcript is the sense that the participants, greatly influenced by the strident position taken by the powerful Defense Minister, Ustinov, truly believed that the actions taken had been proper and appropriate. Not a single voice was raised to question or object. Stung by the U.S. portrayal of their actions as barbaric, they circled the wagons, seeking comfort from the military that proper procedures had been followed and persuading themselves it was all a provocation warranting a tough response.

Ten years after this fateful Politburo meeting, the UN inquiry into the tragedy concluded on June 15, 1993, that Soviet military officials had "assumed" that the South Korean airliner was a U.S. reconnaissance plane, although at least two top officers in the Far East Defense Command suggested about ten minutes before the attack that the plane might be a passenger craft.

In the aftermath, the major issue for Washington was how to respond. Shultz thought it important that he proceed with a meeting in Madrid with Gromyko. Weinberger and others thought he shouldn't go so soon after the shoot-down, but Shultz was adamant and agreed to keep the agenda to KAL-007 and human rights. Reagan sided with Shultz. The exchange between Gromyko and Shultz in Madrid was very tough. Gromyko wrote in his memoirs, "It was probably the sharpest exchange I ever had with an American Secretary of State, and I have had talks with fourteen of them."

In addition to proceeding with the Shultz-Gromyko meeting,

the United States continued its participation in both the INF and START talks, despite strong opposition from a number of people in and out of the administration. In fact, apart from rhetoric, the U.S. response was largely limited to multinational retaliation in the civil aviation arena. Even so, the Soviets thought the U.S. reaction —especially the rhetoric about their barbaric behavior—had been "provocative."

While U.S. official actions in response to the shoot-down were fairly restrained, the powerful public reaction in the United States and official rhetoric added further stresses to an already very strained relationship. Early in 1983, there had been some tentative but behind-the-scenes moves to ease tensions and begin to move forward on issues of mutual interest like arms control. But SDI, KAL-007, and then the deployment of INF and Soviet walkout from the arms control talks all together put U.S.-Soviet relations in the deep freeze. Worse than that, there was real fear building on both sides that the situation was so bad, armed conflict was possible.

"Able Archer"

One of the potentially most dangerous episodes of the Cold War was prompted by a NATO command post exercise during the period November 2–11, 1983. The exercise, to practice nuclear release procedures, came at the moment of maximum stress in the U.S.-Soviet relationship described above. But it also came against the backdrop of Andropov's seeming fixation on the possibility that the United States was planning a nuclear strike against the Soviet Union.

What we know about this is primarily—but not exclusively—from the KGB defector Oleg Gordievsky. He has written that in May 1981, Andropov told a KGB conference that the United States was actively preparing for nuclear war. Those in the KGB familiar with the United States thought this was "alarmist" and suggested that Andropov's "apocalyptic vision" originated with the Soviet military high command and, specifically, Andropov's close associate Defense Minister Ustinov. As early as 1981, directions were sent from KGB headquarters (the Center) to its residencies in NATO capitals and in Japan calling for "close observation of all political, military, and intelligence activities that might indicate preparations for mobilization." This program was called "RYAN"—the Russian acronym for "Nuclear Missile Attack." This was the KGB's top priority in 1982. Andropov's elevation to General Secretary only added to the priority given RYAN.

The threat of a U.S. preemptive nuclear strike, according to intelligence sources, was still taken "very seriously" in Moscow in mid-1983 and even into 1984. Our sources claimed to have seen documents that betrayed genuine nervousness that such a strike could occur at any time, for example, under cover of an apparently routine military exercise. According to one source, "Few officials with direct experience of life in the West took the threat of a U.S. first strike seriously, but in senior party circles such an eventuality was widely perceived."

The Soviet propaganda apparatus cranked up in October 1983, and actually produced a war scare in the USSR. The official line to party and public alike was pessimistic about the chances for arms control, and promoted the notion that the deployment of INF would worsen relations with the United States, which seemed bent on world domination. Personal attacks on Reagan were extraordinary.

All this was even before "Able Archer" began on November 2. According to Gordievsky, the exercise especially alarmed Moscow because (1) the procedures and message formats used in the transition from conventional to nuclear war were different from those used before, and (2) in this exercise the NATO forces went through all of the alert phases from normal readiness to general alert. Further, he says that alarmist KGB reporting persuaded "the Center" that there was a real alert involving real troops. Also, surveillance around U.S. bases in Europe reported changed patterns of officer movement. Thus "the KGB concluded that American forces had been placed on alert—and might even have begun the countdown to nuclear war." This kind of reporting continued throughout the exercise.

But it wasn't just the KGB. Casey met with Reagan on December 22 and advised him that we had learned that in November there had been a GRU (Soviet military intelligence) instruction to all posts to obtain early warning of enemy military preparations so that the Soviet Union would not be surprised by the actual threat of war. All posts were to try to determine "the enemy's" intentions and actions. Finally, GRU elements were to create new agent groups abroad with the capability of communicating independently with GRU headquarters. The DCI told the President on that December day that the KGB and GRU information "seems to reflect a Soviet perception of an increased threat of war and a realization of the necessity to keep intelligence information flowing to Moscow during wartime or after a rupture in diplomatic relations."

Despite Casey's December briefing of the President, we in CIA did not really grasp how alarmed the Soviet leaders might have been until some time after the exercise had concluded—in fact not until our British colleagues issued an assessment in March 1984 saying that the Soviets had thought nuclear war might have been imminent during "Able Archer." The British reviewed Gordievsky's reporting and added that the threat of a preemptive strike was taken very seriously in Moscow in mid-1983 and early 1984.

The assessment noted that in mid-1983, a Czech intelligence officer had confided to a Warsaw Pact colleague that about a year earlier a requirement had been placed on his service to look for any indication that the United States was about to launch a preemptive nuclear strike. There was also an exceptional requirement to monitor with special care major NATO exercises. He continued that the increased state of alert of U.S. bases observed in early November 1983 (very likely due to heightened concern about terrorism after the bombing of the Marine barracks in Beirut in late October) in connection with "Able Archer" had given rise to "exceptional anxiety" within the Warsaw Pact. A genuine belief had taken root within the leadership of the Pact that a NATO preemptive strike was possible.

We later learned more about the Soviet military reaction during "Able Archer." Between November 2 and 11, there had been considerable activity by Soviet and other Warsaw Pact forces in the Baltic Military District as well as by East German, Polish, and Czechoslovak forces in response to preparations for the exercise and the exercise itself. Elements of the air forces of the Group of Soviet Forces Germany had gone on heightened alert because, according to the commander, of the increase in the threat of possible aggression against the USSR and its Warsaw Pact allies during the exercise. Soviet military meteorological broadcasts were taken off the air during the exercise. Units of the Soviet Fourth Air Army had gone to increased readiness, and all combat flight operations were suspended from November 4 to 10.

Because of all this reporting, and the strongly held views of one of our allies, we prepared a special national estimate in May 1984, "The Implications of Recent Soviet Military-Political Activity." The general view of CIA and U.S. military intelligence was that the heightened Soviet concerns were caused by the deployment of INF; it was acknowledged that the reduced warning time caused by the Pershing IIs "could not but have created apprehension" that Soviet vulnerability would increase, thereby forcing the Soviet leadership to seek a means of negating the potentially debilitating effect of reduced warning time. They wrote that there was insufficient evidence to conclude that the Soviets had been worried about a possible attack because of "Able Archer," and said that Moscow's reactions were likely due to military prudence and precautionary measures to ensure that proper readiness levels were maintained.

We wrestled with this controversy for another year, with our own experts divided. The issue was terribly important. Had the United States come close to a nuclear crisis the preceding fall and not even known it? Was the Soviet leadership so out of touch that they really believed a preemptive attack was a real possibility? Had there nearly been a terrible miscalculation? To what degree was our skepticism about the war scare prompted by the fact that our military didn't want to admit that one of its exercises might have been dangerously if inadvertently provocative, or because our intelligence experts didn't want to admit that we had badly misread the state of mind of the Soviet leadership?

Information about the peculiar and remarkably skewed frame of mind of the Soviet leaders during those times that has emerged since the collapse of the Soviet Union makes me think there is a good chance—with all of the other events in 1983—that they really felt a NATO attack was at least possible and that they took a number of measures to enhance their military readiness short of mobilization. After going through the experience at the time, then through the postmortems, and now through the documents, I don't think the Soviets were crying wolf. They may not have believed a NATO attack was imminent in November 1983, but they did seem to believe that the situation was very dangerous. And U.S. intelligence had failed to grasp the true extent of their anxiety. A reexamination of the whole episode by the President's Foreign Intelligence Advisory Board in 1990 concluded that the intelligence community's confidence that this all had been Soviet posturing for political effect was misplaced.

AGGRAVATIONS

Two other developments during 1983, while not nearly as dramatic as INF, SDI, KAL-007, or Able Archer, nonetheless contributed to both superpowers being on edge and worried about the activities of the other, and added to overall tensions.

A serious development in 1983 was more active Soviet involvement in the Middle East (and unrelated disasters there for the United States). After Israel thoroughly thrashed the Soviet-equipped Syrian air force in June 1982, and the Syrians claimed that the Soviet response had been inadequate, later that summer the Soviets delivered to the Syrians the most advanced air defense equipment they had—complete with advisers, technicians, and, finally, SA-5 surface-to-air missiles. Construction of the SA-5 sites in Syria began in October, and by January 9, 1983, the missile complexes were complete. Because Soviet crews had to man the missiles until the Syrians could be trained, suddenly Soviet combat crews were facing the Israelis. There clearly had been a qualitative increase in the Soviet commitment to Syria, with the Soviets running a much greater risk of being drawn directly into the Arab-Israeli conflict. The potential for a real disaster loomed.

Casey advised the Vice President, Shultz, Weinberger, and Clark on January 20 that it was "hard to attribute Soviet actions on the SA-5s to any purpose other than forcing all the parties to reckon with and ultimately deal with the Soviet Union." Nearly everyone in the administration agreed that with the SA-5s, there was a new ballgame, and one possibly allowing the Soviets to force their way into the Middle East equation for the first time since Kissinger and then Carter had sidelined them.

Another episode in 1983 adding to U.S.-Soviet tensions involved the little island of Grenada. In 1979, Jimmy Carter had signed a finding to support resistance to the Marxist leader of Grenada, Maurice Bishop. The Senate Intelligence Committee wouldn't let him implement it, and Bishop proceeded to strengthen his grip over the island and increase the presence and role of Cubans on the island. On October 13, 1983, Bishop was placed under house arrest by his even more radical Deputy Prime Minister Bernard Coard. Several other cabinet ministers were arrested over the next two or three days. On October 19, Bishop's supporters freed him and they all marched to the downtown area. Coard's forces there were able to recapture Bishop, and he and several supporters were executed—murdered.

The situation on Grenada became more confused by the hour. CIA placed a woman on the island who provided troop and weapons locations to a "pleasure yacht" offshore. We were concerned about the visibility of the boat and asked one of our close allies—for whom we had done much in the past—to use its diplomatic pouch to get to the woman a more powerful radio that would reach to Florida, thus allowing the boat to leave. Our ally turned us down flat. We then had to withdraw the woman, and the absence thereafter of any CIA presence on the island hampered efforts to find out what was going on. Meanwhile, contingency planning had been under way for the evacuation of some one thousand American students in medical school on the island. Now the contingency planning at the White House was made somewhat awkward by the fact that the Pentagon wasn't interested in playing. They wanted no military action in Grenada. The JCS representative at the meeting, Vice Admiral Art Moreau, even refused to discuss the subject.

It was my experience over the years that one of the biggest misimpressions held by the public has been that our military is always straining at the leash, wanting to use force in any situation. The reality is just the opposite. In more than twenty years of attending meetings in the Situation Room, my experience was that the biggest doves in Washington wear uniforms. And perhaps that is as it should be. Our military leaders have seen too many half-baked ideas for the use of military force advanced in the Situation Room by hairy-chested civilians who have never seen combat or fired a gun in anger. The generals feel a great responsibility for the servicemen in their charge and are very cautious about throwing them into combat situations on the whim of "feather-merchants" —an old military term for civilians.

All that notwithstanding, this time Reagan—having in hand a request for military help from the Organization of Eastern Caribbean States—met with the JCS on October 24 and shortly thereafter told Weinberger to proceed in Grenada—to rescue the students and prevent a communist takeover. The military assault began on October 25.

Not only was the Grenada operation a great success domestically, it had wholly unexpected consequences elsewhere. Lo and behold, the Nicaraguan Sandinistas soon were behaving better (temporarily) and talking about negotiations. And a variety of bad guys were making an "agonizing reappraisal" of who had power and was willing to use it. The lesson of the successful application of U.S. military force was not lost on the Soviets either, who saw in this use of force all the more reason to worry—against the backdrop of the INF deployment and Able Archer—that this President didn't flinch from tough decisions, or from the use of force.

THE NIGHT OF FEAR

Nineteen eighty-three was a year filled with crises and tensions, a year in which the Soviets truly may have thought that the danger of war was high. While the U.S. government did not share that apprehension, the American people did.

By 1983, many in the United States were worried, even scared. Détente had failed, the Soviet military buildup continued, the Soviets had invaded Afghanistan, conflicts raged elsewhere in the Third World, a massive U.S. rearmament program was under way, new nuclear weapons were being deployed to Europe for the first time in many years, and SDI signaled a whole new arena for the arms race. The political dialogue between Moscow and Washington had collapsed even as both sides were building and deploying new generations of strategic nuclear weapons.

Opponents of Reagan's policies reacted strongly, believing his belligerence was in fact increasing the danger of war. Now nearly forgotten, the nuclear freeze movement—an effort to get both sides to stop building nuclear weapons that became, practically, a call for a unilateral U.S. freeze—posed a serious political challenge to advocates of U.S. strategic modernization, and reached its apogee with "Ground Zero Week." It was also in 1983 that the "nuclear winter" alarm was sounded by a group of U.S. scientists—the theory that the detonation of a certain number of nuclear weapons would trigger severe changes in climate with devastating consequences.

The spirit of the times, of 1983, was captured also in popular entertainment in the United States. One of the big television events of the year was the movie *The Day After*, a graphic fictional account of a nuclear war and its aftermath. The movie aired on November 21, right in the middle of the INF deployments to Europe. The show was considered so politically potent that Shultz and others participated in panel discussions on the air afterward to try to calm people. There were other such movies and television shows during this period.

By the end of 1983, rising tensions between the superpowers, the accelerating arms race, the willingness of both sides to use force, and the absence of any countervailing negotiations or dialogue all contributed to considerable public anxiety—fear—in both countries that matters were getting out of hand. INF. SDI. Able Archer. Spy wars. Lebanon, Syria, and SA-5s. Grenada. Nineteen eighty-three had been quite a year—a "year of living dangerously." Casey and Weinberger were alarmed as they saw more trouble and Soviet assertiveness ahead. They were not wrong.

But Reagan and Shultz, who were just as tough, believed also that something fundamental had changed that year in the U.S.-Soviet relationship, that day by day the United States was getting stronger and the USSR weaker. That for all the stresses and anxieties of the year, the momentum—the "correlation of forces"—had shifted irreversibly in favor of the United States. The administration had passed through the darkness of 1983. The U.S. military buildup was surging forward. INF was being deployed. The economy was beginning to boom. Confidence was high. The alliance was stronger than ever.

After the night, the dawn was coming. By the end of 1983, the West had indeed reawakened. The time had come to begin gathering the harvest.

CHAPTER FIFTEEN

The War in Washington, 1983:
Shultz Against the Field

MY SERVICE IN CIA and at the NSC coincided with the tenure of nine Secretaries of State, seven of whom I was able to observe or know at close hand. George Shultz was, for me, the most complex of them as a person and perhaps the most farsighted as a policymaker. Over six and a half years, he periodically solicited my personal views on developments in the Soviet Union, offered his time to discuss substantive differences between us, and routinely treated me with courtesy, respect, and in a friendly manner. Yet, during the same period, I was more than once the target of his fury on the telephone, and I was told by senior White House advisers to President Reagan that the Secretary of State had tried to get me fired. I saw him demonstrate great kindness and patience, and I saw him act in petty and mean ways. A man of rare success in both private and public life, Shultz was confident and bold. But he was also excessively thin-skinned, sensitive even to implied criticism, and turf conscious to a degree unparalleled at his level in all my years in Washington.

George Shultz impressed the hell out of me from the beginning. He had a wide-ranging intellect, and his interests were quite diverse. He had gathered over the years an extraordinary array of friends and acquaintances in all walks of life, including many of the world leaders with whom he interacted as Secretary. His experience in senior government positions was virtually without equal in his generation.

278

Shultz was, in my opinion, also the toughest Secretary of State I knew. A former marine, he had no hesitancy about the use of military force—perhaps, at times, too little hesitancy. He held no brief for any course of action that suggested American weakness or lack of will, enthusiastically embraced covert action when he thought it useful (fairly often) and sustainable (somewhat less often), and saw no inconsistency between bleeding the Soviets in one part of the world while negotiating with them in another—or the same—part.

Shultz was not a team player unless he could be coach, captain, and quarterback. Unlike Haig, though, he always remembered who owned the team. He acknowledged the primacy of the President, and, between 1983 and 1988, he forged with Reagan one of the most successful partnerships of a President and Secretary of State in modern times. With all others, however, he wanted to call the shots. For Shultz, foreign policy and national security policy were virtually synonymous, and anytime Defense or CIA or anyone else stepped beyond the narrow roles Shultz regarded as appropriate for them, there was hell to pay.

Arms control was the one area where Shultz simply had to make the interagency process work because both Defense and CIA had critical roles to play. And here he did make it work with a harmony that was unique in the administration. Of course, there were continuing disagreements, sometimes bitter ones, but they were fought out above the table with everyone having a chance to be heard. Shultz was in charge, but he treated the different players as a team, included them in his traveling squad, kept them informed, and won—for the most part—their support. I always wondered why a smart man like Shultz didn't look at that unique experience, understand how much of a difference his own leadership and approach made, and apply it to other policy issues. His approach on arms control won him allies in both Defense and CIA, and eased his path considerably, at least in Washington.

In informal settings, I found Shultz engaging, humorous, interesting. There was a certain puckishness about him at times, and you could almost see a funny line or droll comment working its way from brain to voice. He was given to wearing bow ties, especially on weekends, though occasionally on regular workdays, and would show up at his Saturday seminars or Sunday meetings in really outrageous golf clothes totally at odds with his usual businesslike mien. He was constantly at war with his waistline and trying to diet. We would have lunch in his elegant dining room at State, be presented with a several-course meal, and he would sit there eating a piece of toast and cottage cheese or some such while the rest of us stuffed ourselves.

Many people at senior levels in other agencies and departments came to dislike Shultz for some of the reasons I described above. In fact, throughout the government (outside of the State Department, where he was immensely popular), Shultz was more respected than liked. I must admit that, although he was often critical of me and of CIA's work, and despite the fact that he and Casey came to despise each other, I both liked and admired him—even as, from time to time, his knife was being drawn across my throat.

U.S.-SOVIET RELATIONS: THE SHULTZ ALTERNATIVE

To the position of Secretary of State, George Shultz brought extraordinary strategic acumen, dogged stubbornness, and a historical optimism that was at times naïve and at times visionary.

His strategic acumen was demonstrated in his early understanding of the overriding importance of INF and the reality that political conditions had to be created in Europe that would allow the governments of countries where the weapons were to be deployed in fact to do so. Thus his efforts—ultimately successful—to defuse a bitter dispute between the administration and our European allies over the U.S. attempt to prevent them from helping the Soviets build a pipeline to export gas to the West. In a deal orchestrated by Shultz, Reagan lifted sanctions on construction of the pipeline in exchange for European agreement to trade and credit sanctions on the Soviets. This approach eased tensions with the Europeans over the gas pipeline and contributed considerably to repairing the relationship.

The Europeans' agreement to deploy INF also required a serious effort by the United States to negotiate limits on INF. Shultz drove this policy home despite considerable opposition from both the NSC and Defense. Again, Reagan was a realist. While reaffirming his zero-zero proposal on INF (neither side to have any INF missiles), he gave Shultz some bargaining room, which he used effectively to the chagrin of the rest of the Reagan national security team—all, that is, but Ronald Reagan.

In my opinion, the separate national decisions to deploy INF —by the Federal Republic of Germany, Italy, Belgium, and the

Netherlands—would have been much more complicated and some might not have happened at all if it had not been for Shultz's leading role (with Reagan's critical support) in promoting a serious attempt to negotiate limits on INF and repairing the U.S. relationship with the Europeans in 1982–1983. Shultz looked ahead, identified the most important strategic objective, and worked to shape policy to achieve that objective. I don't know any better definition of strategic acumen. And for a supposed ideologue, Reagan's support for Shultz against the advice of so many others during this period of extraordinary tension in the U.S.-Soviet relationship underscores his own farsightedness and grasp of strategic priorities. There can be no argument that without Reagan's support, Shultz's efforts would have crashed and burned in Washington.

Shultz demonstrated just as much strategic vision in terms of how to approach the U.S.-Soviet relationship overall. Most critically, Shultz, virtually alone in the administration's senior foreign policy team, perceived that Ronald Reagan saw America's resurgent military power and its challenge to Soviet assertiveness worldwide as a means to an end—to reduce nuclear weapons and, through a more constructive relationship, to take steps to promote a more peaceful world. When Reagan said these things publicly, most members of his own team, the press, and the public wrote it off as political theater. Only Shultz seems to have grasped that Reagan was really serious and meant what he said. Reagan's idealism—grounded in American economic and military strength—also extended to a dream of eliminating nuclear weapons altogether, a notion dismissed by his advisers, who did not understand that while this was Reagan's dream, it also happened to be one he was serious about achieving.

Strangely enough, Shultz, who did not have as close or as long-standing a personal relationship with Reagan as several other senior members of the administration, seems in retrospect to have been the only member of the national security team who truly had confidence in Reagan and his judgment. Perhaps this was because it served Shultz's policy interests to do so, but I think there was more to it.

I am convinced that a number of Reagan's conservative senior advisers, including Casey, Clark, Weinberger, and Kirkpatrick, did not think the President was particularly smart. Oh, they admired him as a man, fully respected his political skills and his ability to communicate with the American public, and obviously agreed with his broad priorities of getting government out of people's hair, cutting taxes, and strengthening defense. But they did not regard him as skilled in foreign policy and thought he was too easily influenced by those interested in negotiating with the Soviets or in restrained responses to Soviet provocations. At breakfasts and meetings, week after week, Weinberger and Casey would grump about Reagan's unwillingness to "rein in" Shultz or to act more aggressively in one or another situation involving the Soviets.

I never heard the notion expressed by either of them that perhaps Reagan, even as he was totally supportive of Weinberger's military buildup and Casey's covert wars, understood that strength was not an end in itself. I never heard either reflect that there might be no contradiction in Reagan's mind between supporting their respective efforts and being completely "in sync" also with Shultz's vision of how to use the country's resurgent strength. In fact, I think neither they nor others ever grasped the evolving synergistic relationship between Reagan and Shultz—that the Secretary provided the President a practical, hardheaded course of action to translate his hopes for the future of U.S.-Soviet relations into reality.

Because of political realities inside the Soviet Union, Shultz's ambitious ideas for progress in the relationship were premature by at least two years—as Andropov and then Chernenko physically weakened and then died. Only in the last months of Chernenko's tenure and then with Mikhail Gorbachev's accession to power in March 1985 would the Soviet Union be ready to move forward.

It was a tough two years for Shultz. His efforts to make progress in the relationship found no interlocutor on the Soviet side and encountered constant opposition in Washington. With perhaps the exception of quiet support from Nancy Reagan, Jim Baker, and White House aide Mike Deaver, Shultz was alone. Often opposed by Defense and NSC, and he thought also by CIA, more than once he offered to resign out of frustration. What Shultz did not seem to understand was that, while his vision and his strategy were correct, it took two to tango and the other side wasn't yet ready to dance—even with a skilled tripper like George Shultz. As a result, his constant efforts to push the agenda with the Soviets looked hopelessly optimistic and at times even foolish against the backdrop of events both internationally and inside the USSR in 1983–1984.

THE OPPOSITION

Shultz's principal antagonists inside the administration were Weinberger, Clark, and Casey. Caspar "Cap" Weinberger's relationship with Shultz was the most complex of all, because they had worked together both in and out of government, generally with Shultz in the more senior position.

Weinberger was Shultz's primary nemesis on policy issues, and a more unlikely looking foil you would never meet. A short man with an easy and ready smile and a good sense of humor, Weinberger had a low-keyed manner and nonconfrontational style that was misleading. Once decided on a course of action or position, Cap was immovable, the most tenacious opponent around. There was nothing slick or underhanded or subtle or devious about Weinberger. He was every bit as stubborn as Shultz, an implacable, relentless presence. But the nicest implacable foe you will ever meet. Indeed, other than in Congress, I never met anyone—however much he or she disagreed with Weinberger—who did not like him as a person.

Weinberger and Shultz disagreed early on, in August 1982, over the dispatch of U.S. Marines as part of a multinational peacekeeping force in Lebanon. Shultz wanted them there, Cap Weinberger did not. In this case, the NSC was on Shultz's side. Their first disagreement on the USSR came early—on easing the sanctions relating to the Soviet export gas pipeline. Weinberger was against giving up the sanctions, and only after a Shultz-Weinberger confrontation in front of the President on October 15, 1982, did Reagan side with Shultz. They clashed also on arms control and arms sales. They quarreled about meetings with the Soviets and how much Shultz could or should say to Gromyko. After KAL-007, Weinberger wanted very tough action against the Soviets; Shultz wanted strong rhetoric, but little action and, as well, approval for him to go ahead and meet with Gromyko a few days later. Shultz won. So it went from July 1982 until Weinberger resigned in November 1987.

Shultz's relationship with William Clark was less complex. Despite a total lack of experience relating to foreign affairs, Clark had been selected as Al Haig's deputy at State. There he remained until Richard Allen resigned as National Security Adviser in January 1982, and then he moved to the White House to take that job.

The National Security Council was created in 1947 as a mechanism to help the President coordinate the diverse elements of U.S. activities abroad—diplomacy, the military, and intelligence. The only members are the President, Vice President, and the Secretaries of State and Defense. The Director of Central Intelligence and Chairman of the Joint Chiefs of Staff are, by law, advisers to the NSC, and all CIA activities are carried out under its auspices. Since the early 1950s, the staff of the NSC has operated under the Assistant to the President for National Security Affairs (earlier the Special Assistant), also known as the National Security Adviser.

The position of National Security Adviser to the President is a complex and difficult one in the best of circumstances. Presidents have been best served by individuals with substantive expertise and/or experience in the national security arena, practical policy and government experience, the complete confidence of the President, and the confidence of the other members of the national security team. The National Security Adviser should have a personal relationship with the President that allows an open dialogue between them, including debate and disagreement. Cabinet officers must have the confidence that their views will be completely and fairly reported to the President, that options will be presented to him evenhandedly, that all views will be heard, and that no decision will be made behind a principal's back. The National Security Adviser should be a facilitator for Cabinet officers and encourage their access to the President. The National Security Adviser should be as adept at crisis management as at long-range strategic thinking and conceptualization. He should have experience in Washington, preferably in a position that has involved interaction with the Congress. Finally, as an earlier President was told by a prospective candidate for the job, "You need someone who can bring you bad news every day and you still won't grow to hate him." Obviously, no one fits all these demanding criteria completely, but a few (like Brent Scowcroft) have come close.

Sadly, the National Security Adviser did not play such a role during the first six years of the Reagan administration, partly for structural reasons, partly because of the deficiencies of those who would hold the job. Downgraded in 1981, a weak and often incompetent Reagan NSC removed from the bureaucratic equation a powerful protection for the President—a potent personal representative who could bring the national security mandarins together, develop agreements and compromises when possible, and crystallize disputes into manageable alternatives for presidential decision.

There was even more in-fighting, quarreling, back-biting, and jock-eying for advantage among the senior members of the Reagan national security team than in the Carter administration. During the first six years of the Reagan administration, there was no one at the NSC whom Cabinet officers would keep regularly informed of their activities and who could, as necessary, coordinate those activities and make sure all were adhering to the policies determined by the President. End runs to the President by individual Cabinet members bypassing the NSC interagency process were commonplace and caused endless trouble.

When the NSC works, Cabinet officers don't get blindsided, don't have to worry that decisions affecting them will be made in their absence. With a weak NSC during most of the Reagan administration, too often important decisions were made in private meetings with the President without all the key players being present or informed. Both Shultz and Weinberger were victims—as well as perpetrators—more than once. And whenever that happened, the level of mistrust spiked higher, until the Secretary of State was virtually not speaking to the Secretary of Defense or the DCI.

The frustrations involved led at least two Reagan NSC advisers to resign—Bill Clark and Bud McFarlane. Another manifestation that something serious was wrong in the White House: since Eisenhower's time, there has been, on average, one NSC adviser per presidential term, an average tenure of about four years. Reagan would have *six* national security advisers in eight years.

This was, unfortunately, the environment in which Bill Clark found himself. A terribly nice man, Clark fit very few of the criteria necessary for a capable national security adviser. An old California friend of Reagan's, Clark gave it his best, but clearly was out of his element and did not serve the President well. He quickly allied himself with Weinberger, Casey, and Kirkpatrick, and against Shultz. The Secretary's view of him, thus, was not a charitable one. Shultz came to distrust Clark and believed he was trying to usurp the role of the Secretary of state—with the acquiescence of the Secretary of Defense and the DCI.

SHULTZ, CASEY, AND INTELLIGENCE

Casey seemed genuinely pleased, I thought, when Shultz was named to replace Haig. Right after Shultz was named to take Haig's place, Casey bent over backward to send him briefing materials and information to help the Secretary-designate quickly get up to speed. How much it helped or whether Shultz even used it is less important than the fact that it suggested no early animosity on Casey's part. Shultz also seemed to approach the relationship open-mindedly. He set a weekly lunch with Casey and his deputy and, early on, became an aggressive user of intelligence.

But it didn't take long before a chill set in. By late fall 1982, Shultz clearly saw Casey as teamed with Weinberger and Clark in opposition to new initiatives to improve relations with the Soviet Union. As time went on, he was put off by what he saw as Casey's independence of action in various locales around the world. As Casey became more critical of Shultz's handling of policy issues, especially of what he saw as the Secretary's inadequately aggressive posture vis-à-vis the Soviet Union, the Director would more and more often lecture Shultz at lunch on what he ought to be doing. Shultz hated being lectured by Casey, and this, together with the Secretary's unhappiness with the head of intelligence so assertively pushing policy positions, steadily increased the distance between the two men. Distance soon soured into antagonism, animosity, and conflict.

Without parallel in the history of postwar American intelligence, Bill Casey as DCI had his own foreign policy agenda and, as a Cabinet member, pursued that agenda vigorously and often in opposition to the Secretary of State. Indeed, sometimes Casey was boastfully blunt about his use of intelligence. He told intelligence community leaders at an out-of-town conference on December 11, 1983, "Our estimating program has become a powerful instrument in forcing the pace in the policy area." In meetings, he would sometimes offer his own views of a situation overseas without being explicit that they were his personal views and not necessarily shared by CIA's experts or others in the intelligence community. A President is not well-served if his DCI cannot offer views different than those of the intelligence community's analysts, but the DCI should be very clear to distinguish between the two. Casey rarely was.

The bad blood between Casey and Shultz significantly aggravated what, in the best of circumstances, would have been a complicated relationship between CIA's substantive experts and the Secretary of State. Complicated only because there were significant elements of CIA's work that Shultz respected and used.

Although Shultz was often critical of intelligence, I think—perhaps with the exception of George Bush—he was the best senior user of intelligence I ever encountered. One important reason was that George Shultz seemed genuinely to care about what we did and paid attention—even if only because periodically he thought we had something wrong and wanted to stop us from saying it again to others. He spent time with us, tasked and used us, met with our analysts and case officers, was willing to be debriefed by them, all to a degree unprecedented at the Cabinet level.

Shultz discusses intelligence and CIA often in his memoirs, almost always critically. However, at the time, our relationship with him had significantly more positive aspects than he describes. He especially liked much of the work we did on international economic issues and energy, and was continually tasking us for information on these and related subjects. Shultz was an avid user of our information prior to his meetings with foreign leaders, and when he found errors or gaps, he would provide us with better information and his personal insights. He received many briefings on Soviet military, and especially strategic, developments. The Secretary also received detailed CIA briefings on proliferation issues, such as the Pakistani nuclear program. He asked for, and received, many assessments on subjects as diverse as China, technology transfer, the impact of oil spills, the Soviet Union. Even after his relationship with Casey soured, he would ask for stacks of material from us—as, for example, in early 1984 when he asked for a number of specialized reports on Iran and Iraq.

While Shultz and Casey had their disagreements on arms control, Shultz valued the expert assistance CIA provided on the verification elements of negotiating positions, and included Doug George, the head of CIA's Arms Control Intelligence Staff, on all of his trips to meet with the Soviets. He often praised Doug and his successors, and told Casey they could have access to him at any time. In March 1983, Shultz asked for new estimates on Soviet attitudes toward arms control and subsequently spent a great deal of time being briefed by George and others on our capabilities to monitor agreements on Soviet strategic weapons.

Shultz was a critic of intelligence, but he listened even when he didn't agree. He thought our analysis too pessimistic on too many subjects, from El Salvador to Lebanon to Angola, from the danger of an Indo-Pakistani war to developments in the Soviet Union and Soviet foreign policy. He was especially assertive in challenging our experts' views when they could complicate his negotiations, when they provided ammunition to his critics on the Hill and inside the administration, and when he thought them just plain wrong.

Shultz was thoughtful about intelligence. More than once he urged me, for example, to focus our work more on what he called "opportunity intelligence"—identifying issues or problems around the world that offered opportunities for American action and successes. I agreed with this, but also warned him that the line between identifying opportunities and becoming a policy advocate was a very thin one—that it was hard to identify areas for action without being tagged as advocating such action.

After I became Deputy Director for Intelligence, Shultz and I met on several occasions, usually with only one other person present, to discuss his problems with our analysis and to work out difficulties. My hardest "sell" was to try to persuade him from time to time that when our analysts had a different view than his, they were not shilling for Casey or responding to his pressure, but in fact offering their own independent view. Nor were they fronting for the clandestine service and its covert actions. His reaction was often one of open disbelief. As the 1980s wore on, the relationship would not get better. And our differences over developments inside the Soviet Union would fuel the continuing dispute, even after Casey was gone.

U.S.-SOVIET RELATIONS: REAGAN TILTS TO SHULTZ

During the first two years of the Reagan administration, relations between the United States and USSR were locked in ice. There were modest American efforts to reach out to the Soviets in 1981–1982, but they were very modest indeed. Although by midsummer 1982 the two sides were talking on arms control, that was about all. Neither government was in a mood to deal. Thus George Shultz became Secretary of State during one of the coldest periods of the Cold War.

Shultz's first major strategic foray with Reagan was a memorandum, "U.S.-Soviet Relations in 1983," which he sent forward on January 19, 1983. The memorandum called for an intensified dialogue with the Soviets on a four-part agenda: human rights, arms control, regional issues, and bilateral relations (a basic agenda that would guide U.S. policy for the remainder of the Cold War). Shultz would send two further memos to Reagan, both in March, on how to proceed with the Soviets and implement the guidance he had been given by the President—to go forward step by step, based on Soviet responsiveness.

Clark, Weinberger, and Casey did not share Shultz's view that early 1983 was an appropriate time to begin a serious dialogue with the Soviets. They believed that Soviet behavior in the Third World, their continuing military buildup, their efforts to stop deployment of INF, and other actions did not create the proper atmosphere for a change in direction in the relationship.

As a result, at the beginning of 1983 an internecine war began over how to deal with the Soviets that would rage for two years and smoulder for the rest of the Reagan administration. It reached the point that in July 1983, Clark attacked Shultz's management of the Soviet relationship in a memorandum to Reagan and proposed that the President turn the account over to the NSC. The next month Shultz offered to resign because of the continuing conflict with Clark. Reagan refused.

The events of 1983 described earlier, both at the time and in retrospect, make clear that Shultz's hopes for the dialogue during that period were unrealistic. And the positive spin he placed on minor Soviet steps was disproportionate to their continuing obduracy on INF, their egging on the Syrians in Lebanon and providing them with advanced SA-5 missiles, and their actions elsewhere.

WHITHER THE USSR: SHULTZ VS. CIA AND ME (ROUND ONE)

In 1983, a dialogue began between George Shultz and me about where the Soviet Union was headed, a dialogue that would extend over the next five years. At a meeting with Casey on May 13, Shultz asked what was going on in the Soviet Union. At their next meeting, on May 20, I accompanied Casey and briefed on the USSR and Andropov in particular. John McMahon wrote afterward, "It was very well received by the Secretary, who was most attentive." John overstated.

The briefing did not satisfy Shultz, who, on June 13, asked Casey for a "go-around" with CIA on Soviet goals and priorities with the primary focus on their willingness to continue to talk and negotiate. As a result, on the 17th I gave Casey a paper to send to Shultz. In it, I said that Andropov's chief priority was the internal economic situation. I spelled out a number of Soviet economic problems that would be addressed in a series of analytical papers in coming weeks and the impact on Soviet performance. I observed that Soviet economic problems were deep and difficult to correct, and that they derived in part from investment decisions made in 1975, the higher cost of extracting raw materials than forecast, and slower growth in basic industries, agriculture, and so on. I wrote that the Soviet defense effort and industries were not immune to problems caused by these larger economic difficulties and said that it was reasonable to speculate that with such problems, Andropov's interest in arms control was likely enhanced if it didn't disadvantage the USSR militarily. I concluded, "Between them, Andropov and Ustinov have enough power, along with Gromyko, to have great flexibility in foreign policy issues."

The next round in my dialogue with Shultz came in September after he had invited me to attend one of his Saturday seminars on Soviet affairs. At the end of the September 24 seminar, he asked for a memo of my thoughts along the lines expressed at the breakfast.

A CIA briefer each morning would deliver a copy of the *President's Daily Brief* to Shultz (and Weinberger), and I occasionally used this channel to send personal notes or analysis directly to the Secretary of State. I did so on September 27 with my response to his request. I began my analysis by saying that the tone of the bilateral relationship was probably as "pervasively bleak" as at any time since Stalin's death, but that since the Soviets have a long perspective, then so should we. According to the memo, "the halcyon days of détente lasted less than 30 months in the early 1970s and the trend in the relationship was generally downhill under three successive presidents of both parties."

In words that must have struck a chord with Shultz, I noted that every time an opportunity to begin reversing that downward trend presented itself, there had been some event or action in Washington, Moscow, or the Third World that had killed the opening. "In short, the Soviets see problems with the U.S. transcending this administration and this makes overall developments and the future all the more worrisome to them." I said that I thought the Soviets saw the Reagan administration as more dangerous to them than its predecessors not because of its rhetoric and attitudes but because it had been more successful in countering the USSR in three areas: defense, the Third World, and INF.

I offered a forecast that was pessimistic in the short term, but brighter a couple of years out. I wrote: "I believe the Russians still recognize the need to do business with the U.S. and will do it with this administration, but not until 1985. They are prepared to be patient. A range of economic, political and strategic motives *impels* the USSR to cultivate ties with the U.S., though not at any price." I said they would not abandon an active role in the Third World, tolerate attempts to interfere in or change their domestic policies, allow the United States to use arms control to restructure Soviet forces, or abandon their global pretensions or ambitions.

I suggested that for the next year the bilateral prospects were bleak—that KAL-007 would make it difficult for the United States to initiate a dialogue for the rest of 1983. Then INF would be deployed and the Soviets would react to that, and then there would be the U.S. election campaign, "in which the Soviets hope with all their hearts for the defeat of the President." In short, the bilateral relationship would be in the deep-freeze until 1985 when the United States would be in a position to seize the initiative.

The memo concluded that the first problem was "how to get through the next year without a further dangerous increase in tensions." I suggested to Shultz a matter-of-fact response to Soviet measures in response to the INF deployment; proceeding with routine business and meetings, making clear to Moscow our understanding that some lines of communication must be kept open; a new initiative on confidence-building measures; and continuing a businesslike approach at START. I said that this sort of "keeping the lines open" would be the best way to get through the year and set the stage for possibly some improvement in the relationship in 1985.

I ended with a warning: "I mentioned above the times in recent years when a promising dialogue had been cut short by events. There are all too many places these days where such events can take place. It will take considerable skill and luck just to keep things from getting even worse during the next year."

With considerable skill, Shultz, with the support of President Reagan, did prevent the relationship from getting worse in 1984 and began the long road forward. Even in the worst of years, 1983, Shultz had been, to use his word, "gardening"—preparing the soil —with Reagan and the Soviets. He would continue to do so in

1984. And in 1985, he would come into his own. And the dialogue over what was happening in the Soviet Union between the Secretary and CIA—between Shultz and me—would continue, with him often disagreeing, but still willing to talk and to listen.

REAGAN AND SHULTZ: A MEETING OF MINDS

During the darkest days of 1983, George Shultz developed a remarkable meeting of the minds with Ronald Reagan. He would emerge from that difficult period having established a decisive personal and policy advantage with the President over his rivals and critics. After January 1983, Shultz would increasingly emerge on top in the bureaucratic struggle over how to deal with the Soviets, both in a broad sense and in specific situations. He would not win all the bureaucratic battles over Soviet policy, but he would win increasingly often and he would win nearly all of the important struggles.

Reagan listened to Shultz and, at each critical juncture, decided issues relating to the USSR either in Shultz's favor or at least tilted in his direction. Shultz supported the U.S. arms buildup and he supported CIA's covert wars, but he also devised a strategy of engagement with the Soviet Union that the President endorsed and supported if, at times, with reservations. Indeed, Reagan would be pulled this way and that by different members of his national security team, and his desire to be accommodating to people usually produced more conflict than it avoided. But with all the ambiguity, frustrations, and conflict, during 1983 I believe Reagan and Shultz forged a tough-minded yet pragmatic approach on how to deal with the Soviets, an approach that generally pointed in a positive direction, that pointed toward eventual negotiation and agreement on a range of issues once the Soviets were prepared to retreat.

However, another death in Moscow meant they would have to wait a little longer.

CHAPTER SIXTEEN

Central America, 1983–1984: Our Own Worst Enemy

A HOUSE DIVIDED

The United States and Nicaragua. Not since Vietnam had the American government been so bitterly divided and along so many fault lines. Between the Executive Branch and the Congress. Within Congress. Within the Executive. Within the White House. Within State, Defense, and the NSC. Within CIA.

By the end of 1982, the most fundamental division over Central America within CIA was between the career professionals and Casey. At the seniormost levels, the primary motive of opponents of the Central American covert action was neither moral nor political. It was instead recognition that this covert action, more than any of the others, was controversial and that the policy itself lacked a popular or congressional mandate. We had learned a lesson in the investigations of the mid-1970s: when a President asks CIA to undertake a covert action because he cannot get public support for an overt policy, CIA will be left holding the proverbial presidential bag. This skepticism was born of painful experience, and the resulting bureaucratic protectiveness was as realistic as it was parochial. And this self-protectiveness of CIA drove the right wing in Washington, and often Casey, absolutely around the bend.

Both Inman and McMahon were skeptics. Inman was deeply uncomfortable with Casey's penchant for bypassing him and the DO senior management and directly partnering with Dewey Clarridge to manage the Central American program. He had real concerns that both men were inclined to play loosey-goosey with the rules, and Casey's approach on Central America played a critical role in Inman's decision to resign.

McMahon represented the CIA career officials in his belief that an unpopular program such as Central America would end up tarring CIA both with the Congress and with the public at large. While he was loyal to Casey, he pulled no punches in offering his views, criticisms, or advice. He liked Clarridge—Dewey was very hard not to like—but he didn't trust his judgment and felt that Dewey needed close supervision. And McMahon would explode when he found out something was going on he didn't know about. It was a Vesuvian display of sound, light, and vocabulary you could have sold tickets to see and hear.

For example, on January 17, 1983, after such a display aimed at Clarridge, McMahon followed up with a short memorandum to the DDO, John Stein, that—considerably dressed up from the preceding personal dressing down—left little to the imagination. John wrote: "The DCI and I were distressed to learn that Dewey Clarridge was in Panama talking about the Panamanians developing a 250 man paramilitary force without the DCI or I knowing about it. . . . I want to be aware of all major activities within Nicaragua by forces under our sponsorship and give prior approval before any conversation with foreign nationals on any proposed covert action." Of course, Stein almost certainly had not known either.

There were critics of the Central American covert program inside the Directorate of Operations but there were more on the analytical side of CIA—just as there had been over Vietnam. Some resented the way the DO Latin American Division and its Central American Task Force cut them out of information, some thought the effort was doomed, some saw the operation bringing a storm down on the Agency, and some—like certain of their clandestine service colleagues—knew there was a covert action in Central America because the political support was lacking for an open U.S. confrontation with the Sandinistas in Nicaragua. The truest believers tended to be the handful of people that Casey had brought into the Agency from the outside, and those directly involved in running the program.

I was torn. I—along with Inman and McMahon—agreed totally with our analyses of what the Cubans, Soviets, and Sandinistas were doing in Nicaragua and elsewhere in Central America. But the contrast between the administration's apocalyptic rhetoric and the pusillanimous character of its actions, as well as the failure of the administration (and Casey) to keep the Congress on board, made me very uneasy. I wanted to defeat the Sandinistas but I didn't think it could be done with ever more constrained covert action.

By the end of 1984, I concluded that we were kidding ourselves if we thought the Contras might win. I wrote Casey on December 14, and began by saying, "The Contras can't overthrow the Sandinista regime." I continued that we were muddling along in Nicaragua with a halfhearted policy because of the lack of agreement within the administration and with Congress on our real objectives. I urged moving to an overt policy including withdrawal of diplomatic recognition; providing open military assistance and funds to a government-in-exile; imposing economic sanctions, perhaps including a quarantine; and using air strikes to destroy Nicaragua's military buildup—no invasion but no more Soviet/Cuban military deliveries. I concluded, "Relying on and supporting the Contras as our only action may actually hasten the ultimate, unfortunate outcome."

The foulest word in the professional intelligence officer's lexicon is "zealot," and too many associated with the Central American effort, both in and out of CIA, were zealots. And that made a lot of people nervous. They hadn't seen anything yet. On Central America, and there alone, the DCI himself was a zealot.

Casey's zealotry on Central America contributed greatly to creating deep divisions inside the administration. Shultz supported the covert action, but he believed the administration had to have a diplomatic or negotiating track as well in order to succeed in Central America, and also to build congressional and public support. He was very attuned to the growing opposition on Capitol Hill. On the other side, Casey, Clark, Weinberger, and Kirkpatrick fundamentally were opposed to negotiations of any kind.

In an exchange with Casey on February 22, 1983, Shultz went to the heart of his position. He said, with respect to Central America, that the question was whether it was an issue of national security or simply tending to our own backyard. If national security, then we should send in the Marines and have them take care of the problem. If, on the other hand, it was a matter of tending to our backyard, then we should pursue a solution on the political front.

The next several months saw an intensification of conflict between Shultz and the NSC's Bill Clark as they wrestled over who was in charge of foreign policy. The laconic, seemingly low-keyed

Clark was driving the Secretary of State crazy. In late May, in a move to recapture control of Central America policy, Shultz went to Reagan and described his problems with Clark and the NSC, telling the President that "you have a fed-up, frustrated secretary of state on your hands." When the sun went down, Shultz had received Reagan's approval for how Central America policy was to be managed—by George Shultz.

Meanwhile, we had prepared a new intelligence estimate on Nicaragua, "The Outlook for the Insurgency." It did not provide much good news. While acknowledging the growing number of Contras, the assessment noted the small scale of their activities compared to insurgents in El Salvador, the need for a tangible success soon, their inadequate strength and tactical direction, and the lack of a political strategy. It concluded that the Contras had not yet succeeded in capturing or destroying arms shipments from Nicaragua to the guerrillas in El Salvador.

Casey gave the draft estimate to the President on June 25, 1983, with a cover note that said, "We are losing in Central America." He urged strengthening El Salvador's counterinsurgency capabilities, strengthening the Contras and "eliminating their fear of the rug being pulled out from under them," strengthening Honduras, and taking steps to keep additional Cuban military and security forces out of Nicaragua.

Another fight came in July 1983 when, in Shultz's absence, the Department of Defense planned a highly visible U.S. military exercise around Nicaragua, especially in Honduras. Shultz once more was blindsided and on July 25 tried to resign as a result of the NSC's independent actions in both the Middle East and Central America. Shultz and Casey had lunch together on July 29, and the Secretary complained bitterly about being cut out of the exercise proposal, discussion, and decision to deploy the U.S. ships to Central America. Casey said that he, too, had been unaware of consideration of this idea and observed that the Defense Department had clearly made an end run with the NSC on the whole matter. I am confident that Shultz was as skeptical then that Casey had not known as I am today.

Clark had received a lot of press attention that summer along the lines that he had become the dominant figure in administration foreign policy. In reality, whenever Shultz pressed his case with Reagan, he consistently won. And it happened again. Although the confrontation between Shultz and Clark built further in the days following the military exercise, the outcome had already been decided. By early August 1983, once again, arrangements had been sorted out along the lines of Shultz's preference. Clark resigned on October 13.

News of the July military exercise in Central America torched off a tremendous furor in Congress. The net result was that on July 28, the House of Representatives voted to cut off all aid to the Nicaraguan opposition, the Contras. Thus the administration's own fumbling around once more gave valuable ammunition to its critics on Central America.

CONGRESS BALKS

The Reagan administration's reading of the situation in Central America had much in common with that of Jimmy Carter's national security team. Of course, a highly partisan new administration and one so scornful of its predecessor could not bring itself to point out to the public or the Congress that two very different administrations saw the situation, and the dangers of Soviet and especially Cuban meddling, pretty much the same. As described in Chapter 13, Reagan signed two findings in 1981 expanding Carter's "nonlethal" covert actions in Central America. One finding authorized the use of force to interdict weapons and the other provided assistance to the Contras as a way of bringing pressure on the government in Managua to abandon its interventionist activities elsewhere in the region.

By fall 1982, Clarridge appeared to have wrought a bureaucratic wonder. He managed to build a Contra force of nearly 3,500 anti-Sandinista guerrillas—2,300 Spanish-speaking fighters, nine hundred Miskito Indians, and some five hundred men with Eden Pastora. Just as Dewey's early efforts had been aided by taking over support of five hundred Contras funded by the Argentine junta, so, too, was the expansion of that U.S.-sponsored force helped by the ouster of the junta after the British defeated Argentina in the Falklands War earlier in the year. When the junta disappeared, the United States inherited another 2,000 Contras from the Argentinians. It happened so fast we had to scramble to find the funds to support them.

Throughout 1982, congressional mistrust of Casey and Clarridge grew. They originally had proposed a force of five hundred and now it was many times that. Their whole demeanor while testifying conveyed a sense of contempt, of doing the minimum absolutely required, of being there against their will and determination to get the hearing over and go back to doing real work. Many Democrats (and, I suspect, more than a few Republicans) on the oversight committees soon became convinced that—at best—they weren't getting the full picture. A number thought they were being misled and some thought they were being lied to.

As a result of congressional mistrust (and a healthy dose of politics)—and energized by a *Newsweek* article in November 1982 on CIA support for the Contras, the chairman of the House Intelligence Committee, Representative Edward Boland of Massachusetts, submitted an amendment forbidding Defense or CIA from providing military equipment, training, or advice "for the purpose of overthrowing" the Nicaraguan regime. It passed the House on December 8 by 411–0. That could not be seen as a partisan vote.

In late December, two weeks after Senator Moynihan wrote Shultz charging that the administration's covert action program to support the Contras was in violation of the law, Casey told Clark that senior Honduran officials had told Senator Patrick Leahy that the purpose of the U.S. covert action was to overthrow the Sandinista government. Casey warned Clark that this would "add fuel" to the concerns of Moynihan and others whether in fact the U.S. program was legal or illegal.

Next, State weighed in. When Casey and Clark again discussed on January 26, 1983, whether CIA was violating the law with its program, the Director reported that State had suggested raising the issue to the Attorney General for a ruling. Casey said he didn't think that was necessary. Even so, Casey told Clark he would not initiate actions in Central America until he was "directed to do so." Clark instructed him to proceed.

The growing confrontation with Congress over Central America heated up further in April 1983. On April 1, Moynihan was quoted in the *New York Times* as questioning again the legality of intelligence activities in Nicaragua. On the 5th, the chairman of the committee, Barry Goldwater, asked for a hearing on Nicaragua. The same day, Leahy on the Senate floor charged that the administration was supporting, and might be guiding, a large-scale anti-Sandinista guerrilla movement aimed at the overthrow of the government of Nicaragua.

On April 12, Assistant Secretary of State for Latin America Tom Enders testified before the Senate Foreign Relations Committee and the SSCI on a modest program of support for the Contras. In the SSCI, Moynihan and Republican Senator David Durenberger spoke against the program, claiming again that the Agency was violating the Boland Amendment. The Republican-dominated committee disagreed.

On April 18, 1983, Casey warned Clark of a likely confrontation on Central America the next day when the FY 84 budget was considered by the SSCI. He thought the outlook was not bright but that the vote was "winnable." As always, Casey took a tough line. He told Clark, "My vote is to lay it out to the people in a joint session and roll them [opponents of the program]." At the same time, he warned John McMahon, "The possibility of being shot down is strong and perhaps requires some kind of forward thinking to handle that eventuality."

On the same day, Casey sent Reagan a letter urging the President to make a national address on the Central America problem. He urged a strong, bold move to explain to the American people "what we face in Central America." He said the speech needed to be before a joint session of Congress for impact.

The DCI forwarded to the President talking points on what was at stake in Central America that revealed the sources of Casey's own militancy: The Soviets "care about perpetuating instability in the region south of the United States border and distracting the United States from threats in Europe, Africa and Asia. The Soviet-Cuban aim is to destabilize or to control every country from Panama to Mexico and create a flood of refugees by land and by sea, across the Gulf of Mexico, to the borders of the United States. If Central America is lost, our credibility in Asia, Europe and in NATO will go with it. . . . ."

Clark apparently sided with Casey on an effort to use a congressional setting to appeal to the American people over the heads of Congress, because on April 27, 1983, Ronald Reagan appeared before a joint session of Congress to speak about Central America. But, once it was over, it was clear that even Reagan wasn't starchy enough on Central America for Casey. After the President's speech, Casey complained to Weinberger that while Reagan's delivery had been good, the "White House staffers had ruined the text." The speech had no punch line, he said. It did not directly task the Congress.

Casey was still dissatisfied. And so was Congress.

The House Intelligence Committee scheduled a vote on a

second Boland amendment on May 3, 1983. Casey asked to testify before they voted, and Boland agreed. Casey warned them, on the day of the vote, that a cutoff of money to the "Nicaragua Project" would send a message that we were unwilling to defend our legitimate national security interests close to our own border, Panama would return to a more or less openly pro-Cuban policy, Costa Rica and Honduras would seek accommodation with Nicaragua (and there might be a military coup in Tegucigalpa), and a right-wing coup in El Salvador would become very likely when it saw the United States pulling back from Central America. Bill touched all the bases, hit all the scare buttons, but to no avail. The committee voted to cut off all aid to the Contras.

For all his tough talk, Casey was now forced to back off. His "roll 'em" strategy had failed. Now he had to deal. He wrote the President on May 10 and proposed repackaging the Central America program to gain congressional support. Casey suggested a bipartisan commission of Congress, labor, and other segments of American life to formulate recommendations on a comprehensive program to preserve democracy and freedom in Central America. He suggested Senator Lloyd Bentsen to chair the commission and urged the involvement of "nonconservatives" like Lane Kirkland, head of the AFL-CIO. He added that the administration should emphasize that it would aid the anti-Sandinistas only as long as the Sandinistas continued to support the Salvadoran insurgency, should seek a new finding designed to encourage political and civic action as well as paramilitary action, and should create a broader bipartisan umbrella in Congress for the program.

Casey's and the administration's strategy through the summer and fall was to come up with a finding and program that could gain the support of a majority on the Senate Intelligence Committee. The House was lost, voting down aid to the Contras by a vote of 228–195.

On August 10, 1983, Casey forwarded to Shultz and Clark a new draft Central America finding, "to meet what I judge to be acceptable to the Senate Intelligence Committee." The NSC met on September 16 to review the situation in Central America and to discuss the new finding which, among other things, authorized cooperation with other governments in providing support, equipment, and training to the Contras.

The new finding also had been modified to state more explicitly that the objectives of the program were to hamper the Cuban-

Nicaraguan arms supply, to divert Sandinista energies and resources from the export of revolutionary violence, and to induce them to enter into negotiations to cease support of insurgencies. When Casey briefed the Senate Intelligence Committee on September 20, he added a cautionary note: "The new finding . . . no longer expressly authorizes us to conduct paramilitary operations— but rather to provide support to Nicaraguan paramilitary resistance groups. This reflects that we have less of a leadership role and more of a passive role."

Thanks to Barry Goldwater, Casey's strategy worked and the will of the House was thwarted by the Senate. However, a second Boland amendment capped funding for the Contras for the next year (FY 84) at $24 million, a level considerably below what the administration had requested. But the Agency's Central America program got another year to live.

How Do You Sell What People Don't Want to Buy?

Casey had a second burr under his saddle on Central America, in addition to the Congress, and it was the administration's failure in his eyes to persuade the American people that the threat in Central America was real and that the United States had to act. The result was constant pressure from Casey on both Clark and Shultz to do more. For example, on December 22, 1982, he wrote Clark on this, cited a number of directives from the White House to do more, reviewed the lack of progress, and concluded, "It must be obvious to all that the response to these directives has been inadequate if not feeble."

On January 7, 1983, Casey confronted Shultz directly on the subject. He argued that State could do more to sensitize our friends in South America and stiffen them regarding the Cuban and Soviet threat. He then gave Shultz papers listing the public diplomacy initiatives required by various presidential directives. Shultz responded coldly that day that he was trying to convince the Europeans and Latin Americans that the United States was willing to negotiate but not appear weak.

Casey focused special attention on the President. After succeeding in his campaign to get the President to address Congress in April, Casey in June sent him a memorandum setting out a twelve-step program Reagan should undertake "to put on Congress and the people" responsibility for supporting the President and for what needed to be done to save Central America. Casey had graduated from trying to tell Shultz what to do on Central America to telling the President how to do his job.

For all the effort everyone put into declassifying and making intelligence information on Central America available to one and all, there were two fundamental flaws in the administration's and Casey's approach. First, the effort was always haphazard, largely uncoordinated, and irregular. Second, the premise of the approach was just plain wrong. A lack of information was not the problem. There was little disagreement in 1983 across the political spectrum about what was going on in Nicaragua or what the Nicaraguans were doing elsewhere in Central America. The deep fissures were over what, if anything, the United States ought to do about it. And no number of compendia or dazzling briefings of intelligence information could help there.

DISTRUSTING DIPLOMACY

Will Rogers once defined diplomacy as the art of saying "Nice doggie" until you can find a rock. That certainly was Casey's approach to most negotiations. He considered diplomacy on Central America, at best, nothing more than a necessary smokescreen to quiet opposition to the paramilitary program in Congress, among the American people, and in the region. He, along with Clark, Weinberger, and sometimes Kirkpatrick, adamantly resisted Shultz's initiatives to explore the possibilities of negotiation as a complement to the paramilitary program.

In late 1982–1983, Shultz tried to make something of two separate regional diplomatic initiatives. The first was a U.S.-organized meeting in October 1982 that elicited pledges from each regional signatory to the "San Jose Principles"—in brief, to create democratic government, forgo interference in its neighbors' affairs, and limit arms. The second was the Contadora Forum, which involved Venezuela, Mexico, Colombia, and Panama and the other five states of Central America. Representatives of these nine countries—not including the United States—met first on the island of Contadora, off the coast of Panama, in January 1983. The purpose was to attempt to reach a negotiated solution to the conflicts in Central America independent of outside powers. The United States came to support this process.

Casey opposed both the San Jose and Contadora efforts. He

worried that Shultz, and especially his minions, would become so enamored of getting an agreement, any agreement, that they might give away the store, leading to the consolidation of Sandinista power and influence in Central America. He also feared that U.S. support for such initiatives, even looking closely at a negotiated settlement, would unnerve the Contras and persuade them they were about to be abandoned.

Unfortunately, both Shultz and Casey had a point, and their inability to trust each other or to conduct a productive dialogue—not to mention the absence of a neutral National Security Adviser who might have promoted or even forced such a dialogue—resulted in a missed opportunity to have a genuinely nuanced policy that might have garnered more support in Congress and among the public. The internal battles in the administration made many on the Hill believe that negotiations were merely a charade—or that Shultz was outgunned by the hard-liners—and that Reagan and company wouldn't accept a settlement even if it was on their own terms. Here, again, I think Casey had a serious political blind spot. A heavy price would be paid for that.

Nevertheless, by the end of 1983, things weren't going too badly for the United States in Central America. The program to aid the Contras remained alive, and progress was being made in the paramilitary arena. There had been reasonably free and fair elections in El Salvador that gave that country's government new international respectability. The Contadora negotiating process was continuing and showed some modest promise. And, on January 11, 1984, the Kissinger Commission issued its nonpartisan report that gave a lift to administration efforts in Central America.

Still, the covert program to aid the Contras hung by a political thread in the Congress. With the House Democratic majority steadfastly against it, the entire covert program depended on the continued sympathy and support of the Senate Intelligence Committee, and especially its chairman, Barry Goldwater. It would be CIA, not politics or the Senate, that would snap that vital thread in 1984. And it would be done more by inadvertence coupled with political stupidity than by design. Therein would be the tragedy.

Before I turn to that story, though, Casey's strategic and tactical management of the Central American program warrant mention. Two examples from mid-1983 illustrate both his wide reading and strategic approach, and his tactical micromanagement. First, the strategic. At the end of May, he sent a memorandum to Dewey

Clarridge attaching Chapters 33 and 59 of *The Seven Pillars of Wisdom*, by T. E. Lawrence (Lawrence of Arabia). He recounted Lawrence's description of how, during World War I, a tiny Arab force had a real advantage when it stayed away from garrisons of the larger Turkish forces, leaving them there to consume transport and food while the Arabs stayed in a position to threaten and cut off either the influx or outflow of matériel and force. He thought this approach could be applied in Nicaragua: "This may inspire us to shape our finding in a way that places, as Lawrence puts it, the intellectual above the physical yet requires measured force to maintain the access to the target and the constant threat which will shape the target's conduct."

I can't imagine anyone else in all my years of government who would even try to take Lawrence of Arabia's writings on insurgent warfare and attempt to apply them imaginatively to Central America. For all I know, it was all total nonsense, but it was characteristic of Casey's constant search in history, literature, and personal contacts to find new and better ways to do things—a rare openness simultaneously to the old and proven as well as to the new and interesting.

At the other end of the spectrum, in early July 1983, Casey dragged McMahon down to Central America with him to see for himself how things were working and to try to build John's enthusiasm. (McMahon was trying that summer to persuade the government to take the Central America program overt and turn it over to Defense. He saw a train wreck coming and knew CIA was tied to the rails.) When they returned, Casey sent a memo to McMahon, the DDO, and me listing twenty-three actions for follow-up to the trip. This included such minutiae as instructions to get ponchos (raingear) and uniforms for the Contras made in El Salvador, to establish supply caches in the center of Nicaragua to draw the Contras down there, closer coordination of supply routes, and more. And woe be to the officer who thought Casey would let this stuff drop.

CIA AND THE SALVADORAN DEATH SQUADS

Nineteen eighty-four was a bad year for CIA in Central America. It began with allegations in the press that CIA had been involved with the Salvadoran death squads. These right-wing groups had killed a number of opponents of the military government in El Salvador since the 1970s, and their murder of Archbishop Romero and later of four Catholic nuns evoked outrage in the United States. Thus, any link with these cutthroats was anathema. Indeed, during Casey and McMahon's trip to Central America in the summer of 1983, the DCI had been very direct with the Salvadorans that a stop had to be put to the death squads—if for no other reason than the impact on support for El Salvador in the United States.

Efforts by the Directorate of Intelligence to provide information and analysis to policymakers and the Congress on the death squads led to real conflict with the Directorate of Operations early in 1984. I wrote John Stein on February 3:

> There is nothing more irritating in this job than finding out that this directorate has been denied the information needed to do its job. . . . apparently there is DO information available on the death squads which we were not shown. . . . Presumably DO information on the Salvadoran death squads is in such operational traffic. . . . I understand the DO's sensitivities in this matter. We have given considerable deference to the DO in terms of our use of information drawn from their operational traffic on the Contras, probably too much deference. I am willing to limit people in the DI with access to DO operational traffic from Central America to one or two, but we can no longer go down this track with one hand tied behind us.

The situation thereafter improved, but not by a lot.

The allegations of involvement with the death squads continued for several weeks, with bold headlines proclaiming CIA was in cahoots with the Salvadoran murderers and commentators and editorialists flaying us alive. Our only recourse in such situations was to find out the facts and get them out. Unfortunately, that was (and is) a painfully slow process for CIA. In mid-April, CIA's Inspector General found "no basis for concern to date" of a CIA relationship with the death squads. The congressional intelligence committees also looked into the allegations and could find little to substantiate them. But real damage had been done to the Agency in the volatile political atmosphere in Washington during those days, especially on anything involving Central America. Sad to say, the trouble had only begun.

MINING THE HARBORS: A STUDY IN BUREAUCRATIC SUICIDE

On May 28, 1983, the NSC's Crisis Pre-Planning Group considered and approved CIA placing limpet mines on ships in Nicaraguan ports and to mine the river above the port of El Bluff. When Shultz found out about this plan, he hit the roof. He got the plan put on hold, and then reversed by the President at an NSC meeting on the 31st.

Clarridge was undaunted and undeterred. After raids on oil storage facilities at several Nicaraguan ports in the fall of 1983, he raised again the idea of mining the country's harbors, this time with CIA-crafted mines that would do some physical damage, make a lot of noise, and simply scare off the merchant ships that supplied military and civilian goods to Nicaragua. Because the Contras had no idea how to do this, it would be a CIA-run operation, using fast cigarette boats operating from a mother ship off the Atlantic coast of Nicaragua. Casey loved the idea. No one bothered to tell me or to consult with our analysts about the operation.

The House Intelligence Committee was briefed in detail on the mining operation on January 31. In contrast, briefing of the Senate committee was scant at best. In the middle of a long presentation to the committee on March 8 on diverse topics, Casey included the following: "Magnetic mines have been placed in the Pacific harbor of Corinto and the Atlantic harbor of El Bluff as well as the oil terminal of Puerto Sandino." According to the *New York Times*, the committee also was told on March 13 and the staff was briefed on April 2.

In light of the furor in the Senate and then in the press that followed the mining, some context is needed to understand how a senator could be at a committee briefing and not hear or grasp what he or she had been told. First, maddening as it is for a witness, senators come and go all the time during a hearing or briefing. They often come late, step out to take calls, duck out for brief periods to attend hearings of their other committees, work on other business, interrupt the sessions to go vote, talk to staff, talk to each other, sleep, and so on. Their attentiveness while a witness reads a prepared statement or briefing is especially minimal, often because such statements have been provided in advance or drone on endlessly, or the senators have heard most of it before, or they know they can get the text from the record. Add to these circumstances the fact that when Casey was the briefer, he was usually barely understandable or audible, and inclined to brush by potentially controversial parts of testimony. This set the stage for a terrible fight between CIA and the Senate committee over the mining.

All hell broke loose on April 5. A number of ships had hit the mines during March and had been damaged, including one Soviet ship. But the assumption by most was that this was a Contra operation, and so there had been little reaction. However, on April 5 several senators, including Goldwater, learned that CIA had carried out the operation, not the Contras. After brooding over a weekend on what had happened, Goldwater wrote Casey a letter about the mining and how the Agency had handled it, concluding: "It gets down to one, little, simple phrase. I am pissed off." He gave a copy of the letter to the press.

There was a firestorm of congressional and media criticism in response to news about CIA's role. The mining was called an act of war, and an act of utmost stupidity. The United States was roundly criticized by our allies, including Margaret Thatcher. Yet those in the know at CIA felt wronged because they had fully briefed the House committee, and Casey had made his statement to the Senate committee on March 8. Individual senators, like Leahy, acknowledged they had been fully briefed. Even so, Moynihan resigned as vice chairman, recanting only when he got a personal apology from Casey and a pledge to work out procedures to develop full and timely notification of the committees on covert action.

There were three casualties of the mining. First, Dewey Clarridge was reassigned to head the European Division of the clandestine service, no longer to be involved with the Contras—or so it was thought.

Second, events after the firestorm turned Pat Moynihan from a discerning critic of CIA into an implacable foe. The story got about in Washington after the flap that Goldwater hadn't remembered Casey's testimony because with age and health problems, he just wasn't up to the job, that he had "lost it." Moynihan was convinced that such sordid slander originated in CIA, probably with Casey. Moynihan would mention this episode to me time and again in the years to come, and I tried unsuccessfully to find out the source of the story. I don't think it would have mattered. I believe Moynihan was so outraged by the Agency's cursory (and, in his view, nonexistent) briefing of the mining operation and so deeply offended by what he saw as a personal attack on his friend and colleague Goldwater that he would never get over it.

The third casualty was Barry Goldwater's previously unstinting support both for CIA and for Casey. The slender thread that sustained the Contra program in Congress had snapped, as we learned the next fall.

Casey realized he had a very serious problem on his hands on the Hill, and moved to make amends. He sent Goldwater a handwritten note on April 25 apologizing for "misunderstandings and failures in communication." He testified before the Senate Intelligence Committee on the 26th, where he laid out the record of briefings to the Hill on the mining, but in a respectful and regretful manner.

McMahon, a strong supporter of congressional oversight, nevertheless felt that the Agency was getting a bum rap, and disagreed with Casey's decision to eat humble pie. McMahon was traveling abroad at the time, and got a cable from Casey saying that rather than continue to fight with the Senate over whether they had known about the mining, he was going to strike a deal—he would publicly apologize for inadequately briefing them and they would go easy on aid to the Contras. McMahon cabled back a short but characteristically blunt response: "If you're going to start lying now, when are you going to stop?"

Casey had some support on the committee. There was a senators-only committee caucus on the mining issue, and each senator had a briefing book with the transcript of earlier testimony, including the one sentence advising of the mining. Senator Jake Garn pointed out that sentence repeatedly to Moynihan and the others, saying that the failure to follow up and learn more had been the committee's fault. When Moynihan refused to budge or concede any ground at all, Garn lost his temper, threw his briefing book across the room, and shouted at Moynihan that he was "an asshole." There was shocked silence. As Garn told me years later, Moynihan finally looked up over his glasses at Garn and broke the tension by saying quietly, "Smile when you call me an asshole."

In the aftermath, I heard all the arguments, explanations, and self-justifications inside CIA about our briefings and sessions on the Hill relating to the mining. Without questioning them, I still thought we had screwed up, big time. It was a matter of simple logic. If there is only one committee in the Congress that is keeping a program alive, that would argue for bending over backward to ensure that its members had no complaint about being kept well-informed. When the political situation is parlous, tending to congressional allies beyond the bare requirements of the law would seem a given. Failure to do so had now not only endangered the Contra program, it had imposed a terrible political cost on CIA, both in Washington and across the country.

I was angry both that the Directorate of Intelligence—and I—had not had a chance to weigh in on the mining proposal, and that senior Agency people had performed so poorly.

As the costs of the mining mounted for CIA, I thought heads should roll—that a mess so large and so unnecessary demanded firm action in response. As a result, on May 5, 1984, I handwrote on a yellow legal tablet a six-page letter to Casey urging radical surgery at CIA. I never showed it to anyone else. It was long, but it identified problems in the Directorate of Operations that would haunt and damage CIA in the years to come:

> It is my view that keeping the Committees well-informed about covert action *and content that they are well-informed* is a job for the DDO—I mean John Stein. By responding to questions and requests for briefings only when asked and with as little as possible, we invite trouble. We give those who oppose CA [covert action] in one place or another a stick to beat us. And when our friends likewise feel uninformed...! Now, granted chicanery and scoundrels on the Committee staffs—but all the more reason to deny them the weapons to attack us. They get everything anyway—a more aggressive, self-initiated effort by the DDO to engage them in dialogue seems essential to overcome DO's image of reluctance to talk, lack of candor, etc. It's imagery, but as you have seen the last two weeks, it's important.
>
> A second problem I see in the DO is the detachment and weakness of the front office. I don't know how many times I've raised an issue or problem with John [Stein] or Ed [Juchniewicz—Stein's deputy] to find them totally out of the loop—totally uninformed by the division chiefs. . . . When I make an arrangement with John S., he seems often unable or unwilling to make it stick with division chiefs. Senior station chiefs . . . regularly ignore direction or suggestions from their division chiefs. . . . I believe all this is attributable to a loose hand on the DO reins. And *that* has and will continue to cause the Agency problems. . . .
>
> In short . . . the DO's own best interests require a tough new manager who will restore discipline, who controls the directorate, who can protect its interests on the Hill, who can make it more

responsive, and who will try to do something on the political intelligence front. Who is this person? I think he should come from inside CIA. From the DO, only Clair George and Jim Kelly seem qualified to me. . . .

Casey returned the letter to me a week later without a mark on it. I felt badly about criticizing my colleagues, especially since I liked and worked well with Stein. But I felt even worse about the plight of the Agency. In any event, I think I provoked Casey to act. Stein was replaced as DDO a few weeks later, in midsummer, by Clair George. Several other senior personnel changes followed soon thereafter. The mining of the harbors, the furor that followed, and my conviction that far-reaching changes were needed in the way we did business—especially with Congress—claimed several more casualties.

THE "MURDER MANUAL"

In early fall 1984, CIA and the Contra program took yet another major hit. When Casey and McMahon had visited Central America in the summer of 1983, Casey had talked about the Contras' need to pay more attention to political and psychological warfare. The result was the preparation by a contract employee of a little manual entitled *Psychological Operations in Guerrilla Warfare*. The "nom de plume" was "Tayacan," a legendary Central American Indian warrior. Written in Spanish, the manual was never even seen by senior officials at CIA headquarters.

Again, as controversial as the Central American program was, the lack of tight supervision led to disaster. The manual referred to "neutralizing" officials; talked about blackmail, terror, and the use of professional criminals; and was blatant about the objective of overthrowing the Sandinistas. The manual seemed to transgress the Boland Amendments, the prohibition against assassination, and more.

Another firestorm and more hot water for Casey and the Agency. The White House issued a press statement reaffirming the rules against assassination and announcing that the President had asked Casey to have the Inspector General investigate the possibility of improper conduct. The President also asked the presidentially appointed Intelligence Oversight Board to investigate. Casey ordered the IG investigation the next day.

Once again, after getting the facts together, it was apparent that the manual was the product of incompetence, not malign intentions. The Agency was able to report that several of the offending passages had been deleted from the manual before it was circulated to the Contras and that the press characterization of another passage "stretched beyond both its intended and its literal meaning." Ironically, one of the purposes of preparing the manual had been to try to prevent some of the excesses mentioned. Even so, Casey would tell the two oversight committees on October 31 that the manual "was not properly or adequately reviewed." Ultimately, the House Committee attributed the manual to negligence, not an intention to violate the law.

No matter. The Agency got another black eye with the Congress and with the American people. And, if anything, the manual reinforced my belief that command and control in the DO left a lot to be desired.

FUNDING THE CONTRAS: OPERATING AT THE EDGE

Soon after the bruising fight in the fall of 1983 for FY 84 Contra funding and the resulting financial limit on support to the insurgents, the Reagan administration began looking for ways to supplement the funds provided by Congress. What I describe below I learned only in the course of the Iran-Contra investigations.

According to the report of the Iran-Contra Independent Counsel, on January 6, 1984, the NSC approved an effort to get an additional $10–$15 million from domestic or foreign sources to compensate for the reduced level of official U.S. support. Bud McFarlane was given the assignment of arranging this, and in February he raised the idea of encouraging other countries to contribute to the Contras.

On March 27, Casey hand-carried a memo to McFarlane urging him to explore with Israel and other countries the possibility of getting weapons and equipment as well as financial aid for the Contras. Casey also suggested that "after examining the legalities, you might consider urging an appropriate private U.S. citizen to establish a foundation that could be the recipient of nongovernmental funds which could be dispersed to ARDE and the FDN [Contra factions]."

In May, McFarlane persuaded the Saudis to provide $1 million a month to the Contras and directed Oliver North to establish a covert bank account to move the Saudi funds to the Contras.

At yet another NSC meeting, on June 25, 1984, Casey advocated third-country funding, only to have Shultz cite White House Chief of Staff James Baker as saying that such solicitations might be "an impeachable offense." All agreed to get a legal opinion from the Justice Department. The next day, Casey went to Justice and, according to the Walsh report, the Attorney General "determined that third country funding of the contras was legally permissible as long as no U.S. funds were used for the purpose, and as long as there was not an expectation on the part of the third country that the United States would repay the aid."

Casey continued to pursue the third-country funding idea. In a memo he wrote in December 1984 to McMahon, Clair George (by then Deputy Director for Operations), and Alan Fiers (head of the Central American Task Force), the DCI urged, "As in Afghanistan, we need the involvement of other countries which have a stake in checking Communist expansionism in the less developed world." He noted that the Saudis, Moroccans, French, Zaireans, and South Africans were involved in Angola, and that Singapore, Thailand, Malaysia, and China were involved in Cambodia. "In our backyard, we should not, in my opinion, discourage support to check Soviet and Cuban expansionism from these and other countries, including Israel and Taiwan, which have indicated some degree of interest."

The aboveboard effort to gain new congressional authority and funding for the Contra program began in earnest on June 20, 1984, with a meeting convened by Shultz and including Casey, Weinberger, Kirkpatrick, McFarlane, and Deputy National Security Adviser John Poindexter. Clarridge was still around and attended with Casey. The decision was to go "all out" to try to get the Senate to approve $21 million for the Contras and then to fight as long as necessary to get support out of the Congress. Casey, as always, wanted to fight to the death and then, if they lost, blame Congress for the loss of Central America.

Shultz also wanted to look beyond a possible defeat at the hands of Congress on the funding. As Casey informed McMahon, Stein, and Clair George, "Should this fail, I am to convene a meeting to talk about how best to keep the values generated by the Contras in Nicaragua alive; to cope with the problems that spill over into Costa Rica, Honduras and El Salvador; to help those countries in the context of their collaboration in the program; and to keep the spirit of hope in the resistance alive."

Despite a major effort by the administration, on October 10,

1984, the Congress passed the third Boland amendment, this one finally cutting off all U.S. funding to the Contras—*and* prohibiting solicitation from other countries. It was over, or so most of us thought. Little did we know.

1985: Do Something!

Keeping the Contras alive and kicking was a top priority for the administration, and it pursued its goal on three levels. The first, involving only a small number of people at the White House, sought donations from private citizens. The second, known to a broader circle of people at the White House, State, CIA, and Defense, was to solicit money from other governments that might be sympathetic. The third was to get new legislation.

On the first, Casey had suggested the idea of a private foundation to McFarlane in March 1984 and, subsequently, likely had some knowledge about the donors. However, judging from the Independent Counsel report, apart from referring one potential donor to North, it would appear that he kept his distance from the actual "private benefactor" fund-raising. When, in a private meeting on May 23, 1985, McFarlane asked Casey if CIA was "plugged into private efforts to raise $14 million" for the Contras, Casey replied, "We heard something on that but had no details."

With respect to third-country solicitations, Casey was a major proponent, if not the originator, of the idea. In December 1984— nearly nine months after he had recommended that the administration seek the help of third countries—he asked CIA's General Counsel to look at the legality of getting other countries to support the Contras. He didn't like Stanley Sporkin's December 26 answer, and on January 5, 1985, he wrote the General Counsel, the DDO, the chief of the Latin American division, and the chief of the Central American Task Force that their memo didn't get at the issue he was after: "The question is not whether we can deal with other countries on intelligence matters with respect to the Sandinistas. It is whether the State Department or the NSC can legally go to other countries and suggest to them that they provide financial and/or paramilitary support to the Contras." Months after McFarlane had signed up the Saudis, it was just a tad late to be asking for a legal opinion.

The third approach, to get Congress to reconsider and again vote money for the Contras, was not as hopeless as it had appeared at the end of 1984. One of the enduring characteristics of Congress, especially on foreign affairs, is its eagerness to avoid clear-cut actions that will leave the Hill unambiguously responsible if something goes wrong, especially if they have acted contrary to the wishes of the President. Thus, because there was so little real disagreement over what the Cubans and Nicaraguans were doing in Central America, there was also great unease at having left the resistance high and dry. Accordingly, Congress was amenable to restoring some kind of help, even if it was only humanitarian.

In a meeting with McFarlane on March 20, 1985, Casey expressed concern that the administration was going to be content to seek nonlethal aid for the Contras, relying on third countries to supply either arms or money for arms. McMahon chimed in that next year the Congress would try to find out those countries that provided arms or dollars to the Contras and seek to cut off aid or arms sales to them. McFarlane agreed and said he would take it to the President and let him decide, "rather than have another meeting."

By April, new legislation to help the Contras until the new fiscal year was moving forward. As provision of humanitarian assistance became virtually inevitable, the next struggle by CIA was to beat back an effort by the House—at Speaker O'Neill's urging—to cut CIA out of the aid loop. Suspicion of CIA and of Casey was so high in the Congress that State was given responsibility for administering the humanitarian program, though the administration did manage to avoid provisions keeping CIA out altogether. So CIA ended up in a clearly supporting role. Thus it would remain for another fiscal year.

CASEY, CIA, AND CENTRAL AMERICA

U.S. policy in Central America and support for the Nicaraguan resistance would have been controversial even if CIA had done everything in the region and in Washington to perfection. There was real disagreement between many in Congress and the Reagan administration about how to deal with Soviet/Cuban assertiveness and Sandinista communism and interventionism in Central America. And there was continuing discomfort with some of our "friends and allies" in the area.

Casey's contempt of Congress and CIA's mistakes in running

the program, though, gave opponents of support to the Contras the opportunity to evade a direct confrontation with the administration on the gut issue of how to deal with communist interventionism in the region. Instead, the opposition was able to focus on CIA's conduct of the program, and that provided ample ammunition to attack the administration's broader efforts. CIA's sins of omission and commission were more lucrative and easier targets than the hard issue of what to do in Central America.

From the earliest days of the Contra program, Casey had worked outside of normal channels at CIA, establishing direct contact with lower-level officers in the clandestine service and often leaving the Deputy DCI and even the DDO in the dark as to what was going on. As Congress squeezed harder and harder on the CIA-run program, the DCI appears to have been the guiding hand in taking the entire administration Contra program off-line. He suggested to McFarlane in March 1984 the notion of a private "foundation" to support the Contras, and throughout 1984 fed him ideas and suggestions for third-country donors. And as CIA was steadily restricted from assisting and advising the Contras, Casey seems to have encouraged Ollie North to fill the gap in terms of operational guidance.

Although I had heard corridor conversation as Deputy Director for Intelligence about third-country help, virtually all of what I have described above was unknown to me until after Casey's death and the Iran-Contra investigations. Casey never spoke to me about these matters, perhaps because of the memos I already was sending him critical of CIA's management of the program. But he also was a pretty careful old operator. He knew how to run a secure operation—at least for a time. He was, however, running a great risk, jeopardizing the President, himself, and CIA.

Bill Casey's energy, inventiveness, boldness, and operational bent made possible the creation of an increasingly effective armed resistance to the Sandinista regime, a resistance that became preoccupying to the regime and a significant disruptive force in Nicaragua. Casey and those in the DO who helped him did what they had been asked to do, and probably better and quicker than anyone else could have done it. Casey helped keep the Contras alive as Congress turned against them.

But, in the end, well before Iran-Contra, his manner and methods were jeopardizing his considerable successes in Central

America. After the mining and the Tayacan manual, after too many briefings with too little credibility, after his repeated apologies wore thin, even congressional supporters began to walk away. Bill Casey ran a hell of an operation at CIA but, under his management, the overhead costs became very high.

CHAPTER SEVENTEEN
Passages: Last Gasp
of the Soviet Old Guard

THE BIGGEST CHALLENGE at home facing Andropov (and his successors) was the economy. He was aware that the spreading economic crisis was also generating a social—and potentially political—crisis as well. Thus Andropov was convinced of the need to combine firmness toward the population with significant changes in the economic mechanism. The real constraint: the leadership would not consider dismantling the command economy and replacing it with some kind of market socialism.

Just as Andropov's focus was primarily on the Soviet economy in 1983, so, too, did CIA devote great effort to assessing what was happening there.

A major CIA assessment issued in mid-1983 advised that the Soviet economic crisis had been substantially intensified and accelerated by several catastrophic mistakes made by the Soviet leadership since the mid-1970s. The most important error, leading to a remarkable and precipitate decline in industrial production, had been a decision in 1975 to stop massive investment in new plants and equipment and to tie the USSR's economic future to gains in efficiency and productivity—making existing resources produce more. The Agency concluded that the multitude of economic problems that had such a devastating impact on industrial growth from 1976 to 1982 would continue for the rest of the 1980s and might even intensify. Further, major systemic reforms that might provide a solution in the long run were "not yet on the leadership agenda."

Andropov's further plans for leadership change and for reviving the country were altered dramatically when, after less than four months in power, at the end of February 1983, his health failed. Andropov's condition worsened in late January 1984, and he died on February 9. Chernenko was confirmed as new General Secretary on February 13. Mikhail Gorbachev became head of the Party Secretariat (normally the second-ranking job in the Party) and the heir apparent. The old guard was departing. Two down, one to go.

1984: A YEAR OF CONFUSION

If 1983 was a year of tension, crisis, and danger in the U.S.-Soviet relationship, 1984 was a year of confusion. It was, in fact, a year of transition in both countries as personalities and factions within both the Soviet and American governments wrestled over the intentions of the other side, tried to interpret the adversary's internal debates and developments, and attempted to move—however crab-wise—beyond the confrontational approach that had dominated the relationship for nearly a decade.

The debate was especially intense in Moscow, where the debate over resources for the military took place against the backdrop of the mounting Soviet economic crisis. When Chernenko became General Secretary, he fairly consistently defended détente and argued for more resources for the domestic economy and consumer. He was not alone, but clearly there were powerful forces arrayed against him.

As the Soviet leaders faced the economic consequences of their massive military burden, CIA continued its decades-long effort to measure for American policymakers just how big that burden was. Many experts in and out of government believed that CIA's estimates understated the full cost of the Soviet military—and consequently also understated the burden it imposed on the Soviet economy and society.

As an analyst and then as Deputy Director for Intelligence, I was never comfortable with our estimates of Soviet military spending. As a noneconomist, nonstatistician, I was hard-pressed to quarrel with the methodology. But I did see the degree to which military needs dominated the Soviet economy and I believed instinctively that, in this communist variant of Sparta, the burden of military-related spending was far greater than the 14–16 percent of Soviet

Gross National Product that CIA was saying—perhaps somewhere between 25 and 40 percent.

In any event, CIA had been in hot water with Weinberger and Defense since early 1983, when we first reported our judgment that the rate of growth in Soviet military procurement had leveled off, i.e., they were still buying weapons but not as many as before. In the midst of a huge U.S. military buildup that engendered vigorous debate in the Congress and media, the last thing Weinberger needed was CIA analysis that suggested Soviet defense spending was slowing. Worse yet, we said that there had been little or no real growth in Soviet military procurement spending since 1976.

Our analysis was so at odds with the political agenda of the administration that I was treated to repeated lectures at Defense and the White House on the problems we were creating with this analysis. We never backed off one iota, but I was frustrated both because of my own skepticism over our estimates of Soviet military spending, and because I saw members of Congress as well as senior administration officials misusing—and abusing—our analysis, citing it out of context to support their particular agenda. Surprise! Surprise! The problems associated with this arcane but politically sensitive analysis would dog CIA to the end of the Soviet Union and beyond.

THE THIRD WORLD: REAGAN AND CASEY TURN UP THE HEAT

In a year of mixed signals and confusion in terms of future directions of the superpower relationship, there was one unambiguous element: Casey, with some surprising allies, would intensify the pressures on the Soviet Union and its surrogates in the Third World. This expansion of the "Third World" war was replicated on nearly every front.

AFGHANISTAN. Nineteen eighty-four marked a major turning point in the U.S. covert program to assist the Mujahedin in Afghanistan. U.S. help in the preceding five years had been modest, involving several tens of millions of dollars each year. Partly this had been due to a cautious approach by the clandestine service, partly because Pakistani President Zia was reluctant to challenge the Soviets too aggressively, partly because of a U.S. desire to keep the program covert and deniable, and partly because some in the U.S. government were apprehensive that a significantly larger program would provoke the Soviets into a massive reinforcement and result in a terrible slaughter of the Mujahedin. All of these considerations would change in 1984, but the catalyst was not Soviet, or Pakistani, or Afghan, or Ronald Reagan, or even Casey. Rather, the catalyst was a tall, lanky congressman from East Texas, Charlie Wilson. Charlie's motives were fairly uncomplicated—in circumstances where the United States had international opinion and a good cause going for it, he wanted to kill Soviets.

Politically, Charlie was exquisitely placed to get his way in seeking a big increase in covert U.S. support in Afghanistan—he was a senior Democrat on the Defense Appropriations Subcommittee of the House Appropriations Committee. What Charlie knew was that a well-placed Democratic member of the House sitting on the Appropriations Committee who happened to care deeply about an issue could get about anything he wanted. And Charlie wanted $40 million more for the Mujahedin.

One fly in the ointment was that Charlie didn't much like the man in charge of the CIA Afghan program, the chief of the Near East division, Charles Cogan. Cogan was a very capable career operations officer who was quite experienced in Middle East affairs. He had worked and lived in the region for much of his career. But he was from the old school in the DO in the sense that he sought to keep the Afghan program unattributable to the United States, he was sensitive to Pakistani views, and he didn't much relish an outsider from East Texas telling him how to fight an insurgent war in the mountains of Afghanistan.

Chuck Cogan had another strike against him in dealing with Wilson. Chuck was an Errol Flynn lookalike, suave, sophisticated, multilingual, with a thin mustache and a faint mark on his cheek that looked for all the world like a dueling scar; he and Charles Wilson seemed to come from two different worlds. And the chemistry between them was bad. Wilson just steamrollered Cogan—and CIA for that matter.

Wilson believed that CIA's cautious strategy simply would bleed the Afghans (along with the Soviets) until the resistance crumbled. The first step to changing the balance, he thought, was greater firepower and an enhanced antiaircraft capability for the Mujahedin.

Even as Wilson was pushing a $40 million increase in funding for these purposes through Congress, Casey traveled to the Middle East where Pakistan's President Zia raised with him in February the possibility of a "sharp increase" in the volume of arms for the Mujahedin. Also, while Casey was in Saudi Arabia, his hosts agreed to raise their contribution to $75 million for fiscal year 1984 and to go to $100 million in 1985. This commitment now required the United States to increase its own contribution by a total of $50 million—not including Wilson's $40 million transfer from Defense. There was another big increase in spending in the fall of 1984. On October 11, Casey proposed to the Saudis that each country provide $250 million for the next year to handle larger Soviet offensives expected in the spring and to bring increasing pressure on the Soviets—an increase of $150 million over 1984. This was a huge jump. Two weeks later, Casey sent word to the Pakistanis and Saudis that the United States was planning to spend $250 million in fiscal 1985, and was committing $175 million immediately. By the end of the year, Wilson was urging that the U.S. contribution go to $300 million for 1985, even as we were struggling to get to the $250 million mark.

In sum, the character of U.S. policy toward Afghanistan changed dramatically in 1984. Thanks mainly to pressure from Charlie Wilson and Casey's embrace of his support, during the course of calendar year 1984, the size of CIA's covert program to help the Mujahedin increased several times over. During that year, Zia opened the floodgates, taking his chances with Soviet retaliation (and there was a substantial increase in attacks from Afghanistan across the Pakistani border). Further, owing to initiatives from State and Defense, the very purpose of the U.S. program was changed by presidential directive—from increasing the costs to the Soviets to trying to win. Defense put up most of the money. But it was CIA and its clandestine service that took all of this and made it work.

LIBYA. Qaddafi had a busy 1984. On March 16, he carried out a bombing attack against broadcasting facilities near Khartoum, Sudan. It was a kind of hapless affair, involving a single bomber that panicked a lot of Sudanese but did little physical damage. About the same time, he was upping the ante elsewhere in Africa, including an attempt to negotiate a $2 billion loan to Nigeria in exchange for Nigeria's help against Chad and for Ethiopia in its anti-Sudanese efforts. Again, little came of these efforts, but they stirred up Washington.

More seriously, on April 17, Libyans at the Libyan People's Bureau (Embassy) in London provoked a violent confrontation with

British police, during which a policewoman monitoring a demonstration at the People's Bureau was killed. We learned through intelligence sources of Qaddafi's support for this criminal action, including his direction to the People's Bureau to "mobilize the whole revolutionary force, to use all means to go after stray dogs and turn Britain into hell if stray dogs go ahead with [anti-Libyan] demonstrations."

Then, on July 6, a Libyan team of frogmen operating off a cargo ship, the *Ghat*, mined parts of the Red Sea, specifically, in the Gulf of Suez and near the Bab al-Mandeb Strait. In all, nineteen ships were damaged by the mines. Proving Qaddafi's responsibility for the mining was an important CIA success and a classic story of good collection combined with experienced and insightful analysis.

From early 1981 forward, the Reagan administration never abandoned its efforts to block Qaddafi abroad, challenge him militarily, and overthrow him. After the attack on Sudan and the mine-laying by the *Ghat*, CIA intensified its efforts—under way now for some three years—to identify Libyan economic, military, and political vulnerabilities and ways in which they might be exploited.

CAMBODIA. By 1984, five years after Vietnam's invasion, Hanoi had still been unable to deal the Cambodian resistance a decisive defeat. CIA's covert assistance was aimed at building up the political and organizational structure of the noncommunist resistance and setting up broadcast propaganda and information programs. By law, CIA was excluded from providing lethal assistance. The program for fiscal 1984 was $5 million.

The Cambodian covert action was unique in that senior State officials by 1984 were continually pressing us to expand the program. When Casey briefed the NSC on covert action in the Oval Office on March 6, Shultz again spoke up on behalf of more help for the Cambodian resistance. Casey returned to the Agency, called the comptroller, and received assurances that CIA could provide another $2 million. Casey wrote McMahon, "I'm inclined to do that." But State's appetite was large. When the paperwork increasing the Cambodian program finally reached State in July, Shultz told Casey that CIA ought to "think big." I suspect this was one of the few instances in which Shultz urged Casey to become more involved and increase a covert action. Casey did add some money to the program, but he never was an enthusiast for it. He was willing to keep his hand in, but he thought it was money down a rathole.

By the end of 1984, Casey's covert war in the Third World against the Soviet Union and its surrogates was in full swing. Except in Central America, resources were growing, sometimes phenomenally so. As the debate between Chernenko and others in the Soviet leadership raged over future U.S. intentions and the future of the bilateral relationship, Bill Casey's worldwide campaign against the USSR had to be chalked up as an argument for those in Moscow insisting that Reagan's peaceful rhetoric was a ruse and that the United States truly sought to roll back Soviet gains—both militarily and in the Third World.

THE YEAR OF SHULTZ AND GROMYKO

Against a backdrop of leadership politicking in the Kremlin (not to mention in Washington), debates there over resources, and continued competition in the military arena and the Third World, the Soviet and American governments groped through much of 1984 for an opening that might ease tensions and reassure their respective publics. The Soviet side was dominated by Gromyko, who was at the height of his influence and power.

On the U.S. side, the internal battle—especially between Shultz and Weinberger—would rage throughout the year. As usual, Shultz saw himself very much the lonely voice of reason, isolated and embattled against Defense, CIA, and the NSC. It is clear though, at least in retrospect, that Shultz had already won the internecine war. Sure, he would still have to drive the government forward in its relationship with the USSR and there would be continuing argument, press attacks, leaks, and the flak associated with bureaucratic warfare in Washington. And he would lose on disputes over tactics and timing from time to time. But the Secretary of State was clearly in tune with the views and aspirations of the President, as well as the views of others in the White House, who saw Shultz's approach as also serving the President's best interests in his campaign for reelection.

Finally, at least in Reagan's mind, the impression of American political and military weakness had been erased, and he now believed it was possible and desirable to reap the diplomatic harvest of the U.S. military buildup and global effort to hamstring the USSR. As a result, for all the shouting and for all of Shultz's complaining, the Secretary of State would win virtually every significant argument over how to deal with the Soviets from September 1983 on.

Tentative and cautious probes by each side early in 1984 were, however, overwhelmed by other events. From the Soviet point of view, in the first half of 1984, the United States engaged in the talk of peace but acts of confrontation—the damaging of a Soviet tanker and injury to its crew by American mines off Nicaragua; U.S. escalation of its support to the Afghan resistance and other anti-Soviet forces around the world; and U.S. "in your face" military reconnaissance and exercise activity. Meanwhile, the list of worrisome Soviet actions—especially in the military sphere during the first half of 1984 (described in Chapter 15)—made nearly everyone in the U.S. government skeptical of Soviet intentions. Except Shultz.

The Soviet leadership, in early summer 1984, finally recognized that their walkout from START and INF negotiations and their refusal to engage the administration was hurting the USSR far more than the United States—and indeed was helping Ronald Reagan at home. After an opening gambit by the Soviets, the two sides went back and forth during July on the question of resuming arms control negotiations. While ultimately nothing was agreed at that point, the maneuvering showed that each side saw getting back to the table as in its interest—as long as any negotiation was framed in a satisfactory manner. And this set the stage for a long-awaited breakthrough.

Reagan's personal and decisive role at key junctures in U.S. policy toward the Soviet Union during this period was unknown at the time and would have been disbelieved if a White House spokesman had claimed it. Nonetheless, this role was demonstrated again in mid-August, when Shultz told him of indications from the Soviet side that Gromyko might be interested in a meeting with Reagan in Washington in September, when the Foreign Minister was in New York for the UN General Assembly. Shultz put the question to Reagan in a highly tentative way, making clear he was not making a recommendation. According to Shultz's memoirs, Reagan immediately responded that he wanted to have such a meeting.

This would be Gromyko's first meeting with a President since the invasion of Afghanistan in 1979 and his first ever with Reagan. The conservatives in the administration were scared to death at what Reagan might do. Thus the NSC meeting on September 18, some ten days before the encounter, was an important confrontation in its own way. I accompanied Casey.

Casey's opening briefing was surprisingly positive. He reviewed a litany of Soviet woes at home and around the world and observed that they "lacked the creativity, energy or wit to get out of any of these boxes." Casey urged the President to use the meeting and the UN session to lay out an "essentially positive" approach focusing on the future and on arms control. The President should acknowledge that all weapons systems could be considered in negotiations, but should make no specific suggestions and recommendations and agree to no moratoriums.

During the discussion, Shultz got too ambitious, even for the President. His opening remarks about pursuing linked offensive and defensive weapons negotiations were sensible, but he quickly moved to arguing in favor of a concrete proposal and seeking an interim agreement. This time, he *was* utterly isolated. Reagan finally spoke, saying he would not get into specifics with Gromyko, that negotiating specifics in an atmosphere of mutual distrust had been tried. The Soviets had ideological objectives, but there was for them also an element of suspicion and fear of the outside world. He wanted to get into a general discussion and clear the air—that neither side could really gain an advantage, that neither should be a threat to the other. When Weinberger then said that the President should talk, but from strength, Reagan gently but firmly put the Secretary of Defense in his place: "We must follow the Gromyko meeting with specifics and make concessions."

Gromyko's September 1984 meetings with Shultz in New York and Washington and his meeting with Reagan really didn't accomplish much, except to reestablish an earlier pattern of regular contacts at the highest levels that, in turn, conveyed the message that the two superpowers finally were reengaging. Reagan gave a very conciliatory speech at the UN (not reciprocated by Gromyko). That speech, together with his encounter with Gromyko, took the edge off the U.S.-Soviet relationship as a political issue in the U.S. election campaign. But more than that, it marked an important step in Reagan's own approach to the Soviets.

After the September meeting in Washington, momentum began to build. As a result of follow-on talks between Shultz and Gromyko in January 1985, the two sides agreed to convene negotiations on START, INF, and space on March 12. Two days before, on March 10, Konstantin Chernenko had died.

Reagan and Chernenko had both hoped to change the direction of the relationship, but the actions of each government—especially through August 1984—reinforced lingering concerns of the other and made it hard to move. Reagan's aspirations for the relationship tended to collide inopportunely with his equally strong belief that the Soviet system was inherently aggressive and historically doomed. The latter theme in his public statements, at least from the Soviet perspective, made it hard for them to take his loftier hopes for the relationship seriously. This Soviet suspicion and quest for recognition of equality was intensified by the blatant American triumphalism that was so manifest at the Los Angeles Olympics and so integral to Reagan's reelection campaign.

Only when it became apparent to the entire Soviet leadership that their current policies were self-defeating was the willingness to reengage expressed by Chernenko permitted to go forward. By the time he died, the stage had been set for his successor to attempt to get the USSR out of its many foreign policy blind alleys and, in so doing, try to obtain foreign help for the Soviet Union's desperate crisis. It was a tall order but, at long last, both sides would be ready to move forward at the same time.

CHAPTER EIGHTEEN

1985: Reagan and Gorbachev—
the Best of Enemies

CIA AND THE GORBACHEV ASCENSION

CIA had been enthusiastic about Gorbachev since he emerged as Andropov's protégé early in 1983. We knew a lot about him. Even so, it took us several years to understand him—to grasp his boldness and courage, but also the contradictions to the man and the limits to his boldness and courage, and to his vision. We overestimated him in important respects and underestimated him in others just as important. Years later, some of his rightist opponents would allege that he and his buddy Yakovlev had been CIA agents. They weren't, and it's a good thing. We could not possibly have guided him to engineer so successfully the destruction of the Soviet empire.

CIA's enthusiasm over Gorbachev was, needless to say, a curious phenomenon. There were several reasons underlying our interest in him rising to the top. First, we grasped the magnitude of the political, economic, and social crisis in the Soviet Union. The twin dangers of chaos and a possible desperate military lunge for an economic lifeline or diversion from problems at home were a concern. Accession at last of a leader who was prepared to make tough decisions to address that crisis was to be welcomed by the United States.

Second, CIA analysts were convinced that the Soviet economic crisis could not be attacked effectively without significant reductions in expenditures on the military, and many were persuaded that Gorbachev would eventually face up to this reality. Third, CIA professionals were no more immune than other Americans to the feeling that the U.S.-Soviet confrontation had gotten a bit too hot in recent years. A new leadership that might cool things down, and back off around the world, in order to focus on domestic problems —with the help of the West—was to be welcomed.

Finally, after long years of watching every move of a group of aging, colorless, uninteresting Soviet leaders, here was one of flesh and blood, of energy and action, of emotion, a man seemingly determined to change things.

Even so, we had no illusions about Gorbachev. We knew that he had risen to prominence as a standard communist functionary, first in Stavropol, then in Moscow. Party ideologist Mikhail Suslov and KGB Chairman Yuri Andropov—especially the latter—had been instrumental in advancing Gorbachev's career. Gorbachev was appointed party secretary for agriculture in November 1978 and just a year later became a candidate member of the Politburo. He was selected as a full member a year after that, in October 1980. He was forty-nine.

Just as Khrushchev and Brezhnev before him, Gorbachev, too, would not suffer for his failures in the agricultural arena. In fact, during the first four years—1979–1982—that he was Party Secretary for Agriculture, there were four successive bad harvests, resulting in huge purchases of grain abroad. In 1981, Reagan helped the Soviets out of a tough spot by lifting the American grain embargo imposed by Jimmy Carter. The situation was so bad that Gorbachev's performance and his political future almost certainly would have been unfavorably scrutinized at a Central Committee plenum scheduled for November 17, 1982, but Brezhnev's death a week before—and the succession of Gorbachev's patron, Andropov, as General Secretary—saved him. Had Brezhnev lived just two or three more weeks, the whole course of history might have been changed.

We in CIA were convinced early on that Gorbachev would succeed Chernenko. On February 5, 1985, we told the President that the two likely successors to Chernenko were Gorbachev and Romanov (the Leningrad Communist Party chief), with Gorbachev the clear front-runner. We described him as the most pragmatic, most open to fresh approaches to Soviet economic problems. He had little experience in foreign policy, but a demonstrated ability to project an image of flexibility without departing from long-established Soviet positions. We then wrote of the potential for change under Gorbachev: "If Gorbachev is chosen, it could lead to the emergence of a more articulate, self-confident brand of Soviet leadership. He might push for more innovative solutions to Soviet economic problems and greater flexibility and initiative in dealing with opportunities and challenges abroad."

Early in 1985 we also worked to provide policymakers some insight into what Gorbachev might be like. As DDI, I was concerned that we were too captivated by the public Gorbachev we had seen in Canada and Great Britain. Some of the initial draft intelligence assessments on his personality and likely positions on issues read like campaign flyers. What worried me was that we were missing something fundamental about Gorbachev—the toughness, the "iron teeth" that went with the "nice smile," as Gromyko was rumored to have described him. After all, the protégé of Andropov and Suslov could not be all sweetness and light. These had been two of the hardest cases in recent Soviet history. They would not take a wimp under their wing.

I wrote one of our leading Soviet experts, Bob Blackwell, on February 6, 1985, more than a month before Chernenko died: "I don't much care for the way we are writing about Gorbachev. We are losing the thread of what toughness and skill brought him to where he is. This is not some Soviet Gary Hart or even Lee Iacocca. We have to give the policymakers a clearer view of the kind of person they may be facing."

A succession that we in CIA viewed as a coronation was, apparently, a down-and-dirty political struggle between the old Brezhnev faction and the Andropov faction, led by Gorbachev. The latter obviously won. But the nature of his victory was important. No one who helped make him General Secretary owed him anything. Gromyko, whose support for Gorbachev was critical, was independent, and Gorbachev's other Politburo supporters were all Andropov appointees or protégés—like himself. Thus, while Gorbachev may have come to power as the bearer of people's hopes that at last the country had a healthy, able leader who could tackle its problems in traditional Soviet terms, he also came to power with less experience at or near the top of the party than any of his predecessors, and with virtually no Politburo members beholden to him.

Much of what CIA knew in 1985 about Gorbachev's personality and style was from his visit to Canada in 1983 and his visit to Britain in December 1984, where he had been such a hit with Prime

Minister Thatcher. We were embarrassingly hungry for details from our Canadian and British colleagues as well as for the observations of those politicians and others who had spent time with Gorbachev. In both cases, his substantive positions on issues were quite unyielding and followed the official line without any real deviation. But, as we first learned from the visit to Canada, here was a Soviet leader willing to listen, to engage in give and take, who was eager to observe and learn, and who was more skillful than virtually any of his colleagues in defending Soviet positions and in responding to criticisms. His conduct was unremarkable for a Western politician. For a member of the Soviet leadership, it was an unprecedented tour de force.

The same was true in Britain, where he was seen as the likely successor to Chernenko and therefore was more subject to public scrutiny, including on television. He did not disappoint his audiences, abroad or at home—though his colleagues probably were not pleased at his grandstanding and favorable acclaim.

In sum, CIA generally believed that Gorbachev had come to power with broad support and a strong mandate to attack the problems facing the USSR, even though there was no consensus on how to do that. In reality, although specific accounts differ, most now agree that his elevation was contested and that there was no clear mandate. Further, he faced a Politburo half of which comprised old Brezhnev cronies and the other half independent political figures, the newest of whom owed their rapid promotions to Andropov, not Gorbachev. The Central Committee continued to be dominated overwhelmingly by people appointed in the Brezhnev years.

CIA's View of Gorbachev's Agenda

Gorbachev was an innovative, dynamic communist, not a revolutionary. He had chaired various study commissions for Andropov on needed changes and reforms in the economy and society. Yet, while he clearly had ideas and programs, it would soon become apparent that Gorbachev had no strategy. In domestic affairs, Gorbachev was truly a communist believer. He believed that the state created by Lenin was fundamentally distorted and perverted by Stalin and his successors, and that with the right political approach, it could all be fixed—within the framework of a communist state. His view of this, especially with respect to the economy, never changed.

Gorbachev began in March 1985 where Andropov had left off a year earlier. His first policies were restoration of Andropov's vigorous anticorruption and antialcohol campaigns, reassertion of the campaign for greater discipline in the workplace, and rejuvenation of the party through personnel changes. New technology was seen as the key to fixing many economic problems.

As we look back from a post-Soviet vantage point and see how far Gorbachev went to change the system, it is essential to remember that he never intended to go so far. He started modestly and cautiously, and only as one series of moves failed to produce results did he take another step, and then another.... His approach was evolutionary, and I suspect that if he could have seen even in 1985 how far he would be driven or drawn in just two or three years, his approach might well have been very different. He never intended to bring down the system that had brought him to the pinnacle of power.

CIA's first comprehensive look at the new leader's policies was a paper done by the Soviet office in mid-June 1985, "Gorbachev, the New Broom." Casey sent it to the President on June 27. It began with the statement that "Gorbachev is gambling that an attack on corruption and inefficiency, not radical reform, will turn the domestic situation around.... It is his no-holds-barred approach to confronting chronic domestic problems that underscores his new style as a leader." He made clear that his policies were justified by the foreign and domestic problems facing the USSR, and he studded his speeches with language evoking the image of a crisis, a turning point. He warned that accelerating economic growth was imperative due to the need to sustain then-current levels of consumption "while making the investments in defense required by current international tensions."

Our paper to Reagan underscored that Gorbachev's first priority was to push his domestic economic program, but we also pointed out the limitations to his approach. "While some Soviet officials have indicated he is sympathetic to the use of pragmatic methods, including tapping private initiative, his statements and actions underscore his overall commitment to the current economic system and his determination to make it work better."

In foreign policy, we told Reagan that Gorbachev's impact up to that point had been pretty much stylistic, in part because he had no urgent agenda to match his ambitions at home. A variety of sources, we reported, had told us that Gorbachev was not disposed to concessions in arms control, and intended to expand previous efforts to drive wedges between the United States and its allies. Still others told us that Gorbachev was taking a tough line also with the Warsaw Pact. Finally, we advised that Gorbachev's early actions had suggested strong support for key Third World allies. Specifically, Soviet forces in Afghanistan were pursuing the more aggressive tactics we had begun to see in 1984, and Gorbachev met with Nicaragua's Daniel Ortega and promised increased oil deliveries only days after the U.S. Congress turned down Reagan's request for aid to the Contras.

Casey's cover note forwarding this paper to Reagan had a different tone than the analysis. He wrote that Gorbachev and those around him "are not reformers and liberalizers either in Soviet domestic or foreign policy." He told Reagan that the Soviets had to be convinced that the "original Reagan agenda is here to stay: revived U.S. military power, revived alliance leadership, revived engagement in regional security matters, and a revived ideological challenge to the inhuman features of the Soviet system." Casey concluded with a policy prescription that went far beyond the intelligence analysis he was forwarding and beyond what was appropriate for a DCI. He said: "Achieving this Soviet conviction against the doubts that are accumulating in Moscow will require political victories for your policy agenda in the Congress, the U.S. public, and the Alliance. It will require skill and adherence to a durable strategic concept in dealing with all the issues that attach to the U.S.-Soviet superpower struggle. For that, more discipline, persistent and active articulation of our purpose and implementation of policies and initiatives is a necessary condition."

While many of us in CIA—though by no means all—agreed with Casey's appraisal of Soviet motives and strategy, his personally drafted cover notes, such as that quoted above, talking points, and letters did not offer any balance or pretense of objectivity. His transparent advocacy pleased Weinberger, infuriated Shultz, and antagonized others. All in all, there was no line between policy advocacy and intelligence for Bill Casey.

Thus CIA was more than a little schizophrenic during this period, and I more than most. As Deputy Director for Intelligence, I strongly supported the analysts when they had unwelcome information for policymakers, whether to Shultz on Angola or to Weinberger on reductions in the rate of spending on the Soviet military, the Soviets' changed approach to chemical warfare, or new, lower estimates on Soviet nuclear tests, and more. I authorized publication and dissemination of all these and many other controversial assessments without seeking Casey's approval, although in several cases I informed him in advance and warned him to expect trouble. He never saw most of what the DI published until after it was in the hands of senior policymakers, including the *President's Daily Brief*, sent each day not only to Reagan, but also to Bush, Shultz, Weinberger, Crowe, and McFarlane. Despite later allegations that I slanted the DI's work to support Reagan administration policy (Shultz's? Weinberger's? McFarlane's?), the documentary record shows that the Directorate of Intelligence during this period preserved its objectivity and its integrity. We were honest, even if we were not always right.

Life was more complicated and I was much less in control in my second job as chairman of the National Intelligence Council, the group that produces all the national intelligence estimates and represents the entire intelligence community, not just CIA. Traditionally, DCIs often have involved themselves deeply in the preparation of national intelligence estimates. In fact, for many years, DCIs signed the cover page, and the estimates were considered to be the DCI's estimate. Schlesinger and Colby had been active participants in the estimates process, and Turner had been deeply involved in the substantive presentation and conclusions of estimates, especially on strategic forces. So Casey's active engagement was neither unusual nor inappropriate.

Yet he rode the process hard, pushed his own views, and was often very tough for people to deal with or talk to. Under these circumstances, I regarded it as my job to try to ensure that different points of view—including from CIA—were included, to try to resolve interagency disputes or issues that seemed of marginal importance, and to soothe NIOs, analysts, and other agencies offended by either Casey or one of the "outsiders" he appointed to the Council. (When Casey appointed me to the additional position of chairman of the Council, some on the outside thought one person should not be the head of the Council and also head of CIA's analytical component. They were right.)

The old Cold Warrior's skepticism of Gorbachev in June 1985, and his worry that the administration was letting down its guard too soon in response to everyone's hopes of what Gorbachev intended, were based on the actions the new leader had taken in his first few months: more resources for the military, new offensives in

Angola and Afghanistan, and little action at home other than a new, more open tone. Casey, and others of us, would eventually be proved too cautious about Gorbachev's moves to withdraw in foreign policy and to make the USSR more democratic (under Communist Party rule). But our caution during 1985–1987 was consistent with his deeds at the time. It would be to Reagan's credit —with Shultz's support—that he remained tough-minded and skeptical about how far Gorbachev might (or could) go, but was prepared to provide an opening if the new Soviet leader showed flexibility.

WASHINGTON TAKES GORBACHEV'S MEASURE

The general reaction to Gorbachev by virtually all of Reagan's seniormost advisers, including Shultz, in the spring of 1985 was positive but wary. As Ronald Reagan wrote—more honestly than some of those around him—in his memoirs: "I can't claim that I believed from the start that Mikhail Gorbachev was going to be a different sort of Soviet leader." Clearly, however, he was going to be a more difficult adversary than his three dying predecessors over the past thirty-six months.

In reality, there was very little difference at the outset among the various senior officials of the Reagan administration about Gorbachev. He had been an outspoken defender of resources for the military. There was nothing in his speeches to suggest anything less than an aggressive approach in the Third World. He was a protégé of Andropov's, and we knew what kind of relationship we had with the Soviets under him. A new and more innovative approach to dealing with internal problems did not necessarily translate into a similar approach on foreign policy—and it wouldn't for some time.

Shultz, in his memoirs, is openly derisive not only of CIA's analysis of Gorbachev but also of his own Soviet experts at the State Department. Writing about the run-up to Gorbachev's selection as General Secretary, he said, "Our knowledge of the Kremlin was thin, and the CIA, I found, was usually wrong about it." In fact, although CIA (and I personally) would later have serious differences with Shultz about Gorbachev and developments in the Soviet Union, there was a remarkable harmony of views during this early period of Gorbachev's tenure. We had a tough new challenger, but also an interesting one—one with whom eventually progress might be made. That remained to be seen. We all knew, though, that a new era had begun.

EARLY GORBACHEV: REAL CHANGE OR WISHFUL THINKING?

From a post-Soviet, post–Cold War perspective, from perfect hindsight, everything about the Soviet Union seems to have changed with Gorbachev's succession, especially in foreign policy. In reality, for some time, very little changed, except that the Soviet Union had a new, more imaginative, more vigorous leader whose effectiveness and skill were, at least at the outset, undoubtedly over-dramatized in no small measure simply because of the contrast with his three predecessors.

How people in Washington viewed Gorbachev in his early days as General Secretary depended a great deal on where they worked, their own political philosophy, and how much they knew about Russian and Soviet history. Shultz, for example, was pretty realistic about Gorbachev as a dedicated communist who intended to fix—not replace—the system. At the same time, the Secretary had a diplomatic agenda that needed a pragmatic political operator on the Soviet side with similar priorities and a determination to change fundamentally the direction of Soviet foreign policy. Sure enough, that was the Gorbachev he found. Casey, Weinberger, and most Soviet experts in and out of government looked at continuing Soviet actions around the world, the continuing growth of Soviet defense programs, continuing instances of outrageous Soviet be-havior, and the continuities in Russian and Soviet history and found in all these realities a Gorbachev who was simply a new and more clever and subtle proponent of Soviet global imperialism abroad and communism at home. That's what I thought, too. Funnily enough, for some time we were all more or less right because Gorbachev showed us all of these different faces.

THE SOVIET MILITARY JUGGERNAUT ROLLS ON

In many respects, Soviet actions and Gorbachev's approach early on lent credence to the concerns of Reagan administration conservatives. Most importantly, the arrival of a new leader in a Soviet Union enmeshed in deep economic crisis produced no dis-cernible reduction in military research and development, production, force deployments, or spending. Gorbachev would do little during his first three and a half years in power to challenge the inertia of huge military programs approved years before or to reduce the level of military spending. Nineteen eighty-five saw the Soviet Union deploy the SS-25 mobile ICBM; flight-test a rail-launched ICBM, the SS-X-24; continue follow-on programs for the next generation of ICBMs; begin deployment of a modernized ballistic missile submarine, with a new, longer-range, and more accurate missile soon to follow; develop a new air defense fighter; make new advances in precision-guided munitions; launch the first of a new class of aircraft carrier; and test two new kinds of attack submarines, one of which used a new kind of polymer coating on the bow to give it greater speed and on the propeller screws for quieting.

GORBACHEV AND THE THIRD WORLD: GOOD MONEY AFTER BAD

Years later, we would learn—or be told—that one or another turning point had been reached or decision had been made by Gorbachev in 1985 to resolve the conflict in Afghanistan or settle in Nicaragua, or to pull back from conflicts in the Third World. In some cases, this is plausible, in some it probably is true. Even so, no one detected a slackening of Soviet efforts at the time. Quite the contrary.

In Afghanistan in 1985, the Soviets intensified the conflict, pouring in additional assistance for the Afghan government and turning to more aggressive tactics against the Mujahedin. This more aggressive Soviet approach, when combined with the significant increase in our assistance to the Mujahedin during this period, resulted in a significant intensification of the war in Afghanistan in 1985.

The Soviets also cranked up the action in Angola. The Soviets became deeply involved in combat operations, and directed Angolan-Cuban forces in more than one large engagement. So massive and so threatening was their offensive that the South Africans reentered the conflict in substantial numbers and the U.S. Congress reversed the decade-long ban on U.S. covert assistance to Savimbi.

Similarly, in Nicaragua, even as CIA's support to the Contras was increasingly restricted by Congress, and then ended altogether, the Soviets and Cubans tried to build the Sandinistas' advantage with more weapons and equipment and more direct involvement in combat operations. Here, too, their efforts were so blatant as to begin to turn the tide of congressional opinion once again toward help for the Contras.

As CIA's reporting of these "on-the-ground" realities continued through 1985, this portrayal of an even more aggressive Soviet approach to Third World conflict under Gorbachev was increasingly in conflict with Shultz's agenda with the Soviets, in particular the dialogue over regional issues. He accused us of undermining his diplomacy in both Angola and Mozambique, and of pursuing our own agenda.

With Casey's approval, I wanted to set the record straight with Shultz that our analysts were offering their own independent judgments, and had no separate agenda. I had a message delivered directly to the Secretary on December 6, 1985, by way of the *President's Daily Brief*, asking to meet with him to discuss his problems and concerns with our analytical support.

We met on January 9, 1986. I was ushered into his large formal outer office a little after 4:30 P.M., and we settled into two large chairs in front of a roaring fire in the fireplace. I realized almost immediately that I was in serious danger of being roasted twice— once by the Secretary of State and again by his fire. We talked for an hour, covering CIA's analysis of the world, but always coming back to Angola. I tried to explain to him distinctions that mattered greatly to intelligence professionals—between CIA analysis, interagency intelligence estimates and the DCI's role in them, and what the DCI said in meetings at the White House and in his own memos. I stressed that what he read on Angola was the unfettered view of the analysts, and that neither the clandestine service nor Casey meddled with what was said. Nor were their views affected by a covert action CIA might have under way. I described CIA's structure and the differing cultures of the clandestine service and the analysts and the rivalries that existed, and explained that the monolithic, single-minded bureaucratic organism he believed was continually trying to pursue its own policies—and undermine him —did not exist. He went through his criticisms and complaints. It was a long, cordial, serious discussion. I suspect no senior CIA official and Secretary of State had ever had a conversation like it. Unfortunately, I don't think I made a dent in his growing distrust of CIA. But we would talk again.

A KILLING IN GERMANY

Just two weeks after Gorbachev became General Secretary, the Soviet campaign to challenge the Western position in Berlin exploded politically when a Soviet sentry on March 24 shot Major Arthur D. Nicholson, a member of the U.S. Military Liaison Mission. (Under informal, reciprocal ground rules, the U.S., British, French, and Soviet Military Liaison Missions carried out intelligence gathering in much of Germany—the three Western allies in the East. Both sides would from time to time act quite boldly and even aggressively in seeking information.) As Nicholson lay on the ground severely wounded, the Soviets refused to render assistance and allowed him to bleed to death. Everyone was furious at the Soviets, but Weinberger demanded that there be no meetings or other contacts with the Soviets until they had apologized and promised compensation to the family. Shultz, no less outraged, angrily protested to Dobrynin—but also was insistent that the tragedy not derail the overall effort to resolve bilateral problems and pursue arms control. It was the first major test of Shultz's desire to eliminate "linkage" in the relationship. Once again, Reagan leaned toward Shultz, especially after the Soviets grudgingly issued orders to their sentries in East Germany not to use "deadly force" against Americans.

THE SECRET SOVIET TERROR CAMPAIGN

We also learned in March 1985 about a Soviet effort to target U.S. servicemen in West Germany for terrorist attacks that shocked us all. According to information from Soviet sources, Soviet agents had been assigned the task of locating dead-drop sites—hiding places for information being transmitted to and from agents—inside bars and restaurants near American military installations in West German cities. The purpose of these sites, however, was not for dead drops, but for hiding explosive devices that would be set off in a way to make them look like terrorist attacks. The sites included behind vending machines, in a ventilation cavity under a sink, in a bathroom stall over the windowsill, on a wooden beam over a lavatory, under the bottom of a paper-towel dispenser, and so on. CIA checked out fourteen of these reported sites and confirmed the existence of all but one, just as reported. And every location was filled with U.S. servicemen or dependents or was known to be frequented by U.S. and NATO servicemen. We later concluded that the targeting had been done in 1983, probably in connection with the very aggressive Soviet campaign against deployment of the INF missiles.

Casey passed all of this information on to the President, Bush, Shultz, Weinberger, and McFarlane. Needless to say, although the targeting apparently had taken place perhaps two years earlier, the "hawks" in the administration thought that such Soviet ruthlessness was so deeply ingrained that it was unlikely to be significantly moderated merely by succession of a new General Secretary.

SOVIET PERCEPTIONS OF THE UNITED STATES: NO BETTER

If we detected little change in Soviet actions in the military arena or the Third World, the Soviets could have said the same about us.

• On February 1, 1985, the Reagan administration issued another report on Soviet noncompliance with arms control agreements, highlighting their cheating.

• On February 22, three weeks before Gorbachev became General Secretary, Shultz (the administration "moderate") gave a speech in San Francisco in which he spelled out the real content of the "Reagan Doctrine": insurgencies fighting against communist domination across the globe would have American help.

• On March 19, the Senate approved deployment of the MX missile, followed by the House the next day.

• In June, the United States took action to reduce the number of Soviet diplomats in the United States and the number of Soviets working for our embassy in Moscow.

• Reagan decided in June that the United States would adhere to the terms of the expiring SALT II treaty but only provisionally and only after an acrimonious and public debate.

• On August 8, the Congress repealed the 1975 Clark Amendment prohibiting aid to Savimbi in Angola.

• Through the summer, the administration debated whether to announce that it had decided to interpret the ABM treaty in a manner that would allow the SDI program to go forward unfettered, and some even argued for pulling out of the treaty altogether. The issue was finally resolved along the lines of a restrictive interpretation in mid-October, but again only after much public disputation and wrangling with the Congress.

In short, on both sides there still was plenty of evidence that not much had changed in terms of the actions, attitudes, and behavior of either country.

AT LONG LAST, CHANGE: STRAWS IN THE WIND

Even at a time when evidence was plentiful that little had changed in Moscow with the arrival of a new General Secretary, there was an unmistakable change in the tone of the relationship, and signs appeared throughout the first seven or eight months that something new and different was in the wind. Mostly it was Gorbachev's candor at home about the Soviet Union's domestic crisis and the way in which he was approaching the need for far-reaching action. We wrote about this frequently in the *President's Daily Brief.*

But there were clearly signs of something different in foreign policy as well. The frequent exchanges of letters with Reagan, while usually restating old Soviet positions, also conveyed a serious interest in dialogue and in dealing with problems. (Because most of this correspondence was not shared at the time with those of us in intelligence, complaints from some senior policymakers that we missed some of the signals therein ring just a bit hollow. This was not a new problem for us, but it was always frustrating.)

Through the spring and summer of 1985, Gorbachev made a number of arms control proposals. They one-sidedly favored the Soviet Union and were regarded primarily as propaganda by Washington—as they undoubtedly were. Yet they also indicated an adroit political mind at work in the Kremlin, and that in itself offered some hope that things might get better.

Meanwhile, talks on regional issues such as the Middle East, southern Africa, and Afghanistan went forward through the spring, discussions that were controversial in Washington because of fears of State Department concessions but that at least offered a chance for useful dialogue. At an otherwise fairly sterile meeting between Shultz and Gromyko in Vienna in mid-May, the two privately began discussions about a summit that led to the Geneva meeting between Reagan and Gorbachev the following November.

On July 3, the same day the Geneva summit was announced, Gorbachev surprised the world by announcing that Andrei Gromyko would be replaced by Eduard Shevardnadze, the communist leader of Georgia and a man with no foreign policy background.

The departure of Gromyko was universally welcomed and regarded as encouraging. In the biographic paper CIA provided for Shultz, we described Shevardnadze as "anything but a faceless implementer of policy." We described a man with "flamboyant style, courageous, decisive, intelligent, and with an imaginative approach to problem solving." In addition to all this, he had retained a reputation for personal integrity, staying in the same apartment as his career progressed and taking public transportation to work. He also was an innovative economic manager. Our report concluded with this observation about the new foreign minister: "He will eventually leave a distinctive mark on Soviet foreign policy and the conduct of diplomacy." (In his memoirs, Shultz takes CIA to task at every opportunity when he thinks we got something wrong, including biographic information on foreign leaders he encountered. He is silent about important ones like Shevardnadze that we got just right.)

Shultz and Shevardnadze met for the first time at a conference in Helsinki from July 30 to August 1. While little substantive headway was made, the U.S. team was struck by the new Soviet Foreign Minister's different tone and approach. On November 2, Shultz left for Moscow for a final preparatory session with Shevardnadze for the Geneva summit. He met with Gorbachev, and the two of them went at each other on a range of issues, but in a way that pleased Shultz. He had given Gorbachev as good as he got and, more importantly, as he later would write, felt he was connecting with the Soviet leader despite the range of their disagreements.

These and other developments between March and the Geneva Summit in November neither balanced nor overshadowed Soviet actions of real concern during the same period. The positive side of the ledger primarily comprised changes in tone, approach, and thinking—not yet deeds. But these changes did seem to signal a genuine change of direction in Soviet foreign policy that was challenging in some respects and promising in others.

THE ROAD TO GENEVA

Casey, the Directorate of Intelligence, and the National Intelligence Council all became deeply involved in the preparations for the President's meeting with Gorbachev in Geneva. I had been involved in preparing the four previous summits since 1974, and none of those efforts began to compare with the exhaustive process of preparing Ronald Reagan to meet with Gorbachev. As Casey's representative in the interagency meetings relating to the summit, and based on what I was hearing from the contacts of our Soviet office around town, I wrote to Casey on September 3:

> Bill, I think Gorbachev wants and needs a deal so bad he can taste it. I've been involved in preparing a number of U.S.-Soviet summits and I have never seen such an open signaling of a desire to do business. Yet, I detect a defensiveness in the U.S. outlook that is inconsistent with the circumstances. This is not to say we *should* cut a deal on arms or anything else—it just means President Reagan goes to Geneva holding better cards than any president meeting his Soviet counterpart since Eisenhower went to Geneva 30 years ago. Our planning should start from that premise and focus on specific, realistic demands we should make of Gorbachev—not to score debating points, but to advance U.S. interests in concrete ways—from Nicaragua to Angola to Afghanistan to Kampuchea to the Iran-Iraq war to arms control to cultural agreements to human rights. . . .
>
> The meeting is shaping up as a terribly important moment in the Reagan presidency. I fear that the President's staff is approaching the meeting aiming just to survive it and without a clear view of the larger objectives—and opportunities.

That's exactly what they were doing. It was yet another manifestation that few on the President's own staff had much confidence in him or in his ability to deal one-on-one with the dynamic and agile Gorbachev.

At an NSC meeting on September 20, prior to Shultz's meeting with Shevardnadze the next week, Casey forewarned—accurately—that the Soviets would present a proposal in Geneva involving substantial reductions in strategic weapons in exchange for limits on SDI they knew the administration could not accept, with the goal of using the desire of the media and Congress for reductions to build pressure within the United States to eliminate SDI. "In sum, the Soviets see Geneva almost exclusively in terms of the political contest and what they cannot win from you at the bargaining table they intend to win through manipulation of the American media and Congress."

The days before the Geneva Summit were filled with briefings for Reagan and everyone else. CIA sent a ton of background material to Jack Matlock, now the senior Soviet expert on the NSC. On November 7, the President had lunch with half a dozen prominent outside Sovietologists. I attended the luncheon and was struck by the degree of consensus that dramatic changes were under way in the USSR but that none threatened the system itself.

At Casey's suggestion, Reagan agreed to meet with several CIA experts for an hourlong briefing before Geneva, and it took place in the Oval Office on November 13. I'm sure Shultz was both miffed and uneasy about the likely tenor of the briefing, and he made sure to attend. Casey introduced us and I led off.

I described for Reagan the severe domestic problems Gorbachev faced and his need for a respite as well as Western economic cooperation and help. Above all, he needed to avoid major *unanticipated* defense expenditures. I said that I thought Gorbachev was not prepared to pay much for some breathing space with the United States—that he likely saw it coming anyway in the defense arena, especially SDI. I said that the same would be true in the Third World, where support for freedom fighters would decline when Reagan left office. My bottom line: Gorbachev simply intended to outwait Reagan.

Finally, I said that we did not think that Gorbachev's plans to get the Soviet economy working would be successful. We expected the pressures on him to increase steadily "and, at some point— perhaps as early as two or three years—the Soviets must consider real concessions on strategic forces and foreign policy—if the U.S. sustains the pressure in the strategic competition and the third world."

The highlight of the briefing for Reagan, though, was the presentation on internal stresses and pressures in the Soviet Union given by Kay Oliver, an experienced analyst from our Soviet office. She had just drafted the estimate "Domestic Stresses on the Soviet System," and described in detail for Reagan the alienation, alcoholism, drug abuse, and crime problems of the USSR. She also reviewed the decline of popular confidence in the system and the leadership; the pervasiveness of corruption, economic stagnation, and anti-Russian nationalism; and the revival of religion and dissent. Oliver described how in the late 1970s and early 1980s the ruling elite had become stagnant, cynical, outrageously corrupt and ineffective, all protected by Brezhnev's relatively passive policies. She also reported the great impact inside the USSR of information from and about foreign societies and about events abroad, especially in Poland, and how this contributed to overall disgruntlement.

All these were problems Gorbachev had to face. Yet she predicted—as had the estimate—that Gorbachev's domestic policies for the next several years would be relatively cautious and conservative—that he would not go very far in adopting market mechanisms for the economy or legalizing private activity. In her own words, she summarized the most important prediction in the estimate: "We cannot foresee the time, but we can see the tendency for this tension [between social aspirations and regime control] eventually to confront the regime with challenges to its political control that it cannot effectively contain."

I felt Reagan was alert but not very interested in what I and others had to say. However, he was riveted by Oliver's briefing, I think because she described the Soviet Union in terms of human beings, everyday life, and the conditions under which they lived. It was all far more real to the President than the strategic concepts and broad geopolitics the others of us went on about.

There was, however, one point in my briefing when Reagan nearly came out of his chair. I was seated closest to him, and about two minutes into my comments I heard a piercing electrical hum. Reagan's eyes got very wide, and he reached up to his ear to adjust his hearing aid. A couple of minutes later, the hum returned and, since I could hear it, I could only guess how loud it must have been in his ear. At that point, in some disgust, he reached up, pulled the hearing aid out of his ear, and pounded it on the palm of his hand a couple of times. As he replaced it in his ear, he looked at me, smiled, and said, "My KGB handler must be trying to reach me."

That briefing, eight months into Gorbachev's tenure, captured both the strengths and weaknesses of CIA's analysis of the last General Secretary. On foreign policy and defense issues, we simply kept pace with Gorbachev's actions; but after 1986, we more often than not failed to anticipate how far he would go. By the same token, those in and out of the U.S. government at the time who now contend that they foresaw the dramatic changes Gorbachev would make plainly saw more than Gorbachev did because his policies in the foreign and defense arenas were clearly evolutionary, often tactical, and truly did not begin to emerge until the 27th Communist Party Congress, in February 1986. So if we at CIA were slow to detect change, it was because we were tracking Gorbachev's actions at the time. This does not excuse our failure to anticipate where he might go.

On the other hand, we were dead-on accurate about Gorbachev's handling of domestic problems in the Soviet Union and his failure to come to grips with their magnitude or to develop a coherent and workable strategy for coping with them. His measures to democratize the party and to promote glasnost—openness—were stunning departures from the Soviet Union's past. But it was apparent from the beginning that Gorbachev didn't know what he was doing in economic matters or in dealing with the nationalities, and he never would. In addressing these realities, CIA accurately described current developments and correctly forecast his failures. And both the national estimate on domestic stresses in the USSR and Kay Oliver's briefing to Reagan before Geneva foreshadowed a growing threat to continued control by the Soviet Communist Party—*six years* before that control collapsed.

As the participants recorded in their memoirs, little progress was made on substantive issues at Geneva. Both Reagan and Gorbachev talked tough and pursued tough policies suggesting little change from the past. Yet a dialogue began with their correspondence and through their diplomatic champions, Shultz and Shevardnadze, that led to the first summit in six years and a change in attitudes and approach that would eventually change the world. By the end of 1985, Reagan and Gorbachev may not yet have become friends, but they had become the best of enemies. And nearly everyone knew that, with this new Soviet leader, something fundamental had changed between the two superpowers. Even those of us in CIA.

CHAPTER NINETEEN

The Third World Competition, 1985–1986: Washington Pours It On

THE ACID TEST of Gorbachev's seriousness about change in foreign policy for many of us was whether he would cut back Soviet military programs and draw back from aggressive involvement in the Third World. We would not begin to see positive changes in approach on defense—at least changes not easily reversible—until 1987–1988. By the same token, in 1985 and 1986 the competition in the Third World got even hotter as the Soviets poured weapons and military matériel into the hands of its now-threatened clients. This Soviet behavior seemed to many at CIA and to Defense (and to some at the White House) to outweigh significantly the Soviet rhetoric and gestures Shultz found so encouraging. And so, during this same period, the United States and its friends—sensing both a Soviet challenge and Soviet vulnerability—likewise expanded their covert assistance to anticommunist resistance forces all over the world; new money and new weapons cascaded in to them. And all with congressional support, and often in response to congressional pressure.

ANGOLA: A CONGRESSIONAL CHANGE OF HEART

For ten years after Congress in 1975 prohibited U.S. covert support to Jonas Savimbi's UNITA group by passing the Clark Amendment, the United States was a bystander in Angola's civil war. The military advantage seesawed back and forth between

UNITA and the MPLA government for several years, until in the early 1980s the Soviets began very large scale military assistance to the MPLA in addition to the nearly 40,000 Cuban soldiers fighting on the MPLA side. This aid by 1985–1986 totaled several billion dollars. UNITA was kept alive by South African assistance and modest contributions from several other countries, as well as the skill of its fighting men. By 1985, however, UNITA was in difficulty as the Soviets, Cubans, and Angolans steadily pushed Savimbi's forces east and south, back toward his headquarters at Jamba.

The MPLA-Cuban-Soviet offensive in the summer of 1985 was thwarted by a significant infusion of men and matériel from South Africa. Once again, however, Moscow's overreaching in the Third World proved self-defeating. On August 8, 1985, the U.S. Congress repealed the Clark Amendment.

On November 12, 1985, just a week before his first summit meeting with Gorbachev, Reagan signed a presidential finding authorizing covert lethal assistance to UNITA. CIA formed a special task force to administer the program, and weapons and other military equipment were soon flowing to Savimbi—though at a fraction of the level of Soviet assistance to the MPLA. We sent a man to Jamba to serve as liaison with Savimbi, and a CIA representative would remain there, living in a thatch hut, for the next several years. Our airlift was a masterpiece of logistical planning as we often used a single C-130 to ferry goods from our staging base to Jamba—where the plane would remain on the ground only a few minutes while being quickly unloaded.

By mid-December 1985, Casey was pressing to get defensive air and antitank systems into Savimbi's hands. The Soviet SA-7 ground-to-air missile just wasn't good enough. Casey raised this with Weinberger on December 20. By February 1986, the NSC had approved providing both Stinger antiaircraft missiles and TOW antiarmor weapons to Savimbi.

While much controversy would attend whether to provide Stingers to the Mujahedin in Afghanistan, there wasn't much fuss over providing them to UNITA. And we were dumbfounded by the remarkable effectiveness of the missiles and the soldiers using them in Angola. Indeed, until we began getting video pictures and other evidence, the U.S. Army was quite skeptical of the kill rates being reported by UNITA. It is a little-known fact that the extraordinary performance of the Stingers in Angola helped overcome resistance to their use in Afghanistan.

In short, at a time when U.S.-Soviet diplomacy was once again active and hopes were high for change in the relationship as a result of new leadership in the Kremlin, massive Soviet military assistance to a Third World client provoked a new and large U.S. paramilitary covert action. Casey had another war to manage. While the covert action in Angola was never as popular with Congress as Afghanistan, the Agency did it by the book, and the activity retained strong bipartisan support throughout its existence. Most importantly, it provided Shultz the leverage he needed to put pressure on the MPLA—and he did just that.

AFGHANISTAN: THE MAGIC AMULET

The Soviets significantly turned up the temperature in Afghanistan in 1985. Special Spetznaz troops were sent in, and the Soviets resorted to carpet bombing, the use of helicopter gunships, and strong campaigns into the major valleys and strongholds of the Mujahedin. Millions of small mines were strewn by aircraft in order to terrorize the Afghan people. The insurgents resisted the increasing pressure and in the summer of 1985 beat back four major Soviet offensives in the Konar Valley, the Panjshir Valley, Paktia Province, and the city of Herat.

Although by the end of 1984 planning was under way for spending several hundred million dollars in fiscal year 1985 on the Afghan program, an amount to be matched by the Saudis, we were faced with growing competition among the Mujahedin factions for arms. In 1985, old political, religious, tribal, and ethnic conflicts from remote Afghanistan made their way to the corridors of power in Washington—to the White House, State, Defense, Capitol Hill, and the press. It was quite a spectacle as the bearded and robed Mujahedin political leaders went from office to office, building to building, making their personal and parochial cases for greater support. No one should have had any illusions about these people coming together politically—before or after a Soviet defeat. Certainly no one at CIA had such fantasies.

The administration codified its new approach to the war in Afghanistan in March 1985. As more resources were poured into the conflict to help the Mujahedin, there had been growing discontent, particularly at State and Defense, over the traditional covert ground rules being followed by CIA and also with the strategy of simply bleeding the Soviets. These months-long debates came to a head in early 1985 and culminated in a new presidential directive on the war, National Security Decision Directive 166. Signed in March, it set forth a new American objective in Afghanistan: to win. To push the Soviets out.

All through 1985, we poured weapons into Afghanistan—heavy machine guns, SA-7s, and the Oerlikon antiaircraft cannons, all of which began to produce increasing aircraft losses for the Soviets. In addition to large increases in weapons, we improved the logistics base and our ability to bring the weapons, ammunition, food, and clothing to those inside Afghanistan—laying the basis for the extraordinary Mujahedin successes in 1986 and 1987. (This included importing thousands of Chinese mules into Afghanistan to transport weapons. We could not find enough suitable U.S. mules to meet our needs.) Funds for 1986 were increased by more than $125 million over 1985, to be used to buy many more weapons of all kinds.

It was during this period that we began to learn of a significant increase in the number of Arab nationals from other countries who had traveled to Afghanistan to fight in the Holy War against the Soviets. They came from Syria, Iraq, Algeria, and elsewhere, and most fought with the Islamic fundamentalist Muj groups, particularly that headed by Abdul Rasul Sayyaf. We examined ways to increase their participation, perhaps in the form of some sort of "international brigade," but nothing came of it. Years later, these fundamentalist fighters trained by the Mujahedin in Afghanistan would begin to show up around the world, from the Middle East to New York City, still fighting their Holy War—only now including the United States among their enemies. Our mission was to push the Soviets out of Afghanistan. We expected post-Soviet Afghanistan to be ugly, but never considered that it would become a haven for terrorists operating worldwide.

The big issue involving Afghanistan in late 1985 was whether to provide Stinger antiaircraft missiles to the Mujahedin. To that point CIA had opposed providing weapons that were obviously from the United States. The military had opposed providing the Stingers out of fear of technology transfer if and when one of the launchers was captured, and the likely Soviet development of countermeasures. Through most of the year, the problem was sort of a low-grade bureaucratic fever, not a raging argument.

That changed in December. In a breakfast meeting with Casey, McMahon, and Weinberger on December 6, Under Secretary of

Defense Fred Iklé wondered if CIA could use Stingers. McMahon replied that CIA would use every Stinger Iklé provided. A week later, in a meeting at State involving Casey, McMahon, Under Secretary of State for Political Affairs Mike Armacost, and Director of the Bureau of Intelligence and Research Mort Abramowitz, the latter urged getting Stingers into Afghanistan.

A month later, in January 1986, during a Casey visit to Pakistan, Zia told him, "This is the time to increase the pressure." Casey foreshadowed to Zia likely U.S. approval of Stingers. Finally, by mid-February, a decision was made in principle for Defense to provide CIA with four hundred Stingers for use by the Mujahedin.

By September, the Mujahedin were ready to go. On the first day the Mujahedin used the Stingers in combat, they hit three out of four targets. Indeed, it was not too long before they were mounting a devastating antiaircraft campaign against both Soviet and Afghan government aircraft. As losses mounted, the Soviets went to night-flying operations. Then, five months later, when CIA had developed a new sighting system for the Stingers that made them effective at night as well, Soviet and Afghan pilots began to fly higher to avoid the missiles. Thus both the bombing and ground-support roles of the aircraft suffered—to the great benefit of the Mujahedin.

The Stingers were so successful, and the stories about them circulating among the Muj so fanciful, that every group wanted the missiles. We began to hear stories from the field about how those who had the Stingers had become even bolder in combat—how many of the fighters regarded the Stinger as a kind of "magic amulet" that would protect them against the Soviets.

There is little question that providing the Stinger was a major turning point in the Afghan war. It greatly increased Soviet and Afghan aircraft (and pilot) losses and thus the cost of the war to Moscow; it forced changes in Soviet tactics that helped the Mujahedin on the ground; and it was a big psychological boost for the resistance. The huge increases in funding, which vastly increased the flow of all kinds of assistance to the Mujahedin, more sophisticated targeting of Soviet and Afghan installations based on U.S. satellite information, and the flow of Stingers by the end of 1986, had begun to turn the tide. The Soviets had to either reinforce or lose. Because they clearly were not winning.

OBSESSION: TERRORISM AND QADDAFI

Terrorism became a major focus of the Reagan administration in late 1984 and in 1985, especially terrorist acts committed by or on behalf of the governments of Iran, Syria, and Libya. Everyone turned to CIA. In mid-January 1985, Shultz asked Casey what we could do to "develop more aggressive action against terrorists." He wanted "to see some action to let the terrorist groups know that there is risk in this."

Under pressure from the President, Shultz, and Congress, Casey finally got serious about terrorism in early February 1985. At that point, CIA turned dramatically from collection on and analysis of terrorism for warning to preemption and retaliation. On February 14, I sent Casey our first assessment of Iranian, Syrian, and Libyan support to terrorism *and* their respective vulnerability to retaliation.

Our work on the vulnerability of the three major state sponsors of terrorism—Libya, Iran, and Syria—began to provide the administration with information they could use, if only to begin thinking about real action against state-supported terrorism. We did targeting studies of Libyan and Iranian ports and military facilities, and examined similar targets in Syria. We analyzed the potential impact of various kinds of sanctions.

We focused especially on Iran, the worst offender. The downsides of an attack on Iran, to everyone's regret, outweighed how much Iran deserved punishment. We pointed out that failure to hit Iran would ensure that Iranian-sponsored terrorism would continue and even grow, but terrorist-connected targets were near cities and attacks against them would, by themselves, have little impact. We suggested that while sustained military and economic pressure on Tehran might over time strengthen "moderates," it also could drive the Iranians closer to the Soviets for protection. And that was perhaps the single most significant deterrent. Thus Iran proved "too hard"—a limited attack would, as a participant in one meeting indelicately put it, "just piss them off" and make things worse.

Syria was not seriously considered as a target because such action would almost certainly bring a confrontation with the Soviets. Syria had the most effective military, would have to play a key role in any Middle East peace process, and was relatively invulnerable to U.S. economic pressures.

So the process of elimination brought CIA to Libya. Ironically,

Libya had been reluctant to attack the United States directly out of fear of retaliation. But because it was in the poorest position to sustain itself against U.S. actions—military or economic—it became the target for U.S. retaliation against all state-supported terrorism.

The Reagan administration wanted Qaddafi's hide in the worst way. It had been obsessed with him since 1981, and its bill of particulars against the Libyan leader grew longer each day. By early July, 1985, Libya was the clear focus of administration retaliatory action. On July 15, I sent Bush, Shultz, Weinberger, McFarlane, and Joint Chiefs of Staff Chairman General Jack Vessey new updates of our earlier vulnerability and targeting studies on Libya, Syria, and Iran. On the same day, I sent other members of the Crisis Pre-Planning Group—Poindexter, Armacost, Rich Armitage of Defense, Iklé, and Admiral Art Moreau—a paper, "Options Against Qadhafi [Qaddafi]." It assessed the Libyan-Egyptian military balance; Egypt's likely needs and wants if asked to engage against Libya; Libya's warning capabilities; Libyan, Arab, and Soviet reactions to several scenarios; a list of key questions to be answered; and the first draft of a White Paper summarizing Qaddafi's misdeeds.

What McFarlane, Poindexter, and Ollie North had in mind at this point was a combined U.S. and Egyptian attack on Libya, involving the Egyptian army attacking across the desert and entering Libya from the east, while U.S. air and ground forces attacked Tripoli and other targets. It was, to say the least, an ambitious idea. Defense took CIA's paper on Egyptian and Libyan capabilities and drew up contingency plans and the size of U.S. forces required for the NSC-sponsored operation. Because Defense wanted no part of this operation, the plan they prepared looked a lot like the invasion of Normandy on D-Day, 1944. An NSC meeting was scheduled for July 22 to discuss the proposal.

I opposed the plan in my personal memo to Casey before the NSC meeting. I told him on July 19 that the costs and risks included a huge outcry globally against U.S. imperialism, a strong reaction in the Arab world against a U.S. invasion of an Arab country, potentially significant Soviet gains in the Middle East and elsewhere in the Third World, a probable short-term upsurge in terrorism against U.S. citizens and installations, and a potential setback in U.S.-Soviet relations. I concluded that I thought the actions by Libya still were below the threshold for a major invasion of an Arab country and that, in the eyes of many abroad and in the United States, there were actions we could take that would be more proportional.

Not a single principal at the NSC meeting supported the NSC staff's proposal. It was dead. The rest of the year was spent trying to develop options for action against Qaddafi that would win the support of the NSC principals. And since, by now, Shultz was barely speaking to Casey and Weinberger and they in turn were opposed to nearly anything he proposed, the challenge to find an option that would draw the support of all three was daunting.

On March 24, 1986, U.S. aircraft flying over the Gulf of Sidra were attacked by Libyan antiaircraft missiles and, after initial hesitation in Washington, U.S. aircraft sank several Libyan patrol boats and struck SA-5 missile sites in Libya. We learned that in response, Qaddafi had directed several of his "People's Bureaus" in Europe to plan terrorist operations against the United States. On the 27th, the Libyans informed a number of ambassadors in Tripoli that a "state of war" existed with the United States. We quickly began picking up information on Libyan plans to hit us. Qaddafi's operatives were successful on April 5, detonating a powerful bomb in West Berlin at La Belle Disco, a hangout for American servicemen. We had "smoking gun" proof of Libyan responsibility in intercepted communications, which—at Shultz's insistence—we later released.

Reagan met on April 7 with Casey, Shultz, Will Taft (acting for Weinberger), Poindexter, and General John Wickham (representing JCS) to discuss what to do. Casey told the group that we had compelling evidence that since the Gulf of Sidra incident in late March, Qaddafi had organized a widespread terrorist campaign to strike back at the United States. We had specific details on nine separate Libyan attacks tasked or under way. The meeting then turned to targets in Libya and, for once, everyone was in agreement: it was time to act militarily.

Shultz mentions in his memoirs that after the crucial meeting on April 7, Reagan went to Baltimore for the opening game of the baseball season. The President sat in the Orioles' dugout and the catcher, Rick Dempsey, sat down beside Reagan and suggested how to take care of Qaddafi. But Shultz, perhaps out of discretion, told only part of the story. Several of us learned the rest from Orioles' owner Edward Bennett Williams at a farewell dinner Casey gave for John McMahon at the Mayflower Hotel two days later. According to Williams, Reagan listened to Dempsey for a minute or two and then said, "You know what I'd do if Qaddafi were sitting here right now? I'd nail his balls to this bench and then push him over backward!"

Absent that opportunity, on April 14 Reagan sent F-111 bombers from Britain and carrier-based airplanes against Libyan military targets, as well as Qaddafi's residence. Although the damage was less than we had hoped for, it was nonetheless substantial and had a real impact in Libya. We would hear for months that Qaddafi had just left his residence before the attack and had been fairly unhinged by the attacks and his own close call. And, just as after Grenada, the impact of the U.S. action made him much more cautious and probably inhibited others as well—at least for a while. One additional result was to make the Europeans far more willing to cooperate with us on sanctions out of fear that we would respond to Qaddafi again with military force.

Reagan had inflicted a serious blow on another Soviet client. The message was not lost on Moscow that the new relationship developing with Washington would not deter the United States from taking action in the Third World when it saw its interests threatened or a chance to bloody a Soviet surrogate. Because Gorbachev had not yet taken steps to begin withdrawing Soviet support from its Third World minions, Washington was unsure of his intentions in the arena where the relationship had foundered in the 1970s. We would pass up no opportunity to challenge the Soviets and make life hard for them in the Third World until they did withdraw, or negotiate a settlement satisfactory to us, or change their behavior. Thus the Third World competition would be the last element of the relationship to change for the better.

TERRORISM: THE SOVIETS AND THE POPE

Though the attempted assassination of Pope John Paul II in 1981 had no relationship to the U.S.-Soviet competition in the Third World, it was very much regarded as a terrorist act and was constantly on our minds as we challenged the Soviets and their clients in the Third World. From the time the Pope had been shot, CIA had straddled the issue of whether the Bulgarians and thus the Soviets had been involved.

The truth was that we really didn't know. The clandestine service worked hard in Italy, elsewhere in Western Europe, and in

Eastern Europe to come up with more information and, hopefully, "smoking gun" evidence. And we came up with a lot on the trail of the gun that the assailant, Agca, used, and on his travels and arrangements, but nothing on who might have been behind the plot. I had read our own analysis closely enough to know the gaps in the case, and thus remained agnostic on the question. Casey was convinced the Soviets were behind the assassination attempt, and frustrated that we couldn't prove it.

Then, over the winter of 1984–1985, we began receiving from a clandestine source information about the Bulgarian role, and the Soviets', that for the first time seemed to provide an evidentiary base for making a case against them. I suggested to the deputy director of our office analyzing terrorism that they write a paper assessing the possible Soviet role in the attempted assassination in light of the latest agent reporting from Eastern Europe. They did so, in coordination with several analysts in the Soviet office. The draft paper drew together all of the strands suggesting Soviet involvement. It was titled "Agca's Attempt to Kill the Pope: The Case for Soviet Involvement," and was a compelling study, though clearly identifying the tenuous nature of our sources, gaps in information, and the circumstantial nature of much of the information. We sent the paper to only seven people outside of CIA: the President, Bush, Shultz, Weinberger, Vessey, McFarlane, and Anne Armstrong, the chairman of the President's Foreign Intelligence Advisory Board (PFIAB).

It was circulated more widely inside CIA, however, and elicited a very negative reaction from some analysts who had not been involved in its preparation. An analyst in the Soviet office did a critique of the paper and sent it to me on May 20. I sent it to Casey the next day. Then, in June, Anne Armstrong sent the DCI a memo critical of the Agency's overall handling of the "Papal Plot" from the beginning. With these two critiques in hand, on my own, I commissioned an independent review of CIA's analysis of the assassination attempt from the beginning. I got it three weeks later, and shared it with a number of senior managers for the lessons learned.

What I missed at the time was that the evaluation offered a glimpse of trouble in the Soviet office, both in terms of internal discord and, implicitly, dissatisfaction with me on the part of some of the analysts and managers. The evaluation pointed out that until a short time before, that office had not been organized to look at the instruments of Soviet policy but to focus rather on foreign policy in various regions. A number of analysts in the office believed that some of their colleagues and managers still preferred not to consider the "seamy" side of Soviet policy—"wet operations" (assassination) and the like. These analysts believed that initially some of their colleagues had dismissed the possibility of Soviet involvement in the assassination attempt, and they consequently welcomed a paper looking at the case for Soviet complicity. At the same time, the evaluation also pointed out that there was another group within the office with a lingering "malaise" stemming from the conflict in 1981 between Casey and the Soviet office on the Soviet role in terrorism. In short, there were significant substantive differences and factions within the Soviet office, as well as major differences between some Soviet analysts and the DCI and me on what the Soviets were up to around the world.

The paper on the assassination attempt against the Pope published in May 1985 was CIA's last major analytical assessment of that awful event. We never would get additional information from our sources, even after the collapse of the Soviet Union. As a result, the question of whether the Soviets were involved in or knew about the assassination attempt remains unanswered and one of the great remaining secrets of the Cold War.

CHAPTER TWENTY

Intelligence Wars

JUST AS THE CONTINUING intense competition between the super-powers in the Third World complicated their warming dialogue in 1985, so, too, did the activities of their intelligence services. Running covert operations against each other, propagandizing each other's activities, recruiting agents in each other's country, CIA and the KGB tangled around the world in ways that fed the suspicions and skepticism of leaders in both countries. The Cold War of the spies continued unabated.

CIA AND KGB BLACK OPERATIONS: "CAMPAIGN TRICKS"

Both the KGB and CIA in 1985 and 1986 sponsored countless covert activities designed to embarrass the other side and its leaders. Some were fairly serious, and others in retrospect seem more like silly pranks practiced in U.S. political campaigns or on college campuses.

The Soviets were all over the place secretly supporting opponents of continuing INF deployments and then SDI, which they sought to discredit in all possible ways. They created forgeries of documents purportedly signed by Shultz, Casey, and senior U.S. military leaders in hopes of scaring the bejesus out of our friends and allies. In Africa, they accused CIA of creating the AIDS epidemic. In South Asia, the KGB spent a great deal of time and money during this period trying to blame the United States for assassinating Indian Prime Minister Indira Gandhi. (The KGB in January 1985 was assigned as a high priority the task of producing evidence of or "reasonable conjectures about" American involvement in the assassination.) Throughout the Third World, they spread a story that the United States was kidnapping babies there to use their body parts in transplant operations. These efforts certainly created anti-American feelings, and some of these tales would gain a life of their own and still be circulating after the collapse of the Soviet Union.

But CIA was busy as well. For example, on Poland:

• In March, we printed and smuggled into Poland forty thousand postcards with a photograph of Father Popieliusko (the Polish priest who had been beaten to death by the security services) and the texts from some of his sermons. We later heard that the Pope saw some of these and liked them very much.

• In May, we arranged a pro-Solidarity demonstration at a soccer match between Poland and Belgium, including a twenty-foot-wide banner that was clearly seen on Polish (and international) television.

• In June, CIA obtained a copy of the map used by Hitler's Foreign Minister, Joachim von Ribbentrop, and Soviet Foreign Minister V. M. Molotov during their meeting in Moscow in September 1939 that resulted in the partition of Poland. We made hundreds of miniaturized copies and arranged for their infiltration into Poland. On the reverse side of the map, we printed, in Polish, the text of the secret protocols of the meeting.

We were active on other fronts as well.

• In November 1985, CIA pulled out all the stops to make Gorbachev feel unwelcome in Geneva when he had his first meeting with President Reagan. CIA mobilized its assets to participate in a wide range of anti-Soviet demonstrations, meetings, exhibits, and other such activities in Geneva. Our first major effort to publicize the Soviet role in Cambodia was in Geneva at this time, and drew broad media coverage.

• Throughout 1985 and 1986, CIA sponsored many demonstrations, protests, meetings, conferences, press articles, television shows, exhibitions, and the like to focus worldwide attention on the Soviet involvement in Afghanistan. These efforts overseas in which the American hand was hidden complemented the overt coverage of the Soviet role on VOA and through other official U.S. channels.

None of these or myriad other covert propaganda activities

determined the outcome of the Cold War. Some may have been counterproductive by making diplomatic efforts to reach out to the Soviets more complicated or harder. But most, particularly those associated with publicizing the Soviets' human rights record and the cases of specific individuals, and those in support of Poland's Solidarity, served a useful purpose in my view in keeping the world's attention on Soviet behavior and bringing pressure to bear on them to change that behavior. We kept a bright worldwide spotlight on nefarious Soviet activities at home, in Eastern Europe, and in support of Third World surrogates that otherwise would have remained largely unknown or neglected.

Overt Intelligence Operations

CIA also ran openly recognized operations against the Soviets in 1985. The most significant was publicizing Soviet technology theft in the West and Japan. Beginning in 1981, through cooperation with a West European intelligence service, CIA had acquired detailed information on Soviet operations to acquire western technology. We stopped getting information in 1982; two years later we learned that the Soviet source who had been providing the information had been discovered and executed.

The information provided was widely shared among Western intelligence services, and in December 1984, the French service proposed helping Western governments and companies protect their technology by making public what the intelligence services knew. There was full agreement in our government at top levels to publish a document laying out what the Soviets were doing. CIA prepared an unclassified version with the catchy title "Soviet Acquisition of Militarily Significant Western Technology." In July, Vice President Bush took a draft of the paper to France, where he told President Mitterrand of our desire to make it public, and Mitterrand gave his approval. In early September, CIA printed fifty thousand copies of the "White Paper," and State and Defense distributed them worldwide.

Another of our efforts to expose Soviet espionage and covert influence activities originated in a research project carried out in early 1985 by the Directorate of Intelligence on the Soviet presence at the United Nations. One of our analysts tracked every one of the eight hundred Soviet nationals assigned to the UN and showed how they reported directly to Soviet diplomatic missions and were part of an organization managed by the Soviet Foreign Ministry, intelligence services, and the Central Committee of the Communist Party. The study, "The Soviet Presence in the UN Secretariat," described in detail how the Soviets exploited their personnel at the UN to achieve Soviet foreign policy and intelligence objectives. It argued persuasively that about one-fourth of the Soviets in the UN Secretariat were intelligence officers and that many more were coopted by the KGB and GRU.

The paper was a revelation and provoked a real stir. Congress was especially upset, and the Senate Intelligence Committee published its own unclassified version of our assessment in May.

Gorbachev might be a breath of fresh air and have the potential to change the nature of the Soviet Union—but he hadn't done it yet, and the United States wasn't going to ease up until he did. As long as the Soviet intelligence services were still fighting the Cold War, we weren't going to slacken our efforts to counter them.

"HOSTILE PRESENCE"

One area where CIA and State had a common approach was the question of what to do about the huge number of Soviets in the United States, many of them intelligence officers. This became known as "the hostile presence" issue. The career foreign service and CIA's clandestine service were of one mind—they hated the idea of expelling Soviet spies and diplomats. They did so because the Soviets always retaliated for expulsions from the United States by throwing a like number of American diplomats (or spies) out of the USSR. And because there were so many more Soviets in the United States than Americans in the USSR, we always suffered disproportionately.

Because of the attitude of the clandestine service, this was one issue where Casey never pressed Shultz particularly hard. The real pressure came from Congress and from the NSC, which thought the disparity in numbers in Washington and Moscow was outrageous and were determined to bring greater parity to the relationship. Casey played both sides of the street on the issue. While privately blaming State and Shultz for inaction, he was also privately supporting Shultz. For example, he wrote the Secretary on April 26, 1985, that Senators Patrick Leahy and Bill Cohen had come to CIA for help on the Soviet presence because they hadn't liked the response they received from State. Referring to an in-between approach that would require the number of Soviet and United States nationals in diplomatic status to be the same, Casey told Shultz in his note, "I think we are pretty much on the same wave length."

The issue was finally brought before the President on August 7, 1985. After a long and occasionally sharp discussion, the President ultimately approved an approach that would require the Soviets to reduce the size of their UN mission from 275 to 170 by April 1988. State still didn't like the idea and found one reason or another to keep delaying informing the Soviets and beginning the process. Finally, the Soviets were told and the decision was publicly announced on March 7, 1986.

Thus ended the first round on the hostile presence issue. It would not be the last, and George Shultz's heelmarks were all over the canvas.

SPIES: THEY'RE EVERYWHERE!

The aggressive actions of the KGB and CIA around the world trying to advance the interests and policies of their respective governments were only the most visible part of their shadowy activities. The other arena was their war upon each other—trying to recruit each other's officers and trying to prevent such recruitments. Until the mid-1980s, we in American intelligence thought we held most of the high cards in this competition—between defections of KGB and GRU officers, our recruitments among their officers, and our smug confidence that all of our people were loyal. Indeed, we boasted to ourselves that the Soviets had never run an agent in place inside CIA. Sure, William Kampiles, a young CIA officer, had sold the Soviets the manual to our most sophisticated satellite system in the 1970s (for a measly $3,000), but that was a onetime shot. In 1985, we and the rest of the intelligence community got our comeuppance.

CIA and the FBI each took a counterintelligence hit in late 1984 that, in retrospect, foreshadowed deeper problems. On October 2, Richard Miller, an FBI agent, was arrested for espionage, the first such traitor caught in the Bureau. Then, the next month, Karl Koecher, a CIA contract employee—it was carefully underscored at the time that he was *not* a career staff employee—was arrested for working for the Czech intelligence service.

The first major spy case to break in 1985, however, was the

arrest on May 24 of John Walker, who worked for the U.S. Navy. Walker provided the most sensitive cryptographic and other documents to the Soviets over a period of some seventeen years, thereby enabling them to decipher perhaps a million U.S. Navy coded messages. Although it took a long time to determine in detail the extent of the damage, everyone in U.S. intelligence knew instinctively that it had been terrible.

Still, CIA exuded confidence and pride in its security record. However, unknown to anyone in the United States, apparently at about the same time—May 1985—the Soviets recruited Aldrich Ames, a career CIA officer assigned to Soviet operations and counterintelligence. From his recruitment in 1985 until his arrest in 1994, he would provide information on the most sensitive CIA operations against the Soviet Union, in the process condemning to death nine or more Soviet agents recruited by CIA.

In June 1985, there was another setback for CIA when one of our most valuable agents in the Soviet Union, Adolf Tolkachev, who had provided detailed information on Soviet aerospace and other weapons programs, was arrested. Almost immediately, a U.S. embassy officer, Paul Stombaugh, was expelled from the USSR. Tolkachev was tried and executed.

In July and August, the West scored two huge successes in the espionage war. The first was the successful exfiltration in late July from Moscow (and from under the KGB's nose) by the British Secret Intelligence Service of Oleg Gordievsky. Gordievsky, the KGB chief in London at the time of his defection, had worked for the British service since 1974 and had been an extraordinarily valuable agent. He had come under suspicion in the spring, ordered to return to Moscow, interrogated, and was awaiting the KGB's next move when, on July 19, he dressed in jogging clothes, went out, and disappeared. Gordievsky's defection was announced by the British on September 12. (Casey called Reagan the day before to tell him the news.)

It was the turn of the United States to hit the jackpot in the undercover war when, on August 1, Vitaly Yurchenko defected to us in Rome. Yurchenko had just been promoted to general in the KGB before his defection and was responsible for Soviet espionage in the United States. CIA's most sought after target was a KGB or GRU officer, especially one knowledgeable about spy operations in the United States (just as Ames was for them). Such an agent or defector could usually reveal ongoing operations and often finger those in the United States working for the Soviet Union. Thus Yurchenko was regarded as especially useful.

Casey was like a child with a new toy with Yurchenko. Not only was he eager to hear, virtually on a daily basis, about the debriefings: he also could not help bragging about this great CIA coup. He met with Yurchenko, had dinner with him, couldn't get enough of him. By this time, I thought Casey and I (then DDI) were pretty close, yet when I asked to join him for dinner with Yurchenko, the DCI evaded my request and, when I pressed, turned me down cold, saying that the DO thought it might make Yurchenko uneasy. I thought then that it was a strange and, in fact, unbelievable answer, but didn't push. Thus I never laid eyes on Yurchenko while he was in the United States. As widely as Casey briefed and bragged about Yurchenko, it was only a brief time before news of this remarkable defector leaked. I am sure Casey wanted it known—after all, as usual, he was in hot water with the press and Congress, and publicity about a great intelligence success was political helpful.

Come September, it was the Soviets' turn to gloat. One of the Soviet agents in the United States identified by leads from Yurchenko was a former CIA operations officer, Edward Lee Howard. Howard had been hired by CIA in 1981, was assigned to Soviet operations, and was soon selected for assignment to Moscow. He went through all the necessary training and, most important, learned nearly everything about CIA's activities in Moscow, both human and technical. However, a polygraph examination prior to Howard's departure for Moscow revealed drug use, heavy drinking, and more. He was fired. Presumably out of revenge, he began selling secrets to the Soviets.

When Yurchenko's debriefings led CIA's counterintelligence to Howard, the FBI put him under surveillance at his home in New Mexico. To everyone's consternation and the FBI's intense embarrassment, Howard eluded the surveillance and escaped from the United States, finally showing up in Moscow. He had used his CIA training to give the FBI the slip, having his wife drive him away from home, then jumping out of the car, triggering a pop-up dummy dressed like him. This gave the impression that two people were still in the front seat. The whole thing could have taken much less than a minute. Howard was CIA's most devastating counterintelligence setback up to that time. Many of our Soviet operations were compromised and either rolled up by the KGB or shut down by us. It was due to Howard, we believed, that the Soviets arrested, tried, and then executed Tolkachev.

The Howard case was also a terrible political embarrassment for CIA at home. Conservatives, and others, pointed to alleged laxity in counterintelligence since the forced retirement of Angleton in the mid-1970s and demanded action.

Casey personally was embarrassed and angered by the handling of Howard. He commissioned an investigation of the case by the Agency's Inspector General and then was further angered by the IG report, which he wrote on November 11 was "not tough enough" and needed "to pinpoint failures and make specific recommendations." The second draft didn't make him any happier, and he wrote the IG on November 26, "I am troubled . . . by the failure to discuss any specific responsibility for the appalling confusion and inattention to detail . . ." in the DO's handling of the case.

Six months later, after reading the PFIAB investigation of the Howard case, Casey's anger at the Directorate of Operations boiled over. He wrote Clair George a personal memo on June 4, 1986. It was tough: "I am appalled at the DO's handling of the Howard case as described in the recent PFIAB report." He reviewed the warnings ignored, delays in bringing the case to the attention of the FBI, the absence of overall direction, the reluctance to recognize a major counterintelligence problem until too late, "and, above all, an astonishing complacency about, seemingly an unwillingness to accept even as a possibility, a DO officer committing espionage for the Soviet Union." Casey said the organizations involved "deserve censure" and that "Deficiencies in process, organization and attitude that contributed to this catastrophe must be corrected and I hold you personally responsible to do so." I worked closely with Casey for five and a half years. He never wrote a letter that strong to any other CIA officer. In short, his already substantial unhappiness with the clandestine service as an institution was only increased by Howard and the aftermath. (And his criticisms of the DO would be repeated nearly verbatim a decade later after the debacle surrounding Aldrich Ames.)

Unfortunately, Howard was only the first of several terrible embarrassments that fall. First came the "redefection" of Yurchenko on November 2, when he persuaded the security officer assigned to him to go out to dinner in Georgetown, and then simply got up and walked away, going to the Soviet embassy. Yurchenko's return to the Soviet Union prompted serious questioning about whether his defection had been genuine or had been some kind of elaborate deception. The questions about Yurchenko have continued to the present and have become even more complicated in connection with the 1985 recruitment of Aldrich Ames and the possibility of other moles in CIA.

There was more to come. On November 25, Ronald W. Pelton, who had worked in the Soviet section of the National Security Agency for some fourteen years before resigning in 1979, was arrested for spying for the Soviets. Yurchenko had provided the tip that led to Pelton, who had given the Soviets information on some of America's most sensitive (and effective) technical intelligence operations.

While Walker, Howard, Tolkachev, Yurchenko, and Pelton were part of the spy war between the United States and the USSR, the revelations about them in 1985 were accompanied by other, nearly as embarrassing, if not nearly as damaging, spy cases. On July 11, a young CIA officer, Sharon Scranage, was arrested for providing intelligence information to a boyfriend employed by the Ghanaian government. On November 21, Jonathan Pollard, a navy civilian intelligence analyst, was arrested for spying for Israel. Two days later—and two days before Pelton's arrest—a longtime CIA officer, Larry Wu-tai Chin, was arrested for spying for Communist China for many years.

Over the course of 1986, there would be other espionage flaps, but none as embarrassing or as costly to the United States as those in 1985. There was one, however, in the last half of the year that deeply engaged the most senior officials of both governments for more than a month, and led to further bad blood between Casey and Shultz.

On August 23, 1986, a Soviet scientist working for the UN, Gennady Zakharov, was arrested in New York by the FBI for espionage. He did not have diplomatic immunity, and had been the target of an FBI "sting." In retaliation, the KGB was authorized to reciprocate by arresting a nongovernmental American. Nicholas Daniloff, a correspondent for *U.S. News and World Report*, was their target. On August 30, Daniloff met a Soviet contact who was to provide him with information on Soviet activities in Afghanistan. The material was classified and Daniloff was arrested.

Daniloff was not a spy for CIA, and based on Casey's assurances to that effect, Reagan wrote Gorbachev on September 5 repeating the assurances. On September 12, both Zakharov and

Daniloff were released into the custody of their respective ambassadors. When Shevardnadze visited Washington a week later, he and Shultz spent a great deal of time on this case, and the Soviet Foreign Minister provided Shultz with the case against Daniloff the Soviets were prepared to make. A deal was made in which Daniloff was released on September 29 without trial and Zakharov was released the next day after pleading "nolo contendere." The same day Zakharov was released, the Soviet dissident Yuri Orlov and his wife were allowed to emigrate from the USSR. Finally, also on September 30, both governments announced that Reagan and Gorbachev would meet in Reykjavik on October 11–12.

One reason Shultz was eager to work out a deal was that he had learned that CIA had implicated Daniloff in one of its operations without the reporter's knowledge and thus compromised the U.S. position. As Casey informed Shultz on September 8, CIA had received a document from a source in 1981 that was "the most significant document ever received by CIA on Soviet strategic missiles." The Agency was unable to follow up. Then, on January 22, 1985, Daniloff had gotten a telephone call from a "Father Potemkin," who had first visited Daniloff the month before. Father Potemkin told Daniloff he was sending him some materials. Daniloff received an envelope addressed to him at his office on January 24. The inner envelope was addressed to the ambassador and within that a third envelope was addressed to Casey. Daniloff took the letter to the embassy. The handwriting in these materials, and the themes, were identical to the 1981 materials the Agency thought so valuable.

The Directorate of Operations was desperate to establish contact with the source of these materials and thus decided to try to reach him through Potemkin. In a second meeting with Daniloff at the embassy, our station obtained Potemkin's telephone number. Then, on March 23, one of our officers reached a person he believed to be Potemkin, who acknowledged that he had delivered an envelope. Our officer visited Potemkin and left a letter for the source as well as a contact signal. The letter introduced our case officer as a "friend of Nikolai"—thus implicating Daniloff without his knowledge. The source never made contact. In early April, Daniloff told two embassy officials that he had received a call from Potemkin referring to the March 23 letter and telling Daniloff that the arrangements for a meeting were no good. Daniloff told the chargé at the U.S. embassy that he did not want to be involved and was told, in turn, that the government didn't want him involved and was trying to keep him out. On April 18, another CIA source in Moscow reported that the letter had been delivered to the wrong person and had gotten to the KGB.

On September 9, after Casey had informed Shultz of the above information, the two talked again, and Casey agreed to send a message to the Soviet embassy explaining how Daniloff had received an unsolicited package and had delivered it to our embassy. Daniloff had nothing to do with CIA's effort to follow up. The message, in Shultz's view, still was not sufficiently explicit that Daniloff did not work for CIA.

A political firestorm attended all of this, with widespread outrage over the arrest in Moscow of an American journalist. Reagan himself, poorly informed as to what Casey had told Shultz, was angry and even sent a Hotline message to Gorbachev about the matter. Conservatives were demanding that Shevardnadze's trip be canceled, Casey and Weinberger wanted to call off the impending summit, and still others wanted to expel a large number of Soviets from the United States. When the deal described above was announced, Shultz took a lot of flak from conservatives and others for caving in. He was not happy about it, believing that CIA had hopelessly undermined any case the United States might make as to Daniloff's innocence and that publicizing the facts would work against the United States.

The matter did not conclude, however, without an exchange of bitter recriminations between Shultz and Casey. In the middle of the Daniloff episode, Shultz had fulminated to Reagan about CIA's clumsiness and bungling of the case. When Casey heard about this, on October 7, he wrote Reagan, Shultz, Weinberger, Regan, and Poindexter to provide detailed information on CIA's role (as he had done for Shultz a month earlier). After reaffirming the value of the 1981 information, Casey then criticized statements by government officials (Shultz) that the effort to renew this information was "unprofessional" or "bungled."

Finally, in November, Shultz sent Casey a letter referring to the Daniloff case and wondering if new guidelines were needed to protect U.S. private citizens in the USSR—in effect that no CIA or station personnel would make contact with them. Casey wrote back on November 15, saying: "I think the present system is working as well as reasonably could be expected. New guidelines are not warranted. Your point regarding direct contacts with the station is well-taken and instructions will be sent to this effect." That was as close as Casey ever came to admitting to an outsider that the Agency had made a mistake with Daniloff.

In the middle of all this but independent of it (at least technically), on September 17 Reagan ordered, by name, twenty-five KGB officers in the Soviet mission to the UN to leave by October 1. The Soviets retaliated by expelling five Americans, and the United States countered by throwing out five more Soviets and then fifty more. The Soviets then expelled five more American embassy officials and withdrew all 260 Soviet support personnel from the U.S. embassy—chauffeurs, maids, cooks, and so on. The escalating ejections finally stopped in mid-October. But those who had argued the year before for reducing the "hostile presence" in the United States and in our embassy had gotten their way in spades.

I learned a personal lesson from the Daniloff episode. By this time, I had been DDCI for just over four months. As bits and pieces of the Daniloff story and CIA's involvement began to drift in to me in early September, it was clear that CIA did not have a precise record of what had happened in 1985 with "Father Potemkin" and our station. And every time I asked another question, I got an answer that contradicted an earlier answer. I asked Clair George to have his people put together a detailed chronology of what had happened, but even that was confused and contradictory. Finally, frustrated and impatient, I decided the clandestine service couldn't do it and that I would try. So, I gathered all of the involved operations officers in my office one afternoon and methodically went through our information, from the 1981 contact on—sorting out different accounts and reconciling dates and information. At the end, we had a reasonably accurate chronology. But, in light of troubles to come, it was a disturbing harbinger of the operations directorate's haphazard and scattered record of its activities. Compartmentation and security were one thing. Disorganization and confusion were another.

KIDNAPPINGS AND SPY DUST

As the spy wars intensified, each side believed that the other had resorted to violence and dangerous techniques to "acquire" agents or to defend itself. The KGB, for example, was convinced that CIA was drugging and kidnapping its officers. In the private channels of communication between the two spy agencies—the most active of which was "the Gavrilov channel"—the Soviets complained time and again about CIA using thuggery on its agents. They just couldn't believe that all the defections they were suffering were self-motivated. They were wrong.

For our part, Yurchenko told us that for some time the KGB had used chemical tracking and tagging substances against U.S. personnel in the USSR. We had collected samples of a strange yellow powder in Moscow in 1976, 1977, 1979, 1980, and 1982 —identified in 1982 as nitrophenyl pentadiene (NPPD)—but the evidence at the time suggested that exposure was infrequent and unsystematic. We were unaware of any health hazard, in particular the potential for cumulative toxicity, until laboratory tests in 1984 showed potential harm. Eight more samples were collected in the spring and summer of 1985. We were then told that the chemical was potentially carcinogenic and a potential mutagen. According to Yurchenko, new materials were being developed as tracking substances.

Casey wrote the President on August 17 about the tracking powder, calling it "more direct, provocative and ultimately dangerous than the microwave radiations against the embassy." He said that the powder had caused great concern about the health risks and that there had been interagency agreement to lodge a strong protest with the Soviets and to take steps "to advise and protect" our people. Deputy Secretary of State John Whitehead protested to the Soviets in Washington on August 19, and there was a press briefing on the 21st.

Later, there would be allegations that the "spy dust" affair was trumped up as a political tactic, and we did eventually learn that NPPD probably was not harmful. But the outrage—and health concerns—at the time were genuine. And more than a few case officers, and their families, who had served in Moscow spent an anxious period wondering if they had been exposed to a cancer-causing chemical agent. Always looking for a new theme for anti-Soviet propaganda, CIA mounted a major covert campaign exploiting Soviet use of "toxic substances" for tracking.

INTELLIGENCE WARS: THE U.S. SENATE

Casey's relationship with Congress, even independent of Central America, continued to deteriorate in 1985 and 1986, especially as the magnitude of the intelligence losses in 1985 became apparent. The Senate Intelligence Committee—and in particular its chairman, Senator David Durenberger, and vice chairman, Senator Patrick Leahy—was Casey's special nemesis. The Yurchenko and Howard affairs provoked considerable outcry from the committee, and Casey was subjected to withering criticism, some of it outside the hearing room and in public.

Casey was equally impatient in the face of either serious congressional inquiry or congressional grandstanding. Thus, when Durenberger was quoted publicly in November 1985 as critical of CIA's inadequacies in dealing with long-term issues such as the Soviet Union, the Philippines, and other situations, Casey went ballistic. He responded with a blistering letter to Durenberger attacking his "off-the-cuff" approach to oversight, and reviewing the Agency's record on the issues Durenberger had mentioned. Fed up with both Durenberger's and Leahy's public statements about intelligence, he concluded: "Public discussion of sensitive information and views revealed in a closed session of an oversight committee is always damaging and inadvisable. As we have discussed many times, if the oversight process is to work at all, it cannot do so on the front pages of American newspapers. The cost in compromise of sources, damaged morale and the effect on our overall capabilities is simply too high."

Casey's relationship with Leahy was no better, and two letters the DCI wrote to the Senator in early 1986 make the point. He sent the first, but apparently not the second. The first, sent in early February, complained to Leahy about his comments to the press, earlier leaks, and later comments on Casey and oversight. One passage went as follows:

> The other night you referred to the occasion when Senator Moynihan complained that the Committee had not been briefed on the [Nicaraguan] mining, although it had in fact been reported, and you said on television that you had obtained the information [on the mining] and that it had been available to others. I certainly appreciate that but can't give you too much credit. All you did was tell the truth. If Moynihan has not spoken to you since, as you said, it seems to me you have already been amply rewarded.

The second letter to Leahy was drafted on April 1, after Casey had heard from a friend to whom at a dinner party Leahy had denounced the DCI as a liar. Casey wrote that he had read to Leahy's dinner partner the correspondence between them (Casey-Leahy) and this "was sufficient to explain why you would volunteer and indulge in such outrageously false and slanderous talk. . . . As you must be aware, for forty years I have maintained an unimpeachable reputation for reliability and truthfulness in dealing with business, financial and political leaders and with lawyers and other professional colleagues all over America and the world. If I learn of any more such slanderous talk from you, you can count on being hauled into court." I don't think Casey ever sent this letter.

During 1985, the Agency also was under attack from conservatives, especially on arms-control-related issues. In May, Senators Jesse Helms, Steve Symms, and Malcolm Wallop sent a letter to the President with a number of questions relating to CIA assessments, views on arms control monitoring, and the attitudes of its analysts. The thrust of the questions seemed particularly aimed at the head of CIA's Arms Control Intelligence staff, Doug George, and his predecessor, Ray McCrory. A number of the questions were personal and accusatory. Helms wrote the President again in October.

Casey answered all of these letters at once, on December 2, on behalf of the President. The twenty-six-page letter was prepared by the Directorate of Intelligence, but a key paragraph was all Casey's: "I am disturbed by the inferences in your letter of disloyalty at CIA. I have seen no evidence to support charges that past analysis has been affected by a pro-Soviet bias or by penetrations. . . . Suggestions that past shortcomings were due to a pro-Soviet bias or worse are unjustified and unwarranted."

Our critics were multiplying. The chairman and vice chairman of the Senate Intelligence Committee. Conservative senators. Continuing public and media criticism prompted by the "Year of the Spy." Complaints from Shultz. By 1985–early 1986, we at CIA were feeling more than a little bruised. It was therefore with delight that we received at the Agency a letter from a group of nine-year-old boys in Kansas who wanted to start a CIA fan club. We also received at about the same time a letter from a group of Boy Scouts offering to help us fight terrorists—as long as we didn't tell their mothers they had written us. As one senior officer at a staff meeting observed, at least they had a well-developed sense of security.

PART FOUR

1986–1991: Liberation and History's Dustbin

CHAPTER TWENTY-ONE

Gorbachev's Uncertain Trumpet,
1986–1987

IT IS NOT ENTIRELY TRUE that when an intelligence officer "smells the flowers" he looks around for a coffin. But the nature of our business, in both operations and analysis, makes of us great skeptics and pessimists. Especially of rhetoric unmatched by actions. This approach—mind-set—most often puts us at odds with diplomats and negotiators who, when confronting the most intractable problem, can find hope or opportunity in the nod of a head, the wink of an eye, in the slightest change or nuance in language. Their approach, too, is understandable. They must try to solve problems or negotiate agreements, and that requires some measure of optimism, a tendency to look on the bright side, to minimize the bad news or the obstacles.

This clash between intelligence officers and diplomats, between skepticism and hope, was especially intense during 1986–1987, as each tried to figure out what to make of Mikhail Gorbachev. Of course, the breakdown wasn't completely clean. Both schools were represented within State and CIA, and many individuals perceived to be firmly planted in one camp shared some of the views of the other. But Washington politics and the media don't allow for much gray when they line up conflicting factions, nor do the warring egos at the top.

All of this became important in January 1986 as Gorbachev began to move in new and very different directions on both foreign and domestic policy. The moves were still, for the most part, rhetorical. But they were at such odds with the Soviet past that they could not be ignored. The issue in Washington was what it all meant. Were we seeing a basic and lasting departure from the past in Soviet behavior and objectives abroad and governance at home? Or were Gorbachev's moves in both arenas a bold and dramatic attempt to "fix" what wasn't working and thus position the Soviet Union to resume the strategic contest with the United States in the future in a much strengthened posture? And how could we reconcile what he said with what really was happening on the ground inside the USSR and outside its borders? Or understand what he was up to when we learned from agent reporting and even the press that he was telling different audiences different things? These basic questions dominated the debate over Gorbachev inside the Reagan administration, both generally and in response to each new initiative—which followed one after another during the first several months of 1986.

Believing that the U.S. interagency process was too constipated to respond effectively to Gorbachev, Shultz got Reagan's approval in mid-January to create a "steering group" of senior officials to manage the U.S. side of the relationship. The group would meet periodically on Saturday mornings in Shultz's office. Casey told me on January 17 about this idea, and that the participants would be Weinberger and Assistant Secretary Richard Perle from Defense, Poindexter and Soviet expert Jack Matlock from the NSC, Casey and me from CIA, and Shultz and several others from State. There would be no substitutions among the participants. The plan was to meet every Saturday in order to keep on top of and manage the U.S.-Soviet relationship.

Judging from his memoirs, I believe that Shultz apparently considered CIA—and me—to be the greatest skeptics of Gorbachev and the prospects for real change in the Soviet system. I certainly did not doubt for a second that Gorbachev represented a significant change in leadership, that we now faced a much greater Soviet political challenge, or even that Gorbachev intended to make dramatic changes inside the USSR and find a way out of various foreign policy blind alleys. However, as I saw him continue to pump money and weapons into Nicaragua, Angola, and Afghanistan and to sustain Soviet military programs at a very high level, his rhetoric seemed less persuasive to me than his actions. Similarly, his actions at home as of early 1986 represented no serious challenge to the Soviet state and party structure that had existed for decades.

As people write their memoirs and we reflect on the latter half of the 1980s, there is a tendency to run those years together and to suppose that where Gorbachev ended up in 1988–1989 was where he intended to go in 1986. In fact, he was making up strategy as he went along—as he put it, "on the march." I believe to this day my skepticism in early 1986 that he intended to revolutionize both foreign and domestic policy was justified by his actions. Indeed, his lack of strategy, of a plan, combined with his frenetic pace, reminded me of the bumper sticker "I'm lost, but I'm making good time."

The first of Shultz's seminars was on January 25, and I attended without Casey. Needless to say, there was no meeting of the minds between the Secretary and me. He voiced his disagreement with my point of view (and me) on Soviet intentions again at a breakfast and all-morning seminar Shultz hosted on February 1 on Afghanistan, attended by, among others, Brzezinski, Scowcroft, and former Defense Secretary Don Rumsfeld. After two such sessions in a week's time, I wrote Shultz a letter on February 4, 1986, expressing my concern that "we may be talking past one another on Gorbachev and what the Soviets are doing." I went on:

I have the impression you believe we at CIA are too rigidly fixed on the notion of no change in the Soviet approach to the U.S. or their domestic problems and, therefore, that we are missing the importance of current developments and also misreading the shape of things to come in the Soviet Union. . . . I agree with you on Gorbachev's toughness, extraordinary tactical flexibility, creativity and boldness. But all we have seen since Gorbachev took over leads us to believe that on fundamental objectives and policies he *so far* remains generally as inflexible as his predecessors. For example,

• As you pointed out on Saturday, there has been no change in Soviet positions on regional issues or their commitments to their clients.

• At home, all of Gorbachev's moves to modernize the economy have been within the framework set by his predecessors.

• With the U.S., he is trying to re-create the détente atmosphere of the early 1970s on the same premises. As Nitze indicated, the new comprehensive arms proposal, while tactically a clever stroke, did not change any basic Soviet position on SDI or START or provide a realistic approach to INF.

• Gorbachev is determined to address domestic problems, but *so far* he has been very orthodox on the basics at home and abroad.

• One of our highest priorities is to identify at the earliest possible time indications of real changes in key Soviet domestic, foreign and military policies and goals. While we do not see such indications now, we will continue to work this problem open-mindedly.

The Secretary of State probably gagged reading the last sentence of my letter. Even so, he continued the dialogue on Soviet affairs with CIA and with me, if only to know what the "enemy" was thinking.

After Gorbachev had been in power for slightly less than a year, Shultz did not seem to disagree with CIA or with me about what was actually happening in the Soviet Union—from aid to Third World clients to the military budget to little movement on economic reform. But he discerned in Gorbachev's rhetoric and proposals much more potential for fundamental change in Soviet direction than we did. The trouble was that with the sole exception of arms control, Gorbachev's rhetoric of change in foreign policy would far exceed any change in the realities on the ground for nearly two more years—until late in 1987. And because we were in the uncomfortable position of having to point out that ugly reality, we in CIA were cast as the troglodytes.

I MAKE A BIG MOVE UP

On April 16, two days after the U.S. bombing attack on Libya, I was sworn in as Deputy Director of Central Intelligence by Vice President Bush. On February 26, Casey had written President Reagan a letter recommending my nomination as successor to John McMahon, who had decided to retire. He went into my background in some detail, said some flattering things, and noted that he had "counselled with" Bush, Shultz, Weinberger, Poindexter, and Regan. Because Casey already had Reagan's agreement, the usual White House vetting process was skipped. My hearings were held in early April in the secure meeting room of the Senate Intelligence Committee and lasted about two hours. The hearings were businesslike, but friendly, and my nomination was reported to the Senate with unanimous approval of the committee. I was confirmed on a unanimous voice vote in the Senate on April 14. I came away with the sense that this confirmation stuff was pretty easy. Was I in for a surprise!

I did not understand in my first months as DDCI that behind the smiles and cooperative spirit of the clandestine service there was considerable unease about someone from the analytical side of the Agency in the Deputy DCI chair—especially someone as active and involved as they suspected I would be. I think some in the Directorate of Operations saw me as a critic of both the Agency and them, and now I would be their boss, not just an easily ignored head of the analytical directorate. They knew I would involve myself in their business.

Their concerns undoubtedly were increased when on April 23, after only a week in the job, I revived a semiannual review of all covert action programs by a small group of senior Agency officials including the Executive Director (who would be chairman), the deputy directors for Operations and Intelligence, and the Inspector General. The next day, I established the Covert Action Review Group to provide coordinated advice to the DCI and DDCI on all aspects of proposed findings for covert action and changes to existing findings. This group would include the Executive Director, DDO, DDI, General Counsel, Comptroller, and Director of Congressional Relations. While the group was created to streamline and improve the internal CIA coordination process, it was also intended to bring more intrusive oversight of covert action. Later, when he became DCI, Bill Webster would further strengthen this group and formalize its procedures. In any event, the clandestine service—I would later learn—was neither comfortable nor happy with such involvement by other parts of the Agency in its activities.

I began to meet weekly with the heads of the operations task forces on Angola and Afghanistan, and in late summer added the head of the Central American task force in anticipation of our congressionally authorized program scheduled to resume on October 1. I also asked for an early morning briefing by the special assistant to the Deputy Director for Operations on overnight events, as well as problems and issues that I should know about. Years later, I was told by one of those special assistants that, at first, Clair George closely monitored what I was being told and, on occasion, would complain that I didn't need to know something or shouldn't be told something. Over time, the clandestine service seemed to relax somewhat and my morning briefings got longer and longer. At the time, though, I didn't sense any of this and thought things were going pretty well with the DO. I would later understand that like most bureaucratic entities, but more so, the clandestine service was reluctant to share information about internal problems or concerns outside the directorate—especially with the DDCI or DCI, who might decide to help solve the problem from above.

With my strong support, Casey appointed Dick Kerr, who had been my deputy, to move up to Deputy Director for Intelligence. That meant he, rather than I, would represent CIA in interagency policy-making meetings at the White House. I had enjoyed that part of the job, and I would miss it. But Kerr was a first-rate intelligence professional, a good friend, and had a wonderful—though at times bizarre—sense of humor (such as dressing up in a gorilla suit and riding a motorcycle around posh Great Falls, Virginia). Kerr was great to work with, cared deeply about CIA, and always gave me sound advice and counsel, consistently forthright and full of common sense. I would continue to enjoy working closely with him.

MIXED SIGNALS

Gorbachev's first meaningful "rhetoric of change" in the thrust of Soviet foreign policy occurred during the 27th Congress of the Soviet Communist Party, which took place February 25–March 6, 1986. The historic turning point represented by Gorbachev's speech at the Party Congress in March 1986 was apparent only in retrospect because the next months were filled with events that kept suspicion alive on both sides. However, from Gorbachev's speech and the agenda that would flow from it eventually would emerge a radical turn in Soviet foreign policy away from the confrontations of the past and toward international cooperation. The changes came slowly, one at a time, beginning in Europe and with arms control, then involving the United States more broadly, and extending, finally, to the last redoubt of the Cold War—the Third World. March 6, 1986, then, should be marked as the beginning of the end of the Cold War.

Several American histories catalogue a number of U.S. actions during this period hostile to the Soviet Union (Stingers to the Mujahedin, the attack on Tripoli, renewed aid to the Contras, the arrest of the Soviet spy Zakharov, and more). They unfavorably contrast this American "aggressiveness" to Gorbachev's far-reaching arms control proposals in January; his agreement to let Anatoliy Shcharansky leave the USSR as part of a spy swap (he crossed the Glienicke Bridge from East to West Berlin on February 11); his initiative for substantial conventional force reductions in Europe on April 18; his statements at the June Central Committee plenum breaking the linkage between INF and intercontinental strategic systems, thus allowing a separate INF agreement that would ban the missiles in Europe and freeze their levels in Asia; and other actions generally bespeaking an accommodating approach and peaceful intent.

We saw all that, too. But we saw another side of Soviet behavior, a side not mentioned in these books, or by Shultz in his memoirs. In 1986, under Gorbachev, we saw the Soviet Union— whether because of inertia in major military programs, his decisions, or both—continue to deploy the SS-25 mobile ICBM, flight-test their rail- and silo-based SS-24 ICBM, deploy additional Typhoon and Delta IV submarines, begin production of their first strategic bomber in a generation (the Blackjack), begin testing new cruise missiles, deploy the new MiG 29 in forward areas, and send to sea trials the fourth Kiev class carrier. We saw a new Soviet $600 million line of credit extended to Nicaragua, over a billion dollars in new economic assistance to Vietnam, and another $1.5 billion in military assistance for Angola. We received new and worrisome evidence about the Soviet biological and chemical weapons program, including their development of new and devastating biological weapons. In January, we saw what appeared to be a Soviet-sponsored coup in South Yemen led by four pro-Soviet hard-liners. In May, we saw the Soviets unceremoniously dump Babrak Karmal as their minion in Afghanistan and replace him with Mohammed Najibullah.

In his memoirs, Shultz is both derisive and critical of the failure of CIA (especially me) and Defense to appreciate the changes under way in the Soviet Union during this period. He claims that we saw the USSR as "a mighty nation confronting us everywhere —confident, unchanging, determined." That is not true. We had documented better than anyone up to that time the economic and social crisis in the Soviet Union, as well as its lack of political appeal around the world. By this time, the West not only had been in the ascendancy for some years, but was winning nearly everywhere— and we knew that. But we also saw a Soviet Union in deep economic crisis continuing its vast military programs unabated and continuing to shovel money and weapons to clients around the world. Either Gorbachev wasn't truly calling the shots, which we did not believe, or there was a disconnect between his rhetoric and his actions—a disconnect we suspected was due to his unwillingness to take on the military, the KGB, and the still numerous traditionalists on the Central Committee. So, just as in 1984 and 1985, the struggle to develop a new relationship made slow headway amid mixed signals from *both* sides.

GORBACHEV AT HOME: CONTRADICTIONS

Faced with a giant country in the middle of political, economic and social crisis, Gorbachev had no strategy, no plan for "fixing" the system. The idea of *replacing* the Soviet system is nowhere to be found in any Gorbachev speech, writing, or private conversation yet available to the West. His approach both economically and politically was one of experimentation, of trying something, and if that failed, trying something else. He knew that what he saw did not work, but did not have the vision that would have enabled him to see that the basic structure of the Soviet Union itself was the root cause of the crisis. He seemed to believe that his country's problems derived from Stalin's distortion of what Lenin had created, and if the Stalinist legacy could be eliminated—the lack of democracy within the party, central management of the economy, fear—then the socialist state created by Lenin would emerge stronger and "better" politically, socially, and economically, ready to assume its rightful place as a model for the world.

At home, Gorbachev would begin seriously in 1986 and 1987 to confront the three challenges—economic, political, and ethnic —that he would face throughout his time in power. In all three, unknowingly and inadvertently, he would take actions that hastened the destruction of the Soviet Union.

First, the economy. There was much noise about new economic initiatives, and many new programs and policies were announced, but little happened on the ground. By the end of 1987, Gorbachev had not yet begun to kick the struts out from under the Soviet economy—the Stalinist Communist Party administrative structure that was crudely effective in meeting minimal needs—but the welter of policies and proclamations, many of them contradictory, had failed to improve economic performance and had greatly increased confusion and uncertainty. And the confusion and uncertainty had a predictable effect on the bureaucrats that ran the Soviet economy: they became afraid to do anything (much less act boldly) and hunkered down in the hope that this, too, would pass. And the contrast between the storm of new proposals and ideas coming out of Moscow and the lack of action in the countryside became very stark indeed.

What Gorbachev could not then see was that his moves to break down the central management—party management—of the economy *would* work, but that the jumbled, contradictory, half-hearted, and confused mix of measures he tried to put in its place *wouldn't*. His gradual approach to changing the structure of the economy, I said at the time in a speech, was similar to a gradual change from driving on the right-hand side of the road to the left. And the results would be similar. In fact, Gorbachev's ideological blinders would fatally hobble economic reform to the end of his days in power.

Gorbachev's second challenge was political, and here he would find his greatest "success," though his successes sowed the seeds of destruction of the USSR and of his own political career. Here his changes were dramatic and effective. After behaving in the traditional secretive Soviet manner following the Chernobyl disaster, Gorbachev responded in a way that would become typical—he became bolder and upped the ante, especially by expanding "glasnost." This policy of openness had several purposes from Gorbachev's standpoint. A more open approach to information-sharing was needed to gain the support of the intellectual elite—especially the scientists and engineers. Glasnost enabled the regime to compete with foreign and unofficial sources of information and put an official spin on it. Exposing problems in the system, whether corruption or incompetence or simply backwardness, offered the opportunity to build support for his reform efforts. Legitimizing broader discussion of problems and possible solutions contributed to weakening domestic opposition to change and increased Gorbachev's own maneuvering room. Finally, public exposure and condemnation gave Gorbachev a powerful weapon to use against his political opponents—and use it he did.

Reflecting on his travels in Russia in the early 1830s, a French nobleman, the Marquis de Custine, wrote, "A word of truth dropped in Russia is a spark that may fall on a barrel of gunpowder." So it was in the latter half of the 1980s. Communist authority in the Soviet Union depended on myths and lies. It depended not just on the complete control of information about the present but control of history as well. I do not believe Gorbachev understood this, or that by unleashing artists, journalists, and finally the historians, he would undermine the legitimacy and the very survivability of the regime he sought to reform. Glasnost, including especially the truth about Soviet history, along with Gorbachev's turn away from coercion within Russia—his liberation of most Russians from fear—contributed as much as anything else to the ultimate collapse of the Soviet Union.

Gorbachev in late 1986 turned his attention to changing the party. So far, it had been a major obstacle to change, to reform. He felt compelled to make it more responsive, more accountable. Further, officials facing competition for their jobs, he presumably thought, would be more supportive of perestroika—reform and restructuring. He spoke bitterly of the party's role in the stagnation of the country. He described a system in crisis, and scathingly attacked corruption under Brezhnev and the obstructionism of the bureaucracy. He called for multicandidate elections for both governmental and party positions, the secret ballot in party elections, opening senior government positions to nonparty members, and more.

In briefing several congressional committees as Acting DCI early in 1987, I made the following point concerning Gorbachev's political agenda: "The cautious changes thus far instituted are inadequate to achieve his goals and he will therefore have to contemplate more radical, risky and disruptive reform." Did CIA grasp the magnitude of what Gorbachev was doing? Here is how I concluded: "Gorbachev is changing the rules across the board in a society and culture that traditionally has been resistant to change. He is placing tremendous pressure on the system and the changes are significant by Soviet standards. It would be a mistake to underestimate the degree of pressure, tension and turmoil in the Soviet Union today."

Even as the public adulation of Gorbachev, especially in the West, was growing, those of us watching him carefully observed several troubling characteristics. For all of his courageous support of glasnost, the openness during this period did not yet include criticism of Lenin or of Gorbachev. Further, for all of his talk about and promotion of democratization, when it suited his purposes he fell back on the old ways of doing politics in the USSR—purges, denunciation, secrecy, stacked votes, and so on. From the looks of it, glasnost and democratization were for everyone but Gorbachev. Our occasional efforts to point this out were not welcome in most policy quarters in Washington.

Gorbachev's third challenge was ethnic. After at least one failed attempt to boot the leader of Kazakhstan, Dinmukhamed Kunayev, out of the Politburo, Gorbachev finally secured his retirement on December 16, 1986. Traditionally, another ethnic Kazakh would have been selected to take his place. In a move illustrating Gorbachev's ignorance and insensitivity to Soviet ethnic problems, a member of the Chuvash minority (considered Russians by many Kazakhs), Gennady Kolbin, was chosen to take Kunayev's place as Kazakh party secretary. Rioting broke out the next day in the Kazakh capital of Alma-Ata, eventually involving thousands of people and a good deal of violence. Both police and demonstrators were killed. We provided to the White House extraordinary satellite photos of the riots.

Beyond the appointment of someone viewed as a Russian to the First Secretary's post, the uprising was an expression of broader resentment among Kazakhs of Moscow and Russia than recognized in the Kremlin. Gorbachev's anticorruption program was applied with a vengeance in Central Asia and elsewhere on the Soviet periphery, and in many places, like Kazakhstan, was perceived to be a tool to weaken local authority and strengthen that of Moscow. In places it was also seen as ethnically insulting. The result was an increase in anti-Russian, anti-Moscow sentiment, given a boost—ironically—by glasnost at the regional level. Glasnost spread what had happened in Kazakhstan throughout the Soviet Union as well, with important consequences. As one scholar put it, "Alma-Ata revealed that, in Gorbachev's USSR, it had become possible to rise up against Moscow." Long intimidated nationalists in the non-Russian republics of the Soviet Union observed the events in Alma-Ata and began to stir.

AND WHAT DID CIA THINK?

CIA watched events in each of these arenas—economic, political, and ethnic—carefully and reported on them routinely to senior policymakers and to Congress. Our assessments of Gorbachev's economic policies and especially what really was happening—how little was happening economically—were, in retrospect, accurate and realistic. We understood better than Gorbachev the contradictions in his programs, their shortcomings, and the opposition within the bureaucracy. And we provided our information not just in classified publications but in regular unclassified reports to the

Joint Economic Committee of the Congress. We received little criticism at the time on this work.

When it came to political developments, our day-to-day reporting was accurate, but limited by our lack of inside information on politics at the top level—which were still very secretive. We monitored specific events, but too often did not draw back to get a broader perspective on the meaning of those events.

In fact, during this period, there was a growing feeling among a handful of individuals in and out of government that CIA might be missing the forest for the trees, that beyond the Agency's assessments of chronic and worsening economic crisis and political turbulence, something more dramatic and immediate might be happening.

Inside CIA's Soviet analytical office, there was a growing conviction that the downward spiraling Soviet economy could not sustain existing military programs, much less the future weapons programs and deployments we were forecasting. The lack of communication between the economists and the military experts seemed hopeless. The head of that office, Doug MacEachin, wrote to my successor as Deputy Director for Intelligence, Dick Kerr, in April 1986 that the *lowest* force projection in the national estimates would require at least 10 percent growth annually in the cost of Soviet strategic forces for the next five years—a rate no one believed was realistic.

Outside, the concerns about our work in 1986 were growing, too. Senator Bill Bradley, a member of the Senate Intelligence Committee, expressed concern increasingly that we were not giving enough attention to possible dramatic changes in the USSR and what they might look like. In May 1986, Bradley met with analysts from the Soviet office to discuss the future of the Soviet Union, and there would be more such meetings. Bradley at one point asked me in a hearing about more resources for looking at alternative Soviet futures—and I told him we didn't have the resources for such hypothetical analyses. It was not a good answer, nor was it the right one. On August 7, the SSCI held a hearing on intelligence estimates on the USSR. Bradley asserted that the process cast up estimates with little innovation or introspection. He, as well as Senators Bill Cohen and Sam Nunn, expressed concern that the estimative process was not positioned to anticipate possible major changes in Soviet policy. Bradley went further, saying that significant changes might be taking place that the estimates were missing. All questioned the potential for change, wondering if the Soviets' huge economic problems might not force major changes.

Although Shultz, Bradley, and others appeared to view me as an unreconstructed advocate of the view that nothing of consequence was happening in the Soviet Union, I was in fact uneasy with our analysis—however I might defend it externally. In 1985, as Deputy Director for Intelligence, I had funded a study group of outside experts led by Harry Rowen that was critical of CIA's statistical portrayal of the Soviet economy. I complained in a June 11, 1985, memo to the Soviet office about "the unchanging nature of SOVA's prediction that Soviet economic growth will be one and a half to two and a half percent for the rest of the decade. . . . The continuing litany of 2% growth for the 1980s has less and less credibility with me." I said that I did not see in the office's work any reflection of concerns and problems I had set forth in other memos to them on the way we dealt with the Soviet economy, adding, "I'm amazed by the lack of any mention of uncertainties and variables in these conclusions." I ended by saying that "I see *no* progress in terms of the suggestions and comments I have made on how we should begin addressing the problems that I see in our analysis of the Soviet economy and how to make it both more realistic and more lively."

After I left the job of DDI and became Deputy DCI, I expressed my strongest concerns that we were missing something in the USSR. I wrote my successor, Dick Kerr, on October 16, 1986:

> I continue to worry that we are not being creative enough in the way we are analyzing Soviet internal developments. It seems to me we are looking at Soviet domestic (social) and economic issues in terms of straight line projections, based on the methodologies and data sources that have dominated our analyses in the past, without opening new lines of inquiry, asking new questions and exploiting previously under-utilized sources. . . . From talks with émigrés and defectors, I sense that there is a great deal more turbulence and unhappiness in the Soviet Union than we are conveying in anything we have written. . . . To what degree have we failed to give adequate attention to what Gorbachev actually has done? . . . Has he actually done a great deal more than [tinkering with the system] and set in motion even more to create the possibility of qualitative change in the Soviet system over a several year period? . . . . I am concerned

that we are in a rut and may not be recognizing significant change in the Soviet Union even as it is taking place. . . . Everything seems too pat.

Despite my supposed intimidation of the Soviet office, I was remarkably unable to alter at all their approach to the Soviet economy—even to persuade them to acknowledge uncertainty, or to take seriously other points of view. I sure don't claim to have had the right answers in 1986—I was as skeptical as any on how far Gorbachev could or would go at home, and more so than most. But I did feel that we weren't asking some of the right questions and that we were more confident than justified in our statistical projections of the Soviet economy.

SLOUCHING TOWARD . . . CHAOS

In the USSR, by the end of 1987, to most Western eyes, perestroika seemed to be proceeding remarkably well. Changes most never expected to see in the USSR were under way. The system was being criticized and examined and changed. Economic reform was being developed and slowly implemented. Changes in party rules were opening the way to democratization. Leaving aside the remarkable initiatives in foreign policy, Gorbachev was moving ahead dramatically in attacking nearly simultaneously every aspect of the old order in an effort to revive the Soviet Union. But what even the optimists in the West did not fully grasp at the end of 1987 was that, unintentionally and inadvertently, Gorbachev's "reforms" were sowing the seeds of destruction of the Soviet Union.

Gorbachev did not understand the fundamental contradiction that doomed him to fail. Without authoritarian central control of the economy and society—buttressed by myths and fear—the Soviet system could not survive. Yet, in a postindustrial world dependent on the free flow of information and rapid integration of new technology, a centrally controlled economy and society could not survive—at least in a militarily or economically competitive sense. Central control doomed the Soviet economy, yet without that control Soviet communism could not exist. Gorbachev never understood the fundamental error of his approach—the belief that the Soviet system could be "fixed." It could "muddle down," potentially over a number of years, but it was fatally flawed and, ironically, reform would only hasten the end.

And so, as Gorbachev in 1986 and 1987 began to dismantle the house that Stalin built, he unconsciously accelerated the demise of the entire system. Through glasnost and a new look at Soviet history, he exposed the myths and lies that had been central to preserving the authority of the center and the party. Through economic reform, he began to undermine the central administrative structure that met at least the most minimal basic material needs without putting an alternative structure in its place. Through democratization, he revealed the inner workings of the party and over the months proved—including to himself—that the party could not help solve the USSR's problems. Through ignorance and insensitivity, he aroused nationalist passions on the periphery that ultimately could not be contained.

Mikhail Gorbachev in 1986–1987 started a number of political, economic, social, and ethnic fires that he believed would liberate the USSR from its past and freshen the ground for new growth. What was not apparent to him or nearly anyone else back then was that the fires would spread beyond his control, creating ultimately a conflagration that would consume him and the system he tried to save. His trumpet of leadership was uncertain because his vision was limited. He could deliver the peoples of the Soviet Union from their past, but he had not the vision to see the future. This would be Gorbachev's glory, and his tragedy.

CHAPTER TWENTY-TWO

Diversions

THE NIGHTMARE BEGAN just after nine Pacific Time on Tuesday morning, November 25, 1986. By then Deputy DCI for seven months, I was in San Francisco to give two speeches. A CIA security officer knocked on my hotel room door and, when I answered, urgently told me I had better turn on the television, that the Attorney General was holding a press conference: apparently profits from the U.S. sale of arms to Iran had been used—diverted—to fund the Contras in Nicaragua. The arms sales to Iran, "arms for hostages," had become public on November 3. That was a foreign policy disaster. But this latest news changed the character of the whole thing.

I sat down on the edge of the bed, my stomach churning. What had been, up to the time of Meese's press conference, simply a foreign policy debacle, I knew from experience would now become a full-scale congressional inquiry into wrongdoing, possibly even criminal acts, based on what Meese was saying. On November 25, the crisis went nuclear and would soon threaten to destroy Ronald Reagan's Presidency.

The name of the scandal, Iran-Contra, was a misnomer, a product of journalistic shorthand. In fact, as we would see more clearly after the investigations were under way, for all but a few people in the White House, there were really two completely separate disasters, two separate time bombs waiting to go off. The first was the administration's semi-stealthy funding of the Contras through private U.S. citizens and foreign donors, together with the NSC's secret management of the Contra operation—both contrary to the clear intent of Congress when it forbade CIA to support them. (As head of CIA's analytical directorate until April 1986, I knew very little about the fund-raising and virtually nothing about the NSC's operational role. In fact, I thought the NSC's main role was to serve as contact point for the Contra leaders and private fund-raisers and to encourage the efforts of the latter.) The second time bomb was the secret sale of Hawk antiaircraft missiles and TOW antitank weapons to Iran in an effort to secure release of U.S. hostages held in Lebanon. (After January 1986, I knew a good deal about this.) For nearly all senior officials in the Reagan administration knowledgeable about all or pieces of each operation, they remained separate and wholly self-contained until Meese's disclosure of the financial connection.

Because Iran-Contra interrupted the Reagan administration's move toward better relations with the Soviets and, subsequently, in my opinion, significantly accelerated that process as a means of recovering the President's place in history, the scandal warrants treatment here. Because Bill Casey was thought to be at the center of the plot, CIA was inevitably drawn into the vortex of the storm. I was caught in the middle of that storm, and here is how I saw it.

THE CONTRA TIME BOMB

Looking back, an explosion over Reagan administration activities in support of the Contras after the congressionally directed termination of CIA's role was inevitable. The only uncertainty was when it would happen. There were three ingredients that made the Contra program a political time bomb.

The first was Reagan's determination that a way be found to keep the Contra effort alive despite the opposition of a majority of the Congress and increasing legislative restrictions on CIA, culminating in a total cutoff of authority and funds beginning on October 1, 1984. Early in 1984, as the U.S. program to help the Contras began to run short of money, Casey and McFarlane had begun discussing alternative sources of additional revenue. As described in Chapter 16, Casey urged looking to foreign donors first, countries for whom U.S. support was important. Israel and Saudi Arabia were his prime candidates, and the Saudis would come through with millions of dollars for the Contras. Separately, in the fall of 1984, the White House began encouraging private donations to the Contras with Ollie North as the action officer.

As the congressional cutoff of CIA support for the Contras became inevitable during the summer of 1984, operational responsibility for the Nicaraguan resistance passed from the Agency's clandestine service to North on the NSC staff. Because the law proscribed any U.S. "agency or entity . . . involved in intelligence activities" from supporting the Contras, Casey and others presumably believed that the NSC—which was not considered an intelligence agency—was not covered by that statute. From May 1984 on, North was briefed on CIA's operations in Nicaragua and over the summer assumed increasing responsibility for operational direction of the resistance. Thus, by the time the prohibition on CIA began on October 1, 1984, the action on Nicaragua and the Contras had passed from CIA to NSC. The details of all this were known only to a handful of people at CIA headquarters. I was not among them.

The administration was so committed to keeping the Nicaraguan resistance alive that it put its political neck on the line in supporting an off-the-books covert action, yet Reagan and his senior advisers never really made a sustained, serious effort to persuade the American people of the importance of resisting the communists in Central America. Casey was appalled by the contrast between the threat he and others perceived and the administration's feeble response. His efforts to galvanize an open political campaign on behalf of the Contras peaked each spring for three years running —1984, 1985, and 1986. He would buttonhole every senior person in the administration, including the President, to try to get something going, to get them to face the Nicaragua issue head-on politically.

The administration not only would not take the issue to the country; it refused to take a clear stand with the Congress and force the legislature to a straight up or down vote. Instead, it accepted the increasingly restrictive Boland Amendments and other legislative barriers to supporting the Contras rather than veto important legislation to which such amendments were attached. The contrast was stark between the muscular rhetoric about the communist danger in Nicaragua and the administration's temporizing and knuckling under as Congress progressively crippled the program to help the resistance. The Reagan administration stood by and watched the Congress pass legislation that restricted CIA's ability to support the Contras and finally killed it while, by signing these bills, the President allowed the legislature to evade responsibility for the strangulation.

So the first ingredient in the Contra time bomb was an administration unwilling to make a major national political issue of Nicaragua and live with the results, yet so committed to the Contra cause that it would thwart the obvious will of Congress and, unprecedentedly, run a foreign covert action out of the White House funded by foreign governments and private citizens.

The second ingredient was a Congress in which the Democratic majority was opposed—sometimes bitterly so—to U.S. support for the Contras, but equally afraid of being held responsible for Nicaragua and perhaps other countries in Central America "going communist." Thus, rather than simply vote the issue up or down, the Congress over a period of four years passed increasingly complicated restrictions on CIA. What kind of equipment and information CIA's officers in the field could provide was so confused that, at times, even the oversight committees and their staffs could not agree on what they had meant. So memos and legal briefs went back and forth among congressional lawyers and committee chairmen, and CIA's operations officers were constantly taking specific requests from the Contras to the Hill to see if CIA was or was not allowed to respond favorably. At a time when CIA was allowed to help the Contras in certain areas, there was another restriction that forbade CIA officers from going within twenty miles of the Nicaraguan border. In October 1986, the Senate rejected by a vote of 50–47 an amendment that would have required the administration to report to Congress on official involvement with the Contras' private benefactors. What kind of message did that send CIA people in the field? The confusion in Washington did a huge injustice to CIA's officers in Central America by making them accountable for observing complicated rules that at times even the Congress that passed them didn't fully understand. After the Iran-Contra storm, it was apparent that, in fact, CIA had worked hard to comply with the miasma of restrictions, though several officers would become ensnared in Ollie North's operation.

Further, there had been plenty of hints of continuing administration involvement with the Contras in the press during 1984 and 1985. Yet efforts on the Hill to find out more were halfhearted and not pursued with vigor or commitment. Administration denials to inquiries were taken at face value with none of the intrusive inquiry and investigation Congress often brings to bear on Executive activities it wants to know more about. On an issue as controversial and politically sensitive as support to the Contras, apart from close scrutiny of CIA by the intelligence committees, Congress was unusually passive in response to the news stories and rumors going around.

In sum, the second ingredient in the Contra time bomb was a Congress, like the administration, unwilling to take the Nicaragua issue head-on. Instead, it steadily circumscribed CIA's ability to support the Contras but without ever passing legislation that would just kill outright all American assistance to the resistance—a politically risky move that would leave Congress holding a smoking gun if Nicaragua became a Soviet outpost and communist-backed insurgencies threatened other governments in the region.

The third ingredient of the Nicaraguan time bomb was CIA's management of the Contra program and Casey's role. The net effect of the administration's political pusillanimity on Nicaragua and the President's determination—abetted by his DCI—to keep the Contras in the game, together with the Congress's legislated opposition cloaked in ambivalence and confusion, was to place CIA in an awful spot. CIA paramilitary specialists in the field were supposed to implement and observe restrictions that expert lawyers on Capitol Hill sometimes couldn't understand. The guys in the field could help the Contras in some ways, but not in others—and the ambiguities in a clandestine insurgent conflict always are rampant. The men in the field knew where Casey stood, and they knew where the President stood, on helping the Contras. In that light, how to decide the close—and not so close—calls? For several years, Congress had approved lethal help to the Contras. Our officers built up relationships, friendships, with the resistance fighters, sometimes got to know their wives and children. Then politics in Washington required them to abandon those people who had committed themselves to the struggle with the assurance of American help. What was clinically clean and simply another war of words in Washington was up close and personal in Central America. And our government, both Legislative and Executive branches, imposed burdens and decisions and demands on CIA's people in the field that they should never have had to bear. It is a tribute to their professionalism and integrity that so few crossed the line—even inadvertently—under these conditions.

But, in truth, CIA headquarters in Washington made a bad

situation worse. The mining of the harbors, the Tayacan manual, incomplete and evasive briefings on the Hill, contemptuous treatment of Congress, political games, petty deceptions—all these and more eroded confidence on the Hill that CIA was playing straight on Central America and playing with good judgment and skill. The near-total absence of congressional confidence in Casey and his trustworthiness, especially on this issue, simply made the situation worse. And he did, apparently, cross the line on several occasions, such as continuing to provide covert funding for the Catholic Church in Nicaragua after he promised Congress he would stop. The Directorate of Operations also aggravated the difficult circumstances it had been placed in by others by its own acts of omission and commission. And everyone in CIA who was involved with Central America was put in peril by Casey's willingness—indeed, often his eagerness—to play right on the baseline, at the edge. And, in the view of many, to go beyond it.

The final ingredient, then, in the Contra time bomb was a CIA whose top management involved in Central America was playing at the edge of the law, with a leader whose zealotry for the Contra cause was legendary. Dealt a lousy political hand by the President and the Congress, the Agency played it amazingly stupidly. And only because the Agency's senior managers on Central America worked to remain within the law in helping the Contras, even while exploiting its gray areas to the fullest, CIA as an institution would be scorched but not consumed when the firestorm of Iran-Contra came. Some of its officers in the field and at headquarters would not be so lucky.

THE IRAN TIME BOMB

The Reagan administration had two motives in selling arms to Iran. Foremost was the President's hope that the arms sales would lead to the release of the American hostages in Lebanon. We knew most, if not all, were held by Hezbollah, which was heavily funded and politically supported by Iran. The second motive was a growing worry that the Soviet Union had designs on Iran and that therefore the United States had to do something dramatic to try to reestablish its position in Tehran.

As detailed in the Independent Counsel's final report and in Bud McFarlane's memoir, the government of Israel played a major role in the early stages of the arms-to-Iran affair. On July 3, 1985,

David Kimche, a former Mossad officer and by then Director General of the Israeli Foreign Ministry, came to see McFarlane at the White House and advise him about Israeli contacts among the Iranian opposition. Kimche said that these people needed outside support, and wanted it from the United States. To prove their bona fides, they offered to obtain the release of all the U.S. hostages in Lebanon—without any quid pro quo. When Reagan was informed of this, he approved engaging with the Israelis' Iranian contacts *if* all the hostages were released first.

On July 13, McFarlane was told that the Iranian "oppositionists" had decided that if they were going to prove their good faith by getting the hostages freed, the United States should do likewise by providing one hundred TOW antitank missiles. Over the next week or so, the idea was debated among Reagan's most senior advisers, with Weinberger and Shultz strongly against the idea, Regan and Bush "mildly" opposed, and only Casey strongly for, at least according to McFarlane. Reagan ultimately said no to the Israeli proposition, but only reluctantly and still intrigued by the possibility of getting the hostages out through this channel.

On August 2, Kimche asked McFarlane whether the United States would allow Israel to buy replacement weapons from the U.S. if the Israeli government provided their own weapons to Iran. The next day, according to McFarlane, there was a meeting with the President on this proposal. Weinberger remained adamantly opposed to the Israeli proposal, as did Shultz. Casey was not present, but Regan and Bush—again, according to McFarlane—were "mildly supportive" of Israel taking the action. Later that day, August 3, Reagan approved the Israelis going ahead.

By November, the Iranians were seeking Improved Hawk antiaircraft missiles and the Israelis were preparing to meet their demands. Again, Kimche met with McFarlane (November 8), and the next day McFarlane told Weinberger that the hostage release efforts plainly were tied to arms sales to Iran. On November 22, with U.S.—and specifically CIA—help, Hawk missiles were sent from Israel to Tehran. It turned out the wrong Hawks were sent and the Iranians were furious. No hostages were released. When informed after the fact of CIA's support role, McMahon knew immediately that it had been improper without a finding, and insisted on preparation of a finding that would approve, retroactively, the Agency's participation. McFarlane resigned as National Security Adviser on December 4 for personal reasons unrelated to the arms deal.

There was a key meeting involving the President and his senior advisers on December 10 on the dealings with Iran. Casey wrote a memo on it when he returned and sent it to McMahon, eyes only. He said everyone in the meeting had supported remaining in touch with representatives of "the moderate forces" in the Iranian government, "talking and listening on a purely intelligence basis but alert to any action that might influence events in Iran." Casey concluded, as the meeting broke up: "I had the idea that the President had not entirely given up on encouraging the Israelis to carry on with the Iranians. I suspect he would be willing to run the risk and take the heat in the future if this will lead to springing the hostages."

As it turned out, the arms-for-hostages deal would continue, but Israel would drop out of the picture. In January 1986, Reagan approved direct U.S. arms sales to Iran in exchange for the release of the hostages, with CIA officially authorized by a January 17 finding to arrange the logistics. Reagan specifically directed CIA not to inform the congressional intelligence committees. There would be three shipments in 1986.

There seems to me little question that, personally, Reagan was motivated to go forward in the Iranian affair almost entirely because of his obsession with getting the American hostages freed. And that obsession affected Casey strongly. Reagan was preoccupied with the fate of the hostages and could not understand why CIA could not locate and rescue them. He put more and more pressure on Casey to find them. Reagan's brand of pressure was hard to resist. No loud words or harsh indictments—none of the style of Johnson or Nixon. Just a quizzical look, a suggestion of pain, and then the request—"We just have to get those people out"—repeated nearly daily, week after week, month after month. Implicit was the accusation: what the hell kind of intelligence agency are you running if you can't find and rescue these Americans?

Much has been written about Casey and the Iranian arms-for-hostages deal. And while trying to block the Soviets from gaining a foothold in Iran undoubtedly played a part in his nearly solitary support for going forward, I believe the roots of his support were in Reagan's nagging him about finding the hostages—and, less important but nonetheless a factor, his hope to get kidnapped CIA station chief William Buckley out of the terrorists' hands. I think he felt both pressured and vulnerable on the hostages, and by the only guy in government whose views really mattered to him.

There is also a more cynical explanation. By late 1985-early 1986, Casey's relationship with Shultz was really in the cellar. In the continuing contest for influence with Reagan, I think Casey perceived the President's strong desire to play out the Iranian string and decided to cater to it, to ally himself with the President in a risky venture as a means of increasing his clout with the boss on other matters—and so much the better if at Shultz's expense. In conversations with me in the spring and summer of 1986, Casey was fairly open in expressing his view that the Iranians were just jerking us around and that we almost certainly would not get all the hostages back. It was equally apparent that he had no intention of spending his political capital with the President in opposing an operation the President wanted very much to go forward. All in all, pursuing the arms-for-hostages deal was for Bill Casey a win-win proposition. He alone among senior advisers was supporting the President, the operation got the President off his back on locating and rescuing the hostages, and if it went sour, it was not his operation but the NSC's.

As the arms deal went along, a central premise of supporters was that there was a "moderate" faction in Tehran or an "opposition" worth cultivating. This was the view of the Israelis and it was the view the NSC adopted. CIA's Iran experts thought differently, and in the spring of 1985 and consistently thereafter they published analyses acknowledging a faction inside Iran that strictly in terms of internal affairs—especially economic policy—might be called moderate. But there was no such faction when it came to the United States. Toward the United States, they were all radicals. This analysis was provided to McFarlane and the NSC. They chose to believe the Israelis. The notion that there was no CIA intelligence on internal Iranian affairs is incorrect. The intelligence we had simply was inconvenient.

There is little doubt in my mind that Casey advanced views in the meetings that did not reflect CIA's own analysis. Further, North established personal relationships with individual CIA analysts who worked with him on terrorist matters and obtained from them information suggesting that Iran was moderating its support for terrorism. This kind of information was used to justify continuing the arms deal and, when used by Casey or the NSC, would infuriate Shultz.

Unfortunately and mistakenly, first McMahon and then I allowed the NSC to limit how many and even who in CIA would be knowledgeable about the arms deal and the NSC dialogue with the Iranians. Thus we were unable to brief our Iranian analysts and then use their views to try to influence Casey or others. Nor were the analysts filled in on the conversations held by the NIO for Terrorism, Charles Allen, with the Iranian go-between, Manucher Ghorbanifar. I don't think their involvement would have changed anyone's mind—meaning Casey or the NSC—at the end of the day, but our failure to insist on their being brought in was negligent and an abdication of responsibility. Allowing the NSC to set the rules for CIA's involvement in the Iran deal, both operationally and analytically, was a serious mistake. In our defense, though, every time McMahon and I challenged the NSC approach, such as on providing intelligence information to the Iranians, Casey backed Poindexter.

Many shelves of libraries are now filled with books about the Iran affair, some accusatory and conspiratorial, others defensive and self-serving. According to the Independent Counsel's report and McFarlane's memoir, virtually all of the senior figures on Reagan's national security team knew a great deal about the origins and then the ongoing details of the Iranian arms-for-hostages operation. Initial claims by both Shultz and Weinberger not to have known much of what was happening were later apparently belied by notes they or their assistants took at the time. This prompts the question of how the dealing with Iran could go on so long in light of the apparently strong opposition of both Shultz and Weinberger, as well as others at senior levels.

I believe the real answer is the last dirty little secret of the Iran affair: no one thought it was that big a deal. With the huge outcry after exposure of the arms sales to Iran and later charges that the administration not only had subverted our policies toward terrorism but also had tried to subvert the Constitution, no one was willing to admit in late 1986 and 1987 that this whole business had been seen inside the government as a wacko, likely-to-fail NSC operation that the President wanted to pursue—and *no one* was willing to put his job on the line to stop it. Amid summits with the Soviets, INF, a revolution in the Philippines, retaliation against Libya, a pro-Soviet coup in South Yemen, getting rid of the Duvaliers in Haiti, wars in the Third World, and more, the Iran operation didn't seem all that important. And so, as it popped up periodically through 1986, the senior members of the Reagan team monitored developments from one hapless negotiation to the next arms shipment to the release of another hostage to the seizure of more hostages. But no one really paid very much attention.

The arms deal could have been stopped at any time if Shultz or Weinberger had thought it important enough. As I have suggested earlier, beginning in the fall of 1983, Shultz's influence grew steadily with the President, to the point where he lost virtually no important strategic battle he carried to the Oval Office. If, at any point in the Iran operation, Shultz had gone to the President and said, "Either it's over *now* or I'm gone tomorrow—no ifs or buts," I—and others—believe it would have ended. Alternatively, had Weinberger done this, it might also have worked, though this is less certain. And if just once the two of them would have put aside their personal animosity and, on this issue where they agreed, gone in privately to the President together with a joint ultimatum, an end to the operation would have been assured. But it just wasn't that important. Until November 25, 1986.

CASEY'S ROLE IN IRAN-CONTRA

With hardly a friend in the Congress or the media, and numerous enemies in the Executive Branch in December 1986, Bill Casey quickly became the evil genius of Iran-Contra. And after he collapsed in mid-December with a brain tumor, became incapacitated, and then died, not just the media and the Congress fingered him as the bad guy; so, too, did anonymous sources in the White House who saw an opportunity to shift blame and responsibility away from the Oval Office. But now it is possible to judge Casey's role more fairly with all the evidence we will ever get.

With respect to the Contras, there is little doubt that the effort to secure foreign funding beginning in 1984 was Casey's idea or, at minimum, an approach he suggested and encouraged. And while he tried to keep the action out of CIA and let State and NSC carry the ball, there may have been one or more occasions in which that line was crossed and CIA officials approached other governments—such as South Africa. Casey may also have originated the idea of a private fund-raising effort, but subsequently did seem to keep his distance from that, referring potential donors and private benefactors to North.

Casey probably also was instrumental in moving operational

management of the Contras from CIA in the summer and fall of 1984 to the NSC, to North. And there seems little doubt that he advised and helped North during the period CIA was proscribed from involvement. Indeed, once the investigations began, even Casey was surprised to see from the record how often he had met and talked with North.

In short, Casey's zeal for the Contra cause led him to take actions clearly contrary to the intent of Congress beginning in the spring of 1984. Whether those actions were illegal was never tested in court. But his activities put the President and CIA, at minimum, in political jeopardy and CIA officers in harm's way.

With respect to the Iran arms-for-hostages operation, Casey was involved from the beginning and, as suggested above, the only senior official who wholeheartedly backed the idea from the outset. In February 1986, he offered a number of specific suggestions on how to conduct the continuing talks with the Iranians. Casey understood the consequences of the secret talks: "The fact of discussions between the U.S. and Iran could change the whole universe. Iraqi resistance would weaken. The Arab world could go mad unless the discussions are carefully and adequately explained."

Again, in a memo to Poindexter at the end of July, Casey reviewed the situation and concluded: "In summary, based on the intelligence at my disposal, I believe that we should consider what we may be prepared to do to meet [the Iranians'] minimum requirements that would lead to release of the rest of the hostages. . . . I am convinced that this may be the only way to proceed, given the delicate factional balance in Iran."

Casey's support for the arms-for-hostages deal was more than pro forma, more than just in meetings with the President, and much more aggressive than he conveyed to me, his deputy. His motives were mixed, both in terms of his relationship with the President and geostrategically. He felt vulnerable on the hostages and CIA's failure even to find them. He was irritated that we didn't and couldn't do more. Thus he became aggressive in trying to find some way to get them released, and just as aggressive in telling the President all he was doing.

He cared about William Buckley, but I believe he was not motivated primarily in the Iran affair by concern for the kidnapped Beirut station chief, as others have alleged. He was not callous, but neither did he flinch from taking losses in wars against either terrorists or Soviet surrogates.

Finally, for reasons described below, I am convinced his support was not based on the opportunity to use the Iran operation to get more money for the Contras.

What about Casey and the diversion? I believe that the weight of the evidence now, in contrast to 1987, strongly supports the conclusion that Casey probably did *not* know about the diversion of funds from the Iran operation to the Contras.

• First, after a seven-year investigation, the Independent Counsel, Lawrence Walsh, found not a single document nor took a word of testimony to the effect that Casey knew about the diversion—except from Oliver North. Not from Poindexter, McFarlane, retired Air Force general and arms-deal middleman Richard Secord, or anyone else.

• Second, Poindexter testified before the Joint Congressional Iran-Contra Committee in the summer of 1987 that he never discussed the diversion with Casey. The notion that only three people in government knew of the diversion and that North discussed it with Poindexter and Casey separately but that Casey and Poindexter never discussed it at all stretches credulity to the breaking point. Poindexter had every reason in the summer of 1987 to include Casey in the circle of those knowing of the diversion. He had no reason to protect the dead DCI. Thus his testimony is credible.

• Third, in a computer message (PROF note) on May 15, 1986, Poindexter specifically told North not to tell Casey about the diversion. He later testified, "I did not want to put him or anybody else in a position of being evasive in terms of answering [congressional] questions."

• Fourth, all through the spring of 1986, Casey was worried about how the Contras would survive until the congressionally approved CIA program resumed on October 1. Indeed, on May 16 (the day after Poindexter told North not to reveal the diversion to Casey), the DCI told the President in an NSC meeting about the Contras' dire straits. Yet that same day North had advised Poindexter that several million dollars had just been received from the Iran arms deal and made available to the Contras. Casey might be willing to be evasive with the Congress, but would he knowingly mislead the President? With others present, he could have just kept silent.

• Fifth, according to both Attorney General Meese and the Independent Counsel, from the first questioning of North about the diversion (on November 23, 1986) until Casey's death, North never mentioned Casey as one of those who knew about the diversion. Only after the DCI was safely in his grave did Ollie implicate him. Indeed, the Independent Counsel points out, "The credibility of North's testimony is weakened by the fact that he never made such assertions while Casey was alive." Finally, when North told Fiers about the diversion, he did not say that Casey knew. Why not?

• Sixth, North's testimony about Casey is not credible in other respects. He testified, for example, that Casey gave him a poison pill to carry on the trip to Iran with McFarlane in May 1986. Yet there is no record at CIA of such a pill (known as an "L" pill— for lethal) being prepared. Did Casey go down to his basement and prepare this capsule with his home chemistry set? Get one at the drugstore? In more than a quarter century in CIA, I am aware of only one of these pills being authorized for an agent, and the paperwork was extraordinary. After the congressional investigations of the mid-1970s, and revelations of CIA experiments, it would have been unthinkable for CIA's scientific and technology directorate clandestinely to prepare such a pill without a paper trail to protect themselves. Similarly, North claims Casey gave him a ledger to keep track of the monies collected and dispersed through the various bank accounts. Did Casey just walk down to the local stationers and buy it for Ollie? Requisition it from CIA office supplies? Why not simply tell North to buy his own? It doesn't pass the giggle test.

• Seventh, when Charles Allen, the NIO for Terrorism and the CIA officer who first suspected the diversion, told Casey of his suspicions on October 7 in my presence, both Allen and I thought Casey looked surprised. Further, while it means little to skeptics on the outside, Casey told a number of us at CIA in private conversations that he had not known of the diversion, and I think we all believed him.

In sum, I believe Casey bears much responsibility for off-line actions in support of the Contras between 1984 and 1986, actions that in some cases were improper and may have been illegal. Similarly, he was an important and informed advocate of the arms-for-hostages deal with Iran. However, I am convinced he did not know about the diversion that connected the Iran and Contra operations. If true, this in turn means that the so-called Enterprise for unauthorized covert actions beyond Nicaragua funded by the diversion was probably a figment of North's imagination.

CHAPTER TWENTY-THREE
Geneva to Washington

THE ROAD TO REYKJAVIK

Everyone knew by the end of 1985 that Gorbachev desperately needed improved relations with the West, especially with the United States. Because of multiple crises at home, he needed to constrain the arms race, and new U.S. strategic programs in particular, to avoid new Soviet military expenditures and perhaps even allow some reductions in spending. Domestic crises compelled Soviet initiatives to relax tensions.

Throughout 1985 and 1986, Gorbachev tried to achieve that change in atmosphere on the cheap—without paying anything for it. He changed the tone and the face of Soviet foreign policy but not the substance. Military spending remained about the same, and maybe even rose a little. The Soviets continued to pour money into their client states and into their adventures in the Third World. Where Soviet military forces or advisers were directly involved in combat, as in Afghanistan and Angola, operations were intensified and offensives became even more aggressive. From the Geneva Summit in November 1985 through the Reykjavik Summit a year later, Gorbachev attempted to deflect attention from these realities and to kill SDI with dramatic arms control initiatives.

How to respond to Gorbachev and counter the public image of a Soviet Union leaning far forward to reduce the nuclear threat dominated debate in the Reagan administration in 1986. From this distant perspective, there was little difference in the administration on the basic response: don't budge, and keep the pressure on the Soviets everywhere.

However, there was a real difference of views on how to pursue that strategy. Weinberger and Casey, because of their suspicion of Shultz and negotiators in general, were very leery of engaging with the Soviets at all. Shultz, no less unyielding on basic strategy, was convinced that Gorbachev had to move in our direction at some point and believed the United States could accelerate that process by engaging the Soviets on nearly every subject at nearly every opportunity. I think he believed that flexibility and modest concessions on our part would result in major, fundamental concessions on the part of an increasingly desperate Soviet Union. But the core U.S. strategy, agreed by all (though they'd never admit it), was very tough: stand firm on basic U.S. positions in arms control and aggressive actions in the Third World, and let Gorbachev come to us. As Shultz said all the time, "They're moving toward our agenda."

DISTRACTION

The United States, during the first half of 1986, also was preoccupied with Libya, the retaliatory raid after the bombing of La Belle Disco, and the follow-up. The April attack on Libya, a Soviet client, prompted Moscow to cancel the scheduled meeting between Shultz and Shevardnadze in mid-May.

Throughout May and June, there were intense debates in the Situation Room over launching a second air strike against Libya, promoting internal problems in Libya, and economic sabotage— from attacks on refineries to disruption of communications and computers. Casey was partial to the latter.

Internal disagreements in the administration over what to do in Libya that had plagued deliberations in 1985 returned after the bombing attack in April, with the result that—as usual—the action was handed to CIA. Casey sought operations for sabotage, disruption of Libyan communications and computers, and more.

At an NSC meeting on August 14, Casey reviewed what CIA had been doing to stir up trouble inside Libya and to keep Qaddafi off balance. The main purpose of these activities was to demonstrate Qaddafi's internal weakness to the Libyan population and to encourage any opposition to act. Our activities included launching balloons from ships of the Sixth Fleet (on August 23–24 to coincide with the anniversary of Qaddafi's revolution) with messages to overthrow the government. When briefed on this, I said to make sure that the leaflets were specific that it was *Qaddafi* that should be overthrown. CIA's experience with balloons was not unblemished, and I could just see strong winds carrying the balloons with a generic "overthrow your oppressive government" into Egypt where they would be picked up. I didn't think Egyptian President Hosni Mubarak would be pleased. We also launched small empty boats from offshore to give the impression to Qaddafi and his henchmen that commando teams had been landed.

The use of U.S. Navy ships for these operations led to a fight between CIA and Defense that we thought was a joke and they thought was serious. I got a call from my friend Rich Armitage, then Assistant Secretary of Defense for International Security Affairs, who said that Defense would be billing us $4.5 million for use of the ships. Armitage and I were always kidding around and so I thought he was pulling my leg. I told him I didn't realize we had been renting the Sixth Fleet, and if they were trying to catch up on their budget maybe they could rent it out for birthday parties and so on. Rich wasn't kidding. The next week, Deputy Defense Secretary Will Taft told me that they were having trouble collecting their money from us. I told him I regarded the bill as a joke: were we now being asked to pay for essentially routine operations of the Sixth Fleet? Taft then went to his fallback position and asked if we would pay for flying the balloons to the Mediterranean port where they had been loaded on the ship. I finally agreed that the Agency should reimburse Defense $200,000 for that.

Armitage was an unusual person in Washington, one of those individuals at the sub-Cabinet level who wield tremendous influence. One of the most powerful officials in the Reagan Defense Department, Rich Armitage—like nearly everyone in Washington who gets anything accomplished—had a wide array of powerful friends and a few powerful enemies. A down-to-earth, funny guy, he was popular at all levels in Defense, but especially among the lower ranks. Physically intimidating, a sort of human Abrams tank, Rich was also smart and savvy, very knowledgeable about the world and international politics. He was as welcome and comfortable in the palaces of the Middle East and power centers of Asia as he was in the NCO Club. A man totally lacking any kind of ethnic or racial prejudice, he was supremely politically incorrect in his humor, drawing on the largest collection of dirty jokes in Washington. The more effete the company, the more inclined Rich was to dredge up some really gross joke just to see the reaction. He was a great asset to Weinberger and later Carlucci, and brought wisdom, street smarts, and common sense to the highest councils of government.

BACK TO THE SOVIETS

In parallel with planning for the retaliation against Libya and subsequent actions, the administration battled in early 1986 over whether the United States should continue to adhere to the SALT II treaty. This was part of the larger struggle to determine the next steps in—and the overall direction of—the U.S.-Soviet relationship. As before, despite occasional tactical setbacks for Shultz, most often relating to negotiating positions affecting SDI, it became clear that he and the President were on the same wavelength in terms of dealing with the Soviets. Reagan believed, and said in meetings at the time, that Gorbachev was groping for an approach toward the United States, and that it might be that Soviet actions on divided families and other human rights problems were a way of testing what Reagan had told Gorbachev in Geneva—namely, that the U.S. represented no threat and there was no desire to harm them. Reagan said he wanted to give Gorbachev some ammunition to use with the hard-liners by expressing appreciation for those gestures, by pressing for more "collaborative" activities.

Originally, a meeting between Shultz and Shevardnadze in Washington on September 19 had been intended to focus on preparations for a planned summit. Instead, as so often happened in the relationship, the planned agenda had to be scrapped to deal with a dust-up—in this case, finding a way out of the Daniloff affair. Within an hour of final judicial disposition on September 30 of the Soviet spy Zakharov and his release, Reagan announced that he and Gorbachev would meet in Iceland on October 10–12.

REYKJAVIK: HIT OR MISS?

The so-called working summit between Reagan and Gorbachev at Reykjavik remains the most controversial U.S.-Soviet summit of the last half of the Cold War. What seems clear with the advantage of several years' perspective is that Gorbachev took a very high-stakes, high-risk gamble to set up Ronald Reagan, ambush him, and kill SDI. And the measure of how much the

Soviets feared SDI is how much they were prepared to give up to get rid of it.

The Soviet setup began before the summit convened. In the days before the leaders arrived in Iceland, the Soviets took extensive steps to shape U.S. government and public perceptions of their agenda. Publicly and privately, they tried to create the impression that the Soviet focus at the summit would be on INF and nuclear testing. During those days, dozens of Soviet diplomats and intelligence officers around the world told Westerners that the Soviets would be prepared to be flexible on these two issues. Few even mentioned SDI.

For a meeting billed as a "private" working summit, the Soviets took major steps to assure tremendous press coverage from their side. By the end of the day the leaders arrived, October 10, the Soviets already had held half a dozen different press conferences or meetings with the international press corps, and they broke an agreed press blackout on the 11th to announce Soviet offers and proposals of "historic proportion."

During the sessions between the President and Gorbachev and parallel negotiations between Paul Nitze and Marshal Akhromeyev, the Soviets laid out an amazing cornucopia of concessions in nearly every area of arms control. Reagan got into the spirit of the occasion and repeated his July proposal to eliminate all ballistic missiles, and Gorbachev then proposed to eliminate all strategic offensive forces. Then they agreed to eliminate all nuclear weapons. The tabling of Soviet concessions and dramatic proposals previously regarded as pipe dreams left the American participants agog.

Then Gorbachev sprang the trap. Surveying all that was on the table, all the progress that had been made, a smiling Gorbachev said: "This all depends, of course, on you giving up SDI." He had taken Reagan to the mountaintop, showed him a historic achievement, and tempted him. But there was a flaw in the plan—Gorbachev, like so many before him, underestimated Ronald Reagan. The President got mad. He realized he had been set up. He talked a little more about why the Soviets had nothing to fear from SDI and, as Gorbachev remained unyielding, Reagan got even angrier. Finally, as he later wrote, he turned to Shultz and said, "The meeting is over. Let's go, George, we're leaving."

Gorbachev had hoped, and perhaps believed (like many Americans, including government officials), that SDI was a bargaining ploy for Reagan, a means to elicit Soviet concessions, something that could be negotiated. Shultz earlier had learned differently. Reagan truly believed in SDI and that it promised a safer future for Americans and the rest of the world. And what he believed deeply could not be shaken.

Initially, the reaction was that the summit was a disaster. Some were disappointed that the remarkable progress made in nearly every arms control arena seemed to have been sacrificed for SDI. Others, including our allies and many at home, were horrified by Reagan's agreement to eliminate all ballistic missiles and more, thus giving up our deterrent to superior Soviet conventional forces, and deeply relieved that all had come to naught.

Gorbachev's ambush had failed and, in fact, it backfired badly. He had exposed at Reykjavik far-reaching Soviet bargaining positions in arms control that could not be erased or forgotten. We now knew what they could accept and how far they would go. Further, he had learned the hard way that Reagan had meant all along what he had said about SDI—and that the American President would not give it up.

The Soviets had come far toward American positions on INF and START, and we had moved very little. After Reykjavik, most knew that Gorbachev would keep coming because he had no choice.

In his memoirs, Shultz complains that at Reykjavik he saw "once again, how poor the quality of our intelligence was about the Soviet Union. We had no accurate help from the intelligence community about what to expect. . . ." That simply is not true. A few days before the summit, on October 7, Casey briefed at an NSC meeting: "We think Gorbachev will press hardest on limiting SDI. . . . He will have to use the appeal of nuclear reductions to get you to agree to constraints that would effectively block SDI and eventually kill the program. . . ." We also had made the point about SDI being Gorbachev's key issue at the summit at various interagency meetings concerned with arms control.

CASEY'S LAST MONTHS: TRAGEDY AND WHITE HOUSE POLITICS

After the brief moments of euphoria in Reykjavik, the U.S.-Soviet relationship would spiral downward for several months. But if that relationship became a little frosty, Ronald Reagan's Presidency went into the deep freeze after Reykjavik.

It started when the Republicans lost control of the Senate in the election on November 3. Revelation the same day in a Beirut newspaper of the arms sales to Iran and then disclosure three weeks later of the diversion of money from the Iranians to the Contras brought the administration to its knees. The in-fighting became murderous, with Shultz offering for the umpteenth time to resign and Casey sending Reagan an ugly, personally offensive, politically dumb letter demanding that Shultz be fired for not being a team player—"You need a new pitcher!"

But within weeks, it was Casey who was gone, not Shultz. The DCI's collapse, resignation, and death not only affected the outcome of the investigations but also removed from the scene an independent actor in foreign policy and obstacle to faster progress with the Soviets. Because of the importance of his illness and giving up power—and the myths that have grown up around those events —the circumstances are worth recounting.

Casey was able to testify for nearly three weeks before he collapsed. The second week of December 1986 was a difficult one for him. He had several Iran-Contra hearings on the Hill and faced another grueling session with the Senate Intelligence Committee on December 16, this time under oath. As Deputy, I had received reports from the DCI's security officers that Casey had been falling and bumping into things at home for several days. In contrast to allegations later made by others, I had seen no particular change in Casey's behavior in the preceding weeks or months that might suggest he was ill.

On Monday morning, December 15, DCI Security told me that Casey had become even more unsteady on his feet over the weekend, and I noticed a cut on his forehead caused by a fall. He arrived late, about 9:00, and came into my office (which adjoined his) about 9:30. He looked terrible and was very unsteady, moving hand over hand from one piece of furniture to another and sitting down in front of my desk. We talked for a bit and then he went back into his office to prepare for his Senate testimony the next day.

Between 10:00 and 10:15, Jim McCullough, Casey's and my chief of staff, came into my office and told me Casey had just collapsed while an Agency doctor had been taking his blood pressure. I opened the door between our offices and watched as they gave Bill injections and finally put him on a stretcher. I did not know what had happened or the seriousness of the Director's situation, but I had a feeling in the pit of my stomach that he would never be back.

Casey went through tests for three days, including his own demand for a second opinion on the diagnosis of a brain tumor and recommended surgery. The surgery took place on Thursday, December 18.

On December 22, I met with Vice President Bush to fill him in on Casey's condition. He suggested that I stay in touch with him and that he would keep both Don Regan and the President advised. I told the Vice President that I hoped people would wait in terms of Casey's future to see if he would recover sufficiently to resume his duties. I said I thought I could handle things as Acting Director until that time.

I went on to say that, in light of speculation already taking place about a successor, if there was a decision to appoint a replacement I hoped that someone from the outside would be a person of distinction, with clout on the Hill and access in the White House who would move the Agency forward without ripping up what had been accomplished at CIA in the preceding six years. The Vice President added that he also would not want the impression "to gain currency" that a professional could not be DCI.

After the holidays, as speculation resumed in the press about a successor to Casey, I saw Regan and for the first time talked with Carlucci, the new National Security Adviser. At each meeting I repeated the three available options in order of my preference— give Casey time to recover and make his own decision to resign, appoint a distinguished outsider, or appoint a professional.

Casey's recovery, however, was very slow. By mid-January, it seemed clear that he wasn't coming back to the Agency, ever. I was told he could barely speak at all—monosyllables at best. Thus I was very surprised when, on Saturday, January 24, the phone rang and a CIA security officer at the hospital told me the DCI wanted to speak to me. He came on the line and tried to force his gruff and hale "Hi, Bob!" It was garbled but I could recognize what he was attempting to say. It was an awkward conversation. He would try to say something and I would get enough to ask him if such and such was what he was trying to say. He could then reply with a one-word answer, usually a hard-to-distinguish yes or no. In the course of that conversation, we agreed that I would try to come see him—for the first time—on January 26 or 27. When I told all this to Mrs. Casey on the 26th, she said she thought the end of the week would be better.

On January 27, one of the DCI Security officers told me that Mr. and Mrs. Casey had been closeted, had written a number of notes, and were having a very serious discussion. Later, another security officer passed the word that on the morning of January 28 Mr. Casey had started to dictate to one of his security agents the words "I believe the time has come to . . . ," at which point Mrs. Casey cut off the conversation.

Mrs. Casey called me the same morning—the 28th—and asked me to come see Bill that evening. I let Regan know about the meeting, and he urged me to see if I could open the subject of the future with the Caseys. I said I'd try.

I arrived at the hospital about 5:00 p.m. I was struck by how relatively unchanged Casey looked physically—he had lost some weight but not a lot and there were no bandages or scars on his head that I could see. He was seated by the window in a blue bathrobe. He was very happy to see me. We chatted for a few minutes—him uttering a few syllables and Mrs. Casey and I filling in and leading him. I then said that I had some business to discuss with him, and Mrs. Casey left the room. I went through a list of developments abroad and in the Agency that I knew would interest him. As I was talking, he rather abruptly slammed his arm down on the arm of his chair and said in a very hard to understand voice that it was time for him to move on, "to get out of the way," and for me to take over. I told him that was a very sad decision and one I had not wanted to contemplate. I thanked him for wanting me to succeed him, but said that there were other candidates being considered and powerful political crosscurrents at work. I mentioned some of the candidates, and he reacted to each in his own unambiguous way.

He then motioned for me to get a piece of paper and conveyed that he wanted me to write a resignation letter for him. At that point, I decided I'd better get Mrs. Casey in on the discussion and so went out and got her. When she came in she asked him if he was sure he wanted to move so quickly and perhaps he should wait a bit. He was very forceful in indicating that he wanted to act immediately. He made clear to us that he wanted to do the resignation letter and then call the President.

I knew the President would not be able to understand Casey

and told Bill that Regan would have an important role—perhaps I should arrange for Regan to come see him the next day. The Caseys agreed that was a good idea. I then said that I thought it would be a good idea to have someone else present who had independent access to the President and who was a good friend of Bill's—and I suggested Ed Meese. They liked that idea a lot. Bill again pushed the paper at me to write his resignation letter, but I refused. Soon thereafter, I left. I called Meese from my car, and he said he would participate in the meeting the next morning. I then went to the White House to report to Regan. He said he, too, would go.

When I reported to Regan the night of the 28th on my meeting with Casey, I mentioned that Casey's wife, Sophia, had been a very tough lady in all of this; he said that I didn't know the half of it—that he had that problem in spades. A clear reference to Mrs. Reagan, in my view. In any event, Regan asked me to prepare a resignation letter and see if I could get it signed when I saw the DCI again the evening of the 29th.

Regan and I met yet again on the afternoon before I was to see Casey so he could tell me about his and Meese's meeting with him. With respect to a successor, I said again that I hoped an outsider would bring clout and access, be someone who could work with the other national security principals, and someone who would move the agenda forward, looking to the future. I then said that I could not let the occasion pass without saying that I thought I could do as good a job as anyone in the position. I concluded by saying that however the matter was resolved, I wanted him to know that my success in managing the Agency for the preceding seven weeks in rather extraordinary circumstances had been due in no small part to his support and the confidence he had given me that I had whatever access or help I might need. I thanked him for that.

I got up to leave, but Regan said, "Well, just one more thing. Do you really want the job?" And I said that I had mixed feelings about it but yes, I did. He then said, "Well, you got it." He said he had talked to the President that morning and again after the meeting with Casey, and that the President had decided. He said that I had to give him my word that I wouldn't tell anyone, and there would be an announcement on Monday morning.

That same evening, at 6:00, I saw the DCI again. We talked— sort of—for nearly half an hour until Mrs. Casey arrived. This time he was lying in bed. I went out in the hall once she arrived and let her read the short letter I had drafted. She was overcome for a moment, quickly composed herself, and we went back in. I showed Bill the letter and he said it was fine.

We moved to the side of Casey's bed to give him a chance to try to sign the letter with his left hand (his right was paralyzed) or at least initial the letter. We tried for several minutes to get it in a position where he could sign it. After the first attempt, Mrs. Casey kept telling him that he should just let her sign it for him, that he couldn't write. But he kept trying. Finally, impatiently, he handed the letter to her, and she signed it. At that point, she was crying, and he lay back on the pillow with tears in his eyes and said, "Well, that's the end of a career." And I said, "It was never supposed to end like this." I held his hand for a few minutes and left.

I met with Regan the next morning, the 30th, at 9:45. I gave him the resignation letter, which I had signed as witness. We then went to the Oval Office about 10:00. The Vice President was coming out, shook my hand, and whispered congratulations. We went in and first Regan handed the President the letter of resignation. The President read it, sadly acknowledged it, and I told him what Bill had said after Sophia signed it. He then told Regan that there had to be a very nice letter back to the Director. Regan said of course, after the announcement on Monday.

The President then turned to me and said: "I have a decision to make about the Director of CIA. Are you interested?" I said yes, and went on that it was a great honor but I wished it could have been under almost any other circumstances. He acknowledged that. He and Regan then talked to me about both access and the importance of being thoroughly professional, that is, in bringing straight information to the President—that I had to be the one to tell it straight. The President also said that Casey had often brought him particularly interesting pieces of information and that I should feel free to do likewise. I thanked him and told him that it had been a pleasure to serve him and Bill Casey during the first six years of his administration and I hoped we could make the last two as successful as the first six. President Reagan congratulated me again, shook my hand, and Regan and I left. Later, I would have the impression that I had been the second or third choice for the job—a job no one else seemed to want at the end of January 1987. No wonder.

TRIAL BY FIRE: A DATE WITH THE SENATE

On December 3, 1986, I was told by CIA's Office of Congressional Affairs that the Senate Intelligence Committee wanted me to testify the next day on Iran-Contra. I was surprised and a little dismayed. I had been DDI until April, had had virtually nothing to do with the operational side of CIA's activities in Central America (or anywhere else) up to that time, and the Iran operation already was in place and going on well before I became DDCI. From time to time I had weighed in with Casey when I felt the Agency was being harmed by our own mistakes in Central America (e.g., the mining and my recommendation for a change in DDO). I had reviewed findings as DDI and occasionally would be given a chance to comment on proposed activities. Sometimes Casey listened to me; just as often he did not. Similarly, I had gotten a glimpse of the Iran operation in a meeting with McMahon and others in early December 1985, but was more fully clued in at the end of January when the DI was asked to provide intelligence on the Iraqi battle front for Iran. McMahon and I had objected to Casey and had been overruled. At the time, I had no knowledge of Casey's close working relationship with North on Central America or of the DCI's aggressive involvement in the arms-for-hostages dealings.

Finally, to my way of thinking, when things began to come unglued in the fall of 1986, I had been on the side of the angels. Hearing from a senior CIA officer, Charles Allen, of his suspicions of the diversion, I told him to brief Casey. When Casey told him to prepare a paper describing his concerns and I saw the paper, I asked Casey for authorization to fill in CIA's General Counsel and get his advice on what to do. When the General Counsel said to give the paper to Poindexter and tell him to involve the White House Counsel, I persuaded Casey to do that. And, when it came time to prepare Casey's testimony in November on Iran-Contra, I directed full disclosure.

So I went to the Senate Intelligence Committee hearing room, S-219, a bit uneasy but fairly confident that I had acted properly at each step of the way. What I was unprepared for as I entered the hallway leading to the hearing room was the media frenzy. This was a first for me. Scores of photographers, TV cameramen, and reporters shouting and stumbling over one another. Surrounded by security officers, I felt as if I were being taken to the dock for trial —the only thing missing was the handcuffs. It was unsettling, but once inside the hearing room, I calmed down. I had had little time to review my calendars or files, or even search my memory, but had a few notes and dates scribbled on a legal tablet. And the hearing didn't seem to go too badly.

That appearance on December 4 was the beginning of seven years of testimony, public and private, depositions and written responses to countless questions. It was an odd stretch of time, a time of great personal satisfaction as DDCI, then Deputy National Security Adviser, and finally as DCI. But throughout, it was a time punctuated by days of enormous strain and occasional, gut-wrenching fear over the continuing Independent Counsel investigation.

During the period, I testified or gave depositions repeatedly before the Senate and House intelligence committees, other congressional committees, the Iran-Contra Committee, the Tower Board appointed by the President to investigate Iran-Contra, and, worst of all, the Independent Counsel. I always appeared voluntarily and cooperated totally. As DDCI and then as Acting DCI for the first five months of the investigations, I insisted that CIA cooperate completely with investigators and virtually always resolved disputes over access in ways favorable to the investigators.

The congressional inquiries did not ever accuse me of wrongdoing in Iran-Contra. But I was severely criticized on two counts: first, that after becoming DDCI I should have objected more vigorously to the ongoing Iran affair, especially the continuing nonnotification of the intelligence committees (directed by the President), including a willingness to resign if they were not informed; and, second, after being told by Charles Allen of his suspicion of the diversion, I likewise should have reacted much more strongly by demanding that Casey go to the Attorney General (or go myself if he wouldn't) and by demanding full disclosure to the intelligence committees. I was criticized for willfully keeping myself uninformed on what was going on in Central America, and for not aggressively looking into both the Iran and Contra operations once I became DDCI.

In my mind, and as I testified, there were mitigating circumstances—for example, reassurance from Agency lawyers that there was nothing illegal about the Iran operation, including nonnotification of the Congress. Further, I knew John McMahon had been a real stickler for the rules and, had he been aware of any impropriety or continuing questionable actions with respect to either Iran or Central America, I was certain he would have blown the whistle, or at least warned me. I was new to the job and was trying to learn the ropes while all this was going on. And, finally, I had acted in response to Allen's suspicions by going to the General Counsel and by following his advice with respect to informing Poindexter that something didn't smell right.

I would go over those points in my mind a thousand times in the months and years to come, but the criticisms still hit home. A thousand times I would go over the "might-have-beens" if I had raised more hell than I did with Casey about nonnotification of Congress, if I had demanded that the NSC get out of covert action, if I had insisted that CIA not play by NSC rules, if I had been more aggressive with the DO in my first months as DDCI, if I had gone to the Attorney General on Allen's suspicions of a diversion, if . . .

In his testimony before the Iran-Contra Committee, Shultz had said, "I don't give myself an A-plus in all this" and "I looked and asked myself, did I do enough, could I have done more?" I asked myself the same questions and I did not like my answers, despite a sense that whatever I might have done likely wouldn't have changed anything. I had expertly handled foreign policy crises for years. In my first crisis as DDCI, I gave myself a C-minus, but I graded on a curve that included the actions of officials far more senior elsewhere in government. Others were not so generous.

Because I had been close to Casey and at CIA during the period of Iran-Contra, because of my failure to act more vigorously as described above, and because this was at an early stage in the investigations and there were still many unanswered questions about CIA's (and my) role, I ran into a buzz saw from several Republicans and most of the Democrats on the committee when President Reagan nominated me to take Casey's place as DCI. Congress was outraged over Iran-Contra, and I was the first piece of business to greet the new Democratic majority in the Senate on their return to work in February 1987. And I was a great target. As the second day of hearings was getting under way, I was talking with the forty or fifty photographers arrayed in front of the witness table. One of them asked me, "How do you like the job [DCI] so far?" I replied, "You know that country and western song, 'Take This Job and Shove It'?" To my chagrin, it turned out there had been an open television microphone in front of me, and that quote led the news that night on two networks. It accurately conveyed my sentiments, though.

Two days of hearings were planned in mid-February, and at the end it was apparent the nomination would not move quickly—and if it did, it would be defeated. There were just too many unanswered questions about CIA's role and mine. The chairman of the Senate Intelligence Committee, David Boren, told me privately that if the nomination were deferred until fall, after the Iran-Contra Committee reported its findings, it might still be successful. I knew CIA and the intelligence community could not go that long without a confirmed DCI. Further, with Howard Baker as new White House Chief of Staff as of March 2 and Frank Carlucci as new National Security Adviser in December, it was clear my nomination was too easy a target for those who wanted to keep Iran-Contra an open wound for President Reagan. Although I got a call from the White House on Friday evening, February 27, to reassure me—in light of press speculation—that the President still strongly supported my nomination, I knew what I had to do.

I called Howard Baker in Tennessee on Saturday, February 28, and told him that we should meet first thing on Monday—his first day in the White House. We met privately at first in his corner office in the West Wing, and I went through the arguments pro and con for hanging in there, and then told Howard I thought I should withdraw for the good of the country, the President, and the Agency. I also allowed as how I wasn't having a lot of fun personally either, what with the press stories every day and reporters camped out at the end of my driveway. I suspect Howard was immensely relieved that I had taken the initiative, because I am sure it would have been only a short time before he would have had to. He asked Carlucci to join us, I repeated my decision, and offered to remain as Deputy, an offer they quickly took up. Carlucci said I deserved a medal. We then walked to the Oval Office where we told the President.

Within a day or two of my withdrawal, Reagan nominated the then-director of the FBI, Judge William Webster, to be DCI. Webster had been the head of the FBI for nine years and was preparing to retire so his successor would not be selected in the politically superheated atmosphere of a presidential election in 1988. Webster was sworn in as Director of Central Intelligence on May 26.

I had been acting DCI just over five months, throughout the worst of the investigations of CIA's role in Iran-Contra. The personal toll had been heavy, from my hearings and withdrawal as nominee to be DCI, to leading CIA and the intelligence community alone through a bad period. I liked and admired Webster a great deal, and looked forward to his arrival and to working with him.

It was with the feeling of a great weight lifted from my shoulders that I returned to my office after his afternoon swearing-in ceremony—only to learn that my brother was on the telephone holding for me. My father, with whom I had been very close, had died unexpectedly in Kansas at the very moment Bill Webster had taken the oath of office. He had been suffering from heart problems and I believed, then and now, that the strain on him of my DCI nomination, hearings, and withdrawal had hastened his death by months, if not more. The shock of his death, on top of all I had been through during the past six months, was too much. I closed the door to my office, sat down at my desk, and wept.

Webster was a godsend to the Agency and to me. He had a huge reputation for integrity, honesty, and fidelity to the Constitution. After some twenty years as a federal judge and as FBI director, just as he was preparing to return to private life and a deserved opportunity to prosper, he put his reputation on the line for CIA. He agreed, with CIA still under a shadow, to do another public service for his country and his President. Bill would later be criticized from time to time for his lack of expertise in foreign affairs and more—but none of that, in my view, amounted to a hill of beans compared to what he brought to CIA that May: leadership, the respect of Congress, and a sterling character.

Remaining in Washington in a senior official position after withdrawing in controversy from candidacy to a higher position is nearly unprecedented and awkward in the extreme. People don't know what to say, you are embarrassed by what has happened and by all the publicity, you feel like a leper for whom people have sympathy but still don't want to get too close. It was all the more awkward because I would remain Acting DCI for another three months and was thus forced to remain in circulation, rather than do what I wanted—which was just hide.

Funnily enough, my withdrawal had some important positive aspects. I heard from senators across the political spectrum that what had happened was simply bad timing, the nomination coming so soon after the storm of Iran-Contra broke. Suddenly, important and influential people in and out of Washington befriended me. I received countless letters of encouragement and support. And, most important to me, unlike some others touched by Iran-Contra, it soon became apparent that the Congress still trusted me and I developed closer relationships than ever with many members of the House and Senate, both Republicans and Democrats, from left and right. (When I was up for confirmation again in 1991, most of the leaders of the Iran-Contra committee as well as the committee's chief counsel would support me.) I had had to stand up in the middle of a terrible political storm and, very much alone, defend myself and CIA—the White House was nowhere to be seen. I had taken a beating but was willing to remain in the ring, and a lot of people seemed to admire that. And so I came out of the 1987 confirmation experience ending in my withdrawal without any bitterness or hard feelings. But much, much wiser.

From the Jaws of Disaster

Truth be told, Iran-Contra paved the way for the significant advances in U.S.-Soviet relations during the last two years of the Reagan administration. Sure, the immediate impact was negative in that the President was temporarily unhinged, the administration's relationship with Congress battered, his credibility and political strength gravely undermined, and his administration in disarray.

But the aftermath of Iran-Contra also produced a dramatic change of senior officials and the constellation of power in the administration, with significant consequences for foreign policy. Casey, the most vocal and wiliest conservative and Shultz opponent in the national security arena, was put out of action in mid-December by a brain tumor. Poindexter was gone from the NSC and replaced by the experienced, politically savvy, and pragmatic Frank Carlucci, with Lt. General Colin Powell called home from Germany to be his deputy. Soon, Regan, too, was gone, replaced by former Senator Howard Baker and his new deputy, Ken Duberstein.

Meanwhile, Shultz's influence in Washington, already great, soared as his opposition to the Iran arms sales became known. It would grow even more as a result of his testimony before the Iran-Contra congressional committee in the summer of 1987, in which he condemned not only Iran-Contra, but the NSC, CIA, and everyone who had crossed his path. The self-righteous indignation of the most senior Reagan cabinet officer, who much later would be shown to have known so much and yet done so little about the

Iran affair, offended many of George Shultz's colleagues in the administration—many of whom had been as opposed to the Iran operation as he had—even as he was lionized by Congress and the press. But the congressional, media, and public response to Shultz's opposition to the scheme once and for all established him as the dominant voice in the administration. Weinberger, now the lone hard-liner left at the top of the national security team, would not be stilled, but his influence with Reagan on U.S.-Soviet issues was fading fast and within a year, he, too, would be gone.

The other major effect of Iran-Contra on U.S.-Soviet relations was to convince Reagan, his wife, and his closest White House advisers that the terrible stain of the scandal could only be removed, or at least diminished, by the President becoming a peacemaker, by his achievement of a historic breakthrough with the Soviet Union.

Gorbachev, as well, had run into political heavy weather at home. His reform efforts had bogged down, and in December he confronted anti-Russian riots in Kazakhstan. He characteristically seized the offensive, and at the Central Committee Plenum in January 1987 attacked the party bureaucracy and launched a major political reform. He rammed through personnel changes that strengthened his position, and made even more far-reaching personnel changes at another plenum in June.

In sum, after a bad winter, both Reagan and Gorbachev were ready to move ahead by early spring 1987.

On to Washington

On February 28, 1987, Gorbachev announced that the Soviets were willing to abandon their previous, long-held position that tied progress in all the arms control arenas together—the Soviets were willing to detach INF and not hold it hostage to solution of the SDI issue. The lesson of Reykjavik had been learned. Gorbachev's offer, though, was also an important break for Reagan, then floundering in Iran-Contra. For the first time since the scandal broke, he appeared before the press to welcome Gorbachev's offer. On March 6, the United States announced that Shultz would travel to Moscow in April to pursue INF and a possible summit later in the year.

Signs of real change in the Soviet Union appeared one after another during this period. Those we knew about, we understood were important. For example, it was hard to miss the impact of the German teenager Mathias Rust piloting his little plane to a landing on Red Square on May 28 and the sweeping purge of the military that followed. That same day, Gorbachev was presenting to the leaders of the Warsaw Pact in East Berlin a new Soviet military doctrine, a "defensive" doctrine. This new doctrine, announced publicly on May 30, gave priority to preventing war, and declared that the Warsaw Pact would start no conflict unless attacked first, did not see any state as their enemy, had no territorial claims in or outside of Europe, and would not be the first to use nuclear weapons. The Soviets' even more radical steps in the summer and fall of 1987 in allowing on-site inspection made the INF treaty possible.

Contrary to Shultz's complaints at the time (and later) that CIA was oblivious to these and other changes, and their implications, we repeatedly published assessments on the dramatic developments in Moscow. For example, a July 1987 paper by our Soviet office, "Gorbachev: Steering the USSR into the 1990s," predicted that under political pressure at home, Gorbachev would pursue arms control agreements with the Reagan administration, and advance an even more radical reform program. The paper also warned —again, in July 1987—that Gorbachev might get thrown out: "The risks in more radical reform and a rewrite of the social contract are that confusion, economic disruption, and worker discontent will give potential opponents a platform on which to stand. . . . If it suspects that this process [loosening of censorship and democratization] is getting out of control, the party could well execute an about-face, discarding Gorbachev along the way."

On the military side, in June 1988, the Office of Soviet Analysis suggested that Gorbachev "may well try to impose unilateral cuts" in defense spending. Its assessment concluded, "The poor results from Gorbachev's efforts so far to launch economic revitalization suggest that there is, we think, a good chance he will be forced to adopt this course." This forecast of Soviet unilateral defense reductions was made six months before Gorbachev's dramatic announcement at the UN—and it was largely ignored.

These assessments, and others like them, were not just shoved in a file drawer to bring out someday to show we had been on top of the situation. These papers on Gorbachev were often hand-carried to readers of the *President's Daily Brief* from the President on down, often with a cover note from the Deputy Director for Intelligence.

We now know that beyond the events we knew about in Moscow, there were other dramatic developments unknown to us. We didn't know at the time, for instance, that at the Warsaw Pact meeting at the end of May 1987, Gorbachev had also said that the Soviets would not intervene militarily in Eastern Europe—although we would tell policymakers in the spring of 1988 much the same thing, that the Soviets would not invade Eastern Europe to preserve the empire. Nor did we know that when the Afghan leader Najibullah was in Moscow on July 20, 1987, the Soviets told him they would begin withdrawing their forces within a year. (Shevardnadze would later make public that a decision to withdraw had been made in principle in December 1985.)

Thanks almost entirely to continuing concessions from Gorbachev, an INF treaty in 1987 was looking increasingly possible by summer's end. When Shevardnadze arrived in Washington on October 30, he carried a letter from Gorbachev proposing a summit on December 7, at which the INF treaty would be signed.

THE WASHINGTON SUMMIT: A SPY SUMMIT, TOO

Gorbachev's visit to Washington December 7–10 was an extraordinary media event. The INF treaty was signed on the 8th, and important progress was made as well on START. The signing of INF was historic in several ways. Above all, the treaty marked a transition from "arms control" to "disarmament"—now we would begin actually taking down weapons by agreement. That was unprecedented.

Typically, however, what amazed everyone about the summit was not the substance, but the public relations, especially the "Gorby-mania" that seized the capital. Huge crowds lined the streets to catch a glimpse of Gorbachev, and he seemed to revel in the popular reaction to him. Senior officers of government, members of Congress, top media stars, and celebrities of every stripe fell all over themselves to get close to Gorbachev, to shake his hand—to see this unique man who was so different from any of his predecessors and changing so much at home and around the world. In my two decades in Washington, I had never seen anything like it.

There was another summit in Washington at the time of Gorbachev's visit, one that took place secretly, a meeting without precedent in the entire long history of the Cold War. That summit was between the two highest ranking officials of the KGB and the CIA ever to meet.

The afternoon of December 4, before Gorbachev arrived in

town, I took a call from Colin Powell, now the National Security Adviser (Carlucci had replaced Weinberger as Secretary of Defense). Colin was having dinner with Vladimir Kryuchkov, chief of the First Chief Directorate of the KGB—the head of all the KGB's foreign operations. Kryuchkov had arrived before Gorbachev ostensibly to supervise security for the visit. Colin asked if I—then CIA Deputy Director—would like to join them for dinner. I checked with the Directorate of Operations and with Bill Webster, and with their okay, accepted the invitation.

We met at a fancy restaurant downtown, Maison Blanche, at 7:30. I was surrounded by my own security detail and noticed a number of other security people already at the restaurant when we arrived—KGB security. (I kidded that between my thugs, Kryuchkov's thugs, and the FBI, there was no room in the restaurant for anyone else. I joked with Webster later that it was the only time I had ever seen an armed waiter wearing a trenchcoat.) Powell was accompanied by Fritz Ermarth of the NSC staff and Kryuchkov by Soviet Ambassador Yuri Dubinin (Dobrynin's successor), who looked as if he wanted badly to be somewhere else. I was alone. We sat at a table in the center of the restaurant, and it was plain that no one in the room recognized any of us or realized an unprecedented meeting was taking place. I sat next to Kryuchkov, who was wearing a cardigan sweater under his suit jacket and looked every inch an elderly college professor—not at all like a very senior KGB officer. I ordered a martini, he ordered Scotch. When the interpreter ordered Johnnie Walker Red for him, Kryuchkov corrected him— "Chivas Regal." It was clear he was not a man of peasant tastes.

Powell had told the Soviets I was coming only thirty minutes before dinner, and everyone was a bit awkward at first. Then Kryuchkov said, "This is an occasion of historic importance—two such senior officials of the two intelligence services have never met. Others of our services have met under tables in other places, but this is a first." I replied that it was the first time such a face-to-face meeting had taken place, "although each side certainly is intimately familiar with the daily lives of the other in the two capitals."

We then played a little game of showing how much we knew about each other's personal biography, likes and dislikes. From there on, the conversation was generally one of mutual barbs and debating points, punctuated by substantive discussions.

We talked at length about perestroika, with Powell observing the difficulty of keeping the process under control and the difficulty of economic reform in the absence of a money economy and an inability to calculate military costs. Kryuchkov conceded most of Colin's points, but remarked to the general, with no irony, "One should not be too hard on the military." He then turned to me and said he would share a secret—"Perestroika is proceeding much more slowly than we had anticipated two years ago."

We talked about Yeltsin's ouster as Moscow party boss in November. Kryuchkov said that Yeltsin "had simply turned out to be inadequate to his job, seeking to impose reform from above in the old ways." He then asked, "Did you think Yeltsin was some kind of democrat?"

Kryuchkov then made some comments about the United States that I found stunningly revealing. He said, "How powerful the United States seems—you can feel the power." Several times he referred to the wealth and economic power of the United States. At one point he turned to me and, in a statement that admitted much, said, "I hope CIA is telling the U.S. leadership that the Soviet Union is not a weak, poor country that can be pushed around." I responded that we did not underestimate either their power or their pride.

We discussed Afghanistan, and he repeated that the Soviets wanted to get out, but had to find some kind of political solution in order to do so. Kryuchkov expressed concern about the possible rise to power in Afghanistan of another fundamentalist Muslim state, a concern he thought we should share: "You seem fully occupied in trying to deal with just one fundamentalist Islamic state." The conversation then went on to technology transfer and the bugging of the U.S. embassy in Moscow. He said, "You should come to Moscow and see what we took out of our new embassy in Washington."

As we prepared to leave, I told Kryuchkov I would share a secret with him. CIA had been told by State that Gorbachev wanted tapes of the Moscow evening news so he could see every day how the visit was being handled on Soviet television. I said that there was only one place in town that could provide such tapes, and that Kryuchkov should tell Gorbachev that the tapes of the evening news from Soviet television were a gift from CIA to him in the hope of a successful summit. Kryuchkov thanked me and added, "That is probably the only thing you are doing." The Soviet ambassador was very surprised by what I had told Kryuchkov and said he had been told the tapes were being provided by a friendly TV station. I replied, "That is not altogether untrue."

And so ended the "other" summit in Washington, the secret summit. Another highly unusual step in the direction of a different U.S.-Soviet relationship than had gone before. Two committed foes warily circling, making a jab here, a parry there. But also beginning a dialogue between the last combatants of the Cold War. The Washington summits were over. Reagan would now go to Moscow. And Kryuchkov and I would meet again, as well.

Looking back, it is embarrassing to realize that, at this first high-level CIA-KGB meeting, Kryuchkov smugly knew that he had a spy—Aldrich Ames—in the heart of CIA, that he knew quite well what we were saying to the President and others about the Soviet Union, and that he was aware of many of our human and technical collection efforts in the USSR. Webster and I had been told months before that several of the DO's Soviet operations had been compromised, but the clandestine service didn't know whether the cause was a compromise of our communications security, an unrelated series of operational and tradecraft mistakes—or a mole inside CIA. The search for answers was under way but, tragically and unnecessarily, years would pass before we would learn the awful truth about Ames. The only solace, by then, would be that both Kryuchkov and the USSR were history.

CHAPTER TWENTY-FOUR

Ending the "Third World" War

FOR A COUNTRY in serious and growing economic trouble, the cost of Soviet support to its "socialist family," its empire, by the early 1980s had become exorbitant. And these costs grew even faster in the early 1980s, as resistance to Soviet-supported governments intensified. CIA estimated that Soviet costs between 1981 and 1986 to support their clients in Afghanistan, Angola, and Nicaragua alone were about $13 billion. By the mid-1980s, the Soviets were subsidizing and otherwise aiding Castro's Cuba to the tune of another $5–$7 billion annually.

But the economic burden represented only a part of the cost. The war in Afghanistan was a continuing political liability worldwide, especially in Islamic countries. Moreover, although the Soviets privately defended the need to be there to prevent the spread of fundamentalist Islam to its Central Asian republics, ironically, the war was stirring up Muslims living in the USSR. Another cost was in Gorbachev's credibility. It was hard for people in or out of the USSR to take seriously Gorbachev's rhetoric about democratization, "new thinking," a more cooperative Soviet role in dealing with international problems, and so on while more than 100,000 Soviet soldiers continued to devastate Afghanistan. Further, there was growing unhappiness and protest inside the Soviet Union itself over the war in Afghanistan, a problem we in CIA did all we could to magnify. It was easy. All we had to do was tell the Soviet people the truth about what their government had been doing.

Finally, another cost for Gorbachev was that Soviet support of its clients in the Third World was a continuing impediment to a genuine breakthrough with the United States. Both sides could pursue arms control because it was in their mutual interest and helped diminish a colossal danger. But a real change in political relations—not just a repetition of the false détente of the early 1970s—required evidence that the Soviets were serious about changing their adversarial, confrontational approach in the rest of the world. And no one in the Reagan administration was prepared to ease up in challenging the Soviets in the Third World until they did change. No one.

At the same time, we had our own problems in waging covert war in the Third World. Most important, there was a fundamental disagreement within the administration—mainly between Casey and Shultz—over the nature and purpose of our efforts. Casey's goal was simply to defeat the Soviets or their surrogates, or at least bleed them as painfully as possible. Shultz saw our covert paramilitary support as necessary leverage to end each conflict on terms satisfactory to us—but that meant a negotiating strategy was necessary as well as a military strategy. Casey was always leery of these negotiations, fearing that Shultz would sell out the "freedom fighters" or, at minimum, undermine their morale. Thus, while there were no significant differences within the Reagan administration over pursuing these covert actions, there were important disagreements over their purpose.

The great turnaround in the Third World was that regimes the Soviet brought to power or helped keep in power during the 1970s were, by the mid-1980s, themselves facing serious insurgencies sponsored by the United States. In late 1986, Gorbachev was prepared to move to get the Soviet Union out of its foreign blind alleys.

AFGHANISTAN: TO THE TERMEZ BRIDGE

The Politburo, according to Gorbachev, decided in principle in late 1985 to withdraw from Afghanistan. Even so, he apparently agreed to let the military make a last major effort to break the Mujahedin. Thus, during Gorbachev's first eighteen months in power, we saw new, more aggressive Soviet tactics, a spread of the war to the eastern provinces, attacks inside Pakistan, and more indiscriminate use of air power—overall a strong push to turn the corner. Thanks to our massive infusion of assistance during 1985–1986, the Mujahedin were able to withstand the Soviet maximum push. But they felt the pressure. CIA's senior officer on the ground cabled headquarters in July 1986 that the pace and zeal of Muj activity was heartening but that there were longer and more frequent lulls in combat, and he thought their dynamism was very gradually ebbing.

Because of his concerns, I—then Deputy DCI—decided to visit Pakistan in October 1986 to review the Afghan program. I spent a lot of time with senior Pakistani officers involved with the Muj, inspected warehouses of stockpiled weapons, and was briefed by American, Pakistani, and Mujahedin officials. I also met secretly with a close relative of Masood, the very effective Mujahedin commander—an ethnic Tadzhik—in northeastern Afghanistan. He complained that the Pakistanis were holding out on his force and not providing the weapons that were needed, especially Stingers. We talked about the course of the war, Soviet operations in the Panjsher Valley, and the will of the Mujahedin to continue. I was impressed, and later pressured the Pakistanis to give Masood some Stingers.

The next day, we went to a Mujahedin training camp. It struck me as a combination summer camp, military training facility, and Potemkin village. A hundred or so Afghans of all ages were training on heavy machine guns and RPGs (rocket-propelled grenade launchers). When I saw they all had brand-new coats and observed both their demonstrative enthusiasm and their skill, I was immediately suspicious that I was being given "the tour," the standard package offered all senior visiting Americans. Even taking that into account, I saw some very impressive shooting. They had lined up white rocks on a distant hill, several hundred yards away, in the shape of Soviet tanks. Their aim was remarkable (even allowing for the probability I was watching a bunch of crack shots assembled to dazzle the guy who signed the checks) and after each accurate hit, everyone would jump up and down yelling, *"Allah akhbar!"* (God is great!). They introduced me to one kid they said was sixteen, and who they claimed had killed one Russian for every year of his life. The whole show may have been contrived, but there was no mistaking the determination of those soldiers or their hatred of the Soviets.

We now know that on November 13, 1986, the Soviet leadership decided that the war must be ended within one to two years.

They also decided to replace the leader of Afghanistan, Babrak Karmal, with Najibullah. Right on schedule, Karmal was ousted a week later. On December 12, Najibullah was summoned to Moscow and, in the course of his visit, was told to strengthen his position at home because Soviet troops were going to be brought home within one and a half to two years. No one outside of a small circle in Moscow and in Kabul would know of this decision until the fall of 1987.

In the meantime, the impact of the Stingers began to be felt in Afghanistan. We received another report from the field on January 6, 1987, and the tone was markedly different and more upbeat than the assessment of the preceding July. Our senior officer this time reported that the Mujahedin were increasingly successful on the battlefield, inflicting significant losses on Soviet and Afghan government ground and air forces. He reported that the Muj had developed countermeasures to Soviet interdiction tactics, and that the majority of convoys were making it through the mountain passes and into central Afghanistan. He observed that the "most significant battlefield development during the last six months was the introduction of the Stingers."

At their meeting in mid-September 1987, Shevardnadze confided privately to Shultz that the Soviets had decided to leave Afghanistan and the timetable they had in mind. Shultz finally shared that important piece of information with Webster and me in November.

Most of us at CIA did not question that the Soviets badly wanted out of Afghanistan, but we did not think they could or would take out all their forces or do so under conditions that imperiled their client, Najibullah's government. The debate about whether and when the Soviets would withdraw would continue without interruption at our weekly lunches with Shultz, Deputy Secretary John Whitehead, Armacost, and Abramowitz for many months. On December 31, 1987, a jovial luncheon on New Year's Eve was the occasion for one of our most spirited debates. Armacost introduced the subject, and he, Whitehead, and Abramowitz all clearly believed Shevardnadze's statement to Shultz that the Soviets would withdraw in 1988. They also thought it important to get a large Soviet exodus early. Further, they said, we should make it as easy as possible for them to fulfill that objective.

I responded that there was no question the Soviets wanted out, and perhaps had made a decision to get out, but tough decisions were still in front of them—how to get out, when and without losing face. I said that in my opinion, Gorbachev would not take this controversial step prior to the June 1988 Party Conference and perhaps not before the end of the Reagan administration.

At that year-end lunch, I bet Armacost twenty-five dollars the Soviets would not be out of Afghanistan before the end of the administration. I told him and his colleagues at the time that it was a win-win bet for me. I would get twenty-five dollars or have the pleasure of paying twenty-five dollars on the occasion of an early Soviet withdrawal. A small price to pay for a large victory.

I was truly convinced that the Soviets would have difficulty arranging a face-saving way out. Also, the Soviets had not given up a territorial acquisition under military challenge since World War II. The Chinese had a saying about the Soviet appetite for territory and their unwillingness to give it up: "What the bear has eaten, he never spits out." Well, needless to say, I was wrong. Months later, I paid Mike Armacost the twenty-five dollars—the best money I ever spent. I also told myself it would be the last time I'd make an intelligence forecast based on fortune cookie wisdom.

On February 8, 1988, in a nationwide television address, Gorbachev announced that Soviet troop withdrawals from Afghanistan would begin on May 15 and would be completed by March 15, 1989.

I had another long exchange on Afghanistan with Shultz on February 19, 1988, prior to another of his trips to Moscow. He asked what would happen in Afghanistan after the Soviet withdrawal. I said that the analysts were all agreed that the situation would be messy, with a struggle for power among different Mujahedin groups, and that the outcome most likely would be a weak central government and powerful tribal leaders in the countryside. I told them that most analysts did not believe Najibullah's government could last without active Soviet military support.

John Whitehead then said that he thought we had made two wrong assumptions. First, he thought the chances were good that one or another Muj commander would cut a deal with Najibullah to get the inside track to sharing power, thus leaving Najibullah in power longer than many assumed. Second, the assumption that the refugees would return to Afghanistan was questionable. Abramowitz said he agreed with Whitehead—it was premature to assume that the Najibullah government would fall immediately. As it turned out, Whitehead and Abramowitz were right on both counts.

After Shultz's trip, Colin Powell, now National Security Adviser, told me that little had been agreed in Moscow. He then posed the same two questions Whitehead had raised earlier. Could Najibullah last and how long? How good is the Afghan army— under what circumstances might it last longer than we were expecting? He went on that CIA had "very strong assumptions" on these "two givens," and he wanted to make sure we were thinking about alternatives. I did not think that either Powell or Shultz necessarily disagreed with our view that Najibullah wouldn't last long after a Soviet withdrawal—after all, the Soviets lacked confidence themselves on that score (and even tried to persuade Najibullah to escape the country). Yet clearly much was riding on our answers, and they wanted us to make sure we had seriously thought through the other possibilities.

The Geneva Accords on Afghanistan were signed on April 14, with Shevardnadze, Shultz, and the foreign ministers of Pakistan and Afghanistan present. On April 17, again at our lunch with Secretary Shultz, Armacost—who had played a central role in the negotiations with the Soviets—said to us: "Some people are getting public recognition for what has been achieved in Afghanistan and the victory of the Mujahedin. The people who played a principal role in it—CIA—as usual are getting no recognition." It was a gracious statement by one of this country's most skilled diplomats. (And a guy twenty-five dollars richer at my expense.)

The Soviets withdrew on schedule and met the timetable they had accelerated. The Soviet commander in Afghanistan, General Boris Gromov, proudly walked across the Termez Bridge connecting Afghanistan to the Soviet Union on February 15, 1989.

The Soviets and CIA both were to be proven wrong about the staying power of the Afghan government after the Soviet troops left. Najibullah would remain in power for another three years, as the United States and USSR continued to aid their respective sides. On December 31, 1991, both Moscow and Washington cut off all assistance, and Najibullah's government fell four months later. He had outlasted both Gorbachev and the Soviet Union itself.

For a dozen years, under three Presidents, the United States —through CIA—had supplied and armed those who resisted the Soviet invasion of their country. For the first several years, few believed that Afghanistan would ever be liberated. The road to the Termez Bridge in 1989 would be opened by the blood and courage of Afghan patriots, an international clandestine coalition led by the United States, the zeal of President Zia of Pakistan, and the realism of Mikhail Gorbachev and Eduard Shevardnadze. It was a great victory. Afghanistan was at last free of the foreign invader. Now Afghans could resume fighting among themselves—and hardly anyone cared.

ANGOLA: A WIN FOR U.S. DIPLOMACY

The CIA program to assist Jonas Savimbi's UNITA movement approved late in 1985 by President Reagan really didn't get off the ground until early 1986. We provided supplies of various kinds to Savimbi, but the most critical were the Stingers and antiarmor weapons.

Few Americans thought that Savimbi could defeat the Angolans, Cubans, and Soviets in this civil war. The object of our military assistance was to bring enough pressure on the Angolan government to enter into negotiations and for all the parties to find a political solution. A very talented and remarkably persistent Chet Crocker had been pursuing negotiations with all of the participants since early in the Reagan administration. Although Chet, as Assistant Secretary of State for African Affairs, had succeeded in getting the MPLA to accept the concept of the withdrawal of all foreign forces from Angola as early as February 1984, he had been unable to make much headway in the ensuing years mainly because the Angolan government and its Soviet patron saw no need to make concessions. Shultz had supported CIA's covert action as a means of putting pressure on them and changing their minds. It worked.

In January 1988, at the same time the Cubans and Angolans moved on the UNITA forces around Cuito Cuanavale, Crocker persuaded the Cubans to agree that they would withdraw their troops from Angola as part of a settlement—in exchange for being allowed to join the negotiations. On May 3–4 in London, within a matter of weeks after the Cubans, Soviets, and Angolans succeeded in lifting the siege of Cuito Cuanavale, Crocker succeeded in getting agreement that as part of a settlement the Cubans would withdraw from Angola and the South Africans would leave Namibia. By the end of August, the South Africans had withdrawn from Angola and, a month later, a two-year timetable for Cuban withdrawal from Angola had been agreed in principle. The final agreement was initialed by the parties on December 13, and the formal signing ceremony took place on December 22, 1988, in the presence of Shultz and Shevardnadze.

The agreement was a tremendous achievement by Chet Crocker, whom Casey had distrusted for so long, worried that Chet might sell out Savimbi by negotiating a cutoff in outside support to UNITA while allowing supplies to continue to the MPLA during a protracted Cuban withdrawal. Crocker's diplomacy, combined with the pressure brought to bear by U.S.—CIA—weapons support for Savimbi, and a change of heart in Moscow, ended the Soviet and Cuban involvement in Angola that had begun in 1975. A CIA role in trying to get the Soviets and Cubans out of Angola, started by President Ford and Henry Kissinger and quickly extinguished by Congress, had resumed years later and contributed importantly to a successful outcome. Who knows how much sooner the goal might have been achieved had the American team not been benched for a decade?

NICARAGUA: FROM THE JAWS OF DEFEAT

The final phase of the war in Nicaragua was as ugly and as complicated as the rest of it had been, marked by internecine conflict among the Contras, among the Americans, and between Washington and Central and Latin American governments.

As 1986 began, the political climate in Washington had changed again, and the prospects brightened that Congress would approve CIA's reentry into the conflict. On June 25, the House of Representatives approved a $100 million CIA program to help the Contras, along with another $300 million in economic support for Costa Rica, Honduras, Guatemala, and El Salvador. The Senate, as long expected, followed suit on August 13. On October 1, the beginning of the next fiscal year, we were back in business. And over the next year, CIA made great progress in strengthening the Contras and putting significant pressure on the Nicaraguan regime.

With the United States once again helping the Contras officially, the negotiating arena became active. Shultz had enlisted Philip Habib, one of our most distinguished and successful diplomats, just fresh from helping arrange a transition of power in the Philippines, to take on the Nicaraguan problem. In January 1987, the Costa Rican Foreign Minister met with Habib to review what was becoming known as the "Arias plan" (Arias was the newly elected president of Costa Rica). It called for new elections in Nicaragua, a cease-fire and amnesty, and a regional peace treaty. However, despite Habib's best efforts, by summer 1987 it was clear that the diplomatic track was stalled, and the administration was deeply split on what to do next.

CIA's authorized lethal assistance program to the Contras came to an end on September 30. Congress, still angry over Iran-Contra, had—not surprisingly—proved unwilling to authorize a new Contra aid program for another year, thus keeping intact the decade-long U.S. record of not having a consistent policy on Nicaragua for two consecutive fiscal years. As a result, we received legislative authority for our activities month to month. The hope was to get a humanitarian—nonlethal—aid package approved by Congress before their Thanksgiving recess. It was not to be.

At midnight, February 28, 1988, all CIA paramilitary assistance to the Contras ended. For us, the war in Nicaragua was over.

Faced with no continuing U.S. or other support, on March 23, 1988, the Contras signed a cease-fire with the Nicaraguan government at Sapoa. It provided for formal mutual recognition, amnesty, and offered the Contras the opportunity to "incorporate" themselves into the political and civil life of Nicaragua. Shultz told Webster and me the next day that during his just-concluded talks with Shevardnadze, he had the impression that the Soviets had been weighing in with the Sandinistas to go along with the peace settlement.

Webster, Colin Powell, and I discussed the agreement that same afternoon, March 24. Webster and I thought the deal looked pretty good from the Contras' standpoint, given the lack of U.S. support. Powell was very down, and said he thought the Contras had made a terrible mistake. We agreed that the long-term prospects for them were bleak. On the 25th, at breakfast, Carlucci also was downbeat, saying that the Sandinistas had won. Bill and I acknowledged that this was likely but that the Contras had little choice but to cut the best deal they could.

The Contras' circumstances thereafter declined steadily, as the Sandinistas intensified efforts to root them out inside Nicaragua despite the cease-fire. In July, the Nicaraguan government kicked out the U.S. ambassador and his staff, viewing the embassy as a focal point for organized opposition.

But things weren't going well for the Sandinistas either. Soviet assistance, both military and economic, had been declining for nearly a year. With their continuing military activities, economic sanctions remained in place and the economy was in terrible shape. As part of the negotiations, Nicaragua had agreed to elections in 1991. They moved up that timetable to February 25, 1990, confident of victory in a fair election, followed by economic relief. We would all be surprised—except for George Bush—when Violeta Chamorro won the elections, ousting Daniel Ortega. President Bush, in fact, bet his CIA briefer an ice cream cone before the election that she would win. The next morning, the briefer stopped by the White House Mess on his way to the Oval Office and brought the President the spoils of his successful wager—the ice cream.

The end of CIA's involvement in Nicaragua also essentially ended the broader American involvement, except in the political arena and our efforts to get the Soviets to stop Cuban/Soviet military supplies to the Sandinistas. It had been a long, contentious struggle. At the end of February, when we left, we thought we had lost. But the military and political efforts of the Contras; U.S. economic and military pressures both overt and covert; the influence of Nicaragua's neighbors; waning Soviet support, especially economic; the Sandinistas' oppressive political and economic policies; and the courage of the political opposition inside Nicaragua all combined to "keep hope alive." Then, when given the chance by an overconfident regime, the opposition defeated the Sandinistas at the polls. The elimination of Nicaragua as a Soviet outpost in Latin America came less than a year before the end of the Soviet Union itself. The United States had not won in Nicaragua. The Sandinistas just lost.

A Parting Thought

Soviet support of new authoritarian regimes—communist or socialist—in the Third World and its aggression against Afghanistan in the latter half of the 1970s became the hard kernel of the lingering Cold War in the 1980s. When Gorbachev talked "new thinking" in Moscow, continuing and even increased Soviet involvement in Afghanistan, Angola, and Nicaragua became the litmus test of his sincerity and credibility. And, when he finally moved to end Soviet involvement in Afghanistan and Angola more than two years after taking power, it was the final proof that, at least in foreign policy, this was a very different Soviet leader.

We in CIA, and others in Defense and NSC, watching Gorbachev's actions and skeptical of his words, would take him seriously only when the actions matched the words. Thus the Reagan administration kept the pressure on the Soviets both militarily and in the Third World until real change occurred. I am convinced that this helped accelerate the change. Secretary Shultz, more than anyone else in the administration, *felt* that Gorbachev meant what he said even when there was no evidence on the ground to support such faith. While he always supported keeping the military pressure on, he also used diplomacy to help the Soviets find the exits he believed they had to go through. The remarkable thing, looking back, is that the Reagan administration—so riven with conflict and division— so effectively combined overt and covert power with diplomacy to bring an end to the "Third World" war.

CHAPTER TWENTY-FIVE

Gorbachev: Destroying the Soviet System

GORBACHEV BITES THE HAND THAT FED HIM

Mikhail Gorbachev was last seen reveling in his success at the Washington summit in December 1987. The scene would become all too familiar—triumph and acclaim abroad even as the situation at home worsened. He democratized the party internally, only to find that those elected all too often also were little different from those replaced. Apart from glasnost, his political reforms seemed stymied. And the downward spiral of the country's economy was accelerating amid the confusion of his economic policies.

Under these circumstances, and perhaps further motivated by the increasing hostility of conservatives, Gorbachev acted completely in character: he raised the stakes and moved boldly to overwhelm the opposition. He would now use his authority as General Secretary of the Communist Party to dramatically weaken its role and power in governing the Soviet Union—to take it out of day-to-day management of the country altogether. If he could not change the party, he would hobble it and then leave it behind.

It was a fateful turn for Gorbachev and for the Soviet Union. First, through glasnost and liberating the historians, he exposed and shattered the myths that had sustained communist authority. Now, in the second blow, he would accelerate disintegration of the Soviet state by weakening the very structures that had kept it together and running—however badly. In the first part of the nineteenth century, Alexis de Tocqueville wrote of the period before the French Revolution, "The most dangerous time for a bad government is when it starts to reform itself." So Gorbachev would learn. His attempt to reform what could not be reformed hastened the day of ultimate reckoning.

At a rare party conference in June 1988, Gorbachev condemned the party as incompetent (there was a revelation!), and it paid by giving up its authority and control. Weighted with a long tradition of party discipline and deference to the General Secretary, the party delegates voted, teeth grinding, to begin their steep descent from power.

Voting for the first Congress of People's Deputies in March 1989 marked the first relatively free election in Russia since 1918, and the results shocked the party. One after another, senior party members lost, including some running unopposed. The election dramatically revealed popular attitudes toward the party and its leading officials. Yet, even after that, they did not realize that they stood at the threshold of a revolution.

The first Congress of People's Deputies met from May 25 through June 9, 1989, its proceedings televised at Gorbachev's direction. Gorbachev obtained the structural changes he wanted. The Supreme Soviet was elected and Gorbachev was chosen as president. But far beyond the importance of the votes taken was the unforeseen psychological impact on the country. The peoples of the Soviet Union seemed to sense that this was a historic moment. And so the entire country sat down in front of the television and watched. It was a transforming experience. For the first time, real politics came to the Soviet Union. A spellbound national audience saw Gorbachev, the party, even the KGB, subjected to direct, withering criticism. They saw the arguing and the debates. They saw the leadership in the flesh—angry, scornful, disputatious, egotistical, rude, and divided. The communists who had run the country from behind Oz's curtain for so long were exposed to the entire country—and to the world—as venal, petty, squabbling bureaucrats.

The effect of all this was unforeseen by Gorbachev, and unforeseen by CIA. Both still thought of politics in the Soviet Union as taking place within the walls of the Kremlin. But CIA saw, as Gorbachev did not, that the political revolution he instigated had now overtaken him and would soon leave him behind.

The Congress of People's Deputies met again in March 1990 and approved strong presidential powers, elected Gorbachev as president for five years, approved his proposal to create a presidential council—a cabinet effectively displacing the Politburo—and a federation council comprising the heads of all the republics. Paradoxically, the man who claimed that only a popularly chosen government could implement painful economic reform was now expanding the powers of the new presidency in order to impose economic reform from the top—while still lacking any popular mandate of his own.

By May–June, events were moving beyond Gorbachev and his plans. At the end of May 1990, Yeltsin became the popularly elected president of the Russian Supreme Soviet. Two weeks later, on June 12, Russia declared its sovereignty, followed within weeks by virtually every other republic.

Unable to overcome the obstructionism of the party, to reshape it into an instrument of change and reform, or to bend it to his will, Mikhail Gorbachev shattered its power. Beginning in May 1988, he created an alternative political structure, the system of elected councils, steadily strengthening it at the expense of the party. Displacing his old ally Gromyko as president in September, Gorbachev made himself head of the new structure and dramatically strengthened his power within that structure. While he would remain head of the party until the last, by May 1989 what power he continued to have he exercised primarily through the new presidency. He remained as General Secretary only to deny that position to any potential rival.

In the space of a year, Gorbachev had carried out a political revolution, radically transforming the political life and structure of the Soviet Union. He attacked and crippled the very organization —the Communist Party—that had elevated him to supreme power. Even more significantly, he liberated the peoples of the USSR from the Stalinist past, from the Communist Party, and from fear. This liberation was, and would remain, his greatest achievement. But the alternative political system he created would not and could not last because of his political mistakes, Yeltsin's personal hostility to him, his failures in economic and ethnic policy, and because his alternative rested on the fast-disintegrating foundation of the old Soviet Union.

GORBACHEV AND ECONOMIC REFORM: A TIMID COMMUNIST

Gorbachev's initial economic reform policies and promises of more to come, together with somewhat improved economic performance in 1986, had heightened expectations among the public that their lives would begin to get better. However, Gorbachev was only tinkering at the margins with an economic system he intended to preserve, at least in its essential elements. None of his measures seriously addressed the hard issues of price reform, collectivized agriculture, centralized management, the governing role of the state and the bureaucrats in Moscow, and more. None acknowledged the reality that the system itself was the basic problem. The limited measures Gorbachev announced failed to offer any realistic prospect for improvement in the economy. More important, his weakening of the structures that at least met minimal individual and industrial needs, however badly, together with disruptions caused by the reform program and contradictions and deficiencies in the reform program itself, virtually guaranteed that the long Soviet economic slide would quickly gain momentum.

In both classified and unclassified assessments, CIA (and the Defense Intelligence Agency) documented Gorbachev's economic failures, problems, and the consequences:

• Gorbachev had to retreat on the antialcohol program because it was largely ineffective, there had been huge losses in tax revenue from reduced official sales of vodka, and moonshining on a massive scale had both undermined the campaign and created a widely publicized sugar shortage.

• Despite large new resources for investment in modernizing industry, there was little to show for it either in terms of productivity or quality.

• New machines failed to meet world technological standards, and the Soviet technological lag behind the West was growing (fifteen years in mainframe computers and supercomputers; ten years in advanced microcircuits and fiberoptic equipment; nine years in computer-operated machine tools).

• Implementation of the 1987 economic reform package proved to be disastrously disruptive.

• Worst of all, daily life was getting harder for many citizens. There were food shortages and widespread consumer unhappiness. And what goods were available, both food and nonfood, cost more.

Not surprisingly, as life got harder, the public rebelled. This became evident to Gorbachev and to the world when, in July 1989, Siberian coal miners went on strike. Demands for increased pay, improved working conditions, and political reform were not surprising. But, in one of those small details that can reveal so much, the miners' demands included soap. This "superpower" could not even provide soap to its workers. CIA reported that the number of strikes reported in the Soviet press rose from a couple of dozen involving a few thousand workers in 1987–1988 to more than five hundred strikes involving hundreds of thousands of workers during the first seven months of 1989.

By the end of 1989, the Agency was reporting that Soviet economic problems had reached near-crisis proportions, with severe consumer goods shortages, inflation, and rising social and ethnic violence. Widespread breakdowns in transportation and distribution systems interfered with the delivery of all kinds of goods from producers to consumers. CIA traced the Soviet economic "stall-out" in 1989 to economic policy mistakes, changes in the political system, and in part to the abandonment of "administrative methods"—centralized coercion—traditionally used to direct the economy from the center without waiting for the "economic levers" needed to guide decentralized decisionmaking to be put in place. In the face of economic crisis, Gorbachev procrastinated and temporized.

An unclassified CIA assessment in May 1990 underscored the danger of the situation. It raised the possibility of a sharp economic deterioration even beyond the crisis at hand, and forecast that "a single major event could lead to a substantial drop in output and bring about chaos in the distribution of both producer and consumer goods." The economy was in such trouble that even one more thing going wrong could transform crisis into headlong crash.

While CIA's statistics were not as alarming as its overall analysis, they, too, underscored a continuing decline in Soviet economic performance. For all the later criticism of CIA's statistical work on the Soviet economy, the Agency repeatedly and explicitly warned during this period that statistical analysis was "much less informative now than in the past" with the deterioration in the stability of the Soviet economy. The dynamics, it said, of structural and systemic changes, as well as natural and man-made catastrophes, ethnic violence, and indecision and mistakes "cannot be captured in a summary measure of national output. Comparing economic performance in the late 1980s with that in other periods by comparing rates of growth of GNP misses too much of the story." CIA urged, instead, focusing on qualitative assessments of the Soviet economy as more revealing than the statistics. Policymakers at the time heeded this advice and grasped the magnitude of the crisis we were describing. How ironic that critics later would use the statistics CIA warned against relying upon as evidence that it had missed the crisis altogether!

As late as the summer of 1990, even as the Soviet Union was collapsing around him, Gorbachev—perhaps understanding his own unpopularity at home—feared taking bold economic steps. Facing massive discontent because of declining living conditions, strikes, ethnic conflict, and awesome centrifugal forces, he may have believed that radical economic reform would cause an explosion that could not be contained. Further, it is clear that he simply could not accept important elements of economic reform—from breaking up the collective farms to selling off large state-owned enterprises. However radical his political changes, on economic matters he remained a committed communist. The irony is that Gorbachev did not grasp that his changes in the existing political structure made preservation of the economic structure impossible. Political reform eliminated the mechanisms to manage a centralized economy but, unlike the political realm, Gorbachev was incapable of developing an alternative. Political change, coupled with the inadequacies and contradictions of Gorbachev's on-again, off-again economic reforms, plunged an economy in crisis into a free fall.

THE DEBATE IN WASHINGTON OVER GORBACHEV AND REFORM

I didn't know just how bad a temper George Shultz had until the morning of October 17, 1988. Three days before, I had given a speech to the American Association for the Advancement of Science on Gorbachev and perestroika, and I had been quite pessimistic about his prospects at home. About nine in the morning on the 17th, Shultz called me on the telephone. He was livid. He said neither Webster nor I had any business giving substantive speeches and that he believed this one would be read as an administration pronouncement on Gorbachev. He said that I had caused him a lot of trouble and that what I had to say about Gorbachev was nothing but speculation.

My heart pounding—even the Deputy Director of CIA can't

be oblivious to an angry Secretary of State—I reminded him as evenly and calmly as I could that I had passed copies of all my speeches to him, Powell, and Carlucci in advance of delivery for over ten months and that no one had registered the view that I shouldn't be giving this kind of speech. I said the talk was not at all anti-Gorbachev, but a description of the problems he was facing.

I had not begun to bank the fires of his fury. Shultz concluded by saying that he was "deeply disappointed" in me as a professional for delivering the speech. He said that CIA had been wrong consistently during the Gorbachev period and that he was, across the board, "a very dissatisfied customer."

I learned later that Shultz had raised the speech with Powell and Carlucci at breakfast and demanded that I be fired, but I was told that Colin was not unhappy and that Frank had been amused. More significantly, I was told that Shultz had gone to Reagan to try to get me fired. However, after this conversation ended, Reagan had observed to others that he generally agreed with me. With his approval, Marlin Fitzwater, the press secretary, went out and said in response to a press question that my remarks were consistent with what the President and Secretary of Defense had been saying.

What was I saying that so infuriated the Secretary of State? On economic reform, I said that Gorbachev's program did not go nearly far enough, cited the numerous problems and contradictions in his approach, and concluded: "While important battles have been won in principle, the war to change fundamentally the Stalinist economic system at this point is being lost. After three years of reform, restructuring and turmoil, there has been little, if any, slowing in the downward spiral of the Soviet economy."

On political reform, I said that Gorbachev had decided to circumvent the party to force greater political and economic change, and observed: "While Gorbachev's bold political moves and radical rhetoric have shaken the Soviet system, he has not yet really changed it. . . . It is by no means certain—I would even say it is doubtful—that Gorbachev can in the end rejuvenate the system."

I think what really angered Shultz—beyond my speaking publicly about these matters in the first place—were the implications I drew from those developments for Soviet foreign policy, and for the United States. I said that Gorbachev sought a far-reaching détente with the West to obtain technology, to encourage investment and trade, and above all to avoid large increases in military spending. I also pointed to the continuing "extraordinary scope and sweep of Soviet military modernization and weapons R & D" continuing under Gorbachev—"At this point, we see no slackening of Soviet weapons production or programs." Finally, I reviewed the Soviets' continuing support of clients in the Third World—to the tune of nearly $12 billion in 1987 in economic and military aid and massive subsidies just to Cuba, Angola, Nicaragua, and Vietnam. I acknowledged Gorbachev's willingness to abandon costly and losing involvements in the Third World, such as in Afghanistan, and Moscow's more cooperative approach in places like Angola and Cambodia. But I also said that Soviet objectives in the Third World —"as demonstrated by Gorbachev's recent proposal to trade Cam Ranh Bay for our bases in the Philippines"—remained adversarial and sought to diminish U.S. global influence and reach.

I did not neglect the magnitude of what Gorbachev was trying to do, or pretend that nothing had changed: "What Gorbachev already has set in motion represents a political earthquake. . . . He is a figure of enormous historical importance." But I also said that he intended improved Soviet economic performance, greater political vitality at home, and more dynamic diplomacy to make the USSR a more competitive and stronger adversary in the years ahead.

In an attempt to defuse Shultz's anger toward me, I wrote him a note after the episode apologizing for any difficulty I had caused him and assuring him that I was not trying to cause him trouble. Several colleagues around the government whom I told about the note thought it unnecessary and too accommodating. For my part, I respected Shultz and did not want a hostile relationship with him —either from a personal standpoint or in terms of the Agency's best interests. I did not, however, recant anything I had said about developments in the USSR.

Others in the administration shared my concerns about those developments. A number of senior officials at CIA, Defense, and the NSC did not question the political changes Gorbachev was making at home, his efforts to improve the economy, or even the magnitude of his changes in Soviet foreign policy. But these officials —including me—had two persistent concerns. First, how much of this was an effort to get some "breathing space," a period of a decade or so in which the Soviet Union could try to get back on its feet without having abandoned its long-term ambitions?

Second, even granting Gorbachev's sincerity and seriousness in changing Soviet international behavior and objectives, everything at that point depended solely on him. For the United States to take irreversible military and political steps in response to Soviet initiatives which at that point could still be reversed and the implementation of which depended entirely on Gorbachev's remaining alive, and in power, seemed premature. We would begin to see changes in Soviet military programs and deployments, and in the core structure of their empire, that we considered hard—if not impossible—to reverse only at the end of 1988. Until then, in 1988 just as in 1985, but with a new Secretary of Defense, National Security Adviser, and DCI, the U.S. government still was divided over how to assess developments in the Soviet Union, with Shultz more optimistic about the prospects for Gorbachev and reform, most of the rest hopeful but wary. As Carlucci told me in August 1988 after he visited the Soviet Union, the Soviet military leaders "still carry around some dumb ideas for relatively mature, well-educated and thoughtful leaders."

Shultz tended to put the best face on developments in the Soviet Union across the board, even on the economy. Here, too, he disagreed with CIA's analysis. As late as spring 1988, he urged us to be "cautious" in drawing the conclusion that Gorbachev's economic reforms would not work. At our lunch on April 28, he had told Webster, Dick Kerr, and me that we "should not underestimate the impact of simply stopping doing dumb things and the leavening effect of that on an economy." He concluded that we shouldn't "be misled by the decline in GNP or specific statistics—that while GNP might be declining, the number of usable and useful products may be growing compared to the past. I repeat, an economy can get a boost simply if people stop doing dumb things."

Shultz returned to this theme only a week later, on May 5. He asked our assessment of the Soviet economy, and when we gave a gloomy outlook he and Whitehead initially agreed. But then the Secretary offered an alternative possibility. Gorbachev, he said, had little alternative to reforming the economy. He (Shultz) was "not all that certain that some progress could not be made over the long haul." He went on, "I only recently realized how underdeveloped the USSR is, and even minor improvements in areas such as agriculture could make a significant difference." Clearly, he and CIA were far apart.

While I am sure Shultz and probably others thought CIA had its head buried in the sand and refused to look open-mindedly at developments in the Soviet Union, in fact we understood that the importance of events under way in the Soviet Union made it imperative for us to have the benefit of the thinking of a wide range of views—and that meant bringing in outside experts. As Deputy DCI, on November 29, 1988, I wrote to the head of the National Intelligence Council and CIA's Deputy Director for Intelligence and urged them to organize a conference involving non-CIA experts to look at the future of the Soviet Union. My memo observed that we had not anticipated many of Gorbachev's moves: "A problem we have acknowledged is how often Gorbachev has surprised us with the range and scope of his proposals for change in the Soviet system. . . . We have often been behind the power curve and reacted to events."

CIA had no false pride during this period that we had the best answers or the right answers. And we knew the stakes were unimaginably high.

THE RELUCTANT REVOLUTIONARY

By the end of the Reagan administration, Gorbachev and the forces he set loose had shattered the myths and the fear that sustained the rule of the Communist Party. He had broken the political monopoly of the party and its apparatus, had removed the party from day-to-day administration of the Soviet Union, and had created an alternative structure of power and political legitimacy in the country. Step by tactical step, he had carried out one of the most far-reaching, and bloodless, political revolutions in history. Finally, his political revolution undermined and then largely destroyed the administrative structure that had managed the Soviet economy. Prepared at the end to change radically the Soviet political system, Gorbachev was unprepared and unwilling to reject communism or the doomed economic system that was its creation.

Toward the end, Gorbachev faced two paradoxes. First, the man who went so far, so single-handedly, to democratize Soviet politics was never willing to place his own fate in the hands of voters, with the result that a political process he set in motion finally passed him by. Perhaps this is because, for him, democratization was consistently a means, not an end—a politically useful way to defeat his opponents in the party and force change, but not a reflection of true belief. Second, in trying to fix the Soviet system, he accelerated its inevitable demise. Especially in the realm of the economy, his ideological blinders and personal limitations, together with political opposition and Russian culture and history, prevented creation of any alternative structure. The result was that in 1987–1988 the Soviet economy, as its old mechanisms of economic control were weakened or eliminated by Gorbachev long before new mechanisms were in place, began to collapse. And economic hardship would enormously intensify the other crises afflicting the regime, especially in the non-Russian republics.

As Henry Kissinger would observe about Gorbachev's course during an Agency briefing in the fall of 1989, "If you were setting out to destroy the Soviet Union, would you do it any differently?"

CHAPTER TWENTY-SIX

The "Velvet Revolutions" of 1989: The Avalanche of Liberation

EASTERN EUROPE: FORESHADOWINGS

Truth be told, the American government, including CIA, had no idea in January 1989 that a tidal wave of history was about to break upon us. Sure, we knew dramatic change was under way in the Soviet Union, but it was unclear whether the future held further reform or a return to repression as economic crisis and assertive nationalism undermined institutions and social order. We also knew that pressures for change were building once again in Eastern Europe, pressures intensified by dramatic changes under way in the USSR. And while some people have become very wise and far-sighted in their recollections, I know of *no one* in or out of government who predicted early in 1989 that before the next presidential election Eastern Europe would be free, Germany unified in NATO, and the Soviet Union an artifact of history. It was easy to say that these things were inevitable. Saying when—saying *now*— was impossible, and no one East or West did.

The Soviet empire in Eastern Europe was maintained by force. Again and again—in 1953, 1956, 1968, 1970, and 1980—the peoples of Poland, Hungary, East Germany, and Czechoslovakia rose against Soviet puppet regimes and were brutally repressed by those regimes or by Soviet troops. The Soviet satrapies seethed, Moscow's dominion secured only by fear.

In Eastern Europe, as in the Soviet Union itself, it was Mikhail Gorbachev who broke the fear. It is a measure of Gorbachev's

449

ideological conviction—and his nearly unbelievable naïveté—that he believed reform in both Eastern Europe and the USSR would lead to stronger, more legitimate communist governments. I think he never dreamed, and certainly never intended, that his actions would destroy the world he knew.

Beginning in 1985, Gorbachev began signaling that times had changed, that Moscow would no longer use force to hold its empire in Eastern Europe. Perhaps Gorbachev's starkest message to the old guard in Eastern Europe was his declaration at the UN on December 7, 1988, that, with respect to Eastern Europe, "To deny a nation the freedom of choice, regardless of the pretext or the verbal guise in which it is cloaked, is to upset the unstable balance that has been achieved. . . . Freedom of choice is a universal principle. It knows no exceptions."

CIA AND EASTERN EUROPE

Casey's original reluctance to involve CIA more aggressively in Eastern Europe and especially in Poland over time diminished, and we became more active in supporting the underground resistance movement in Poland and dissidents in other East European countries. Our covert programs focused on sending in printing presses, copiers, and other materials for the underground to publish newsletters and papers and to otherwise publicize their cause, as well as spiriting out speeches and articles by underground leaders and either publishing them and smuggling them back into Eastern Europe or transmitting them over radios. The other main thread of our effort was a worldwide propaganda effort to publicize the repression of these groups and of human rights in Eastern Europe by the regimes—and to make known the work of the resistance. As Gorbachev's reforms began to open cracks in Eastern Europe, thus making communication of our message easier, we intensified our efforts.

We were most active in Poland. We slowly increased our clandestine support of Solidarity, mainly by providing printing equipment and other means of communication to the underground. They were not told that CIA was the source of the assistance, although there must have been suspicions. As Solidarity's activities increased, so, too, did the aggressiveness of the Jaruzelski regime in cracking down on underground publishing and opposition activities. Several of our shipments were seized early in 1986.

As traditional avenues of communication became more heavily watched, we tried new approaches. One such was to use a technique for clandestine television broadcasting that we had developed earlier for use in Iran. We provided a good deal of money and equipment to the Polish underground for this—actually to take over the airwaves for a brief time. The effort was effective, and in June 1987 included the underground overriding Warsaw's evening television news on the eve of the Pope's visit with a message urging Solidarity activists to participate in public demonstrations.

We learned in the spring of 1987 that books we were sending into Poland clandestinely were reaching their target audiences. In May, Radio Solidarity, which we sponsored, broke the regime's monopoly on the media and began making announcements of future opposition events and reporting news items.

By late spring, 1988, we were taking advantage of less stringent border controls to infiltrate equipment and material through Hungary to Poland and to Czechoslovakia. We also were making use of the growing network of cooperation among the East European opposition groups.

In October 1988, CIA arranged the first satellite telecast into Poland from Western Europe, a ten-minute program covering recent labor unrest in Poland. We got a strong, positive reaction from Solidarity leaders. By November we were advised that nearly every factory committee in Poland had the capability to publish a newsletter and that recent labor unrest had led to increased publishing requirements that were pushing the equipment to the limit.

TRANSITIONS

Fate—or Murphy's Law—was against Bill Webster and me on August 26, 1988. We were in Boston at President Reagan's request to give a worldwide intelligence briefing to Democratic presidential nominee Michael Dukakis. We wanted our presence to be low-key and to attract as little attention as possible—no sirens or flashing red lights. We told the security detail to leave plenty of time to get from the Ritz Carlton Hotel, where we spent part of the day going over our material, to Dukakis's house in Brookline. They did so, coordinating with the Boston police. We left the hotel on time and ran immediately into a huge traffic jam—the Red Sox had a makeup game that day at Fenway Park that somehow had escaped the planners' notice. We had no choice—on went the red lights and siren as our car and police escorts wended their way through traffic. As we slowed passing the ballpark because of the number of pedestrians crossing the street, a middle-aged lady stuck her face up against Webster's window and, looking straight at him, shouted with disgust, "It's that goddamn Lloyd Bentsen!"—Dukakis's running mate. Webster smiled and waved warmly at her.

We finally arrived at the house and were greeted by Madeleine Albright, then Dukakis's adviser on national security issues, and with whom I had worked in the Carter administration. We entered the house and in the foyer shook hands with Governor and Mrs. Dukakis and then with Lloyd Bentsen (we did not share our ballpark experience) and his wife, and Congressmen Lee Hamilton and Lou Stokes. Webster and I knew everyone but the Dukakises well and began chatting and gossiping old Washington stuff. I suddenly realized that Dukakis had retreated beyond the circle, an outsider in his own home among the old Washington hands.

The briefing lasted two hours. Dukakis was alert, but I thought uninterested. We unloaded an overwhelming amount of information on him, and I was not surprised that his eyes glazed over. (It was the last time I would see him in person until the national education summit at the University of Virginia on September 27, 1989. The dinner was held at Monticello, Thomas Jefferson's incredible mountaintop home, and there Marlin Fitzwater and I found Dukakis alone in one of the rooms, again the outsider, even among his fellow governors. Feeling sorry for him, we stayed and drank with him for a while.)

After Bush won the election, Webster and I knew he would be an interested and informed user of intelligence—after all, he had once been DCI. But we did not know if the new President would keep Webster as DCI. I don't think it mattered a lot to Bill whether he stayed—he had been ready to retire from government in 1987 when appointed DCI. But he cared a great deal that if he were to depart, it be done with courtesy and dignity, and not through some press story. As it turned out, he was asked to stay. Bush apparently wanted to try to reestablish the apolitical nature of the DCI's job and demonstrate that it would not necessarily turn over with a change in Presidents.

I planned to stay on as well, although with small enthusiasm. I had a great relationship with Webster and we were a strong team, but I knew I would not get a second chance at being DCI and thus was looking at eight more years as deputy before I could retire. The thought appalled me.

Then, on December 15, while I was eating lunch in the Agency cafeteria, one of my security officers told me I had a call from Brent Scowcroft. I took the call at a security guardpost just outside the cafeteria. Brent had been appointed as Bush's National Security Adviser and asked me to be his deputy. It was a bolt from the blue. We agreed to meet the next day.

I was torn. Scowcroft was a workaholic for whom fourteen-to-sixteen-hour days were common. I had already worked at the NSC —including in the front office—for three Presidents and knew that behind the façade of pomp and power was the reality of endless frustrations, bureaucratic battles, internal politics and backbiting, and a lot of grunt work. And it would mean resigning from CIA, my professional home since graduate school. On the other side, I was not looking forward to continuing indefinitely as Deputy DCI, Scowcroft was an old friend, I thought I knew how to make the interagency process work, and I liked George Bush. Further, Scowcroft said he wanted me to serve as his alter ego—what he knew I would know, I would have a lot of time with the President, I would be a real participant and adviser. I told Scowcroft on December 16 that I would accept his offer on one condition—I wouldn't keep his hours. I had two kids at home and wanted to see them more than just on Sundays. I wanted to get out for school events and ballgames and so on. Scowcroft readily agreed. What a joke. He knew that once involved, I would do the job regardless how long it took.

I would have no regrets, though. Through my entire career, I never had more fun or enjoyed as much personal and professional satisfaction as during the nearly three years I spent in the Bush White House as Deputy National Security Adviser. Talk about being in the right place at the right time to watch history unfold and even get to help make it!

Other than Scowcroft, the members of the Bush national security team I knew were the President; Defense Secretary Dick Cheney, whom I had known through his membership on the House Intelligence Committee; Admiral Bill Crowe, chairman of the JCS, and later his replacement, Colin Powell; and Larry Eagleburger, James Baker's deputy at State. I did not know Baker except in passing, Quayle, or John Sununu, the White House Chief of Staff.

Of the six Presidents for whom I worked, I was lucky that

George Bush was the one with whom I got to work most closely. He was immensely well-versed in foreign affairs, his instincts were sure, and he had an uncommon—near-unique—grasp of the importance of personal relationships among leaders in achieving important goals. He devoted ample time to working the problems. He was an eager learner and interested in reaching out beyond government experts for insights and information. He listened. He was often bold and always courageous. And he was personally kind and generous. His weaknesses in foreign policy were reflections of his strengths: he was at times too patient and too forgiving of the ambitions and game-playing of both foreign leaders and some of his own people. He was at times loyal to some who did not deserve it or return it. But, all in all, it is hard to imagine a President better suited to dealing with the extraordinary events that would transpire during his term of office.

On the really big issues, Bush was not much one for elaborate briefing papers and options laid out in a formal way. On German unification, the Gulf War, the intervention in Panama, his decision process was encompassed in small, frequent meetings of trusted advisers and an open dialogue with former senior officials and others, from whom Bush encouraged different views and debate. Most of his senior advisers operated the same way, each turning to a small coterie of trusted aides. It was in this way that the advice of people like Paul Wolfowitz and Steve Hadley at Defense, Bob Zoellick and Dennis Ross at State, and Bob Blackwill, Condoleezza (Condi) Rice, and Richard Haass at NSC proved so influential. It was a process that put a premium on quality people—and reflected the long experience of all involved that while the bureaucracy was very important, new initiatives and the path to bold decisions were not to be found there.

Bush was a delight to work for. He was very funny and tolerated—even aided and abetted—kidding and shenanigans among his senior national security team that cemented personal friendships and a level of collegial teamwork perhaps unparalleled in postwar American government. Bush was constantly savaged by the cartoonist Garry Trudeau, whose strip "Doonesbury" often featured the President's invisible other self—"President Skippy"—as an asterisk. One morning when Bush stepped out of the Oval Office during a briefing, we had a photographer come in and take a picture of Scowcroft, Sununu, and me all talking and gesturing vehemently at an empty presidential chair. We later presented a large framed copy of the photo to him, inscribed "To President Skippy, from the Gang that knows you best." He loved it, and promptly decided to show it to the press. When he strode into the press room, there was nearly a riot—no advance warning, no indication whether a national disaster had occurred. He showed them the picture, said there was clearly a plot against him inside the administration, and then attributed the whole idea to Marlin Fitzwater. He was always game for a good practical joke, like substituting an explosive golf ball for Scowcroft's ball on the tee or many others. You could always get his attention with a good dirty joke—as long as it wasn't really gross, and as long as only men were present.

Bush was a gentleman in an age when not much premium is placed on that quality. He treated everyone alike—gardeners, the staff in the residence, the Secret Service, clerks, and Cabinet officers—in an open, friendly, and dignified manner. He would joke with them, ask about their families—and none of it was artificial or insincere. There was a reason a lot of longtime White House people cried when he lost in 1992. Bush had a temper, though he showed it rarely, and, in private, he could swear with skill and even some poetry when provoked.

George Bush was tough. He could take a punch and get back up. There are numerous examples from his public life. The most vivid one for me was in his personal life. I was with him and Mrs. Bush when they first saw their home in Kennebunkport after it had been devastated by a storm. As we approached it, we could see that their most treasured belongings—family pictures, mementos, and the like—were either lost to the sea or strewn all over the grounds, stuck in shrubs, most of them ruined. The entire seaward side of the house had been gouged open by the waves and the wreckage was everywhere. But George Bush didn't flinch. His jaw tight, the President of the United States put on waterproof pants, grabbed a shovel, and set about salvaging what he could of his home.

He was often sentimental, especially about others. At the memorial service for the crewmen who were killed as a result of the explosion on the battleship *Iowa*, some of the press were critical because he raced through his remarks. What they didn't know was that if he hadn't, he would never have made it through at all. I saw this time and again, from meetings with dying children for the Make a Wish Foundation to the parents of servicemen who had been killed—he felt these things very deeply.

I saw Bush in the arena where he thrived, where the issues

seemed clear, where he was most skilled, where he felt most comfortable with the team around him. That is the George Bush I describe here. The George Bush often portrayed in the press I did not recognize; the political and domestic policy George Bush I did not often see.

Baker was a real piece of work. Former campaign manager for Ford, Reagan, and Bush; former White House Chief of Staff; former Secretary of the Treasury, Baker brought to the position of Secretary of State uncanny political acumen about Washington, a decades-long close personal friendship with the President, and not much experience in foreign affairs. But what he didn't know about dealing with—and manipulating—the press was hardly worth knowing. Baker was a skilled negotiator abroad and at home. Watching him work his counterparts abroad, members of Congress and the press, and even Scowcroft and Cheney, was to see a master craftsman of the persuasive and backroom arts at the peak of his powers. I respected Baker and came to like him. I also was always glad he was on our side.

With all his strengths, two aspects of Baker's way of doing business bothered me. The first was that he demanded more loyalty of the President than he gave in return. It was a complex friendship, and they both resented journalists who tried to put their relationship "on the couch," to psychoanalyze it. But when Baker would go beyond his brief, get in a jam, or get the President in hot water, he would call Scowcroft to insist that the President stand behind him. On the other hand, when convenient, he would at times take credit that in fact belonged to the President—or occasionally, in difficult circumstances, distance himself from the President.

Second, Baker had a rarely displayed but formidable temper. Once I sat in for Scowcroft during one of Baker's private meetings with the President. Sununu, who routinely sat in on these sessions, made some characteristically disparaging remark about the State Department's efforts with the Congress. Baker blew his top. He turned to Sununu and, oblivious to the President (and to me), unloaded on him in the most graphic and scathing terms for the better part of several minutes—beginning with how a chief of staff should conduct himself. President Bush and I just looked at our shoes, embarrassed.

Another example: Housing Secretary Jack Kemp really got under Baker's skin, and could aggravate him with only a word or two. One morning, Kemp entered the Oval Office after a meeting in the Cabinet Room to accompany the President on a trip to St. Louis. Baker was clear across the Oval Office from Kemp, walking toward the door to return to his office. Kemp made some cutting wisecrack to Baker, to which the Secretary of State responded—in the Oval Office—by shouting across the room, "Fuck you, Kemp!" Kemp rushed across the room, chased Baker down the hall, and I thought there was going to be a fistfight right there in the West Wing of the White House. They confronted each other right outside Marlin Fitzwater's office. Just as the President told me to go get Kemp, that the helicopter was leaving, the Secretary of Housing and Urban Development returned and we left. I was later told there had been no violence.

These episodes were notable for me because they were rare as far as I knew. Normally, Baker was smooth as could be, good-humored, and a pleasure to work with. Except, I guess, for those he disliked or did not respect.

Cheney was very impressive. He was a team player and, while he presented his views forcefully and consistently, when he lost he didn't leak or try to play games behind people's backs. He and Powell (who became Chairman of the Joint Chief of Staff in the fall of 1989) were a strong team, and when they disagreed—which was rare—Dick would encourage Colin to offer his views to the President. Cheney was quite conservative, and a forceful advocate for Defense both publicly and on Capitol Hill. He was always very steady, unflappable. He could also be very stubborn, especially when Defense Department interests were at stake. Cheney was the only senior member of the administration more skeptical than I that Gorbachev would be successful at home.

Finally, I come to Scowcroft. During the six Presidencies of my career, some National Security Advisers were liked and others were respected. Only three were both liked and respected by their peers in government—Carlucci, Powell (each of whom was in the job only about a year), and Scowcroft (who served two Presidents as National Security Adviser for a total of nearly six years). A dogged defender of the Presidency, Scowcroft's lack of egotism and his gentle manner made possible the closest working relationships with other senior members of the national security team. Further, the strong individuals who ran State, Defense, CIA, and the other key institutions of national security trusted Scowcroft as no other National Security Adviser has been trusted—to represent them and their views to the President fairly, to report to him on meetings accurately, to facilitate rather than block their access to the President. Scowcroft ran the NSC and its process as it should be run.

By the same token, on substantive issues, Brent had his own views and he would advance and defend them stubbornly. Neither Cheney, Baker, nor Powell would ever think of Scowcroft as a soft touch on the issues. Scowcroft was less flexible than Baker in negotiating, but more radical in his thinking on future military force structures and arms control than Cheney; there were some battles royal in Scowcroft's corner office. But nearly all ended in good humor and friendship.

I never worked more intensively for as long with any person as I did with Scowcroft. I never argued as much with any person. I never got more frustrated at times with any person. But, when I became DCI and left the White House, I considered Brent Scowcroft my closest friend in the world.

Scowcroft's loyalty toward and affection for Bush was reciprocated. I suspect there has never been such a close personal bond between a President and his National Security Adviser. With all the game-playing and maneuvering that goes on in every White House, no one would have dared utter a criticism of Brent to George Bush —substantive issues apart. And his friendship with Barbara Bush was equally strong. Scowcroft was, in fact, as close to family as you could get with the Bushes and not be blood kin. While under other Presidents and other circumstances, this could have been a problem, during this period it was an advantage for the country— and for the world.

I benefited from Brent's relationship with the President. I attended virtually all meetings of the principals in the Oval Office and elsewhere, I traveled routinely with the President on his domestic trips, I had the same easy access to him that Brent did. And I, too, would have the friendship and support of Mrs. Bush.

My main job, apart from support to the President and Scowcroft, was to oversee the interagency NSC process—policy and contingency planning, the development of policy options, the decision-recommending and decision-making process, and the management of day-to-day national security operations. All administrations have had a senior-level interagency group to carry out this function, with varying degrees of success. Ours, called the Deputies Committee, included Robert Kimmitt, the Undersecretary of State for Political Affairs and a close adviser to Baker; Paul Wolfowitz, Under Secretary of Defense for Policy and a Cheney appointee; Dick Kerr, who replaced me as Deputy DCI; and Air Force General Robert Herres, Vice Chairman of the Joint Chiefs of Staff, later replaced by Admiral Dave Jeremiah. This group, supplemented at times by others, would develop the medium- and long-range objectives of U.S. policy and would manage U.S. policy day to day through one of the most remarkable periods in modern history. After a failed coup attempt in Panama in the early fall of 1989, the Deputies Committee also was assigned by the President to handle crisis management for the American government.

The personal chemistry was right, the talent was there, the group had the confidence of our superiors, all were experienced hands, egos were under control, and everyone had the final key ingredient to success—a great sense of humor. What is hard for historians to discern from dry documents is the importance of these flesh-and-blood relationships in making government work. The friendships—and trust—that developed among the core members of the Deputies Committee in 1989–1991 not only made the NSC process work, but cut down dramatically on the personal backstabbing and departmental jockeying that had been so familiar. Also, we never forgot that it was our bosses and ultimately the President who made the final decisions, not us.

Reflecting on both the personal relationships among the "principals" and the part played by the Deputies Committee, I believe it was the nation's good fortune that at a critical time in history, the great departments of the American government pulled together more effectively and more harmoniously than ever before.

So that's the cast of characters and the basic structure of the Bush administration as we began the extraordinary run of events from the liberation of Eastern Europe to the unification of Germany to the Gulf War to the collapse of the Soviet Union and its empire. It was to be one hell of a ride.

JUMPING ON A MOVING ROLLER COASTER

Every new administration begins with a review of developments and U.S. policies around the globe. However, because Bush had been Reagan's Vice President, there was a widely held assumption that continuity would be the order of the day in national security affairs and that such reviews either were unnecessary or would be pro forma. But this was a new President who felt a personal and political need to move out of Reagan's shadow and establish his Presidency in his own right. Moreover, and more importantly, there were many of us who believed that Shultz's hope to reach a new strategic arms agreement in 1988 (opposed by Bill Crowe and the JCS) had sped past both the U.S. military's analysis of the strategic implications and the ability of U.S. intelligence to monitor any such new agreement. Finally, Bush, Scowcroft, and I all believed that Gorbachev confronted serious challenges at home and in Eastern Europe. We thought, therefore, that it would be wise to take a few weeks at the beginning of the administration to weigh all this, let the permanent government catch its breath from 1988, have the new team become familiar with the situation and the issues, and then proceed.

There was never much expectation that the policy reviews would result in a dramatic departure from the basic forward-looking and conciliatory approach of the Reagan administration toward the Soviet Union. We did hope that the bureaucracy might come up with some new initiatives or approaches with respect to events in the Soviet Union and Eastern Europe—a triumph of hope over experience. In this, we were predictably disappointed.

There was much criticism in the spring of 1989 in the press, Congress, Europe, and the USSR (and now by historians) about this "pause" and what it meant. Scowcroft and I, perceived as the administration hard-liners, were cast as the villains in an effort to derail the Reagan-Shultz approach to the USSR. The reviews, however, were nothing more or less, in our view, than an orderly process for assessing where we stood, bringing everyone up to speed, probing the bureaucracy for ideas, and setting directions for the future. At the end, there were no dramatic departures from previous policies, but we were far better prepared for the rush of events both in Eastern Europe and the USSR that were upon us by spring. The exercise also confirmed once again that new ideas would come from Bush, Baker, Scowcroft, and their respective inner circles working in harness together.

What was new at the end of the reviews was that for the first time in memory the inner circles around the Secretary of State and the National Security Adviser actually had become partners and collaborators, however uneasy at times. This group—Bob Zoellick and Dennis Ross at State, and Bob Blackwill and Condoleezza Rice at NSC—would provide much of the intellectual and political imagination guiding administration policy toward Eastern Europe and the USSR. Out of this group came many of the ideas for helping the newly liberated East European states economically, the "beyond containment" strategy toward the USSR, the "two plus four" concept for managing German unification, and much more. It is to the credit of Bush, Baker, and Scowcroft that they turned to these remarkable "young" people, listened to them, and fashioned their ideas into American policy.

Their contribution, coupled with Bush's experience and instincts, Baker's political savvy and negotiating skill, Scowcroft's strategic and historical perspective, and my management of the interagency process, would allow the United States to play a sure-footed leadership role in the liberation of Eastern Europe, the unification of Germany, and the final collapse of the Soviet Union. This team, joined in the spring by Dick Cheney and in the fall by General Colin Powell, guided the policies and actions of the victorious superpower through the end of the Cold War and breakup of the Soviet Union—surely some of the most dramatic moments of a bloodthirsty century. And when we were done, there were more or less democratic governments in nearly all of the former communist states, an ancient and heavily armed empire was dismantled, and a revolution in world affairs had been accomplished, all virtually without bloodshed.

Together, we boarded the roller coaster in January 1989. Experts all, we had no idea what lay in store for us sooner than we could imagine.

GETTING SOVIET TROOPS OUT OF EASTERN EUROPE

Bush had stoutly defended the NSC review process for two months—the "pause"—but by mid-spring he was getting antsy. The perception in the West was growing that Gorbachev was much fleeter politically and gaining the advantage in Europe as the new Bush administration dawdled.

To regain the political initiative in Europe and to respond to developments in both Eastern Europe and the USSR, Bush indicated early on that he wanted to make a bold proposal for force reductions in Europe at the NATO summit in late May. In an Oval Office meeting on March 30, Bush told us that he believed Gorbachev had eroded U.S. leadership in Europe and that he wanted a series of proposals to put the United States out front again.

Scowcroft, as arranged beforehand with the President, then

tabled a radical idea: how about setting a goal of removal of all U.S. and Soviet ground troops from Europe by the turn of the century? (Scowcroft had been needling Bush since before Christmas 1988 about making such a proposal, primarily to lighten the Soviet troop presence in Eastern Europe.) Cheney looked at Scowcroft as if he'd lost his mind. He countered with the idea of challenging Gorbachev to open up military information. Baker threw out another idea—let's propose getting rid of all the tanks in Europe. Cheney came back again, arguing that this was not the time to get out front on withdrawals from Europe because of uncertainty about what was going to happen in the USSR. Bush ended the meeting grumpily. His last words: "If we don't regain leadership, things are going to fall apart."

Despite Bush's evident unhappiness, none of the President's chief advisers offered any new ideas in the ensuing weeks. Bush's sense that he had to do something bold was reinforced by Scowcroft, by allied leaders, and by the press. He knew the best opportunity would be at the NATO summit at the end of May, and time was running out. His frustration was apparent during our morning meetings.

Finally, he moved. On May 15—with only two weeks to go before the summit—he convened a meeting of his principal advisers to discuss a new initiative Scowcroft had developed for troop cuts in Europe. A new feature was that the troop reductions would apply only to U.S. and Soviet forces, not those of their allies. And, obviously, most of the Soviet reductions would be in Eastern Europe.

The Secretary of Defense didn't like it. Cheney argued that NATO was a "goosey coalition," that the United States was "the rock," the troop proposal would "unhinge the Alliance," and "the British and French would go crazy." He complained that, in an effort to get out in front politically, "we would be making a big move that was not well thought out." General Bob Herres, representing the Joint Chiefs, said he thought the Chiefs could accept some form of Scowcroft's proposal.

The President was the most forward leaning of all. He again hit on the need "to seize the offensive" with a dramatic reduction, and at one point in the meeting spoke of cutting our force levels by half if the Soviets would meet us at that level. (Even Baker said he thought that was unrealistic.) The meeting ended with the President wanting to move forward in refining the proposal. JCS was sent off to do the homework.

The next two weeks were intense. Bush was to host French President Mitterrand at Kennebunkport, the President's home in Maine, on May 20. The day before, all of the key players involved in the new U.S. conventional forces proposal flew up to Maine for further discussions. A dozen or so of us met in the President's living room, a light airy place looking out to the ocean, and continued the internal negotiation that precedes any major new initiative. But one thing was clear: there would be such an initiative. We were now ironing out the details. After the meeting, the President hauled us all out to the lawn for a press conference. Everyone, even Cheney, was in good humor, and there was a lot of kidding and horse-play. It was easy to forget the magnitude of the issues we were addressing.

We met again with the President on the afternoon of May 22. A blizzard of numbers, percentages, phases, phrases, and acronyms swirled through the Oval Office that afternoon, and the give and take continued even after. Finally, Bush made his decisions. Our proposal included significant reductions in tanks, armored personnel carriers, and combat aircraft, but the heart of it was a ceiling of 275,000 troops for both the United States and the Soviets (outside their national territory, thus requiring a Soviet reduction of some 325,000 troops in Eastern Europe compared to a U.S. reduction of about 30,000 in Western Europe). Finally, we proposed accelerating the timetable for reaching agreement from the five years proposed by the Soviets to six months to a year.

Just two days before the NATO summit, Deputy Secretary of State Larry Eagleburger and I were dispatched to Europe to explain and sell this proposal to NATO leaders. Larry and I took on the toughest challenge first. We figured if we could get past Margaret Thatcher, the rest would be easy. We were ushered into the Prime Minister's sitting room and directed to two easy chairs. Larry gave her a letter from the President explaining what he wanted to propose. She scanned it quickly, set it aside, and frostily asked us to explain it to her. We did so, with Eagleburger doing most of the talking. We both felt like schoolchildren called before the principal for committing some unspoken dastardly act. She asked pointed, informed questions, and expressed her concerns and reservations crisply. She knew the subject, and its details, thoroughly. She probably understood what was being proposed better than some of the Americans who had helped formulate it. The airpower reduction especially bothered her. And yet, at the end, and just as crisply, she said that of course she would support the President of the United States in this initiative.

Exhausted from the ordeal, but relieved, our small traveling circus then went to Germany, where we met with Chancellor Helmut Kohl. He was joined by his national security aide, Horst Telschik, and Foreign Minister Hans-Dietrich Genscher. We sat on the patio of Kohl's official residence (called the "Bungalow"), with the lawn sweeping down to the Rhine River. There was a plate of cakes on the table, and Kohl devoured nearly the entire thing—challenged only by Eagleburger—as we talked. He was ecstatic over the proposal, praised the President's boldness and vision, and pledged his full support. This was just what he had been hoping for.

On, then, to Rome to see Prime Minister Giulio Andreotti, and then to Paris, to meet with President Mitterrand. Impassive, he listened carefully. He expressed concern, like Prime Minister Thatcher, over the airpower reductions. But then he, too, promised his support. Finally, on to NATO headquarters to see Secretary General Manfred Woerner, to The Hague to meet with the Dutch cabinet, and finally home. We arrived only a couple of hours before the President departed for the Summit on May 28.

The U.S. proposal for reductions was a political triumph. The alliance leaders heaped praise on the President for his bold initiative and even his vision. And the proposal, and European praise for it, prompted a very positive reaction in the United States. It was a winner.

But, as Scowcroft originally intended, there was another audience for the proposal—in Eastern Europe. And the message to that audience was that, in all likelihood, after more than four decades, the Soviet army of occupation—or at least most of it—was going home in the foreseeable future.

NINE MONTHS THAT REMADE THE WORLD

By fall 1988, CIA's reporting made clear that economic problems in Eastern Europe were spawning political difficulty—including increasingly frequent demonstrations and strikes—for the communist governments, especially in Hungary and Poland. Also, the radical changes Gorbachev was making in the Soviet Union were not being made in most of Eastern Europe, thus making the latter regimes more conservative and isolated than their mentor. By the end of 1988, Gorbachev's message had penetrated: the regimes in Eastern Europe were increasingly insecure because there would be no more help from Moscow to suppress subjects who were becoming unafraid.

The "roundtable" dialogue between Solidarity and the Jaruzelski government that began in January 1989 concluded on April 5 with an agreement to hold new elections for the Polish senate, to allow a free opposition press, and to permit other opposition parties to participate in the election.

We needed to respond to these developments. There was an NSC meeting on aid to Eastern Europe on March 24, and on April 17—the same day Solidarity was legalized—Bush laid out administration policy toward the region in a speech in Hamtramck, Michigan. This was the first of several major speeches on foreign policy Bush made in April and May, and all were essentially ignored by the American press. It seemed that only the Europeans took them seriously. In Hamtramck, Bush reviewed developments in Poland and Hungary, declared that what was happening in Poland deserved U.S. support, and announced a number of steps the United States would take to encourage the reform process. Because of their technical nature, these measures had little sex appeal to the U.S. audience, but they were important to the Poles and signaled Bush's recognition that what was happening in Eastern Europe was real and deserved support. The speech also established the principle that U.S. aid would be linked to the forward progress of the reform process in Eastern Europe.

Even these measures required considerable muscling of the bureaucracy. Treasury hated the idea of debt relief because it might give other debtor governments unwelcome ideas. Commerce was uneasy with tariff concessions that might create trade problems with other countries. In short, virtually all the measures—none of which was exactly earthshaking—we put forward as part of the Polish initiative ran into flak. There was little accommodation, and Bush ended up making the key decisions.

On June 4—the same day the Chinese government crushed the demonstrators on Tiananmen Square—Poland held new elections for its parliament, as had been agreed at the "roundtable" talks in April. The communists were routed. Solidarity and allied candidates won ninety-nine out of one hundred seats in the upper house. Jaruzelski asked Walesa to join a coalition. He refused and, as a result of another round of negotiations, another election was scheduled in July to fill the remaining lower house seats. There was little doubt what the outcome would be.

On July 7, Gorbachev met with the leaders of the Warsaw Pact in Bucharest. In effect, he told them he accepted the political changes taking place in Poland and Hungary. The Soviet Union would not intervene to stop the changes under way.

From July 9 to 13, Bush visited Poland and Hungary. For his East European audience, the message was one of support and encouragement for the reform process. What many critics saw as Bush's excessive sympathy for the old guard on the trip was an attempt to grease their path out of power by showing respect and pretending—at least where he could with a straight face—that they were playing a constructive role in the unfolding of their nation's history. If violence was avoided, we knew reform would inexorably proceed. Bush's friendly, solicitous approach to soon-to-be-ousted leaders, for example in Poland, was intended to smooth transitions and to avoid providing them or their regimes any pretext for a dying orgasm of bloodletting. And so he ensured that both Jaruzelski and Walesa were at the luncheon he hosted at the U.S. embassy residence in Warsaw—and had pictures taken of the three of them, just one big, happy family.

Bush's second audience was the Soviets. Just as he tried to help ease the passage from power of old leaders in Eastern Europe by treating them respectfully and by seeming to make them partners in the process of change, so, too, did he give the impression that countries easing out of the Soviet orbit were doing so with Moscow's help, and that this was to the Kremlin's self-perceived advantage.

At the time, not knowing what was to come in the months ahead in Eastern Europe, journalists and other observers saw little remarkable in the Bush trip. Only in retrospect could people see that an American President traveled to Eastern Europe in mid-July 1989 with an unvarnished message of support for political freedom and national independence. He departed a few days later having boosted reform and blunted the fears of those most threatened. Only later would anyone, including those of us involved, see that it had been a remarkable high-wire balancing act in which a misplaced step could have been catastrophic. And, truth to tell, if we had known all that was to come, for fear of such a misstep the trip might never have taken place.

After the trip, events began to gather momentum. In Poland, following the June elections and runoffs, there had been prolonged jockeying between Solidarity and the Polish government over the nature of a coalition government. The communists could not stand the thought of relinquishing power after more than forty years.

Once again, Gorbachev played a critical role, and a positive one at that. On August 22, he telephoned Polish communist leader Rakowski and, in a forty-minute conversation, persuaded him to participate in a Solidarity-led coalition government. Thus, on August 24, at the urging of a Soviet leader, the Polish communists handed over the reins of power to a noncommunist government led by Solidarity.

On August 23, the day after Gorbachev's historic call to Rakowski, Hungarian Foreign Minister Gyula Horn decided to open the Hungarian border to the West for East Germans to escape their country. (As early as May 2, the Hungarians had begun dismantling the barbed wire and obstacle fence along their border with Austria.) On September 10, the Hungarian government formally announced the opening of the border.

East Germans wasted no time in taking advantage of this opportunity, and during the next three weeks or so, tens of thousands left for West Germany, most by way of Hungary, though also through Czechoslovakia. East German leader Erich Honecker tried on October 3 to close the border with Czechoslovakia, but succeeded only in inflaming the situation. When, on October 6, Gorbachev visited East Germany, he was greeted by huge demonstrations.

CIA received the same reports heard by journalists: that Gorbachev told Honecker during the visit that Soviet troops would not be used to restore order. There were even stories that Gorbachev urged other East German communists to oust Honecker, an avowed opponent of perestroika. Gorbachev returned home on October 7.

The same day, the Hungarian Socialist Workers Party—the Communist Party—abandoned Leninism and, as their leaders had foreshadowed to Bush on July 12, became the Hungarian Socialist Party. Thus Hungary became the second East European state in seven weeks to throw off communism.

Honecker in East Germany was a tough case. On October 9,

he ordered the use of force to break up a demonstration of 70,000 marchers in Leipzig, but local leaders refused to obey. A week later, on the 16th, there was another huge demonstration in Leipzig, this time perhaps 150,000 people. Another East German communist leader, Egon Krenz, made common cause with the marchers, joining the revolt. He was able to force Honecker to resign on October 18, and became his successor.

A week later, Gorbachev announced in Helsinki that the Soviet Union had no right to interfere in Eastern Europe. Of all the "green lights" Gorbachev flashed to the East Europeans, this was the most explicit. On October 31, Gorbachev told Krenz to open the East German border to West Germany. Four days later, 500,000 people demonstrated in East Berlin, and Prime Minister Willi Stoph and his entire cabinet resigned. East German communism was tottering, but not yet gone.

On November 9, a transitional East German government announced that the country's citizens could leave without special permission. Almost immediately, surging throngs crossed through the previously heavily fortified checkpoints and passages in the Berlin Wall, and soon the Wall itself was breached.

No one who watched on television will ever forget the images of crowds of East and West Germans dancing on the top of the Wall, hacking away bits of it for souvenirs, and finally dismantling whole sections with construction machinery. If ever there was a symbolic moment when most of the world thought the Cold War ended, it was that night in Berlin.

Those of us who had fought that war saw, in our mind's eye, the U.S.-Soviet tank confrontation in 1961, the days when the Wall went up, countless confrontations and crises over divided Berlin, the bodies of young East Germans riddled with bullets as they tried year after year to escape, the countless novels and movies set in Berlin amid the bleakness of the long stalemate. Most of us, I think, that night watched this celebration silently, moved beyond words at this unforgettable moment in the epic story of human freedom. This great, ugly serpentine Wall of concrete and steel, a Wall of death, was killed that night. And that part of the world that did not rejoice must have shuddered, knowing that their time, too, was drawing nigh.

Indeed, that same day, in Sofia, the communist leader who had ruled Bulgaria for thirty-five years, Todor Zhivkov, was ousted in a coup led by his own foreign minister.

On November 10, Gorbachev, who in many ways had set these changes in motion and at key points encouraged critical actions, including opening the Wall, wrote to the leaders of the three other governing powers in Berlin. To Bush, Thatcher, and Mitterand, he amazingly expressed alarm at the speed of events in East Germany. It was as if, having set his own house afire, he discovered it actually was burning.

Now it was Czechoslovakia's turn. A student rally on November 17 was attacked by police. On the 19th, 10,000 attended a protest in Prague. On the 20th, the marchers numbered 200,000. On the 22nd, 250,000. On November 24th, 350,000. The message was clear, and that night Czech General Secretary Milos Jakes and his entire Politburo resigned.

On December 3, the East German Politburo resigned. Thus, when the Warsaw Pact leaders met on the 4th, all of them were new except Gorbachev and Ceausescu of Romania. They condemned the 1968 invasion of Czechoslovakia and declared the Brezhnev doctrine dead.

In Czechoslovakia, Husak resigned as president on December 10. And, at long last, the Romanian people had enough of Nicolae Ceausescu. There was an uprising on December 19 and considerable violence. As the tide turned against the government, Ceausescu and his wife were captured trying to escape Bucharest. They were tried by a military court and executed by firing squad on Christmas Day.

CIA moved quickly in late 1989 and early 1990 to establish contact with the security services of the new, democratic governments in Eastern Europe. The object was partly to obtain information on Soviet espionage operations run in concert with the spy organizations of the old Warsaw Pact organizations, partly to provide assistance as the new services tried to establish their independence of the KGB, partly to gain access to military and KGB communications equipment, partly to get access to Soviet military equipment, and partly to lay the foundations for future cooperation.

If anything, Scowcroft and I tried to slow the Agency down a little. We wanted to know if those services with whom they were establishing a relationship were still spying on the United States or still acquiring American technology. We also wanted to know more about their relationship with their own new governments. We also didn't want to have the Agency so far out in front in Eastern Europe that it might create an embarrassment for Gorbachev—or for Bush.

By the same token, CIA's ability to help some of the new East European leaders develop communications networks and personal security forces was an important asset for us and a real help to those leaders. Another historic milestone was passed when the director of CIA, Bill Webster, visited Hungary, Czechoslovakia, and Poland in November 1990.

BUSH, GORBACHEV, AND EASTERN EUROPE

Over the space of nine months, with the sole exception of Romania, a bloodless revolution—a "Velvet Revolution," as Czechoslovakia's Vaclav Havel called it—swept Eastern Europe. Denied resort to the Soviet army to sustain illegitimate and hated regimes, every communist government save Albania was forced from power by the anger of its own citizenry. And the Soviet empire in the West collapsed in the twinkling of an eye. The Cold War that began in Eastern Europe was over, and now Europe, the Soviet Union, and the United States would turn to the last piece of unfinished European business, the unification of Germany.

How had all this happened? Clearly, there were historical and economic forces at work. The Soviets had done everything possible to avoid military intervention in Poland in 1956, 1970, and 1980, each time turning to a Polish communist who promised to restore order and each time ceding more autonomy to Warsaw. But 1980 had been different. This was a revolt by an organized opposition of workers, encouraged and morally sanctioned by the new Polish Pope. They would be suppressed in December 1981, but the price to the Soviets and to the Polish government was high. And, while the workers' movement might be suppressed for a time, the government proved incapable of dealing with an economic crisis that day after day sapped its power. Elsewhere in Eastern Europe, groups spawned by the Helsinki process became increasingly vocal, and communist governments, as in Poland, were equally incapable of managing the homegrown political and economic crises. These were rotten governments, kept in power solely by the image of Soviet tanks—by fear.

And, in Eastern Europe as in the Soviet Union, it was Mikhail Gorbachev who stripped away that fear. He thought the result would be more democratic, more effective communist governments. Governments with legitimacy. In Eastern Europe, as in the USSR, he was wrong. With the fear gone, the utter moral and political bankruptcy of the regimes—and their weakness—were exposed.

Why did Gorbachev act as he did? Because he knew that military action would destroy his relationship with the West and any chance of help for economic revival in the USSR. Because Moscow had never faced trouble in most of the East European states simultaneously, and repression through military force thus became a genuinely massive undertaking with incalculable costs. Because he knew that military suppression in Eastern Europe would destroy perestroika in the Soviet Union. Because he had no grasp of the deeply held nationalist passion of the East Europeans and their resentment of Russian domination. And, I think, because he had no stomach for the bloodletting that would be required. Forced either to fight or let Eastern Europe go, he let it go. Finally, I believe he did not act decisively because the speed and magnitude of events, the rush of history, overwhelmed him.

George Bush's contribution to the success of the "Velvet Revolutions" in 1989 was in what he did not do as well as in what he did. He did not gloat. He did not make grandiose pronouncements. He did not declare victory. He did not try to accelerate events in any of the East European countries. He did not join the dancers atop the Berlin Wall. He did not immediately invite new East European leaders to Washington. He did not threaten or glower at tense moments. He did not condemn those who were under pressure to let go the levers of power.

What he did was play it cool. In extensive and continuing personal contacts with different factions, and through promises of support and assistance, he helped grease the skids on which the communists were slid from power. There was little Bush might have done to promote or speed the revolutions of 1989. There is much an American President could have done to derail or at least complicate those revolutions. Bush played it just right, as virtually all of the leaders of the new democracies in Eastern Europe would later attest. But, even considering all of the many historical factors at work in 1989, Bush also grasped that many of the changes in Eastern Europe and, above all, the lack of bloodshed during these revolutions were due to the leader of the Soviet Union, Mikhail Gorbachev. It was, at the end of the day, a Soviet leader who let an empire slide away peacefully.

CHAPTER TWENTY-SEVEN

Together at Last: Bush and Gorbachev

ON MONDAY, JANUARY 23, 1989, three days after George Bush took the presidential oath, a gray, unmarked van approached the Northwest Gate of the White House. The driver told the Secret Service he had been asked to deliver a large box shipped from the Soviet Union to the new President. He had no idea of the contents of the box, which he said had been flown to the United States by Aeroflot, the Soviet airline. There was no message on the box, no card, nothing. The Secret Service contacted Condi Rice of the NSC staff, and she called the Soviet embassy. They had no knowledge of any gift or shipment. It was all very mysterious, and a little worrisome. Taking due precaution, the Secret Service took the box to one of their facilities in Anacostia in Southeast Washington, where explosives experts carefully opened the box.

It was a cake. A five-hundred-pound cake. But from whom? Thus began the great cake caper, the first challenge in Soviet-American relations of the Bush administration. Rice played detective. She tracked the cake back to a collective of bakers in the Soviet Union who had wanted only to express good wishes to Bush in their own way. When I filled in the President on this gift—with some irreverent humor, I admit—he was quite taken with the effort involved and decided that we should arrange to have a picture taken of a member of his family standing next to the cake and send it to the collective. By the time we were able to arrange this—several weeks later—the cake was much the worse for wear (and the rats at

472

the Secret Service facility much fatter). As the cake deteriorated, I tried several times just to forget the whole thing, but Bush never let me off the hook. He insisted on that picture and nice note to the bakers.

It was this human touch that made Bush so effective in dealing with foreign leaders, his concern for their feelings and pride, his ability to understand their circumstances and point of view, to see things from their perspective. This was especially true with Mikhail Gorbachev. And that rare ability would prove critically important during the momentous events of 1989–1991.

FACTIONS

Journalists at the time and historians writing subsequently have made much of the lack of in-fighting and contention in Bush's national security team, particularly in contrast to preceding administrations. In fact, there were disagreements, sometimes harsh ones, all the time and on almost every problem we faced. Unlike my Bush-appointed colleagues, I had worked in all of those earlier administrations and thus could pinpoint what made the Bush team different. Nearly all of the major players had known and worked with one another off and on for up to twenty years or even more. Nearly everyone had his ego under control. No one had to worry about his views not getting to the President straight and unvarnished—either in person or on paper or through the NSC. Everyone at the top level could get access to the President on short notice by phone or in person. And, above all, everyone was loyal to the President and knew how much he hated—hated is the right word —having disagreements played out in the press. Bush was an old Washington hand, and knew how to read between the lines in press stories to figure out the source, if not the person then the department. He had help in this from his press secretary, Marlin Fitzwater. The result was a remarkable, though thanks mostly to State by no means perfect, discipline at the top level of the administration in containing disputes and self-serving leaks. It was quite a change for me from the Carter and Reagan years.

From the beginning of the administration, there was little disagreement about developments in the Soviet Union or about Gorbachev's strengths and limitations. Everyone, from Bush on down, was skeptical about Gorbachev's chances for success in reforming the Soviet system. There was a clear understanding of the Soviet economic crisis and the ineffectiveness of Gorbachev's efforts to deal with it. There was no disagreement about continuing Soviet military power or Gorbachev's ability politically to complicate our lives with the allies and others when it served his purposes. There was full recognition of the magnitude of the reforms he already had accomplished, and what he might still do, but there were no false hopes either.

The fault line in the administration was in the prescription of what to do—how to deal with the Soviets so as to maximize the chances for further change favorable to our interests. Bush, Baker, and Scowcroft were more or less committed to working with Gorbachev, saw him as the best person to continue and manage change in the USSR, and I think hoped there was a chance he could see the process through to a successful end. They were far from naïve and had no false expectations. They were just open-minded about the possibility.

Dick Cheney, Larry Eagleburger, and I were the most skeptical that Gorbachev could permanently wrench the Soviet Union away from its philosophical and historical roots and build a new structure based on democratic values and a market economy. To change fundamentally, the Soviet Union had to abandon communism, and we three believed, whatever Gorbachev's inclinations, he already had shown he could not—would not—go down that path. He really thought the existing system could be fixed. We thought that, unless and until the Soviet Union abandoned communism, no matter how much Gorbachev did, many of his actions could be reversed and the USSR would continue to be a major potential security problem for the United States.

For my views, a May 28, 1989, article in the *Washington Post* said, "Gates has become to the world of Sovietology what Eeyore is to Pooh Corner—someone capable of finding a dark lining in even the brightest cloud."

With the possible exception of Cheney, all—including me—agreed that however skeptical we might be about Gorbachev's prospects (or those of his policies), we could not stand pat. As Reagan and Shultz had shown, much could be accomplished with Gorbachev that would advance Western security, a more peaceful international environment, arms control, and welcome changes in the Soviet Union itself. Baker best stated the theme that unified the key players in the administration on Soviet issues: we don't know what will happen there, but we should move quickly to lock in all the gains we can while Gorbachev is still around. Whatever our differing degrees of skepticism, this we could agree on.

PERSONAL CONNECTIONS

Gorbachev clearly was eager to get off on the right foot with Bush. On the morning of the inauguration, the Soviet ambassador in Washington called Scowcroft and said that Gorbachev wanted to be the first foreign leader to congratulate the new President after the ceremony. Arrangements were made for Gorbachev's call to be put through to the Capitol. However, Murphy's Law overrode the arrangements and the contact could not be made. Thus, on January 23, Bush called Gorbachev.

Bush's penchant for picking up the phone and "reaching out to touch someone" was unprecedented on the international scene, and became an important new instrument of foreign policy. We all knew that most correspondence between leaders was written by their staffs and thus had an impersonal, stilted sameness no matter who was writing to whom. Bureaucratese translates much the same in every language. Bush's use of the telephone established a personal connection with other leaders.

There were risks. Spontaneity is not always desirable in communications among world leaders. An offhanded remark, a verbal misstep, a poorly interpreted colloquialism, even someone getting annoyed, all could lead to trouble. And the hazards were magnified in dealing with a Soviet leader.

But Bush's experience and personal touch allowed him to avoid these pitfalls. Instead, over the months, he got a better sense of Gorbachev as a person, and learned much from listening to him explain his problems and positions. And this, in turn, helped Bush say and do things at key moments that made it easier for Gorbachev to abandon long-held Soviet positions—whether in Eastern Europe, Germany, or the Persian Gulf. As suggested in Chapter 26, Bush's attentiveness to Gorbachev the man and the politician certainly contributed to the peaceful liberation of Eastern Europe.

Similarly, I watched Jim Baker establish his own connection with Eduard Shevardnadze. They first met in early March in Vienna. Baker had a hard act to follow in that Shultz and Shevardnadze had met dozens of times and had developed a very strong relationship. Even so, Baker reached out to Shevardnadze in a personal way and with such evident personal regard that a real partnership grew over time. Obviously, it also says much about Shevardnadze that he was able to work so closely and even become friends with two men as different as Shultz and Baker.

"Innocent Abroad": A Spy in Moscow

I made my own personal connections with the Soviet leaders, though at a very different level and in a different way. Baker continued Shultz's practice of taking a large interagency contingent with him for talks with the Soviets, and so in May 1989, after working on Soviet and Russian affairs my entire adult life, I first set foot in the Soviet Union. A reporter asked me at a U.S. delegation press conference in Moscow how I liked the USSR. I replied that after all these years, it was nice to see it from the ground level. I had been warned that my room at Spaso House, the U.S. ambassador's residence in Moscow, probably was bugged, and as I prepared for bed the first night, I said aloud for the benefit of the listeners that I would be going right to sleep, had no companionship planned, would be in bed all night, and so they could take the evening off. I thought I heard a chuckle, but undoubtedly imagined it.

While in Moscow, I met secretly a second time with Vladimir Kryuchkov, by now head of the KGB. I stepped into a Soviet Chaika limousine in front of Spaso House at 5:00 P.M. I was driven to a KGB safe house in downtown Moscow. It was an old, prerevolutionary merchant's house and had been redecorated in the elaborate but dowdy fashion one might associate with a very elderly but wealthy maiden aunt. I was later told that the house had once belonged to Lavrenti Beria, Stalin's sadistic and homicidal secret police chief. Kryuchkov invited me to join him for dinner, and we went in to a dining room with one of the most elaborate spreads of delicacies I had ever seen. There was food enough for a dozen people, all set out for the two of us with interpreters. I was impressed, but mostly with how many hungry Russians that food might have fed that night.

Our conversation at this second meeting was less historical and philosophical than our first encounter in Washington seventeen months earlier. He talked at length about mistakes of the past, the misuse of power, the period of stagnation under Brezhnev, and the need for perestroika. He described how he was bringing perestroika to the KGB and trying to establish it as a "law-governed" service. In the course of speaking about Soviet ethnic problems, he asked how our federal system worked, who resolved disputes between the states and the central government, and so on. It was all fairly standard boilerplate, but it did seem to me that he was strongly supportive of Gorbachev and perestroika, and, further, that his job was to convince me that even the KGB was on board.

We then turned to the spy business. A Soviet scientist, Vladimir Aleksandrov, had disappeared in Spain, and the KGB was convinced CIA had kidnapped him. (We had learned in the late summer of 1988 that the KGB had gotten so exercised about what it believed was CIA drugging and kidnapping of their officers and other Soviet citizens that it was planning to retaliate against some of our officers. To head off an ugly incident, as Deputy CIA Director, I had taken the unprecedented step of sending a message to Kryuchkov denying that we had been involved or that we used these methods.) This came up at our dinner in Moscow, and I tried, without success, to persuade him that we knew nothing about Aleksandrov and that the others had come to us of their own free will. We talked about other cases as well. Finally, I urged him to free the family of Oleg Gordievsky, the KGB resident in London who had been a British agent for some years and defected in the mid-1980s. He was unyielding, saying that the family would never be allowed to leave but that if Gordievsky came home, he would not be punished, would be reunited with his family, and would be given a job and an apartment. I told him, "No chance." On this note, our second meeting ended.

The next day, I met Gorbachev for the first time when Baker invited me to participate in the plenary session with the General Secretary. I was impressed with Gorbachev's energy and, given all his problems by then, amazed by his confidence. In his introductory comments, he noted my presence and commented to Baker that he had heard that I was in charge of a "cell" at the White House with the purpose of discrediting him. He made a few other comments and then told Baker that if they succeeded in their efforts to improve the relationship, then perhaps "Mr. Gates would be put out of a job." I was embarrassed at being singled out in this way, especially by a man for whom I had developed considerable respect and regarded as a figure of great historical importance. When the meeting was over, and we were leaving, as I shook Gorbachev's hand he leaned over and said quietly to me that he understood Kryuchkov and I had had a very useful meeting. I agreed and then told him that no one in the administration was opposed to him—

we all admired what he was trying to do but wanted to be realistic about the challenges he faced.

On the way back to Spaso House, I thought about the fact that in the space of eight months, both an American Secretary of State and the leader of the Soviet Union wanted me fired. At least I didn't mess around with the "mattress mice"—lower-level officials— when it came to making enemies. But I did wonder how a mild-mannered kid from Kansas had managed to get on so many high-level hit lists.

ROADSHOW: THE SOVIETS SEE WYOMING

Nineteen eighty-nine was the year of Eastern Europe, and much of the U.S.-Soviet dialogue that year was focused on the dramatic changes there. Even so, there was considerable progress made in other areas of the relationship, particularly in two high-level meetings in the most unlikely places.

Prior to those meetings, however, the administration was treated to a visit by Boris Yeltsin. Some of us thought that we ought to be reaching out to establish contact with reformers other than Gorbachev. Yeltsin was coming to the United States to lecture under private sponsorship, and Condi Rice and I thought he ought at least to be received at the White House. (I vividly remembered President Ford's snub of Solzhenitsyn in 1975.) The President and Brent were worried that Gorbachev would be miffed by a formal Oval Office meeting with the President with all the press trimmings, so they decided to have Yeltsin meet with Scowcroft and me in Brent's office, and the President would "drop in."

Yeltsin's trip to the United States that September was not good for his reputation. He apparently drank too much, gave a poor account of himself in a speech at Johns Hopkins University, and was generally boorish. So it was at the White House when he visited on September 12. He had been told that he probably would see the President but because we wanted as low key a visit as possible he was not given absolute assurance. He was brought in to the White House complex on a side street, West Executive Avenue, out of sight of the press. Condi Rice greeted him and escorted him through the West Wing basement entrance. When he was inside, he balked, and refused to go any farther until assured he would see the President. After a brief but rather tense discussion between him and Rice, the slight young woman took Yeltsin by the elbow and essentially propelled him up the stairs to Scowcroft's office. Then he balked again because he could not bring all of his aides into the meeting. That resolved, he finally sat down with Brent, Rice, and me to talk. Looking him over, I noticed he was missing a couple of fingers. I was told later they had been blown off when he was young and was playing with a grenade. I thought to myself that he was still playing with grenades, but they were political ones now—and a lot more dangerous.

Yeltsin went through a long, excruciatingly monotonous presentation of ten proposals on how the United States could help the Soviet economy. As he droned on, I saw that Brent was getting sleepier and sleepier, and finally we lost him altogether. He was snoozing as Boris Yeltsin described how the Soviet Union ought to be run. Yeltsin, self-absorbed, seemed wholly oblivious to the impact he was having on his audience.

His whole demeanor changed when the President came in and sat down. Chameleonlike, Yeltsin was transformed. He came alive, was enthusiastic, interesting. Plainly, in his view, someone had arrived worth talking to—someone really powerful. So, for twenty minutes or so, Bush and Yeltsin had a good conversation, the spirit of which was not dampened when the President reaffirmed his support for Gorbachev. After Bush left, Vice President Quayle dropped by, everyone getting a photo taken with Yeltsin as we went along.

Shevardnadze came to Washington nine days later for the again-routine meeting between a Soviet Foreign Minister and the President when the former attended a UN General Assembly session. The meeting was on the 21st and was very cordial. Bush told Shevardnadze and later the press that he supported perestroika, was convinced the reform process would continue, and that the United States would not exploit the changes under way in Eastern Europe.

Now it was time to get down to nuts-and-bolts issues. Rather than simply move over to the State Department, Baker shepherded Shevardnadze onto a U.S. Air Force plane and they and their teams all flew to Jackson Hole, Wyoming, one of the most spectacular outdoor settings in the United States. And there we were in coats and ties buried in the arcania of arms control.

However, Baker's initiative in choosing a nontraditional setting for the meeting was inspired, and I think helped cement a strong relationship between him and Shevardnadze that had begun to take shape when they met in Paris the preceding July. They talked for hours on the flight westward about problems inside the Soviet Union, and especially about the economic difficulties. Shevardnadze had brought with him a reform economist, Nikolai Shmelyov, and the two of them, Baker, Zoellick, and Ross sat in Baker's cabin sharing concerns and ideas. I was seated a few feet away and heard most of what was said, and I was struck by the very fact of the exchange and who was involved. Baker pushed hard on the need for fundamental reform, including price reform and moving as quickly as possible to a market economy. As former Treasury Secretary, his advice was sound and credible.

During the Wyoming talks, real progress was made toward getting the Soviets to dismantle their illegal radar at Krasnoyarsk, in delinking START and SDI, and on eliminating chemical weapons. Just as important, there was a relaxed atmosphere that encouraged making the kind of human connections that are so rarely noted by historians but which, in real life, count for so much in dealings between nations. There was a candor in the informal discussions that I had never seen before. Shevardnadze would play a critical role in the next fifteen months, particularly in the reunification of Germany and in Soviet participation in the coalition against Saddam Hussein. I believe the connection he and Baker made in Wyoming was of crucial importance in the part Shevardnadze would play. Even if their short fishing trip at the end of the meeting was something of a bust. And I suspect that, upon returning home, he never went out in public wearing the hand-tooled cowboy boots Baker gave him.

ANOTHER SPEECH PROBLEM

A month after the Wyoming meeting, I was scheduled to give a speech at Georgetown University. I prepared a draft again focusing on developments in the Soviet Union. As with previous such speeches, it was full of praise for Gorbachev yet realistic about the internal crisis in the Soviet Union. I sent the draft to Defense, State, and CIA for comments and corrections. Baker objected strongly. Under the circumstances, Brent had no choice but to tell me not to use the speech. After all the effort, I was really steamed at being silenced. However, after sulking a day or two, my anger passed because I grudgingly realized Baker had been right.

That fall, the Secretary of State gave two speeches laying out U.S. policy toward the Soviet Union and discussing events there.

Given my reputation as a "hard-liner," the differences in tone and nuance between our speeches would have been used to show a split in the administration, an internal conflict—just the kind of thing the President disliked so intensely. It was the kind of story the press would love, the White House versus State.

Unfortunately, Baker or his staff created the very problem I thought had been averted by my not delivering the speech. Either Baker or one of his close advisers leaked to the *New York Times* that he had squelched my speech because it was too hard on Gorbachev. This was widely reported and prompted the very speculation about a split on Soviet policy I thought we had been trying to avoid. Conservatives, never very fond of Baker, were especially up in arms. I kept quiet and refused the pleadings of a number of journalists, columnists, and others to give them the undelivered draft speech. I told Scowcroft that, thanks to State, the speech had gotten a hell of a lot more attention ungiven than if I had gone ahead and delivered it. Though I had played by the rules all along, I felt badly about provoking the problem in the first place. For a second time, a speech—this time even an undelivered one—had gotten me in hot water with a Secretary of State.

MALTA

After the NATO summit and his trip to Poland and Hungary in July 1989, Bush better than the rest of us understood how fast events were moving in Eastern Europe, in arms control, and in the Soviet Union itself, and he concluded that it would be a mistake to wait to meet personally with Gorbachev until the formal summit planned in Washington in 1990. He thought a more personal relationship and a direct dialogue essential in light of the momentous changes under way. Given what was to come, it was a wise judgment. Thus, on his way back from Eastern Europe, he wrote Gorbachev a personal note suggesting a meeting late in 1989, either at Camp David or at Kennebunkport. Gorbachev responded that he did not want to go back to the UN in the fall—giving him a pretext to meet with Bush in the United States—since he had just been there the preceding December. Bush then proposed Alaska and, when Gorbachev finally made clear he couldn't come to the United States, the President suggested Malta. This initiative was an extremely tightly held secret in the government, with only six or seven of us aware.

Bush was very clear about the kind of meeting he wanted. He disliked set-piece meetings with other leaders, far preferring an informal setting conducive to a relaxed but candid exchange of views. He wanted, therefore, to avoid all the diplomatic formalities in Malta and focus on just talking with Gorbachev. Announcement of an early December meeting in Malta was made on October 31.

November was a frenzy as we prepared for the Malta meeting. The Berlin Wall came down and the East German government teetered on the brink of extinction. The Czechoslovak communist government collapsed. The Soviet Transcaucasus was in an uproar. And, in the middle of all this, we were trying to prepare for an important summit meeting. Bush wanted to cover the widest possible range of subjects but, more important, he wanted to put on the table a laundry list of initiatives and actions the United States was prepared to undertake as a manifestation of confidence in the reform process and in Gorbachev. When Bush left for Malta, he had a package of seventeen proposals to put on the table. We all knew that none of them individually amounted to much. But, taken together, we thought they represented a significant political investment in Gorbachev and perestroika.

The Malta meeting was a great success from Bush's perspective. There was progress in START, Conventional Forces in Europe (CFE), and other arms control negotiations, including real headway in the sensitive area of on-site inspection. There had been direct talk about Soviet aid to Nicaragua and Cuba. Gorbachev had described the situation in the Soviet Union in detail, including what he was trying to do and what his problems were. There had been a candid discussion of the Baltic states, with Bush urging Gorbachev to avoid violence and assuring him that if he did so, the United States would respond with restraint. Bush further reassured Gorbachev that the United States would not try to exploit the changes in Eastern Europe. And Gorbachev told Bush that the USSR wanted U.S. troops to remain in Europe.

In a sense, the extraordinarily turbulent seas at Malta and the storms at the time of the meeting symbolized the political turbulence and storms then raging in Eastern Europe and the Soviet Union. There was a revolution under way in the most heavily armed region of the world. Malta provided reassurance to the world that Bush and Gorbachev would work together to keep the process of change under way and to keep it peaceful. For Bush's part, he had arrived in Malta strongly supportive of Gorbachev and what he was trying to accomplish. When he left, this remained unchanged but now was complemented by a new personal relationship on both sides that would prove important in the coming months.

"BY FAITH ALONE": THE REUNIFICATION OF GERMANY

In retrospect, it is astonishing how events of historical significance crashed upon us one after another during this time. Historians too often impose an order, a sequence, to great events that fails utterly to capture the real-world confusion, the challenge of juggling several different problems at once, the physical stamina required to run flat-out for months on end, the difficulty of orchestrating the actions of the many elements of the American government, and the intellectual energy required to come up with ideas that you know—for good or ill—will have profound consequences. And when you are confronting challenges that you know will alter the course of history, it can become downright scary. From 1989 to 1991, we shot the rapids of history, and without a life jacket.

It was in this atmosphere that just as Eastern Europe was breaking away from communism in the fall of 1989, the issue of German unification came to the fore. There had been discussion of the issue before, but the opening of the Hungarian border on September 10 and the outpouring of East Germans headed for West Germany made a hypothetical political issue into a real one.

In September 1989, most Europeans and many Americans didn't think much of the idea of the Germans getting back together again. The French and British were nearly as opposed as the Poles and the Soviets. Memories of the last time there had been one Germany were long and very painful. But George Bush, himself a veteran of combat in World War II (though in the Pacific), had a different view.

That view was first expressed clearly in a most unlikely place. Bush was on a domestic trip to the American West, and on September 18 gave a press conference in the House of Representatives chamber of the Montana statehouse. I accompanied Bush on nearly all of his domestic trips, and was there on that beautiful fall day, standing in the back of the chamber. Bush was asked whether he thought a reunified Germany would be a stabilizing or destabilizing force in Europe. He answered as follows:

I would think it's a matter for the Germans to decide. But put it this way: If that was worked out between the Germanys, I do not think we should view that as bad for Western interests. I think there's been a dramatic change in post–World War II Germany. And so, I don't fear it. And I notice that the Chancellor had something to say on this the other day—I might need help on this from Bob [Gates]. But nevertheless, this is something that should be for them to determine. But I think there is in some quarters a feeling—well, a reunified Germany would be detrimental to the peace of Europe, of Western Europe, some way; and I don't accept that at all, simply don't.

Alone among the leaders of the Western alliance and the Soviet Union, George Bush believed in his heart that the Germans had changed, and he was prepared to gamble a very great deal on that faith. He would cast his lot with Helmut Kohl and the German people. He knew, too, that American leadership in bringing Germany together would establish an even more powerful political bond between the two countries. His straightforward answer that day in Helena, Montana, would guide U.S. policy for the next year.

At the end of November, in a speech to the West German Bundestag (parliament), Chancellor Kohl offered a ten-point program for achieving German unity. It was a gradual, step-by-step approach that was based on the assumption that unification would take several years. But it defined a path and made the goal clear. In a phone conversation the next day, November 29, Bush offered Kohl his support for the program. The chancellor received no such call from Gorbachev, who was unhappy at the Kohl proposal and publicly spoke of the enduring reality of two Germanys.

Two days later, at Malta, Bush and Gorbachev talked about the future of Germany. Bush played Gorbachev just right on the issue. He talked about the changes under way in Eastern Europe and East Germany and urged Gorbachev to accept them. He made clear American support for reunification but in a low-keyed, nonthreatening manner, noting how he had acted with restraint. He had tried not to put Gorbachev on the spot and said he would continue to avoid "jumping on the Wall." Gorbachev explained his concerns about a reunified Germany and suggested that everything be done within the context of Helsinki (CSCE). But Bush, ever the fisherman, played the line: he started leading Gorbachev to the hook—German reunification—without scaring him off. Most important, he avoided any statement or question relating to reunification to which Gorbachev had to answer "no."

Bush had an equally challenging task at a NATO summit in Brussels on his way home from Malta. In the second, afternoon session, Bush endorsed German reunification based on four principles: (1) pursuit of self-determination without prejudice to the outcome; (2) unification in the context of Germany's continued commitment to NATO and the European Community; (3) unification as a peaceful, gradual, and step-by-step process; and (4) on the question of borders, support for the principles of the Helsinki Final Act. Despite concerns expressed by Prime Minister Andreotti of Italy and Prime Minister Thatcher, the alliance endorsed Bush's approach. NATO was now on record on unification, although Gorbachev soon made clear he still wasn't.

Events on the ground in East Germany during December 1989 and January 1990 soon accelerated everyone's German timetable. Most significant, the East German government was collapsing and could not provide the basis for a Soviet approach to the German question radically different from that of the West. East German elections were moved up from May to March 18. By the end of January, the Soviets were discussing how to proceed on reunification, not whether to do so. And, in the United States, the inner circles at State and NSC were drawing up proposals not just for the rapid reunification of Germany, but how to keep that Germany in NATO. Now that, in Blackwill's parlance, was indeed a "big idea."

The "how" of unification was the brainchild of Ross and Zoellick at State. It was their idea to use the postwar Four Power mechanism (United States, United Kingdom, France, and the USSR) to deal with the external aspects of German unification and add to it a forum in which the East and West Germans could negotiate the internal aspects of unification independent of the Four. At the same time, the Two would be included in the discussions of the Four.

This political arithmetic started from the premise that the Soviets had to be involved in the unification process in any case and the Four Power mechanism was one that would appeal to them. Such a forum also would ensure that reunification was not the result of a deal between the Soviets and Bonn in which the FRG's tie to NATO would be jettisoned as the price for Soviet agreement. Finally, it allowed for German pride in determining their own future, but within a controlled environment. Thus was born the "Two Plus Four" arrangement to bring about German unification.

As German reunification became likely and the Warsaw Pact collapsed as a military alliance, we again turned to the question of

American troop levels in Europe. There were several reasons to consider a new initiative. First, some members of Congress were beginning to question the need for a large American presence in Europe, given the liberation of Eastern Europe and the growing crisis in the Soviet Union. Second, practically speaking, with pressures on the Defense budget and in light of events in Europe, how large a force did we really need in Europe? Third, we were pushing to complete the CFE treaty in 1990, including the proposals Bush had made at the NATO summit the previous May, and the Soviets were muttering in the negotiations about removing all foreign troops from German soil. We—and NATO—needed an agreement sanctioning a residual U.S. military presence in Germany. Finally, we needed a well-reasoned approach to troop levels that would provide a sustainable basis for a U.S. military presence in Europe after the end of the Cold War. We had to establish a floor for our presence—a level we would not go below.

Senior officials at Defense, State, and NSC again went into high gear to develop alternative ideas. Now in January 1990, as had happened the preceding May, Bush's national security team met repeatedly in the Oval Office—Quayle, Baker, Cheney, Powell, Scowcroft, Sununu, and me. I was the notetaker in each meeting, and what is readily apparent from the discussion is the fact that Bush and Scowcroft together and alone consistently pushed for bolder initiatives, especially in arms control, and were resisted equally consistently by Baker, Cheney, and Powell. Cheney resisted because he hated arms control in principle and, paradoxically, saw it as an obstacle to arms reductions. Baker resisted because he was nearing agreement with the Soviets on proposals already on the table and any modification to U.S. positions would spoil the chances of early and successful conclusion to these negotiations. Powell was worried about the impact on the alliance and the military's ability to carry out the missions still assigned to it by the political leadership of NATO. These debates underscore the disagreements within the administration, but also how Bush prodded his senior advisers into bolder and bolder actions. Out in front of everyone else on his team on German reunification, including Scowcroft, contrary to his public image, Bush now would push hard to respond to new opportunities in arms control. If "prudent" was supposedly one of his favorite words in public, his vocabulary of choice in private as he looked to Europe and the USSR was "boldness" and "opportunity."

The first meeting was on January 4 and, when the discussion turned to CFE, the President and Scowcroft pushed for a bold new initiative. Scowcroft took the lead, saying: "We could go to the Allies and say we want to negotiate a bilateral cut to 200,000 [from the 275,000 proposal of the preceding May]. We can get ahead of the Congress and establish a sustainable level."

Baker spoke first, expressed his reservations, and made a counterproposal: stick with the current U.S. position, get agreements at the June summit, and at the summit announce we will seek a troop-level goal of 200,000 in CFE II. Then Cheney chimed in. He said that his first day at NATO headquarters during a recent trip had been spent "putting out fires." Significant U.S. reductions were trouble. The East Europeans, Soviets, and West Europeans all wanted us to stay. "All but Congress. . . . This only gives us a bigger problem on the Hill."

Finally, Bush spoke up. In response to Cheney, he said a little impatiently:

> Isn't this all good news? So we are sitting with 270,000 troops? Offering no reaction to Soviet actions? The world is changing and we're going to change with it. . . . Why do we always need the same number of troops and bombs? Let's test the Soviets. Ask them to do something that they would never do. Otherwise, we'll have passed up an opportunity, we'll have to make unilateral cuts, and we'll get nothing for it. Let's not have slight, begrudging change, but respond boldly. We have an enormous opportunity to do something dramatically different. . . . I don't want to miss an opportunity.

Despite Bush's pushing, the debate within the seniormost level of the administration on a new initiative would continue inconclusively for more than two weeks. It is a measure of how fast events were moving in Europe that by the time of the next meeting, on January 22, the whole tenor of the discussion had changed. The East Europeans were calling for more reductions to get the Soviets out and were worried that CFE would be used as an excuse not to draw down. Powell, just back from Europe, said he thought that the Germans would go for the additional reductions, although we wouldn't know for sure until the President talked to Kohl. The British would object and the French would be uneasy. Colin said that "all are expecting significantly lower troop levels than 275,000, and all agree this is in our interest."

The President, obviously pleased, observed that this was "a big step along the lines of Brent's proposal." He then said the United States would need to get someone to go talk to Thatcher and Kohl.

Cheney signed up, saying: "I can feel the sand running out. Let's get 'em out of Eastern Europe. Colin and I have a problem on the Hill regardless. . . . It's hard for us to argue against the proposal if the allies feel the way they do."

Bush then said the next step was for Eagleburger and Gates to go see Thatcher and Kohl with the proposal and specifics. I winced. Thatcher had been tough enough the previous May. This would be no fun at all.

Thanks to Bush's phone calls to the European leaders, we had a pretty good idea of what we'd encounter. Kohl, as we expected, was enthusiastic. Mitterrand had no particular objection to the proposal but was worried about the Germans, in their eagerness to reunify, moving toward neutrality and getting all foreign forces out of their country. Thatcher's concerns, too, related to Germany as much as to the Soviets, but she also was worried about a German wish to denuclearize their country.

Larry Eagleburger and I, accompanied by Air Force Lt. General Lee Butler (who would later become Commander of the Strategic Air Command), arrived in London early on January 29 on our second secret mission. We cleaned up after an all-night flight and then were driven to 10 Downing Street. The Prime Minister greeted us in the same sitting room and, motioning us to the same chairs we had sat in the preceding May, said with more than a tinge of sarcasm, "Won't you take your accustomed places?" Once again, we knew this was our toughest meeting. She knew more about U.S. military deployments and NATO strategy than Eagleburger, any of her own advisers, or I did. Nonetheless, with Larry doing most of the talking, we presented the U.S. proposal and why we thought it provided a basis for sustaining U.S. forces in Europe for the long term. In his inimitable way of blending humor, finesse, and hard-nosed strategic good sense, Eagleburger was very effective—as least sufficiently so that we didn't get thrown out. And, at the end, it was clear to us that, however reluctantly, the British Prime Minister would go along with the President.

As we rose to leave, Mrs. Thatcher was quite friendly to the two of us, saying as we departed, "You two will always be welcome here." Then the smile was replaced by a hard look, and she continued, "But never again on this subject." She would later refer to our meetings with her as visits from "Tweedledum and Tweedledee."

Our other meetings, including with Kohl and Mitterrand, went smoothly and with no hiccups. On January 31, Bush called Gorbachev to inform him about the proposal, and then made it public that night in his State of the Union address to the Congress.

We had come a long way in just a few weeks. Communist governments had been replaced throughout Eastern Europe. We had put forward a plan for U.S. troop withdrawals from Europe in keeping with the radical strategic transformation of the continent during the preceding months (and, obversely, an approach that would give us a strong position at home for keeping a sizable force in Europe indefinitely, as sought by our allies, the East Europeans, and the Soviets). And we had developed a process for bringing about German unification in NATO on our terms—the Two Plus Four. Now all we had to do was sell that mechanism to our allies and the Soviets.

Baker carried the major burden in this. The British and Germans agreed to this approach without much difficulty. Baker departed Andrews Air Force Base near Washington for Eastern Europe and the USSR on February 6. On his way, he met with French Foreign Minister Roland Dumas in Shannon, Ireland, during a refueling stop for Baker's plane and got a sympathetic reaction to the Two Plus Four approach.

Finally, on to Moscow and critically important discussions on German unification. In early February 1990, Gorbachev and Shevardnadze were dodging political bullets. Gorbachev was in the middle of the crisis with Lithuania. Two weeks before our meeting, riots and killings had occurred in Baku. As we arrived in town, Gorbachev had just concluded a major Central Committee plenum that agreed to creation of a new executive presidency and significant changes in party structure. But at the plenum there also had been bitter attacks on Shevardnadze, blaming him for the loss of Eastern Europe and for mismanaging foreign policy in general.

So, on February 9, 1990, Gorbachev was a man with a lot on his mind. And yet he still seemed confident and even relaxed. Baker already had spent considerable private time with Shevardnadze on Germany, and it had been hard going. We were not optimistic about Gorbachev. After about ninety minutes, Gorbachev ended the plenary session and everyone left but Baker, Shevardnadze, and notetakers. It was time to talk about Germany.

Following the session, Baker called Zoellick, Margaret Tutwiler (Baker's press—and political—adviser), and me to his hotel suite and he and Ross (who had been notetaker) filled us in on what had happened. The session had lasted for two hours, from 12:30 to 2:30 P.M. Gorbachev led off by describing domestic circumstances —"It is not boring"—and what had happened at the Central Committee plenum. He spoke of the need for radical economic reform and said that the plenum represented a "radicalization of perestroika."

Baker led off on Germany, saying that a mechanism was needed to manage the external aspects of unification and to avoid German nationalism. He then explained the Two Plus Four approach. He reassured Gorbachev that the United States sought no unilateral advantage, but that no one favored a neutral Germany—a neutral Germany would not necessarily be a nonmilitary Germany.

Gorbachev was surprisingly conciliatory. He told Baker: "Basically, I share the course of your thinking. Stability in Europe must be maintained. We can't be passive if we are to ensure stability in Europe. There is nothing terrifying in the prospect of a unified Germany." He spoke of concerns in Eastern Europe about "a new Reich," and the concerns in Britain and France as well. He said it was important to channel the process of unification, and the "mechanism of Four Plus Two or Two Plus Four is suitable." After more discussion, Gorbachev said he would be giving thought to all of the options they had discussed, but emphasized: "Any extension of the zone of NATO is unacceptable. The presence of U.S. troops could have a constructive role. What you've mentioned is possible. We don't want Germany to arm itself like after Versailles—we need to create a process which constrains Germany within the European structure." Reflecting the situation at home, he concluded, "Don't hold me to this as a bottom line."

But Baker had made important headway. He, like Bush at Malta, had by his manner and reassurances led Gorbachev further toward accepting a unified Germany in NATO without giving him a pretext to say no. The road ahead would be very bumpy, but we had a map and all the lights were either green or at least a cautionary yellow.

On a more human level, after the evening session with Shevardnadze on Friday the 9th, the Foreign Minister asked to speak to me privately. This was a first, and I was uneasy. Both he and Gorbachev seemed to believe that I was somehow responsible for U.S. intelligence, a view not hard to understand. He told me that a former colleague of his was writing an ugly book about him that would say many untrue things and that this book was to be published in the United States. Could I do anything to stop it? Marveling at the Soviets' belief in the power of the CIA—presumably reflecting the role in the USSR of the KGB—I told Shevardnadze I would do what I could. In fact, I was trying to be polite but knew there was nothing I would or could do to help him. At our next meeting, in May, Shevardnadze would come up to me and thank me profusely for my successful efforts on his behalf. Apparently, either the author or publisher had decided unilaterally not to proceed with the book and Shevardnadze attributed this decision to me. I smiled and accepted his warm thanks, thinking I now had a brownie point with the Soviet Foreign Minister that might someday come in handy.

During that Moscow meeting, I also had my third and last secret meeting with Kryuchkov of the KGB. It was quite unsettling, even to a pessimist like me on Soviet domestic developments. This time, no safe house, no sumptuous dinner. Instead, we met in his office—Andropov's old office—at KGB headquarters. His tone, demeanor, and whole approach were very different. More formal and stiff, less candid. No more talk about the need for reform or support for perestroika. He spoke at length of problems in the USSR, of the nationalities and the dismal conditions in Russia. He said, "The people are dizzy with change" and it was therefore time to slow down, to reestablish order and stability. Kryuchkov seemed to have written off Gorbachev and concluded that perestroika had been a terrible mistake. We talked for about an hour or so, and I took my leave. As I told Baker on my return to the hotel, Kryuchkov was no longer a supporter of perestroika and Gorbachev had better watch out. And I later told Condi Rice I thought this was an important and even dangerous turn of alliances in Moscow. I was particularly struck by the fact that Kryuchkov would be so open with me about his change of heart—he was openly opposing Gorbachev in a meeting with a senior American official, and a perceived hard-liner to boot. I decided I would not meet with him again.

We knew from both open and secret sources that Gorbachev was under great pressure from the political right in Moscow that late winter and spring. But Gorbachev's more conservative approach in both foreign and domestic policy was not just a reaction to pressures from others. The economic situation was continuing to deteriorate, and he faced a crisis in Lithuania and in the other two Baltic states. The idea of creating a strong executive president had been his, and he sought more and more power in order, he said, to move reform along. But he also was determined to hold the Union together and to restore order.

These difficulties inevitably affected the Soviet approach on Germany, and the spring was filled with new ideas, proposals, and negotiations. As nettlesome as they were at the time, in retrospect it seems clear that they did not long delay unification. On May 14, Kohl announced that an all-German election might take place in 1990, and, on the same day, his aide, Horst Telschik, traveled secretly to Moscow where he told Gorbachev that the Germans would be prepared to pay the costs of maintaining Soviet troops in East Germany after unification until their withdrawal and then build housing for them back in the Soviet Union.

Baker arrived in Moscow the next day, and this visit was dominated by Lithuania and tough negotiations on arms control. His private session with Gorbachev on Germany did not go particularly well, and the Soviet leader seemed much more negative on a unified Germany in NATO than in February. The Germans already had offered the Soviets a number of financial and political goodies, and now the United States informally offered a number of political commitments to reassure them—from changes in NATO strategy, an enhanced role for CSCE, and no German possession of nuclear, chemical, or biological weapons, to settlement of Germany's future borders—nine proposals in all.

"Inducements" and "incentives" were nice diplomatic words. In truth, we were trying on two levels to bribe the Soviets out of Germany. First, knowing of their desperate economic circumstances, West Germany was offering them a pile of money to agree to unification in NATO. Also, the Soviets approached us for loans and, while pleading that it would be hard to get political support in the United States for aid while they were trying to suppress the Lithuanians, we did not say no—thus leaving open the possibility. Second, without compromising or yielding on key issues relating to our security or German sovereignty, we were trying to develop a number of proposals that would both make unification in NATO acceptable to Gorbachev and give him some important Western concessions on Germany and European security that he could use at home.

The U.S.-Soviet summit in Washington from May 30 to June 2 was an important turning point on German unification. While there were extended conversations on the subject, the key moment came during a plenary session in the Cabinet Room the afternoon of May 31, when Bush observed that under the CSCE principles, each nation had the right to choose its own alliance. So shouldn't Germany have the right to decide for itself? When Gorbachev agreed with this, there was quiet consternation on the Soviet side.

Later that day, Bush took Gorbachev to Camp David for talks on regional issues and relaxation. After the discussions, Bush and Gorbachev set out to tour Camp David by golf cart, with Gorbachev driving. Marlin Fitzwater and I were sitting on the porch of one of the cabins when the two presidents came by in their cart. Both looked up and waved at us, at which point a distracted Gorbachev nearly drove the golf cart into a tree, lurching sharply to avoid it and nearly turning the golf cart over. Marlin and I speculated as they drove away about the international implications of the two presidents being in such a bizarre accident and joked that our financial futures would have been comfortably assured if it had happened and we had exclusive photographs.

June was a busy month. On June 12, Gorbachev told the Supreme Soviet he would go along with a unified Germany in NATO as long as there was a transition period for the military forces in East Germany. Nine days later, the East and West German legislatures endorsed a swift economic union, and vowed to sign a treaty confirming the postwar borders with Poland. On June 22, in a Two Plus Four meeting in Berlin, Shevardnadze took a very tough line on Germany. He made clear that much depended on the NATO summit scheduled for July 5 in London and the message that would be sent by NATO about changes to the alliance in keeping with a new situation in Europe and a changed relationship with the USSR. He also made clear that nothing would happen until after the 28th Soviet Communist Party Congress, scheduled for July 2–13.

Developing the changes in NATO that Shevardnadze was looking for as a precondition for German unification within the Western alliance fell to a new, high-level committee that I chaired, called the European Strategy Steering Group. It included the closest and most trusted advisers of Baker, Cheney, Powell, Scowcroft, and Webster. Somewhat unwieldy, the Group—an expanded version of the Deputies Committee—still worked well together, and provided a mechanism for translating the ideas of Zoellick, Blackwill, and their colleagues into government policy or crisp options for the principals and the President to consider.

The Group met constantly in the White House Situation Room between June 4 and the NATO summit in early July. It was critical to come up with a package of initiatives with respect to reappraising and changing the role of the alliance. Expectations of dramatic proposals to alter NATO were very high both in Europe and in the Soviet Union. The Steering Group was no less than a way to bypass the U.S. bureaucracy on reshaping the NATO alliance. There was little time and a need for bold departures, at least from the way the American government had thought about the alliance up to then. This was one of the times in which my own close relationship with and easy access to the President—together with wide knowledge of that relationship in the bureaucracy—was important. It was important that when I began a Steering Group meeting, the participants knew that what I said reflected the President's thinking and the direction he wanted to go. And, on one or two occasions when we were deadlocked, it helped when I could interrupt the meeting, go see him, and return with guidance.

Once again, the intellectual heavy lifting was done by Zoellick, Blackwill, Philip Zelikow (also of the NSC), Rice, and Ross, with a lot of help from others as well. It is a tribute to the quality of the people sitting around that table in the Situation Room that, in the space of three weeks, we produced a draft NATO summit declaration that would change much about the four-decade-old alliance and set its face toward a very different future.

The reaction to the draft in the alliance overall was positive, although Thatcher remained skeptical. Kohl was overjoyed. But, most important, Gorbachev found the NATO declaration a real help. With a positive NATO declaration in hand and the Party Congress behind him, Gorbachev agreed on July 15, during a visit by Chancellor Kohl, to a united Germany in NATO, "if that is its choice." He announced this the next day at a press conference.

Negotiations continued over the rest of the summer, sorting out all of the details associated with reunification. On September 12 in Moscow, the Four Powers who had been in Germany since 1945 blessed the reunification, and two weeks later in New York they signed a declaration giving up their special Four Power rights at the moment of unification. The declaration became effective on October 3, 1990.

This was a remarkable achievement. The challenge before George Bush as Eastern Europe liberated itself was to encourage the final outcome, to offer inducements for further "reform," to try to keep the change peaceful, and especially to conduct the American government so as to avoid giving the Soviet Union any pretext to try to interrupt the process. We were coaching from the sidelines, but not actually running the plays on the field.

With respect to the reunification of Germany, George Bush was coach and quarterback. Without his faith in the Germans, the skill he and Baker brought to the effort with the Europeans and especially with Gorbachev, and the contributions of the rest of his team, I believe the odds are high that German reunification would have been delayed—perhaps significantly—and may well have taken place outside of NATO. At the time, and later, Helmut Kohl would attest to this historic role by the President of the United States.

HEDGING OUR BETS IN MOSCOW

By midsummer 1990, Bush had developed strong admiration for Gorbachev and an appreciation for his courage in bringing change to the USSR, his restraint in letting Eastern Europe go, and his willingness to let Germany unify in NATO. In Bush's view, Gorbachev was owed for the part he had been playing in making history. Further, in arms control and other arenas, there was more to be accomplished, and he, Baker, and Scowcroft saw Gorbachev as the leader best able to deliver the Soviet Union in these endeavors.

I did not disagree with any of this, but as I saw the Soviet Union tearing itself apart, I thought we were placing all our bets on a man who had about run out his political string. Continued support for Gorbachev in Bush's and Scowcroft's view—mine, too —was not causing us to forgo or miss concrete opportunities to advance our own or alliance interests. To the contrary. Even so, I thought we needed to reach out to other reformers and establish new relationships for the future. Especially with the President of the Russian Supreme Soviet, Boris Yeltsin. I knew that Cheney, Eagleburger, and Condi Rice agreed with this view.

On July 13, 1990, I sent the President a memorandum urging a change in the U.S. approach. I said that, at home, Gorbachev is increasingly viewed unfavorably by the public at large—as indecisive, a "chatterbox," a leader who offers no way out of the present sorry state to which he has brought the USSR. . . . He remains, in his heart of hearts, a Communist—and continues to say so. . . . And, as more reform leaders emerge in the USSR as a result of elections, he is becoming more and more a symbol of the old way of doing business. . . . His effort to meld state socialism and "regulated" markets . . . and the incoherent mishmash of reform measures all have produced economic catastrophe. And, there is no indication that, in fact, he has the faintest idea of a way out.

Then I got to the core of my argument:

Gorbachev has successfully carried out a political revolution and, in so doing, has broken the USSR's tie to the past. Thanks to him, the country is able to contemplate a different future economically, politically and structurally. But, like Moses, having brought his people out of bondage, it is increasingly evident that Gorbachev cannot lead them over into the Promised Land. Delivered by Gorbachev from the past, the peoples of the USSR seem destined now to wander in the desert awaiting a Joshua to take them into the future.

I then proposed to "depersonalize" our support for reform in the Soviet Union, to focus more on support for the process of reform and to give visibility to other reform leaders, advocates of democratic and market reforms, and key reform measures themselves.

I concluded: "Gorbachev has earned his place in history but history now seems to be moving beyond him. It would be a pity for you, Mr. President, as you boldly and confidently lead the West into the future, to be seen in the Soviet Union as wagering everything on a man whose vision at the end of the day does not reach far enough."

The President's reaction was ambivalent. He wrote, "Brent/Bob—Good thought paper. The advice . . . is sound, however, Gorby seems, at least so far, to be a survivor."

I don't know how much influence my memo had, and there were others like Eagleburger and Cheney making the same case. In any event, when Baker saw Shevardnadze in Paris on July 18, he advised him that the United States intended to start reaching out more to Yeltsin and other reformers.

THE LAST DANCE TOGETHER: THE GULF WAR

Never underestimate the role of luck in the affairs of nations. It was very lucky that on August 2, 1990, when Saddam Hussein invaded Kuwait, Baker was with Shevardnadze in the USSR. To reciprocate for the Wyoming meeting, Shevardnadze had invited Baker and his delegation to Irkutsk. When the news arrived, Baker urged Shevardnadze to have Gorbachev join an arms embargo on Iraq. Though Shevardnadze decided to return at once to Moscow, Baker decided to proceed as previously planned to Mongolia for meetings—and a much-anticipated hunting trip. Ross and Zoellick returned to Moscow, another lucky break, because they flew with Shevardnadze and used the opportunity to press for a joint U.S.-Soviet stand against the aggression—a joint statement, which Baker's two brain-trusters wrote.

While Shevardnadze liked their draft statement, he ran into a buzz saw with others in the Soviet government. There were powerful elements of the Foreign Ministry, the military, and the KGB opposed to any Soviet action that might sever their long relationship with Iraq.

When Baker arrived in Moscow, he told Shevardnadze that the proposed statement finally acceptable to the Soviets was inadequate. They worked it over at the airport and, as read by Baker, the two governments jointly called for an arms embargo against Iraq. Shevardnadze had taken full responsibility on his own shoulders for agreeing to the American proposal. As on Germany, he was well out in front of Gorbachev and the rest of the Soviet government.

From the first days after the Iraqi invasion of Kuwait, Bush had to balance two equally desirable but occasionally incompatible objectives: the first was the effort to put together the largest possible international coalition against Saddam Hussein and obtain widely supported international sanctions against Iraq; the second was to protect U.S. military freedom of action against encroachment from that political coalition. The Soviets were important to the first objective and a danger to the second. Baker was in charge of the first, Cheney the second. It was our job at the White House to keep the two in tandem.

A tough early clash between our diplomatic and our military strategies came on August 20, when we found out that an Iraqi oil tanker was steaming toward South Yemen. A U.S. warship fired a warning shot, but the tanker steamed on. The question was whether to disable the ship. I was in Kennebunkport with the President at the time, and on the phone constantly with Scowcroft, still in Washington. Baker wanted to hold off striking the ship and use that as leverage to get the Soviets on board for a UN resolution authorizing military action to enforce the sanctions. The President summoned his key advisers on the war to Maine a couple of days later, and Eagleburger (representing Baker, who was vacationing in Wyoming), Cheney, Powell, Scowcroft, Sununu, and I sat around a small table on the deck of Bush's house to thrash out the issue. Cheney, Powell, Scowcroft, and I all supported hitting the ship— that we couldn't let the Soviets hold our military actions or perceptions about our will hostage to their political maneuvering. After all the tough U.S. rhetoric about Saddam, this was the first real challenge, and we were deeply worried about suggesting to Saddam that we were unwilling to use force when lines we had drawn were crossed.

It was a tough call and, again, Bush's instincts led him to the right decision. He gave Baker more time to get Soviet support for an enforcement resolution, and Jim used it effectively. After a last-ditch Soviet effort to get some conciliatory move out of Saddam, Shevardnadze sent a message to Baker on August 24 indicating that the Soviets would support the resolution. Those of us who had supported an immediate attack on the ship had been wrong. From then on, Bush would weave his way through the political/diplomatic and military decisions, leaning one way or the other depending on the issue. During the next five months, he would make nary a misstep.

We all knew that Gorbachev was a lot shakier on cooperation with us against Iraq than was his Foreign Minister. We also figured that other than the two of them, there was no one at the top of the Soviet government who favored this collaboration. Under these circumstances, Bush again took the initiative, inviting Gorbachev to a face-to-face meeting in Helsinki on September 8. The purpose of the meeting was to nail down the Soviet position on Iraq. At the Helsinki meeting, Bush offered Gorbachev something to take home —American agreement to joint sponsorship of an international conference on the Middle East after the confrontation with Iraq was over. A joint statement was issued that avoided directly linking the conference with Soviet cooperation against Saddam. More important was the appearance and the reality of that cooperation. Bush had gotten what he came to Helsinki for.

On November 8, Baker was again in Moscow, and this time he used the opportunity—as he had on Germany—to start Gorbachev thinking about the possible use of force against Iraq and UN authorization for it. Gorbachev spoke of two UN resolutions, one to authorize the use of force after a grace period and a second to go to war. Baker countered with one resolution, with a built-in grace period. At the end, once more Gorbachev had not said no and seemed to be leaning in favor. After further talks with the Soviets on November 18 in Paris, where the CFE agreement was signed, the UN Security Council passed a resolution on November 29 authorizing the expulsion of Iraq from Kuwait using "all means necessary." Bush and Baker had worked Gorbachev and Shevardnadze skillfully.

Agreement at Helsinki notwithstanding, Gorbachev would continue trying to play both sides of the street between Washington and Baghdad until the eleventh hour. He called Bush on January 11, four days before the UN deadline expired, to urge postponement of the attack. Siding with Baker in not wanting to risk driving Gorbachev out of the coalition at this late hour, Bush soft-pedaled concerns on the Baltics, and would continue to do so—though he already was headed toward postponement of the summit scheduled for February. Condi Rice and I thought the President should have reacted more strongly on the Baltics and told Scowcroft so.

The air war began the night of January 16. Bush had managed not only to get the UN Security Council to approve launching the war but had also won the support of both houses of the U.S. Congress, though narrowly in the Senate. These votes, at home and at the UN, were immensely useful politically, but had they turned out differently, I don't think it would have made any difference in the President's decision to go to war. I heard him say on several occasions that he was prepared to be impeached to get Saddam out of Kuwait. For George Bush, the issue was not jobs or oil, though those were important. The real issue was a "naked aggression" after the end of the Cold War that had to be reversed or it would set a precedent that would thwart any hope of a more peaceful world. He was coldly implacable toward Saddam. George Bush was going to throw that son of a bitch out of Kuwait and there was never any doubt about it—regardless of what the Congress or the UN said.

The period was not all stress and tension, though. One Saturday afternoon, when the "Gang of Eight" was meeting in the Oval Office, it was cold in the room and Bush lit a fire in the fireplace.

The flue, operated electronically, was closed, and smoke quickly filled the historic office. It was really very funny as we all tried to be cool and pretend nothing was wrong—that is, until we began choking. Cheney went out to get the Secret Service and a fire extinguisher. The Secret Service finally got the flue open, but to get rid of the smoke, we threw open all the doors to the President's office in February—and nearly froze.

Gorbachev tried again to stop the ground war on February 21. He called the President around 6:00 P.M., and Bush took it in his office on the second floor. I raced over from the West Wing at his request. He and Gorbachev talked for quite a while as the Soviet leader tried out yet another variant of his peace plan. When the conversation ended, the President headed out to Ford's Theatre in black tie. He asked me to gather the "Gang of Eight" for a meeting after the performance. The purpose of the meeting was how to respond to Gorbachev, and opinion was split. Baker wanted to play him along and keep the Soviets on board. Cheney wanted to tell him where to get off. In the end, Bush called Gorbachev the next day and the President and Baker sweet-talked him for nearly an hour and a half, but also set forth an ultimatum for Saddam. The President was resolute in not letting Saddam get out of the trap he had laid for himself. And Gorbachev reluctantly went along.

GAME'S END

Throughout his leadership, Gorbachev had always tried to balance between reformers and more conservative elements of the old regime. This middle ground was comfortable political territory for him in that it permitted temporizing, compromises, and halfway measures consistent with Gorbachev's own uncertainty about moving into the future. Beginning in 1988, that broad middle ground on which he pursued perestroika began steadily to dwindle as he moved forward and the Soviet political spectrum polarized. He had first tried to lead both reformers and the old guard. Then he tried to balance between the two. And finally, in his last two years in power, he jumped between them—first taking dramatic actions on reform, then turning to the right and repression, then back to reform, and so on. His own chief of staff, Boldin, described him as running "from one side of the sinking ship to the other, confusing everybody and hiding his true intentions." As a result, Gorbachev was discredited with both factions by the spring of 1991. By March, he was walking a tightrope, with politicians, nationalists, "tradition-alists," reformers, and institutions all figuratively throwing things at him and waiting for him to slip just once. His time was run-ning out.

Condi Rice and I believed this wholeheartedly, while Brent—and, I think, the President—were more hopeful. Rice and I could see that the reactionaries in Moscow—the military, the KGB, the party—were dominant at the center. At the same time, we saw that the republics were moving beyond the gravitational pull of that center, and were themselves leaving Gorbachev behind. Thus the sands were running out on the man who had done so much to change the Soviet Union—and the world. And, the Bush adminis-tration was under increasingly heavy fire for not abandoning Gor-bachev in favor of the new leaders of the reform movement.

In fact, the Bush administration was engaged in a balancing act of its own. Most of us understood that Gorbachev had taken reform as far as he could, and either had to ally with the reformers and give others their head or be pushed aside. Since the summer of 1990, the U.S. government, with State in the lead, had reached out ag-gressively to make contact with reform leaders other than Gorba-chev and to talk to leaders of the republics. By early 1991, a steady stream of these people were coming to Washington and meeting with officials at various levels, up to and including the President. The really tough decision as new and unknown leaders from the different republics showed up in Washington was which U.S. offi-cial should see each one, and deciding whom the President should see. He couldn't see them all—most weren't that important, and we did not want to devalue the important coinage of a presidential meeting. It was difficult to sort out who was worth listening to—and who should do the listening. Rice and I, for example, thought it essential that Scowcroft see the new leader of Kazakhstan, Nur-sultan Nazarbayev. He was an important figure, but that didn't protect us from Scowcroft's scorn after a meeting in which Nazar-bayev quoted production statistics for an hour.

Even as we reached out to others, Bush, Baker, and Scowcroft thought we could still accomplish some important business with Gorbachev, specifically finally wrapping up the CFE treaty (that the Soviet military was trying to destroy) and finishing the START treaty. Also, the administration greatly feared instability in the crumbling Soviet Union and wanted to do all we could to promote an orderly process of change. Cheney and I wanted to see the Soviet

Union broken up, thereby significantly reducing the chance it could ever threaten our security again. Scowcroft privately shared this view but thought it was bad politics and bad policy to say so publicly. Our approach was summarized crisply in a statement Scowcroft made to the President in the Oval Office during our national security briefing on May 31. He said, "Our goal is to keep Gorby in power for as long as possible, while doing what we can to help head them in the right direction—and doing what is best for us in foreign policy." This approach would guide us until August 19, 1991.

Three high-level Soviet visitors came to Washington in May and June. The Chief of the General Staff, General Mikhail Moiseyev, came on May 20–21 as a result of Bush's suggestion to Gorbachev (on the recommendation of Scowcroft, NSC staff member Arnold Kantor, and me) and brought with him a proposal to resolve a major problem with the CFE treaty caused in the first place by the Soviet military.

Then, on May 27, also at Gorbachev's request, our old "friend" Yevgeniy Primakov—who had earned our cordial dislike by his game of footsie with Saddam Hussein in January and February—rolled into town to talk about economic reform and, especially, Western economic assistance. He brought with him Deputy Prime Minister Vladimir Shcherbakov and the economic reformer Grigori Yavlinsky. Prime Minister Pavlov in April had produced his "anticrisis" economic plan, which made some positive noises but essentially kept the central government as final authority on economic matters. The idea that this plan had much positive in it or that Primakov had anything of value to say on the economy struck all of us as ludicrous. It was a measure of Bush's continuing respect for Gorbachev, and his bottomless well of courtesy, that he agreed to see Primakov at all. And Scowcroft, Zoellick, Ed Hewitt (who had taken Rice's place on the NSC Staff when she returned to Stanford), and I urged Bush to ask questions directly of Yavlinsky—whom we were confident Primakov was bringing only for show.

Why Gorbachev ever dreamed that Primakov could sell the Bush administration anything is a puzzle. He could hardly have chosen someone more personally unwelcome or substantively less qualified. The result was predictable: Primakov and Shcherbakov both made apparent that the Soviet government had no idea what it was doing on the economy and that any Western aid would be money down a rathole. The meeting in the Cabinet Room on May 31 was as sharp and unfriendly an exchange as I could remember, as our side asked hard questions and the Soviets had no answers. Yavlinsky might as well have sat on our side of the table for the critical observations he made and his obvious lack of support for his government's program.

The third visitor was Boris Yeltsin. All spring, we had been wrestling with how to treat with Gorbachev's main rival. We (and he) had come a long way since his poor performance at the White House in September 1989, although administration officials continued to criticize and dismiss him long after that unfortunate meeting. Some eight months after Yeltsin's meeting with the President, Scowcroft, and me in Scowcroft's office, and a week after he was elected president of the Russian Supreme Soviet in May 1990, I had written Bush a memorandum on the new Russian leader. In the short memo, dated June 6, 1990, I warned that we might have underestimated Yeltsin as a result of the 1989 meeting. I said, "He has proved himself remarkably adept at using the new rules of the system to re-emerge as a political leader. He appears to be an effective and popular politician, however erratic. . . ." I concluded with this recommendation: "He's going to be a major player, at least for a while, and we ought to avoid further negative public comments about him—we may someday find ourselves across the table from him." Bush wrote in the margin, "I agree with this."

While the negative tidbits largely faded after that, Bush, Baker, and Scowcroft remained skeptical of Yeltsin and worried that any major overture toward him would both anger and weaken Gorbachev. Cheney and I were probably the strongest proponents of reaching out to him. The bad blood between Yeltsin and Gorbachev and their blunt attacks on each other didn't help in either Moscow or Washington, and contributed to an unwillingness in the White House to embrace Yeltsin.

CIA was another cheerleader for Yeltsin, not in so many words but through a series of assessments highlighting his popularity in and out of Russia, his reform initiatives, and his approach to dealing with the nationalities. The two strongest CIA voices speaking positively about Yeltsin were George Kolt, head of the Soviet analytical office, and Fritz Ermarth, chairman of the National Intelligence Council. I had brought Kolt to CIA and reenlisted Ermarth and, not surprisingly, was much influenced by their thinking. Scowcroft, on the other hand, tended to write off CIA as hopelessly pro-Yeltsin and did not take seriously any CIA assessment on Yeltsin or the Yeltsin-Gorbachev relationship.

I believe that an influential factor in changing Bush's and Scowcroft's approach toward Yeltsin was Richard Nixon's visit to Moscow in late March and personal report to Bush in April. Nixon had met with Yeltsin, and because of the respect both Bush and Scowcroft had for the former President's acumen in assessing foreign politicians and events, I think his appraisal of Yeltsin counted for a lot. It didn't cause an abrupt change, but it did at least change the climate. Yeltsin was elected to the new position of president of Russia (an executive presidency, not a parliamentary chairman or president) on June 12.

Only days later, on June 17, Prime Minister Valentin Pavlov told the USSR Supreme Soviet that foreign assistance and market reforms were part of a Western conspiracy, and then he and other speakers attacked Gorbachev, Yeltsin, Shevardnadze, and all aspects of reform. Pavlov urged Gorbachev to take a rest and transfer to him many of the president's powers. We watched from Washington in surprise as men whom Gorbachev had raised up tried through a "constitutional coup" to bring him down.

In the middle of this crisis in Moscow, Yeltsin came calling at the White House. He met with Bush on Thursday, June 20. This was a "new Yeltsin." He plainly had grown with his responsibilities. He was well-dressed, his demeanor dignified and serious. He acted like a man to be taken seriously and one who expected to be taken seriously. Even Scowcroft was grudgingly impressed, as I nudged him and pointed out the changes.

There was a flurry of excitement surrounding the meeting. Our ambassador in Moscow, Jack Matlock, had been warned by the reform mayor of Moscow, Gavril Popov, that there would be a coup attempt by the reactionaries the next day to throw out Gorbachev. He wanted Yeltsin warned. CIA had been warning us about such a coup attempt for weeks, and we took Popov's warning very seriously. So, after the waves of press left the Oval Office, Bush told Yeltsin about the warning. Yeltsin seemed to me to be concerned but not alarmed and suggested that they call Gorbachev and tell him. I was struck by the strange picture of the presidents of the United States and Russia calling the president of the Soviet Union from the White House to warn him of a possible coup attempt. In any event, they could not reach Gorbachev, and Bush had Matlock request an urgent meeting in Moscow to do so. Gorbachev was even less worried than Yeltsin.

And, sure enough, the next day, June 21, the Soviet president went before the Supreme Soviet, took on his opponents, and emerged with a strong vote of confidence. The "constitutional coup" was over. He walked out of the session with Pavlov, Kryuchkov, and Interior Minister Boris Pugo as though all were forgiven and they were buddies again. In Washington, we thought he was a fool to keep these men in their posts. The danger they posed would remain great.

The last act on the international stage for Gorbachev, and for the Soviet Union, began at the London Economic Summit on July 21 and concluded with Bush's trip to Moscow at the end of the month. When Gorbachev was changing Soviet foreign policy, withdrawing from adventures abroad, making arms control deals or unilateral reductions in military forces, letting Eastern Europe go, and striding across the world stage as an agent of radical and positive change, he often left other leaders breathless and always dazzled. His final appearance on that grand stage, however, put the spotlight on his greatest weakness and his greatest failure: to grasp the magnitude of the Soviet economic disaster and then to take decisive, dramatic, market-oriented steps to deal with it. At the London Economic Summit, the G-7 were left shaking their heads sadly. Gorbachev had been unable to persuade an already skeptical audience that he knew what he was doing, understood the right path for the Soviet Union, and could put the country on that path. When it came to the Soviet economy, he was as big a disappointment in the international arena he had once dominated as he was at home.

Eight days later, on July 29, George Bush arrived in Moscow for what was to be the last formal U.S.-Soviet summit. (Bush and Gorbachev would meet just once more, at the Middle East conference in Madrid on October 30, 1991.) The major substantive piece of business was to sign the START treaty that had been under negotiation for a decade.

Bush's trip was notable for several reasons. First, the signing of the START agreement. Second, agreement on a number of bilateral cooperative arrangements, as well as agreement to cosponsor an international conference on the Middle East in October. Third, the constant jockeying between Gorbachev and Yeltsin in an effort to upstage each other—with Yeltsin's behavior more clearly that of the parvenu. The game-playing did neither of them credit, and reminded us of the "old" Yeltsin.

The fourth and final important element of the visit was Bush's trip to Ukraine. Bush was warmly welcomed in Kiev, with large and enthusiastic crowds. The high point was to be his speech to the Ukrainian parliament. The speech draft showed plainly Bush's own hand and Scowcroft's significant influence. Intended to promote a peaceful evolution of relations between the center and the republics, the actual language suggested to many listeners in Ukraine— and in the United States—a sales pitch for Gorbachev's approach to the future shape of the union. Especially offensive to Ukrainian listeners were these lines: "Americans will not support those who seek independence in order to replace a far-off tyranny with a local despotism. They will not aid those who promote a suicidal nationalism based on ethnic hatred." The effect was much more negative than intended. We were very much concerned at that point with the growing civil war in Yugoslavia and the civil war in Soviet Georgia, and saw the potential for Soviet disintegration that would be both highly destabilizing and very dangerous. The message thus was generic but, delivered in Kiev, sounded aimed at the Ukrainians specifically. The result was an unhappy one.

How had the skilled team around Bush failed to anticipate the reaction? First, his statements were taken out of context. More important, though, was that we did not fully grasp the emotional fever in Kiev, in Ukraine, by that time and understand that the Ukrainians would examine every word Bush uttered through the prism of their zeal for independence.

Gorbachev had dealt with two American Presidents, Reagan and Bush. Reagan had left office after two terms in January 1989. Bush would survive Gorbachev in power by only a year. Yet, in those six years, the three changed the world. Focused on day-to-day events, Americans would not grasp the potential dangers of the revolution under way in the Soviet Union or understand the statecraft involved in laying to rest a vast and ancient empire and midwifing new governments, and doing it all peacefully. Bush's greatest achievement with Gorbachev was in bringing about the unification of Germany, because the President's role was so central. But the imagination reels at the thought of a less experienced and skilled President trying to exploit the liberation of Eastern Europe or dealing with the final crisis and death throes of the Russian and Soviet empire. Bush manipulated and used Mikhail Gorbachev to achieve foreign policy goals critical to the West, to the United States, to the republics of the former Soviet Union—*and* to a democratic Russia. As the communist bloc was disintegrating, it was George Bush's skilled, yet quiet, statecraft that made a revolutionary time seem so much less dangerous than it actually was.

CHAPTER TWENTY-EIGHT

Destruction of the "Evil Empire"

BLINDNESS

Mikhail Gorbachev had three blind spots that assured his failure at home and accelerated the collapse of the Soviet Union: (1) he believed that communist rule in the Soviet Union could be reformed, made more competent, and sustained in power; (2) he believed the Soviet economy could be revived while preserving central control, industrial socialism, and collectivized agriculture; and (3) he believed that the East Europeans and non-Russian nationalities in the USSR would want to remain part of a reformed and more democratic Soviet empire.

Because Gorbachev, by his own admission, remained a dedicated communist to the end of his days in power, he was blind to the reality that Soviet communism had been imposed on the Russian empire and was sustained by coercion, fear, and myths. It is a measure of the depth of his belief that he thought he could eliminate these three pillars of communist power and make reform communism legitimate and acceptable in Russia, the non-Russian republics, and Eastern Europe. His blindness to the real foundations of Soviet communist power gave rise to policies that helped destroy that power. And Gorbachev's blindness to the realities of the relationship between non-Russian nationalities and Moscow, as well as the extent of their hostility toward the center by the late 1980s—his third blind spot—precipitated and accelerated the actual breakup of the Soviet Union.

Glasnost created an environment in which ethnic and nationalist sentiment could be expressed openly and grow quickly. However, other aspects of perestroika, such as the anticorruption campaign and regional purges of the party and government, antagonized the non-Russians, convinced them they were being singled out for especially harsh treatment, and fanned the flames of anti-Russian feeling. Deepening conviction of their declining status and influence in Moscow, the lack of representation of significant ethnic groups and nationalities at senior levels in the Kremlin, Russifying policies in the non-Russian republics, economic hardship, Moscow's inability to mediate successfully between conflicting ethnic groups, and Gorbachev's own obtuseness toward nationalist pleas and demands all greatly aggravated the situation.

In late 1987, CIA warned about growing ethnic conflict in the USSR. The Agency argued that ethnic conflicts in separate Soviet republics had larger implications for the Soviet Union as a whole —that the potential was growing for ethnic crises in different republics to combine and produce an overall crisis of central control in the non-Russian republics. The intelligence bureau at the State Department adamantly disagreed, contending that each separate crisis was unique and explainable in local terms. According to State, there would be no cumulative or contagious effects. When CIA's warning was published as an article in the *National Intelligence Daily*, State insisted that the article note explicitly their view that CIA's assessment was "alarmist."

After three years of forswearing the use of coercion as an instrument of change inside the Soviet Union, Gorbachev's resort to force to maintain order and control in the non-Russian lands turned their festering resentment and anger into full-blown rebellion. By then, even the Soviet military could not quell the spreading drive to leave this "prison house of nations."

ARMENIA AND AZERBAIJAN

The final act of the seventy-year-old Soviet tragedy began in a remote mountainous area of the Caucasus called Nagorno-Karabakh. The region, ethnically more than 90 percent Armenian, had been an ancient source of conflict between Armenia and Azerbaijan. Despite the ethnic affiliation to Armenia, Soviet authorities in the 1920s, for political reasons, had made Nagorno-Karabakh an autonomous region within neighboring Azerbaijan. Neither the inhabitants of Nagorno-Karabakh nor Armenia ever forgot; nor did they ever give up their dream of attaching Nagorno-Karabakh to Armenia. And when perestroika came along in the mid-1980s, the residents decided that if "restructuring" meant looking into every aspect of Soviet life, then their status should be reviewed as well. Gorbachev and the center ignored them for a long while and then summarily rejected their request that the borders be redrawn to incorporate the region into Armenia.

Real trouble began on February 11, 1988, with demonstrations in the capital of Nagorno-Karabakh, and in the Armenian capital of Yerevan. Inevitably, violence erupted. Late in February, Armenians attacked Azeris in Nagorno-Karabakh, and this, in turn, provoked prolonged and bloody retaliation by Azeris against Armenians living in Baku, the capital of Azerbaijan. Moscow sent in troops from the Ministry of Internal Affairs to reestablish order. But the troops could not suppress fear, and large numbers of Armenians fled Azerbaijan and many Azeris fled Armenia. The violence, and the fear and hatred, made compromise or a political solution impossible. War had broken out in the Caucasus.

CIA was watching the situation in the region as well as it could. Our efforts had long been focused on events in Moscow, and we were only beginning to realize how small and inadequate were our collection capabilities and expertise on the non-Russian republics and ethnic groups. For the first time, the press in places like Yerevan and Baku was important as a source of information, and yet it took us weeks to get copies of newspapers. We had virtually no human sources and, apart from monitoring military actions, our technical collection systems were of marginal value. We had countless pictures of demonstrators, but that wasn't much help in learning about or understanding the decisions and actions being taken on the ground. It wouldn't be the last time CIA would get basic information from CNN. They could comfortably go openly where we could not. And we had not even gone there secretly.

That said, we did have good analysts and they understood early the significance of developments in Armenia and Azerbaijan, not just for those two republics, but for the Soviet Union as a whole. DCI Webster and I were impressed by what they had to say, and beginning in mid-June 1988 began warning Colin Powell, then the National Security Adviser, that Moscow was losing control in the Caucasus.

The situation on the ground got worse in the first months of

1989 as first the Armenians and then the Azeris tried to blockade and isolate towns and outposts of the other. Both in geography and support structure, the Azeris had the advantage, and soon Armenia was nearly totally cut off from the rest of the Soviet Union. Trains were attacked, bridges were mined, roads were blocked, energy supplies were cut off, and even relief supplies for Armenian earthquake victims were intercepted.

In late April 1989, Bill Webster provided to senior policymakers another CIA warning about the Soviet internal situation. It said the situation in the Soviet Union was grim—less stable than at any time since the great purges of the 1930s—and that it was "far from certain that Gorbachev will be able to control the process he has set in motion." It described in detail the growing threat from nationalism and warned that Gorbachev's policies "could unleash centrifugal forces that will pull the Soviet Union apart or create such serious tensions among nationalities that the ensuing social and political chaos will undermine Gorbachev's reforms." His economic program was a "near disaster," and the analysts promised that the next few years would be "some of the most turbulent in Soviet history." Finally, it warned explicitly about the possibility of a conservative backlash and the possibility of a coup attempt.

In May, the National Intelligence Council prepared an interagency paper on Gorbachev's chances for survival. CIA was by far the most pessimistic, and in fact formally dissented, predicting that unless Gorbachev changed his current policies, he could not survive.

By fall 1989, civil war raged in the Transcaucasus. Gorbachev ordered an end to the blockades and restoration of transportation links, and he was ignored. The USSR Supreme Soviet issued the same order, and it, too, was ignored. In September, both Azerbaijan and Armenia declared their national sovereignty. The central government had lost control of the region.

Georgia's Turn

The Soviet republic of Georgia had an ancient history as an independent country before its conquest by the Russians and subsequently the establishment of Soviet authority after the 1917 Revolution. Strongly nationalistic, Georgia was a persistent source of neuralgia for the Soviet leadership. To help control Georgian nationalism, Stalin had moved non-Georgian ethnic groups to the republic in the 1920s. The largest of these was the Abkhazians, who were given their own area of Georgia. Naturally, the Abkhazians wanted to be independent of Georgia and go their own way. In June 1988, the Abkhazians petitioned the 28th Soviet Party Congress for the right to secede from Georgia. Nothing came of this except to worsen the situation inside Georgia. There were demonstrations in the Georgian capital of Tbilisi during February and March 1989.

Disaster struck in early April when a new round of demonstrations took place in a number of Georgian cities involving many tens of thousands of marchers. Whether on orders from Moscow, a decision by local authorities, or for some other reason, Soviet Interior Ministry troops moved into Tbilisi on April 9 to suppress the demonstrations and restore order. There would be debate over the number of casualties, but they were high, and there was strong evidence that the troops had used debilitating chemicals and even shovels in attacking the crowds. It was ugly and it happened on Gorbachev's watch. The result was a great intensification of anti-Russian, anti-Soviet feeling in Georgia and strengthened determination to press for independence.

Finally, in September, Georgia declared its sovereignty and, on November 18, 1989, the Georgian Supreme Soviet voted that Georgia had the right to reject any federal—Soviet—law that did not serve the interests of the republic. Tbilisi was challenging the unitary nature of the Soviet state. Thus it joined Azerbaijan and Armenia in rebellion against Moscow, which all three believed was pursuing ethnic policies threatening their national existence.

THE BALTICS: LITTLE DAVID SHATTERS AN EMPIRE

The Baltic states were a different matter both for Gorbachev and for the United States—politically, diplomatically, and legally. The independence of Lithuania, Latvia, and Estonia fell victim to the Hitler-Stalin Pact of September 1939, which provided for the Soviet takeover of the three countries. The United States and nearly all other Western countries never legally or diplomatically recognized the incorporation of the three into the Soviet Union, and all retained "legations" in the United States. Moreover, unlike the nationalities in the Caucasus, considerable numbers of refugees from the Baltic states fled to the United States and, over time, became an influential political force warranting the attention of successive Presidents and the Congress. Thus, when these three "republics" began to move toward independence, attention had to be paid—and Gorbachev would get less sympathy from Washington.

The first Baltic "Popular Front," Saiudis, was formed in Lithuania on June 3, 1988. Its objectives were to seek greater autonomy for Lithuania, defend the Lithuanian culture and language, and to protect the environment. Saiudis supported perestroika, but wanted to take it beyond Gorbachev's ideas. The new front held its first demonstration in Vilnius on the next day. The Popular Front idea caught on. The Estonian Popular Front was formed on October 1 and a Latvian Popular Front on October 8.

On November 16, 1988, the Estonian Supreme Soviet declared that country to be sovereign—the first Soviet republic to do so. This meant that it would exercise control over its own natural resources and decide on its own economic policies, and that it rejected the notion of federal supremacy. This declaration of sovereignty by little Estonia—preceding Georgia's by some ten months—set in motion a sequence of actions by other republics that ultimately would bring down the Union of Soviet Socialist Republics. As one scholar put it, "By its bold move, Estonia had in one blow shattered the whole system, which Moscow now had to rethink from top to bottom."

On July 10, 1989, the Lithuanian Communist Party issued a new platform calling for Lithuanian independence. Less than three weeks later, Latvia joined its Baltic neighbors in proclaiming its sovereignty and rejecting the supremacy of the Union. On August 22, the Lithuanian parliament denounced the 1939 Hitler-Stalin protocols and declared the 1939 annexation illegal. The next day, the world was treated to an extraordinary spectacle: a human chain formed from Vilnius, the capital of Lithuania, to Tallinn, the capital of Estonia—a chain of perhaps a million or more people stretching hundreds of miles. It was a protest demonstration but it also was a demonstration of solidarity and defiance, a demonstration of commitment to independence. A tough statement came out of Moscow, a warning really. But the Kremlin couldn't take on everyone in the Union outside of Russia. Greater autonomy, sovereignty, independence: the words, the ideas were contagious and irrepressible. The center was too late. The empire was beginning to dissolve before its eyes.

First the Caucasus, then the Baltics, and then similar moves to organize popular fronts in Belorussia and Moldavia. In September 1989 came the next major blow. In the Ukraine, the second largest republic outside Russia and an integral part of the empire for centuries, the Popular Front for Perestroika was formed in Kiev on September 9–10. Known by the Ukrainian acronym RUKH, it would press for Ukrainian autonomy and for protection of the Ukrainian culture, language, and environment. Shortly thereafter, Azerbaijan declared its sovereignty, followed within days by Armenia and Georgia.

The non-Russians finally had the Kremlin's attention. Gorbachev had first called for a Central Committee plenum on the nationalities problem in February 1988. It finally took place eighteen months later, on September 19–20, 1989. And it showed just how out of touch Gorbachev was. While calling for a "radical transformation" of the Union including greater autonomy for the republics, he reinforced the primacy of the Russian language, declared that the connection between the Baltics and the USSR was beyond discussion, and ruled out secession.

That September, the same month as the Central Committee plenum, CIA's Soviet office issued an assessment entitled "Gorbachev's Domestic Gambles and Instability." The paper, by Grey Hodnett, an analyst in the Soviet office for whom I had developed enormous respect, was extremely influential in shaping thinking at the White House at this time—especially mine. It certainly validated my earlier proposal that we very secretly begin contingency planning for the possible collapse of the Soviet Union.

Hodnett's assessment said, "Conditions are likely to lead in the foreseeable future to continuing crises and instability on an even larger scale in the form of mass demonstrations, strikes, violence and perhaps even the localized emergence of parallel centers of power." He predicted growing pressures for a crackdown, and forecast that Gorbachev's most far-reaching concessions to the non-Russian nationalities would not satisfy them. Hodnett concluded that whether or not Gorbachev remained in power, the United States for the foreseeable future would confront a Soviet leadership facing "endemic popular unrest" and that this instability would "prevent a return to the arsenal state economy that generated the fundamental military threat to the West in the period since World War II." A number of other analysts in the Soviet office disagreed with the paper, saying it was much too pessimistic. And so it carried a caution to readers that it was "a speculative paper drafted by a senior analyst." What was important was that the paper was issued. It made a difference.

IMPERIAL MELTDOWN

The final phase of Soviet history began in December 1989. On December 7, the Lithuanian Supreme Soviet voted to drop Article 6 of the republic's constitution—the article guaranteeing the political monopoly of the Communist Party. The Lithuanian Communist Party endorsed and supported the change. Two weeks later, on December 20, the Lithuanian Communist Party declared its independence of the Communist Party of the Soviet Union. This was too much for Gorbachev, and he reacted harshly. He convened a special plenum of the Central Committee on December 25–26 to discuss the Lithuanian crisis. He was not in a mood for compromise. The Lithuanians would have to back off.

Now, however, problems were appearing in several places at once. Preoccupied with Lithuania, Gorbachev was forced in early January 1990 to send troops to intervene on the border of Azerbaijan and Iran to restore order. There were demonstrations in Moldavia for reunification with Romania. Armenia asserted the right to veto Soviet laws. And this was all just in the first part of January. On the 11th, Gorbachev made his famous trip to Vilnius, where he tried over several days to persuade both leaders and citizens not to press for independence, reminding them of their economic interdependence with the rest of the Union. It was a courageous thing to do, but even his powers of persuasion had no effect on the Lithuanians. He just didn't understand the non-Russian desire for independence.

No sooner had Gorbachev returned to Moscow from Vilnius than anti-Armenian riots broke out again in Baku, with rapidly spreading violence in both Azerbaijan and Armenia. Gorbachev sent in more and more Interior Ministry troops, and when they proved unable to restore order, he sent in the army to reinforce them on January 18, 1990. On January 19, the Soviet army fought its way into Baku against organized and stiff resistance by the Popular Front. The battle for Baku, and the Azeri casualties involved, ignited tremendous anger in Azerbaijan toward both Gorbachev and the Union. The situation finally began to calm, mainly because the Armenians and Azeris accepted an offer by Baltic officials to mediate. Moscow was bypassed.

Even as Gorbachev was creating a presidential system, strengthening his own power, and revolutionizing Soviet politics in those first months of 1990, events outside the Kremlin underscored that all his maneuvering was increasingly surreal and meaningless in the Soviet Union as a whole. He was still a master at political maneuvering in the Party and in Moscow, but that was a steadily narrowing realm. Just from February to April, a period encompassing elections to the new Congress of People's Deputies and its first session, the nationalities crisis intensified.

Elections throughout the Soviet Union for the Congress showed how far the communists had slipped and the growing strength of the nationalists. In the elections in Lithuania on February 25, the Popular Front won a huge victory. On March 4, elections in Ukraine and Belorussia resulted in major defeats for the communist apparat and victories for the Popular Fronts. In the elections in Russia, Yeltsin won his important victory in Moscow. The elections, especially outside of Russia, showed that the fronts formed during 1988 and 1989, which seemed at the time to many inside and outside the Soviet Union to be small groups hoping only to promote local language and culture, had in fact provided a noncommunist organizational base in most republics from which to resist Moscow. And they were able to organize slates of candidates and promote them for election to the Congress. While the apparat would continue to dominate the Congress and events in Moscow for yet a while, political power in most of the republics, including Russia, was passing to people who genuinely represented popular sentiment. And that sentiment was increasingly focused on autonomy or even independence from the Soviet Union.

On March 1, 1990, CIA yet again called attention to the growing Soviet crisis. The Agency described a Soviet leadership facing "a general inability to implement its directives in many national republics, a loss of control over society in general, and the precipitous decline of the Communist Party of the Soviet Union, secessionist movements in the Baltic Republics and elsewhere, serious interethnic strife and continued economic deterioration." It concluded, "[I]t is likely that political instability, social upheaval and interethnic conflict will persist and could intensify."

On March 12, Gorbachev convened the Congress of People's Deputies. The tone for the Congress was set by the Lithuanian Supreme Soviet's declaration of independence the day before. Gorbachev again was unyielding, condemning the declaration of independence, saying there would be no negotiations on the issue, threatening military measures, and declaring that he would preserve the political and territorial integrity of the Soviet Union. On the 15th, the Congress endorsed Gorbachev's position that there would be no recognition of Lithuanian independence.

On March 16, Gorbachev issued an ultimatum to Vytautas Landsbergis, who had been elected chairman of the Lithuanian Supreme Soviet: the declaration of independence had to be renounced by March 19. When this was not done, Gorbachev turned to the military and the KGB. Paratroopers occupied buildings belonging to the Lithuanian Communist Party, tanks rumbled past the Lithuanian parliament building, and other intimidating moves were carried out. Perhaps in part because of pressures from Bush, Thatcher, and other Western leaders, Gorbachev at the end of March offered a dialogue with Landsbergis if the declaration were repealed. The offer was refused.

With the Lithuanian crisis still on the front burner, on April 4, the Congress of People's Deputies passed a law on procedures for secession. It should have been called the law on nonsecession. The complicated new law set forth such sweeping requirements to be implemented over such a long time that it was hard to mistake the message: there would be no secession.

On April 10, Gorbachev told the Lithuanians that he would not insist on repeal of the declaration of independence if they would just stop passing laws contradictory to Soviet law. Three days later, he threatened an economic blockade. On the 17th, he warned that natural gas supplies to the republic would be shut off in forty-eight hours, and late on the 18th he carried out his threat.

While attention was focused on Lithuania, Soviet pressures there did not intimidate the other two Baltic states. On April 11, Estonia abolished Soviet conscription of its citizens for the Soviet army. (Lithuania had done this in March.) On May 4, Latvia declared its own independence.

Now Russian politics significantly complicated Gorbachev's life. Russia held its own elections on May 29, and Yeltsin was running for chairman of the Russian Supreme Soviet. He ran on a highly nationalistic platform, pledging to pursue total Russian sovereignty, sweeping economic reforms, and restoration of the role of the Russian Orthodox Church. Foolishly, Gorbachev put his prestige on the line against Yeltsin, and actually went before the Russian parliament to urge that he not be elected. Gorbachev failed, and then had to face the consequences of his actions.

In June 1990, CIA issued its most pessimistic warning yet: "The recent acceleration of political events in the USSR could soon produce major discontinuity in Soviet policy and substantial changes in the top leadership. President Gorbachev is losing control over the political process and will be under increasing pressure to make a dramatic move to the left or right to try to regain the political initiative. . . . The period of measured reform, directed by the central authorities in Moscow, is coming to an end." The paper again raised the possibility of a coup attempt.

On June 12, the Supreme Soviet of Russia declared Russian sovereignty. Uzbekistan declared its own sovereignty on June 20, Moldavia on June 23, the Ukraine on July 16, and Belarus (Belorussia) on July 27. The Soviet Union was looking more and more like a hollow shell.

The same day that Russia declared its sovereignty, June 12, 1990, Gorbachev faced reality, met with the presidents of the three Baltic Supreme Soviets, and promised to negotiate with them if they would just freeze their declarations of independence. Lithuania did so on June 29—for one hundred days. The next day, the economic embargo was lifted.

Even as negotiations got under way on a new Union Treaty, a new round of conflict began between the republics and the center. Gorbachev met with the leaders of eleven republics on October 13, but there was no agreement on how to proceed. Then came the "war of the laws." On October 24, both Russia and the Ukraine declared the supremacy of their laws over Soviet law. The same day, the USSR Supreme Soviet declared the supremacy of federal law over the laws of the republics. In effect, the republic leaders were taking matters into their own hands, and not awaiting the outcome of any reform or negotiations to alter the relationship between the center and the republics.

Realization that the Soviet Union was slipping away from him, just as Eastern Europe had, at this point prompted a radical shift of political position by Gorbachev, who now made common cause with conservatives. On November 23, 1990, Gorbachev presented a new union plan that would rebuild the federation from the center. Four days later he authorized the Defense Minister, General Dimitri Yazov, to use force to defend government installations around the country. A few days later he fired the reform-minded Interior Minister, Vadim Bakatin, and replaced him with Boris Pugo.

On December 17, Gorbachev opened a session of the Congress of People's Deputies with a tough new line on the nationalities, and called for twelve to eighteen months of executive rule. His rhetoric was strong: "The most essential thing now to overcome the crisis is to restore order to the country. This boils down to a matter of power. . . . Strong executive power is needed at all levels. . . . The situation is, as one calls it, taking us by the throat. And we must act." On the 20th, Shevardnadze resigned as Foreign Minister, warning darkly of a coming dictatorship.

Gorbachev's sharp right turn politically was manifested primarily in the use of force against the non-Russian republics. During the first ten days of January 1991, Interior Ministry "Black Beret" troops seized the Lithuanian Communist Party headquarters, printing presses, and other facilities. Paratroopers were dispatched to the Baltic states, Armenia, Georgia, Moldavia, and the Ukraine to enforce the law on army conscription. More troops were sent into Lithuania to restore Moscow's control. They attacked the Lithuanian television tower on January 13, and on the 19th, Black Berets shot their way into the Latvian Interior Ministry. Seeing the danger to the republics (and their leaders) should Gorbachev reestablish central control, Yeltsin proceeded to sign a mutual support pact with the Baltic states, traveling to Tallinn to do so.

In fact, though, Gorbachev had no stomach for repression. At the end of January 1991, the additional troops sent to the Baltics were ordered withdrawn; on February 1, he appointed negotiators to sit down with the Baltic leaders. On February 9, the Lithuanian people voted for independence; on March 3, Latvia and Estonia followed suit.

At the Congress of People's Deputies in December 1990, Gorbachev had won approval for a national referendum on the new Union Treaty. The referendum was scheduled for March 17, 1991. A new version of the draft treaty was published on March 7; it gave the republics new responsibility and authority in areas such as defense, foreign relations, and the budget—the changes from the preceding draft represented real concessions to the republics. The result was a strong vote in favor of the Union and the treaty, although the vote was boycotted in the Baltics, Georgia, Armenia, and Moldavia. Gorbachev claimed to have won this round.

CIA's stream of forecasts of an impending political and economic crisis of major proportions became even more stark in April and May 1991. On April 25, in a paper entitled "The Soviet Cauldron," the Agency informed policymakers, "Economic crisis, independence aspirations and anti-communist forces are breaking down the Soviet Empire and system of governance." It stated that the centrally planned economy had broken down irretrievably, that Gorbachev's credibility had sunk to near zero, that the economy was in a downward spiral with no end in sight, and that in such a situation of growing chaos, "explosive events have become increasingly possible." Among the possibilities cited was that "the reactionary leaders, with or without Gorbachev, could judge that the last chance to act had come and move under the banner of law and order." The paper observed that if there was a coup, its long-term prospects would be "poor, and even short-term success is far from assured." The message from the Agency was unmistakable: serious trouble was coming quickly in the Soviet Union.

In May 1991, CIA told the President and his senior advisers that Gorbachev's domination of the Soviet political scene had ended and "will not be restored." The Agency predicted, "Whether or not he is in office a year from now, a major shift of power to the republics will have occurred unless blocked by a traditionalist coup." It concluded: "In short, the Soviet Union is now in a revolutionary situation in the sense that it is in a transition from the old order to an as yet undefined new order. Although the transition might occur peaceably, the current center-dominated political system is doomed. As happened in Eastern Europe over the past two years, the ingredients are now present in the USSR that could lead not only to a rapid change in the regime, but in the political system as well."

This CIA alarm in May 1991 predicted again that for the hard-liners to take the tough steps they believed necessary to forestall a reformist victory, they might organize a conspiracy to remove Gorbachev and install their own regime—and that "there is a possibility that they could act against Gorbachev at any time." It also suggested that they would prefer to oust Gorbachev with a legal veneer by getting him to agree to step down and installing their own candidate. That is, of course, apparently what happened a few months later.

At the same time the referendum on the Union took place in March, the Russians had approved direct election of an executive president—not just the chairman of the Supreme Soviet—and

Yeltsin was elected to that position on June 12, 1991. With his support, the Russian Supreme Soviet approved the draft Union Treaty and by mid-July all of the other eight republic Supreme Soviets except the Ukraine had done so, as well as the USSR Supreme Soviet. The Ukraine set its vote for December 1. The draft treaty was published on July 23, and it was announced that signature of the treaty would take place on August 20.

CIA warned us at the White House that once the signing date was set, a deadline of sorts would be established for the conservatives to act. The changes that would follow signature, together with public sentiment, would make action after that date much more difficult. Scowcroft and I had always split Bush's August vacation in Maine, with me taking the first half. Thus it fell to me on August 17 to hand the President his CIA *President's Daily Brief*, which warned of the strong chance that the conservatives would act within the next few days. It said, "The danger is growing that hardliners will precipitate large-scale violence" and described their efforts to prepare for an attempt to seize power. We were sitting on the deck of Bush's house looking out to the Atlantic. He asked me if I thought the situation was serious and if the Agency's warning was valid. I explained the meaning of the August 20 signing ceremony, and said I thought he should take the *PDB* warning quite seriously.

I returned to Washington the next day, a Sunday, and Scowcroft took my place in Kennebunkport. He always stayed up late, and at about 11:30 P.M. called me to say he had heard on CNN about a possible coup in Moscow. Had I heard anything and would I check with CIA? Through the night, we learned more about the house arrest of Gorbachev and the identity of the coup leaders. The leaders of the military, KGB, Interior Ministry, and the party all seemed involved.

Success of the coup seemed assured based on past events in the USSR. By Monday morning, August 19, French President Mitterrand had publicly as much as accepted the coup as a done deal. Bush's first statement, early in the morning, was equivocal but disapproving. The realities of power were (and are) such that there was no point in needlessly antagonizing a new and potentially unstable government with tens of thousands of nuclear warheads. Bush decided to return to Washington.

As the morning progressed, however, our sense in Washington was that something didn't smell right, something was amiss in Moscow. Why were all telephone and fax lines in and out of Moscow still working? Why was daily life so little disrupted? Why had the democratic "opposition" around the country—and even in Moscow —not been arrested? How could the regime let the opposition barricade themselves in the Russian parliament building and then let people come and go? We began to think the coup leaders did not have their act together and that maybe, just maybe, this action could be reversed.

Mid-morning, about the time the President's plane left for Washington, at the White House I received a letter to Bush from Yeltsin, by now inside the parliament building, declaring his determination to resist and urging that the President support opposition to the coup. It was a powerful letter, and I called Scowcroft on *Air Force One* to read it to him. After consulting with the President, Brent then went to the back of the aircraft to the press section and made a statement much more critical of the coup leaders than Bush had made first thing that morning based on the fragmentary information then available.

Meanwhile, Viktor Komplektov, the Soviet ambassador in Washington, asked to come to the White House and deliver a message to the President or Scowcroft as soon as possible. I told him I was the only one there and he could see me or no one. He came in shortly after noon. He had just seen Eagleburger at State. I offered no pleasantries or polite conversation and tried to make the atmosphere as cold as possible. I wanted him to find no reassurance or warmth to report to the coup leaders. He read me a note to the President from the coup leaders offering reassurances about relations with the United States, their peaceful intentions, their intention to continue with reform, and Gorbachev's well-being. He asked for U.S. understanding of the situation. I told him I would deliver the message and, without any further comment, ended the meeting. It was clear Komplektov welcomed the coup and, from the moment the coup failed, I knew we could destroy his career with a single phone call. I relished the prospect.

Around midday, I chaired a Deputies Committee meeting in the Situation Room to prepare a much stronger statement for the President to deliver that night, a statement condemning the coup and indicating a refusal to recognize or work with its leaders. By that time, it was apparent that the coup had not yet succeeded, although its leaders still seemed to hold the stronger hand in Moscow—especially with the apparent support of the KGB and the army. Even so, Yeltsin's defiance and the prospect of a major battle at the Russian parliament building were the focus of worldwide attention. It was the kind of confrontation, in the presence of CNN and other media, that the coup leaders did not want and that began to highlight their personal and political weaknesses.

The statement we put together was a strong one, referring to the coup as illegitimate and unconstitutional. It called for Gorbachev's restoration to power, and warned against the use of force against the other republics or Eastern Europe. After the meeting, Steve Hadley of Defense followed me back to my office and called my attention to the fact that, while the statement was strong, nowhere did it actually "condemn" the coup. I reread it and said, "Well, everyone will read it that way." Steve countered, "But it doesn't say that." Steve was right. So I inserted a sentence specifically condemning the coup, and checked it out with Scowcroft. It was okay with him.

I reconvened the Deputies Committee in the Roosevelt Room at about five for a final look at the statement. The President had indicated he wanted to meet with us that afternoon to go over the statement and to get an update on events. Thus I chaired a unique Deputies meeting, with the President, Scowcroft, and then Cheney joining us. CIA's Dick Kerr repeated for them what he had told us —all the reasons why this was at best an incompetent coup and the very real possibility it would fail. After further discussion of the situation in Moscow, we went through the statement again, and then adjourned.

That evening, all of the television networks led with the news that the administration had "condemned" the coup. Steve Hadley could chalk up a "save."

The next morning, as the confrontation in front of the Parliament building intensified, Bush tried to call Gorbachev and failed. He decided to try to reach Yeltsin in the parliament building, although we were all very skeptical he would be successful. To our astonishment, the call went right through. The coup leaders hadn't even cut the phone lines to the parliament building. Bush's call was a boost to Yeltsin and the others, and the now united and strong Western condemnation of the coup undoubtedly helped the opposition, both by bolstering their morale and courage and by raising doubts among the coup leaders themselves.

That Tuesday afternoon and evening, August 21, was a long period of tense waiting as we all watched CNN to see if the Soviet military would attack the parliament building. Although there was some violence as citizens confronted the tanks in front of the parliament, and three protesters were killed, the battle did not escalate. The Deputies Committee (influenced importantly by Dick Kerr and CIA's analysis) early on had the sense that the coup attempt might well fail—one of the reasons for our pressing a tougher administration response. Our confidence in this view, and the confidence of others, grew as the night passed without an all-out attack. It seemed to me that Yeltsin had been heroic and now stood alone in stature as leader of the democratic, reform forces in the Soviet Union.

By contrast, after surviving the reactionary coup attempt August 19–21, Gorbachev sealed his own fate upon returning to Moscow from his Black Sea dacha where he had been under house arrest. We watched in amazement from the White House as he ignored Yeltsin's role and the courageous resistance at the Russian White House—without which he would no longer have been president. Gorbachev then completed his own political destruction in a press conference on August 22 when he declared that he remained a communist—though he resigned as General Secretary of the party—and, worse, seemed not to understand that everything had changed as a result of the coup attempt. Over the preceding eighteen months, he had presided over an increasingly hollow shell of a Union, but still with at least nominal control of the levers of state power—the army, the KGB, and the Interior Ministry. Now even those were gone, their leaders under arrest, the institutions either drifting or under new, reform leadership.

The coup attempt snapped the last threads of authority of the Soviet government, and led directly to a countercoup by Yeltsin. The Communist Party was banned and Yeltsin began seizing the levers of power of the former central authority, including on August 28 the State Bank and Ministry of Finance. Cleverly, even brilliantly, Yeltsin moved quickly and adroitly to exploit the August 19 failed coup to destroy the central government and transfer to the Russian government—and himself—its authority and powers.

Soviet communism, already dying, committed suicide on August 19, 1991, and in so doing also finally destroyed the Soviet Union at the same time. Latvia declared total independence on August 21, Ukraine on August 24, and most of the other republics in quick succession. The Congress of People's Deputies met on September 2 and acknowledged that the state structure of the Soviet Union had disintegrated. By the end of September, in reality, Gorbachev was all that was left of the Soviet Union.

On October 28, 1991, Russia formally took control of the institutions of the old central government and, in November, Russia adopted its own plan for economic transformation—thus killing the idea of an economic community by saying the others had to follow Russia or get left behind.

The Soviet Union was laid to rest in December 1991. Yeltsin of Russia, Kravchuk of the Ukraine, and Shushkevich of Belarus met on December 7 in Minsk and there announced formation of the Commonwealth of Independent States, and a week later five Central Asian republics joined. The determination of the Ukrainians to be independent, and Yeltsin's acceptance of that reality, was critical to this historic development.

On December 17, Gorbachev announced that the USSR would cease to exist at the end of the year. On Christmas Day 1991 he resigned, and the Soviet flag was lowered from the Kremlin for the last time.

Washington's Role

The rebellion of the republics against the Soviet Union was the result of long-suppressed nationalist and ethnic passions, economic hardship, the liberating environment of perestroika and associated dissipation of fear, and Gorbachev's blindness and mistakes. Overall, neither the United States nor any other outside force (except for developments in Eastern Europe) played a significant role in arousing those nationalist and ethnic passions. Apart from some covert propaganda infiltrated into Central Asia in the mid-1980s highlighting Soviet repression of Islam and Central Asian culture, CIA did not stir up trouble for the central government. The Agency proposed to do so, but neither the Reagan nor the Bush administration would go along.

We knew early in the Bush administration that change was coming fast in the Soviet empire, so fast that we worried about an explosion or widespread instability. Thanks to analysis and warnings from CIA, we at the White House began in the summer of 1989 to think about and prepare for a Soviet collapse.

The first thorough look inside the White House at the growing nationalist crisis and the implications for us was a memorandum

I prepared and sent to the President on July 18, 1989. Based on the stream of reporting and assessments I had seen from CIA, my memo was entitled "Thinking About the Unthinkable: Instability and Political Turbulence in the USSR." It said:

"The odds are growing that in the next year or two there will be popular unrest, political turmoil, and/or official violence in the USSR on such a scale as to affect Gorbachev's position, his program and current western policies. . . . We must begin to think about the possibility that that reality will include significant political instability." I reviewed recent ethnic/nationalist and labor turmoil, and observed, "The prospect of the failure of reform and fear of disorder—from ethnic or economic origins—can affect Gorbachev directly, either by forcing him out or by forcing him to act: whether by retreating from reform, by reimposing order and the authority of the center, or by resorting to draconian measures in response to economic disaster."

I concluded:

As we look out to 1990 and 1991, we should not be confident of Gorbachev remaining in power, of the continuation of reform as presently structured (with or without him), or of the continued manageability of widespread turmoil and even violence. We should not be taken by surprise. . . . What are the implications for us of such a prospect? . . . In terms of the future, we should very quietly begin some contingency planning as to possible U.S. responses, actions and policies in the event of leadership or internal policy changes or widespread ethnic violence and repression—and consider the implications for us of such developments.

Bush agreed to the contingency planning I had first considered in the spring, and in September 1989, I asked Condi Rice to gather a group of people and in very great secrecy begin this work. When I met with her to explain the task, I told her that I thought the planning was very important because the situation in the Soviet Union could go bad in a hurry, and the U.S. government was on "autopilot" when it came to thinking about such dramatic developments. Her group included Dennis Ross at State; Fritz Ermarth and Bob Blackwell from CIA; and Paul Wolfowitz and Eric Edelman from Defense. This group commissioned a number of studies by CIA and used them in reviewing and planning U.S. options. While no such effort can prescribe in detail policies based on specific future events, this work served us to great advantage in dealing with events over the next two years, and especially as the Soviet Union imploded in 1991.

Subsequently, the President and his senior advisers were kept current and well-warned on developments in the Baltics and the Caucasus by CIA, primarily through the *President's Daily Brief*. But, in truth, the nationalities problem was not high on the White House agenda. The problems in the Caucasus were seen in 1989 and 1990 primarily as interethnic conflict, with Moscow trying to maintain order, prevent additional bloodshed, and bring calm.

There was considerable sympathy at senior levels of the administration with the multiple challenges facing Gorbachev, and he continued to be regarded as—and then *was*—the driving force of reform in the USSR. Further, his stock had risen even further by late 1989 because of his willingness to let the East Europeans abandon communism rather than call out the troops.

The Bush administration's unwillingness to push Gorbachev harder on the Baltic states through the summer of 1990 was influenced significantly by what was regarded as the much higher priority of effecting the reunification of Germany. There Gorbachev's attitudes and actions were critically important. Thus, when Soviet paratroopers were sent into Lithuania in March 1990, Bush and Thatcher would agree privately that further public pressure on Gorbachev would not be productive even though Bush would again send a private letter to Gorbachev on the need to defuse the situation and to avoid violence. When Baltic push came to Soviet shove in late April, Bush would decide not to retaliate against the Soviets for their actions in Lithuania. However, he did make clear to Gorbachev that the trade agreement the Soviet leader wanted desperately to sign at the Washington summit in late May would not be concluded without resolution of the Lithuanian crisis. When Gorbachev promised in Washington to resolve the situation peacefully and pass an emigration law, Bush went ahead and signed the agreement, and the Soviet embargo against Lithuania was lifted at the end of June.

Journalists and historians alike sometimes fail to give due credit to the role of Murphy's Law in affairs of state. Such was the case when Lithuanian Prime Minister Kazimera Prunskiene came to see Bush in the White House on May 3, 1990. He had been under heavy pressure to see her for some time and finally agreed. When her car arrived at the Northwest Gate of the White House, however, the electronic gate would not open. As a result, she had to get out of the car and walk up the driveway to the White House and her meeting with the President. Baltic groups, egged on by the *New York Times*, were very critical of the fact that Bush had made the Lithuanian Prime Minister ignominiously walk to the meeting —clearly a terrible slight. To our protestations that the gate had broken, they pointed out that it had worked fine just two hours before when Jamaican Prime Minister Michael Manley had called on the President. Nevertheless, it was true. The gate broke down, and the result was a domestic and foreign policy flap. The real explanation was just too simple and ordinary to be believed.

There was one other consideration as we looked at the Baltics. Gorbachev was clearly under huge pressure from the right to crack down hard there. We were concerned that coming down on him too strongly might provoke the hard-liners to move against him or might even drive him to join them. A constant question before us was how much pressure the system could take without a rightist backlash (something we all worried about)—which could erase many, if not most, of the internal and external changes (what Cheney and I worried about).

By early 1991, there also was a widely held view at senior levels of the administration that Gorbachev was doing what we wanted done on one major issue after another—from his willingness to let Germany be reunified in NATO to his partnership with us in taking on Iraq. There was no desire to jeopardize that. There also was growing worry that any fragmentation of the Soviet Union other than whatever might be worked out politically and by agreement would provoke civil war and dangerous instability in a country with tens of thousands of nuclear warheads. As a result, even after the tragedies in Tbilisi and later in Baku, the Bush administration approach was to react in a low-key way, so as not to add to Gorbachev's difficulties.

Still, in early 1991, both publicly and privately—even as we neared the launching of the Gulf War—the Bush administration admonished the Soviets about the Baltics. When we learned in early January 1991 from CIA sources that Soviet paratroopers were being ordered into the Baltics to enforce the military draft, the administration issued a public statement saying that the Soviet government was guilty of provocation in the Baltic states. Scowcroft was nervous about the reaction in Moscow to the statement as war approached in the Gulf. Since Rice and I had argued for the statement, he let us know his feelings when the "ABC Evening News" led its program that night with the story that the administration had slapped the Soviets with a strong statement on the Baltics.

We did more. After the Soviet attacks in Vilnius a week later, the President sent a private letter to Gorbachev threatening to withdraw all American aid to the Soviet Union if Moscow did not cease and desist in Lithuania. The letter had an impact, as I saw Soviet Ambassador Alexander Bessmertnykh in the Oval Office shortly thereafter begging the President not to follow through. Further, beginning with the Soviet-Lithuanian confrontation in January 1990, Baker maintained a steady but private dialogue with Shevardnadze, encouraging negotiations and stressing the importance of dealing with the Baltic states peacefully.

While far from oblivious to the fate of the Baltic states and the other republics, the administration believed it had much larger fish to fry with the Soviet government in 1990 and early 1991, and very limited ability to influence events. Nearly everyone in the administration believed that the breakup of former communist states risked violence and instability if not carried out in an orderly, peaceful way and through a political-legal process that would limit future blood feuds and passion for revenge or reconquest. This would be Bush's policy on both the Soviet Union and Yugoslavia.

After the reactionaries' failed coup and Yeltsin's successful countercoup that finished off a badly wounded Soviet government, we in Washington mainly watched the events in the former Soviet Union from the sidelines. We didn't have much choice or many options. But we did worry a great deal about whether the country that had been the Soviet Union would hold together and who would control the nuclear arsenal.

The "Gang of Eight" first debated these issues in the Oval Office on September 5, 1991, two weeks after the coup attempt. Cheney was the most aggressive participant, saying, "The breakup of the Soviet Union is in our interest. If it is voluntary, some sort of association of the republics will happen. If democracy fails, we're better off if the remaining pieces of the USSR are small." Baker countered, "*Peaceful* breakup is in our interest, not another Yugoslavia." We then argued back and forth about how to deal with the republic leaders, whether to wait for a new Union treaty, whether we could deal with a weak center—and whether a weak center could control the military.

The President was concerned about the volatility of the situation: "Tomorrow the situation will change. Each day there is a new development.... We don't know enough to develop an aid program." When Scowcroft cautioned that all aid from Europe, the G-7, and the United States was premised on a strong center, Cheney responded, "That's old thinking!"

Colin Powell came down somewhere in the middle of the debate. He said he wanted to see the dissolution of the old Soviet Union, but wasn't sure that meant "sixteen republics walking around.... Some confederation is in our interest, and then seek bilateral relationships." When asked about Soviet nuclear weapons, Colin replied: "I'm comfortable with *where* they are. *Who* has them is more important. The Red Army has them now. If they are moved back to Russia, who will control them?"

The President finally moved to the real agenda—how to respond to the dramatic events of the preceding two weeks. He had resolved late in August, after the coup attempt, to propose a whole new series of initiatives to reduce arms further. He had run into doubts from Cheney about going further at this point. Now, in this meeting, he asked if there was anything we could do militarily to save money and to signal that we recognized there was a new world out there. The President concluded by urging a "dramatic statement" of initiatives that would give the United States the offense in global perceptions of the changes under way. An intensive effort to develop such initiatives culminated three weeks later in a presidential address to the nation, in which Bush described a number of proposals to reduce military forces and ease the military standoff—including a proposal to eliminate all MIRVed missiles, as Scowcroft had wanted to do at Malta.

The "Gang of Eight" met again on October 11, 1991. The issue was still whether to encourage the emergence of a central authority in Russia or devolution of authority to the republics. It was still Cheney against the field. When he said, "Support for the center puts us on the wrong side of reform," Baker countered that he was not arguing for central control but for a transformation according to a principled road map. "To say that support for the center makes you against reform is too simplistic. The guys in the center *are* reformers. The President of Georgia is *not* a democrat and yet is the most outspoken for independence." Baker ended the meeting with this statement: "We should not establish a policy of supporting the breakup of the Soviet Union into twelve republics. We should support what *they* want, subject to *our* principles."

Events and expediency overtook a principled approach. In a meeting with Ukrainian-Americans on November 27, Bush announced he would recognize Ukrainian independence after the referendum. As expected, the Ukraine voted for independence on December 1.

Historians may criticize the Bush administration for not taking a more aggressive stand in support of the independence movements among the non-Russian republics of the Soviet Union between 1989 and 1991. Certainly, Baltic-Americans were critical at the time. It is useful to remember, however, that during that period the President was faced with the liberation of Eastern Europe, the reunification of Germany, a revolution in the Soviet Union, and the danger of an explosion there as a result of either economic crisis or centrifugal forces. The challenge was to promote these changes —and to arrange it in the case of Germany—keep them peaceful, and to try to have them carried out in a way that did not guarantee future conflict. We also fought the Persian Gulf War, in which Soviet political help was important. As in Eastern Europe, perhaps George Bush's greatest contribution was in knowing both what to do as these events took place, and what *not* to do.

At the same time, there is little doubt that Bush's strong stand at the time of the August 19 coup attempt played a part in its collapse—Yeltsin himself attested to this shortly afterward. Further, behind the scenes, there was constant pressure on Gorbachev from Bush and Baker to avoid the use of force in the Baltics and elsewhere, to end the use of force and of economic sanctions quickly when Gorbachev resorted to such coercion, and to set in motion a process of negotiation to resolve disputes.

The collapse of the Soviet and Russian empire was one of the most significant events of an eventful and bloody twentieth century. That it took place with relatively little violence was a miracle. A miracle in which important parts were played by Mikhail Gorbachev, Boris Yeltsin, a dozen or so nationalist leaders in the republics —and George Bush.

CHAPTER TWENTY-NINE

A Joyless Victory

IN HIS FAREWELL ADDRESS to the nation on January 15, 1953, President Harry Truman made this statement of faith and prophesy:

> As the free world grows stronger, more united, more attractive to men on both sides of the Iron Curtain—and as the Soviet hopes for easy expansion are blocked—then there will have to come a time of change in the Soviet world. Nobody can say for sure when that is going to be, or exactly how it will come about, whether by revolution or trouble in the satellites, or by a change inside the Kremlin.
>
> Whether the Communist rulers shift their policies of their own free will—or whether change comes about in some other way—I have not a doubt in the world that a change will occur.
>
> I have a deep and abiding faith in the destiny of free men. With patience and courage, we shall some day move on into a new era.

At the end of 1991, the world moved into that new era prophesied by Truman nearly four decades earlier. The struggle between the Soviet Union and the United States in the interval was the greatest armed contest the world had ever seen. The destructive power assembled by each side dwarfed that of any previous arms race or war. The rivalry pushed into every corner of the globe, no matter how remote. The cost was as epic as the conflict itself, in excess of two trillion dollars just on the American side. It was a struggle of irreconcilable ideas as well as arms, a competition of opposing philosophies rooted in no less a concept than the nature of man and the relationship between citizen and government. While the two sides might "coexist" militarily, they could not do so politically.

The danger of nuclear apocalypse prevented all-out war between the two principal adversaries, either by strategic nuclear attack on each other's homeland or by war on the soil of their respective allies in Europe. Thus the conflict was channeled into three arenas: (1) a strategic competition in which each side expanded the size of its strategic arsenal exponentially even as it sought a scientific breakthrough that would give it some usable military advantage; (2) a struggle for political and economic influence or control in the Third World, an area where direct military confrontation—and the associated risk of global conflagration—could be avoided; and (3) less obvious, a contest of the will and ability of each side to sustain the struggle decade after decade.

Why the Soviets Lost

Political and historical revisionism notwithstanding, no one in the American government—in Congress or the Executive—believed that the imminent collapse of the Soviet Union was a real possibility until very late. The inevitability of collapse was, in the West, an article of faith politically and of analysis intellectually. But the reluctance to forecast specific timing was born simply of uncertainty and political self-preservation. No one wanted to look the fool.

How did the Soviet Union go from a slow descent into history's waste bin to quick immolation? I am convinced it was because of decisions and actions taken in Moscow and Washington. While others like Brezhnev, Nixon, and Ford would set the stage, Gorbachev, Carter, and Reagan played the critical roles in hastening the Soviet Union into an early grave—transforming gradual decline, "muddling down," into precipitate collapse.

The Soviet economic decline was intensified and accelerated during the last decade of Brezhnev's tenure by strategically disastrous investment and other policy decisions; adventurism in the Third World that over time became hugely expensive and politically costly at home and abroad; the explosive growth of corruption; the triumph of party and government bureaucrats in prolonging the tenure in office of legion incompetent officials; continued repression of dissidents and suppression of the free exchange of information; and the utter failure to pursue any meaningful reform. Public cynicism and alienation, and an accompanying social crisis, worsened. Further, as the economy steadily slowed, massive expenditures on the military continued to grow. The leadership recognized this drain, and its interest in pursuing arms control with the United States beginning in the late 1960s was fueled primarily by a desire to slow U.S. programs and to avoid unanticipated new military expenditures—even as they continued with their own long-planned military modernization programs. While the rate of growth in the Soviet military budget, especially in procurement, slowed in the late 1970s–early 1980s, the role of the military and its allies in the party hierarchy was so powerful that neither Andropov, Chernenko, nor Gorbachev (until 1988) was ever willing or able to begin reducing the huge military budget. Thus, as the economic crisis deepened, military spending and continued large expenditures on Third World clients and adventures became an increasingly heavy drag anchor. By the time this changed, it was too late. Still, as late as 1986, the Soviet economic crisis remained chronic—a wasting disease, not yet life-threatening.

Gorbachev changed all that. First, his inadequate, confused, and contradictory efforts to reform the economy significantly worsened the crisis. These efforts, including his dismantling of the old administrative and economic structures without creating new ones, as well as a mounting financial crisis, turned gradual decline into a headlong plunge. His continuing promises of change for the better even as daily life became harder intensified already pervasive public cynicism and bred a growing sense of betrayal.

Second, his political reforms stripped away the pretenses and myths of the past, increasing another kind of feeling of betrayal among the populace—betrayal by the party for such misrule, and betrayal by Gorbachev of those whose only hope and justification for continuing sacrifice was the myth of the historical mission and success of communism. Even more important, Gorbachev's reforms took away the fear that had kept so many silent and acquiescent for so long. He made the expression of grievances and opposition relatively safe, but at a point in history where there was no way to address those grievances. Thus long-standing Russian social discipline also began to erode, and massive strikes and public manifestations of opposition became commonplace.

Third, and most significantly, worsening economic conditions,

Gorbachev's political reforms, and his misguided nationalities policies unleashed the long-pent-up hostility of the vast non-Russian
parts of the country. One nationality after another took advantage
of the new political environment to proclaim its grievances against
Moscow and to demand more freedom. Gorbachev's mishandling
of the ethnic challenge, and especially his haphazard and ineffective
repression of nationalists, from Alma-Ata, Baku, and Tbilisi to the
Baltic states, enraged the nationalities without intimidating them
and transformed demands for greater autonomy to declarations of
sovereignty and, ultimately, independence. In the end, it was not
the economy that precipitated the collapse of the Soviet Union,
however much it contributed, but the determination of the nationalities—most especially the Ukrainians and, finally, the Russians
themselves—to abandon a Soviet system and government that had
brought economic catastrophe and that was no longer able to hold
them by fear and force. The economy was racing downhill, but it
was the multinational political structure that collapsed first. In another irony, it was a Russian—Boris Yeltsin—who administered
the coup de grace. (And lest we think too exclusively in terms of
cosmic causes, it is worth remembering that an important motive
for Yeltsin was his personal enmity for Gorbachev and desire to
push him from power.)

A Soviet Communist Party greatly weakened by Gorbachev
suffered a grievous self-inflicted wound as a result of the August 19,
1991, coup attempt. However, it was Yeltsin's actions in the weeks
afterward to exploit the communists' failure that actually termi-
nated the life of the Union of Soviet Socialist Republics. A Bolshe-
vik coup in 1917 brought the communists to power in Russia;
Yeltsin's countercoup nearly seventy-five years later pried their
fingers from the last vestiges of power and ended Soviet rule.

If Gorbachev's actions and decisions between 1985 and 1991
took the Soviet Union from worsening crisis to collapse, the United
States between 1970 and 1985 played a significant role in intensifying the Soviet crisis and in forcing actions and decisions in Moscow that led ultimately to the collapse.

First, perhaps the most important and lasting benefit of the
Europeans' and then Nixon's reaching out to the Soviets through
détente was to begin the process of opening up the Soviet Union
on a continuing basis to contacts with and information about the
West. Especially from 1972 on, a growing stream of Western officials, journalists, businessmen, scientists, cultural groups, and fi-

nally tourists visited the Soviet Union and touched the lives of Soviet citizens, especially government and party officials and the intelligentsia. Arms control negotiations not only increased contacts between the two governments and the militaries but, over time, led to greater public knowledge on both sides about the military capabilities of the other. On the Soviet side, the government's monopoly on information was weakened.

Over the period, this process was broadened overtly by an end to Soviet jamming of Western radios such as the BBC, the Voice of America, and others, and by greater access, particularly in Eastern Europe and the Baltic states, to Western television. They could compare their lives under communism to life in the West, admittedly idealized, and it was no contest. Covertly, CIA steadily expanded its infiltration of books, periodicals, cassettes, and even videotapes into Eastern Europe and the Soviet Union, an effort that brought to Soviet citizens the words of their own dissidents such as Solzhenitsyn, information about the misdoings of their own government, and literature about democracy and national cultures. All of these avenues helped many in the Soviet elite and in the scientific and technical community to grasp the backwardness of the Soviet Union and the contrast between their government's words and its deeds. These efforts laid the foundations for glasnost and contributed to the erosion of the myths that had sustained the Soviet government at home. Time and technology left Soviet information control in tatters.

Second, beginning with the Helsinki Declaration in 1975—including President Ford's much-criticized signing—the West began openly to attack and undermine the legitimacy of the Soviet government at home. As the Declaration was publicized, the gap between Soviet rhetoric and Soviet practice was brought home to more and more Soviet citizens. Groups such as Helsinki Watch in the USSR, Charter 77 in Czechoslovakia, and many others were founded, independent of the party and government, and were determined to publicize their governments' failure to adhere to international human rights standards they had pledged to uphold.

President Carter's human rights campaign, including his public support of Andrei Sakharov, further served to highlight the contrast between Soviet declaratory policy and repression of its own citizens. Also, the Carter administration's covert actions in Eastern Europe and the Soviet Union contributed to undermining the legitimacy of the Soviet regime in the eyes of its citizens.

Finally, President Reagan's intensification of the ideological war, and his unwillingness to accord the Soviet government legitimacy and acceptance (the "evil empire") denied the regime the respect and "equality" it so long craved, and contributed to internal developments in the USSR in the early to mid-1980s exposing the party's and government's weaknesses.

Taken together, the overt policies and public disdain, and the covert programs, pursued and expressed consistently through the Carter and Reagan administrations, helped fray the cloak of internal and international respectability and legitimacy so important to the Soviet regime's status at home, and gave comfort and support to those inside the Soviet Union seeking to promote change and challenge the system. The approaches of these two Presidents, one a Democrat and the other a Republican, described at length in these pages, were markedly different and more aggressive in this respect than those of any of their predecessors.

Third, these same two Presidents pursued economic warfare against the Soviet Union. Export controls had been established long before the mid-1970s, but had been pursued erratically and usually ineffectively. Major efforts to promote bilateral trade and commercial relations had been undertaken as part of Nixon's détente policies. Despite powerful bureaucratic and business opposition, the Carter White House (and especially the NSC) began to strengthen enforcement of export controls and, as a result of Afghanistan, imposed severe restrictions on U.S.-Soviet trade—both agricultural goods and industrial technology.

These measures were further strengthened and expanded by the Reagan administration, except for its lifting of the grain embargo imposed by Carter. Indeed, considerable effort was made by the Reagan administration not only to broaden restrictions in every way possible to aggravate Soviet economic difficulties, but also to enlist the support and participation of the other industrial democracies. Highly controversial at home and among our allies, these efforts nonetheless enjoyed considerable success. Thus, at a time of worsening Soviet economic crisis, the United States in 1977 began pursuing a campaign of economic warfare intended to aggravate that crisis and force painful economic and political decisions on the Soviet regime, a campaign that was dramatically intensified after 1981.

Fourth, in 1975, even as North Vietnamese troops were seizing Saigon, President Ford continued the American effort to challenge the Soviets in the Third World. While the initial U.S. covert action in Angola failed because of congressional opposition, as early as the spring of 1979 in Afghanistan and the summer of that year in Central America, the Carter administration had begun to lay the foundations of covert U.S. opposition to Soviet clients and to support Third World groups resisting the Soviets and their minions.

This effort was expanded after the Soviet invasion of Afghanistan and became a vast worldwide campaign under Ronald Reagan. In country after country, what had appeared to be long-term Soviet gains in the Third World in the mid- to late 1970s became major economic and political liabilities to the Soviet Union as internal resistance increased and client states pursued self-destructive economic policies according to the Soviet model. By the early 1980s, in Afghanistan, Nicaragua, Angola, Cambodia, and elsewhere, Soviet clients were being challenged at home and demanding more and more help from Moscow. This did not stop the Soviets from searching for new opportunities up through the mid-1980s in the Middle East, the Caribbean, and Africa, but the "correlation of forces" in the Third World had shifted in favor of the United States and those it supported.

Thus it was that, almost without pause after Vietnam, the United States resumed its efforts to thwart Soviet expansionism and adventures in the Third World, acting primarily covertly to sustain its long policy of containment. At a time when the use of American military power in the Third World had been discredited, successive Presidents resorted to the hidden hand of U.S. power—CIA and covert action.

Fifth, and finally, contrary to conventional political wisdom, the United States continued to challenge the Soviets in developing military power without interruption after Vietnam, even though in the 1970s U.S. defense budgets were reduced and readiness declined. Strategic weapons modernization programs begun under Johnson, Nixon, and Ford were nearly all continued under Carter. The development of strategic and tactical cruise missiles continued, along with Trident submarines, the MX missile, and important new measures to strengthen NATO, including the decision to develop and deploy to Europe new intermediate nuclear forces—the Pershing II ballistic missile and ground-launched cruise missiles. New programs, most importantly Stealth fighters and bombers, were begun. The Soviets noticed, even if most Americans did not. The

Kremlin found little solace or relief in the defense policies of the Carter administration.

But they hadn't seen anything yet. If the Carter years offered no respite in the military competition, the Reagan administration represented a new and significant challenge to the Soviets. A modest increase in defense spending under President Carter in 1980 swelled to huge proportions in the early Reagan years as strategic programs were continued, accelerated, and expanded, and the modernization of conventional forces was robustly funded—making the post-Vietnam "hollow army" of the 1970s a bad memory.

The continuing U.S. military modernization program in the 1970s and then the massive military buildup of the 1980s put enormous pressure on the Soviets and compelled them to sustain and even selectively increase spending on their military at a time of growing economic crisis lest they lose the ground in the arms race they had sacrificed so much for fifteen years to gain. By 1983, already panting hard as they tried to keep pace with current and prospective U.S. military developments, the Soviet leaders were left breathless by one U.S. military initiative that, in its ambition and implications, truly horrified them—Reagan's determination to build a space-based ballistic missile defense, the Strategic Defense Initiative.

For the Soviets, SDI symbolized the resurgent and diverse strength of the United States—economic, technical, and military—and highlighted their disadvantage in this technology-based competition. Accordingly, constraining SDI became the single most important object of Soviet diplomacy and covert action after 1983.

Even to Soviets skeptical that SDI would work, it also became important, if symbolic, evidence of the desperate need to modernize the economy if the Soviet Union was to remain a militarily competitive superpower. Changes were needed in the system—economic reforms were needed. On this, everyone in the leadership came to agree. And this was the beginning of the end, for the Soviet system could not truly be reformed without sowing the seeds of its own destruction.

In short, coincident with a significant worsening of Soviet economic and social conditions in the mid- to late 1970s and early 1980s, the United States became markedly more aggressive in exploiting and attacking the most important vulnerabilities of the Soviet system: the economy, a technology-based arms race, the illegitimacy of the regime and its repression of its own citizens, the growing discontent of the diverse peoples of the Soviet Union, and the contest in the Third World. These simultaneous pressures on a regime already reeling from its own mistakes and inadequacies contributed significantly to the realization in the Kremlin in the early 1980s that change—real, far-reaching reform—was urgently needed to sustain dominion at home and superpower status abroad. And once that decision was made, the ultimate, inevitable doom of the Soviet system was greatly accelerated. Change and challenge from within the Soviet Union were the direct causes of imperial implosion, but greatly intensified economic, political, and military pressures from the West, from the United States, in my view played a critical part in creating the perceived need for immediate reform.

In Victory—Debate

When President Bush summoned me to his cabin on *Air Force One* on May 8, 1991—just over two weeks after the "Nine Plus One" meeting at Gorbachev's dacha—I suspected it was to ask me to take Bill Webster's place as DCI. He had always had high regard for intelligence professionals, and I think he welcomed the opportunity for the first time in nearly twenty years to appoint a professional to the DCI position. There, in his cabin, he asked, and I accepted.

I was flattered and honored, and did not hesitate, but I did have very mixed feelings. To again be offered the nomination to be DCI by a second President was incredibly satisfying—I had been certain in 1987 when I withdrew my nomination that the opportunity to be Director would never come again. To have the brass ring come around a second time for that position was the sort of thing that just didn't happen in Washington. Moreover, to be a career intelligence officer—and an analyst—and become Director was unprecedented. I had many ideas for change and reform at CIA and in the intelligence community, and would now have the chance to implement them.

There were, however, downsides to the offer. It meant leaving the most satisfying job I'd ever had. Working closely with Bush and Scowcroft as Deputy National Security Adviser through the momentous changes since 1989 had been a once-in-a-lifetime experience. I once told Scowcroft that he and I were alike in at least one respect—our egos were no smaller than those who had highly visible positions; we just satisfied ours in a different way, through the private exercise of influence. Being at the right hand of the President—of this President—was about as gratifying as it could get. I would be giving up that constant contact, and the great fun we all had besides, even in the tough times.

There was another big downside: the confirmation process. I had no illusions about the difficulties that lay ahead. Only two career intelligence officers had been DCI in CIA's forty-four-year history—Richard Helms and William Colby—and no career officer had been nominated since 1973 (except for my happy experience in 1987). While I told the President that I was confident of being confirmed, I cautioned him that the process was going to be like adding a room to a house—it would take longer, be more costly and more painful than expected, and we would both be lucky if at the end of the day a subcontractor didn't run off with the money and materials.

I also knew something no one else could know: there would be no turning back, no withdrawal if it got ugly. I had withdrawn in 1987 because I thought it was the right thing to do. I would never withdraw again, no matter what the cost.

I believe I was the most realistic person around about how difficult confirmation would be. In 1991, the only career civil servant who had risen to become head of a major department for a generation was Frank Carlucci (who was appointed Secretary of Defense for Reagan's last year in office), and he had been out of government service for several years before returning as National Security Adviser and then as Defense Secretary. Any career person, especially one who had operated at senior levels and had strong views, was bound to pick up unwanted political baggage—enemies. (I reminded Scowcroft of the Washington adage, "Friends may come and go, but enemies accumulate.") I also had served with some controversial and, in some quarters, despised people—Kissinger, Brzezinski, Turner, and, above all, Casey. For nearly a quarter century, I had been involved in or on the periphery of some of the most hotly debated and divisive issues in American foreign policy. Under these circumstances, I'm not sure *I* would have nominated me to be DCI.

Moreover, Iran-Contra was not dead. I was still on the agenda of the Independent Counsel. At the outset of Lawrence Walsh's investigation, I had been told I was simply a witness. I met with the

Independent Counsel staff lawyers and with Walsh whenever they asked. I first testified before the grand jury in early summer 1987, because they wanted me on the record before congressional hearings (and immunized testimony) began. I heard from them from time to time after that. Some months after I resigned from CIA to become Deputy National Security Adviser early in 1989, they asked to see me again, and I now learned that I was a "subject," meaning simply, they told me, that my actions in 1986 fell within the scope of their investigation.

In the spring of 1991, a team of people from Walsh's office came to see me in the White House. Before, I had had the sense that the attorneys interviewing me were objective and fair-minded, genuinely seeking just to find out what had happened and if any laws had been broken. This time they had a new leader, and his arrogance and rudeness filled my office. This was a different kind of lawyer, an attack dog, and he left me very uneasy. I had that feeling again in early May when I testified once more in front of the grand jury—most of whom seemed barely awake.

Only days after that testimony, the President had offered me the position of DCI. Before any announcement was made, I insisted that Scowcroft find a way to learn whether I was in Walsh's crosshairs. I did not want to embarrass the President. The word Brent got back through a go-between was that my status was "unchanged from the beginning of the investigation"—ambiguous but somewhat reassuring.

Even so, throughout the summer it appeared that Iran-Contra still would be my greatest obstacle to confirmation. Indeed, catastrophe loomed when, in July, I got word privately that Alan Fiers, chief of CIA's Central American Task Force in the mid-1980s, had reached a plea-bargain agreement with the Independent Counsel. The lowest point in my life came the day before the plea bargain was announced by Walsh. I received phone calls from two people saying that I would be implicated in some way by Fiers's statement. I knew that would mean that Walsh was coming after me, too. It likely also would put a quick end to my nomination to be DCI, but that was secondary in my mind to potential legal trouble. I was distraught. Confident that I had done nothing wrong and that I had told the truth, and confident as well in the fairness of our system of justice, I had never hired a personal lawyer in all the preceding years of the Iran-Contra investigations. I was probably stupid—or at least insanely naïve—not to have gotten personal counsel. Anyway, that day before the Fiers plea bargain, I asked Russell Bruemmer, who had been CIA General Counsel under Webster, to come see me at the White House, and I asked him if I should now get a lawyer. He said that I should wait and see what Fiers said.

As it turned out, Fiers did not mention me, and from that moment on I began to relax a little, feeling certain that if Walsh could have found a way to implicate me, the Deputy Director of CIA in 1986, he would have. The stories I had heard (from lawyer friends) about the tactics of the Independent Counsel's office and about their zeal overriding good law and even ethics, and seeing what they did to people whom I knew and who I felt had been on the periphery and done no criminal wrong, altogether had left me for years with a deep, gnawing unease. As one government attorney once told me, "A grand jury could indict a pig." I did not know what people put under the threat of going to jail might say to avoid that fate. I came to believe fairness had little part in the Independent Counsel's agenda and worried that I might be indicted for something I didn't do. That would ruin my family financially, not to mention my reputation—all without a case or a conviction. It was the not knowing that became so scary.

(In fact, I had reason to be worried. Walsh apparently came to believe that I had known more about North's operational activities in Central America than I had testified, and that I had been told of the diversion a month or so earlier than I testified. However, he acknowledged in his report that he could not prove either allegation, in part because key individuals would not so testify. I challenged the allegations in my response to his report, noting that the reason key witnesses would not testify to the allegations was that they could not do so truthfully. The nightmare that began for me on November 25, 1986, in San Francisco ended nearly seven years later, on August 4, 1993, when Lawrence Walsh's final report was issued. It had been a searing experience for me, but I knew it had been even worse for some fine and honorable friends.)

As it turned out in the confirmation process, both in secret sworn testimony or depositions, and in public session, everyone in CIA remotely connected with either the Iran or Contra controversies either substantiated what I had said about my role or could not materially contradict it. Three questions about my role were put to Clair George in writing. I was later told that his lawyer had advised the Senate Intelligence Committee that, while Clair would not testify since he was under indictment, his answers to the questions would have been negative if he had testified, and thus not damaging to me.

(The big issue in the press was how Casey and Clair George, the then-Deputy Director for Operations, would know about activities in Central America that the Deputy DCI—between them in the Agency hierarchy—did not know. The answer was simple in my view: I never believed Clair knew either, despite Fiers's testimony against him. Given the way Casey operated outside normal bureaucratic lines on Central America and the loose way the DO was managed, I found it totally plausible that George was much more in the dark than alleged by the Independent Counsel.)

In any event, once the statements were taken, Iran-Contra evaporated as a serious issue in my confirmation, although the committee would publicly and under oath march me through exhaustive questioning on the subject.

I had expected controversy over Iran-Contra, but was totally surprised by the diversity and intensity of other attacks on me. From the beginning, people unrelated to Iran-Contra began coming out of the woodwork to attack me and make other allegations against me. Even Gorbachev got into the act in late May, heatedly asking our ambassador on the 25th the meaning of my nomination —as a known "hard-liner"—to be head of CIA.

Gorbachev was the least of my worries. I was accused on television and in the print media by people I had never spoken to or met of selling weapons to Iraq, of walking through Miami airport with suitcases full of cash, of being with Bush in Paris in October 1980 to meet with Iranians, and on and on. My initial amusement at the ridiculousness of it all gave way to frustration and then anger at seeing a bunch of gunrunners and international lowlifes appearing on television—some of them interviewed from jail cells—to blacken my name. One accuser was so relentless and got so much airtime that his attacks prompted several foreign governments to advise the U.S. government (and the Senate) officially of their earlier encounters with him and his record of fabrications.

The allegations of meetings with me around the world were easily disproved for the committee by my travel records, calendars, and countless witnesses, but of course this usually failed to catch up to the initial public accusations. All summer long, one set of accusers would appear and their allegations would be disproved by the FBI or the committee, only to be followed by yet another. An ardent and consistent foe of conspiracy theories, I began nevertheless to wonder if some group at home or abroad was orchestrating all this. I would conclude not, that what I was experiencing was the magnetic attraction of media attention in drawing out all manner of very strange people.

In this maelstrom, I was very fortunate that, compared to 1987, I had strong allies and friends. Foremost was the President. Repeatedly, I was heartened, yet embarrassed, when he felt pressed to defend me publicly, sometimes with great feeling. Scowcroft was an invaluable source of perspective, humor, and comfort. He kept warning me not to give up my "day job." There were many others, such as Bob Inman, Eli Jacobs, and Stan Moskowitz (CIA's Director of Congressional Affairs), who were a source of support and counsel.

But apart from the President, my most important ally and friend was Senator David Boren, chairman of the Senate Select Committee on Intelligence. Boren and I had developed a strong mutual trust and friendship (along with the committee Vice Chairman, Senator Bill Cohen) in the aftermath of Iran-Contra when, as Acting Director, I worked with him to build a new relationship between CIA and the Congress. He had confidence that I was a true believer in congressional oversight and that I played straight and honest. And so David took it as a personal challenge to get me confirmed. His strategy was simple. Tackle every accusation and allegation head-on *before* beginning the hearings. Take sworn testimony, gather the facts, establish the truth. There were to be no surprises in the hearings. The long delays through the summer of 1991 in getting hearings under way were deliberate as Boren, his staff director George Tenet, and Vice Chairman Frank Murkowski and his lieutenant, John Moseman, went laboriously through every charge. If I was truthful in every instance, the strategy would likely result in confirmation. If I was not, Boren would feel betrayed and confirmation would be impossible. Throughout, he managed the process with objectivity and thoroughness. But it was a comfort knowing that he privately favored my confirmation so strongly.

So September came. I cannot recommend a controversial confirmation as an experience to be relished. Indeed, I reached the point in early September where I didn't care if I was confirmed—I only desperately wanted to have the opportunity, after months of silence, to defend myself and wipe away the dirt and smears of unjustified allegations and calumnies.

The hearings began on Monday, September 16. The preceding

weekend provided me an opportunity to put the entire process in proper perspective. On Saturday morning, we attended the funeral of one of my best friends, Doug George, mentioned often in these pages in connection with arms control. Doug, in his late forties, learned he had cancer in the spring. From his sickbed, he offered me advice and help in the confirmation process. He lost his fight the week before the hearings began. As I sat in the church for Doug's funeral, I reflected on him, on the unpredictability of life, and about what was important. After the funeral, my eleven-year-old son Brad and I drove up into the Blue Ridge Mountains to hike and camp for the rest of the weekend. I figured that was much better preparation for the battle beginning on Monday than anything else I could do.

The committee held hearings three days that first week, and then again on September 24. After the preliminaries—opening statements by all the senators and by me—those four days were spent going through all of the allegations against me. I testified the first two days, and other witnesses—supporters, opponents, and those the committee wanted to hear (like Alan Fiers) filled out the other two days. It wasn't fun. The sheer physical effort involved in sitting in a straight chair, facing banks of television lights, and too often being forced to try to figure out the question as well as the answer for many hours at a stretch is an extraordinary challenge. During the breaks, like a prizefighter, I would retire to a neutral corner—a holding room—and get a snack or a can of soda and my coaches would, figuratively, wipe the blood off and get me ready for the next round. God, I came to dread pulling up out of the chair to go back out there. Before it was all over, I would—by the committee's reckoning—answer nearly nine hundred questions in open session, not to mention those in closed sessions and in writing.

Many people later would ask me how I kept my temper as those opposed to my nomination assailed me. The answer is simple and not very idealistic: I knew I had to keep focused on the reason I was there—to get confirmed. The President by that time had invested considerable political capital in me as had others on the committee, both Republicans and Democrats. To lose control, to lash out, to respond in kind would have been both unprofessional and stupid. I had no intention of being either. But boy, was the temptation ever there.

Bubbling in the political background as one after another of the now familiar allegations against me were dealt with was another crisis, the only one in my view that truly imperiled my confirmation. Fittingly, as we watched the Soviet Union disintegrating even as the hearings droned on, this issue dealt with my views on the Soviet Union and the Soviet threat. In the first instance, the issue was whether I had exaggerated the Soviet threat in the first half of the 1980s and suppressed analysis at CIA that disagreed with my view. As the issue mushroomed, however, the debate in the hearing room and in the press came down to the old fight about the nature of the Soviet Union, how we should have dealt with the Soviets, and whether CIA overstated Soviet strength and failed the critical test of foreseeing the Soviet crisis.

For weeks, I had heard rumors that several former analysts in CIA's Soviet analytical office were whispering to the committee staff accusations that I had "politicized" or slanted intelligence analysis on the Soviet Union to support my "hard-line" views and the political agenda of Casey and the Reagan administration. I had scoffed at the idea that this was serious—after all, I knew of too many instances, a number of them mentioned in this book, where CIA, under my direction or with my approval as Deputy Director for Intelligence, had told the Reagan administration things it did not want to hear about the Soviets. Including Soviet vulnerabilities. I thought there were just too many examples of our conveying unwelcome news and resisting policy pressures to change our analysis for this kind of allegation to be taken seriously. I was wrong.

The replay of many old battles in Washington during the Cold War began for me late in the evening on September 25, when I received a call of alarm from Stan Moskowitz, CIA's chief of congressional affairs. During a closed evening session of the committee to hear from several disgruntled analysts, one of my oldest friends in the Agency, Mel Goodman, had testified that I had corrupted the analytical process and ethics of intelligence in exaggerating the Soviet threat, "including the case for Soviet involvement in the Papal plot, international terrorism, and Soviet–Third World relations." He also accused me of ignoring and suppressing "signs of the Soviet strategic retreat, including the collapse of the Soviet empire, even the Soviet Union itself." A little later the same evening, another old friend and colleague, Harold Ford—a veteran and much-liked analyst—had surprised the committee staff by changing his testimony and joining in the attack against me. Their testimony, according to those who were present, was high drama, especially when Ford confounded expectations and spoke against me.

The night of that closed session we were celebrating my forty-eighth birthday at home. It was a birthday I won't forget. I was stunned and sickened by the telephoned account of what had happened at the hearing. Neither man had ever come to me to express concern or disagreement. Goodman and his family had been close friends of our family for nearly twenty-five years. Mel and I had had spirited but friendly debates for years over Soviet intentions and policies, but he had never suggested that I was toeing someone else's line or lacking in integrity. After I became DDI in 1982, we saw little of each other, but I had promoted him and certainly had no sense he bore me ill will. I was dumbfounded by Ford's testimony, especially since he would later acknowledge he had no personal experience of my slanting analysis or riding roughshod over analysts.

My friends on the committee staff were worried. Powerful ammunition had been given to my antagonists on the committee—especially Senators Metzenbaum and Bradley—and critical fence-sitters like Senator Sam Nunn had been deeply concerned at what they had heard. In short, I had a big problem from a totally unanticipated quarter. After dealing with Iran-Contra and a multitude of false allegations and suspicions from critics and adversaries both known and unknown, I had been sucker-punched by two old friends who had turned against me. The confirmation process was beginning to resemble a soap opera.

A number of senators, especially Nunn, insisted that what they had heard that night in closed session should be heard in public testimony. The result was four full days of testimony on CIA's analysis of the Soviet Union. It was not pretty. Goodman, Ford, and another analyst I did not know (or remember) repeated their allegations against me. Then a number of Agency Soviet experts testified on my behalf. They acknowledged that while they had not always agreed with me, I had not pressured them to change their analysis and, in fact, that I had encouraged the presentation of alternative views and disagreements. Several testified about occasions when I had disagreed strongly with their analysis and still approved its publication, while others told about the times I had gone to bat for assessments that evoked considerable criticism and pressure from policymakers. At some point, the witnesses began quarreling with one another and refighting even more old battles surrounding our work in the Soviet Union. The disputation and finger-pointing could not have presented the Agency in a worse light. What on a more elevated plane was the give and take of ideas and opinions so essential to good intelligence analysis, under the glare of television lights and provocation from the committee degenerated into an intellectual and bureaucratic food fight. It was also inconclusive in terms of the allegations made against me.

What my friends and supporters tried to point out to the committee was that virtually all of the allegations against me had come from a handful of people, most of them from one subunit of the Soviet office—the one dealing with the Soviets in the Third World that Mel Goodman had headed. In short, this was a more localized dissatisfaction than the hearings had conveyed. (Indeed, in not one of the areas even more prone to controversy—the Soviet military and strategic programs, the economy, or internal developments—was there a single allegation by analysts against me.)

After two full days of this, it was plain that I had to do something fairly dramatic to salvage confirmation. There were two challenges: I had to refute the allegations against me authoritatively and I had to persuade the committee that after all the rancor, I could still lead the Agency.

I had anticipated the first of these challenges immediately after the night session of September 25. I urgently asked the Agency for scores of intelligence assessments relevant to the issues raised by my accusers. The afternoon of Friday, September 27, I accompanied the President and Mrs. Bush to St. Simons Island, Georgia, where they planned to spend a relaxing weekend. I carried two huge briefcases of documents with me on *Air Force One.* When I arrived at the resort, I closed the drapes in my room and spent the next forty-eight hours handwriting my response to the allegations, drawing on the stacks of intelligence assessments provided by CIA and copies of sworn statements by analysts provided by the committee. I summarized each allegation and then drew on assessments or the sworn statements of those directly involved in their preparation to show that the allegations against me were false. When we flew back to Washington, I was ready. What's more, I had finally gotten mad.

I testified on the third day, and read my handwritten statement. In response to each allegation, I not only documented how I had dealt with the issue personally, but then provided lists of CIA assessments that showed how the Agency had dealt with it—in each case showing through the documents that the allegation was false and, in most cases, based on unfounded rumor or ignorance of the facts. The last of twenty allegations I addressed was that Casey and I "created an agency view of the USSR that ignored Soviet vulnerabilities and weaknesses and failed to recognize the pluralistic political culture that Gorbachev had developed in a relatively short period of time." I reminded the committee of a memo I had sent to the then-DDI in 1986 expressing the worry that our analysis was understating the turbulence in the Soviet Union as well as the degree of change that Gorbachev had brought about—"that we are in a rut and may not be recognizing significant change in the Soviet Union even as it is taking place." I pointed to other memos and directives demonstrating that, within the Directorate of Intelligence, I had pressed vigorously for analysts to look at the Soviet Union in a new light, more open-mindedly and with a view to avoid underestimating the nature of the changes under way there. I reminded the committee of the conferences I had called for with outside specialists on the future of the Soviet Union and on instability in the USSR.

I concluded: "Overall, from the early 1980s to 1987, the Soviet office provided a considerable body of analysis about Soviet problems, weaknesses and vulnerabilities as well as the prospects for major change. It highlighted early Gorbachev's disposition to reform and continued to track the radicalization of his reformist agenda through 1987 when the advent of democratization unleashed the forces that ultimately undermined the old system."

After I had dealt with the specific allegations, I told the committee:

> ... A careful review of the actual record of what was published and sent to policymakers demonstrates that the integrity of the process was preserved. We were wrong at times, but our judgments were honest and unaffected by a desire to please or to slant. Our review process wasn't easy. But it was far from closed. It was rigorous. But it was fair. People who wanted to be heard were heard. I was demanding and blunt. Probably sometimes too much so. I had and have strong views. But . . . I'm open to argumentation and there was a lot of that. And I never distorted intelligence to support policy or to please a policymaker.

I then turned to the issue that concerned Senator Nunn and others—whether after this bureaucratic Donnybrook I could still lead the Agency. I presented to the committee eight different initiatives that I would take to safeguard the objectivity of the analytical process and to deal with the perception among some analysts of more senior officers slanting assessments.

We then spent the rest of that day, and part of the next, going over many of the allegations that had been made. The focus was on the Agency's analysis of the Soviet Union, my part in that, and my own views on Soviet affairs. Through it all, my responses to the twenty allegations relating to Soviet analysis held up—after all, I had known they would be dissected and thus bent over backward to cite documents evenhandedly.

My every action and word as a senior official for the preceding decade was placed under a microscope, and in the existing political environment, the focus was predictably on the warts—not the actions, ideas, judgment, and skills that had led to my unprecedented ascent through the bureaucratic ranks or made me the choice of two Presidents to be Director of Central Intelligence. Through it all, my most determined and aggressive public defender was Senator Warren Rudman, assisted in the background by Senator Bill Cohen. Rudman was especially effective in making readily apparent that Goodman's allegations against me were wrong or based on rumor and hearsay, not direct experience or knowledge.

After the hearings concluded, I took one other initiative. Sam Nunn was a close friend of Boren's but, at the end of the hearings, was still undecided on the nomination. So, I handwrote a long private letter to him intended to provide reassurance that I could provide effective leadership for CIA, outlining new initiatives I hoped to take, and making clear that I would address the concerns that had been expressed.

As the hearings wound down, and I was feeling pretty battered, my old friend and colleague Dick Kerr—then Acting DCI—called to tell me he was going sailing by himself on Chesapeake Bay. He said, "You have been accused of many things recently but I am going to add one more." Kerr said, "I am going to put a note in my wallet in case I fall off the boat and drown. The note will say, 'Bob Gates did it.' " I think I laughed.

On October 18, the committee voted 11–4 to recommend confirmation to the full Senate. Before the Senate voted on November 5, Boren would personally visit more than thirty Senators to urge that they vote favorably. The final vote was 64–33, although I had the votes of the three Senators who were not present. Most important, those voting in favor spanned the political spectrum, from right to left, and included a substantial number of Democrats as well as Republicans. I had always felt that a bipartisan vote would be important. I regretted losing the votes of two senators I had always respected and liked—Bill Bradley and Pat Moynihan.

Within a month of my swearing-in as Director of Central Intelligence on November 12, Yeltsin and others would create the Commonwealth of Independent States as successor to the Soviet Union.

The debate in the last weeks of my confirmation hearings in many respects captured the essence of the larger and long-standing debate in the United States about the Soviet Union. My hearings became an opportunity for some to plant successfully the notion— a terribly mistaken notion—that CIA had failed catastrophically by missing the final crisis and collapse of the USSR, and to continue the political argument that the huge sums spent on defense in the 1980s had been unnecessary, that the Soviet Union was weak and would have collapsed on its own. That debate continues to this day.

Because in December 1991 there was no agreement in Washington that the United States had, in fact, helped push the USSR into an early grave, there was no sense of victory. Because the Cold War itself had been waged in shades of gray, there was little definition or sharpness to its conclusion. It, too, was gray. Did we win or did the Soviets just lose? Or was it both? Further, because there was so much unfinished business with Russia, the American government itself was subdued. George Bush, who refused "to dance on the Wall," was not about to declare victory in the Cold War. There was no national celebration such as would follow the Persian Gulf War.

The old fights over dealing with the Soviets continued to be refought and we, as a people, quickly turned to a long-neglected domestic agenda, partisan politics, and the 1992 presidential election. And so the greatest of American triumphs—a triumph of constancy of purpose and commitment sustained over four decades at staggering cost—became a peculiarly joyless victory. We had won the Cold War, but there would be no parade.

Reflections

THE MOTORCADE SCREAMED down the streets of Moscow, and shot through the Kremlin gate. It was October 1992 and I, now Director of Central Intelligence for nearly a year, was on my way to meet with President Yeltsin of Russia. As I looked out the window of the ambassador's limousine, my mind raced across the years of the Cold War from Vietnam to the Soviet collapse. I thought of the Presidents I had known and served, of the years at CIA and the White House. I remembered the endless hours in the Situation Room in the White House basement as crisis followed crisis. I reflected on more than twenty-five years of waging war—secret and not-so-secret war—against the Soviet Union, a communist empire that, from graduate school days and my recruitment by CIA, I always had believed to be evil.

Now I was going to see Boris Yeltsin and in that meeting, once and for all, write finis to CIA's forty-five-year battle against the Kremlin. Of course, the Cold War by then had been over for some time, and CIA had long since begun to dismantle our anti-Soviet propaganda apparatus and other covert programs. Even so, the first visit to Moscow by a CIA director somehow brought closure, a formal end to our role. As a gesture of intent, a symbol of a new era, I carried with me the Soviet naval flag that had shrouded the coffins of the half dozen Soviet sailors whose remains the *Glomar Explorer* had recovered when it raised part of a Soviet ballistic missile submarine from deep in the Pacific Ocean in the mid-1970s. I also was taking to Yeltsin a videotape of their burial at sea, complete with prayers for the dead and the Soviet national anthem—a dignified and respectful service even at the height of the Cold War.

Throughout my visit to Russia, my mind reeled with the ironies. Of my visit to Ysenovo, the suburban headquarters of the KGB's First Chief Directorate—its foreign intelligence arm—and the many KGB employees standing at the windows staring at the motorcade bringing the chief of their longtime enemy onto their home turf. Of toasts with veteran KGB leaders, CIA's bitterest enemies, as their previous chief and my old dinner partner, Kryuchkov, languished in jail for his part in the coup attempt. Of my trip to St. Petersburg, and a visit to the summer palace of the czars outside the old capital—riding out in the Zil limousine I was told had once belonged to the head of the Communist Party in Leningrad. Of being greeted at the palace by a band dressed in czarist army uniforms and trying manfully to play "The Star-Spangled Banner," and later piping me into the palace to the strains of "St. Louis Blues"—I think. It was at once moving and hilarious. As my motorcade made its way around Moscow and as I visited St. Petersburg, it sometimes seemed that the ceremonies not held in Washington celebrating the end of the Cold War and the Soviet collapse were, in the final irony, provided for the last Cold Warrior head of the CIA by the Russians. I could only guess at the thoughts of my KGB hosts.

GORBACHEV

The collapse of the Soviet Union was not inevitable in 1991, but was precipitated by Mikhail Gorbachev, a leader who set out to save the Soviet Union and who, instead, destroyed it. His tenure as the last Soviet leader was the embodiment of the law of unintended consequences. He did not intend to weaken and then dismantle the Soviet Communist Party. He did not intend for Eastern Europe to become independent of the Soviet Union. He did not set out to unify Germany and then to allow it to remain in NATO. He did not intend to preside over the disintegration of the Soviet Union. And yet his policies and actions, intended to correct the economic and political mistakes of his predecessors and give new life to a reformed Soviet Union, surely sealed its fate and accelerated its doom. Though we obviously can never know with certainty, I believe that if Andropov had been younger and healthier, the odds are great that we would still be face-to-face with the Soviet Union, still militarily powerful though still doomed eventually—steadily declining, weakening. However severe the hardship of the peoples of the former Soviet Union today, they owe Gorbachev a great debt, for he destroyed the Soviet state and gave them choices about their future.

What if Gorbachev had taken the Chinese path, focusing on economic change and modernization before political reform? First, the historical and cultural circumstances of Russia and China are very different. As just one example, Gorbachev would still have faced a formidable challenge from the entrenched party apparatus —an apparatus that in China had been largely destroyed by the Cultural Revolution. Second, even had Gorbachev successfully taken the Chinese economic path, I believe it would have only postponed the day of reckoning—as it has only been postponed in China. A market economy and communist rule are fundamentally incompatible. One must eventually give way. China faces its own rendezvous with this reality.

How to Deal with Moscow

Whether to bring new pressures to bear on the Soviet Union, and how to apply those pressures, whether to reach out in a spirit of cooperation or to be confrontational—how to deal with the Soviet Union was enormously controversial in the United States throughout the last half of the Cold War. Nixon's opening to Moscow, especially strategic arms control, was resisted fiercely by conservatives, yet his efforts to keep alive U.S. strategic modernization in the light of a massive Soviet strategic buildup were just as fiercely resisted by liberals. Strategic deployments so proudly trumpeted by the Reagan administration survived infancy in the Nixon administration by only a few votes.

Broadening disenchantment with détente in 1974–1975 made Gerald Ford's decision to go to Helsinki and sign the Declaration very controversial, especially with conservatives and Americans of East European descent. But even as that disenchantment grew and as Soviet aggressiveness in the Third World mounted, Ford's efforts to sustain U.S. defense spending and covertly to contest the Soviets in Angola were thwarted by the liberals.

Carter's human rights campaign against the Soviets was nearly universally condemned by foreign policy gurus and pundits alike as inappropriate and inevitably unsuccessful interference in Soviet internal affairs. Conservatives attacked his arms control initiatives as dangerous and naïve, but liberals opposed his decision to deploy INF to Europe and to proceed with MX and other strategic programs. As Soviet aggressiveness in the Third World grew, the Carter administration split asunder over how to respond—with the issue settled finally only by the Soviet invasion of Afghanistan. American businessmen, in partnership with the liberals, opposed Carter's initiatives to apply new and tougher controls on exports to the Soviets. And, even after Afghanistan, many would urge Carter to respond mildly so as not to undermine arms control.

The liberals bitterly criticized Reagan's arms buildup, fiery rhetoric, economic measures, and failure to engage a succession of dying Soviet leaders. But conservatives leapt on their supposed champion (and especially his Secretary of State) when he finally did reach out to engage Gorbachev—the President's closest friends and allies worried he would sell out on SDI to the clever Soviet leader, even as that Soviet leader yielded ground, step by step, on every important issue.

Finally, the liberals—ironies abounding—would criticize Bush for taking too long to resume Reagan's forthcoming approach to the Soviets, especially on arms control. Later, Bush would be belabored by conservatives and liberals for being too conciliatory to Gorbachev, for lacking requisite triumphalism as the Soviet empire began to dissolve, and for sticking to the old communist leader too long. No one ever really identified what opportunities were missed or lost by continuing to work with Gorbachev. And no one considered that failure to do so might have resulted in his leading the August coup—with who knows what consequences for Yeltsin and the other reformers.

CONTINUITY AND BIPARTISANSHIP, QUIETLY KEPT

In reality, all five Presidents juggled their critics on the left and right, all five displeasing both wings fairly regularly, threading their way through political minefields at home to pursue a policy course toward the USSR that blended confrontation and conciliation. The mix and emphasis would vary from administration to administration, depending on personal predilection, domestic politics, and Soviet actions. But the policies of all five would have elements of pressure and accommodation.

Indeed, the secret all five of the Presidents and their political advisers hid from the American public was the extraordinary continuity in U.S. dealings with the Soviet Union from administration to administration. Hidden because, regardless of philosophy, the public approach of challengers in our politics is usually to tear down rather than to promise to build upon the work of incumbents— especially if the incumbent is in the other party.

In truth, the roots of Nixon's SALT negotiations and his strategic programs were, for the most part, in the Johnson administration. Ford embraced Nixon's détente until Soviet actions forced a change. Carter's human rights campaign built on Ford's signature of the Helsinki Declaration. He continued all but one of Nixon's strategic weapons programs as well as, ultimately, Ford's approach to SALT. Reagan's strategic programs, covert confrontation with the Soviets in the Third World, economic pressures, eventual engagement on arms control, and attacks on the legitimacy of the Soviet government itself built on Carter's efforts in each arena— even though partisans of both Presidents would rather have their tongues turn black and fall out than admit to this.

It was always a disappointment to me that each President could not, would not, acknowledge his debt to his predecessor, and acknowledge that essential continuity—even as each brought a different tone and character as well as new initiatives to the relationship with the Soviets. Because, when the rhetoric is stripped away, there was throughout the last half of the Cold War—just as in the first half, before Vietnam—a bipartisan continuity to U.S. policy toward the USSR that was one of its greatest strengths. Indeed, I believe that the conventional wisdom that Vietnam shattered the American consensus in foreign policy was not borne out by experience. Just as specific presidential policies regarding the Soviet Union in the first half of the Cold War were often controversial, so, too, was that the case in the second half. In retrospect, however, what is startling is how little Vietnam affected subsequent U.S. policy, actions, and strategic weapons programs as they related to the Soviet Union.

Rhetoric notwithstanding, the bipartisan consensus sustaining the competition remained strong as each President based support for his policies on the political center and then carved enough additional votes from the left and right to prevail—most of the time. I believe the most important continuity of all was between Carter and Reagan as, from 1977 on, the United States steadily increased the pressure on a weakening Soviet Union—economically, militarily, politically, and, in the Third World, covertly. And those increased pressures hastened the inevitable collapse of the Soviet Union.

THE ROLE OF CONGRESS:
THE GOOD, THE BAD, AND THE UGLY

Congress was a fickle and difficult partner for all five Republican and Democratic Presidents as they waged the last half of the Cold War. The good news was that, pushed and prodded and pressured by Presidents—who were helped by individual members and some leaders in both Houses—Congress generally followed the presidential lead and supported presidential policies, both politically and with resources. It was, after all, Democrats in Congress who provided Reagan the critical votes on defense spending and for covert actions in Afghanistan, Angola, and even in Central America (a fact that neither Democrats nor Republicans like to acknowledge). Often Presidents won by a whisker—like Nixon with ABM or Reagan with the Angola covert action—but straight-out defeats on major initiatives were rare.

The bad news was that members of Congress at times created some of the crises Presidents had to spend time and political capital to dampen. From time to time, one or another in Congress would lose all sense of proportion and seize upon a single incident, event, or problem, build it up, and envelop it in political hoopla, and then leave it to the President to figure out how to bring the United States back off the limb Congress climbed out on. The furor over the would-be defector Simas Kudirka in the Ford administration, Frank Church and the "brigade in Cuba" as well as the "MiGs in Cuba" flap under Carter, the compromise of embassy security in the mid-1980s under Reagan—in these and many other instances members of Congress would get all worked up and then demand that the President do something unwise or precipitate. And working our way out of these messes was always ugly.

The first instinct of the Congress through the years was to be critical of any presidential use of force. At the time of the *Mayaguez*, Desert One, Grenada, Libya, and other military actions, the first reaction was nearly always negative—and then, as in Grenada and Libya (twice), the reaction turned positive when the Congress saw the popularity of the actions among the American people. There *was* a Vietnam syndrome insofar as the use of force was concerned, but it affected primarily some in the Congress and the Joint Chiefs of Staff. Certainly not Presidents.

Another problem with Congress was that, after years of Republican Presidents, the Democratic majority in Congress moved increasingly often to enforce its will and its preferences in foreign policy by enacting laws—laws too often signed by Presidents for various tactical and political reasons. A crude and often shortsighted approach to making foreign policy, such laws not only complicated decision-making and a strategic approach but also contributed to the "criminalizing" of political differences between the Congress and the Executive—not just in Central America but in other areas as well. A statutory approach to making foreign policy was not a healthy development and weakened those in both branches of government seeking bipartisanship.

In the final analysis, though, for all its obstructionism, criticism, and complicating actions, Congress approved the weapons programs, covert actions, arms control agreements, and other measures requested by Presidents to pursue—and control—the struggle with the Soviets. Congressional continuity was, in fact, a reflection of the broad consensus of the American people. And this enduring broad public support was the great underlying strength of the United States in the long struggle with the Soviet Union.

The obstructionism and complicating role of Congress, however, did have a useful function. I sat in the Situation Room in secret meetings for nearly twenty years under five Presidents, and all I can say is that some awfully crazy schemes might well have been approved had everyone present not known and expected hard questions, debate, and criticism from the Hill. And when, on a few occasions, Congress was kept in the dark, and such schemes did proceed, it was nearly always to the lasting regret of the Presidents involved. Working with the Congress was never easy for Presidents, but then, under the Constitution, it wasn't supposed to be. I saw too many in the White House forget that.

CIA

The Agency, like the Presidents it served, was under political attack from both conservatives and liberals from the early 1970s on. Liberals generally opposed its operational activities and the conservatives its assessments of the Soviet Union, which they considered too soft and too supportive of arms control. CIA was, like the Presidents it served, more or less constantly embattled through nearly all of the last half of the Cold War. Yet its record in retrospect is far better than its critics of all political hues will admit.

Operationally, it had important successes. The greatest of them all was the war in Afghanistan where, under CIA management, the United States and its partners funneled billions of dollars in supplies and weapons to the Mujahedin. The resistance was thus able to fight the vaunted Soviet army to a standoff and eventually force the political decision to withdraw. And both the costs and the stalemate had a real and broad political impact domestically in the Soviet Union. Similarly, covert actions in Angola and even in Nicaragua produced sufficient pressure on Soviet clients to make them seek a political solution. Elsewhere in the Third World, CIA worked successfully with governments friendly to the United States to combat subversion by the Soviets or their surrogates. We waged the war of ideas and a covert human rights campaign inside the Soviet Union and supported the growing opposition in Eastern Europe, especially in Poland. CIA carried out a propaganda war against the Soviet regime, publicizing to the world Soviet abuses inside the USSR and aggressions beyond its borders. With our own surrogates, we challenged Soviet clients such as the Libyans, Cubans, and even the Vietnamese.

The Agency's clandestine successes went beyond covert action. We secretly acquired a wide array of Soviet military equipment for the U.S. military to dissect and study that enabled the preparation of countermeasures. We stole Soviet weapons manuals, recruited scientists and engineers who told us about weapons in research and development, and developed agents who revealed much about Warsaw Pact war plans and military capabilities. We developed and emplaced astonishingly advanced technical devices that yielded much information on the Soviet military and its operations.

The operational record, though very strong, was obviously far from perfect. We made significant mistakes in Central America, nearly all of them in Washington, and failed to dislodge Qaddafi in Libya. We were duped by double agents in Cuba and East Germany. We were penetrated with devastating effect at least once—Aldrich Ames—by the Soviets, and suffered other counterintelligence and security failures. We never recruited a spy who gave us unique political information from inside the Kremlin, and we too often failed to penetrate the inner circle of Soviet surrogate leaders.

And, for too long, our support to military operations was unsatisfactory, plagued by bureaucratic rivalries and turf wars on both sides, and by a cultural gap that grew too wide after Vietnam.

The Agency was criticized from time to time, and often after the fact, about the character of individuals and governments we helped, or who cooperated or worked with us. It is a sad fact of life that at no point in the Cold War were there many democratic governments in the Third World. As a result, during the global struggle against the Soviet Union, CIA (and the United States more broadly) ended up with some strange and often unsavory bedfellows. Most you wouldn't bring home to meet Mom. But, especially after the mid-1970s, foreign agents and governments were told our rules and, if they didn't play by them, our policy was to walk away. The Agency's record in this respect was far from perfect, but it was better—and we worked harder at it—than is usually understood.

Similarly, on occasion, our operations—for example, in Afghanistan—had lingering and dangerous aftereffects. The paramilitary training and weapons we provided, after the conflicts ended, sometimes were put to unwelcome purposes and even used in actions hostile to U.S. interests. We always were conscious of this likelihood and, indeed, had warned policymakers about this possibility during the debate over whether to use Stingers in Afghanistan.

All in all, CIA—uniquely among world intelligence services—endeavored to conduct its activities during the last half of the Cold War according to presidential directive, under the rule of law, and, in every way possible, consistent with American values. No one can or will deny that there were lapses and failures—and the Agency paid a high price for them. But in a shadow war that ranged across the globe, such failures were remarkably few and far between.

In sum, CIA generally was successful in carrying out the operational missions assigned by the President. Though I have revealed in these pages many CIA clandestine activities (both successful and unsuccessful) for the first time, others remain secret to protect agents still living or methods still in use. I would have my differences with the clandestine service over the years, and probably was regarded by many of its officers as operationally inexperienced and overly critical. But their record of accomplishment in the last half of the Cold War has no equal and far surpassed that of their Soviet opposition. They were the effective hidden hand of American Presidents in the shadow wars of the last half of the Cold War.

In the area of technical collection, CIA and the U.S. intelligence community scientists and engineers were brilliant. The American people—indeed, the West in general—owe a huge debt to the unsung technical experts of U.S. intelligence (and those in industry who worked with them) who figured out how to obtain information from a distance of hundreds or even thousands of miles, who designed and built unique technical systems to monitor missile testing and deployments, and who could make sense out of a bewildering array of squiggly lines, rows of numbers, and, at least at the beginning, fuzzy pictures. If ever legends and stories of American technological genius were deserved and not yet realized, they would be about the scientists and engineers—the wizards —of CIA who pioneered reconnaissance aircraft like the U-2 and SR-71 (Blackbird) and photographic satellites from the KH-4 to the KH-11, people like Les Dirks and many others who worked anonymously to serve their country. As they dealt with the most secretive country in the world, it is a tribute to these remarkable men and women that, after the 1960s, there were virtually no Soviet military surprises of broad strategic importance.

The great continuing strength and success of the analysts of CIA and the intelligence community was in describing with amazing accuracy from the late 1960s until the Soviet collapse the actual military strength and capabilities of the Soviet Union. Liberals long argued that CIA overstated Soviet military power and the conservatives argued just as stridently that we underestimated. But we located and counted with precision the number of deployed aircraft, tanks, ships, and strategic weapons. And these numbers and capabilities would be relied upon, with confidence, by the Executive Branch (including the Defense Department), the Congress, and our allies both in arms control negotiations and in military planning.

Perhaps the intelligence community's greatest contribution was that during the last half of the Cold War, there were no significant strategic surprises—no more "bomber gaps" or "missile gaps" as in the 1950s. Further, our detailed knowledge of Soviet forces and capabilities after the middle 1960s made it virtually impossible for the Soviets to bluff us, and this helped prevent miscalculations and misunderstandings that could have destroyed the world.

Similarly, CIA's work on the Soviet economy stands up far better than hindsight criticism suggests. CIA's record—literally thousands of assessments, briefings, and monographs, public and classified, over a thirty-year period—makes clear that the Agency:

• from the late 1960s onward accurately described the growing economic, political, and social weaknesses of the Soviet Union and its worsening systemic crisis;

• accurately portrayed the futility of tinkering with the system and pointed out how Gorbachev was undermining the foundations of the old system without embracing a new one; and

• by 1988–1989, was warning of deepening crisis, the potential for a rightist coup, and possible collapse of the entire system.

These successes were highlighted by an outside panel of scholars asked in 1991 to evaluate the Agency's work on the Soviet economy at the direction of the House Intelligence Committee. The panel's report, sent to the committee late in 1991, observed that CIA's economic work on the USSR "has been presented periodically to the scholarly community for review, criticism and recommendations. There has been very little criticism of this work, and CIA estimates have been accepted as authoritative throughout the world, including the Soviet Union. . . . We conclude . . . the CIA's reports have been of high quality, timely and useful to policymakers."

In analysis, as in operations, the record was not perfect. On the military side, we were occasionally surprised by the technical capabilities of specific Soviet weapons, for example, the speed of the Alpha-class submarine. We would, from time to time, both over- and underestimate specific characteristics of Soviet weapons. We were constantly revising our estimates of exactly how many Soviet troops were stationed in Warsaw Pact countries. Further, perhaps as a reflection of the criticism (and reality) of our underestimates of future Soviet strategic forces in the late 1960s–early 1970s, during the mid-1980s our projections of the military forces we thought the Soviets would deploy five to ten years into the future were too high. While we saw no slackening in military expenditures or the vigor of Soviet weapons research and development and modernization programs, the already huge Soviet deployed forces in the 1980s did not grow as quickly as we had predicted.

Even so, for a quarter century, American Presidents and the Congress negotiated and made decisions with confidence in our knowledge of the adversary's actual military strength—a confidence that was justified. The existing Soviet military capabilities that we described were real, and those capabilities were created—to a considerable degree—at the cost of bringing an already fundamentally flawed economic system to its knees. The Soviet military helped destroy the system it was built to defend.

In the economic arena, CIA in its statistics overstated the size of the Soviet economy and relatedly underestimated the burden of military expenditures on that economy and society. CIA's statistical analysis of the Soviet economy, while the best available East or West, in absolute terms described a stronger, larger economy than our own interpretive analysis portrayed and existed in reality. Our quantitative data failed adequately to capture the growing disparity between the Soviet economy and economies in the West. CIA fell short and opened itself to criticism in its efforts to compare the U.S. and Soviet economies and the two countries' military expenditures.

Finally, CIA came late to the realization that the entire Soviet structure might collapse. Until early 1989, CIA did not contemplate that a Soviet communist apparatchik—Gorbachev—once in power would unintentionally set in motion forces that would pull the props from under an already declining economic system and bring down the entire political and imperial system in the process. To be fair, the Agency had a great deal of company in this regard—in the United States, elsewhere in the West, *and* in the Soviet Union.

Most important, though, by early 1989, CIA was warning policymakers of the deepening crisis in the Soviet Union and the growing likelihood of a collapse of the old order. The gloom and doom of these assessments had two concrete results. First, at the White House, I took them seriously and, because of them, established a contingency planning effort to prepare for the possibility of collapse. Second, these reports helped consolidate the judgment in the Bush administration by the summer of 1989 to move quickly to lock in as many accomplishments in our national interest as soon as possible. Preventing surprise was CIA's mission and it fulfilled that mission two years ahead of time. That was considerably more warning than Gorbachev got. Prophecy beyond that was not in CIA's charter and, in the real world, speculation of a Soviet internal apocalypse much before then would have been ignored, if not ridiculed, by decision-makers.

CIA has been accused of failing in the 1980s to warn of Soviet limitations, vulnerabilities, and weaknesses. The accusations are not supported by the facts and by documents. The Agency's record on the Soviet economic and social crisis is well-documented. In the military arena, after many a hard-fought debate, CIA warned about Soviet shortcomings and the limitations of specific Soviet weapons systems. On issues ranging from the declining rate of growth in Soviet military spending in the early 1980s to problems of morale and the unreliability of the USSR's Warsaw Pact allies, to economic crisis, we described Soviet problems and vulnerabilities, often providing analysis policymakers did not want to hear. While we reminded our government of continuing Soviet interest in opportunities in the Third World and the large sums Moscow was still spending to support Cuba, Angola, Nicaragua, Vietnam, and others well into Gorbachev's tenure, we also advised them of strains in those relationships and the dissatisfaction of Soviet clients with much of the aid they received. The Agency's analysis accurately portrayed Soviet policies and activities in the Third World at the time the assessments were prepared. On Soviet involvement with international terrorism, in retrospect, if anything, we now know CIA understated Moscow's role.

In sum, CIA made an important contribution to victory in the Cold War. The American sword in the surrogate wars of the Third World, a source of help and sustenance for dissidents and oppositionists in the Soviet Union and Eastern Europe, worldwide purveyor of the realities of Soviet repression and subversion, gatherer of critical military information, accurate appraiser of Soviet military strengths and weaknesses, chronicler of the growing Soviet crisis at home, and, by 1989, herald of potential systemic collapse—in all these roles CIA successfully if not perfectly carried out the missions Presidents assigned to it in the last half of the Cold War.

What about my personal analysis of Soviet developments during these last years? From 1985 through 1987, I believe my skepticism of Gorbachev's economic reforms and belief that he would fail to revitalize the economy were right on the mark. My view that he remained a committed communist and would not weaken the party through genuine political reform also was accurate through 1987. Finally, my observation that, if anything, he was upping the ante in the Third World and continuing Soviet military programs apace also was accurate for that time period. I would remain correct on Gorbachev's doomed economic program until he fell from power, and on the military side until late in 1988.

That said, when Gorbachev began his radical internal political reforms in 1988 aimed at weakening the party and at democratization, I underestimated how far he would go. Beginning late in 1987, he would begin making changes in Soviet foreign policy and behavior in the Third World that were much more dramatic than I anticipated. And, at the end of 1988, he would move boldly in making unilateral military reductions, the importance of which I accepted immediately but which I had not expected. In sum, my assessments of Gorbachev were, I think, pretty accurate across the board for the first three years of his rule, but I was slow to appreciate his dramatic change of course in late 1987 in foreign policy and willingness to leave behind the Communist Party in 1988. I, like many others who had studied Russian and Soviet history, failed to reckon on a Soviet leader who would retreat abroad and destroy the Soviet system at home. At the same time, my view from 1985 onward that Gorbachev could not "reform" the Soviet system and that he was aggravating its crisis would prove consistently correct.

I saw Gorbachev as a traditional but reform-minded Soviet leader who wanted to repair a system he regarded as essentially sound. While he remained in that mold, which was longer than many U.S. policymakers at the time and later observers acknowledged, my analysis was sound. During 1988, when, unintentionally, he became a revolutionary and began, unknowingly, to dismantle the Soviet system, I underestimated how far he was prepared to go.

I remained convinced throughout Gorbachev's rule that his goal was to restore the Soviet Union to good health politically and economically and thereby allow it to retain its place as a superpower with global interests and ambitions, a communist superpower in more dimensions than military strength. I still believe that.

PRESIDENTS AND CIA

At a private dinner in the White House, President Johnson once was discussing intelligence with World War II "wise man" John J. McCloy. According to the then-DCI Dick Helms, Johnson told McCloy things were going well in intelligence and then went on:

> Let me tell you about these intelligence guys. When I was growing up in Texas, we had a cow named Bessie. I'd get her in the stanchion, seat myself and squeeze out a pail of fresh milk. One day, I'd worked hard and gotten a full pail of milk, but I wasn't paying attention and old Bessie swung her shit-smeared tail through that bucket of milk. Now, you know, that's what these intelligence guys do. You work hard and get a good program or policy going, and they swing a shit-smeared tail through it.

CIA is a uniquely presidential organization. Virtually every time it has gotten in trouble, it has been for carrying out some action ordered by a President—from Nicaragua to Iran. Yet few Presidents have anything good to say about CIA or the intelligence they received. How come?

The most significant reason is intelligence failure. Whether Nixon's unhappiness over poor estimates of projected Soviet ICBM deployments, Carter's anger over failure to forecast the Iranian revolution or untimely upward revisions of North Korean troop strength, or Reagan's dismay that CIA could not find the hostages in Lebanon, in these and other cases Presidents and their advisers believed intelligence either contributed to policy disasters or made the Presidents vulnerable to criticism. (From the intelligence officer's perspective, some so-called failures of intelligence forecasting resulted from Presidents taking warnings to heart and either changing their policy or taking an action that altered the predicted outcome.)

Presidents also dislike controversy within the Executive Branch, something intelligence often provokes. They and their senior advisers also do not like intelligence assessments that suggest their policies are not working at all or as well as they want to believe —especially when those assessments go to the Congress. This is the reality behind Johnson's story of Bessie's "shit-smeared tail."

Over the last twenty years, Presidents have regarded with jaundiced eye the growing direct relationship between Congress and CIA. Indeed, Mort Abramowitz, the head of intelligence for the State Department under Shultz, once told me that one of the Secretary's reasons for having a jaded view of intelligence was his perception that we "too frequently ran to the Hill" with information that could have been delivered at a later time without compromising Executive Branch policy formulation. "He [Shultz] thinks you forget who your real master is."

Finally, Presidents and their senior advisers usually are ill-informed about intelligence capabilities. Therefore, they have unrealistic expectations about what intelligence can do for them, especially when they see examples of some of the truly remarkable things we *can* do. And when they do learn the limitations, they are inevitably disappointed. Presidents usually learn the hard way that, although intelligence can tell them a great deal, it only rarely—and usually in crises involving military forces—provides the kind of unambiguous and timely information that can make day-to-day decisions simpler and less risky. Presidents expect that, for what they spend on intelligence, CIA should be able to predict coups, upheavals, riots, intentions, military moves, and the like with great accuracy. In the early morning hours, when the National Security Adviser must repair to the President's study with the usually bad news about such events, the Chief Executive will not unnaturally wonder why his billions for intelligence do not spare him surprises.

For all their unhappiness and complaining, Presidents keep CIA around for two simple reasons. First, the unending river of information that flows from intelligence about the military, economic, political, and even social developments constantly taking place around the world. Sure, they get a lot from CNN and myriad other sources. But that's not where they find out about North Korean or Iranian nuclear programs, or cheating on arms control or economic agreements by other countries, or so much more that they need to know to make informed decisions. It's not the long-range estimates or speculations about the future that bind CIA to Presidents—it is the politicians' mother's milk of factual, accurate information.

Second, Presidents also always want to retain the option of covert action in dealing with problems abroad. Every President has turned to covert action either as the best or politically only available option for dealing with tough problems abroad. Because the national interest, as perceived by the President, sometimes can be protected or advanced only by action in the gray areas—somewhere between the politically acceptable and unacceptable—Presidents always turn to the only governmental organization that can operate in that world of ambiguity and shadows: CIA. In the real world, if CIA were to disappear, Presidents would create some entity to take its place. And one, to be sure, not as constrained by Congress and the law.

HAWKS AND DOVES

While the eagle may be the American bird, there aren't many of those to be found in or around Washington, D.C. Instead, during the Cold War, the most common sightings by political ornithologists were of hawks and doves. In the political shorthand of the Cold War, hawks were those who favored toughness, putting pressure on the Soviets, military strength and preparedness, a willingness to use force, and a general skepticism of negotiation in dealing with them. The doves preferred to emphasize negotiation, restraint, and an effort to find common ground for cooperation; consistently promoted arms control; often opposed U.S. military programs and U.S. military actions; frequently attributed crises or confrontations or missed opportunities to U.S. shortsightedness or mistakes; and saw Soviet behavior often as reactive to U.S. actions. Both characterizations are obvious oversimplifications, but were widely used at the time and remain convenient terms of art.

American doves since the end of the Cold War have proudly proclaimed that they had been right all along about the Soviet Union—that it was rotten to the core and would (and did) collapse without a push from the United States. That "the Soviet threat is not what it used to be" and "that it never was." The hawks have just as confidently asserted that the U.S. military buildup—especially SDI, wars in the Third World, and economic warfare— brought down the Soviet Union. The doves were always worried about making U.S.-Soviet relations worse by applying pressures or by taking actions, while the hawks tended to be unwilling to wait on developments in Moscow or to settle for the status quo. So who was right? I believe both were and, further, that successful U.S. policy over nearly three decades depended on the continuing influence of both hawks and doves in the decision process in Washington.

I believe that the influence of the hawks—to build up our military, to take on the Soviets in the Third World, to challenge them at home, to wage economic war, and to proceed cautiously on arms control—was critical in bringing to bear on the USSR the panoply of pressures that forced its leaders to begin making changes at home, changes that ultimately brought down the whole shaky structure. On the other hand, initiatives generally favored by doves —the negotiating track, the promise of trade and credits, expanded bilateral contacts, the effort to find issues where the two adversaries could cooperate, arms control, and so on—even in the darkest days, kept the U.S.-Soviet relationship from getting out of control and kept alive a dialogue critical to continued peace. These efforts—by both the United States and the USSR—kept the Cold War "cold." Dialogue and negotiation with the West also made the risk of proceeding with internal changes acceptable to the Soviets.

If Presidents had listened only to the hawks, U.S. belligerence and aggressiveness would have been so overwhelming that the Soviets would have been afraid to undertake changes in their system, to have let down their guard at all. The danger of direct conflict would have been much higher. If Presidents had listened only to the doves, not only would the Soviets have seen many opportunities to gain strategic military advantage and new influence in the Third World; there would have been significantly less pressure on them to change. Those who argued, and I heard them many times, that the Soviets would have responded to U.S. restraint with their own restraint would have done well to remember the observation of Harold Brown, Carter's Secretary of Defense: "We build, they build. We stop, they build."

The terms "hawks" and "doves" do oversimplify the contending factions in the American government from 1969 to 1991. Indeed, three of the most effective senior U.S. officials during the period—Kissinger, Brzezinski, and Shultz—were in my view basically hawks who drew extensively on the ideas and initiatives of the doves. All were eager advocates of the use of military force and covert action, but each also was a strong proponent of arms control and dialogue. The important thing is that all five Presidents during this period pursued both confrontation and conciliation, conflict and dialogue with the Soviet Union. And it was their crude balancing of these twin strands of policy that sustained congressional and public support in the United States, the support of our European allies, and brought pressures to bear on the USSR that forced them to begin changing internally—and the reassurance that they could do so with limited risk of the U.S. taking undue advantage.

Each President needed and drew upon advisers who gave particular emphasis to one or the other of these strands. The differences between these advocates—both personal and philosophical—in the real world of Washington politics were interpreted, correctly, by public and press alike as manifestations of division in the Executive Branch. What was so superficial, even silly, was that this was treated as unusual or as a sign of presidential weakness and indecision. Kissinger and Rogers, Kissinger and Laird, Kissinger and Schlesinger, Vance and Brzezinski, Brzezinski and Carter, Brown and Vance, Haig and everyone at the White House, Haig and Weinberger, Weinberger and Shultz, Shultz and Casey, Baker and Cheney, Scowcroft and Baker—these disputes were neither unusual nor weakening. They represented, in fact, a healthy contention of ideas and approaches that, however messy and discomfiting to us on the inside at the time, helped Presidents make better and more balanced decisions, even as the disputes made life harder for them personally and sometimes politically. Presidents needed both hawks and doves, because this aviary mixture allowed the Presidents, more often than not, to be the "owls."

PRESIDENTS

I served under six Presidents, and knew five of them. Johnson was forced out by Vietnam. Nixon was almost impeached and re-signed. Ford served only two and a half years before being defeated. Carter was dismissed by the people after one term, with the econ-omy in a shambles and the perception of weakness in foreign policy. Reagan served two terms, but was nearly destroyed by Iran-Contra. And Bush served but one term, defeated after winning great victo-ries abroad but viewed by the electorate as unable to deal with domestic affairs. No wonder the Eisenhower years looked so tran-quil. What is astonishing in retrospect is that during a period of such turmoil in domestic politics—the post-Vietnam, post-Watergate era during which the American political environment became meaner year by year—we preserved so much continuity in our approach to the Soviet Union.

While I entered government under Johnson, I never met him. I knew the next five Presidents in varying measure—Bush best, followed in order by Reagan and Carter, Ford at a distance, Nixon remotely and mainly after he left the Presidency. Five very different men, with very different staffs and styles. I watched them all in action, and here is a thumbnail view of them from the trenches.

Richard Nixon has been examined and psychoanalyzed by so many historians, political scientists, journalists, and filmmakers that I can add little. He was, in my view, by far the most liberal President of the five in both domestic and foreign policy, contrary to the perceptions of many. I cannot think of an American President per-ceptions of whom were more at variance with reality, whose public words and private actions were in such contrast, or who made more of a fetish of talking tough while shrinking from personal confron-tation and reaching out to old foreign enemies. No stranger man in American history dominated our politics and our lives for so long.

Conservatives never forgave Ford for embracing Kissinger and détente, and many across the political spectrum never forgave him for pardoning Nixon. He was a good man and a good President. Never was this more evident than in the first days and weeks after he took office in the wake of Nixon's unprecedented resignation, as he reassured the nation and the world and quickly restored faith in the Presidency and in the government. One of our most athletic Presidents, he was portrayed by the press as clumsy and fumbling as they watched vulturelike for him to stumble or trip or otherwise fit the niche to which he had been assigned. And somehow the image of physical clumsiness was meanly extended to his intellectual capabilities. Smart enough to impress the likes of Chancellor Schmidt of West Germany and President Giscard d'Estaing of France with his knowledge of politics and economics, here, too, his public persona at home was unjust. I had not known Ford before he became President, but in the ensuing two and a half years, from my NSC perch at the White House, I would grow to admire his common sense, his personal touch, his successful relationships with Congress and foreign leaders alike, and his courage—as when he went to Helsinki.

Carter was the first President I would see often, as I sat in the West Wing of the White House. There was never a President who worked harder at the job—who read more, worked longer hours, or who was more conscientious. He was by far the most fiscally conservative President I served. In contrast to Nixon, he was much tougher in private than in public. He was not afraid to be sharp with his most senior advisers and Cabinet officers. And when he established a priority—like the Panama Canal Treaties or Camp David Accords—he would demonstrate unshakable determination and political skill until victory was won. Casey would often point to the political campaign to win ratification of the Panama Canal Treaties as an extraordinary example of political maneuver and organization worthy of emulation.

Carter's record in dealing with the Soviet Union, as I have shown in these pages, was far more complex and successful than commonly believed at the time or since. Indeed, he was the most consistently—if often unintentionally—truculent President in relations with the Soviets since Harry Truman. Unlike Reagan, for Carter there would be no reconciliation with the Soviets at the end of his term. Bedeviled with an economy marked by extraordinarily high interest rates and high inflation, as well as with the hostage crisis in Iran, Carter's defeat in 1980—and the rhetoric of that campaign—clouded a foreign policy record that had a number of important successes. If people had known what he was doing secretly to take on the Soviets, perceptions of his record likely would have been different.

I believe that, eventually, the historians' view of Ronald Reagan will be very different from the perception of many contemporary observers. At some point, someone will acknowledge that Reagan, twice elected governor of California and twice elected President, was a hell of a lot better politician than actor—and uniquely combined the two arts. He had focus on his priorities and went straight for the ideological throat. Reagan carefully used his political strength—while he talked the talk of social conservatives, he rarely spent a political chit to help them achieve their agenda. He kept a distance between himself and even the most senior members of his administration. Mrs. Reagan is given credit for being the tough one, the one who would undermine a senior official and ease him out. But in a team as close as the two of them, who is to say that there was not more than a little deception of others in this—that his hand was very much there, if hidden? The conventional wisdom is that Reagan paid attention to two or three big issues and stayed above the fray (or was uninterested) on the rest. I don't believe it, at least not in the first term. Based on my observations, that "Aw, shucks," easygoing manner masked one of the toughest and shrewdest political minds of our time—again, at least for the first four or five years of his administration. Historians, like too many politicians and journalists before them, in my view make the error of underestimating Reagan, only the second two-term President in half a century.

Others who knew him better and saw him more closely than I did may disagree, but I believe Reagan began to fade bit by bit beginning in late 1985–early 1986. In the first five years or so, I would watch Reagan in the Situation Room, see him listen to complex options or problems and then tell a story that would transform those complicated ideas into something the average citizen could understand. His stories were Lincolnesque and often would capture the point of the discussion with precision. It was an amazing thing to observe. However, as the second term wore on, we would hear a story told over and over, often told with no point at all. I thought he was still on top of the issues, at least the major ones, but a quality I believed to be fairly magical was waning, day by day. Both when he offered me the job as DCI in 1987 and when I later told him I was withdrawing, I had the sense he could not have recalled my name five minutes later. Even so, he was a man of courage and conviction, and I was always proud to work for him.

I always thought it was George Bush's tragedy that his best

advisers were in the national security arena—where he needed them least. Baker, Cheney, Powell, Scowcroft, Eagleburger, and others—this was the best national security team since the Truman administration. But it was Bush who set strategy, who decided to push for German reunification, who decided how to deal with revolution in Eastern Europe, who decided how to cope with a collapsing Soviet empire. He also was the master of tactics, from when to call a foreign leader to the need to make a splash with a new arms control proposal. His instincts were sure and, mostly, the rest of us did what he told us to. Sadly, in the arena where he was less sure, where his instincts were not as finely tuned—domestic affairs—he did not have advisers of the same caliber. And as they disagreed and pulled him this way and that, as he made tactical decisions on the budget and other issues without a larger strategy, no coherence emerged, no theme to persuade the American people that the President who had led them to victory in the Cold War and in the Persian Gulf could also lead them successfully in tackling domestic problems. He was my President and my friend, and I ached for him.

Ford, Carter, Reagan, and Bush were all good men, men of character and strength. I saw them, warts and all, and I liked what I saw. I saw how much they cared about the country, how much they loved it. I saw how much of themselves they gave to it. I saw how they were moved by the majesty of their office and by the awesome majesty of the American people. Each, in his own way, was a modest man. Each was determined to do his best, and I saw each consciously make decisions that would cost him politically— maybe even reelection. For each, the country came first. They were all worthy. And it saddened me to see three of them defeated, rejected by the people for whom they had given their all. Public service in a rough-and-tumble American democracy is not for the weak or faint of heart.

The White House is a poignant place. I spent more years working there than any President but Franklin D. Roosevelt. And it seems to me that for those who live and work there, if they are completely honest with themselves, with rare exception the most vivid memories are not of victory and joy but of crisis and defeat —and, for a fortunate few, of one or two occasions of historical importance. This is why character counts for so much in a President. In the White House, the elation of victory is fleeting and the burden of responsibility is enduring.

FINAL THOUGHTS

The Soviet Union *was* an evil empire. As more documents are released from Soviet archives, we are learning not only that the communists in the Kremlin committed virtually all of the atrocities long suspected, but even more that were controversial, doubted, or even unknown in the West. The Soviets stand proven guilty of crimes against humanity by their own records and those of their satellites. We are now learning that however badly we thought of them, they were even worse.

I never dreamed in 1966 that the long struggle with the Soviet Union would be over in my lifetime. Two generations of us accepted George Kennan's 1947 analysis that if Soviet expansionism could be contained, eventually the fundamental contradictions in the Soviet system would bring it down. Even so, we expected the struggle to continue for generations. The Cold War, and its recurrent crises, were a fact of life—and death. Indeed, while nuclear conflagration was avoided, on countless battlefields people died to resist Soviet communism or its local satraps. From the Berlin Wall to the mountains of Afghanistan, the central Sahara, the jungles of Cambodia, Angolan battlefields, the forests and hills of Nicaragua, and the factories of Eastern Europe, people died rather than submit, died in the struggle against Soviet communism. Inside the Soviet Union itself, from ancient nationalities to Russian dissidents and other men and women of conscience, people went to the camps or died rather than submit. It was for all these people that Americans fought. It was to contain a truly evil empire that for so long we armed ourselves and others, and waged political, economic, and covert war across the globe. Even after Vietnam, with the leadership of President after President, Congress after Congress, the American people paid the price to match the empire's military might, to resist its grasping for new conquests, to keep the hope of freedom alive—all in the belief that, denied new conquests, the inherent weaknesses of Soviet communism ultimately would bring it down. We were right.

It was a glorious crusade.

Notes

22   According to a senior KGB defector: Christopher Andrew and Oleg Gordievsky, *KGB: The Inside Story* (New York: HarperCollins, 1990), p. 530.

PART ONE
1969–1974: Détente—
THE YEARS OF SMOKE AND MIRRORS

ONE: Washington and Moscow: 1969

31   "Whose team is CIA on?": Russell Jack Smith, *The Unknown CIA* (McLean, Va.: Pergamon–Brassey's International Defense Publishers, 1989), p. 208.

PART TWO
1975–1980: THE MASK OF SOVIET ASCENDANCY

THREE: American Paralysis

59   The subsequent compilation: William Colby, *Honorable Men* (New York: Simon and Schuster, 1978), p. 340.
59   According to Colby: *Ibid.*

FOUR: The "Third World" War

65   The Soviets remained consistent: Gerald R. Ford, *A Time to Heal* (New York: Harper and Row, 1979), p. 252.
67   The first planeload: Cord Meyer, *Facing Reality* (New York: Harper and Row, 1980), p. 257.
68   CIA estimated: *Ibid.*, pp. 259–63.
77   The real breakthrough: Andrew and Gordievsky, *op. cit.*, p. 551.

FIVE: Planting Lethal Seeds

85   As then–Soviet Foreign Minister Andrei Gromyko: Andrei Gromyko, *Memories* (London: Hutchinson, 1989), p. 282.
87   Bill Hyland, years later: William G. Hyland, *Mortal Rivals* (New York: Random House, 1987), p. 128.
87   According to Lech Walesa: Lech Walesa, *A Way of Hope* (New York: Henry Holt, 1987), pp. 97–98.
89   When he first met: Jimmy Carter, *Keeping Faith* (New York and Toronto: Bantam Books, 1982), p. 146.
90   Hyland later wrote: Hyland, *op. cit.*, p. 199.
90   Indeed, Gromyko: Gromyko, *op. cit.*, p. 291.
94   In a 1977 interview: Abraham Brumberg, "A Conversation with Andrei Amalrik," *Encounter*, June 1977, quoted in Meyer, *op. cit.*, p. 138.
95   Brzezinski would later write: Zbigniew Brzezinski, *Power and Principle* (New York: Farrar Straus Giroux, 1983), p. 300.

SEVEN: Defense and Arms Control: Advantage USSR

109   Carter says in his memoirs: Carter, *op. cit.*, pp. 222–23.
109   Early in the administration: Hyland, *op. cit.*, p. 212.

EIGHT: 1979: Cold War, Hot War—East War, West War

133   Starting on Christmas Eve: Andrew and Gordievsky, *op. cit.*, p. 575.

NINE: Carter Turns to CIA

136   The new President had campaigned: Carter, *op. cit.*, p. 143.
137   He found no: Stansfield Turner, *Secrecy and Democracy* (Boston: Houghton Mifflin, 1985), pp. 23–24.
161   Walesa said of that time: Walesa, *op. cit.*, p. 85.
161   According to Walesa, "the decisive moment": *Ibid.*, pp. 104–105.
162   According to Walesa, "Solidarity": *Ibid.*, p. 123.

PART THREE
1981–1986: THE RESURGENCE OF THE WEST

ELEVEN: The Reawakening

193   In fact, he wrote White House counsel Edwin Meese: Caspar Weinberger, *Fighting for Peace* (New York: Warner Books, 1990), p. 41.
194   As he later wrote: Ronald Reagan, *An American Life* (New York: Simon and Schuster, 1990), p. 267.

THIRTEEN: Turning the Tables

235   A final attempt: Walesa, *op. cit.*, pp. 196–98.

FOURTEEN: 1983: The Most Dangerous Year

268 Interestingly, confirmation: George Shultz, *Turmoil and Triumph* (New York: Charles Scribner's Sons, 1993), p. 364.
269 Gromyko wrote in his memoirs: Gromyko, *op. cit.*, p. 300.
270 What we know about this: Andrew and Gordievsky, *op. cit.*, p. 583.
271 According to Gordievsky: *Ibid.*, pp. 599–600.

FIFTEEN: The War in Washington, 1983:
Shultz Against the Field

288 Shultz's first major strategic foray: Shultz, *op. cit.*, p. 162.

SIXTEEN: Central America, 1983–1984: Our Own Worst Enemy

296 In late May: *Ibid.*, p. 306.
311 According to the report: Lawrence E. Walsh, *Final Report of the Independent Counsel for Iran/Contra Matters*, Washington, D.C., August 4, 1993, Vol. I, p. 80.

EIGHTEEN: 1985: Reagan and Gorbachev—
the Best of Enemies

334 As Ronald Reagan wrote: Reagan, *op. cit.*, p. 614.
334 Shultz, in his memoirs: Shultz, *op. cit.*, p. 507.

NINETEEN: The Third World Competition, 1985–1986:
Washington Pours It On

353 Shultz mentions in his memoirs: *Ibid.*, p. 684.

TWENTY: Intelligence Wars

367 On September 9: *Ibid.*, p. 735.

PART FOUR
1986–1991: LIBERATION AND HISTORY'S DUSTBIN

TWENTY-ONE: Gorbachev's Uncertain Trumpet,
1986–1987

376 Judging from his memoirs: *Ibid.*, p. 703.
381 In his memoirs: *Ibid.*, pp. 703, 710–711.
383 Reflecting on his travels: Marquis de Custine, *Empire of the Czar* (New York: Doubleday, 1989), p. 615. (First published as *La Russie en 1839.*)
385 As one scholar put it: Hélène Carrère d'Encausse, *The End of the Soviet Empire*. Translated by Franklin Philip (New York: Basic Books, 1993), p. 45.

TWENTY-TWO: *Diversions*

395   On July 3, 1985: Robert C. McFarlane, *Special Trust* (New York: Cadell & Davies, 1994), p. 20.
402   Indeed, on May 16: Joseph Persico, *Casey* (New York: Viking, 1990), p. 501.
403   Indeed, the Independent Counsel points out: Walsh, *op. cit.*, p. 212.

TWENTY-THREE: *Geneva to Washington*

408   Then Gorbachev sprang: Reagan, *op. cit.*, p. 677.
408   Finally, as he later wrote: *Ibid.*, p. 679.
409   In his memoirs, Shultz: Shultz, *op. cit.*, p. 780.
417   In his testimony: *Ibid.*, p. 922.

TWENTY-SEVEN: *Together at Last: Bush and Gorbachev*

500   His own chief of staff: Valery Boldin, *Ten Years That Shook the World*. Translated by Evelyn Rossiter (New York: Basic Books, 1994), pp. 211–12.

TWENTY-EIGHT: *Destruction of the "Evil Empire"*

513   As one scholar put it: d'Encausse, *op. cit.*, p. 149.

REFLECTIONS

569   That "the Soviet threat . . .": *Time*, January 1, 1990, p. 69.

Index

Aaron, David, 69, 71, 72, 75, 91,
124, 125–26, 127, 136, 142,
144–45, 150, 151, 167, 192, 227
ABC, 71
"ABC Evening News," 529
"Able Archer" exercise, 270–73,
274, 276
Abramowitz, Mort, 350, 430, 431,
567
Abrasimov, Pyotr, 88
Abu Nidal organization, 204
Afghanistan, 130, 150, 178, 197, 231,
236, 242, 250, 256, 276, 324,
332, 334, 336, 340, 347, 425,
427, 538, 556, 558, 560, 561,
575
  antiaircraft campaign in, 349–
  350
  Carter administration and, 143–
  149
  Casey and, 251–52, 349–50
  China and, 174, 175
  Geneva Accord signed on, 432
  growing Soviet involvement in,
  131–34
  SCC meetings on, 144–47
  Shultz and, 432
  Soviet campaigns in, 144–48, 149,
  252, 348, 350
  Soviet invasion of, 118, 133, 147

  Soviet withdrawal from, 428–
  432
  Turner and, 131–33, 143, 145,
  146, 147–48, 149
  U.S. covert programs in, 251–52,
  319–21, 348–50, 358
  U.S. sanctions and, 177, 537
AFL-CIO, 164, 237, 300
Agca, Mehmet Ali, 239, 241,
355
Agnew, Spiro, 41
AIDS epidemic, 357
Albania, 470
Albright, Madeleine, 452
Aleksandrov, Vladimir, 477
Algeria, 129, 349
Allen, Charles, 399, 403, 415, 416–
417
Allen, Lew, 164
Allen, Richard, 166, 193, 219, 238,
283
Alma-Ata riots, 385
Alvor Accords (1975), 66
Amalrik, Andrei, 94–95
American Association for the
  Advancement of Science, 443
Ames, Aldrich, 16–19, 22, 362, 364,
365, 560
Amin, Hafizullah, 132, 133
Amin, Idi, 77

Andreotti, Giulio, 464, 485
Andropov, Yuri, 187, 271, 330, 534, 554–55
  background of, 189–90
  Brezhnev replaced by, 188–89, 257
  Brezhnev's ouster sought by, 185–186
  Gates's assessment of, 189–90
  Gorbachev and, 328, 329, 334
  illness and death of, 259, 282, 318
  Shultz's meeting with, 188–89
  U.S. and West mistrusted by, 102, 266, 270
Angleton, James Jesus, 32, 34, 209, 364
Angola, 58, 60, 73–74, 75, 76, 77, 78, 86, 105, 118, 124, 125, 148, 174, 175, 287, 312, 332, 334, 336, 337, 339, 348, 376, 379, 381, 445, 538, 558, 560, 565, 575
  Congress and, 68, 346–47
  Cuba and, 66, 68, 433
  final agreement on, 423–24
  Soviet Union and, 65–69
anti-ballistic missile system (ABM), 558
  SDI and, 264, 265, 339
  Soviet Union and, 37–38
Arafat, Yasir, 129
Argentina, 245, 297
"Arias plan," 434–35
Armacost, Michael, 350, 352, 430, 431, 432
Armenia, 509–11
Armitage, Richard, 352, 406–7
arms control, 17–18, 30, 45, 184, 187, 194, 279, 289, 324, 332, 380, 404–5, 421, 482, 569
Armstrong, Anne, 355
Assad, Hafez al-, 129
Association of Southeast Asian Nations (ASEAN), 255, 256
Austria, 32, 467
Azerbaijan, 509–11

Bakatin, Vadim, 519
Baker, Howard, 157, 418, 420

Baker, James, 219, 282, 312, 453, 458, 460, 461, 462, 474, 480–481, 486, 487, 490, 491, 492, 493, 495, 501, 503, 530, 531, 570, 574
  Bush's relationship with, 456
  Gulf War and, 497, 498–99
  Kemp's confrontation with, 456–457
  personality of, 456
  Shevardnadze and, 475–76, 479–480, 496, 497, 529
  Wyoming talks and, 479–80
Baltic states, 512–15
Baltimore Sun, 99–100
Bay of Pigs, 58
Bazargan, Mehdi, 128, 129, 130
BBC, 536
Beirut bombing, 272
Belgium, 261, 262, 280–81, 358
Belorussia, 514
Bentsen, Lloyd, 300, 452
Beria, Lavrenti, 476
Berlin issue, 39, 85, 338
  détente and, 44–45, 48
Berlin Wall, 482, 575
Bessmertnykh, Alexander, 529
Bishop, Maurice, 125, 126, 143, 274–75
Blackwell, Robert, 185, 189, 392, 526
Blackwill, Robert, 454, 460–61, 485, 494
Boland, Edward, 246, 298, 300
Boland Amendments, 247, 298, 299–300, 310, 313, 392
B-1 bomber, 106, 109, 110, 111, 177, 178
Boren, David, 418, 545, 551
Bowie, Robert, 92, 138
Bradley, Bill, 386–87, 548, 551, 552
Brandt, Willy, 44
Brezhnev, Galina, 186
Brezhnev, Leonid, 37, 38, 82, 90, 132, 134, 166–67, 171, 174, 196, 234–35, 252, 328, 329, 343, 384, 476, 533
  Andropov and, 185–86, 188–89, 257
  death of, 188, 189
  physical decline of, 116–17
Bross, John, 191, 222

Brown, Harold, 75, 91, 109, 110, 115, 133, 141, 142, 152, 156, 159, 163, 166–67, 242, 570
Bruemmer, Russell, 543
Brzezinski, Zbigniew, 73, 77, 88, 95, 109, 110, 112, 113, 119, 121, 123, 126, 133, 135, 136, 146, 148, 149, 152, 155, 176, 192, 193, 222, 238, 242, 377, 541, 570
   Aaron's confrontation with, 127
   Algiers conference and, 129–30
   anti-Soviet propaganda campaign and, 90–92, 93, 94
   character and personality of, 69–71
   covert action and, 142–43
   Cuban-Soviet cooperation and, 123–24
   NORAD false alarm and, 114–15
   Polish crisis and, 163, 164–67
   Shah issue and, 129–30
   Soviet aggression as seen by, 74–76
   spy crisis and, 100, 101, 102, 103
   Turner and, 140–42
   Vance's conflicts with, 71–74, 158–59
Buckley, William, 397, 401
Bulgaria, 239, 354, 355, 468
Burt, Richard, 227
Buryata, Boris, 186
Bush, Barbara, 455, 458, 549
Bush, George, 19, 81, 106, 113, 137, 189, 192, 219, 253, 287, 333, 339, 352, 355, 378, 396, 411, 436, 452, 453, 460, 461, 471, 493, 501, 502, 503, 504, 517, 521, 549, 571
   assessment of, 573–74
   August coup and, 523
   Baker's relationship with, 456
   broken gate incident and, 527–28
   CFE and, 462–63, 487
   collapse of Soviet Union and, 526, 528–31
   "Doonesbury" cartoon and, 454–455
   Eastern Europe visit of, 466, 469
   Gates named DCI by, 540
   German reunification endorsed by, 483–84, 485, 495
   Gorbachev's relationship with, 475, 506–7
   great cake caper and, 472–73
   Gulf War and, 498, 499
   Hamtramck speech of, 465
   media and, 454–55, 456
   Moscow visit of, 505–6
   personality and style of, 454–56, 475
   Poland visited by, 466, 470
   Scowcroft's troop withdrawal proposal and, 462–63
   Ukraine speech of, 506
   Yeltsin's phone conversation with, 523
   Yeltsin's U.S. visit and, 479
Bush administration, 453–59
   collapse of Soviet Union and, 525–31
   contingency planning for Soviet collapse, 525–27
   factions in, 473–75
   Gorbachev supported by, 500–501, 527
   policy review period ("pause") of, 460–61
Butler, Lee, 488
Byrd, Robert, 157

Callaghan, James, 111, 183
Cambodia, 27, 30, 57, 60, 64–65, 174, 242, 312, 322, 358, 445, 538, 575
   Vietnam's invasion of, 255–56
Camp David Accords (1979), 82–83, 572
Canada, 329, 330
Caribbean Joint Task Force, 159
Carlucci, Frank, 126, 137–38, 144, 146, 149, 251, 407, 411, 420, 424, 435, 444, 446, 457, 541
Carter, Hodding, 155
Carter, Jimmy, 19, 70, 71, 74, 75, 77, 79, 99, 118, 126, 128, 129, 130, 154–55, 163, 167, 173, 191, 219, 227, 239, 242, 243, 251, 256, 262, 263, 328, 533, 539, 566, 570, 571, 574
   Afghan finding signed by, 146, 178
   Annapolis speech of, 102

Carter, Jimmy, *continued*
  anti-Soviet propaganda campaign
    and, 90–96
  assessments of, 176–79, 572
  Camp David Accords and, 82–83,
    572
  Central America findings signed
    by, 150–51, 178
  and China's invasion of Vietnam,
    119, 120–21
  CIA and, 136, 141–42
  CIA covert actions and, 142–53,
    178, 191, 242, 251, 256, 297,
    536, 538
  defense and, 108–15
  Deng and, 120–21
  Grenada findings signed by, 178,
    274
  Guadeloupe summit and, 111–12
  human rights and, 89–91, 94, 95–
    96, 536, 555–58
  Middle East finding signed by, 150
  personality of, 72–73, 110
  public perception of, 178, 197
  Reagan's continuation of policies
    of, 113, 115, 177, 178, 179,
    557–58
  Sakharov letter of, 90, 95
  SALT II and, 115–17
  Soviet brigade in Cuba fiasco and,
    155, 156, 159
  Soviet-Cuban relationship and, 124
  Soviet perception of, 178–79
  Turner's relationship with, 141–42
Carter, Rosalynn, 73
Carter administration, 74, 79, 80, 95,
    119, 136, 142, 150, 172, 193,
    242, 285, 297, 536
  Afghan insurgency and, 143–49
  Cuba and, 123–25
  DI and, 94
  fall of Soviet Union and, 537,
    538–39
  Poland and, 228, 237
  Reagan administration's
    perception of, 195–96
Carter Doctrine, 113
Carver, George, 191, 192
CAS (Covert Action Staff), 91–92
Casaroli, Cardinal, 240, 241
Casey, Sophia, 411–14

Casey, William J., 128, 186–87, 188,
    198, 260, 264, 271–72, 277,
    283, 285, 305, 310, 335, 348,
    351, 355, 356, 357, 362, 378,
    379, 399, 405, 409, 417, 420,
    434, 450, 541, 544, 549–50,
    570, 572
  Afghanistan conflict and, 251–52,
    349–50
  analysis and, 202, 207
  Angola conflict and, 347
  arms-for-hostages deal and, 391,
    394, 395, 396, 397–98, 401, 415
  background and personality of,
    199–200, 216–18
  Boland Amendment and, 247
  Cambodia conflict and, 255–56
  Cambodia covert action and, 322
  Central America covert actions
    and, 242–44, 245, 246–48, 294,
    295, 297–98, 299, 300, 301–3,
    313, 315–16
  CIA changes by, 202–3
  Congress and, 213–14, 217, 220,
    225, 297–98, 314–15, 369–70,
    395
  Contadora Forum opposed by,
    302–3
  Contras and, 311–12, 313, 394,
    400–401
  Danilov spy case and, 367
  death of, 400, 402
  described, 215–16
  Directorate of Intelligence and,
    192, 201–2, 221, 248, 333, 341
  Directorate of Operations and,
    208–13, 256, 364
  estimates process and, 333
  front office of, 221–22
  Gates's relationship with, 222–23,
    224
  Gorbachev appraised by, 332–34
  hostile presence issue and, 360–61
  Howard spy case and, 364
  illness of, 410–14
  Inman and, 219–20
  intelligence "style" of, 200–201
  Iran-Contra role of, 400–403
  KAL shoot-down and, 267, 268, 269
  "Lawrence" memorandum of, 303–4
  Leahy and, 370–71

Libya and, 254–55, 351, 353
management style of, 200–203
martini episode and, 198
media and, 213, 214–15
Meese and, 219
Middle East memorandum of,
    250–51
Nicaragua mining operation and,
    306–8
NIEs and, 202, 203–4
in North's congressional
    testimony, 402–3
OSS and, 199–200, 208, 209, 225
Polish crisis and, 229, 231–32,
    233, 237, 238, 241
press leaks and, 214–15
private sector initiative of, 212
proposed Reagan-Gromyko
    meeting and, 324–25
Reagan advisers and, 281–82
Reagan's appointment of, 192–93
Reagan's relationship with, 218–
    219
resignation letter of, 411–14
SA-5 missiles episode and, 274
San Jose Principles opposed by,
    302–3
Shultz's relationship with, 219,
    280, 286–87, 289, 301–3, 353,
    365, 398, 410, 428
Shultz's steering group and, 376–
    377
Soviet-terrorism connection and,
    202–5
terrorism estimate and, 202–6
Third World strategy of, 249–51
Yurchenko defection and, 363
Zia's meetings with, 251–52, 320–
    321, 350
Castro, Fidel, 59, 68, 83, 124, 125,
    157, 242, 243
"CBS Evening News," 60
Ceausescu, Nicolae, 252, 469
Central America, 242–49, 256, 293–
    316
    Boland Amendments and, 247,
        298, 299–300, 310, 313, 392
    Congress and, 293, 295, 297–301
    Contadora Forum and, 302–3
    covert action debate and, 242–44,
        245, 246, 293–94

Cuba and, 150–53
Kissinger Commission and, 303
Nicaragua and, 244–46
Reagan administration and, 151,
    243, 244, 294–95
Reagan and, 242, 247, 297, 301–2
San Jose principles and, 302–3
Shultz and, 295, 296, 301–4
Soviet strategy in, 152–53, 158–
    160
see also Nicaragua
Central American Task Force, 248,
    312, 313, 542
Central Command, U.S., 113
Central Intelligence Agency (CIA):
    analysis quality of, 563–64
    assessments of, 223–24, 561–62
    bureaucracy of, 33–35
    career training program of, 21–22
    directorates of, see specific
        directorates
    "family jewels" era of, 58–63
    headquarters of, 19–20
    military arena and, 564–65
    policy making process and, 56
    popular perception of, 27–28
    Presidents and, 31–32, 566–68
    private sector and, 212
    successes and failures of, 560–61
    technical collection by, 562
    see also specific individuals and topics
CFE, see Conventional Forces in
    Europe
Chad, 77, 254, 256, 321
Chamorro, Violeta, 436
Chamran, Mustafa Ali, 129
Chaos, Operation, 59
"Charter 77 movement," 89, 536
Cheney, Dick, 453, 456, 457, 458,
    461, 462, 463, 474, 486, 488,
    493, 495, 496, 497, 498, 499–
    502, 503, 523, 528, 530, 570,
    574
Chernayev, Rudolf, 100, 101, 102,
    103
Cherne, Leo, 200
Chernenko, Konstantin, 186, 187,
    282, 318, 323, 328, 329, 330,
    534
    death of, 325, 326
Chernobyl disaster, 383

Chin, Larry Wu-tai, 365
China, People's Republic of, 30, 38,
    40, 44, 49, 83, 116, 117, 132,
    146, 167, 287, 312, 365, 555
  Afghan resistance and, 174, 175
  Angola conflict and, 65, 66
  economic reforms in, 174–75
  Soviet Union's border clashes
    with, 35–36
  Tiananmen Square
    demonstrations in, 465
  Turner's secret visit to, 123
  U.S. normalization with, 119, 123
  U.S. relationship with, 174
  U.S.-Soviet Relationship and, 80–
    82
  Vietnam-Cambodia conflict and,
    255
  Vietnam invaded by, 119–21, 174
Christian Democratic Union,
    German, 184
Christoper, Warren, 163, 164
Churbanov, Yuriy, 186
Church, Frank, 59, 157, 158, 558
Church Committee, 59, 60, 136
Clancy, Tom, 107
Clark, Bill, 219, 238, 241, 247, 260,
    268, 274, 286, 295, 298, 299, 300
  Reagan as seen by, 281–82
  resignation of, 297
  Shultz and, 283–84, 285, 289, 296
Clark, Dick, 68
Clark Amendment, 68, 339, 346, 347
Clarridge, Duane "Dewey," 244,
    245, 246, 247, 248, 293–94,
    297, 303–4, 307, 312
Clift, A. Denis, 55, 56
CNN, 510, 521, 523, 566
Coard, Bernard, 274–75
Codevilla, Angelo, 191
Cogan, Charles, 320
Cohen, Bill, 360, 386, 545, 551
Colby, William, 32, 59, 60, 61–63,
    68, 135, 333, 541
Colombia, 302
Commerce Department, U.S., 465
Committee for Defense of Workers
    (KOR), 161
Commonwealth of Independent
    States (CIS), 525, 552
Communist Party, East German, 261

Communist Party, Lithuanian, 513,
    515, 517, 519
Communist Party, Polish, 87, 164,
    175, 233, 235
Communist Party, Portuguese, 65
Communist Party, Soviet, 188, 345,
    380, 515, 516, 524, 535, 554, 566
  Gorbachev's undermining of,
    438–40, 447
Communist Party, West German, 262
Congo Republic, 66
Congress, U.S., 28, 40, 82, 94, 106,
    116, 118, 143, 151, 154, 156,
    157, 158, 160, 171, 178, 184,
    191, 211, 241, 244, 265, 284,
    319, 420, 513, 562, 567
  Angola conflict and, 68, 346–47
  anti-military mood of, 46, 47, 105
  Casey and, 213–14, 217, 220, 225,
    297–98, 314–15, 369–70, 395
  CIA covert operations and, 293,
    295, 297–301
  Clark Amendment repealed by,
    339, 347
  Colby and, 61–63
  collapse of Soviet Union and,
    558–59
  Contra funding and, 311, 312–14,
    315, 332, 336, 391, 392–94,
    434–35
  defense budget and, 46
  Ford's tenure and, 58
  Gates's DDCI nomination and, 378
  Gates's first DCI hearings and,
    417–18
  Gates's second DCI hearings and,
    545–52
  Gulf War and, 499
  hostile presence issue and, 360
  Nicaraguan mining operation and,
    306–10
  Presidency challenged by, 56–58,
    64, 172, 559
  and President's control of CIA,
    60–61
  and Salvadoran death squads, 305
  SDI and, 342, 343
  Vietnam War and, 64–65
  Watergate affair and, 57–58
  see also House of Representatives;
    Senate, U.S.

Congress of People's Deputies,
  Soviet, 516–17, 519, 524–25
Conservative Party, British, 183
"constitutional coup," 504–6
Contadora Forum, 302–3
Contras, 245, 248, 295, 296, 297,
  306, 307, 308, 380, 402, 410
  Casey and, 311–12, 313, 394,
    400–401
  Congress and funding for, 311,
    312–14, 315, 332, 336, 390–94,
    434–35
  murder manual episode and, 310–
    311
  Senate Intelligence Committee
    and, 298–301, 303
Conventional Forces in Europe
  (CFE), 485–89, 499, 502
  Bush and, 462–63, 487
  Malta conference and, 482
  Scowcroft and, 461–62, 487–88
  Thatcher and, 463–64
Costa Rica, 127, 246, 247, 300, 312,
  434, 435
Covert Action Review Group, 379
Covert Action Staff (CAS), 91–92
Cox, Archibald, 41
Crawford, Jay, 101, 102
Crisis Pre-Planning Group (CPPG),
  188, 306, 352
Crocker, Chester, 433–34
Crowe, William, 333, 453, 460
Cuba, 29, 40, 43, 49, 142, 174, 178,
  201, 243, 244, 246, 347, 427,
  445, 482, 560, 565
  Angola conflict and, 66, 68, 433
  Carter administration and, 123–
    125
  Central America involvement of,
    150–53
  Ethiopia conflict and, 73–74, 75
  Grenada and, 125–26, 143, 150
  Nicaragua and, 126–28, 150–52,
    242, 336–37
  Soviet brigade fiasco and, 155–61
  as Soviet proxy, 66, 68, 73–74, 75,
    78–80, 83, 124
Cuban Missile crisis, 28
Cultural Revolution, 555
Custine, Marquis de, 383
Cutler, Lloyd, 160

Cyprus, 58
Czechoslovakia, 37, 93, 164, 165,
  175, 449, 451, 469, 470, 482
  communists deposed in, 469
  Soviet invasion of, 23, 37

Daniloff, Nicholas, 365–68, 407
Danish-Soviet Friendship
  Association, 261
Day After, The (film), 276
DCI/DDCI Executive Staff, 222
Dean, Robert, 158, 162–63, 165
Deaver, Mike, 282
defense, 105–17
  Carter and, 108–15
  Guadeloupe summit and, 111–12
  Reagan buildup and, 196–97
  SALT II and, 115–17
  window of vulnerability and, 106–
    108
Defense Department, U.S., 17–18,
  31, 33, 92, 114, 127, 152, 191,
  193, 228, 251, 252, 260, 279,
  280, 282, 293, 296, 298, 304,
  313, 319, 321, 346, 348, 352,
  359, 376, 457, 486, 562
Defense Intelligence Agency (DIA),
  205, 267, 441
Defense Ministry, Soviet, 230
deGraffenreid, Kenneth, 191
Democratic Party, U.S., 190, 214,
  298, 393, 417, 420, 558, 559
Dempsey, Rick, 353–54
Denend, Leslie, 141
Deng Xiaoping, 120–21, 122, 123
Denmark, 261
Deputies Committee, 458–59, 494,
  522, 523
Desert One, 154, 558
Desert Storm, Operation, 196
détente, 28, 29, 37, 38, 39–52, 69,
  148, 184, 188, 194, 318, 535,
  537, 555, 557, 571
  Berlin issue and, 44–45, 48
  CIA and, 44–45
  Helsinki Accords and, 86, 87
  linkage and, 39, 44, 48
  Middle East and, 39–41, 43, 49
  Nixon and, 29–30, 46, 47–49
  SALT and, 44–47, 49
  Soviet military buildup and, 41–43

Directorate of Administration (DA), 32
Directorate of Intelligence (DI), 32, 192, 221, 248, 305, 309, 333, 341, 359, 371, 415, 550
  Carter administration and, 94
  OSS tradition of, 33
  Turner's tenure and, 139–40, 201–2
Directorate of Operations (DO), 94, 144, 147, 158, 221, 248, 305, 395, 417, 424, 544
  Arabian peninsula and, 149–50
  bureaucratic culture of, 32–33, 379–80
  Casey and, 208–13, 256, 364
  Covert Action Staff of, 91–92
  Daniloff case and, 366–67
  double-agent damage to, 18–19
  Gates's criticism of, 309–10
  Howard case and, 364
  Hugel's tenure at, 210–11
  Schlesinger's "purge" of, 42
  Soviet/Eastern Europe (SE) Division of, 91–92
  Turner's "purge" of, 138–39
  Yurchenko defection and, 363
Directorate of Science and Technology (DS&T), 32
Dirks, Les, 562
Dobrynin, Anatoly, 79, 89, 101, 102, 103, 158, 338
Dodd, Christopher, 246
Donovan, William J., 199–200, 217
"Doonesbury" (Trudeau), 454–55
"dual track" decision, 259
Dubcek, Alexander, 23
Duberstein, Ken, 420
Dubinin, Yuri, 424
Dukakis, Michael, 451–52
Dulles, Allen, 30
Dumas, Roland, 489
Durenberger, David, 299, 370

Eagleburger, Lawrence, 453, 463–464, 474, 488, 495, 496, 498, 522, 575
Eastern Europe, 17, 38, 48, 94, 176, 188, 201, 449, 461, 560
  Bush's visit to, 466, 469
  CIA and, 450–51, 469–70
  Helsinki Accords and, 86, 87–89, 175
  Polish crisis and, 164, 237
  Soviet reforms and, 463–64, 468
  Soviet troops in, 461–64
Edelman, Eric, 526
Egypt, 40, 71, 77, 78, 82, 144, 250, 352, 406
Eisenhower, Dwight D., 179, 285, 342, 571
elections:
  of 1960, 30
  of 1968, 23
  of 1974, 58, 64
  of 1976, 69, 89
  of 1980, 72, 152, 175, 190–91, 197, 210, 218, 219, 572
  of 1984, 323, 325, 326
  of 1986, 409–10
  of 1988, 452
  of 1992, 455
Ellsberg, Daniel, 58
El Salvador, 127, 150–51, 152, 178, 242–43, 245–46, 248, 249, 287, 296, 300, 303, 434
  death squads in, 304–5
Enders, Thomas, 298–99
Enger, Valdik, 100, 101, 102, 103
Enhanced Radiation Weapon (ERW), 109–10, 142, 178
Eritrea, 73
Ermarth, Fritz, 43, 424, 503
Estonia, 512–15, 517
Ethiopia, 69, 73–74, 75, 76, 77, 78, 83, 105, 118, 122, 124, 125, 148, 174, 178, 242, 243, 250, 321
European Community, 485
European Strategy Steering Group, 493–94
Evans, Roland, 79
"evil empire" speech, 262–63, 266
Executive Intelligence Review, 217
Export-Import Bank, 228

Falklands War, 297
Federal Bureau of Investigation (FBI), 100, 125–26, 361, 363, 364, 365, 418, 419, 544
"Ferret, the," 54–55
Fiers, Alan, 312, 403, 542, 543, 544, 546

INDEX / 589

Filatov, Anatoliy, 99
Fitzgerald, C. C., 117
Fitzwater, Marlin, 444, 452, 455,
    457, 473, 493
Ford, Gerald, 19, 54, 58, 62, 67, 77,
    82, 95, 96, 98, 111, 174, 192,
    434, 456, 478, 533, 536, 537–
    538, 555, 557, 574
  assessment of, 571–72
  Helsinki Accords and, 86–87, 89
  media and, 572
  Nixon pardoned by, 64
Ford, Harold, 548
Ford administration, 109, 193, 558
Foreign Intelligence Capabilities
    Group, 206–7
Foreign Ministry, Israeli, 396
"40 Committee," 66, 67
France, 23, 32, 183–84, 185, 312,
    359, 462, 483, 485, 487
Free Democratic Party, German,
    184
Free Trade Union (Poland), 162

Gandhi, Indira, 167, 358
"Gang of Eight," 499–500, 529,
    530
Garn, Jake, 308
Geer, Debbie, 217
General Staff, Polish, 233, 235
Geneva summit (1985), 340, 341–42,
    358, 404, 407
  Reagan's briefing for, 343–45
Genscher, Hans-Dietrich, 184, 464
George, Clair, 221, 310, 312, 364,
    368, 379, 543–44
George, Douglas, 260, 287, 371, 546
Georgia, Soviet, 506, 511–12, 513,
    514, 519
German Democratic Republic
    (East), 37, 164, 166, 175, 449,
    482, 484, 485, 492, 493, 560
  Helsinki Accords and, 87–88
  Hungary's open borders and, 467–
    468, 483
  terrorism and, 206
German reunification, 483–90
  Bush's endorsement of, 483–84,
    485, 495
  Gorbachev's opposition to, 484,
    490, 492, 493, 494

Moscow talks on, 489–90
NATO and, 485, 489, 490, 492–
    494
"Two Plus Four" arrangement
    and, 485, 489–90, 493–95
  Washington summit and, 493
Germany, Federal Republic of
    (West), 23, 32, 37, 44, 88, 184,
    185, 261, 262, 467, 483, 485,
    493
  INF deployment and, 280–81
  Soviet terror campaign and, 338–
    339
Germany, Nazi, 213
Ghana, 365
Ghorbanifar, Manucher, 399
Giap, Vo Nguyen, 129
Gierek, Edward, 37, 87, 161, 163
Ginzberg, Aleksandr, 90, 99, 177
Giscard d'Estaing, Valéry, 111–12,
    167, 173, 183, 572
glasnost, 345, 383–84, 385, 389, 438,
    509
Glemp, Archbishop, 235, 236
Glomar Explorer, 553
Goldwater, Barry, 219–20, 298, 301,
    303, 307–8
Gomulka, Wladyslaw, 37
Goodman, Melvin, 547, 548, 549, 551
Gorbachev, Mikhail, 185, 318, 339,
    342, 354, 358, 360, 366, 367,
    378, 404–5, 425, 432, 433, 460,
    461, 462, 466, 485, 491, 503,
    513, 533, 544, 550, 556
  Afghanistan withdrawal and, 431
  Andropov and, 328, 329, 334
  Armenia-Azerbaijan conflict and,
    510
  ascension of, 327–30
  August coup and, 521, 524, 525
  background of, 328–29
  "blind spots" of, 508–9
  Bush administration's support of,
    500–501, 527
  Bush administration's view of,
    473–75
  Bush's relationship with, 475,
    506–7
  Casey's appraisal of, 332–34
  CIA assessments of, 330–34, 385–
    388, 422, 436–37, 514–15

Gorbachev, Mikhail, *continued*
  collapse of Soviet Union and, 384,
    447–48, 508–9, 511, 514–15,
    518–19, 521, 524, 525, 528,
    529, 531, 564
  Communist Party as undermined
    by, 438–40, 447
  "constitutional coup" and, 504–5
  "defensive" doctrine of, 422
  domestic strategy of, 330–31, 340,
    343, 375–76, 381–84
  Eastern Europe policies of, 423,
    449–50, 470–71
  economic reform and, 421, 438–
    439, 441–47, 492, 500–501,
    508–9, 534
  ethnic crisis and, 385, 509–10,
    514–17
  flawed approach of, 388–89, 508–
    509
  foreign policy and, 331–33, 335,
    346, 375–76, 377, 380
  Gates's assessments of, 495–96,
    554–55, 565–66
  Gates's first meeting with, 477–78
  German reunification and, 484,
    490, 492, 493, 494
  glasnost and, 383–84, 385
  Gulf War and, 498–500
  INF and, 381
  Lithuania crisis and, 489–90, 492
  at London Economic Summit, 505
  at Malta conference, 481–83
  1986 Party Congress speech of,
    380
  political right turn of, 518–19, 528
  public adulation of, 384, 438
  Reagan administration debates on
    reforms of, 443–47
  Reagan administration's reaction
    to, 334–35
  Reagan's correspondence with,
    340, 345, 365
  resignation of, 525
  at Reykjavik Summit, 407–9
  Shultz's view of, 334, 335
  Soviet military buildup and, 335–
    336, 381
  Third World policies of, 336–37
  Vilnius trip of, 515
  Yeltsin and, 505–6, 517–18, 535

"Gorbachev, the New Broom"
  (CIA), 331
"Gorbachev: Steering the USSR
  into the 1990s" (CIA), 422
"Gorbachev's Domestic Gambles
  and Instability" (Hodnett), 514
Gordievsky, Oleg, 270, 271, 272,
  362, 477
Gorshkov, Sergei, 129
Graham, Daniel O., 264
Great Britain, 185, 251, 262, 272,
  297, 329–30, 462, 483, 485, 487
  Libya and, 321–22
  Thatcher's emergence in, 183
Greece, 58
Grenada, 174, 277, 354, 558
  covert action and, 143, 151, 178,
    558
  Cuban involvement in, 125–26,
    143, 150
  JCS and, 275
  Reagan and, 275
  U.S. invasion of, 274–76
Gromov, Boris, 432
Gromyko, Andrei, 85, 88, 90, 117,
  159, 185, 189, 283, 324, 329,
  340–41, 440
  Reagan's meeting with, 325
  Shultz's meetings with, 269–70,
    325, 380
"Ground Zero Week," 276
GRU, 271–72, 360
Guadeloupe summit, 111–12
Guatemala, 151, 434
Gulag Archipelago, The
  (Solzhenitsyn), 177
Gulf of Sidra incident, 353
Gulf War, *see* Persian Gulf War

Haass, Richard, 454
Habib, Philip, 434–35
Habre, Hissen, 254
Hadley, Steve, 454, 523
Haig, Alexander, 59, 193, 203, 204,
  219, 238, 242, 245, 251, 253,
  255, 261, 279, 283, 286, 570
  CIA as seen by, 243–44
Haile Selassie, Emperor of Ethiopia,
  73, 83
Haiti, 399
Hamilton, Lee, 452

Hart, Gary, 329
Havel, Vaclav, 470
Helms, Jesse, 371
Helms, Richard, 30–32, 42, 44, 61, 62, 142, 541, 566
Helsinki Accords, 85–89, 161, 484
    détente and, 86, 87
    dissidents and, 87–88, 90, 99
    Eastern Europe and, 86, 87–89, 175
    East Germany and, 87–88
    Ford and, 86–87, 89
    human rights and, 85–86, 88, 90
    Poland and, 87, 88, 175
    Soviet Union and, 88, 90
    U.S. opposition to, 87, 89
Helsinki Declaration, 87, 88, 536, 555, 557
Helsinki Final Act (1975), 95, 96, 161, 177, 485
Helsinki Watch Group, 90, 99, 536
Herres, Robert, 459, 462
Hersh, Seymour, 59, 68
Hewitt, Ed, 502
Hezbollah, 395
High Frontier Project, 264
Hineman, Evan, 224
Hitler-Stalin Pact (1939), 512, 513
Ho Chi Minh, 81
Hodnett, Grey, 185, 514
Honduras, 151, 247, 296, 300, 312, 434
Honecker, Erich, 87, 88, 467
    resignation of, 468
Horelick, Arnold, 76, 78, 92, 131, 132, 145, 148, 158, 159
Horn, Gyula, 467
Hoskinson, Sam, 34
hostage rescue mission, 153–55
"hostile presence" issue, 360–61, 368
House of Representatives, U.S., 151, 297, 301, 303, 314, 339, 420
    Appropriations Committee of, 320
    Intelligence Committee of, 217, 245, 246–47, 254, 298, 299–300, 306, 307, 311, 416, 563
Howard, Edward Lee, 363–64, 365, 370
Hugel, Max, 210–11, 214, 221

human rights, 99, 161, 177, 178, 269, 289, 560
    Carter and, 89–91, 94, 95–96, 536, 555–58
    Helsinki Accords and, 85–86, 88, 90
    Soviet Union and, 85–96
    U.S. anti-Soviet propaganda campaign and, 90–94
Hungary, 449, 451, 464, 465, 466, 470
    borders opened by, 467–68, 483
    communism deposed in, 467
Hunt, Howard, 58
Hunt for Red October, The (Clancy), 107
Husak, Gustav, 469
Hussein, Saddam, 480, 497, 498, 500, 502
Hyland, William, 55, 85–86, 87, 90, 98

Iacocca, Lee, 329
Iklé, Fred, 350, 352
Ilichev, Leonid F., 81
Inderfurth, Rick, 136
Indo-Pakistan War (1971), 40, 43
inflation, 172
Inman, B. R., 133, 158, 192, 203, 215, 221, 222, 223, 224, 225, 244, 246, 249, 293, 294
    Casey and, 219–20
Intelligence Oversight Board, 310
Intermediate Nuclear Forces (INF), 112, 236, 270, 271, 273, 274, 276, 277, 289, 324, 325, 339, 357, 399, 408, 409, 421, 422, 556
    allied deployments and, 262, 280–281
    Gorbachev and, 381
    NATO and, 177–78, 259–60, 261, 262
    NSC and, 260
    peace movement and, 260–61
    Reagan's zero-zero proposal and, 280
    Shultz and, 259–60, 262, 280–81
    signing of, 423
    Soviet covert operations against, 260–61
    Washington Summit and, 423

Internal Affairs Ministry, Soviet, 510, 512, 515, 519, 524
Iowa, 455
Iran, 35, 116, 118, 122–23, 128–31, 147–48, 175, 196, 197, 239, 251, 252, 287, 351, 352, 410, 415, 451, 515, 568
  hostage rescue mission and, 153–155
Iran-Contra affair, 62, 199, 311, 315, 390–403, 435
  aftermath of, 420–21
  Casey's role in, 400–403
  Contras funding and, 392–94
  Gates's DCI nomination and, 541–45
  Gates's testimony in, 415–17
  Israel and, 395–97
  media and, 393, 415–16
  North's testimony on, 402–3
  NSC and, 400, 401
  public disclosure of, 410
  Reagan and, 392, 396, 397, 420, 421
  Shultz and, 420–21
Iran-Contra Committee, *see* Senate Intelligence Committee
Iraq, 239, 287, 349, 415, 497–99, 528
Isma'il, Abd-Al-Fattah, 149–50
Israel, 82, 239, 250, 274, 311, 312, 365, 391
  arms-to-Iran affair and, 395–96
Italy, 32, 241, 280–81, 354
Izvestia, 101–2

Jackson, Henry M., 87
Jacobs, Eli, 545
Jakes, Milos, 469
Jallud, Abdul Salam, 77
Jamaica, 175, 178
Japan, 176, 270, 359
Jaruzelski, Wojciech, 229, 230, 232, 233, 234–36, 238, 450, 465, 466
Javits, Jacob, 157
Jeremiah, David, 459
John Paul II, Pope, 96, 167, 232, 358, 451, 470
  attempted assassination of, 239–241, 354–56

Johnson, Lyndon B., 19, 23, 31, 36, 57, 58, 397, 538, 566, 567, 571
Johnson administration, 105–6, 557
Joint Chiefs of Staff (JCS), 167, 284, 353, 457, 460, 462, 463, 559
  Grenada operation and, 275
Joint Congressional Iran-Contra Committee, 402
Joint Economic Committee (JEC), 184, 385–86
Jones, David, 75, 167
Jordan, 40, 82
Jordan, Hamilton, 119
Juchniewicz, Ed, 309
Justice Department, U.S., 215, 312

KAL-007 shoot-down, 266–70, 274, 283
  Shultz-Gromyko meeting and, 269–70
Kampiles, William, 361
Kania, Stanislaw, 163, 165, 168, 226, 229, 230, 232, 233, 234–35
Kantor, Arnold, 502
Karmal, Babrak, 381, 430
Kaunda, Kenneth, 67
Kelly, Jim, 310
Kemp, Jack, 456–57
Kennan, George, 575
Kennedy, John F., 28, 30, 198
Kennedy, Robert F., 23
Kenya, 74
Kerr, Richard, 380, 386, 387, 446, 458–59, 523, 551
KGB, 22–23, 93, 99, 100, 102, 110, 114, 116–17, 133, 186, 188, 190, 203, 206, 230, 272, 357–58, 382, 439, 469, 497, 517, 554
  August coup and, 522, 524
  CIA's "spy wars" competition with, 16–19, 361–65
  perestroika and, 476–77
  RYAN program of, 270–71
  "spy dust" affair and, 368–69
  Washington summit and, 423–26
Khmer Rouge, 60, 65, 255
Khomeini, Ayatollah, 128, 132, 217
Khrushchev, Nikita, 328
Kimche, David, 395–96
King, Martin Luther, Jr., 23
Kirkland, Lane, 164, 237, 300

Kirkpatrick, Jeane, 219, 249, 268, 281–82, 295, 312
Kissinger, Henry, 29, 30, 32, 33, 39, 40, 41, 44, 47, 48, 49, 55, 57, 67, 70, 71, 72, 82, 85, 87, 95, 98, 121, 129, 192, 193, 274, 434, 448, 541, 570, 571
Kissinger Commission, 303
Koecher, Karl, 361
Kohl, Helmut, 184, 464, 484, 487, 488, 489, 492, 494, 495
Kolbin, Gennady, 385
Kolt, George, 185, 503
Komplektov, Viktor, 522
Koppel, Ted, 155
Korea, Democratic People's Republic of (North), 22, 568
Korea, Republic of (South), 110
Korniyenko, Georgi, 102
Kosygin, Aleksei, 35, 37, 38, 79, 80, 176
Kravchuk, Leonid M., 525
Krenz, Egon, 468
Kroesen, Frederick, 206
Kryuchkov, Vladimir, 424–26, 476–477, 491, 505, 554
Kudirka, Simas, 558
Kuklinski, Ryszard, 227, 229, 230, 231, 234–35, 238, 239
Kulikov, Victor G., 233, 234, 236
Kunayev, Dinmukhamed, 385
Kuwait, 497, 499
Kvitsinskiy, Yuli, 259

La Belle Disco bombing, 353, 405
Laird, Melvin, 29, 30, 31, 46–47, 570
Lam Song 719 operation, 31
Landsbergis, Vytautas, 517
Laos, 31
Lapham, Tony, 103
LaRouche, Lyndon, 217
Latvia, 512–15, 517, 519, 524
"Lawless" (case officer), 212
Lawrence, T. E., 304
Leahy, Patrick, 298, 307, 360, 370–371
Lebanon, 78, 242, 277, 283, 287, 289, 391, 395, 396
LeMay, Curtis, 20
Lenin, V. I., 330, 382, 384

Libya, 80, 174, 201, 239, 250, 256, 399, 407, 558, 560
    Casey and, 254–55, 351, 353
    Great Britain and, 321–22
    Gulf of Sidra incident and, 353
    NSC and, 352–53
    Reagan administration and, 351–352, 405–6
    Reagan and, 353–54
    terrorism and, 253, 255, 351–54
    U.S. raid on, 354, 378
Lindsay, Frank, 224
linkage, détente and, 39, 44, 48
Lippmann, Walter, 96
Lithuania, 239, 489, 492, 512–15, 516–17, 518, 519, 527–28, 529
London Economic Summit, 505
Lon Nol, 30
Lumumba, Patrice, 59
Luns, Joseph, 261

McCloy, John J., 566
McCone, John, 198
McCrory, Ray, 371
McCullough, Jim, 410
MacEachin, Doug, 386
McFarlane, Bud, 285, 311, 312, 313, 314, 315, 333, 339, 352, 355, 391, 395, 396–97, 399, 402, 403
McMahon, John, 138, 192, 204, 212, 218, 220–21, 224, 244, 246, 249, 289, 293, 294, 299, 304, 305, 308, 314, 322, 349, 350, 353, 378, 396, 397, 399, 415, 416–17
Madrid conference (1991), 505
Malaysia, 312
Malta conference, 481–83
Manley, Michael, 151, 528
Mansfield Amendment, 47
Mao Zedong, 35, 36, 80–81, 174
Mariam, Mengistu Haile, 73
Masood (Mujahedin leader), 429
Matlock, Jack, 342, 376, 504–5
Mayaguez, 60, 558
media, 40, 211, 244, 319, 375, 421, 460
    August coup and, 521, 523
    Bush's Eastern Europe trip and, 466–67
    Casey and, 213, 214–15
    CIA and, 59–60

media, *continued*
    Ford and, 572
    Gates's DCI nomination and, 544
    Iran-Contra affair and, 393, 415–416
    MUTS issue and, 98
    Nicaragua mining operation and, 307
    Reykjavik summit and, 408
    SDI and, 342
    Soviet brigade in Cuba fiasco and, 155, 158
    Soviet campaign against, 99–100
    Vietnam War and, 57
    Washington summit and, 423
Meese, Edwin, 193, 219, 390, 391, 402, 413
Metzenbaum, Howard, 548, 551
Mexico, 299, 302
Middle East, 76, 201, 256, 340, 538
    Camp David Accords and, 82–83
    Casey's memorandum on, 250–51
    détente and, 39–41, 43, 49
    SA-5 missiles episode and, 274, 277, 289
    Soviet Union and, 82–83
    see also specific countries
Miller, Richard, 361
Mitterrand, François, 183–84, 359, 463, 464, 469, 488, 489, 521
Mobutu, Joseph, 67
Moiseyev, Mikhail, 502
Moldavia, 514, 515, 518, 519
Mondale, Walter, 72, 75, 121, 136, 141, 156
Morocco, 250, 312
Molotov, V. M., 358
Moreau, Art, 275, 352
Moscow Unidentified Technical Signal (MUTS), 97–98
Moseman, John, 545
Moskowitz, Stan, 545, 547
Movement in Defense of Human and Citizen Rights, 87, 161
Moynihan, Daniel Patrick, 247, 298, 299, 307, 308, 552
Mozambique, 174, 254, 337
MPLA (Popular Movement for the Liberation of Angola), 65, 66–67, 68, 347, 348, 433, 434
Mubarak, Hosni, 406

"murder manual," 310–11
Murkowski, Frank, 545
Muskie, Edmund, 141, 166, 242

Nagorno-Karabakh, 509–10
Najibullah, Mohammed, 381, 423, 430, 431, 432
Namibia, 254, 433
National Association of Evangelicals, 262–63
National Defense Council, 230
National Foreign Assessment Center, 138, 139
National Front for the Liberation of Angola (FNLA), 65, 66, 67–68
National Intelligence Council (NIC), 184, 192, 248, 314, 315, 324, 333, 341, 447, 511
    mining operation and, 306–10
National Intelligence Daily (CIA), 41, 509
National Military Command Center (NMCC), 114
National Security Agency (NSA), 133, 155, 220, 365
National Security Council (NSC), 17, 53, 55, 94, 125, 143, 146, 147, 220, 229, 249, 267, 280, 282, 289, 293, 296, 306, 312, 313, 322, 324, 342, 347, 360, 405, 417, 445, 465, 486, 537
    arms-for-hostages deal and, 391, 392, 398, 399
    Deputies Committee of, 458–59, 494, 522, 523
    40 Committee of, 66, 67
    INF and, 260
    Iran-Contra affair and, 400, 401
    Libya operation and, 352–53
    Poland meeting of, 167–68
    Reagan administration and, 193, 283–85
National Security Decision Directive 166, 349
National Union for the Total Independence of Angola (UNITA), 65–68, 175, 346–47, 433, 434
Nazarbayev, Nursultan, 501
Netherlands, 261, 262, 280–81
Neto, Angostinho, 65, 66

neutron bomb, 110, 142, 260
New Caledonia, 256
Newsom, David, 144, 156, 157, 227
Newsweek, 298
New York Times, 59, 68, 87, 99–100,
   102, 268, 298, 306, 481, 528
Nicaragua, 72, 174, 175, 178, 201,
   205–8, 256, 293–94, 295, 296,
   302, 304, 336, 376, 381, 393,
   394, 398, 445, 482, 538, 560,
   565, 575
   Arias plan and, 434–35
   Boland Amendments and, 247,
     298, 299–300, 310, 313, 392
   Casey's covert action proposal for,
     242–43
   cease fire in, 434–35
   Central American insurgencies
     and, 244–46
   Congress and, 246, 247, 248, 249
   Cuban involvement in, 126–28,
     150–52, 242, 336–37
   Grenada operation and, 275–76
   mining operation and, 306–8
   1990 election in, 436
   Patora and, 245–46
   Reagan and, 242–43, 332
   see also Contras
Nicholson Arthur D., 338
Nigeria, 321
Nikolaev, C. G., 235
"Nine Plus One" meeting, 540
Nitze, Paul, 40–41, 259, 377, 408
Nixon, Richard M., 19, 23, 27, 28,
   36, 39, 40, 41, 46, 56, 57, 58,
   62, 72, 82, 95, 111, 121, 173,
   174, 191, 192, 224, 397, 533,
   535, 537, 538, 555, 557, 558,
   566, 572
   ABM treaty and, 37
   assessment of, 571
   CIA disdained by, 30–33
   détente and, 29–30, 46, 47–49
   Ford's pardon of, 64
   Gromyko's recollection of, 85
   Moscow visit of, 504
   resignation of, 53
   Soviet-German relations and, 44
   U.S.-Soviet relationship and, 29–
     30, 85
   Yeltsin's meeting with, 504

Nixon administration, 30, 106, 193
North, Oliver, 311, 313, 315, 352,
   392, 393, 398, 415, 543
   Iran-Contra testimony of, 402–3
North American Air Defense
   Command (NORAD), 114
North Atlantic Treaty Organization
   (NATO), 101, 111, 112, 113,
   114, 270, 299, 528, 538
   Able Archer exercise and, 271–72,
     273
   CFE debates and, 486–87
   "dual track" decision and, 259
   German reunification and, 485,
     489, 490, 492–94
   INF and, 177–78, 259–60, 261,
     262
   modernization of, 177–78
   Polish crisis and, 227–28, 231, 236
Norway, 262
Novak, Robert, 79
Novotny, Antonin, 23
nuclear freeze movement, 263, 276–
   277
Nunn, Sam, 386, 548, 550, 551

Odom, William, 114, 117
Office of Congressional Affairs, 415
Office of Management and Budget,
   47
Office of Soviet Analysis (SOVA),
   203, 205, 387, 422
Office of Strategic Services (OSS),
   32, 199–200, 201
Ogorodnik ("Trigon"), 103
Oliver, Kay, 185
   Reagan briefed by, 343–44, 345
Olszowski, Stefan, 235
Olympic Games:
   of 1980, 147
   of 1984, 326
Oman, 150, 250, 254
O'Neill, Thomas P. "Tip," 157, 314
Organization of Eastern Caribbean
   States, 275
Orlov, Yuri, 90, 366
Ortega, Daniel, 332, 436

Pakistan, 144, 146, 148, 149, 175,
   250, 251, 252, 287, 320, 350,
   428, 429, 432

Palestine Liberation Organization (PLO), 243
Panama, 127, 244, 294, 299, 300, 302, 454, 459
Panama Canal Treaties, 572
Pastor, Robert, 125
Pastora, Eden, 245–46, 247, 297
Pavlov, Valentin, 502, 504, 505
peace movement, 260–61
"Peace Program," 38
Pelton, Ronald W., 365
Pentagon Papers, 58
perestroika, 384, 388, 424–25, 443, 471, 476–77, 491, 509
Perle, Richard, 376
Pershing II ballistic missile, 259, 262, 538
Persian Gulf War, 113, 454, 497–500, 528, 531
Persico, Joseph, 199
Pforzheimer, Walter, 191
Philippines, 370, 399, 434, 445
Pienkowski, Jerzy, 229
Pike committee, 60
Piper, Harold, 99–100
Poindexter, John, 312, 352, 353, 367, 376, 378, 399, 401, 402, 415, 420
Poland, 37, 86, 92, 162–68, 242, 256, 343, 449, 450–51, 464, 493, 560
  Bush's visit to, 466, 470
  CIA propaganda actions and, 358–359
  communism deposed in, 465–66, 467
  Helsinki Accords and, 87, 88, 175
  1980–81 crisis in, see Polish crisis of 1980–81
  NSC meeting on, 167–68
Policy Review Committee, 75
Polisario Front, 254
Polish crisis of 1980–81, 226–41
  attempted assassination of Pope and, 239–41
  Brzezinski and, 163, 164–67
  Cardinal Wyszynski episode and, 232–33
  Casey and, 229, 231–32, 233, 237, 238, 241

  CIA assessment of, 231–32
  CIA in aftermath of, 236–38
  Eastern Europe and, 164, 237
  martial law implementation and, 236–37, 238, 259
  martial law threat and, 229, 230–231, 233, 234, 235
  NATO and, 227–28, 231, 236
  Reagan administration and, 227, 228, 230
  Rural Solidarity incident and, 229–30, 231
  Solidarity and, see Solidarity
  threat of Soviet intervention and, 226–29, 230, 231, 233, 234–235
  Turner and, 162–65, 166, 167, 168–69
  U.S. contingency planning and, 227–28
Pollard, Jonathan, 365
Pol Pot, 255
Popov, Gavril, 504
Popular Front for Perestroika (RUKH), 514
Popular Fronts, 513–14, 515, 516
Popular Movement for the Liberation of Angola (MPLA), 65, 66–67, 68, 347, 348, 433, 434
Portugal, 65, 66, 67, 138
Popieliusko, Father, 358
Potemkin, Father, 366, 368
Powell, Colin, 420, 424–25, 432, 435, 444, 453, 457, 458, 461, 486, 487, 488, 493–94, 498, 510, 530, 574
Powell, Jody, 113, 119
Pravda, 234
President's Daily Brief, 30, 73, 267, 268, 290, 333, 337, 340, 422, 521, 527
President's Foreign Intelligence Advisory Board (PFIAB), 273, 355, 364
Primakov, Yevgeniy, 502–3
Prime, Geoffrey, 23
Prunskiene, Kazimera, 527–28
Pueblo, 22
Pugo, Boris, 505, 519

Qaddafi, Muammar al-, 77, 129, 212, 217, 253–55, 321–22, 351, 353–354, 406, 560
Quadripartite Agreement (1971), 44
Quayle, Dan, 453, 479, 486

Radio Free Europe, 94
Radio Liberty, 94
Radio Solidarity, 451
Rakowski, Mieczyslaw F., 467
Ramparts, 35
Rapid Deployment Force (RDF), 113
Reagan, Nancy, 219, 282, 413, 421, 573
Reagan, Ronald, 80, 87, 166, 183, 188, 210, 213, 216, 239, 244, 249, 253, 271, 277, 291, 303, 323, 324, 331, 333, 334, 358, 362, 366, 367, 378, 410, 414, 444, 456, 474, 533, 538, 567, 571
    arms-for-hostages deal and, 392, 396, 397
    assessment of, 537, 556, 573, 574
    Carter's policies as continued by, 113, 115, 177, 178, 179, 557–58
    Casey appointed by, 192–93
    Casey's relationship with, 218–19
    Central America and, 242, 243, 297, 301–2
    Clark's view of, 281–82
    Contra funding and, 242–43, 245
    Doctrine of, 256, 339
    election of, 190–91
    "evil empire" speech of, 262–63, 266
    foreign policy practice of, 194
    Geneva Summit briefing of, 343–345
    Gorbachev's correspondence with, 340, 345, 365
    Grenada operation and, 275
    Gromyko's meeting with, 325
    INF and, 280
    Iran-Contra and, 392, 396, 397, 420, 421
    KAL shoot-down and, 268, 269
    KGB officers expelled by, 368
    Libya raid and, 353–54
    Nicaragua and, 242–43, 332
    Oliver's briefing of, 343–45
    at Reykjavik Summit, 407–9
    Shultz's relationship with, 279, 281–82, 292
    Shultz's Soviet agenda and, 288–289
    Soviet grain embargo lifted by, 328
    Webster nominated DCI by, 418–419
    zero-zero proposal of, 280
Reagan administration, 94, 153, 289, 297, 311, 339, 537, 539
    Carter administration as seen by, 195–96
    Central America and, 151, 243, 244, 294–95
    CIA as perceived by, 191–92
    debate on Gorbachev's reforms in, 443–47
    Gorbachev assessed by, 334–35
    Libya and, 351–52, 405–6
    NSC and, 193, 283–85
    peace movement and, 261–62
    Polish crisis and, 227, 228, 230
    position of National Security Adviser in, 193, 283–85
    Soviet perception of, 290–91
    Soviet succession and, 188
    transition period and, 191–94
Reagan Doctrine, 256, 339
Red Army Faction, 204, 206
Regan, Don, 219, 367, 378, 396, 411, 413, 414, 420
"Report on International Broadcasting" (Carter administration), 94
Republican Party, U.S., 190, 214, 298, 409–10, 417, 420, 558
Research Institute of America, 200
Reykjavik Summit (1986), 404, 407–409, 421
Rhodes, John, 157, 167–68
Rhodesia, 76
Ribbentrop, Joachim von, 358
Rice, Condoleezza "Condi," 454, 460–61, 472, 478, 479, 491, 494, 495, 499, 501, 526, 528
Roberto, Holden, 65, 66, 68
Rockefeller, David, 128
Rogers, Will, 302

Rogers, William, 30, 570
Romania, 23, 86, 164, 252, 469, 470, 515
Romanov, Grigory, 185, 328
Romero, Archbishop, 305
Roosevelt, Franklin D., 574
Ross, Dennis, 454, 460–61, 480, 485, 490, 494, 497, 526
Rowen, Henry "Harry," 184, 201, 208, 387
Rudman, Warren, 551
RUKH (Popular Front for Perestroika), 514
Rumsfeld, Don, 377
Rural Solidarity, 229–30, 231
Russia, 440, 491, 524, 525, 555
    sovereignty declared by, 518
Rust, Mathias, 421–22
"RYAN" program, 270–71

Sadat, Anwar, 41, 71, 239
SA-5 missiles, 274, 277, 289
Saiudis Popular Front, 513
Sakharov, Andrei, 90, 95, 536
SALT (Strategic Arms Limitation Talks), 39, 40, 60, 72, 74, 86, 123, 124, 557
    détente and, 44–47, 49
    Senate and, 115, 116, 155–56
SALT II, 101, 103, 109, 339, 407
    Carter and, 115–17
    Senate and, 175
    Soviet brigade in Cuba fiasco and, 155–56, 157, 160
    telemetry encryption issue and, 115–16
    Vienna summit and, 116–17
"San Jose Principles," 302–3
Saudi Arabia, 74, 144, 148, 149, 150, 175, 251, 311, 321, 348, 391
Savimbi, Jonas, 66, 68, 175, 336, 339, 346, 347, 433, 434
Sayyaf, Abdul Rasul, 349
Schlesinger, James, 34, 59, 81, 333, 570
    CIA "purged" by, 42–43, 61, 62, 63, 142
Schmidt, Helmut, 88, 110, 111, 167, 173, 174, 184, 572
Schneider, Mark, 191
Schorr, Daniel, 59–60

Scowcroft, Brent, 55, 62, 98, 284, 377, 453, 454, 455, 456, 460, 464, 469, 474, 475, 480, 486, 493–94, 495, 497, 499, 506, 521, 522, 523, 528, 530, 541, 542, 545, 570, 574
    assessment of, 457–58
    CFE and, 461–62, 487–88
    CIA as viewed by, 503–4
    on Soviet collapse, 501–2
    troop cuts proposal of, 461–62
    Yeltsin's visit to, 478–79
Scranage, Sharon, 365
Secord, Richard, 402
Secret Intelligence Service, British, 362
Secret Service, U.S., 472–73
Select Committee to Study Governmental Operations with Respect to Intelligence Activities, 59
Senate, U.S., 68, 190, 199, 247, 369–370, 393, 409–10, 420, 434
    Appropriations Committee of, 59
    Armed Services Committee of, 59
    Contra funding and, 312
    defense budget and, 175
    Foreign Relations Committee of, 156, 298–99
    Gulf War and, 499
    Intelligence Committee of, see Senate Intelligence Committee
    MX missile deployment approved by, 339
    Nicaraguan mining operation and, 306–7, 308
    SALT and, 115, 116, 155–56
    SALT II and, 175
    Trident vote in, 106
Senate Intelligence Committee, 191, 241, 360, 410
    Carter's Grenada finding and, 143, 274
    Contras and, 298–301, 303
    Gates's DDCI nomination and, 378
    Gates's first DCI hearings and, 417–18
    Gates's Iran-Contra role and, 415–18, 543–44

Gates's second DCI hearings and, 545–52
mining operation and, 306–7, 308
spy wars and, 370–71
Seven Pillars of Wisdom, The (Lawrence), 304
Shcharansky, Anatoliy, 90, 99, 102, 103, 177, 380–81
Shcherbakov, Vladimir, 502–3
Shevardnadze, Eduard, 340, 345, 366, 367, 405, 407, 423, 432, 433, 434, 489, 493, 499
 Baker and, 475–76, 479–80, 496, 497, 529
 Gates and, 490–91
 resignation of, 519
 Shultz's meetings with, 341, 342, 430, 435, 475
 Wyoming talks and, 479–80
Shevchenko, Arkady, 68–69
Shipler, David, 99
Shmelyov, Nikolai, 480
Shulman, Marshall, 156
Shultz, George, 202, 238, 241, 242, 247, 249, 274, 276, 277, 298, 300, 332, 333, 338, 339, 343, 345, 346, 348, 352, 357, 387, 399, 405, 407, 421, 431, 434, 437, 443, 446, 460, 570
 administration foes of, 283–85
 Afghan conflict and, 432
 Andropov's meeting with, 188–89
 Angola conflict and, 433
 arms deal and, 396, 400
 Cambodia and, 322
 Casey's relationship with, 219, 280, 286–87, 289, 301–3, 353, 365, 398, 410, 428
 Central America operations and, 295, 296, 301–4
 CIA disdained by, 287–88, 337, 381–82, 409, 422, 444, 567
 Clark and, 283–84, 285, 289, 296–297
 Contadora Forum and, 302–3
 Daniloff episode and, 366, 367
 foreign policy and, 323–24
 Gates and, 289–92, 377–78
 Gorbachev as seen by, 334, 335
 Gromyko's meetings with, 269–270, 325, 380
 hostile presence issue and, 360–61
 INF and, 259–60, 262, 280–81
 Iran-Contra affair and, 420–21
 KAL shoot-down and, 267, 268–270
 Libya and, 351, 353
 personality and character of, 278–280
 Reagan's relationship with, 279, 281–82, 292
 Reykjavik summit and, 408–9
 San Jose principles and, 302–3
 Shevardnadze's meetings with, 341, 342, 430, 435, 475
 Soviet gas pipeline issue and, 280, 283
 steering group created by, 376–77
 U.S.-Soviet relationship and, 280–281, 288–92
Shushkevich, Stanislau S., 525
Singapore, 312
Siwicki, General, 233, 234
Sixth Fleet, U.S., 253, 405–6
Slocombe, Walt, 92, 144–45
Social Democratic Party, German, 184
Socialist Workers Party, Hungarian, 467
Solidarity, 37, 162, 165, 168, 175, 231, 235, 238, 239, 358, 359
 Cardinal Wyszynski episode and, 232–33
 CIA and, 450–51
 implementation of martial law and, 236–37
 legalization of, 465
 Rural Solidarity incident and, 229–30
 strike moratorium of, 226–27
Solzhenitsyn, Alexander, 177, 478, 536
Somalia, 73, 78, 250, 254
Somoza, Anastasio, 72, 126, 245
Sonnenfelt, Helmut "Hal," 55
South Africa, 66, 175, 336, 347, 400, 433
SOVA (Office of Soviet Analysis), 203, 205, 387, 422
"Soviet Acquisition of Militarily Significant Western Technology" (CIA), 359

Soviet/Eastern Europe (SE) Division, 91–92
"Soviet Forces for Intercontinental Conflict Through the Mid-1980s" (National Intelligence Estimate 11–3/8–76), 106–7, 108
"Soviet Goals and Expectations in the Global Power Arena" (national intelligence estimate), 74–75, 171–72
"Soviet Options in Southwest Asia after the Invasion of Afghanistan" (Turner), 147–48
"Soviet Presence in the UN Secretariat, The" (CIA), 360
"Soviet Role in Revolutionary Violence, The" (national intelligence estimate), 205–6
"Soviet Strategic Programs and Détente: What Are They Up To?" (Special National Intelligence Estimate 11-4-73), 43
Soviet Union, 22, 58, 173, 250, 251, 287
    Able Archer exercise and, 271–73
    ABM and, 37–38, 265
    Afghanistan campaign of, 144–48, 149, 252, 348, 350
    Afghanistan invaded by, 118, 133, 147
    Afghanistan withdrawal of, 428–432
    Alma-Ata riots in, 385
    Angola conflict and, 65–69
    anti-media campaign of, 99–100
    August coup in, 521–24, 529, 535
    Carter as perceived by, 178–79
    Central America strategy of, 152–153, 158–60
    China's border clashes with, 35–36
    CIA's performance against, 562–563
    Cold War as lost by, 533–40
    collapse of, see Soviet Union, collapse of
    Communist Party of, see Communist Party, Soviet Union
    "constitutional coup" and, 504–5
    corruption and malaise in, 188
    Cuba as proxy of, 66, 68, 73–74, 75, 77–80, 83, 124
    Cuban brigade fiasco and, 158–160
    Czechoslovakia invaded by, 23, 37
    "defensive" doctrine of, 422
    détente and, 39, 49–50
    dissidents in, 90–96, 99–100
    domestic affairs of, 330–31, 343–345
    double-agent reporting and, 16–19, 361–65
    economy of, 36–37, 116, 173, 177, 184–85, 187, 190, 194–95, 266, 317–19, 327–28, 381–84, 386, 502–3, 533–35
    Ethiopia conflict and, 73–74
    ethnic unrest in, 93–94, 385
    first free election in, 439
    gas pipeline of, 280, 283
    Gates's assessments of, 176, 289–291
    glasnost and, 383–84, 385
    Gorbachev's failed reforms and, 441–43
    Gorbachev's structural changes and, 438–40
    Grenada operation and, 276
    Gulf War and, 497–500, 528
    Helsinki Accords and, 88, 90
    hostile presence issue, 360–61
    human rights issue and, 85–96
    INF opposed by, 260–61
    Iranian revolution and, 130–31
    KAL shoot-down and, 266–70
    leadership succession in, 185–88, 329
    Middle East and, 82–83
    military buildup of, 28–29, 41–43, 170–72, 187, 335–36, 381
    papal assassination plot and, 239–240, 354–56
    "Peace Program" of, 38
    Polish crisis and, 163–67, 226–29, 230, 231, 233, 234–35
    Reagan administration as seen by, 290–91
    Reagan's military buildup and, 194–96, 197
    Rust airplane episode and, 421–22

RYAN program of, 270–71
SA-5 missile episode and, 274
Salvadoran insurgency and, 243
SDI impact on, 264–66, 539
Sino-Japanese treaty and, 113
Sino-Vietnamese conflict and,
    121–22
spy crisis and, 99–104
Stalinist legacy of, 381
Syria and, 274
terrorism and, 338–39, 565
United Nations and, 359–60
U.S.-China relationship and, 80–
    82
U.S. Congress and, 558–59
U.S. continuity and bipartisanship
    and, 556–58
U.S. feared by, 288–89
U.S. human rights campaign and,
    90–96
U.S. military buildup and, 194–
    196, 197
U.S. as perceived by, 113–14,
    339–40
U.S. radio campaign against, 94–
    95
Vietnam War and, 28, 39, 48, 65
war scare in, 271–73
Western influence on, 535–36
West Germany and, 44
Soviet Union, collapse of, 508–31
    Armenia-Azerbaijan conflict and,
        509–11, 514–15, 519
    August coup and, 521–24, 529
    Baltic States and, 512–17, 518,
        519, 524
    Bush-Yeltsin phone call and, 523
    CIA warnings of, 510–11, 514–15,
        518, 519–20, 526
    Congress of People's Deputies
        and, 516, 519
    final act of, 525
    Georgia and, 511–12, 513, 514,
        519
    Gorbachev and, 384, 447–48,
        508–9, 511, 514–15, 518–19,
        521, 524, 525, 528, 529, 531,
        564
    human chain episode and, 513
    Moldavia and, 514, 515, 518, 519
    perestroika and, 510, 513

Popular Fronts and, 513–14, 515,
    516
Russia and, 440, 518, 524, 525,
    555
Ukraine and, 516, 518, 519, 520,
    524, 525, 531
Union Treaty and, 518, 529
U.S. role in, 525–31
"war of the laws" and, 518
Yeltsin and, 516, 517–18, 519, 529
Yeltsin's countercoup and, 522–
    524, 525, 529
Soyuz, Exercise, 240
Spain, 477
Special Coordinating Committee,
    79, 91, 92, 93, 116, 126–27,
    142, 144, 163, 167
Sporkin, Stanley, 218, 313
"spy dust" affair, 368–69
SR-71 program, 138
SS-20 ballistic missile, 259, 262
Stalin, Joseph, 190, 233, 290, 330,
    382, 389, 511–12
START, 270, 291, 324, 325, 377,
    409, 423, 480, 482, 505
Stasi intelligence service, 206
State Department, U.S., 33, 40, 56,
    67, 76, 91, 92, 93–94, 125, 127,
    128–29, 131, 145, 146, 150,
    151, 164, 167, 193, 227, 255,
    280, 293, 301, 313, 314, 321,
    322, 334, 340, 348, 359, 360,
    375, 400, 425, 457, 486, 509
    bugged embassy episode and,
        100–101
    and Soviet brigade in Cuba fiasco,
        156–57
State Planning Commission
    (Gosplan), 230
Stein, John, 207, 211, 212, 221, 241,
    244, 246, 294, 305
    Gates's criticism of, 309–10
Stevens, Sayre, 138
Stinger antiaircraft missile, 347,
    349–50, 429, 430, 561
Stoertz, Howard, 44
Stoessel, Walter, 98
Stokes, Louis, 452
Stombaugh, Paul, 362
Stone, Richard, 156, 157
Stoph, Willi, 468

Strategic Defense Initiative (SDI), 38, 262–66, 274, 276, 277, 357, 377, 404, 421, 480, 539, 556, 569
  ABM Treaty and, 264, 265, 339
  Congress and, 342, 343
  media and, 342
  Reykjavik summit and, 407–9
  Soviet fear of, 264–65, 539
Strauss, Robert, 72
Strike Command, U.S., 113
Sudan, 74, 77, 78, 250, 254, 321, 322
Sununu, John, 453, 454, 456, 486, 498
Suriname, 256
Suslov, Mikhail, 185–86, 328, 329
Symms, Steve, 371
Syria, 83, 250, 274, 277, 289, 349, 351, 352

Taft, Will, 353, 406
Taiwan, 312
Taraki, Nur Mohammad, 131, 132, 143, 145
Tarnoff, Peter, 125
telemetry encryption, 115–16
Telschik, Horst, 464, 492
Tenet, George, 545
terrorism, 203, 204–7
  East Germany and, 206
  Libya and, 253, 255, 351–54
  Soviet Union and, 338–39, 565
  in West Germany, 338–39
Thailand, 312
Thatcher, Margaret, 173, 183, 190, 307, 329–30, 469, 485, 488, 494, 517, 527
  CFE proposal and, 463–64
"Thinking About the Unthinkable: Instability and Turbulence in the USSR" (Gates), 526
Tiananmen Square demonstrations, 465
Tocqueville, Alexis de, 438–39
Tokyo economic summit, 126
Tolkachev, Adolf, 362
Toon, Malcolm, 79
Tower Board, 416
Treasury Department, U.S., 465
Trudeau, Garry, 454
Trujillo Molina, Rafael, 59

Truman, Harry S., 95, 178, 532, 572
Tsvigun, Semion, 186
Tunisia, 250
Turkey, 58, 60
Turner, Stansfield, 69, 70, 75, 78, 91, 100, 103, 116, 124, 126, 127, 128, 151, 152, 154, 171, 176, 191, 192, 198, 201–2, 222, 242, 541
  Afghan conflict and, 131, 132–33, 143, 145, 146, 147–48, 149
  Brzezinski and, 140–42
  Carter's relationship with, 141–142
  CIA under, 135–38
  DI and, 139–40, 201–2
  DO and, 138–39
  Polish crisis and, 162–64, 166, 167, 168–69
  secret China visit by, 123
  Soviet brigade in Cuba fiasco and, 155–56, 158, 159
  Soviet economy described by, 173–74
Tutwiler, Margaret, 490
"Two Plus Four" arrangement, 485, 489–90, 493–95

Uganda, 77
Ukraine, 91, 239, 516, 518, 535
  Bush's visit to, 506
  Popular Front of, 514
Union Treaty, 518, 529
UNITA (National Union for the Total Independence of Angola), 65–68, 175, 346–47, 433, 434
United Kingdom, 184, 261
United Nations, 146, 219, 268, 324, 325, 365, 422, 450
  Gulf War and, 498, 499
  KAL shootdown and, 269
  Soviet covert activities and, 359–360
United Press International, 98
"United States Global Presence" (Presidential Review Memorandum 43), 75–76
U.S. News and World Report, 365
"U.S.-Soviet Relations in 1983" (Shultz), 288–89

"U.S. Strategy for Non-Military
  Competition with the Soviet
  Union" (Presidential Review
  Memorandum 42), 75, 76
Ustinov, Dmitri, 82, 117, 185, 186,
  269, 270, 290
Uzbekistan, 518

Vance, Cyrus, 71, 73–74, 75, 77, 79,
  82, 90, 91, 101, 102, 109, 113,
  114, 121, 124, 126, 129, 141,
  155–59, 166, 178, 570
Vatican, 237, 240
Veil (Woodward), 199, 214
Venezuela, 302
Vessey, John W., Jr., 352, 355
Vickers, Bob, 248
Vienna summit, 116–17
Vietnam, 80, 83, 174, 201, 243, 381,
  445, 565
  Cambodia invaded by, 255–56
  China's invasion of, 119–21,
    174
  Soviet Union and, 122
Vietnam, Democratic Republic of
  (North), 28, 58, 60
Vietnam, Republic of (South), 60,
  64
Vietnam syndrome, 65, 558–59
Vietnam War, 21, 27, 28, 29, 57, 60,
  64–65, 77, 83, 172, 557
Voice of America, 94, 358, 536
Vorontsov, Yuli, 98

Walentynowicz, Anna, 162
Walesa, Lech, 87, 161, 162, 231,
  232–33, 235, 466
Walker, John, 22–23, 362, 365
Wallop, Malcolm, 371
Wall Street Journal, 87
Walsh, Lawrence, 402, 541–43
Walters, Dick, 237
Warsaw Pact, 163, 164, 168, 226,
  227, 228, 234, 238, 240, 272,
  332, 485
Washington Post, 211, 214, 474
Washington Summit, 423–26, 438
  German reunification and, 493
  INF and, 423
Watergate affair, 41, 42, 54, 57–58,
  62, 105, 172

Webster, William, 377, 418–19,
  424, 430, 435, 443, 446, 451–
  452, 470, 494, 510, 511, 540,
  543
Weinberger, Caspar, 193, 202, 219,
  220, 237, 238, 241, 242, 245,
  251, 252, 253, 260, 268, 269,
  274, 275, 277, 281–82, 283,
  285, 286, 289, 290, 295, 299,
  312, 319, 323, 325, 332, 333,
  335, 338, 339, 347, 349, 352,
  353, 355, 367, 376, 378, 396,
  399, 400, 405, 407, 421, 424,
  570
Welch, Richard, 60
Wells, William, 138, 139
Whitehead, John, 430, 431, 432, 446
White House:
  ambience of, 119–20
  broken gate incident and, 527–28
  working environment of, 53–55
Whitney, Craig, 99–100
Wickham, John, 353
Williams, Edward Bennett, 353
Wilson, Charlie, 320–21
"window of vulnerability," 106–8
Woerner, Manfred, 464
Wojtyla, Karol, *see* John Paul II, Pope
Wolfowitz, Paul, 454, 458, 526
Woodward, Bob, 199, 214
World Peace Council, 261
World War II, 32, 199
Wyszynski, Cardinal, 232–33

Yavlinsky, Grigori, 502, 503
Yazdi, Ibrahim, 129
Yazov, Dimitri, 518
Yeltsin, Boris, 425, 440, 495, 531,
  552
  August coup and, 522–23, 524
  collapse of Soviet Union and, 516,
    517–18, 519, 522–23, 524, 529
  "constitutional" coup and, 505–6
  elected president, 520–21
  first U.S. visit of, 478–79
  Gates's assessment of, 503
  Gates's visit to, 553–54, 556
  Gorbachev and, 505–6, 517–18,
    535
  Nixon's meeting with, 504
  Scowcroft visited by, 478–79

Yemen, People's Democratic
Republic of (South), 76, 149–
150, 174, 175, 178, 250, 381,
399, 497
Yemen Arab Republic (North), 74,
149–50, 174, 175, 178, 250
Yom Kippur War (1973), 40, 41, 82
Young Poland Movement, 161
Yugoslavia, 23, 86, 93, 506, 529
Yurchenko, Vitaly, 352–65, 369, 370

Zagladin, Vadim, 240
Zaire, 66, 67, 73, 312
Zakharov, Gennady, 365–66, 380,
407

Zambia, 67
"Zero, Commandante," 245
zero-zero proposal, 280
Zhivkov, Todor, 468
Zia ul-Haq, Mohammad, 146, 148,
250, 433
Casey's meeting with, 251–52,
320–21, 350
Zimbabwe African National Union
(ZANU), 76–77
Zimbabwe African Peoples Union
(ZAPU), 76–77
Zoellick, Robert, 454, 460–61, 480,
485, 490, 494, 497, 502
Zumwalt, Elmo, 81